Mistake, Fraud and Duties to Inforı European Contract Law

This examination of twelve case studies about mistake, fraud and duties to inform reveals significant differences about how contract law works in thirteen European legal systems and, despite the fact that the solutions proposed are often similar, what divergent values underlie the legal rules of these jurisdictions. Whereas some jurisdictions recognise increasing duties to inform in numerous contracts so that the destiny of mistake and fraud (classical defects of consent) may appear to be uncertain, other jurisdictions continue to refuse such duties as a general rule, or fail to recognise the need to protect one of the parties where there is an imbalance in bargaining power or information. Avoiding preconceptions as to where and why these differences exist, this book first examines the historical origins and development of defects of consent, then considers the issues from a comparative and critical standpoint.

RUTH SEFTON-GREEN is a lecturer in law at University of Paris 1 (Panthéon-Sorbonne). She has received a Master's degree from the University of Oxford, and was awarded her PhD in Law from the University of Paris 1 (Panthéon-Sorbonne).

CONTRIBUTORS

Florence Bellivier, Laura Caldwell, John Cartwright, Isabelle Corbisier, Craig Coyle, Eva Grassl-Palten, Martijn Hesselink, Philippe Jouary, Armand Kacenelenbogen, Damien Keaney, Roswitha Kundi, Albéric Luciani, Raimund Madl, Luis Menezes Leitao, Alberto Musy, Helmut Ofner, Elisabeth Poulou, Stéphane Reifegerste, Francisca Sanchez Hernanz, Martin Josef Schermaier, Ruth Sefton-Green, Lasse Simonsen, Joe Thomson.

The Common Core of European Private Law

For the transnational lawyer the present European situation is
equivalent to that of a traveller compelled to cross legal Europe using
a number of different local maps. To assist lawyers in the journey
beyond their own locality *The Common Core of Europe Private Law Project*
was launched in 1993 at the University of Trento under the auspices
of the late Professor Rudolf B. Schlesinger. This is its fifth completed
book.

The aim of this collective scholarly enterprise is to unearth what is
already common to the legal systems of European Union member
states. Case studies widely circulated and discussed between lawyers of
different traditions are employed to draw at least the main lines of a
reliable map of the law of Europe.

Books in the Series

Mistake, Fraud and Duties to Inform in European Contract Law
Edited by Ruth Sefton-Green
0 521 84423 1 Hardback

Security Rights in Movable Property in European Private Law
Edited by Eva-Maria Kieninger
0 521 83967 X Hardback

Pure Economic Loss in Europe
Edited by Mauro Bussani and Vernon Valentine Palmer
0 521 82464 8 Hardback

The Enforceability of Promises in European Contract Law
Edited by James Gordley
0 521 79021 2 Hardback

Good Faith in European Contract Law
Edited by Reinhard Zimmermann and Simon Whittaker
0 521 77190 0 Hardback

Mistake, Fraud and Duties to Inform in European Contract Law

edited by

Ruth Sefton-Green

CAMBRIDGE
UNIVERSITY PRESS

CAMBRIDGE UNIVERSITY PRESS
Cambridge, New York, Melbourne, Madrid, Cape Town, Singapore, São Paulo, Delhi

Cambridge University Press
The Edinburgh Building, Cambridge CB2 8RU, UK

Published in the United States of America by Cambridge University Press, New York

www.cambridge.org
Information on this title: www.cambridge.org/9780521844239

First published 2005
Reprinted 2006
This digitally printed version 2008

A catalogue record for this publication is available from the British Library

Library of Congress Cataloguing in Publication data
Mistake, fraud and duties to inform in European contract law edited by Ruth
Sefton-Green.
    p.   cm. – (Cambridge studies in international and comparative law)
Includes bibliographical references and index.
ISBN 0 521 84423 1 (hardback)
1. Mistake (Law) – European Union countries.   2. Fraud – European Union countries.
3. Contracts – European Union countries.   I. Sefton-Green, Ruth.   II. Series.
KJC1063.M57   2004   346.402–dc22   2004051802

ISBN 978-0-521-84423-9 hardback
ISBN 978-0-521-09310-1 paperback

Contents

General editors' preface

This is the fifth book in the series *The Common Core of European Private Law*. The *Common Core of European Private Law* Project was launched in 1993 at the University of Trento under the auspices of the late Professor Rudolf B. Schlesinger. The methodology used in the Trento project is novel. By making use of case studies it goes beyond mere description to detailed inquiry into how most European Union legal systems resolve specific legal questions in practice, and to thorough comparison between those systems. It is our hope that these volumes will provide scholars with a valuable tool for research in comparative law and in their own national legal systems. The collection of materials that the Common Core Project is offering to the scholarly community is already quite extensive and will become even more so when more volumes are published. The availability of materials attempting a genuine analysis of how things are is, in our opinion, a prerequisite for an intelligent and critical discussion on how they should be. Perhaps in the future European private law will be authoritatively restated or even codified. The analytical work carried on today by the almost 200 scholars involved in the *Common Core Project* is a precious asset of knowledge and legitimization for any such normative enterprise.

We must thank the editors and contributors to these first published results. With a sense of deep gratitude we also wish to recall our late Honorary Editor, Professor Rudolf B. Schlesinger. We are sad that we have not been able to present him with the results of a project in which he believed so firmly. No scholarly project can survive without committed sponsors. The Dipartimento di Scienze Giuridiche of the University of Trento, its past and present directors and its excellent staff must be thanked. The European Commission has partially sponsored some of our past general meetings, having included them in their High

Level Conferences Program. The Italian Ministry of Scientific Research is now also funding the project, having recognized it as a 'research of national interest'. The Istituto Subalpino per l'Analisi e l'Insegnamento del Diritto delle Attività Transnazionali, the University of Torino, the University of Trieste, the Fromm Chair in International and Comparative Law at the University of California and the Hastings College of Law have all contributed to the funding of this project. Last but not least, we must thank all those involved in our ongoing Trento projects in contract law, property, tort and other areas whose results will be the subject of future published volumes. Our home page on the internet is at http://www.jus.unitn.it/dsg/common-core. There you can follow our progress in mapping the common core of European private law.

General Editors:
MAURO BUSSANI (University of Trieste)
UGO MATTEI (University of Turin and University of California, Hastings College of Law)

Honorary Editor:
RUDOLFO SACCO (University of Turin)

Late Honorary Editor:
RUDOLF B. SCHLESINGER (Cornell University and University of California, Hastings)

Editorial Board
James Gordley, Cecil Turner Professor of Law, University of California, Berkeley; Editor in Chief of the American Journal of Comparative Law
Antonio Gambaro, Professor of Law, University of Milano; President of the Italian Society of Comparative Law
    Franz Werro, University of Freiburg and Georgetown University Law Center
    Rodolfo Sacco, President of the International Association of Legal Science (UNESCO)

Preface

This project was conceived in Paris at a meeting with Jacques Ghestin, Horatia Muir Watt and myself at the request of Mauro Bussani. The original cases were formulated by Horatia Muir Watt, Stéphane Reifegerste and me in June 1996. Our questionnaire become the subject of a brainstorming session in Trento in July with all the members of the contract group present which was most useful. I subsequently became editor of the project.

I am indebted to Jacques Ghestin for formulating the theme of the project and to Horatia Muir Watt for her initial contribution and constant encouragement. I would like to record my thanks to Stéphane Reifegerste for his active participation in the early stages of the project and particularly the group work he carried out with the students of the DEA de droit anglais et nord-américain des affaires at the University Paris I (Panthéon-Sorbonne) in the years 1997–98. I am also grateful to Muriel Fabre-Magnan for her friendly counsel and consistent support.

Above all, I would like to record my warmest thanks to the national reporters of this project with whom I would like to think we have formed a team. I would like to make special mention of the friendships and discussions which have ensued by e-mail and in our annual meetings in Trento and notably the intellectual and moral support I received from John Cartwright and Martijn Hesselink. I am immensely grateful to John Cartwright for contributing a paper on 'The rise and fall of mistake in the English law of contract' and also to Martin Schermaier for his contribution on 'Mistake, misrepresentation and precontractual duties to inform: the civil law tradition'. The team was greatly helped by our round-table discussions held at the UMR de droit comparé of the University Paris I in May 1999. I am very grateful to the director of the UMR (then Mireille Delmas-Marty) and her co-directors (Hélène Ruiz-Fabri and

xiii

Horatia Muir Watt) for having made this meeting possible. The meeting was extremely valuable for all who attended. Several people helped with the organisation of our two-day meeting: my thanks once again to Sophie Guy for her administrative assistance and Martine Kloepfer and Maxime Dequesne for their material and intellectual support and hard work.

Last, but certainly not least, I would like to thank the general editors of the Common Core of European Private Law Project, Ugo Mattei and Mauro Bussani, for their hospitality and support. They are of course the original inspiration for this particular project in the widest sense. My participation in the Common Core Project has enriched my understanding and teaching of comparative law and its methodology and encouraged these to evolve continually. For this I owe them an incommensurable debt for it is in action that our understanding grows.

The reports were all originally written in the period 1998–2002, but where possible reporters have updated their reports to reflect the law as at March 2004.

Ruth Sefton-Green
Université Paris 1

March 2004

Contributors

The case studies have been prepared:

for Austria by *Eva Grassl-Palten, Raimund Madl, Roswitha Kundi* and *Helmut Ofner*, University of Vienna

for Belgium by *Isabelle Corbisier*, Bruxelles

for England by *John Cartwright*, Christ Church, Oxford

for France by *Stéphane Reifegerste* (University of Maine), and *Ruth Sefton-Green* (University of Paris 1 Panthéon-Sorbonne) with the assistance of *Florence Bellivier* (University of Paris X), *Philippe Jouary, Armand Kacenelenbogen* and *Albéric Luciani*, Comparative Law Research Group, University of Paris 1 (Panthéon-Sorbonne)

With thanks to the students of the DEA de droit anglais et nord-américain des affaires 1997–98, University of Paris 1.

for Germany by *Martin Josef Schermaier*, University of Münster

for Greece by *Elisabeth Poulou*, University of Athens

for Ireland by *Damien Keaney*, Barrister-at-Law, Dublin

for Italy by *Alberto Musy*, University of Piemonte Orientale, Novara

for the Netherlands by *Martijn Hesselink*, University of Amsterdam

for Norway by *Lasse Simonsen*, University of Oslo

for Portugal by *Luis Menezes Leitao*, University of Lisbon

for Scotland by *Laura Caldwell, Craig Coyle* and *Joe Thomson*, University of Glasgow

for Spain by *Francisca Sanchez Hernanz*, Abogado, member of the Madrid Bar

The rise and fall of mistake in the English law of contract by *John Cartwright*, Christ Church, Oxford

Table of legislation and international instruments

(including CISG (United Nations Convention on Contracts for the International Sale of Goods (1980)), EC Directives, PECL (Principles of European Contract Law) and UNIDROIT Principles of International Commercial Contracts)

Note: (t) after a page number indicates where the text of that part of the legislation under discussion may be found.

Austria
Civil Code (*ABGB*) 1811 (including
   subsequent amendments)
  351(a) 90
  370 225
  380 248–9
  863 248, 249
  870 131, 193–4, 220, 268–9,
    327, 342–3
  871 (1811/1916) 55
  871 18 n. 66, 40, 63, 89, 129,
    131, 164–5, 189, 224–5, 285,
    308–9, 343, 353, 355, 382, 383
  872 224–5
  872 (1811/1916) 55
  873 342–3, 353, 355
  874 132, 194–5
  875 309
  876 (1811/1916) 55
  877 224–5

901, 1st sentence 248
901, 2nd sentence 20, 248
901 268–9, 343
914 ff. 248–9
918 249
923 ff. 225
932 195–6, 222, 225
933 225
934 54, 55, 89–90
1167 225
1295 63–4, 196, 221–2,
  285
1435 225
1874 161 n. 91
Consumer Protection Law
  (*Konsumentenschutzgesetz*)
  (*KSchG*) 1986
  3 284–5
  6(1)(14) 285
  25c 309

**PECL (Principles of European
Contract Law)**

Portugal

Table of cases

France

The Netherlands

Abbreviations

Austria

ABGB	*Allgemeines bürgerliches Gesetzbuch*
BGBL	*Bundesgesetzblatt*
ecolex	*Ecolex – Fachzeitschrift für Wirtschaftsrecht*
EvBl	*Evidenzblatt der Rechtsmittelentscheidungen des Obersten Gerichtshofs*
JBl	*Juristische Blätter*
Klang	H. Klang, *Kommentar zum ABGB* (Vienna, 1968)
Koziol/Welser	H. Koziol and R. Welser, *Grundriß des bürgerlichen Rechts* (10th edn, Vienna, 1995)
MietSlg	*Sammlung mietrechtlicher Entscheidungen*
NJW	*Neue Juristische Wochenschrift*
NZwG	*Notariatszwangsgesetz*
ÖBA	*Österreichisches Bankarchiv*
OGH	*Oberster Gerichtshof*
ÖJZ	*Österreichische Juristenzeitung*
RG	*Reichsgericht*
Rspr	*Rechtsprechung*
Rummel	P. Rummel (ed.), *Kommentar zum ABGB* (2nd edn, Vienna, vol. I 1990, vol. II 1992)
SZ	*Entscheidungen des österreichischen Obersten Gerichtshofes in Zivilsachen*
WBl	*Wirtschaftsrechtliche Blätter*
ZAS	*Zeitschrift für Arbeits- und Socialrecht*

Belgium

Act. dr	*Actualité du droit*
Ann. dr. Louvain	*Annales du droit de Louvain*

Ann. Fac. Dr. Lg.	*Annales de la faculté de droit de Liège*
Amén	*Aménagement*
Cass	*Cour de cassation*
Chron. D.S.	*Chronique Dalloz-Sirey*
DC/CR	*Droit de la consommation/Consumentenrecht*
De Page, *Traité élémentaire*	H. De Page, *Traité élémentaire de droit civil belge* (3rd edn, Paris, vol. I 1962, vol. II 1964; vol. IV 1938, vol. V 1941, vol. VIII/1 1944)
JJP	*Journal des Juges de Paix*
JLMB	*Jurisprudence de Liège, Mons et Bruxelles*
JP	*Justice de paix*
JT	*Journal des tribunaux*
JTT	*Journal des tribunaux du travail*
Limb. Rechtsl	*Limburgs Rechtsleven*
Meinertzhagen-Limpens, *Traité élémentaire*	A. Meinertzhagen-Limpens, *Traité élémentaire de droit civil belge* (Brussels, 1997)
Pas	*Pasicrisie belge*
RCJB	*Revue critique de jurisprudence belge*
RDCB	*Revue de droit commercial belge*
Rechtspr. arb. Br	*Rechtspraak van de arbeidsgerechten van Brussel*
Res Jur. Imm.	*Res et Jura Immobilia*
Rev. not. b.	*Revue du notariat belge*
RGAR	*Revue générale des assurances et des responsabilités*
RGDC	*Revue générale de droit civil belge*
RW	*Rechtskundig weekblad*
T. Agr. R	*Tijdschrift voor agrarisch recht*
T. not.	*Tijdschrift voor notarissen*
TPR	*Tijdschrift voor privaatrecht*
Trib. civ.	*Tribunal civil*
Trib. comm.	*Tribunal de commerce*
Trib. trav.	*Tribunal de travail*

England

AC	Law Reports, Appeal Cases (from 1891 to date)

All ER	All England Law Reports (from 1936 to date)
Bing.	Bingham's Reports
CA	Court of Appeal
Ch	Law Reports, Chancery Division (from 1891 to date)
Ch D	Law Reports, Chancery Division (1875–1890)
Chitty on Contracts	J. Chitty, *Chitty on Contracts* (28th edn, London, 1998)
CLR	Commonwealth Law Reports
DLR	Dominion Law Reports
HL	House of Lords
KB	Law Reports, King's Bench (1901–52)
LQR	*Law Quarterly Review*
LR	Law Reports
NZLR	New Zealand Law Reports (from 1883 to date)
QB	Law Reports, Queen's Bench (1881–1900, from 1952 to date)
P & CR	Property and Compensation Reports (formerly Planning and Compensation Reports)
SGA 1979	Sale of Goods Act 1979
SGSA 1980	Supply of Goods and Services Act 1980
SI	Statutory Instrument
Treitel, *Contract*	G. H. Treitel, *The Law of Contract* (11th edn, London, 2003)
v.	*versus*
WLR	Weekly Law Reports (from 1953 to date)

France

Ass. Plén.	*Assemblée plénière*
Bull civ	*Bulletin civil de la Cour de cassation*
Cass	*Cour de cassation*
CCC	*Contrats, concurrence, consommation*
ch.	*chambre*
Chr.	*Chronique*
Civ	*Cour de cassation, Chambre civile*
Com	*Cour de cassation, Chambre commerciale*
D	*Dalloz*
Def	*Répertoire du Notariat Defrénois*

DH	*Dalloz, Recueil hebdomadaire de jurisprudence (1924–40)*
DP	*Dalloz Périodique*
Gaz. Pal.	*Gazette du Palais*
Ghestin, *La formation*	J. Ghestin, *Traité de droit civil, Le contrat, La formation* (3rd edn, Paris, 1993)
IR	*Informations rapides*
JCP	*La Semaine juridique*
Juris-classeur	*Juris-classeur (1950, updated annually)*
Req.	*Cour de cassation, chambre des requêtes*
RTDCiv	*Revue Trimestrielle de droit civil*
RTDCom	*Revue Trimestrielle de droit commercial*
S	*Recueil Sirey*
Soc.	*Cour de cassation, Chambre sociale*
somm.	*sommaires*
Terré, Simler and Lequette, *Les obligations*	F. Terré, P. Simler and Y. Lequette, *Droit civil, Les obligations* (8th edn, Paris, 2002)

Germany

AcP	*Archiv für die civilistische Praxis (Munich)*
AP	*Nachschlagewerk des Bundesarbeitsgerichts – Arbeitsrechtliche Praxis (Munich)*
BAG	*Bundesarbeitsgericht*
BB	*Betriebsberater (Heidelberg)*
BGB	*Bürgerliches Gesetzbuch (1900)*
BGH	*Bundesgerichtshof*
BGHZ	*Entscheidungen des Bundesgerichtshofs für Zivilsachen (= official report of the Bundesgerichtshof, Cologne)*
D.	*Digesta Justiniani*
DB	*Der Betrieb (Düsseldorf)*
EG	*Europäische Gemeinschaft(en) (European Community)*
Erman	W. Erman (Founder), *Handkommentar zum Bürgerlichen Gesetzbuch*, 11. Aufl. Münster 2003
EuGH	*Europäischer Gerichtshof (European Court of Justice)*
EWiR	*Entscheidungen zum Wirtschaftsrecht (Cologne)*

Flume, AT	Werner Flume, *Allgemeiner Teil des Bürgerlichen Rechts, Band 2: Das Rechtsgeschäft* (4. Aufl., Berlin, 1992)
FS	*Festschrift*
Inst.	*Institutiones Justiniani*
Jura	*Juristische Ausbildung (Berlin)*
JuS	*Juristische Schulung (Munich)*
JZ	*Juristenzeitung (Tübingen)*
KG	*Kammergericht*
Larenz/Wolf, AT	Karl Larenz and Manfred Wolf, *Allgemeiner Teil des Bürgerlichen Rechts* (8th edn, Munich, 1997)
LG	*Landgericht*
LM	*Lindenmaier/Möhring, Nachschlagwerk des Bundesgerichtshofs in Zivilsachen (Munich)*
LZ	*Leipziger Zeitschrift für Deutsches Recht (Leipzig)*
MDR	*Monatsschrift für Deutsches Recht (Cologne)*
MüKo	*Münchener Kommentar zum Bürgerlichen Gesetzbuch* (3. Aufl., Munich, 1995–1999, 4. Aufl., Münster, 2000–2003)
MuSchuG	*Mutterschutzgesetz*
NJW	*Neue Juristische Wochenschrift (Munich)*
NJW-RR	*Neue Juristische Wochenschrift – Rechtsprechungsreport (Munich)*
OLG	*Oberlandesgericht*
Palandt	*Beck'scher Kurzkommentar zum Bürgerlichen Gesetzbuch, founded by Otto Palandt* (62. Aufl., Munich, 2003)
RabelsZ	*Zeitschrift für ausländisches und internationales Privatrecht, founded by Ernst Rabel ('Rabels Zeitschrift', Berlin)*
RAG	*Reichsarbeitsgericht*
RG	*Reichsgericht*
RGRK	*Das Bürgerliche Gesetzbuch mit besonderer Berücksichtigung des Reichsgerichts und des Bundesgerichtshofes* (12. Aufl., Berlin, 1976–2000)
RGZ	*Entscheidungen des Reichsgerichts in Zivilsachen* (= official report of the the Reichsgericht)
RL	*Richtlinie (directive)*
Soergel	*Bürgerliches Gesetzbuch (Kommentar)* (12. Aufl., Stuttgart, 1987–2000, 13. Aufl., Stuttgart, 1999–2002)

Staudinger	*J. v. Staudingers Kommentar zum Bürgerlichen Gesetzbuch, 13 Bearbeitung Berlin (ab 1993)*
UWG	*Gesetz gegen den unlauteren Wettbewerb (1909)*
WM	*Wertpapiermitteilungen, Zeitschrift für Wirtschafts- und Bankrecht (Frankfurt a. M.)*
ZIP	*Zeitschrift für Wirtschaftsrecht und Insolvenzpraxis (Cologne)*

Greece

AK	*Civil Code*
AP	*Areios Pagos (Supreme Court of Civil Law)*
ArchN	*Archio Nomologias (Archive of Court Decisions)*
Arm	*Armenopoulos (a journal)*
EEN	*Ephimeris Hellinon Nomikon (a journal)*
Erm	*interpretation*
Them	*Themis*

Ireland

| IR | *Irish Reports* |

Italy

Cass	*Corte di cassation sezione civile*
DL	*Diritto del lavoro*
FI	*Foro italiano*
FP	*Foro padano*
GI	*Giurisprudenza italiana*
GC	*Giustizia civile*
Merito	*Giurisprudenza di merito*
NGCC	*Nuova giurisprudenza civile commentata*
RCDP	*Rivista critica di diritto privato*
RDC	*Rivista di diritto civile*
RDCo	*Rivista di diritto commerciale*
Riv. dir. lav	*Rivista di diritto del lavaro*
Riv. trim. dir. proc. civ	*Rivista trimestrale di diritto e procedura civile*
TR	*Temi Romani*

The Netherlands

| AA | *Ars Aequi* |

Asser/Hartkamp II (2001)	A. S. Hartkamp, *Mr C. Asser's handleiding tot de beoefening van het Nederlands burgerlijk recht, Verbintenissenrecht* (The Hague, 2001)
Asser/Hijma 5-I (2001)	J. Hijma, *Mr. C. Asser's handleiding tot de beoefening van het Nederlands burgerlijk recht; Bijzondere overeenkomsten, Deel I Koop en Ruil* (6th edn, Deventer, 2001)
Asser/Clausing/Wansink, (1998)	P. Clausing, J. H. Wansink, *Mr. C. Asser's handleiding tot de beoefening van het Nederlands burgerlijk recht*, Vol. 6: *De verzekeringsovereenkomst* (Deventer, 1998)
Bakels/Asscher-Vonk/Fase (2000)	H. L. Bakels, P. Asscher-Vonk, W.J.P.M. Fase, *Schets van het Nederlands arbeidsrecht* (16th edn, Deventer, 2000)
BW	*Burgerlijk Wetboek* (Civil Code)
HR	*Hoge Raad des Nederlanden*
MJ	*Maastricht Journal of European and Comparative Law*
NJ	*Nederlandse Jurisprudentie*
NJB	*Nederlands Juristenblad*
NTBR	*Nederlands Tijdschrift voor Burgerlijk Recht*
RvdW	*Rechstspraak van de Week*
WPNR	*Weekblad voor Privaatrecht, Notariaat en Registratie*

Norway

NJA	*Nytt Juridiskt Arkiv avd.I*
NJA	*Nytt Juridisk Arkiv* (contains all judgments pronounced by the Supreme Court in Sweden *Høgsta Domstolen*)
Ot. prp.	*Odelstings proposisjon* (a bill or proposition from the government to the Norwegian parliament)
RT	*Norsk Retstidende* (contains all judgments and rulings pronounced by the Norwegian Supreme Court *Høyesterett*)
TfR	*Tidsskrift for Rettsvidenskap* (a periodical for the Scandinavian countries)

Portugal

BMJ	*Boletim de Ministerio da Justiça*
CJ	*Colectânea de Jurisprudência*
STJ	*Supremo Tribunal de Justiça*

Scotland

All ER	All England Law Reports (from 1936 to date)
SC	Session Cases
SLT	*Scottish Law Times*

Mistake, misrepresentation and precontractual duties to inform: the civil law tradition

ABGB	*Allgemeines bürgerliches Gesetzbuch* (1811)
AcP	*Archiv für die civilistische Praxis* (Tübingen)
ALR	*Allgemeines Landrecht für die preußischen Staaten* (1794)
Annali Palermo	*Annali del seminario giuridico dell'università di Palermo* (Palermo)
Aristot. *Eth. Nic.*	Aristoteles, *Ethica Nicomachaea*
BGB	*Bürgerliches Gesetzbuch* (1900)
C.	*Codex Justiniani*
Can.	*Canon*
cap.	*capitulum*
CC	*Code civil* (1804)
CIC	*Corpus iuris canonici* (1918)
Cic. *off.*	Marcus T. Cicero, *De officiis*
D.	*Digesta Justiniani*
fol.	*folium*
FS	*Festschrift*
Index	*Index. International Survey of Roman Law* (Naples)
Labeo	*Labeo. Rassegna di diritto romano* (Naples)
lib.	*librum*
n.	*nota*
NWB	*(Nieuw) Burgerlijk Wetboek* (1992)
PECL	*Principles of European Contract Law*
pr.	*principium*
qu.	*quaestio*
r.	*recto*
repr.	*reprint*

RIDA	*Revue international des droits de l'antiquité* (Bruxelles)
rubr.	*rubrica*
SDHI	*Studia et documenta historiae et iuris* (Roma)
Thomas, STh.	Thomas Aquinas, *Summa theologiae*
TR	*Tijdschrift voor Rechtsgeschiedenis* (Den Haag)
ZEuP	*Zeitschrift für Europäisches Privatrecht* (München)
ZSSt	*Zeitschrift der Savigny-Stiftung für Rechtsgeschichte, romanistische Abteilung* (Cologne/Vienna/Weimar)

Other sections

CISG	United Nations Convention on Contracts for the International Sale of Goods 1980
CLJ	*Cambridge Law Journal*
Harv. LR	*Harvard Law Review*
LQR	*Law Quarterly Review*
MLR	*Modern Law Review*
OJLS	*Oxford Journal of Legal Studies*
RIDComp	*Revue international de droit comparé*
RLR	*Restitution Law Review*
YLJ	*Yale Law Journal*

1 General introduction

Ruth Sefton-Green

What is at issue in the law of mistake, fraud and duties to inform?

Why did we choose to look at mistake, fraud and duties to inform? At first sight, the choice appears straightforward: in order to examine the world of European contract law it is quite logical to start at the beginning with contract formation. The general theory of defects of consent provides a safe starting place.[1] The title indicates perhaps that civil law[2] inspires this enquiry. These three initial assumptions will be examined shortly. Before turning to the heart of this study however, a preliminary terminological explanation is required. Mistake has been adopted for the sake of consistency throughout even though it is the term for an English legal concept; 'mistake' thus covers the Scots law of *error*, as well as *erreur* (French and Belgian law), *errore* (Italian law), *erro* (Portuguese law), *Irrtum* (Austrian and German law), *dwaling* (Dutch law) and *plani* (Greek law). It was generally agreed that the use of an English legal term was innocuous in this instance. Likewise, fraud has been used to refer to *dol* (French and Belgian law), *dolo* (Italian law), *dolo* (Portuguese law), *arglistige Täuschung* (Austrian and German law), *bedrog* (Dutch law) and *apati* (Greek law). In contrast, the term 'duty to inform' has been chosen so as to avoid using specifically English legal concepts (misrepresentation and duties of disclosure) to denominate concepts existing in other legal systems where such a transposition would be both erroneous and misleading. Thus the term 'duties (or duty) to inform' has

---

[1] However, no attempt to be exhaustive has been made since this study only examines some defects of consent.

[2] See H. P. Glenn, *Legal Traditions of the World* (Oxford, 2000), ch. 5 on the civil law tradition (reference is also made to the civilian tradition). On the meaning given to 'civil law' see also fn. 65 below.

been coined. Of course, a choice of terms is never innocent: there is an obvious semantic difference between 'disclosing' and 'informing', perhaps connoting a tacit conceptual choice made by the various national laws.[3]

First then is it accurate to assume that a study of mistake, fraud and duties to inform is confined to contract formation? Far from being limited to remedies for contract formation, as opposed to contractual non-performance or breach of contract, we will see that mistake, fraud and duties to inform cross this conceptual bridge (which is, in any event, more accentuated in certain, notably civil law, systems, than in others), in a very significant way. Indeed, this overlap – between remedies under the heads of defective consent and breach of contract – is common to all national systems examined and brings to the forefront a commonality of approach, at least in this particular respect. The historical foundations of mistake will explain, to some extent, this apparent incoherence.[4]

Secondly, can we likewise assume that mistake, fraud and duties to inform fit into a general theory of defects of consent? Four criticisms can be levelled at this assumption. In the first place is it actually true that a general theory of defects of consent exists in all of the legal systems examined? Two exceptions of a different nature exist: Scandinavian[5] contract laws contain general invalidity regulations[6] that are not based on defects of consent. The emphasis on invalidity is not linked to a vitiated will.[7] More specifically, the invalidity rules of Scandinavian contract law have primarily been developed with the intention of remedying the abuse to which contractual freedom might lead.[8] This has

---

[3] If a person is under a duty to disclose, the assumption is he has something to hide, the law thus obliges him to reveal something he may not have chosen to reveal himself; if a person is under a duty to inform, he is under a positive duty to help or behave transparently towards the other contracting party. The emphasis is slight perhaps, but nevertheless important.

[4] Cf. Martin Josef Schermaier, in 'Mistake, Misrepresentation and Precontractual Duties to Inform: the Civil Law Tradition', pp. 39–64.

[5] Scandinavia is used here to refer to Danish, Norwegian and Swedish law. There are many similarities in the law of obligations and property and it should be recalled that the Contract Act and the Sale of Goods Act have been constructed on a cooperative basis by Denmark, Norway and Sweden.

[6] See for example §§ 33 and 36 of the Norwegian Contract Act.

[7] Reference is made to an 'invalid declaration of will' (ugyldige viljeserklæringer) or an 'invalid juridical act', cf. PECL, ch. 4, notes to art. 4: 101.

[8] A Norwegian jurist, Stang (1867–1941) developed a specific theory about invalidity rules, called densynbare viljesmangel (obvious lack of consent), see in particular the

partly been accomplished by establishing rules concerning bad faith and dishonesty on the part of the promisee,[9] and partly by rules concerning unreasonable contracts. These rules are not based on 'a general theory of defect of consent'. However, concepts expressing this kind of thinking do exist, for instance in the rules relating to 'fraud' and 'lack of capacity'.[10] England, Ireland and Scotland provide another exception. These legal systems do have a theory of defects of consent – it might be more controversial to assert, however, that there is such a thing as a general theory. Controversy about the existence of a general theory in the common law can take two forms: either it can be submitted that there is no general 'theory' since the common law does not work in this way, according to general (deductive) principles,[11] or that there is no underlying trend constituting a 'theory' as such.[12]

In the second place, in the legal systems which do admittedly contain a general theory of defects of consent, namely France, Belgium, Germany, Greece, Italy, Spain, Portugal and the Netherlands, further preliminary questions arise: what is the content of such a general theory and even more simply, what is its function? In other words, why does the law need a general theory of defects of consent?[13] It is precisely this question which enables us to focus on the choice made in this enquiry. Contract formation (at least apparently) and defects of consent have been chosen to test the truthfulness of the various assumptions outlined above. Moreover, we will attempt to demonstrate that even if the enquiry is inspired by civil law preoccupations, it is certainly not limited to them, to the exclusion of other national legal systems. In the third place, a theory of defects of consent is old-fashioned, because it is based on the assumption

condition that 'the other party knew of or should have known of the error'.
A development of this theory is that it is (probably) not required that the person concerned possesses knowledge of the condition. It is sufficient that he ought to have possessed such knowledge. The rule, in other words, has been made normative. However, the doctrine was never awarded much general support.

[9] There is also in Scandinavian law a non-statutory doctrine of failed contractual assumptions. For a further explanation of the doctrine of failed contractual assumptions, see the Norwegian report in Case 1.

[10] In order to indicate in which way § 36 of the Contract Law (the 'General Clause') differs from § 33, the latter is sometimes referred to as 'the little General Clause'. I am grateful to Lasse Simonsen for making this clear.

[11] G. Samuel, *The Foundations of Legal Reasoning* (Antwerp, 1994).

[12] *Contra*, J. Cartwright, *Unequal Bargaining* (Oxford, 1991).

[13] By analogy, see the enquiry made by E. Savaux as to the truthfulness of the existence of general theory of contract in French law, in *La théorie générale du contrat: mythe ou réalité?* (Paris, 1997). According to this author, such a general theory is nothing other than a doctrinal construction.

that the binding force of contracts is based on will, intention[14] and autonomy and thus represents a nineteenth-century conception of contract law. In the fourth place, some may submit that the theory of defects of consent is *politically* wrong because it is based on the assumption that the binding force of contract is based on party autonomy (free consent), whereas the binding force of contract is (also) based on solidarity.[15]

Thirdly, what is the source of inspiration of our enquiry? We will take as our starting point a pattern which has emerged in say French law with regard to the development of the duty to inform (*l'obligation d'information*), which will help to explain the seeds of our enquiry. French case law has increasingly recognised the duty to inform since 1958.[16] A twofold development can now be identified in case law: the existence of the duty was first brought to light by penalising active fraudulent behaviour in failing to disclose information which would have had a material effect on inducing a party to contract. Then, passive fraudulent behaviour, that is silence, became reprehensible in certain contexts, thus giving rise to the idea that a positive duty to inform pre-existed, since otherwise the silence would not be subject to challenge. An extension of this fraudulent concealment (*réticence dolosive*) has enabled the law to identify the circumstances in which a duty to inform exists, absent all allegations of fraud.[17] As a starting point this phenomenon raises a number of comparative challenges and a central theme of our enquiry is to examine whether or not this development is a common occurrence in Europe, and if so, to what extent.

---

[14] See K. Zweigert and H. Kötz, *An Introduction to Comparative Law* (translated by T. Weir, Oxford, 1998), p. 423, who suggest that 'the doctrine of intention, traces of which still lurk in Continental rules relating to mistake, is socially inappropriate'.

[15] I am indebted to Martijn Hesselink for objections three and four. For a discussion of the theory that the binding force of contracts is also based on solidarity, cf. T. Wilhelmsson, *Social Contract Law and European Integration* (Aldershot, 1995); B. Lurger, *Vertragliche Solidarität, Entwicklungschancen für das allgemeine Vertragsrecht in Österreich und in der Europäischen Union* (Baden-Baden, 1998); J. B. M. Vranken, 'Over partijautonomie, contractsvrijheid en de grondslag van gebondenheid in het verbintenissenrecht' in J. M. Barendrecht, M. A. B. Chao-Duivis and H. A. W. Vermeulen (eds.), *Beginselen van contractenrecht: Opstellen aangeboden aan B. W. M. Nieskens-Isphording* (Deventer, 2000); C. Jamin, 'Plaidoyer pour le solidarisme contractuel', in G. Goubeaux et al. (ed.), *Études offertes à Jacques Ghestin; Le contrat au début du XXIe siècle* (Paris, 2001); M. W. Hesselink, 'The Principles Of European Contract Law: Some Choices Made by the Lando Commission' in M. W. Hesselink, G. de Vries, *Principles of European Contract Law* (Deventer, 2001), pp. 5–95.

[16] Cass civ, 19 May 1958, Bull civ I, p. 198; cf. for a detailed explanation, J. Ghestin (ed.), *Traité de droit civil, La formation du contrat* (3rd edn, Paris, 1993), no. 566, pp. 535 ff.

[17] See the synthesis in Ghestin, *La Formation du contrat*, no. 626, p. 610.

Legal theories about mistake: protection versus legal certainty

Mistake has common origins deriving from Roman law and the Aristotelian scholastic tradition. Nonetheless, even though it may be contended that mistake has developed uniformly, in comparison with say the duty to inform,[18] a closer look at mistake shows that this contention must be qualified. It is of course true that mistake has developed along with theories about contractual validity and in this sense, mistake is a good pointer for theories about contract law in general. However, it will be seen that from these common roots a diversity of legal theories about mistake, and consequently contract law theory, has evolved. In this respect, it will be seen that even though civilian legal systems share a common origin, the evolution of the concept of mistake in the French and German legal traditions has been very different. As far as the English concept of mistake is concerned, even if it has been suggested that English law 'borrowed' from Pothier and the natural lawyers in the nineteenth century to give a theoretical foundation to mistake based on the autonomy of the will,[19] so that it could be argued that English law shares common Roman law origins with civilian legal systems, the comparison stops short. The English concept of mistake is in fact very different from its civilian counterparts[20] and recent developments show that this continues to be the case.[21] In other words, the European legal systems considered do not share the same conception of mistake today despite its common origins. In order to get a flavour of these differences, two historical enquiries have been included.[22] This eclectic choice fails to be representative of all the legal systems considered but concentrates on contextualising and explaining the historical background of certain themes essential to our study.

It is somewhat trite to assert that mistake is inextricably linked to the question of consent and the validity of contract. The first obvious issue that mistake raises is the following; if it can be inferred from a mistake

---

[18] Cf. Schermaier in 'Mistake, Misrepresentation and Precontractual Duties to Inform: the Civil Law Tradition', pp. 39–44.

[19] A. W. B. Simpson, 'Innovation in Nineteenth Century Contract Law' (1975) 91 LQR 265–9: J. Gordley, *The Philosophical Origins of Modern Contract* (Oxford, 1991), pp. 142 ff.

[20] See John Cartwright, 'The Rise and Fall of Mistake in the English Law of Contact', see below pp. 65–86.

[21] See, for example, *Great Peace Shipping v. Tsavliris Salvage (International) Ltd* (2002) 4 All ER 689.

[22] See Schermaier in 'Mistake, Misrepresentation and Precontractual Duties to Inform: the Civil Law Tradition' (see pp. 39–64) and Cartwright, 'The Rise and Fall of Mistake in the English Law of Contact' (see pp. 65–86).

that the parties have not consented, then there is no contract. In the simplest sense, this is a question of fact: have the parties agreed and on what? If not, there is no agreement. The mistake is one of essence,[23] it touches on the heart of the matter: it is said that mistake destroys the parties' consent.[24] This theoretical explanation of mistake can be traced back to Roman law but also to Aristotelian and Thomistic analyses that the essence or end-purpose of the contract (what kind of contract, what is the object of the contract?) does not exist if a mistake has been made.[25] This is expressed in the idea that there is no *consensus ad idem*. French law, for example, has identified this sort of situation by the doctrine of *erreur-obstacle*.[26] To simplify, we could say that this type of mistake affects the existence of the contract. An interrelated question that mistake raises is that of the will and intention of the parties: in the event of a material mistake or misapprehension, the voluntariness of the act of one or both contracting parties is at stake. Medieval jurists thus added on the question of autonomous intention and will to the Roman law conception of mistake. Ibbetson suggests that Pothier confounded these two logically distinct situations in order to arrive at 'an apparently unified theory'.[27] This type of mistake does not destroy consent: it merely negatives consent, or to simplify again, the mistake concerns the validity of the contract. The second issue is clearly highly problematic for the will theory of contract that became increasingly important for legal theory in the nineteenth century.[28]

The advent of the will theory marks a more clear-cut divergence of mistake theories in European legal systems. If the 'real task of contract law (is) to enforce the will of the parties', then mistake as a legal doctrine confronts this issue head-on since it addresses the question of the parties' consent.[29] In France, for example, contractual validity and consent were amalgamated into an enquiry as to the subjective intention of the parties. French nineteenth-century jurists pursued, *inter alia*, a distinction

---

[23] In the Aristotelian sense of the word, *ousia*.

[24] Gordley, *The Philosophical Origins of Modern Contract*, p. 187; D. Ibbetson, *A Historical Introduction to the Law of Obligations* (Oxford, 1999), pp. 225 ff. G. H. Treitel, *The Law of Contract* (11th edn, London, 2003), uses the expression that the mistake nullifies consent, pp. 286–98.

[25] Gordley, *The Philosophical Origins of Modern Contract*, pp. 85 ff.; pp. 187 ff.

[26] P. Gaudefroy, *L'erreur-obstacle*, PhD thesis (Paris, 1924); Ghestin, *La formation du contrat*, no. 495, p. 459.

[27] Ibbetson, *A Historical Introduction to the Law of Obligations*, p. 226.

[28] P. S. Atiyah, *The Rise and Fall of Freedom of Contract* (Oxford, 1979).

[29] Gordley, *The Philosophical Origins of Modern Contract*, pp. 186–7.

between mistakes as to substance and as to *qualities substantielles*[30] but more crucial is the fact that mistake became embedded in the will theory in which overriding value is given to the protection of consent and the subjective intention of the parties. By the same token, it is suggested that the law focuses on the parties' subjective intention when it enquires whether the subject matter of the mistake was important for the mistaken party.[31] In England, the situation became increasingly complex where, apart from being influenced by a French version of mistake,[32] certain writers on contract, Chitty for example, adopted an objective interpretation of the contract, in accordance with Paley's theories.[33] It is hard to fit the two theoretical bases into one coherent theory.[34] The line of development traceable in French law contrasts nicely with the evolution of the concept of mistake in German law. This latter development represents a real divergence in theory and outlook. Following Savigny's theory, a mistake did not affect consent in that a party had actually consented to the contract but an analysis had to be made at a prior stage in the proceedings: what counted for Savigny was the distinction between the will and what preceded the outward declaration of the will. In his view, in the event that the internal will of the party does not correspond with the outward declaration of his will, giving relief for the subsequent mistake will be justified.[35] This analysis is linked to the declaration of will being considered as the legal foundation for contracts as juristic acts (*Rechtsgeschaft*). The emphasis is put on the communication of intent (a shift from the intent *per se*) and, more importantly, on the subsequent and objective reliance on that declaration by the other party.[36]

---

[30] Gordley suggests, *ibid.* at p. 193, that this sort of reflection led to a 'mystical' analysis about the characteristics that determine the species of an object.

[31] See below on unilateral, mutual and shared mistakes, p. 18.

[32] See A. W. B. Simpson, 'Innovation in Nineteenth Century Contract Law' (1975) 91 LQR 247 at pp. 265 ff.

[33] Ibbetson, *A Historical Introduction to the Law of Obligations*, p. 221.

[34] Indeed criticism of the incoherence of the rules of mistake in English law has attributed the cause to the evils of legal transplants: see Simpson, 'Innovation in Nineteenth Century Contract Law', p. 268 who refers to 'an unhappy piece of innovations' and the more vigorous criticism of H. Collins, 'Methods and Aims of Comparative Contract Law' (1991) 11 OJLS 396, at p. 398 who comments '. . . hopelessly confused – a confusion which could have been avoided if English law had resisted the meddlesome transplants of Victorian contract lawyers'.

[35] Gordley, *The Philosophical Origins of Modern Contract*, pp. 190–7 at pp. 190–1.

[36] See Schermaier, 'Mistake, Misrepresentation and Precontractual Duties to Inform: the Civil Law Tradition', see below pp. 39–64, who suggests that this is a result of theories of language developed by Hobbes and Puffendorf.

To summarise, two distinct strands can be identified: the first relates to a conception of the will theory and the subjective intention of the parties as opposed to the second that emphasises the declaration of the will of the parties and analyses their intention objectively. A tension exists between these two distinct sets of values, as the will theory (*Willenstheorie*) of subjective intention versus the theory of declaration (*Erklärungstheorie*) of objective reliance. It is contended that the English view of mistake does not fit either of these theories perhaps because mistake in England has developed in isolation and in somewhat different contexts.[37] The fact that a large majority of English (common law) cases on mistake concern commercial contracts no doubt explains these differences since the judges' immediate concerns about mistake arose in fact-specific situations giving rise to a need for adjudication, where priority had to be given to finding a balance between giving relief and protecting commercial interests.[38] In other words, the little theorising about mistake that was done happened during or as a consequence of litigation.

An aim of this enquiry is therefore to examine to what uses mistake, fraud and duties to inform are put today in European contract law and what light this sheds on contemporary theories of contract law.

The meaning and scope of protection

What is the purpose of a theory of defects of consent? A simple answer may be that its aim is to protect a party's consent to the contract. One of our aims is to consider empirically and critically whether the protection offered by mistake and fraud suffice in European contract law today. In this respect, it is therefore also necessary to examine the significance of the emergence of duties to inform and its relationship with mistake and fraud. We will need to enquire as to the purposes of duties to inform: are they protective, efficient and useful? It has been submitted that three distinct categories of defects of consent can be identified,[39]

---

[37] See Gordley, *The Philosophical Origins of Modern Contract*, pp. 142 ff. who points out that English judges were preoccupied by a variety of practical concerns such as the innocent reliance of the mistaken party or the healing power of Equity etc.

[38] See also H. Beale, 'The "Europeanisation" of Contract Law' in R. Halson (ed.), *Exploring the Boundaries of Contract* (Aldershot, 1996), pp. 23 ff. at p. 40, who suggests that common lawyers' conception of mistake is closely linked to the sort of commercial cases they are used to see being brought before the courts.

[39] M. Fabre-Magnan, 'Defects of Consent in Contract Law' in A. Hartkamp, M. Hesselink, E. Hondius, C. Joustra and E. du Perron (eds.), *Towards a European Civil Code* (2nd edn, Nijmegen, 1998), p. 219.

two of which are of interest to us.[40] The first, mistake, is to protect a mistaken party to a contract. The second, fraud, is to punish the behaviour of a party who has fraudulently induced the other party to contract. The term 'punish' requires a parenthesis. Its connotations, e.g. of punitive damages, which may come to the mind of lawyers whose jurisdictions recognise such a concept, must be discarded. It is submitted that in some legal systems legal rules clearly have moralistic[41] overtones, so that it may not appear surprising to talk of 'punishing'[42] a person's fraudulent behaviour. Admittedly, this idea does not transpose very well into English legal terminology and may lead to misleading and unfortunate associations.[43] It is not just the signifier that is at issue; it is the signified. It may therefore be less controversial to say that the law treats fraudulent behaviour with greater severity, because of the fraud.[44] This detail reveals a difference in legal mentality since it can be inferred from the law's severe treatment of fraudulent behaviour that fraud should be discouraged, not punished. The end-purpose is somewhat different.[45] From the aggrieved party's point of view it may be more helpful to see the remedies given for defects of consent as a form of protection. Annulment is deemed to be a protective measure although of course the efficacy of such *post hoc facto* protection is subject to doubt. In the event that fraud has operated, a reinforced protection for the aggrieved party will be given in the form of compensatory damages. This protective approach, admitting of degrees, may be used as a starting point. In order to examine the meaning of protection it must be considered whether the focus of the law is on protecting the aggrieved party and/or taking the other (non-mistaken) party's behaviour into account. Legal systems diverge on this point. We will see that some protect the mistaken party regardless of the other party's behaviour. Reasons for not protecting the mistaken party arise from, *inter alia*, the mistaken party's behaviour.[46] Others do

---

[40] The third relates to the concepts of duress, violence, threat, abuse of circumstances etc. summarised by the concept of 'undue pressure', *ibid.*, p. 222.

[41] See G. Ripert, *La règle morale dans les obligations civiles* (4th edn, Paris, 1949).

[42] The appropriate term in French is '*sanctionner*', which in a non-penal context can be both repressive and compensatory – cf. G. Cornu (ed.) *Vocabulaire juridique* (8th edn, Paris, 2000).

[43] For example, 'punishment' is generally reserved for criminal law, 'punishing' along with damages leads to 'punitive damages' etc.

[44] I am grateful to John Cartwright for having pointed out this semantical confusion to me.

[45] A twofold end-purposes analysis may be insufficient.

[46] See French and Belgian reports in Case 1 on the issue of excusability. Of course, protection may be refused for other reasons e.g. the security of transactions.

take the non-mistaken party's behaviour into consideration. Illustrations of the latter viewpoint can be found in the Austrian and German view of mistake, for example, where the end-purpose of protection is recognised by granting the remedy of annulment but such a right is qualified by a duty on the mistaken party to compensate for the annulment (German law) or even as an objection to annulment (in Austrian law) where the non-mistaken party's protection prevails.

In contrast, when a mistake is induced by fraudulent behaviour the aggrieved party has a choice: he[47] can base his claim on mistake or fraud. French law, to take one example, will allow the aggrieved party to claim annulment[48] on the basis of defects of consent (mistake under art. 1110 and fraud under art. 1116 *Code civil*). In addition, should the claim be based on fraud, an additional claim for damages for tortious liability may be founded under arts. 1382–3 of the Civil Code.[49] Another example may be given by German law since §123 BGB (called 'fraudulent misrepresentation') provides that where a mistake has been caused by fraud, the mistaken party seeking annulment does not have to compensate the other contracting party for its reliance interest, unlike the claims under §119 and §122 of the BGB for mistake. Such a remedy may be considered justified by the fraudulent behaviour of the non-mistaken party who has thus lost all entitlement to protection. Here it could be said that protection is not opposed to taking the other party's behaviour into account: on the contrary it is precisely because of that other party's (fraudulent) behaviour that protection is reinforced. Sometimes, however, we will see that these two priorities do conflict when there is no fraud; some legal systems enhance protection exclusively whereas other systems try to find a balance between protection and weighing it up against the attitude or state of mind of the non-mistaken party. The reliance of that other party is used to denote this idea. This is important to bear in mind when looking at the law's attitudes towards duties to inform.

If it is accepted that the overall end-purpose of mistake is to protect a mistaken contracting party; of fraud to grant even greater protection

---

[47] For the avoidance of doubt, where the masculine is used throughout to refer to a person, it is deemed to include the feminine.

[48] It should be noted that we have chosen to use the term 'annulment' throughout this study as it was considered to be the most neutral term. We have thus set aside other terms such as rescission or avoidance.

[49] This is not to exclude the possibility of making a claim for damages in addition to annulment for mistake where the presence of a *faute* has been identified, though it is rare in practice. See Ghestin, *La formation du contrat*, no. 519, p. 481; no. 623, p. 605.

to the party upon whom fraud has operated, or conversely to treat the fraudulent behaviour with severity, the duty to inform clearly straddles these two identifiable objectives of defects of consent. Three reasons of a different order may help to explain why this is so. The first two question the nature of the objectives of defects of consent. The third asks whether the duty to inform truly belongs to the realm of defects of consent.

First, it is submitted that the duty to inform is also a highly protective measure. Suppose that a party's fraudulent behaviour is characterised by giving, or failing to give, information. Fraudulently informing the party with whom one is contracting clearly falls into the category of fraud (*dol* in French law, fraudulent misrepresentation in English law, German law § 123 BGB etc.) and is treated harshly by the law. However, a duty to inform is often imposed for the very purpose of protecting one of the contracting parties – from the other party's position of superiority, whether in terms of bargaining power, knowledge etc. (for an example, see Case 2).

Secondly, a related reason for suggesting that the aim of a duty to inform is protective is deduced from the types of behaviour it covers. The duty to inform goes further than fraud since it covers not only fraudulent behaviour (whether active or passive) but also negligent behaviour (for an example, see Case 3). Recognising duties to inform may be an admission that mistake and fraud are insufficient to remedy all types of behaviour. For example, under French law the recognition of duties to inform has clearly played a role in highlighting negligently[50] caused mistakes. Negligently caused mistakes arise when incorrect information is provided (not through dishonesty but through negligence). Such mistakes are covered in English, Irish and Scots law by the law of misrepresentation as has already been pointed out.[51]

Thirdly, the duty to inform does not just belong to the realm of defects of consent. To add weight to this assertion, a further distinction is required. To qualify the duty to inform, precontractual duties to inform (duties to inform during the precontractual stage) must be distinguished

---

[50] For the sake of accuracy, it should be noted that 'negligently' or 'negligence' is being used here to cover *faute* or *culpa*. Such behaviour involves carelessness but not intention.

[51] Zweigert and Kötz, *Introduction to Comparative Law*; H. Kötz and A. Flessner, *European Contract Law, Formation, Validity, and Content of Contract; Contract and Third Parties* (translated by T. Weir, Oxford; 1998) vol. I; O. Lando and H. Beale (eds.), *Principles of European Contract Law, Parts I and II* (The Hague, 2000).

from contractual duties to inform (duties to supply information during the course of the contract). Consequently, the former kind of duty to inform may also have the effect of extending the concepts of defective consent into what is recognised today as the larger field of precontractual liability, for example, by using the doctrine under German law of § 242 BGB *culpa in contrahendo* (now §§ 311 II, 241 II, 280 I), or the use of the general principle of art. 1382 of the French Civil Code. Recognising this shift is important for an analysis of the objectives of duties to inform and is linked to the kind of remedies available. As already mentioned, the remedy of annulment can be analysed as a protective measure but it is often criticised as being a drastic all or nothing remedy. Examining duties to inform with mistake and fraud thus extends the scope of the enquiry since looking at awards of damages arising out of a breach of a duty to inform raises a whole series of questions, not only as to their purpose and efficacy, but as to their quantum, means of evaluation and the nature of their liability (contractual or precontractual). Furthermore, this enquiry enables us to examine in depth the precontractual/contractual nature of duties to inform since it will be seen that legal systems often choose one or the other or use both, depending on the circumstances. This choice may be determined by reason of conceptual coherence and of procedural issues. Investigating the presence of duties to inform in European contract law leads us to question what is meant by protection and to show that protecting the aggrieved party may be counterbalanced by an awareness of the other party's behaviour. This awareness represents an important change of attitude for some legal systems.

The search for underlying values in mistake, fraud and duties to inform

Finally, the above rests on the assumption that the objectives of mistake, fraud and duties to inform hinge on traditional legal values attached to contract making – protection of a party's consent in accordance with the will theory, or upholding the moral duty of honesty and telling the truth. This assumption is simplistic for a number of reasons. First, these traditional legal values are open to debate now that the foundations of the will theory (freedom of contract, freedom to contract,[52] party

---

[52] A distinction between freedom of contract, freedom to contract and even freedom from contract may be made; see for example, R. E. Barnett, 'The Duty to Disclose

autonomy etc.) are highly contested.[53] Secondly, these legal values are no doubt more complex than those that are assumed. Nineteenth–century legal values have been displaced not only by twentieth–century legal values introducing numerous other contract law theories as an analytical basis to explain contract law[54] but also by economic analyses[55] which thus deviate from classical legal values of contract and contract-making. It is not of course suggested that economic analyses are in any way more meaningful, or useful than traditional analyses, but their existence cannot be ignored.

This enquiry enables us to unearth a set of formants and values which go far beyond those traditionally assigned to defects of consent. A primary objective of our enquiry is then to attempt to identify the values used by the national legal systems in reply to fact-specific situations which may give rise to mistake, fraud and/or duties to inform. One of our objectives is to examine exactly how each legal system makes use of these values: i.e. to identify what priority is given by which legal system(s) and in what circumstances. Furthermore, this leads us on to question the underlying values in the law of contract since it is important to ascertain how legal theory and values correspond. Sometimes we will see that legal systems have recourse to legal concepts (other than mistake, fraud and duties to inform), perhaps to promote certain values. This, in itself, reveals something about legal policy. It should be noted that these values are not always made explicit by the courts or legal doctrine. It should also be pointed out that many of these values conflict with one another, but this is not surprising for the comparativist.

It is of course somewhat difficult, if not foolhardy, to try to establish an exhaustive list of the values imbedded in mistake, fraud and duty to inform. A list, the aim of which is simply to enumerate some major ideas and to highlight the undercurrent issues follows. The list is not ordered taxonomically.

Information and the Liberal Conception of Fraud' in R. E. Barnett (ed.), *Perspectives on Contract* (Boston, 1995), p. 342.

[53] The literature is far too abundant to cite in full: see e.g. the seminal thesis of E. Gounod, *Le principe de l'autonomie de la volonté en droit privé; Contribution à l'étude critique de l'individualisme*, PhD thesis (Dijon, 1912); Atiyah, *The Rise and Fall of Freedom of Contract*.

[54] Citation of the numerous contract law theories that have appeared in the twentieth century would be hazardous and inevitably selective.

[55] A. T. Kronman, 'Mistake, Disclosure, Information and the Law of Contract' (1978) 7 JLS 1; R. Posner, *Economic Analysis of Law* (2nd edn, Boston, 1979); M. Fabre-Magnan, *De l'obligation d'information dans les contrats, Essai d'une théorie* (Paris, 1992).

  i.   Protecting the consent of the parties.

  ii.   Upholding the security of transactions.

  iii.   Controlling contractual fairness. This can be subdivided into two parts:

    a.   Controlling procedural unfairness in the event that an injustice or abuse by one of the parties leads to damage being suffered by the other.

    b.   Regulating the inequality of exchange through an Aristotelian view of commutative justice which can be referred to as substantive fairness.

  iv.   Upholding the moral duty to tell the truth. Two corollaries follow:

    a.   Dishonesty should be discouraged and treated severely.

    b.   It is immoral to hold a mistaken party to the contract.

  v.   Protecting or compensating the innocent reliance of a mistaken party: this means that the other party is liable for the consequences of that reliance.

  vi.   Imposing or regulating standards of behaviour expected by contracting parties for normative purposes.

  vii.   Setting objective standards in relation to the content of the contract.

  viii.   Allocating risks under the contract.

This study examines the hypothesis that mistake has traditionally been bound up with the validity of contract and consent whereas fraud and duties to inform focus on contractual fairness and liability. How these two approaches fit together is central to our enquiry.

From the beginning, this study aims to discover empirically if there is a trend towards recognising or imposing duties to inform[56] in European contract law, and if so, whether the national laws under enquiry seem to be raising the standard of behaviour expected from the parties in relation to providing information to one another. In fact, one of the things this enquiry sets out to do is to discover whether imposing duties to inform provides a new kind of protection of a party's consent – the suggestion being, to take the medical metaphor of remedies to its limits, that the protection arises through prevention rather than cure. If this is the case, it may well be that the side effect of these developments is to change the face of mistake and to some extent fraud. The relationship between mistake and duties to inform must be examined in depth. Is mistake becoming a subsidiary or residual remedy as a result of duties to inform? Can it be inferred that duties to inform are taking over or have replaced the more traditional concept of mistake?

---

[56] As explained, such duties can be qualified as precontractual or contractual.

Alternatively, it is necessary to investigate whether the relationship between mistake and duties to inform is not one of substitution but of competition.[57]

This study focuses therefore on describing the standards of behaviour of contracting parties by examining when is a duty to inform incumbent and why; when is a party's mistake recognised and remedied by the law.[58] Clearly however, what is of most interest is to uncover the patterns of behaviour the law expects from contracting parties at the precontractual stage and in particular, the remedial approach adopted enables us to ascertain the degrees of protection given, should the parties break such standards. What are the legal concepts used in each of the legal systems under enquiry to exercise such a protection? In other words, does each country use the same or different tools and to what degree? For the avoidance of doubt it should be recalled that there is no presumption that the hypotheses this study sets out to examine can be proven monolithically, indeed it is much more probable that the results will reveal different patterns in the various legal systems under consideration. Moreover, it is recognised that it would be harmful to start from a presumption of similarity,[59] in other words, it is envisaged that it will be necessary to highlight the variations, of nature and degree, of protection given under each national law, and to analyse the reasons for the differences.

The methodological approach of our enquiry has been to induce from the case studies which the national reporters have been asked to solve. The method is essentially casuistic as opposed to deductive. The focus on extracting the law and its formants from case studies lies at the centre of the Common Core of Private Law Project. The project aims to 'search for what is different and what is already common . . . in

---

[57] On the efficiency of competing legal concepts, see U. Mattei, *Economic Analysis and Comparative Law* (Ann Arbor, 1998).

[58] See D. Kennedy, 'The Methods and Politics of Comparative Law' in M. Bussani and U. Mattei (eds.), *The Common Core of European Private Law* (Boston; London, The Hague, 2003), pp. 131–207, at p. 149 who calls this generating a plausible causal account of what has been mapped. See also H. Collins (quoted by Kennedy), 'Methods and Aims of Comparative Contract Law' (1991) 11 OJLS 396, at p. 398 who suggests that it is almost impossible to achieve this method as the comparativist always leaves out one of the dimensions (culture, society, history, politics and legal logic) in his explanation. We would point out that we are self-critical of the method adopted.

[59] Zweigert and Kötz, *Introduction to Comparative Law*, p. 39. For a strong criticism of this presumption, see the abundant writings of P. Legrand, who insists on the differences, not the similarities. See e.g. P. Legrand, *Fragments on Law-as-Culture* (Deventer, 1999).

order to draw a reliable map of the law of Europe'.[60] Its method aims to be descriptive and critically neutral; there is no intention of striving for uniformity or even harmonisation. Likewise at the other extreme, although recognising that cultural diversity is an asset, no desire to be preservationist or chauvinistically conservative is present.[61] Even within the project, a certain degree of pluralism of opinion is both recognised and welcomed.[62] The aim of this work is to identify similarities and differences as induced from the practical appplication of legal rules in relation to fact-specific situations, as already stated; this enterprise is relatively neutral, at first sight. Consequently, our enquiry attempts to trace the patterns identifiable in mistake, fraud and duties to inform in the legal systems examined. Our enquiry remains sceptical both as to the significance of the common core and also as to the neutrality of its approach.[63] To put it simply, even if we attempt to be neutral, experience has shown that this is not entirely possible. In a sense, this does not matter as long as one is under no illusions. Lastly, our research aims at including in the description of the lie of the land a critical analytical explanation (where possible) of why we have found the picture shown. It is perhaps this enquiry as to underlying values, outlined in the comparative observations at the end of each case, which may fuel scepticism about neutrality. This is somewhat inevitable since a comparative exercise that merely describes will no doubt be insufficient and an attempt to explain slides into an exercise which cannot be wholly neutral. With that in mind, our comparative aim is to compare and contrast,[64] for the purposes of increasing our awareness. This can only occur through practice.

To summarise, this study aims therefore to test whether a theoretical shift from contractual validity (a procedural question) to contractual fairness (a substantive question) is taking place in European contract

---

[60] For a recent restatement of the project's aims; see Bussani and Mauro (eds.), *The Common Core of European Private Law*, pp. 1–9.

[61] On culturalism and chauvinism, see the debates at the Amsterdam conference on European critical legal theory in Eur. Rev. Priv. Law 1 (2002).

[62] Bussani and Mattei, *The Common Core of European Private Law*, pp. 2–3.

[63] For a discussion about what he calls 'methodological eclecticism and political neutrality', see D. Kennedy, 'The Methods and Politics of Comparative Law' in M. Bussani and U. Mattei (eds.), *The Common Core of European Private Law*, pp. 131–207; R. Sefton-Green, 'Le défi d'un droit commun des obligations' in M. Delmas-Marty, H. Muir Watt and H. Ruiz-Fabri (eds.) *Variations autour d'un droit commun* (Paris, 2002), pp. 443 ff. See also our comparative conclusions below.

[64] See R. Sefton-Green, 'Compare and Contrast: Monstre à deux têtes' (2002) RIDComp 85 ff.

law. It is submitted that this shift can be demonstrated, *inter alia*, by the emergence and increasing emphasis given to duties to inform. In order to investigate the lines of enquiry outlined above, three guidelines should be borne in mind:

i. Is the law focusing on the standards of behaviour expected of contracting parties rather than on the parties' consent?

ii. Is it true to contend that the content of the contract is scrutinised according to objective standards?

iii. Is the process of concluding the contract (i.e. the precontractual phase) taking precedence over the consent of the parties?

In order to understand what is meant by mistake, fraud and the duty to inform in this study, it may be helpful to identify and describe the conceptual classifications present in the national laws, which may appear more radically divergent than they actually are in practice. For this purpose it will be our aim to see whether some preconceptions about differences and similarities (civil law versus common law?) can be knocked down.[65]

Identifying the heart of the matter

The heart of this study needs to be identified; what is meant by mistake, fraud and duties to inform? What does European contract law mean? Starting with the second question, the thirteen European countries whose laws have been examined are the following: Austria, Belgium, England, France, Germany, Greece, Ireland, Italy, The Netherlands, Norway, Portugal, Spain and Scotland. The Norwegian report includes an overview of Swedish and Danish law as well, and for comparative purposes reference is sometimes made to Scandinavia. The reports of each country are presented in alphabetical order. Our aim is to carry out an inductive empirical enquiry. In order for the reader to familiarise himself with the three main concepts that form the heart of the enquiry, these are introduced briefly.

---

[65] In this respect we should point out that the civil law/common law divide is not an assumption relied on in this study. Quite the reverse. Nevertheless, the labels 'civil law' and 'common law' are used sometimes for the sake of convenience. Using such labels has often led to a realisation of how false the assumption is, which has led to an attempt to eliminate them as far as possible. Furthermore, for those versed in comparative legal study, it is apparent that the very terms are devoid of significance. What is a 'civil law' country? A country that has a codified legal system perhaps. Within such countries the term 'civil law' means something quite different since civil law is opposed to commercial law or some other branch of the codified system.

Mistake

To understand the contours and the colours of mistake some of the central issues raised by the doctrine of mistake, which need to be examined in this enquiry and have been implemented in the cases, are underlined. No attempt to define mistake will be made, since each national reporter in Case 1 has done this.

What kinds of mistake are operative?

The classification of mistake as fundamental

France, Belgium, Spain, Italy, The Netherlands and Portugal deriving mistake from the Roman law conceptions of *substantia* and *qualitas*, present an apparent similarity of approach. Moving from the mere textual definition, requiring mistake to pertain to the essence or the substance of the thing or the person, an extension has been made by case law to include essential or substantial qualities of the thing or the person. German law makes a further distinction since § 119 BGB is divided into two definitions: the first clause covers the so-called 'mistake in declaration or expression' as to meaning or to content, comparable to the Dutch 'mistake improper' (*oneigenlijke dwaling*), the second 'mistake as to subject matter' or *error in substantiali qualitate*.[66] Austrian law also frames mistake about the content of the declaration relating to an essential thing. Greek law distinguishes two instances of fundamental mistake: (i) mistake as to the declaration (art. 140 AK) which is due to a discrepancy between the will and the declaration and (ii) mistake as to the qualities of a person or thing (art. 142 AK). Norwegian law specifically governs only a 'mistake in transaction'.[67] Scots law contains a complex categorisation of mistake.[68] In order to harmonise this idea, and avoid an excessive variation of vocabulary, we have agreed to call such a mistake fundamental.

Unilateral, mutual and shared mistakes

In England, Ireland and Scotland, the main categories of mistake are distinguished according to whether the mistake is unilateral[69] (made by

---

[66] Of course, these two subsections represent the tension between the theory of declaration (*Erklärungstheorie*) and the will theory (*Willenstheorie*) respectively. The same tension is found in § 871 ABGB.

[67] Section 32, The Norwegian Contract Act, see Case 12 for an example.

[68] See Scots report, Case 1 where the conditions are set out in full.

[69] Cartwright, *Unequal Bargaining*, p. 4, explains this as where the parties are at cross-purposes.

one party only), mutual[70] (both parties make a mistake but not the same mistake) and shared or common[71] (both parties make the same mistake). At first glance, this conceptual classification seems to differentiate the civil law and common law approaches. On one interpretation, civil law admits unilateral mistakes relatively easily. This is no doubt because greater emphasis is given to protecting the aggrieved party, sometimes at the expense of legal certainty.[72] Here is an example of how legal terminology can be misleading. In most civil law countries 'unilateral mistake' may also be opposed to a 'common mistake'. A unilateral mistake is thus one where the non-mistaken party does not know that the mistaken quality is important; a common mistake is therefore one where the non-mistaken party knew, or should have known of the importance of the mistaken quality.[73] A further qualifier is necessary since it has been pointed out that Dutch law does not attach the so-called civil law meaning to 'common mistake', for it has the same meaning under Dutch law as the so-called common law terminology.[74] It should be clear at once that although the same terms are used, their meaning is entirely different. According to the common law terminology, unilateral (and indeed mutual) mistakes are cross-party mistakes, but there is absolutely no onus on the non-mistaken party to be aware of the importance that the mistaken quality represents to the mistaken party.

Mistakes as to the person

This category of mistake is recognised but not often admitted in practice in nearly all the systems examined. This kind of mistake has not been considered in great depth although it raises the following important question: in what type of contract is the identity of the contracting parties important? A potential mistake as to the person can be identified in Case 12.

---

[70] Cheshire, Fifoot and Furmston's *Law of Contract* (14th edn, London, 2001); see also Treitel, *The Law of Contract*, pp. 298–310, who calls this a mistake negativing consent.

[71] J. Beatson (ed.), *Anson's Law of Contract* (28th edn, Oxford, 2002) calls these mistakes 'mutual'. For Treitel, these are mistakes which negative consent.

[72] See above at pp. 5–8.

[73] Ghestin, *La formation du contrat*, no. 524, p. 488. However, although the signified is clearly present the term unilateral mistake (*erreur unilaterale*) is not actually used; see below p. 21 for the condition in Italian law etc. that the mistake be recognisable, see also Kötz and Flessner, *European Contract Law*, p. 188.

[74] Again, my thanks to Martijn Hesselink who pointed this out to me; this simply proves the point that civil law and common law labels lead to confusion and mistakes! Moreover, it should be recalled that art. 4:103 PECL on mistake adopts the so-called common law terminology.

What kinds of mistake are inoperative?

By contrast, non-fundamental and consequently inoperative mistakes, may be of two types: either relating to motive, or to the value of the thing.

Mistake as to motive

German, Greek and Austrian law all make use of this distinction explicitly and reject mistakes as to motive as non-fundamental.[75] This rejection is said to reflect Savigny's theoretical distinction between two stages in contracting, the moment when the party is forming his intention and actually expressing it.[76] Other civil law systems share this idea though it is not expressed in the texts: French law does not admit a mistake *sur les simples motifs*,[77] or more positively requires that the importance of the 'mistaken quality' has entered into the contractual field.[78] Obviously this cannot be the case if the mistake rests in the unexpressed intention of the mistaken party.

Mistake as to value of the subject matter

No legal system admits mistakes as to the value of the subject matter. These too are non-fundamental mistakes. A much-criticised distinction is drawn between a mistake as to the value of the subject matter of the contract and a mistake as to the qualities of the thing which affects its value,[79] the former being non-fundamental, the latter fundamental. It has been suggested that the distinction is artificial and that a more appropriate formula is to examine the mistake in terms of apportionment of risk.[80] Clearly, not even the most protective of systems will admit that all mistakes are operative otherwise the consequences for the security of transactions would be disastrous.

---

[75] § 119(1) BGB, art. 143 AK, § 901 line 2 ABGB.

[76] Kötz and Flessner, *European Contract Law*, p. 182, nn. 46–7. See German and Greek reports for criticisms, in Case 1.

[77] Ghestin, *La formation du contrat*, no. 507, pp. 472 ff.

[78] See the French report in Case 1 for a more detailed explanation.

[79] Kötz and Flessner, *European Contract Law*, p. 183.

[80] Note that the distinction is not universally criticised, see e.g. German and Greek law where such criticisms are made. Contrast with French law, for example, a mistake as to mere value can be conceptually distinguished from a mistake as to the qualities or substance of the thing affecting its value. When the latter constitutes an erroneous economic assessment arising from exact data it is qualified as a fundamental mistake (*sur la substance*). See Ghestin, *La formation*, p. 474.

Bars to recognising operative unilateral mistakes

Numerous bars or limits on unilateral mistake can be identified; the first relates to the behaviour of the non-mistaken party. In France, Belgium, Spain, and Italy (inspired by French case law before the 1942 Italian Civil Code, but also today) judges use a bar, developed as a result of case law, that excludes annulment if the mistake has occurred as a result of the mistaken party's behaviour, described as inexcusable. It may be appropriate to term this the fault or negligence of the mistaken party[81] but we have preferred to use the language of excusable and inexcusable behaviour. The second limit on a mistake is the knowledge (constructive knowledge may be inferred) of the non-mistaken party of the mistake made by the mistaken party. Austrian, Italian[82] Portuguese[83] and Dutch law make use of this criterion.[84] In other words, if the non-mistaken party did not know about the mistake, the mistaken party cannot plead his mistake. This may be another version of a unilateral mistake.[85] The

---

[81] Kötz and Flessner, *European Contract Law*, pp. 185 ff.

[82] Article 1431 of the Italian Civil Code phrases this in the requirement that the mistake must be recognisable (*recognisibile*), see the Italian report, Case 1.

[83] It is noticeable that the majority of Portuguese scholars have rejected the requirement of the excusability of the mistake on the basis that this would restrict contracts from being annulled for mistake and that most mistakes are usually based on at least negligence by the mistaken party. See J. Tavares, *Os princípios fundamentais de Direito Civil* (Coimbra, 1928), vol. II, p. 501; C. Gonçalves, *Tratado de Direito Civil* (Coimbra, 1931), vol. IV, pp. 304–5; M. De Andrade, *Teoria geral da relação jurídica* (Coimbra, 1960), vol. II, p. 240; F. Correia, *Erro e interpretação na teoria do negócio jurídico* (2nd edn, Coimbra, 1968), pp. 294 ff.; R. De Alarcão, 'Breve Motivação do Anteprojecto sobre o negócio juridico na parte relativa ao erro, dolo, coacção, representação, condição e objecto negocial' in (1964) BMJ 138, pp. 71–122, at pp. 88–90; V. Serra, Anotação ao Ac. STJ3/7/1973, in RLJ 107 (1975), pp. 219–23, and 228–32, Anotação ao Ac. STJ 14/3/1979, RLJ 112 (1980), pp. 267–8, and 274–5; P. De Lima and A. Varela, *Código Civil Anotado* (4th edn, Coimbra, 1987), vol. I, p. 233; C. Mendes, *Teoria geral do Direito Civil* (Lisbon, 1985), vol. II, pp. 91 ff.; O. A. Ascensão, *Teoria Geral do Direito Civil* (Lisbon, 1992), vol. III, pp. 109–10; C. Mota Pinto, *Teoria geral do Direito Civil* (3rd edn, Coimbra, 1985), pp. 511 ff.; C. Fernandes, *Teoria geral do Direito Civil* (2nd edn, Lisbon, 1996), vol. II, pp. 131 ff.; P. Mota Pinto, *Declaração tácita e comportamento concludente no negócio jurídico* (Coimbra, 1995), pp. 406 ff., n. (440). Portuguese law appears to be very protective of the mistaken party and only a small minority of scholars have suggested that the excusability of the mistake should be considered but this view has not been accepted by the courts: see B. Dos Santos, *A simulação em Direito Civil* (Coimbra, 1921), vol. I, pp. 55–6; L. Cabral De Moncada, *Lições de Direito Civil* (4th edn, Coimbra, 1995), p. 619, n. (2), and p. 628; G. Telles, *Manual dos Contratos em Geral* (3rd edn, Coimbra, 1965), pp. 80–1 and M. Cordeiro, *Da Boa Fé no Direito Civil* (Coimbra, 1984), vol. I, pp. 516 ff.

[84] As does art. 4:103 PECL.   [85] See at (ii) above.

third identifiable criterion is the assumption of risks, a consideration used by German law[86] and Dutch law for example.[87] Other factors, such as causation of the mistake by the other party may be used as a criterion. Scots law, for example, refers to an 'uninduced unilateral error'.[88] Austrian law also examines whether or not the non-mistaken party caused the mistake.[89] Likewise, misrepresentation in English (and Scots) law is nothing other than that: a mistake induced by a statement or conduct of the other party. If the other party (the misrepresentee) also made the same mistake as the misrepresentor, it is (i) innocent misrepresentation and (ii) common mistake. If the other party (the misrepresentee) did not make the same mistake as the misrepresentor, it is (i) misrepresentation and (ii) unilateral mistake.[90] Finally, the absence or presence of reliance of the non-mistaken party on the contract may likewise exclude[91] or qualify[92] the annulment, whereas in some national systems, reliance is not a significant factor.[93]

Miscellaneous concepts other than mistake

We have not deliberately set out to find functional equivalents[94] for mistake. Intuitively, the national reporters have suggested other remedies

---

[86] See Case 1 for an example. Kötz and Flessner, *European Contract Law*, pp. 184–6, suggest that the question of whether or not a mistake falls into the sphere of risk of the mistaken party can be equated with taking into account the fault of the mistaken party.

[87] Article 6:228(2) BW (Dutch code). See Case 1. and the analysis of the Kantharos case.

[88] See Case 1, Scots report.

[89] If the non-mistaken party has caused the mistake, he is not entitled to protection and annulment will be granted (§ 871 ABGB). See Case 1, Austrian report for a full explanation.

[90] I am grateful to John Cartwright for formulating this idea. It is noteworthy that few English contract law books make the association between mistake and misrepresentation. See however, R. Goff and G. Jones, *The Law of Restitution* (6th edn, London, 2002), ch. 9 and J. Cartwright, *Misrepresentation* (London, 2002); whereas the overlap between mistake and misrepresentation is much more obvious to comparative lawyers or civil lawyers generally. See for example, Zweigert and Kötz, *Introduction to Comparative Law*, pp. 419–21; Kötz and Flessner, *European Contract Law*, p. 173.

[91] See Austrian report, Case 1. Likewise Dutch law considers whether a mistake was due to a statement by the other party (art. 6: 228a BW).

[92] See German and Greek reports, Case 1.

[93] For example in systems closely linked to the will theory of contract, e.g. France and Belgium.

[94] For an account of functionalism as a methodology used by comparativists, see D. Kennedy's explanation of Zweigert and Kötz's methodology, in 'The Methods and Politics of Comparative Law', pp. 170–5.

when attempting to find the solution to cases since they were asked to consider all available remedies on offer for the claimant. By identifying these other remedies we are not in any way presuming that they are functional equivalents. However, it is necessary to introduce a number of concepts to familiarise the reader with the panoply of available remedies. The comparative observations after each case point out what role these other remedies actually play.

German law has sometimes referred to the doctrine of 'the failure of the basis of the transaction'[95] (now called *Geschäftsgrundlage*[96]), originally traceable to the customary law *rebus sic stantibus*.[97] Greek law has also been influenced by German law,[98] as has Italian law with its doctrine of *presupposizione*.[99] The Netherlands uses a concept called *dezelfde onjuiste veronderstelling* (shared mistaken assumptions) under art. 6:228 (c) BW which is however part of the mistake doctrine. It also has a doctrine of change of circumstances (*onvoorziene omstandigheden*), which only applies in case of 'mistake' with regard to assumptions relating to the future. In Scandinavian countries, also influenced by German legal theory, a doctrine of contractual assumptions was developed principally through Danish writing.[100] A common term is 'failed contractual assumptions' (*sviktende forutsetninger*).[101]

Two important provisions of Scandinavian law must be emphasised: in the common Scandinavian contract legislation from the early 1900s, a general rule with respect to honest behaviour and good faith on entering into agreements was accepted (cf. the Contract Act § 33.4). In the 1980s, a remarkable expansion of the invalidity regulations in Scandinavian law took place by the adoption of the Contract Act § 36, the so-called General Clause, which applies to 'unreasonable contracts'.

---

[95] The concept has been developed by B. Windscheid, *Die Lehre des römischen Rechts von der voraussetzung* (1850), pp. 80 ff.

[96] P. Oertmann, *Die Geschäftsgrundlage – ein neuer Rechtsbegriff* (1921), p. 37. 'The basis of the transaction is the assumption or expectation of one party or the mutual assumption or expectation of several parties which arises at the conclusion of the contract relating to the existence of the intervention of those circumstances constituting the basis for the intention underlying the transaction and the importance of which is recognised and not objected to by the other party.' I am indebted to Martin Schermaier for this explanation.

[97] See more specifically, in Chapter 2, pp. 39–64 below.

[98] For examples, see Case 1, German report; Case 6, Greek report.

[99] See the Italian report for an illustration, Case 1.

[100] A more recent description of the doctrine is found in the monograph, B. Lehrberg, *Förutsettningsläran* (Uppsala, 1989).

[101] See the Norwegian report, Case 1 for a full explanation.

French and Belgian law have sometimes referred to the concept of *absence de cause*, as an alternative remedy to that under the head of mistake. Italian law also uses the concept of *causa*.[102] The cause of the contract is an essential condition of its validity and is thus distinct from defects of consent.[103]

Finally, the concepts of *laesio enormis*[104] and *lésion qualifiée*[105] have been considered.

Fraud

Fraud is relatively straightforward as a concept, its main component being an intention to deceive. What actually constitutes fraud is possibly more complicated and is left to discussion in the cases. Fraud gives the right to annulment and damages. In some cases it will deprive the fraudulent and non-mistaken party of his right to damages for negative interest,[106] as already discussed. The reason why fraud is not treated in much detail as a separate concept is that it tends to overlap with duties to inform.[107] It is because of the overlap that fraud has been included in this study. It is impossible to treat either mistake or duties to inform without touching on fraud.

Duties to inform

The common and civil law systems divide over the precontractual obligation to provide information. Very generally, civil law countries impose a precontractual duty to inform more liberally than their common law

---

[102] See for example, Case 9.   [103] See Case 12 for an example.

[104] Under Austrian law, see Case 1.   [105] Under Belgian law, see Case 1.

[106] 'Negative interest' can be roughly explained as follows: although the aggrieved party may be entitled to annul the contract, his remedy is counterbalanced by his liability to the non-aggrieved party for the harm which the latter has suffered as a result of relying on the validity of the contract. These damages are also called 'reliance interest', based on the idea that reliance underlies the contractual relationship. The idea belongs to German law and other systems influenced by German law also recognise it (Italy, Greece, Portugal and Spain). See the seminal article of Fuller and Perdue, 'The Reliance Interest in Contract Damages' (1936) 46 Yale LJ 52; p. 373 which suggests that reliance interest is also contained, although not explicitly recognised, by American law.

[107] An objection raised by M. Hesselink suggests that duties to inform overlap with mistake (as under Dutch and German law) but the same argument was not mentioned above; this might be begging the question since this study sets out to examine this triangular overlap and it is certainly not obvious for all national systems considered that duties to inform overlap with mistake.

counterparts.[108] It appears trite to state that the common law does not recognise a general duty of disclosure; on the contrary some would say that it discourages such a principle on the grounds of *inter alia* economic-based analyses.[109] The presence of a duty to provide information can be ascertained first by examining its negative aspect, which is most clearly seen by the differing attitudes towards silence. For example, French law's attitude to silence is that it can be penalised if framed in terms of a fraudulent concealment.[110] Other national laws call this negative fraud.[111] In Dutch law this is framed as a mistake, caused by a breach of the duty to inform. The mere existence of the duty implies that silence is reprehensible. It may even be more accurate to suggest, as already mentioned, that a positive duty to inform has been inferred from silence.[112] According to Nicholas, such a method of induction-deduction from and to general propositions runs contrary to the grain in English law since the latter develops propositions of law incrementally.[113] In contrast, the common law's view of silence is that no remedy is available unless a positive statement has been made. Thus, misrepresentation, a common law concept, cuts straight across mistake and the duty to inform. Moreover, misrepresentation cannot be equated to a duty to inform since the duty to tell the truth does not arise at the same point in time. Whereas a duty to inform imposes a positive duty to tell the truth (and sometimes a negative duty not to conceal the truth), misrepresentation does not impose a duty (positive or negative) to make an initial statement. The point of misrepresentation (including conduct, half-truths and active fraudulent concealment) is that when statements are made, they must be truthful.

Furthermore, the importance of (fraudulent) concealment as a means of identifying a positive duty to inform should be highlighted. It has been suggested that imposing a duty to inform may raise the standard

---

[108] See P. Legrand, 'Pre-Contractual Disclosure and Information, English and French Law Compared' (1986) 6 OJLS 322; J. Ghestin, 'The Pre-Contractual Obligation to Disclose Information: French Report', pp. 151 ff. in D. Harris and D. Tallon (eds.), *Contract Law Today: Anglo-French Comparisons* (Oxford, 1989) and B. Nicholas, *ibid*. English Report, pp. 166 ff.

[109] B. Rudden, 'Le juste et l'inefficace, pour un non-devoir de renseignement' (1985), RTDCiv, 91 ff.

[110] On the notion of *réticence dolosive*, see the French report, Case 2.

[111] Spanish law refers to negative fraud (see Cases 2 and 6), whereas the Italian reporter suggests the concept may be useful although it is not yet recognised (see Case 2).

[112] See Ghestin, 'The Pre-Contractual Obligation to Disclose Information: French Report'.

[113] See Nicholas, 'The Pre-Contractual Obligation to Disclose Information: English Report'.

of behaviour expected of contracting parties.[114] Let us examine how this can be done.

At first sight, it seems possible to identify four distinct foundations of the duty to inform, the first two of which are related:

The first foundation is fraud, i.e. an intention to deceive constituting an autonomous concept categorised for the most part as a defect of consent. We could describe this as a fraudulently induced mistake. All systems have some version of this concept. The common law version is found in the concept of fraudulent misrepresentation, subject to the observations made earlier about the exclusive scope of the duty to inform and misrepresentation. Under Scandinavian law, this may be covered by more general invalidity rules.[115] We have called the German concept under §123 BGB 'fraudulent misrepresentation'. The immediate remedy is annulment. It may be possible to cumulate this ground with a claim for damages[116] or else the fraudulent behaviour of the non-mistaken party will preclude the annulling party from paying compensation for negative interest.[117] Alternatively, it is possible in some systems to claim damages exclusively, without claiming annulment, if the latter is barred because of time limitations or because the contract has been confirmed.[118] In English law, bars operating to preclude annulment may connote a similar idea.

The second foundation could be called more generally precontractual liability. In French law, for example, the obligation to act in good faith in the formation of contracts is deemed to be encompassed in the general provisions on delict and quasi-delict (arts. 1382–3 *Code civil*). The generality of these provisions (reference is made to *faute*) means that a negligent breach of duty to inform is covered here as well as fraudulent breach. Damages are the only remedy subject to the proviso below. This foundation may be cumulated with fraud, where appropriate (including

---

[114] The suggestion will be tested in the rest of this study.

[115] Section 30, para. 1 of the Contracts Act states: 'If a declaration of will is obtained by means of fraud on the side of the other party, the said declaration shall not be binding for the person who has made it. The same applies in cases where a third party has obtained a declaration of will by means of fraud, and the second party was, or should have been, aware of the fact.'

[116] For example, in France and Belgium this is possible under arts. 1116 and 1382–3 of the Civil Code.

[117] This is the position in Austrian, German and Greek law, for an example, see Case 4.

[118] French and Belgian laws have a doctrine of 'confirmation', see the Belgian report, Case 4, for an example.

fraud by omission or fraudulent concealment) so that the claimant may ask for annulment and damages. It is logically sound[119] that the remedy is tortious since either the contract is annulled and retrospectively void; or else, if the contract is not annulled, the breach took place at a moment in time when the contract did not yet exist.[120] Other versions of precontractual liability exist, the most famous being the doctrine of *culpa in contrahendo* under § 242 BGB (now §§ 311 II, 241I, 280).[121] This action gives rise to a claim for damages or termination as damages *in specie*. This doctrine is also recognised in Austria, Greece, Italy and Portugal.

It may be submitted that negligent and innocent misrepresentation in English, Scots and Irish law is also a form of precontractual liability. This does not totally exclude fraudulent misrepresentation being treated within this category. This suggestion is made on the basis that damages for misrepresentation are based on tortious liability and make the misrepresentor liable for his actions prior to the contract's conclusion. Treating misrepresentation as a form of precontractual liability is therefore relatively uncontroversial. A further objection, that has already been mentioned, may however arise. It is not entirely accurate to present misrepresentation within the general category of a duty to inform and the statement requires qualification. Misrepresentation is rather a duty to tell the truth – that the information provided be accurate – which is not exactly the same thing as a duty to inform, since the breach of the duty is only remedied at a second later stage, once the information has been given. There is no onus to supply information in the first place.

The third foundation is a duty, which might be qualified as arising by operation of law, thus imposing a norm of behaviour. The meaning of this expression is twofold. Either the duty arises as a result of special legislative provisions (*lex specialis*) e.g. insurance law, consumer protection, banking law etc.[122] or case law says that the duty exists as a result of usage, business practice according to one of the following criteria: the particular contractual relationship, the status of the parties, the inequality of the parties: an inequality as to informational power or an

---

[119] Logic is of course not the sole criterion in law; it is also conceivable that such liability be considered *sui generis*.

[120] Ghestin, *La formation du contrat*, no. 665, p. 646.

[121] See the German report, Case 6 for an example.

[122] See for examples in insurance contracts Case 10; for consumer protection generally, see Cases 6 and 8; for guarantee contracts, see Case 9.

asymmetry of bargaining power etc.[123] It is submitted that a similar idea is expressed in the general clauses of the Norwegian Contract Act (sections 33 and 36) which allow the contract to be put aside when contrary to good faith or when considered unreasonable, where regard should be given, among other factors, to good business practice.[124] Moreover, the main emphasis in Scandinavian law lies in the question of 'unreasonableness'; 'good business practice' constitutes only one, albeit significant aspect. Arguably, promoting unreasonableness as a major criterion for interpretation is the strongest evidence of imposing a norm of behaviour. An underlying rationale may be found in the expression of a special relationship of trust or even reliance between the parties. Such a relationship may help explain why such a duty is found to exist. This hypothesis will be tested in a number of different contractual relationships illustrated in the cases.

Plausibly, the common law version of a duty of disclosure may well fit into the third category. As a general principle no duty to inform arises in common law systems according to the adage *caveat emptor*. However, a duty of disclosure may arise in exceptional circumstances. In these specific and limited circumstances, it may be submitted that the duty to disclose starts to resemble the civil law version of a duty to inform, since a positive duty lies on the person who has the relevant information and the condition of a relationship of trust is inevitably present. It is therefore necessary to identify when and why such a special duty arises, e.g. in insurance law and contracts *uberrimae fidei*. Furthermore, it is becoming easier to question the primacy of the general principle *caveat emptor* in English law.[125] The cases in this study illustrate usefully the extent to which the principle still exists.

The fourth foundation is of course mistake, i.e. causing a mistake by (negligently) omitting to inform. Such a foundation exists in Dutch law[126] and gives rise to a remedy in addition to damages since the contract can obviously be annulled on this ground.

It is crucial to consider the relationship between mistake, fraud and duties to inform, now that they have been presented separately: to what extent are they cumulative legal bases? Is one preferable to the other

---

[123] Dutch law relies on art. 6:228 BW, s. 2; Austrian law uses the criterion of business usage; Greek law uses good faith in art. 288 AK. See for an example of the parties' inequality of bargaining power and knowledge, Case 2.

[124] See the Scandinavian report, in Case 2.

[125] Nicholas, 'The Pre-Contractual Obligation to Disclose: English Report'.

[126] See for Dutch law, Cases 2 and 6 for example.

as far as the innocent party is concerned? This raises an important and related issue as to whether duties to inform are going to swallow the older more traditional concepts, such as mistake and fraud. To put it another way, we need to investigate whether duties to inform strictly belong to defects of consent and contract formation.

If it is true that mistake, fraud and duties to inform are in the process of evolution, arguably this is a reflection of a change in underlying legal values of contract; in any event this study will enable us not only to identify these changes but also to attempt to ascertain what are the reasons for their occurring. One obvious answer may lie in the fact that the procedures and the circumstances in which contracts are made are changing, to take but one example used in this study,[127] contracts qualified as door-step sales are subject to special protective legislation, and this surely has a profound effect on the requirements of consent in contracting.[128] Another reason for the shift lies in the fact that expectations about contract-making and contracts in general are changing. This may lead to an enquiry into the relationship between contract-dynamics (contract-making) and contract-products (the end result).[129] Inevitably, a study, which examines the lie of the land as to the former, cannot neglect the latter or the relationship between the two. In other words, examining defects of consent requires a description and inspection of both procedural and substantive fairness in contract.[130]

Such questions will have the effect of bringing others to the surface. Two phenomena, that of specialisation of contracts and that of specific legislation[131] (the two being subject to mutual exclusivity and overlap) have to be considered in the development of defects of consent. Do defects of consent still have a remedial role to play in the general

---

[127] See Case 9.

[128] This has been the subject of discussion in French law for example; controversy has arisen over the influence that the 'cooling-off period' has had on the time of formation of the contract as well as the nature of consent, since the sanctity previously attached to giving one's consent is subject to a change – one can always (within time-limits) take it back! See for example, J. Calais-Auloy, 'L'influence du droit de la consommation sur le droit civil des contrats' (1994) RTDCiv 239 ff.; C. Thibierge-Guelfucci, 'Libres propos sur la transformation du droit des contrats' (1997) RTDCiv 357 ff.

[129] See for example on the distinction between contract as a dynamic and static process – G. Rouhette, *Contribution à l'étude critique de la notion de contrat*, PhD thesis (Paris, 1965).

[130] On procedural and substantial fairness, see for example, P. S. Atiyah, 'Contract and Fair Exchange' in *Essays on Contract* (2nd edn, Oxford, 1990), pp. 329 ff.

[131] See further on this point, p. 36 below.

theory of contract[132] and/or in specific contracts?[133] Is the role traditionally assigned to defects of consent now residual in the face of increasing
leges speciales?[134] Is the role of defects of consent diminishing or increasing in European contract law? This study purports to answer such critical
questions.

Choice of remedial approach: cutting across legal concepts

Choosing a remedial approach has had the effect of uniting systems
that would otherwise seem to display quite extraordinary conceptual
differences. However, if an opposition is to be made between a conceptual and remedial approach, it is also important to consider the relationship between legal concept and remedy under each national law.
Remedies must be examined in the light of two dichotomies: prevention
versus annulment and/or compensation; annulment versus damages.
Finally, attention should be paid to whether the remedies offered are the
result of general rules or specific legislation. Our remedial choice can be
justified in a number of ways.

First, on a purely pragmatic level, and to put it rather bluntly, what
counts at the end of the day is the possibility of action for a 'victim',[135]
either of a mistake or of a duty to inform. Examining mistake and duties
to inform from a more theoretical conceptual point of view would not
only fail to meet the standards of the Trento common core approach but
would moreover fall prey to the criticisms of a construction along the
lines of a *cas d'école* – which is very far from our objectives. Secondly and
more critically, even if it may be alleged that our remedial approach is
not entirely neutral, it is believed it was the only sensible line of investigation. This line has put the factual approach to the forefront while
bringing up to the surface the conceptual mixtures which do not divide

---

[132] This begs the question of whether a general theory of contract exists or ever existed,
Savaux, *La théorie générale du contrat: mythe ou réalité*.

[133] By specific contracts, reference is made to the civil law distinction between nominate
or special contracts, as opposed to the general theory of contract. The term is not
unknown to English law since it is the title of Chitty on contracts, volume II.

[134] It should be noted that the interpretation given to the concept of *lex specialis* varies
among the legal systems considered. For example, German law adopts a strict view of
lex specialis in the law of sales which means that mistake, but not fraud, may be
excluded by remedies under the law of sales, see the German report in Case 3 for an
example and further explanation.

[135] The term is perhaps another example of the moralistic connotations used by the law,
see above.

simply into common law and civil law opposites, as may at first sight be presumed. Finally, it has been suggested it is important to examine the relationship between legal concepts and remedies in each national law. What needs to be borne in mind here is the initial crucial question of whether and to what extent *ubi ius ibi remedium* or inversely *ubi remedium ibi ius*. In other words, remedies shape their legal counterparts – the concept or institution – and vice versa. This is an additional reason why the remedial approach has had the advantage of refining an examination of legal concepts, such as mistake, fraud and duties to inform. It reveals perfectly the stratification of formants[136] (legal and extra-legal), which the Trento common core methodology emphasises. Sometimes we will see that the disparity between the stated black letter rule of the law and the reality is flagrant – and this gap is most accurately revealed by our remedial approach. Thus, our enquiry uncovers a highly textured tapestry and unravelling the different coloured threads is a rewarding challenge.

More concretely, the cases have been designed to display the wide range of choice of remedies available and to emphasise a number of determining factors, which may influence the claimant's choice. To mention but a few examples, these may turn on the evaluation of damages, time limits, evidential difficulties, the effectiveness or adequacy of the remedy, the retrospective nature of annulment and its consequences in the law of restitution, the retrospective nature (or not) of termination, the passing on of property to innocent third parties and whether this excludes annulment or whether the monetary equivalent can be the object of restitution etc. The remedies available for mistake, fraud and duties to inform are not limited to annulment and damages but can also include rectification and adjustment of the contract. All these factors operate and produce convergence and divergence in the national laws under consideration.

In what fields of law have we applied this approach in our study of mistake, fraud and duties to inform?

A conscious choice was made right at the beginning to avoid the pitfall of narrowing the inevitable link between mistake and contracts of sale. Mistake and the duty to inform inevitably cover a much wider range of contracts; a fact which is sometimes forgotten in the classical textbook approach setting out the legal rules. In this sense, reliance has been

---

[136] R. Sacco, 'Legal Formants: A Dynamic Approach to Comparative Law' (1991) 39 AJCL 1 ff.; 343 ff.

placed, on the one hand on the theory of defective consent as part of the general rules of the theory of contract and, on the other hand, on the important contribution played by special contracts to illustrate and derogate from the general rules. Although this approach may at first glance seem more influenced by civilian systematic considerations, since the common law does not consciously analyse in categories of special contracts to the same extent, it is believed that this approach is useful and appropriate for a number of reasons, not least because it represents a common reality. In other words, conceptual explanations aside, it is first relevant to categorise the various illustrations of mistake and the duty to inform according to the nature of the contract for the very reason that in the presence of differing conceptual analyses, the nature or type of contract must be a common denominating factor in all national systems (barring disagreement about characterising the nature of the contract, no minor matter indeed). Secondly, this approach enables a comparative enquiry to be made into the varying degrees of influence that specific legislation, be it purely internal or inspired by European Directives, may have on the core of traditional general rules of contract. Comparative analyses can therefore follow without being biased by national legal conceptions of the geographical lie of the land. In our view, clearly, the initial methodological choice will determine, although it is hoped not excessively predetermine, the results of the research undertaken.

It is now helpful to set out more precisely how the cases chosen can be categorised into special contracts. Once again, it should be noted that the choice was not purely theoretical but was largely influenced by existing case law from a number of legal systems. In fact, it should be possible to avoid the criticism of having used unrealistic case studies, since every case is drawn from empirical research.

Description of cases

To describe each case in turn it will become apparent that the cases were designed in clusters to treat different issues that may arise in each type of contract. Cases 1 to 3 (Anatole v. Bob, Célimène v. Damien, Emile v. Far Eastern Delights) concern contracts for the sale of goods and in particular sales of works of art. The variety turns on the status of the contracting parties (their knowledge, their bargaining capacity), the content and manner in which precontractual information is given as well as the availability of the range of remedies. Case 4 (Mr and Mrs Timeless v. Mr and Mrs Careless) also treats a contract of sale but this time the subject matter of the sale is land and hinges on, *inter alia*, the relevance of a mistake being qualified as fact or law as well as on the question of concealing relevant and material information concerning the quality of the land before the contract's conclusion. Cases 5 and 6 deal with sales of second-hand goods but constitute variations on a theme, in that the enquiry focuses on precontractual statements or silence. Is the same standard expected in relation to the content of information given, in view of the fact that the subject matter of the sale is not new? Is the same standard required when the sale concerns a professional seller and non-professional buyer? Case 5 (Bruno v. The Local Garage) concerns a fairly common occurrence, that of the sale of a second-hand car, between a consumer and professional where a false statement was made. This case is a good illustration of the overlap between contractual remedies for non-performance, or breach of contract and remedies for defective consent. Case 6 (Emmanuel v. The Computer Shop) concerns a contract of sale between consumer and professional for an object that requires specialised knowledge. The question raises not only the seller's silence about material facts which induced the buyer to contract but also the question of how to qualify a duty to inform when the information given has a decisive effect on the performance of the contract. In other words, is it accurate to describe as precontractual a duty to inform which has a long-term effect on the contract as well as inducing a contracting party to contract? The relevance of the reason for qualifying the duty in some systems is that such a qualification will affect the appropriate remedy.

From the sale of business to company law, Case 7 (Cinderella) owes its particularity to the nature of the market in question (shares quoted on the stock market). Thus company law disclosure requirements and regulations may interfere, although as we shall see, this is not necessarily the case.

Cases 8 and 9 examine a contract of loan and a contract of surety respectively. Case 8 (Estella v. Uriah Heep) concerns both a door-step sale and a door-step contract of consumer credit (as between a consumer and a professional). Here, the overlap between general remedies for defective consent and special consumer protection is particularly accentuated. Case 9 (Nell v. Scrooge Bank) concerns a contract of guarantee in a particular context: the fairly frequent case of surety given by one spouse for another to guarantee business interests. This case was inspired by the somewhat abundant case law in English law,[137] whereas it has not

---

[137] *Barclays Bank plc* v. *O'Brien* [1994] 1 AC 180. Of course the German case law is important too, see German report, but it did not in fact directly inspire this case.

necessarily been a subject of so much speculation in other national systems. That said, it is not a matter of purely English law interest but is
perhaps an example where English law has set a new trend in relation to
the duty to inform in a bank–client relationship. This is worth highlighting for its rarity, since more generally the concept of a duty to inform is
less highly developed in the common law than in the civil law systems.

Examining a completely different area of the law, that of insurance
contracts, Case 10 (Zachary) examines a mistake which results in a double insurance – although there is an obvious mistake it will be seen that
the remedy available is not always legally categorised under the concept
of mistake.

Case 11 (Monstrous Inventions Ltd v. Mary Shelley) looks at the possibility of mistakes arising in a settlement agreement. This case treats a
settlement agreement in employment law where the dishonesty of an
employee may provide a sufficient reason to invalidate what would otherwise be a valid contract. Here there is an overlap between two types
of *leges speciales*, although in the common law countries, this question
would be still considered under the general rules of contract.

Case 12 (Lady Windermere v. Angel) concerns a mistake in relation to
a gift *inter vivos*. Obvious differences between civil law and common law
rules arise since only in the former is a gift qualified as a contract. This
issue is not crucial here. Moreover, at the end of the day, the qualification
of the mistake itself – is it a purely material mistake? Is it a mistake as
to the person? – may not be very relevant. If neither legal classification
is of utter significance, there is one distinguishing feature of the case
that differentiates it from the others. The case concerns a gift and we
will see that the gratuitous nature of the transaction turns out to be
the most significant common denominator coupled with the fact that
this necessitates a formal requirement in most countries.

Identifying the limits of the approach: the cases that were abandoned

Finally it may be worthwhile recording the various cases that do not
appear in this report for a number of reasons.

First, an attempt was made to include a case on the sale of land where
the buyer knew of the existence of important minerals under the land,
of which the seller was unaware.[138] This case is obviously inspired by

---

[138] The facts were as follows: Oriol, a farmer, agreed to sell his land to Andermatt, a
water mineralogist, for a reasonable market price. Unknown to Oriol, Andermatt had
been carrying out extensive enquiries into the surrounding area and had reason to
believe that a source of mineral water existed under the land to be sold. If exploited,

American law and the law and economics approach to the disclosure of valuable information.[139] However, since the fact-hypotheticals did not correspond to any real cases under the national reporters' systems and did not throw up any new legal issues which the other cases had not treated, the attempt was abandoned on the grounds that a set of facts which were both unrepresentative of legal reality and redundant did not deserve further attention. The attempt is mentioned since unfruitful research is in itself revealing: two conclusions are possible – either one may indeed deduce that the law is lacunose on this point or that such cases never get taken to court, which does not mean that they do not happen in practice. Next, if it were shown that the law were defective in this area, it might be necessary to consider why no special remedy, or in some cases why no remedy at all, would be available.

Secondly, a set of hypotheticals[140] which attempted to examine the overlap of mistake in the law of what common law lawyers call restitution (and also here an illustration of *condictio indebiti* or the action in French law of *répétition de l'indu*) was also set aside after some discussion amongst the majority of national reporters. The point is mentioned since it touched a raw nerve as to the difficulties that can be encountered in comparative legal research. The case raised a conceptual hubbub – most national reporters did not want to conceptualise this area as mistake. To put it simply it was generally felt that this was simply not a question of mistake in contract law. Once again, the omission is worth mentioning since it was felt that we had pushed the limits of factual categorisation too far. At some point, and this was the very point, all national reporters showed the desire or need to classify legally the set of facts before them into some sort of coherent order.[141] Too much chaos or disturbance was therefore not entirely appreciated. This example is perhaps illustrative

> the source could be used both for setting up a thermal establishment and for bottled drinking water. After the sale Andermatt did indeed dig up a new source of water which obviously increased the value of the land beyond Oriol's imagination. What remedy, if any, is available to Oriol?

[139] See for example, Kronman, 'Mistake, Disclosure, Information in the Law of Contract', who uses as a criterion the distinction between casually acquired information and information acquired at a cost.

[140] The facts were as follows: Unknown to one another, Janet Keats and John Keats, brother and sister, both took out motor insurance with Eagle Life. Janet had an accident and claimed on her policy. John opened a letter adressed to 'J. Keats' and banked the cheque enclosed. What remedy, if any, is available to (i) Janet and (ii) the insurers?

[141] For an appraisal of the need for legal doctrine to classify, see S. Smith, 'Taking Law Seriously' (2000) 50 *University of Toronto Law Journal*, pp. 241 ff.

of the limits within which the Trento common core project lies. Apparently, it is difficult, if not impossible, to strip national law reporters of all their legal prejudices!

Thirdly, it has already been suggested that *leges speciales*, particularly those made to transpose European directives in consumer law, have had a considerable impact on the parties' consent at the contract's formation. The rules about when the contract is formed and when the parties' consent becomes definitive have been subject to change as a result of European legislation about long-distance sales. Two cases treating these questions as well as the effect of misleading advertising on the parties' consent were originally included in this report.[142] In a sense these cases prove perfectly the point that mistake is being pushed to the background in the face of protective legislation, thus rendering defective consent a subsidiary remedy. Methodologically, after consideration it seemed difficult to justify the presence of cases which do not test one of the hypotheses of this enquiry but rather beg the question.[143] Moreover, in view of the increasing specialisation of consumer contracts[144] it may be inappropriate to make inferences about mistake in general from such contracts which contain specific rules.

Likewise, cases which concern certain contracts regulated by law and often considered as belonging to distinct branches of the law (e.g. employment contracts) have been mostly excluded from the scope of this study. This exclusion is both unfortunate and necessary. During our

[142] The facts were as follows: (a) The television-watching public is regularly reminded of 'Eternal Youth', a cosmetic manufactured and advertised on television by the White Lie Company with the slogan 'makes your skin look as new as a baby's'. But when Candida, after using the cream to no avail for a whole year, complained of her bitter disappointment to the White Lie consumer department, she was informed that 'Eternal Youth' could not possibly work miracles on vintage skins, and that she should have begun the applications many years ago. What remedy, if any, is available? (b) The Nutshell Bed Company's catalogue advertises a new concept in bedroom design: 'beds that fit anywhere, specially designed to be assembled and disassembled in small spaces'. But when Mr and Mrs Dove received a double bed after ordering it by mail directly from the Nutshell Bed Company, it soon became clear that it would never adapt to the nooks and crannies of their little artist's studio. What remedy, if any, is available?

[143] The existence of a common core is self-evident in this sort of situation since European harmonisation has imposed a common core.

[144] It is quite justifiable, when looking at the law of contracts today in the light of European legislation, to ask whether there is not one law of contract for consumer contracts and another for contracts between parties who are both acting in the course of business. This assertion comes as no surprise to jurists whose legal system has a separate Consumer Code.

investigations it was observed that specific rules in relation to nominate contracts sometimes have the effect of distorting the answers. It
then becomes easy to particularise the solution as a result of specific
legislation. The unfortunate aspect of this exclusionary choice is that
inevitably it also warps the neutrality of the enterprise, which is why it
has already been pointed out that the neutrality of a comparative investigation must be treated with caution. Methodological considerations
apart, the choices in this study reveal the paradoxes of comparative law.
Examining mistake, fraud and duties to inform together has, no doubt,
revealed a number of surprising comparative challenges.

2 Mistake, misrepresentation and precontractual duties to inform: the civil law tradition

Martin Josef Schermaier

Introduction

When comparing the law on mistake in modern legal systems, it is not immediately obvious that their provisions, although very different in some respects, are in fact the same in nature. This also applies to pre-contractual duties to inform that today are discussed in different contexts. And yet both fields of law spring from the same source, namely Roman law and the Aristotelian-scholastic theory of contractual acts. Nevertheless, there exists a fundamental difference between these two fields: whereas the law on mistake has developed uniformly and without significant interruption, the so-called 'precontractual duties to inform' coalesced from very different starting points and even today, have still not been grasped in a systematic fashion but are discussed in completely different fields of law.

At least in the legal systems of continental Europe, the two legal institutions of mistake and precontractual duties to inform may, to a certain degree, be separated. A mistake made when concluding a contract enables the mistaken party to free himself from a given declaration of intent, a promise or a contract – provided certain conditions have been fulfilled. A breach of duties to inform, however, gives rise to either the annulment or amendment of a contract already concluded or imposes a duty to compensate incumbent on the party bound to inform. Despite this major difference, both aspects of law are also partly connected. All legal systems require that the aggrieved party be unaware of the defects in the thing delivered (i.e. he 'was mistaken') before warranty claims may be asserted. At the same time, the legal definition also latches on to the 'contractual nature' of the goods, i.e. the kind and nature of the goods as agreed by the parties. In this respect, it is decisive on the one hand, how the vendor (lessor, manufacturer) has described the goods and, on the other, whether he has remained silent as to features that are important for the mistaken party. Sometimes the law on mistake itself also takes into account whether the other party has given flawed or incorrect information: accordingly § 871 of the Austrian ABGB, art. 1302 of the Spanish Civil Code and art. 6:228 (a) of the Dutch BW recognise a mistake where it was induced by the other party.[1] This example shows precisely that 'mistake' and 'duty to inform' mark the range of the two poles between which every civilian set of values lies to determine contractual validity and duty: between taking into account the parties' (subjective) intention and the (objective) value of the parties' communication of intent or – to put it simply – between intention and reliance.

Roman law

From a historical viewpoint too, it is not always possible to separate these two aspects of law; rather, one observes how they compete with each other in different areas. Nevertheless, the debate concerning the significance of mistake and duties to inform during the course of the history of private law is to a considerable extent governed by the limits laid down by Roman law: the significance of intention for the validity of legal acts is dealt with in the law on mistake and in the interpretation of declarations of intent; neglected duties to inform play a role in establishing and determining contractual liability.

Mistake

The portrayal of the Roman law on mistake passed down to us in Justinian's Digests under the name of Domitius Ulpianus (Ulp. D. 18,1,9; 11 and 14) continues to exercise a profound influence over European discussion today.[2] Using sale as an example, the question whether a mistake

---

[1] Further commentary on comparative law may be found in E. A. Kramer, *Der Irrtum beim Vertragsabschluß. Eine weltweit rechtsvergleichende Bestandsaufnahme* (Zürich, 1998), pp. 52 ff.

[2] On the text's significance to legal history, see R. Zimmermann, *Law of Obligations. Roman Foundations of the Civilian Tradition* (Oxford, 1996), pp. 587 et seq. Less fitting is P. Haupt, *Die Entwicklung der Lehre vom Irrtum beim Rechtsgeschäft seit der Reception* (Weimar, 1941). But, see also J. A. C. Thomas, 'Error in persona and error in substantia' in *La formazione storica del diritto moderno in Europa III* (3 vols., Florence, 1977), vol. III, pp. 1203 et seq.; B. Schmidlin, in: *Berner Kommentar zum schweizerischen Privatrecht, Vol. IV: Obligationenrecht, 1. Abt.: Allgemeine Bestimmungen*, 2. Tbd. 1 b: Mängel des Vertragsabschlusses, art. 23–31 OR, Lieferung 1: Kommentar zu art. 23–7 OR (Vorbemerkungen und Kommentar), (Bern, 1993); now M. J. Schermaier, *Die Bestimmung des wesentlichen Irrtums von den Glossatoren bis zum BGB* (Vienna/Cologne/Weimar, 2000).

concerning the object of sale and its qualities prevents a contract being validly concluded is decided in the Digests,[3] according to the value given to various categories.[4] *Error in corpore* and *error in substantia* or *materia* vitiate the consensus of the parties and are therefore substantial, whereas an *error in qualitate* does not affect contractual consent.

Although Ulpian refers to the older Marcellus in his decision, we must proceed on the assumption that a mistake concerning circumstantial facts was only placed at the centre of legal opinion in this way relatively late. That is to say, in older texts a 'mistake' of the purchaser is only referred to as ignorance of a material defect[5] or impossibility of performance;[6] therefore leading only to the question whether warranty remedies would be available or whether the rules governing impossibility would be applicable. With Ulpian however, the question whether the contractual consensus is itself invalid due to a substantial mistake moves centre stage. Older debates are concerned with the validity of a transfer of ownership where the parties are at odds over its legal basis (*causa traditionis*)[7] and the question whether the contracting parties have reached a valid agreement if both have intended a different purchase price.[8] However, such cases do not concern mistakes relating to factual

---

[3] For the Roman context of D. 18,1,9 ss. cf. P. Voci, *L'errore nel diritto romano* (Milan, 1937), pp. 109 ff.; J. G. Wolf, *Error im römischen Vertragsrecht* (Cologne/Graz, 1961); U. Zilletti, *La dottrina dell'errore nella storia del diritto romano* (Milan, 1961); T. Mayer-Maly, 'Bemerkungen zum Aspekt der Konsensstörung in der klassischen Irrtumslehre' in *Mélanges Philippe Meylan* (2 vols., Lausanne, 1963), vol. I, pp. 241 et seq.; F. Wieacker, 'Irrtum, Dissens oder gegenstandslose Leistungsbestimmung?' in *Mélanges Philippe Meylan*, vol. I, pp. 383 et seq.; J. Miguel, 'Una aportación al estudio del "error in substantia" en la compraventa' in *Annuario de derecho civil* (1963), pp. 79 et seq.; P. Cornioley, 'Error in substantia, in materia, in qualitate' in *Studi in onore di Giuseppe Grosso* (6 vols., Turin, 1968–74), vol. II, pp. 249 et seq.; P. Apathy, 'Sachgerechtigkeit und Systemdenken am Beispiel der Entwicklung von Sachmängelhaftung und Irrtum beim Kauf im klassischen römischen Recht' (1994) 111 *Zeitschrift der Savigny-Stiftung für Rechtsgeschichte, romanistische Abteilung* (= ZSSt) 95 at pp. 137 et seq.; for further commentary see M. Schermaier, 'Auslegung und Konsensbestimmung. Sachmängelhaftung, Irrtum und anfängliche Unmöglichkeit nach römischem Kaufrecht' (1998) 115 ZSSt 235 at pp. 244 et seq.

[4] Valuated according to contemporary philosophical concepts, cf. M. J. Schermaier, *Materia. Beiträge zur Frage der Naturphilosophie im klassischen römischen Recht* (Vienna/Cologne/Weimar 1992), pp. 109 et seq.

[5] For example, in: Ulp. D. 21,1,1,6; Pomp. D. 21,1,48,4; Marcian. D. 18,1,45; perhaps also in Paul. D. 19,1,21,1.

[6] For example in: Mod. D. 18,1,62,1; Pomp. D. 18,1,6 pr.; Lic. Ruf. D. 18,1,70; Paul. D. 18,1,34,3; Paul. D. 18,1,57.

[7] Iul. D. 41,1,36 (in the Middle Ages: *error in causa*).

[8] Pomp. D. 19,2,52 (in the Middle Ages: *error in pretio*).

circumstances, as for example in Ulp. D. 18,1,9, but solely the parties' mistakes in understanding;[9] nevertheless, both in the latter and the former, the question of an effective consensus is of prime importance.

Application of the *condictio indebiti* requires a mistake relating to the existence of an obligation to perform (*causa solutionis*),[10] yet this requirement – although it may have been the subject of early discussion – is never compared to mistake at the conclusion of a contract. Indeed, even under the heading of *De iuris vel facti ignorantia*,[11] created by Justinian, there is nothing in the text which analyses mistakes made at the conclusion of a contract. Nonetheless, the legal concept of a mistake impeding consensus and those cases which Ulpian was the first to grasp conceptually (*error in corpore, substantia, qualitate*) experience an astonishing success in later European history and are responsible for the fact that all European legal systems are familiar with and – subject to different requirements – take contractual mistake into account.

Misrepresentation

'Naturaliter concessum est . . . invicem se circumvenire' (individuals are naturally permitted to overcharge one another), so Julius Paulus, a scholar of the late-classical period and Ulpian's contemporary, on the question whether one may deal in a thing at a greater or lesser value than it is worth.[12] Only if a contractual party had acted with fraudulent intent, i.e. if he wanted to injure the other party by providing intentionally incorrect information, would he be bound to compensate the loss arising therefrom. Accordingly, only *dolus malus* restricts the liberal pursuit of profit propagated by Paulus.[13] Apart from malicious acts, a vendor or lessor is also liable for the presence of certain features if he had given an express warranty to that effect (*dictum*), or if they were due on account of a special, formal covenant (*promissum*).[14]

---

[9] For this, see at present: Schermaier, 'Auslegung und Konsensbestimmung' (1998) ZSSt 115 at pp. 253 et seq.

[10] Ulp. D. 12,6,1,1; Pomp. D. 12,6,7; Pomp. D. 12,6,16; Pomp. D. 12,6,19,2 u. 3; Ulp. D. 12,6,26,2; Ulp. D. 12,6,26,12; Paul. D. 12,6,27; Ulp. D. 12,6,31; Marc. D. 12,6,40 pr.; Cels. D. 12,6,47; Papin. D. 12,6,59 and especially Pomp. D. 12,6,50.

[11] D. 22,6; C. 1,18.

[12] Paul. D. 19,2,22,3; similarly Ulp. D. 4,4,16,1 citing Pomponius. For an analysis of this see: A. Wacke, 'Circumscribere, gerechter Preis und die Arten der List' (1977) ZSSt 94 at pp. 184 et seq.

[13] Cf. Ulp. D. 4,3,1,2: 'Dolum malum Servius quidem ita definit machinationem quandam alterius decipiendi causa, cum aliud simulatur et aliud agitur.'

[14] For an analysis of this see: A. L. Olde Kalter, *Dicta et promissa. De ansprakelijkheid van de verkoper wegens gedane toezeggingen betreffende de hoedanigheid van de verkochte zaak in het klassieke romeinse recht* (Utrecht, 1963).

Where the vendor merely praised the thing or also where he made reference to alleged qualities, such statements were held not to be binding. Thus, determining the boundaries of an informal but binding *dictum* was therefore just as important and difficult for legal practice then as it is now: 'Ea quae commendandi causa in venditionibus dicuntur, si palam appareant, venditorem non obligant', according to Florentinus.[15] The application of this rule – which is still valid today – was far from a simple matter in a given case:[16] if the vendor said, for example, that the slave (for sale) was handsome, then he was not liable, if he said however, that the slave was especially educated, healthy or not prone to escape, then he was liable for such assurances.[17] This distinction nevertheless only makes sense if the object of purchase is present at the time the contract is concluded.[18] If things are sold, which the purchaser himself cannot see, then the seller must probably answer for every statement relating to their quality which was of significance to the conclusion of the contract. Only this may explain why, according to Labeo and Marcian, someone who sells used clothes as new,[19] is liable for their newness.

Duty to inform

An important step exceeding the obligation to comply with warranties was taken within the sphere of liability for defects in quality imposed by the *aediles curules*. One power of this magisterial body, which was responsible for supervising the market in Rome, included the judicial control of disputes which arose during the course of market trading. It ordered that protection be given to the purchaser who had purchased slaves or cattle which later displayed certain defects. The edict contained a list of typical, recurring defects which the vendor had to answer for independently of his own knowledge.[20] The list of defects presumably only

---

[15] Flor. D. 18,1,43 pr.: 'That which is said during a sale for promotion purposes does not bind the vendor if one thereby only promotes that which is obvious in any case.'

[16] Cf. also Ped./Ulp. D. 21,1,19 pr.

[17] Numerous examples of warranties given in the purchase of slaves may be found in D. 21,1 (e.g. Ulp. D. 21,1,17,20; Gai. D. 21,1,18,1–2; Ulp. D. 21,1,19).

[18] Cf. Flor. D. 18,1,43,1.

[19] Lab./Marc. D. 18,1,45; it is debated whether Labeo and Marcian proceed on the basis of an express or implied warranty of the vendor or rather on the basis of the vendor's *dolus*. Cf. for example: G. Impallomeni, 'Applicazioni del principio dell' affidamento nella vendita romana' (1995) 21 *Studia et documenta historiae et iuris*, pp. 166 et seq.; H. Honsell, *Quod interest im bonae fidei iudicium* (Munich, 1969), p. 94; Olde Kalter, *Dicta et Promissa*, pp. 64 et seq.

[20] The view that originally this liability also depended on a promise of the vendor (which could certainly be obtained by force), to the effect that the slave/cow is free from defect was unsettled by the work of Éva Jakab; cf. E. Jakab, *Stipulationes aediliciae*

referred to features which could not possibly have escaped the attention of the vendor as previous owner of the slave.[21] However, in a dispute the question whether the vendor knew or must have known of the defects was not regarded as decisive.

This model of liability under a warranty was also adopted as a starting point for other contracts of sale and even, to a certain degree, for other barter transactions. Provided the claim of a purchaser (lessee, customer) was measured against *bona fides* however, one was able to establish the vendor's liability only by means of a breach of good faith. Originally, a breach of this nature was only perceived to exist where the presence of defects was fraudulently withheld. If, for example, the vendor knew that the house was due to be pulled down by an official order,[22] that a piece of land was encumbered by an easement[23] or that it was subject to taxation,[24] then he was bound to communicate this to the purchaser. If he remained silent despite being aware of the defect, then he was liable on the basis of the *actio empti* (the purchaser's complaint) to compensate the purchaser's expectation in the complete satisfaction of the contractual obligation ('positive interest'). The question as to which facts the vendor was bound to communicate and those which he could withhold was scarcely debated. As far as the decided cases reveal however, Roman lawyers had a fine sense of judgement for the thin dividing line between permissible and illegal *circumvenire*.[25]

Cicero's critical eye also reveals, however, that the contemporary understanding of *bona fides* was infused with value concepts which we would hardly share today. One known example is that of the corn merchant who sells his produce to the famished Rhodian. He certainly knows that more ships are on course for Rhodes, to provide for the starving masses, but, in order to obtain the highest possible price for his corn, he withholds this fact.[26] From this example, reports Cicero, an argument ensued between Diogenes and his pupil Antipater about whether an advantage of knowledge held by one party is not ethically acceptable

---

(Szeged, 1993) and E. Jakab, *Praedicere und cavere beim Marktkauf – Sachmängel im griechischen und römischen Recht* (Munich, 1997).

[21] From different sources – for example, Ulp. D. 21,2,31 pr. – the lists of possible defects of a slave may be reconstructed in the following way: 'ut sanus est, erro, fur, noxius, fugitivus, vispellio non est' ('That he is sound in body and mind and is no loiterer, thief, is free from convictions, is not prone to escape and is not deceitful').

[22] Cic. *off.* 3,66; Val. Max. 8,2,1.   [23] Ulp. D. 19,1,1,1.   [24] Paul. D. 19,1,21,1.

[25] Cf. once more Wacke, 'Circumscribere, gerechter Preis und die Arten der List', pp. 185 et seq.

[26] Cic. *off.* 3,50.

in barter transactions. Whilst Antipater believed that the vendor may not withhold from the purchaser any information that he possesses,[27] Diogenes argued that the vendor is not bound to surrender all that knowledge which would be useful for the purchaser.[28] Thereby Diogenes – as he himself emphasised – stood in the camp of contemporary civil law, whilst Antipater represented the ideal of the *vir bonus*, oriented around the common good. The argument between the two philosophers may not have been of direct importance for the practical application of law.[29] Nevertheless, it may be deduced from Cicero's description, that basically no distinction was made between fraudulent misrepresentation and the withholding of correct facts.

However, practice and science expanded the vendor's liability in another way: for as part of liability imposed by the *aediles curules* the vendor was required to reveal defects in the object of sale which were normally of concern to the purchaser. If he withheld them, then he would be liable on the basis of the *actio empti* even where he could not be accused of *dolus* or even negligence. However, the vendor – within the sphere of the aedilian edict – was only liable to reduce or refund the purchase price. Herein the distinction of Salvius Julianus, a jurist of the age of Hadrian, gained currency: this demanded that the vendor who was aware of the defects has to compensate additionally the loss which might occur from the defect. If, for example, a defective girder had been sold and used in the construction of a house which then collapsed, the seller who himself was unaware that the girder was defective was only liable for the depreciation in the girder's value. If, however, he had sold a defective girder intentionally, then he was bound to replace the whole value of the loss suffered by the purchaser.[30] Understandable as this differentiation is, it is surprising to make the unaware vendor liable on the basis of an action (*actio empti*) supported by good faith (*bona fides*). The only explanation for this is that his unawareness was equated with a breach of duty of care: he as owner should have been the first to

<hr />

[27] Cic. *off.* 3,51: '. . . ut ne quid omnino, quod venditor norit, emptor ignoret' ('. . . so that the buyer does not in the least ignore, what the seller knows').

[28] Cic. *off.* 3,52: 'Sed non, quicquid tibi audire utile est, idem mihi dicere necesse est'; ('I do not have to tell you everything that would be helpful for you to know').

[29] The formula advocated by Cic. *off.* 3,57 himself nevertheless provides a practical pretext: silence for the sake of profit is reprehensible and contravenes good faith ('neque enim id est celare, quicquid reticeas, sed cum, quod tu scias, id ignorare emolumenti tui causa velis eos, quorum intersit id scire').

[30] Jul./Ulp. D. 19,1,13 pr. Julian's distinction obviously convinced his contemporaries and successors; cf. also Ulp. D. 19,1,11,15; Marc. D. 18,1,45; Ulp. D. 19,2,19,1.

recognise the presence of a defect and could have drawn the purchaser's attention to it.[31] The decisions in the well-known cases concerning the leasing and sale of wine vessels probably convey the same concept: if a person had leased or sold leaky wine vessels, then he was always liable for the loss which arose to the purchaser or the lessee. Therefore even if he had not been aware of the defect he would still be bound – besides termination of contract or reduction of the purchase price – to compensate the purchaser or lessee for the loss arising from the leakage.[32] This did not stipulate any special 'liability under warranty' but rather took the vendor's typified breach of the duty of care into account. Perhaps it was normal practice for the vendor to ensure that the vessels were properly sealed beforehand.[33]

Duties to inform in the modern sense therefore only existed in Roman law where it was apparent that silence amounted to a breach of *bona fides*. Only in the field of warranty law did one proceed on the basis of a typified definition of liability which approached fraud.

Reception and common law (1200–1800)

The concept and theory of the Roman law on mistake and warranty underwent little change in legal science of the middle ages and the early stages of the modern era. One change, however, concerned the arguments both for the invalidity of a contract tainted by mistake and for granting remedies in the case of poor performance. The law on mistake together with the law on defective declarations of intent fell under the regime of the scholastic doctrine of will and the law on warranties was now judged under the aspect of fair exchange (*iustitia commutativa*).[34] Moreover the concept was developed, from some rudiments in

---

[31] In this sense also Zimmermann, *Law of Obligations*, pp. 366 et seq.

[32] Pomp. D. 19,1,6,4; Ulp. D. 19,2,19,1.

[33] Nevertheless, *dolia* were vessels made of clay, which were inserted into the ground for use; at least in the leasing of such vessels testing their water-tightness was a laborious process for the lessor and was therefore not expected. For different explanations see: T. Mayer-Maly, *Locatio conductio* (Vienna, 1956); M. Kaser, 'Die natürlichen Eigentumserwerbsarten im altrömischen Recht' (1957) 74 ZSSt 166; Honsell, *Quod interest im bonae fidei iudicium*, p. 134; K. Luig, 'Zur Vorgeschichte der verschuldensunabhängigen Haftung des Vermieters für anfängliche Mängel nach § 538 BGB' in G. Baumgärtel (Hrsg.), *Festschrift für Heinz Hübner zum 70 Geburtstag* (Berlin, 1984), p. 129, p. 132.

[34] On this see mainly: J. Gordley, *The Philosophical Origins of Modern Contract Doctrine* (Oxford, 1991), pp. 30 et seq.

Roman law, that exploiting an individual's position of necessity with the aim of gaining profit was reprehensible and that transactions of this kind were accordingly void. Typical characteristics of this new social ethic could be found, for example, in spiritual and temporal limits on interest rates[35] or the theory of fair price developed from the *iustitia commutativa*.[36]

Mistake

It was probably the law of mistake which experienced the most fundamental innovation since its creation. Medieval jurists no longer perceived in the mistake of one or both parties solely a problem of consensus – as did the Roman sources – but, following the Aristotelian-scholastic doctrine of imputation, a problem of autonomous intention.[37] A mistake causes an erroneous perception and impairs the formation of intent; an act which is made on this basis and directed by intention is thus not attributable to its author.[38] Admittedly, offer and acceptance in the creation of a contract and other legal transactions are first grasped conceptually in the eighteenth century as *actus iuridicus*,[39] but the concept that only the intention of the parties formed without impairment may produce the contractual consensus may already be perceived in early doctrinal forms developed by medieval jurists. Thus, one begins to grasp different guises of 'mistake' relating to factual circumstances

---

[35] For an analysis of this see: H. Siems, *Handel und Wucher im Spiegel frühmittelalterlicher Rechtsquellen* (Hannover, 1992), pp. 551 et seq. and pp. 591 et seq.; M. Giacchero, *L'attegiamento di concili in materia d'usura dal IV al IX secolo* (Perugia, 1981), pp. 305 et seq.

[36] See for example: J. W. Baldwin, *The Medieval Theories of the Just Price. Romanists, Canonists and Theologians in the Twelfth and Thirteenth Centuries* (1959); K. S. Cahn, 'The Roman and Frankish Roots of the Just Price of Medieval Canon Law' in (1969) 6 *Studies in Medieval and Renaissance History*, pp. 6 et seq.; R. de Roover, *La pensée économique des Scolastiques. Doctrines et méthodes* (Paris, 1971); Gordley, *Philosophical Origins*, pp. 65 et seq.; further comment in: Zimmermann, *Law of Obligations*, pp. 259 et seq. and C. Becker, *Die Lehre von der laesio enormis in der Sicht der heutigen Wucherproblematik: Ausgewogenheit als Vertragsinhalt und § 138 BGB* (Cologne/Berlin/Bonn/Munich, 1993), pp. 27 et seq. and Siems, *Handel und Wucher*, pp. 764 et seq.

[37] On the distinction see recently: M. Schermaier, 'Europäische Geistesgeschichte am Beispiel des Irrtumsrechts' (1998) ZEuP 60, pp. 68 et seq.; for further comment see: A. Dihle, *The Theory of Will in Classical Antiquity* (Berkeley/Los Angeles/London, 1982), pp. 54 et seq.

[38] Especially Aristot. *Eth. Nic.* III, 1109 b 30 ff.

[39] By C. Wolff and in the Wolff-school, probably first in: D. Nettelbladt, *Systema elementare universae iurisprudentiae naturalis, Halae Magdeburgicae; pars I: Introductio in iurisprudentiam naturalem* (1757), §§ 256 et seq.

surrounding the creation of a contract as a problem of mistake at the conclusion of a contract. For example, cases of initial impossibility are described as *error in existentia rei*,[40] common problems of guarantee portrayed as *error in materia, error in corpore* or *error in qualitate*.[41] Whilst jurists are initially occupied with summarising and systemisation and wish to measure the significance of a mistake according to whether it concerns the *essentialia* or merely the *accidentalia contractus*,[42] there emerges in the imputation theory of St Thomas Aquinas an important catalyst for later development.

The importance of Thomas (1225–74) for the modern theory of the creation of a contract and the declaration of intent stems from two requirements. On the one hand, Thomas proposed – on the basis of Aristotle's texts which were by now made available in Europe, handed down by Arabian scholars[43] – a systematic doctrine relating to acts and attribution[44] and actually applied these doctrines to the case where a mistake had been made in the creation of a marriage contract.[45] On the other hand, his doctrine of imputation, passed on by Spanish late scholasticism, became the basis of the natural law theory of intent. The main issue of this theory of attribution (or imputation) is the rule that only acts which the actor has done without an error occurring in his perception (mistake, fraud committed by another)[46] are voluntary acts and are therefore imputable. In legal contexts this means that contractual dealing is only effective and thus leads to a valid contract, if the parties know how, with whom and to which end they are contracting. This can be learned from Thomas' decision of the case of mistake in a marriage

---

[40] On the occasion of D. 18,1,57; cf. Odofredus, *Praelectiones in secundam Digesti veteris partem (Lectura super Digestum vetus)* (Lugduni 1552 reprinted: *Opera iuridica rariora II 2*, Bologna, 1968), ad D. 18,1,9 (fol. 95 v.); in Azo, Gl. *in quo alio* ad D. 18,1,9 still '*error in essentia*'.

[41] Also vice versa; the described cases of mistake are portrayed and treated as problems relating to guarantee.

[42] For example, in Baldus de Ubaldis, *In secundam digesti veteris partem Commentaria* (Venice, 1615), ad D. 18,1,34 pr. (fol. 105 r.).

[43] The classic period of Scholasticism (Aquinas, Duns Scotus, Ockham) owes its growth to the fact that the writings of Aristotle that had only been partially supplied were available from the early thirteenth century in Europe (and most importantly: in Latin); among the writings that were only just available were also those of the two Ethicans (the Nicomachean and Eudemian Ethics), which were crucially important for the development of the scholastic imputation theory.

[44] Primarily Thomas, STh. I–II, qu. 6–7.   [45] Cf. Thomas, STh. suppl. III, qu. 51.

[46] Thomas, STh. I–II, qu.6, art. 3.

contract. Accordingly, if someone makes a mistake relating to the *essentia matrimonii*, then the conclusion of the marriage contract is invalid if the mistaken party would not have concluded the marriage had he not made the mistake. Even contemporary jurists had already made a distinction as to whether a mistake affected the *substantia* of a contract or not.[47] Yet, in contrast to those who drew upon objective, formal criteria with which to determine the *substantia contractus* (price, goods, type of contract), Thomas measured the 'nature' of marriage or indeed contracts in general according to the meaning and purpose of the contract. The principle *error qualitatis in personam redundans*[48] was developed according to this and is still to be found in the Codex Iuris Canonici.[49]

In Roman common law this concept is initially taken up either tentatively or not at all. As the first, Franciscus Connanus (1508–51), a French jurist of the school of Bourges believed that the assessment of a mistake depended not on the *substantia rei*, i.e. the significance of the facts about which one had been mistaken, but rather on the *substantia contractus*, i.e. the nature of the contract which one intended to conclude.[50] However, he initially remained alone in this view.

Despite being partly influenced by innovations of natural law,[51] the doctrine of Roman common law – whether in the *elegantia iuris*, in the *Usus modernus* or in the late *Mos italicus* – could not free itself from the Roman categories of mistake. Jurists discussed the cases known from the sources up to the nineteenth century and only simplified the casuistry (as it was customary to do since the middle ages) by distinguishing cases where the mistake had affected the *substantialia* or merely the *accessoria* of the contract. Accordingly, discussion shifted to the question concerning which elements of the contract belonged to the categories of

---

[47] For example, Rogerius, *Summa Codicis*, ad C. 2,3, nn. 18 ff. (edition: Scripta Anecdota Glossatorum, vol. 1 (Bologna, 1913)); Placentinus, *Summa Institutionum sive Elementorum D. Iustiniani*, ad C. 2,3 (p. 43 of the edition: Moguntiae, 1535); Azo, *Summa Codicis*, ad. C. 4,38,3 and ad C. 4,54, n. 1 (edition: Papiae, 1506). Comprehensively on this see Gordley, *Philosophical Origins*, pp. 61 et seq.

[48] Thomas, STh. suppl III, qu. 51, art. 2, ad 5.

[49] CIC 1983, Can. 1097, § 2: *Error in qualitate personae, etsi det causam contractui, matrimonium irritum non reddit, nisi haec qualitas directe et principaliter intendatur.*

[50] F. Connanus, *Commentaria iuris civilis* (Basiliae, 1562), lib. VII, cap. VI, n. 4 (704 C of the edition).

[51] On this below at pp. 55–60, many authors of the late seventeenth and eighteenth centuries can in fact only be attributed to one of the two main movements with some difficulty. This applies for example to: W. A. Lauterbach, Heinrich and Samuel Cocceji or Jean Domat.

substantialia or *accidentalia*.[52] Even the tendency to treat problems relating to the law on defective performance – for example, cases of initial impossibility, cases of defective delivery – as problems of contractual mistake continued in later common law. In the Dutch and German *Usus modernus* this tendency was even exaggerated in that the mistaken party was granted a claim in damages against the party who was not mistaken: the Roman jurists oblige the vendor who had known of the defect in the goods sold to compensate the loss to the purchaser's property resulting from the defect. Because the purchaser was regarded as the 'party under a mistake' and the seller as the 'party not under a mistake', the rule was accordingly developed that the mistaken party could bring a claim in damages against the party who was not mistaken.[53] This duty of compensation does not have anything to do with modern liability for negligent misrepresentation,[54] rather, it resulted from an amalgamation of the laws on defective performance and mistake.

Declaration of intent and mistake in declaration

From a present-day perspective, the curious rule granting the mistaken party a claim of damages against the non-mistaken party may be traced back to two flaws in the Roman-common law doctrine of mistake: first, one did not consider that such a claim could only exist if the non-mistaken party was bound to point out that mistake which the other party was making. Second – and herein lies the fundamental problem of the doctrine of mistake until the nineteenth century – one did not distinguish between cases of mistake and cases of breach of contractual obligations. If the vendor supplied the purchaser with goods worse than the latter had expected, one may wonder whether the vendor had fulfilled his contractual obligation at all or whether the purchaser had made incorrect assumptions as to the object of sale. In the first case,

---

[52] Cf. for example: B. Altimarus, *Tractatus de nullitatibus contractuum*, tom. 3 (Colonia, 1720), rubr. I, qu. IX pr., n. 19 ff.; J. Hoppius, *Commentatio succinata ad Institutiones Justinianeas* (Francofurti ad M. 1698), lib. III, cap. XXIV, § 2; G. Noodt, *Commentarius in D. Justiniani sacr. princ. libros XXVII Digestorum seu Pandectarum* (Lugduni Batavorum, 1724), ad D. 18,1 (pp. 386 et seq. of the edition); F. G. Struve, *Dissertatio inauguralis juridica de effectu erroris in contractu empti venditi*, resp. J. A. Hankoph (Kiloni, 1749), thes. pp. 13 ff. Even J. Domat, W. A. Lauterbach and S. Pufendorf use this distinction.

[53] G. Frantzkius, *Commentarius in XXI libros Pandectarum* (Argentorati, 1644), ad D. 18,1, at pp. 52 et seq.; H. Zoesius, *Commentaria ad Digestorum seu Pandectarum juris civilis libros L.* (Coloniae Agrippinae, 1736), ad D. 18,1, n. 9; H. Hahn, *Observata theoretico-practica, ad M. Wesenbecii* in: *L. libros Digestorum Commentaria* (Helmstadii, 1659), vol. I, ad D. 18,1, n. 6.

[54] For an overview – for example, of the legal situation in Austria, Italy, France and England – see Kramer, *Der Irrtum beim Vertragsabschluß*, pp. 134 et seq.

the purchaser may demand termination or reduction of the purchase price and, under certain further conditions, claim damages on the basis of non-performance. In the second case, he may claim the contract is invalid and refuse to pay the purchase price. This alternative exists in almost all Roman texts which were adopted in the middle ages in relation to the law on mistake: for example, the case of the purchaser, who, instead of the gold bracelet he expected, only received one of gold-plated bronze.[55] Is he to demand the delivery of a gold bracelet from the vendor or is the contract to be invalid owing to the mistake relating to the substance of the bracelet?

This question can only be decided by examining whether a validly concluded contract for a gold bracelet had actually been made. If – as with the Roman jurists – the conclusion of the contract depended on the internal consensus of intention,[56] then every significant mistake would have to be capable of frustrating the conclusion of the contract (*cum non consentiant qui errent*).[57] Only in the case of formal promises (*stipulationes*) or wills was it usual to deduce the true intention from the intention expressed (either orally or in writing).[58] In the doctrines of Canon and Roman common law, one laid greater store by the objective significance of declarations. Owing to the idea that *interni actus per se spectabilis non sunt*,[59] the medieval law on evidence already examined how internal processes – such as the *dolus* of one party – or the correctness of a fact supported by oath became believable by external signs. At the end of the

[55] Ulp. D. 18,1,14; most recently on this, Schermaier, *Materia*, pp. 121 et seq. with further comment.
[56] Pap. D. 50,16,219: 'In conventionibus contrahentium voluntatem potius quam verba spectari placuit.'
[57] Cf. Ulp. D. 2,1,15; on this rule A. Wacke, 'Errantis nulla voluntas. Grenzen der Konludenz stillschweigender Willenserklärungen' (1994) 22 Index, pp. 267 et seq. On the intersection of error and consent Apathy, 'Sachgerechtigkeit und Systemdenken', pp. 95 et seq. and Schermaier, 'Auslegung und Konsensbestimmung', pp. 235 et seq.
[58] On the dichotomy of *verba* and *voluntas*, cf. for example: G. Gandolfi, *Studi sull'interpretazione degli atti negoziale in diritto romano* (Milan, 1966), pp. 288 et seq.; R. Astolfi, *Studi sull'oggetto dei legati in diritto romano* (2 vols., Palermo, 1969), vol. II, pp. 163 et seq.; M. Kaser, *Römisches Privatrecht*, 1st section: *Das altrömische, das vorklassische und klassische Recht* (2nd edn, Munich, 1971), pp. 234 et seq.; P. Pescani, 'Potentior est quam vox mens dicentis' (1971) 22 Iura, pp. 121 et seq.; B. Albanese, 'Vox e mens dicentis' (1973) 34 Ann. Palermo, pp. 79 et seq.; P. Cerami, 'Verba e voluntas in Celso figlio' in *Studi in onore di A. Arena I* (Palermo, 1981), pp. 477 et seq.; Zimmermann, *Law of Obligations*, pp. 622 et seq.
[59] Hugo Grotius, *De iure belli ac pacis* (Traiecti ad Rhenum, 1773), lib. II, cap. XVI, § I 1. For more detail on the following see: Schermaier, *Die Bestimmung des wesentlichen Irrtums*, pp. 173 et seq.

sixteenth century, it had become generally accepted that where divergences over the content of a contract occur, the most important forms of evidence for deducing the intention of the parties were the words and signs exchanged: 'in pacto verba ad aliud non requiritur, praeterquam ad probandum voluntatem contrahentium'.[60] A doctrine of interpretation in the modern sense was unknown; jurists certainly developed a canon of interpretative rules[61] according to the Roman example, but the contents of a declaration of intent did not depend on its objective meaning. Although the words were regarded as the door to the intention of the speaker, the speaker's will was not judged according to the objective meaning of its declaration but the declaration gave evidence of what the speaker claimed to have intended.

Only natural law in the seventeenth and eighteenth centuries placed the objective meaning of a declaration at the centre of interpretation. The content of a declaration is determined according to how an averagely informed and prudent recipient of a declaration would understand it. Grotius had already demanded an interpretation which was oriented around the usual meaning of the words.[62] Due primarily to Pufendorf[63] this concept becomes established on the basis of Hobbes' social contract

---

[60] Andrea ab Exea, 'Tractatus de pactis' in *Trias receptarum praelectionum et discussionum de pactis* (edition: Basiliae, 1624), at p. 24. The distrust of the meaning of words exchanged is especially noticeable in this statement. The reasons for this are probably the narrowly interpreted Roman sources that only require consensus in intention of the parties for the validity of a consensual contract (or a *pactum*); cf. for example, Ulp. D. 2,14,1,2 f.; I. 3,22,1.

[61] The most well-known is perhaps the rule: *in dubio contra proferentem/creditorem*; on the history of this rule cf. C. Krampe, 'Die ambiguitas-Regel: Interpretatio contra stipulatorem, venditorem, locatorem' (1983) 100 ZSSt, pp. 185 et seq.; C. Krampe, *Die Unklarheitenregel* (Berlin, 1983), pp. 14 et seq.; Zimmermann, *Law of Obligations*, pp. 639 et seq.; generally also: H. Coing, *Europäisches Privatrecht* (Munich, 1985), vol. 1: *Älteres Gemeines Recht (1500–1800)*, pp. 410 et seq.

[62] Grotius, *De jure belli ac pacis*, lib. II, cap. XVI, § 1 and lib. II, cap. IV, § III. On this, for example: M. Diesselhorst, *Des Hugo Grotius Lehre vom Versprechen* (Cologne, 1959), pp. 55 et seq.; H. Hübner, 'Subjektivismus in der Entwicklung des Privatrechts' in D. Medicus and H. H. Seiler (eds.), *Festschrift für Max Kaser zum 70 Geburtstag* (Munich, 1976), pp. 720 et seq.; K. Luig, 'Franz Zeiller und die Irrtumsregelung des ABGB' in W. Selb and H. Hofmeister (eds.), *Forschungsband Franz Zeiller* (Vienna, 1983), pp. 158 et seq.; E. A. Kramer, 'Der Pflichtgedanke bei der Vertragsschließung: Zur vernunftrechtlichen Grundlage der Vertrauensdoktrin' (1971) *Österreichische Juristenzeitung*, p. 121 at p. 125; F. Wieacker, *Privatrechtsgeschichte der Neuzeit unter besonderer Berücksichtigung der deutschen Entwicklung* (2nd edn, Göttingen, 1967), p. 293; H. E. Troje, 'Ambiguitas contra stipulatorem' (1961) SDHI 27 106.

[63] S. Pufendorf, *De jure naturae et gentium*, lib. IV, cap. I, §§ 4–5 (edn Francofurti/Lipsiae, 1759); S. Pufendorf, *De officio hominis et civis iuxta legem naturalem*, lib. I, cap. X, § 2 (edn Cantabrigiae 1682; repr. New York 1937).

theory:[64] because members of a society have to communicate in a single language in order to be able to live together then every member must be able to rely on the meaning of certain words and signs. In the law on mistake,[65] this principle serves basically to excise the appellant's claim that a mistake had been made, i.e. the claim that something else was intended than that which was expressed. In general contract theory, it allows a distinction to be made between intention and declaration of intent and the latter becomes the nucleus of contractual acts.[66] This distinction later enabled Savigny to portray the declaration of intent as the product of the internal formation of intent. However, due to the fact that the act (declaration of intent) – pursuant to the scholastic theory of acts – is only attributable if it has been supported by a corresponding intention (intention of declaration), Savigny is able to transfer the problem of mistake into the dualism of intention and declaration: an operative mistake only occurs where someone declares that which he did not intend.[67]

Fair price and laesio enormis

From late Roman casuistry and the moral-theological theory of fair price, Canon and Roman common law developed an objective instrument to impose sanctions on breaches of precontractual duties of disclosure: if one party promises a performance the value of which is more than 100% of the value of the return performance, the promise (the contract) is invalid.[68] The decisions of the Emperors Diocletian and Maximian[69] from the years AD 285 and 293 that land acquisitions are invalid if the purchase price does not amount to even one half of the value of the land

---

[64] For more detail on this see Schermaier, 'Europäische Geistesgeschichte', pp. 78 et seq.

[65] On this see immediately below at pp. 57–58.

[66] This systematic advance was fully realised in the school of Christian Wolff; Wolff's proposal was itself decisive but it was only Nettelbladt who formulated the new concept. Cf. for example: D. Nettelbladt, *Systema elementare iurisprudentiae positivae germanorum communis* (edn Halae, 1781) §§ 76 and 193; D. Nettelbladt, *Systema elementare universae iurisprudentiae naturalis, pars I: Introductio in iurisprudentiam naturalem* (edition: Halae Magdeburgicae, 1757) §§ 265 et seq.

[67] For the consequences of this starting point on the Pandect law on mistake see below at pp. 60–62.

[68] See generally for the history of *laesio enormis* for example, E. Bussi, *La formazione dei dogmi di diritto privato nel diritto commune* (2 vols., Padua, 1937), vol. II, pp. 37 et seq.; R. Dekkers, *La lésion énorme* (Paris, 1937); Zimmermann, *Law of Obligations*, pp. 259 et seq.; Becker, *Die Lehre von der laesio enormis*; Siems, *Handel und Wucher*, pp. 764 et seq.

[69] C. 4,44,2 and 8.

were reached on the basis of social and economic reasons.[70] Since the middle ages[71] jurists had recognised *laesio enormis* by relying on the theory of fair price as a moral-theological development of Aristotle's *iustitia commutativa*.[72]

Hobbes already opined that prices are formed by the degree of demand[73] and thereby vary from case to case. Thus, § 935 ABGB also restricts the possibility to dissolve a contract on the basis of *laesio enormis* (§ 934 ABGB) where someone intends to acquire a thing 'owing to a special predilection for an extraordinary value'.[74]

Besides the debate which surrounds the question whether and how a 'fair price' (*pretium verum/iustum*) may be deduced at all, there lies behind the application of *laesio enormis* the justified concern to prevent or at least to impede usurious exploitation. Not without good reason do medieval sources[75] already recognise *dolus ex ipsa re* ('deceit in the thing itself') in cases where someone allows a disproportionately high return performance to be promised in return for his own. Modern German

---

[70] Rural exodus, the perishing of farmers and high inflation may have motivated the decisions; for background information and the discussion concerning the authenticity of the sources, see: Zimmermann, *Law of Obligations*, pp. 259 et seq. Additionally, for example: K. Visky, 'Die Proportionalität von Wert und Preis in den römischen Rechtsquellen des III. Jahrhunderts' (1969) 16 *Revue international des droits de l'antiquité*, pp. 374 et seq.; K. Hackl, 'Zu den Wurzeln der Anfechtung wegen laesio enormis' (1981) 98 ZSSt, pp. 147 et seq.; A. J. B. Sirks, 'La laesio enormis en droit Romain et Byzantin' (1985) 53 *Tijdschrift voor Rechtsgeschiedenis*, pp. 291 et seq.; H. T. Klami, '"Laesio enormis" in Roman Law?' (1987) 33 *Labeo*, pp. 48 et seq.; M. Pennitz, 'Zur Anfechtung wegen laesio enormis im römischen Recht' in M. Schermaier, M. Rainer and L. Winkel (eds.), *Iurisprudentia universalis. Festschrift für Theo Mayer-Maly* (Vienna, 2002), pp. 575 et seq.

[71] Cf. on this: Gordley, *Philosophical Origins*, pp. 65 et seq., with commentary from Azo, Accursius, Hugolinus and Baldus; already in Brachylogus iuris civilis ,13,8) from the middle of the twelfth century the decisions from C. 4,44 are extended to all things capable of forming the subject of a transaction. Siems, *Handel und Wucher*, pp. 764 et seq. can follow an unbroken tradition of *laesio enormis* from the late Roman time up to the middle ages.

[72] Aristot. *Eth. Nic.* 5,3 f. (1131 a–1132 b); Thomas Aquinas, STh. II–II qu. 61. See on this, for example Gordley, *Philosophical Origins*, pp. 13 et seq.; T. Mayer-Maly, 'Der gerechte Preis' in G. Frotz (ed.), *Festschrift Heinrich Demelius zum 80 Geburtstag* (Vienna, 1973), pp. 139 et seq.

[73] T. Hobbes, *Leviathan* ch. XV in W. Molesworth *English Works of Thomas Hobbes of Malmesbury* (London, 1839), vol. III, p. 137.

[74] The concept of the *pretium affectionis* is already familiar to Roman jurists (Paul. D. 35,2,63 pr.), however in this form it may be traced back to C. A. von Martini, *De lege naturali positiones in usum auditorii vindobonensis* (Vienna, 1772), § 515 and § 521, and may probably be followed via Thomasius and Pufendorf to Hobbes.

[75] Azo, *Summa Codicis*, ad C. 2,20, n. 9; Rogerius, *Summa Codicis*, ad C. 4,44. Gordley, *Philosophical Origins*, p. 66, in this respect, cites as the oldest source: Vacarius, *Liber pauperum*, lib. IV, cap. LI, ad. D. 18,2,23,3.

case law couples the concept of *laesio enormis* – although it has not been codified – to elements of the usurious and therefore invalid transaction, by arguing that a gross disparity between value and price indicates that the advantaged party has exploited the weaknesses of the opposite party.[76] Frequently, it is an advantage of information, disapproved of by law, which allows this party to obtain an especially good bargain. Today, as then, it is not the deduction of the 'true value' of the thing sold which presents the judge with a difficult hurdle to overcome but rather the question which information should be exchanged and which should not be.[77] Its renaissance in German case law[78] shows especially that the values which underlie *laesio enormis* cannot be reduced to the value–price relationship. The exploitation of the other party's inexperience or position of necessity, i.e. the intention to exploit his weaknesses for the purpose of self-enrichment, is, however, difficult to prove. That said, controlling the contents of contracts cannot end in the mere observation of determined value–price relations. Both codification of *laesio enormis*[79] and codification of elements constituting pure usury[80] therefore demand judicial reduction or extension.

Late scholasticism and natural law (1550–1800)

The late scholastics, mostly Spanish theologians who wrote commentaries on Thomas Aquinas' *Summa theologica* (therein mainly the *quaestiones* 'De iustitia et iure' of the Secunda secundae), developed from Thomas' theory of imputation and Roman law[81] a general theory of

[76] Most recently BGH, Judgment of 2 February 2000, VIII ZR 12/99 (reported in EBE 2000).
[77] See for example, Cic. *off.* 3,50 (above at fn. 26) on the one hand and AG (Amtsgericht) Coburg, NJW 1993, 938: in this case, someone had sold old notes and note books at a flea market. The obviously expert purchaser acquired for a few pennies several pages, among them an autograph of W. A. Mozart. The court did not allow the vendor to rescind the contract. Nevertheless, the judgment did not reduce the *ratio decidendi* to the crucial question of whether the purchaser was bound to have drawn the vendor's attention to the high value of the autograph but proceeded – in formal phrases derived from the case law of superior courts – to the requirements of a rescission for mistake.
[78] See also T. Mayer-Maly, 'Renaissance der laesio enormis?' in C.-W. Canaris (ed.) *Festschrift für Karl Larenz zum 80 Geburtstag am 23 April 1983* (Munich, 1983), pp. 395 et seq.
[79] § 934 ABGB; art. 1674 French Civil Code.
[80] For example, § 138 II BGB; art. 1448 Codice civile it.
[81] In this, they primarily relied on the works of Italian glossators and commentators (*mos Italicus*). They do not appear to know the French school, in particular, contemporary humanism. In contrast to this, Jacobus Cuiacius for example, quotes the *theologi*, as he calls them (J. Cuiacius, *Commentarii in lib. XLIV Pauli ad edictum*, ad D. 22,6,1; in: *Opera omnia*, Mutinae 1778–82, vol. V, 617 B).

consensus and contract at perhaps the same time as Connanus. They consistently judge the significance that defects in intention have on the valid conclusion of a contract according to the principle of subjective causality. Therefore, if the mistaken or deceived party would not have concluded the contract in full knowledge of the real facts, then as far as he is concerned, the contract is invalid. Mainly the proposals of Dominicus de Soto (1494–1560), Diego de Covarruvias y Leya (1512–77), Ludovicus Molina (1535–1600) and Leonardus Lessius (1554–1623) decisively influenced the school of natural law in the seventeenth and eighteenth centuries.[82] The Dutchman Hugo Grotius (1583–1645) is regarded as the founder of this school: his work *De iure belli ac pacis* (1625) also made the new contractual theory popular in legal discussion.

Mistake

In Grotius' view too, every defect in intention that has a causal connection to the making of a promise is significant.[83] Samuel Pufendorf (1632–94), Jean Barbeyrac (1674–1744) and Christian Wolff (1679–1754) adopt this principle but, under the still immense influence of Roman sources, re-model it in various respects. Above all, they attempt to keep the purely subjective criterion of the causative nature of a mistake under control by means of objective criteria, in order to make general statements about the significance of certain mistakes. Titius and – following him – Barbeyrac opine for example, that only mistakes which are made with regard to a *res necessaria contractus* are operative; these may be factual circumstances which are typically significant in the case of a contract of this type or those which the parties have made fundamental to the conclusion of their contract[84] as part of a condition.[85] Only in the case of a mistake concerning the identity of the contractual partner (*error in persona*) are Titius and Barbeyrac among those who continue to be guided by the question whether the mistaken party in

---

[82] For more details on this, see: Gordley, *Philosophical Origins*, pp. 85 et seq. and now Schermaier, *Die Bestimmung des wesentlichen Irrtums*, pp. 124 et seq.

[83] Grotius, *De iure belli ac pacis*, lib. II, cap. XI, § VI.

[84] Cf. G. G. Titius, *Observationes ratiocinantes in compendium juris Lauterbachianum* (Lipsiae, 1703), observatio 511: '. . . ea, quae vel negotii natura vel paciscentium destinatio tempestiva ac declarata requirit'; similarly J. Barbeyrac, *Trad. de Pufendorf: Le droit de nature et des gens, ou systeme general des principes les plus importans de la morale, de la jurisprudence, et de la politique* (Amsterdam, 1706), ad lib. I, cap. III, § 10, n. 2.

[85] On the important role of the condition (in particular of the *conditiones tacitae*) in the theory of contract law below at pp. 58–60.

a given case would have also concluded the transaction had he not made a mistake. This serves to explain on the one hand, the theory of mistake contained in the Prussian Allgemeine Landrecht (ALR 1794)[86] and, on the other, that of Pothier and the Code civil (1804),[87] which, as concerns a mistake relating to the subject of the contract, are guided by whether it is 'objectively' significant, whilst they judge mistake as to the person of the contractual partner according to its 'subjective' significance.

Perhaps at the same time, a fundamentally new proposal of the general theory of contract (and thereby the theory of mistake) arises – again passed on by Pufendorf[88] – from Hobbes' social contract theory:[89] from the concept that every member of every society must be able to rely on the meaning of certain words and signs, Christian Thomasius concludes that no one can assert the claim that his intention diverged from his declaration. Thus, he also decided, logically, that every mistake had to injure the mistaken party himself.[90] The principle drawn from this – *error nocet erranti* – quickly becomes popular in the discussion on the law on mistake, but is refined by the younger natural law jurists pursuant to its origin in the theory of reliance: only if the recipient of the declaration could rely on the intention inferred therefrom, did the giver remain bound to his declaration. However, if the recipient knew of the diverging intention of the giver or if he should have known of it then he cannot rely on his *iusta expectatio*, i.e. his reliance on the declaration.[91] This principle of reliance theory was first anchored in statute

---

[86] ALR, 1. Theil, 4. Titel: § 75. A mistake relating to significant elements of a transaction or in the main subject of the declaration of intent makes the same invalid. § 76. A similar situation applies to a mistake in the identity of the one for whom a right is to arise from the declaration of intent as soon as it becomes clear from the circumstances that without this mistake the declaration would not be given in its existing form.

[87] Article 1110 of the Civil Code: 'L'erreur n'est une cause de nullité de la convention que lorsqu'elle tombe sur la substance même de la chose qui en est l'objet. Elle n'est point une cause de nullité lorsqu'elle ne tombe que sur la personne avec laquelle on a intention de contracter, à moins que la considération de cette personne ne soit la cause principale de la convention.'

[88] Pufendorf, *De jure naturae et gentium*, lib. IV, cap. I, §§ 4–5; *De officio hominis et civis iuxta legem naturalem*, lib. I, cap. X, § 2 (Edition: Cantabrigiae, 1682; repr. New York, 1937).

[89] For more detail on this: Schermaier, 'Europäische Geistesgeschichte', pp. 78 et seq.

[90] C. Thomasius, *Institutiones jurisprudentiae divinae* (Edition: Halae Magdeburgicae, 1720), lib. I, cap. I, § 72.

[91] Thus, for example: J. A. H. Ulrich, *Initia philosophiae iusti seu iuris naturae socialis et gentium* (Ienae, 1790), §§ 215 ff.; G. Hufeland, *Lehrsätze des Naturrechts und der damit verbundenen Wissenschaften* (Jena, 1790), §§ 255 f.

in the ABGB's law on mistake in 1811.[92] The Pandect doctrine of the late nineteenth century seizes on this principle and refines it further. Its core however, originates from the late natural law discussion of the Hobbes–Pufendorfian theory of language. Today – taking into account the corresponding regulations of the Principles of European Contract Law and the UNIDROIT Principles – it forms the maxim of a modern regulation of the law on mistake.[93]

Clausula rebus sic stantibus *and* conditio tacita

Many natural law jurists fell victim to the temptation to deal with mistakes concerning present circumstances or incorrect expectations relating to future circumstances through the legal concept of *conditio tacita* (implied condition). Grotius had already believed, in his treatment of mistake, that every promisor only gave his promise on the condition that all circumstances would turn out as he had imagined them.[94] In support of this, he relied on the classical and medieval *clausula* doctrine.[95] According to this an obligation assumed in contract ceases following a change in the external circumstances pursuant to which the contract was concluded. The problem had already formed the subject of discussion in classical philosophy: Cicero cites the case where someone had taken a sword for safe-keeping and the depositor, who had in the meantime turned mad, demanded its return. The custodian did not breach his obligation to return the object in custody if he refused to surrender the sword.[96] In this respect, even medieval jurists had referred

---

[92] Sections 871, 872, 876 ABGB 1811; these provisions were re-enacted in 1916. § 876 in the 1811 edition stated for example: 'If the promisor himself and alone is at fault with regard to his mistakes of whatever kind, the contract remains valid; unless the circumstances were such that the promisee must have recognised the prevailing mistake.'

[93] Article 4.103 PECL; art. 3.5 UNIDROIT Principles; cf. also art. 6:228 of the Dutch BW.

[94] Grotius, *De iure belli ac pacis*, lib. II, cap. XI, § VI 2: 'Similiter ergo dicemus, si promissio fundata sit in praesumtione quadam facti quod non ita se habeat, naturaliter nullam ejus esse vim: quia omnino promissor non consensit in promissum, nisi sub quadam conditione quae re ipsa non extitit.'

[95] This connection was hitherto disputed, cf. for example: Diesselhorst, *Des Hugo Grotius Lehre vom Versprechen*, p. 92; R. Feenstra, *De oorsprong van Hugo De Groot's leer over dwaling*, in: *Met eerbiedigende werking. Opstellen aangeboden aan Prof. Mr. L. J. Hijmans van der Bergh* (Deventer, 1971), pp. 96 et seq.

[96] Cic. *off.* 3,94 et seq. On this and other sources of the *clausula* doctrine see: R. Feenstra, 'Impossibilitas and clausula rebus sic stantibus' in A. Watson (ed.), *Daube noster. Essays in Legal History for David Daube* (Edinburgh/London, 1974), pp. 77 et seq.; M. Beck-Mannagetta, 'Die Clausula rebus sic stantibus und die Geschäftsgrundlage in der Dogmengeschichte' in *La formazione Storica del Diritto Moderno in Europa* (3 vols.,

to a condition which is 'impliedly' included at the conclusion to every contract.[97] Grotius came across the *clausula* doctrine in both scholastic theory[98] and Roman common law.[99] Grotius' innovation lies in the connection between the law on mistake and the *clausula* doctrine, which he created with help from the legal concept of the *conditio tacita*.

According to this, the promisor's mistake ought to be operative due to the fact that he had only given his promise under the (implied) condition that his expectations are met. If the meaning of a promise (*promissio*) is judged according to the promisor's intention,[100] the construction of an 'implied condition' is largely unproblematic. This has to be viewed from Grotius' doctrine of *promissio*, which was guided by the moral theory of the scholastics how to impute human actions: a promise is – in Grotius's doctrine – the nucleus of legal acting and the main task of the law of contract is to elaborate rules for 'imputing' this sort of action: therefore the questions, what kind of promise it is, to whom it is addressed or what its contents are, can only be answered by the promisor's will and intention. The assumption of a *conditio tacita* becomes difficult however, if the justified expectations of the recipient of the promise are considered, especially if the mistake is examined at the conclusion of the contract. Pufendorf had already conceded that a mistake relating to *promissiones*, could only be taken into consideration if the mistaken party recognisably 'expressed' his (incorrect) expectations.[101] In the case of mistake relating to the creation of a contract (by exchanging two or

Florence, 1977), vol. III, pp. 1263 et seq.; G. Gieg, *Clausula rebus sic stantibus und Geschäftsgrundlage. Ein Beitrag zur Dogmengeschichte* (Aachen, 1994).

[97] Joh. Teutonicus, Gl. *furens*, ad C. 22, q. 2, c. 14; for further comment see: R. Zimmermann, '"Heard melodies are sweet but those unheard are sweeter . . ." Conditio tacita, implied condition und die Fortbildung des europäischen Vertragsrechts' (1993) 193 AcP, pp. 134 seq.; Feenstra, 'Impossibilitas and clausula rebus sic stantibus', pp. 80 et seq.

[98] In this Grotius may have drawn directly from Lessius, *De iustitia et iure ceterisque virtutibus cardinalibus . . . ad secundam secundae D. Thomae* (edn: Venice, 1608), lib. II, cap. XVII, dub. V, n. 33.

[99] M. Rummel presents numerous sources of legal theory of the middle ages and early modern era: *Die clausula rebus sic stantibus* (Baden-Baden, 1991).

[100] Also Pufendorf, *De iure naturae et gentium*, lib. III, cap. VI, § 6; C. Wolff, *Jus naturae methodo scientifica pertractatum* (edn Halae Magdeburgicae, 1744, repr. Hildesheim/New York, 1972), pars IV, § 569; also on this: Zimmermann, '"Heard melodies are sweet but those unheard are sweeter . . .'", pp. 146 et seq.

[101] Pufendorf, *De jure naturae et gentium*, lib. III, cap. VI, § 6: 'Verum si promissio praesentiam aut absentiam alicuius qualitatis tanquam conditionem prae se non tulerit, licet fortasse ea facta non fuisset, ubi de illa promissori constitisset; promissio nihilominus valida erit.'

more promises), he even stipulated that only those circumstances which at the outset the mistaken party had communicated to the other in the form of a condition would constitute a basis for the contract.[102]

Despite these restrictions, the model of the *conditio tacita* did not lose its popularity; it played an important role, to a lesser or greater degree, in Continental-European law on mistake until the end of the nineteenth century. It may be found both in Windscheid's *Voraussetzunglehre* as an 'undeveloped condition'[103] and in Leonhard's doctrine of mistake.[104] The doctrine of the implied condition has also assumed a special role in English law on mistake since *Couturier* v. *Hastie*.[105]

Pandectism (1800–1900)

The historical school of jurisprudence – or, as it is also known, the 'Pandectist' movement according to its major subject of observation the Pandects (Digests) of Justinian – is primarily a German phenomenon. However, the influence that this school had, particularly in France, Austria, Switzerland and Italy, justifies its treatment as a European phenomenon. It also carries the second European wave of codification[106] – just as the natural law of the eighteenth century carried the first – owing to which, its more important results are contained in rules still applicable today.

Mistake

The Pandectist law on mistake is dominated by the legal concept of Savigny's 'mistake in declaration'. This legal concept described the

---

[102] Pufendorf, *De jure naturae et gentium*, lib. III, cap. VI, § 7; for present analysis on this: Schermaier, *Die Bestimmung des wesentlichen Irrtums*, 4.2.2.3.

[103] B. Windscheid, *Die Lehre des römischen Rechts von den Voraussetzung* (Düsseldorf, 1850), pp. 80 et seq.

[104] R. Leonhard, *Der Irrthum bei nichtigen Verträgen nach römischem Rechte. Ein Beitrag zur Vereinfachung der Vertragslehre* (Berlin, 1882/1883), p. 512: 'Those mistakes of a contracting party relating to circumstances are significant when his correct expectation thereof has been displayed in a manner recognisable to the other party as a necessary pre-condition of the contract's validity.'

[105] *Couturier* v. *Hastie* (1856) 5 Clark's Reports, HL 673; for further information and comment on this see: Zimmermann, '"Heard melodies are sweet but those unheard are sweeter . . .'", pp. 149 et seq.; P. S. Atiyah, '*Couturier* v. *Hastie* and the Sale of Non-Existent Goods' (1957) 73 LQR 340 et seq.

[106] Swiss OR (1881) and ZGB (1907); German BGB (1900); 3rd partial re-enactment of the Austrian ABGB (1916); Soviet ZGB (1922); Turkish Civil Law Code/Law of Obligations (1926); Italian Codice civile (1942); Greek ZGB (1946).

situation where someone made a mistake relating to the content of his declaration (judged according to an objective standard) and was termed by Savigny an 'unreal mistake',[107] yet it became the hub of the doctrine of mistake of the nineteenth century. Savigny himself, but more strongly his pupils and supporters – above all Brinz and Zitelmann – had already placed the operative mistake in declaration in conceptual antithesis to an inoperative mistake in motive.[108] This distinction also has its roots in the scholastic doctrine of contractual acts. Zitelmann divided the 'psychological' process of making a declaration of intent into three stages: first of all, someone makes the decision on the basis of his perception to make a declaration of intent (=motive); this decision develops into an actual intent to declare (=intention) and this is once more expressed in a declaration of intent undertaken on this basis (=declaration). The law, in Zitelmann's view, may only take mistakes into account which result from the declaration perceived by the recipient diverging from the intention of the declarer; for example, where someone intends to say '10,000 euros' but in fact only says '1,000 euros'. Mistakes in the formation of intention – mistakes therefore which influence an intention to declare and which the declarer would not have formed had he known of the true circumstances – had to remain insignificant as mere 'mistakes in motive'. Accordingly, whosoever believes a bracelet to be made of gold and wishes to purchase it for this reason, is therefore only committing a 'mistake in motive' because his intention to purchase was formed on the basis of a defective perception.[109] It logically follows from Zitelmann's theory that all mistakes concerning the underlying state of facts – i.e. concerning the foundations of the contract – are insignificant being mistakes in motive. The old cases of *error in corpore*, *in substantia*, *in materia* or *in qualitate* – provided they did not cause a mistake in declaration – could therefore no longer be taken into account.[110]

[107] F. C. v. Savigny, *System des heutigen römischen Rechts* (7 vols., Berlin, 1840), vol. III, pp. 99 et seq.; for a comprehensive analysis and further comment see: Schermaier, *Die Bestimmung des wesentlichen Irrtums*, 9.2.2.

[108] A. Brinz, *Lehrbuch der Pandekten* (4 vols., 2nd edn, Erlangen/Leipzig, 1892), vol. IV, §§ 315 et seq.; E. Zitelmann, *Irrtum und Rechtsgeschäft. Eine psychologisch-juristische Untersuchung* (Leipzig, 1879), pp. 329 et seq., pp. 373 et seq.

[109] Cf. Zitelmann, *Irrtum und Rechtsgeschäft*, pp. 328 et seq., pp. 441 et seq. For this reason, regard is paid to the case of the *viriola aurea* in Ulp. D. 18,1,14.

[110] So indeed: Zitelmann, *Irrtum und Rechtsgeschäft*, pp. 461 et seq., pp. 490 et seq., pp. 549 et seq.; in summary: Schermaier, *Die Bestimmung des wesentlichen Irrtums*, pp. 521 et seq.

Although Zitelmann himself later believed this 'psychological' doctrine of mistake to be an unsuitable basis for a statutory regulation,[111] and despite many other critical opinions,[112] modern German legal theory still holds fast to the distinction between mistake in declaration and mistake in motive.[113] Due to the insecurity concerning the apparently conclusive evidence that mistakes relating to the facts of the case are always insignificant, certain provisions were adopted in § 119 II BGB and in art. 24 I 4 of the Swiss Code of Obligations which categorise mistakes relating to quality or the basis of the contract as operative mistakes.

Culpa in contrahendo

Among the various elements which serve to sanction the neglect of duties to inform in modern private law systems, the enduring obligation to pay damages is the most interesting from a dogmatic point of view. This legal concept establishes both an obligation that the mistaken party pay damages and the obligation that a party compensate the loss suffered by his contractual partner – whom he was bound to have informed of certain circumstances. Its history begins in Roman law as a form of precontractual liability for *dolus in contrahendo*: in some decisions liability arising from a contract is also approved if a contract has not even come into existence (especially where this is due to initial impossibility).[114] In such cases, Roman jurists allowed the contractual complaint without utilising any particular fictions and arguments[115] and in so doing, extended the standard of contractual *bona fides* to the precontractual relationship of the parties. Rudolf v. Jhering generalised these rudiments into the principle that the party, whose fault causes the conclusion of

---

[111] E. Zitelmann, from discussions during the second session of the first section, 12 September 1889, *Verhandlungen des Zwanzigsten Deutschen Juristentages*, published by the Schriftführer-Amt der ständigen Deputation (Berlin, 1889), vol. IV, pp. 101 et seq.

[112] Foremost amongst contemporary criticism: E. Pfersche, *Zur Lehre vom error in substantia* (Graz, 1880).

[113] Cf. for example: W. Flume, *Allgemeiner Teil des Bürgerlichen Rechts* (4th edn, Berlin/Heidelberg/New York, 1993), vol. 2: *Das Rechtsgeschäft*, pp. 449 et seq., pp. 472 et seq. For a summary, see for example: Zimmermann, *Law of Obligations*, pp. 614 et seq.; Kramer, *Der Irrtum beim Vertragsabschluß*, pp. 34 et seq.

[114] For example, Ulp. D. 11,7,8,1 (sale of a *locus religiosus*); Mod. D. 18,1,62,1 (sale of *loca sacra/religiosa/publica*); Ulp. D. 18,4,4 (sale of a non-existent debt); Paul. D. 19,1,21 pr. (sale of a non-existent *partus ancillae*).

[115] V. Arangio-Ruiz, *La compravendita in diritto romano* (2 vols., 2nd edn, Naples, 1961; rist. 1976), vol. I, 209 n. 1 (210) makes reference to a 'validità del contratto (come putativo)'; see also: P. Stein, *Fault in the Formation of Contract in Roman and Scots Law* (Edinburgh/London, 1958); Y. Ben-Dror, 'The Perennial Ambiguity of *culpa in contrahendo*' 27 (1983) *American Journal of Legal History*, pp. 142 et seq.

a contract to fail, is bound to compensate the other's loss arising from his reliance on a futile promise ('negative interest').[116] In particular, the unsatisfactory solution which Savigny's doctrine bestowed (due to the fact that it regarded every mistake in declaration as significant, no matter whether the recipient of the declaration had relied on the validity of the declaration), led Jhering to make the following generalisation: that the mistaken party may indeed be able to free himself from his declaration but he is obliged to compensate the loss which the recipient of his declaration of intent has suffered due to reliance on its validity.[117]

Even this solution was not new; Grotius had already held the mistaken party liable to compensate loss where he was negligent *in re exploranda vel in sensu suo exprimendo* (i.e. in investigating the circumstances of the contract or in communicating information to the other party).[118] Here, and also in Jhering's case, the liability of the mistaken party due to his own *culpa in contrahendo* is thus the price of being able to rely on the mistake and annul the contractual obligation. Legal systems which only take unavoidable or excusable mistakes into account,[119] or those which make the mistaken party's ability to annul dependent on whether the recipient of the declaration suffered loss arising from his negative interest,[120] do not recognise such a connection.

In Germany, Austria and Switzerland,[121] but also in Italy and France,[122] the legal concept of *culpa in contrahendo* has conquered a new and broad field branching off from the law on mistake in that it enables infringements of duties to inform of one party in general to be punished. Due to the fact that German law on delict usually only allows damages

---

[116] R. v. Jhering, 'Culpa in contrahendo oder Schadenersatz bei nichtigem oder nicht zur Perfektion gelangten Verträgen' (1863) 4 *Jherings Jahrbücher*, pp. 1 et seq.

[117] As is the case today: § 122 BGB.

[118] Grotius, *De iure belli ac pacis*, lib. II, cap. XI, § VI 3.

[119] As is the case with the French, Belgian and Spanish practice; cf. the comments in Kramer, *Der Irrtum beim vertragsabschluß*, pp. 61 et seq.

[120] Cf. for example, § 871 ABGB, which only allows annulment on the ground of mistake if the non-mistaken party did not suffer any loss despite relying on the validity of the declaration of intent (*res integra*).

[121] However, also in the USA for example, cf. F. Kessler, 'Der Schutz des Vertrauens bei Vertragsverhandlungen in der neueren amerikanischen Rechtsprechung' in H. C. Ficker (ed), *Festschrift für Ernst von Caemmerer zum 70 Geburtstag* (Tübingen, 1978), pp. 873 et seq.; F. Kessler and E. Fine, '*Culpa in Contrahendo*, Bargaining in Good Faith, and Freedom of Contract: A Comparative Study' (1964) 77 *Harvard Law Review*, pp. 401 et seq.

[122] See once again the comments in Kramer, *Der Irrtum beim Vertragsabschluß*, pp. 134 et seq.

where certain objects deserving of legal protection are infringed but that 'property' is not protected as such an object,[123] liability for *culpa in contrahendo* has even established itself as the third track of the law on liability besides contractual and delictual liability. The attraction of a legal institute which was not regulated in statute until 2002, thereby offering practice and science sufficient freedom for expansion and distinctions, has led to conventional rules governing liability for disclosure (e.g. the law on mistake and fraudulent misrepresentation, the law on unconscionable transactions, usury or on liability for defects in quality) being somewhat pushed into the background. The incursion of *culpa in contrahendo* into the field of mistake may lead us to enquire whether it is possible to fit it into the established set of values of civil law countries or whether it is going to eat up the older legal concepts.[124]

---

[123] Especially not by § 823 I BGB, the central rule of the German law on delict. Matters are different in French and Austrian law for example, which recognise both delictual general clauses; cf. art. 1382 of the French Civil Code and § 1295 ABGB.

[124] For the German discussion cf. most recently: W. Krüger, 'Eine Linoleumrolle und die Folgen' in G. Brambring (ed.), *Festschrift für Horst Hagen* (Cologne, 1999), pp. 409 et seq.; H. C. Grigoleit, *Vorvertragliche Informationshaftung. Vorsatzdogma, Rechtsfolgen, Schranken* (Munich, 1997).

3 The rise and fall of mistake in the English law of contract

John Cartwright

For the comparative lawyer the doctrine of mistake in the English law of contract is a topic of particular interest – and especially for the comparative lawyer with an eye to the historical development of the doctrine and the continental influences on it. No doubt the story is not yet over. But in the light of the most recent decisions on mistake in the Court of Appeal[1] and the House of Lords[2] we can now trace the development of the doctrine of mistake in three centuries, as it passed through the hands of some key members of the judiciary. For the purposes of this discussion, the first life of mistake is in the nineteenth century, born of the common law but with civil law influences through, notably, the insight of Lord Blackburn. The second life is the twentieth century, first growing into a doctrine of mistake at common law with the assistance of Lord Atkin and then in the second half of the century further developing into a doctrine of mistake in equity under the watchful tutelage of Lord Denning. The third life is just beginning, in the twenty-first century. The growth in mistake which was promoted by Lord Denning is being cut back. Mistake is not dead, but its place in the law of contract is being reassessed. Its future will depend on how this century's judges in the higher courts see the nature of contract in English law and their own role in intervening (or not) to protect either the mistaken contracting party or a third party affected by the contract.

The scope of the discussion

This discussion focuses mainly not on the kinds of mistake which prevent the parties having come to an agreement on the same terms, but on

---

[1] *Great Peace Shipping Ltd* v. *Tsavliris Salvage (International) Ltd (The 'Great Peace')* [2002] EWCA Civ 1407, [2003] QB 679 (common mistake as to facts).
[2] *Shogun Finance Ltd* v. *Hudson* [2003] UKHL 62, [2003] 3 WLR 1371 (mistake of identity).

the case where there *is* agreement on the terms but on a wrong assumption by one or both parties as to the facts or surrounding circumstances of their transaction: cases, therefore, where the mistake may 'nullify' (rather than 'negative') the consent.[3] Towards the end of this paper there will also be a brief discussion of one form of mistake which negatives consent – mistake of identity.

The starting point is clear: even in the period when mistake was at its most developed, under Lord Denning, there has been some reluctance to allow a party to escape a contract on the basis of his own mistake. This is not to say that English law has difficulties with the very notion of mistake: in the case of payments made under a mistake, the courts have been rather more open to admitting remedies.[4] Or where a gratuitous transaction, such as a deed of gift, is entered into under a mistake the courts have more easily found a remedy.[5] But when the claim is that the mistake is sufficient to avoid a *contract*, that is a different matter. Judicial instinct seems to rise against the claim. If both parties in fact assented to the contract, why should one party now be allowed to revoke his assent? That would injure the other party (the defendant, let us assume) – who either did not share the mistake (so why should he lose the benefit of the bargain, just because the claimant now shows that he misunderstood something about the subject matter of the contract, or the circumstances surrounding the transaction?) or shared the mistake but does not want to complain (so why should the claimant be able to do so, and deprive the defendant of the bargain?). English law does not generally see mistake as part of a unified theory of (defects of) consent;[6] and the judges tend to start from the position that if one party has, by providing consideration, bought into a bargain he should not easily be deprived of the benefit of it.[7] The other party's consent might have been vitiated by the mistake; but it takes more than that to justify his avoiding the consequences of having given his consent. There is a balance to be struck: the claimant's mistake against the security of the defendant's bargain. If the defendant caused the claimant's mistake, then the scales tip in favour of the claimant: the defendant can no

---

[3] General Introduction to this volume, Part I, section 1. Amongst the principal English textbook writers the language of 'negativing' and 'nullifying' consent is used only by G. H. Treitel, *The Law of Contract* (11th edn, London, 2003), p. 286 taken from Lord Atkin's judgment in *Bell v. Lever Brothers Ltd* [1932] AC 161, p. 217.

[4] R. Goff and G. Jones, *The Law of Restitution* (6th edn, G. Jones, London, 2002), chapter 4.

[5] *Gibbon v. Mitchell* [1990] 1 WLR 1304 at p. 1309; Goff and Jones, *Law of Restitution,* §§ 4-020–4-022.

[6] General Introduction, p. 3.   [7] Goff and Jones, *Law of Restitution,* § 4-005.

longer insist on the bargain being protected.[8] But then we are in a different chapter of the English contract books: misrepresentation. Amongst
English textbook writers the failure to make the link between mistake
and misrepresentation – a consequence of the failure to see mistake and
the other vitiating factors as a coherent theory – has tended to isolate
mistake. If the defendant did not cause the mistake, then he is entitled
to insist on his bargain. The strongest version of this theory is found in
one of the cases from the first life of mistake, *Smith* v. *Hughes*,[9] in which
the court was clear that a party could insist on the contract even where
at the time of its formation he *knew* that the other party was labouring
under a mistake as to the subject matter of the contract, just as long as
he did nothing to cause it and made no contractual promise that the
facts were as the claimant mistakenly believed them to be. This strong
view has so far survived through the development of mistake, although
it might not survive forever.[10] It is closely linked to the reluctance in
English law to impose duties of disclosure and information. A legal system that allows a party to avoid a contract by reason of his mistake can
more easily also admit that, where the other party did not cause the mistake but *could* have disabused him of it, then he *should* have done so –
there was a duty to inform. But a system, such as English law, that is
reluctant to allow mistake to vitiate the contract, and even allows a party
to remain silent when he knows the other party is making a mistake, is
naturally reluctant to embark on the development of a general duty to
inform.

The first life of mistake: the nineteenth century

It is well-documented[11] that the rise of the doctrine of mistake in the
English law of contract begins in the nineteenth century under the
influence of the civil law, both ancient and modern. The early cases, so
far as they involved an issue which can be recognised now as within the
general principles of mistake,[12] tended to reason not from a doctrine of
mistake, but from the construction of the terms of the agreement. There

---

[8] J. Cartwright, *Misrepresentation* (London, 2002), § 1.02.
[9] (1871) LR 6 QB 597.   [10] Cartwright, *Misrepresentation*, § 3.76.
[11] A. W. B. Simpson, 'Innovation in Nineteenth Century Contract Law' (1975) 91 LQR 247;
   D. Ibbetson, *A Historical Introduction to the Law of Obligations* (Oxford, 1999), chapter 12.
[12] The language of mistake comes late into the cases because of the restriction, before
   the middle of the nineteenth century, on the parties giving evidence (and therefore
   on giving evidence as to their understandings): Ibbetson, *Historical Introduction to the
   Law of Obligations*, p. 226.

is an implied contract, or an implied condition, as to the absence of the mistake.[13] The reasoning is sometimes also based on total failure of consideration: where the transaction was void as a result of the mistake, but money had been paid under it, then the money is recoverable.[14] The judges who reasoned along these lines generally made little or no comparative use of the civil law. But there were other cases in which an appeal was made to Roman or French law to explain the reasoning.

Lord Blackburn was not alone in making the comparison with the civil law, but he appears to have been the judge of the period with the strongest inclination to use comparative law techniques – and he was influenced not only by Roman law but also by French law and, in particular, by Pothier.[15] When still at the Bar he wrote an authoritative treatise on the contract of sale, in which he drew heavily on French law ideas and in particular on Pothier's treatise on sale.[16] He maintained

[13] Simpson, 'Innovation', p. 268; *Barr v. Gibson* (1838) 3 M & W 390 at pp. 399–400, 150 ER 1196 at 1200 (contract for sale of ship which had already been lost: Parke B: the sale 'implies a contract that the subject of the transfer did exist in the character of a ship'); *Couturier v. Hastie* (1856) 5 HLC 673 at p. 681, 10 ER 1065 at p. 1069 (contract for sale of corn which had already been sold in Tunis because it was not fit to bring to London: Lord Cranworth LC: 'The contract plainly imports that there was something which was to be sold at the time of the contract, and something to be purchased'); *Pritchard v. Merchant's and Tradesman's Mutual Life-Assurance Society* (1858) 3 CB(NS) 622 at p. 640, 140 ER 885 at p. 892 (life insurance policy renewed on date when insured had already died: Williams J: 'the premium was paid and accepted upon an implied understanding on both sides that the party insured was then alive. Both parties were labouring under a mistake, and consequently the transaction was altogether void').

[14] *Strickland v. Turner* (1852) 7 Ex 208 at p. 219, 155 ER 919 at p. 924 (purchase of life annuity on a date when annuitant had already died: Pollock CB: 'the annuity became the property of Strickland, and the money the property of the vendors. The money, therefore, which was paid, was paid wholly without consideration, and may now be recovered back from the defendant . . .'); *Pritchard v. Merchant's and Tradesman's Mutual Life-Assurance Society* (1858) 3CB(NS) 622 (purchase money recoverable as paid under a mistake of fact – i.e., a mistake as to the validity of the contract).

[15] For an account of the influence of Pothier on the common law generally see B. Rudden, 'Pothier et la Common Law' in J. Monéger (ed.), *Robert-Joseph Pothier, d'hier à aujourd'hui* (Paris, 2001), p. 91, who notes (at p. 97), on the evidence of the English Reports 1220–1865, that Pothier was cited more than 400 times by judges or counsel in the English courts in the first half of the nineteenth century. Using the electronic text available at www.justis.com a search of domestic (i.e., not Privy Council) cases in the Law Reports in the nineteenth century after 1865 also yields a picture of numerous citations of Pothier by counsel and a wide range of judges, but includes more citations by Lord Blackburn than any other judge (eight citations, compared with four by Pollock CB, three by Fry LJ and one or two by a range of other judges).

[16] C. Blackburn, *A Treatise on the Effect of the Contract of Sale on the Legal Rights of Property and Possession in Goods, Wares and Merchandise* (London, 1845), with cross-references to

consistently that the use of the civil law was not as an authority (in the common law sense of the word) but to illustrate and inform the legal argument.[17] And, as Blackburn J, he developed the foundations of the modern law of frustration in a way which kept faith to the common law view of a contract – that the doctrine of frustration should be founded *in the contract*, so that if the supervening event justified its termination this could be held to be the consequence of a condition implied into the contract – but also claimed that this was consistent with the Roman law and French law approach:[18]

> . . . where, from the nature of the contract, it appears that the parties must from the beginning have known that it could not be fulfilled unless when the time for the fulfilment of the contract arrived some particular specified thing continued to exist, so that, when entering into the contract, they must have con-templated such continuing existence as the foundation of what was to be done; there, in the absence of any express or implied warranty that the thing shall exist, the contract is not to be construed as a positive contract, but as subject to an implied condition that the parties shall be excused in case, before breach, per-formance becomes impossible from the perishing of the thing without default of the contractor.
>
> There seems little doubt that this implication tends to further the great object of making the legal construction such as to fulfil the intention of those who entered into the contract. For in the course of affairs men in making such contracts in general would, if it were brought to their minds, say that there should be such a condition.
>
> Accordingly, in the Civil law, such an exception is implied in every obligation of the class which they call obligatio de certo corpore. The rule is laid down in the Digest . . . The general subject is treated of by Pothier, who in his Traité des Obligations, partie 3, chap 6, art 3, §668 states . . .
>
> Although the Civil law is not of itself authority in an English Court, it affords great assistance in investigating the principles on which the law is grounded.

<hr/>

French law at pp. 112–13 (code de commerce), pp. 170–200 (a chapter on the difference between English law and the 'civil law' on the transfer of property without delivery, with extensive quotations from Pothier's *Contrat de vente*) and 202–4.

[17] E.g. *McLean v. Clydesdale Banking Company* (1883) 9 App Cas 95 at p. 105 (an appeal from Scotland: 'We constantly in the English Courts, upon the question what is the general law, cite Pothier, and we cite Scotch cases where they happen to be in point; and so, in a Scotch case you would cite English decisions, and cite Pothier, or any foreign jurists, provided they bore upon the point'); *Westropp v. Elligott* (1884) 9 App Cas 815 at p. 827 (an appeal from Ireland, and citing Pothier's *Du Contrat du Louage*: 'Though the effect of the purpose being shewn may be different in the foreign law from that which it has in English law, yet the reason and the sense of the thing is very often to be found in the writings of the great Roman and foreign jurists').

[18] *Taylor v. Caldwell* (1863) 3 B & S 826 at pp. 833–5, 122 ER 309 at pp. 312–13.

It is therefore perhaps not surprising that, when faced with an argument about mistake in contract, Blackburn J should similarly have
blended civil law concepts with the traditional common law approach.
In giving the judgment of the court in *Kennedy* v. *The Panama, New Zealand
and Australian Royal Mail Co Ltd*[19] it was Roman law, rather than Pothier,
that he used to explain how the common law's approach to mistake is
really the same as that of the civil law – starting from the proposition
that, in the absence of fraud[20] or warranty, the contract can be avoided
by a party making a mistake as to the subject matter only if the effect of
the mistake was so serious as to constitute a failure of consideration: if
the thing delivered was not at all in substance the thing that the parties
had contracted about:

> There is . . . a very important difference between cases where a contract may
> be rescinded on account of fraud, and those in which it may be rescinded on
> the ground that there is a difference in substance between the thing bargained
> for and that obtained. It is enough to shew that there was a fraudulent rep-
> resentation as to *any part* of that which induced the party to enter into the
> contract which he seeks to rescind; but where there has been an innocent mis-
> representation or misapprehension, it does not authorize a rescission, unless
> it is such as to shew that there is a complete difference in substance between
> what was supposed to be and what was taken, so as to constitute a failure of
> consideration . . .
>
> The principle is well illustrated in the civil law, as stated in the Digest, lib 18,
> tit 1 De Contrahenda Emptione, leges 9, 10, 11 . . . And, as we apprehend, the
> principle of our law is the same as that of the civil law; and the difficulty in
> every case is to determine whether the mistake or misapprehension is as to the
> substance of the whole consideration, going, as it were, to the root of the matter,
> or only to some point, even though a material point, an error as to which does
> not affect the substance of the whole consideration.
>
> Some cases were referred to on the argument, in which the question was,
> whether a stipulation in a contract was a condition precedent or not. Those
> cases are, no doubt, analogous, as the question in such cases very much depends
> on whether the stipulation goes to the root of the matter or not; but they are
> only remotely analogous; and after all, the decisions can never do more than

---

[19] (1867) LR 2 QB 580 at pp. 587–8 (contract for purchase of shares in company where the
directors had – without fraud – made false statements relevant to the company's
business; purchaser sought to obtain a return of the price paid as money had and
received).

[20] In this case, in 1867, it was natural to limit the reference to fraudulent
misrepresentation: the common law gave no remedy for innocent misrepresentation.
After *Redgrave* v. *Hurd* (1881) 20 ChD 1 (also, therefore, after the fusion of the common
law and equity jurisdictions) it became clear that any misrepresentation, fraudulent
or innocent, could render the contract voidable.

illustrate the principle, and the question must depend on the construction of the contract and the particular circumstances of the particular case.

It was misleading for Blackburn J to say that his doctrine of mistake was the same as the civil law,[21] and it would be better to say[22] that Blackburn J borrowed from Roman Law the *general principle* that a contract can be void for a mistake as to the substance of the consideration – the fundamental characteristics of the subject matter of the contract. At just the same time, English textbook writers were similarly using civil law references to explain the newly discovered doctrine of 'mistake' in the law of contract.[23] The first substantive discussion of the principles of mistake appeared in Leake's *Elements of the Law of Contracts* in 1867,[24] which introduced the topic by reference to Roman law, the French *Code civil* and Pothier but expounded the English cases[25] and their familiar principles: the question is one of construction of the contract; 'whether the agreement is made absolutely, or only conditionally upon and with reference to the state of circumstances supposed by mistake, so that upon the real state of circumstances the agreement is inoperative and void'. The second edition of *Leake*[26] kept the same structure and ideas to explain mistake, but added in the citation of Blackburn J's judgment in *Kennedy*.

---

[21] F. de Zulueta, *The Roman Law of Sale* (Oxford, 1945), pp. 26–7; *Associated Japanese Bank (International) Ltd v. Crédit du Nord SA* [1989] 1 WLR 255 at p. 268.

[22] Ibbetson, *Historical Introduction to Law of Obligations* pp. 227–8. It should be noted that, by the time of these developments in England, French law had developed beyond the Roman Law principles and even beyond Pothier's own view of mistake as to the subject matter of the contract, by enacting in the *Code civil* of 1804, arts. 1110 and 1117, that a mistake as to the *substance même de la chose* can give rise to *nullité* but does not automatically make the contract *nul*; *nullité* only follows upon an *action en nullité* (although there is a question whether this was an intentional shift beyond Pothier: J. Gordley, *The Philosophical Origins of Modern Contract Doctrine* (Oxford, 1991), p. 188). Roman Law and Pothier however remained the principal points of comparison for English law, no doubt because of their currency amongst the English judiciary.

[23] Simpson, 'Innovation' p. 267; Ibbetson, *Historical Introduction to Law of Obligations* p. 227.

[24] Chapter 1 ('The Formation of Contracts'), section VI, § 1 ('Mistake'). Benjamin's first edition of his treatise on sale in 1868 explicitly drew on the civil law, as even its title made clear: *A Treatise on the Law of Sale of Personal Property with References to the American Decisions and to the French Code and Civil Law*. Without, however, cross-referring on this point to French or Roman law, it stated a limited doctrine of mistake and just cited the common law cases such as *Strickland v. Turner*: pp. 38–9, 303.

[25] Including *Barr v. Gibson, Couturier v. Hastie, Strickland v. Turner* and *Prichard v. Merchant's and Tradesman's Mutual Life-Assurance Society*, above, fns. 13 and 14.

[26] Pages 344–5.

The second life of mistake: the twentieth century

There were two landmark cases in the law of mistake in the twentieth century. The first was the decision of the House of Lords in *Bell* v. *Lever Brothers Ltd*;[27] the second the decision of the Court of Appeal – and, in particular, the judgment of Denning LJ – in *Solle* v. *Butcher*.[28]

Bell is a difficult case to interpret,[29] but it is clear from the case that we can now speak of a doctrine of mistake in the English law of contract. Even if the parties both assented to the same terms, the contract will still be void if one party made a sufficient mistake of the other's identity; or if both parties made the same mistake about the existence of the subject matter or a sufficiently serious mistake about its quality.[30] Interesting for our purposes is the continuity of this decision with the cases of the nineteenth century. Lord Atkin relied[31] on two key decisions of Blackburn J as the 'authoritative expositions of the law': *Kennedy* v. *Panama*[32] and *Smith* v. *Hughes*.[33] And he presented the law of mistake in a way which follows naturally from the common law view of the earlier cases: the first question is always to examine the terms of the agreement itself and see whether one party has contracted to bear the risk of the mistake.[34]

Looking back to how mistake was developed in the second half of the nineteenth century we can see that there was always an inevitable tension. The 'will theory' of contract, based on a subjective meeting of the minds of the parties, competed with the objective theory of contract formation.[35] For a contractual theory based on the subjective intentions of the parties, a mistake is the principal obstacle to a valid contract:[36]

---

[27] [1932] AC 161.   [28] [1950] 1 KB 671.

[29] The question was whether contracts to terminate two employees' contracts of employment with severance payments were void because neither the employer nor (as the jury found) the employees had it in their minds that the employees had committed prior breaches of duty which would have justified the employer dismissing them without payment. The House was divided on the outcome (the majority held the termination contract valid, not void); and gave differing reasons. But it appears that the real difference – and the difficulty of interpretation of the case – was only in their Lordships' analysis of the facts and therefore the application of the law to the facts: in effect, they disagreed about what mistake the parties made. See J. Cartwright, '*Solle* v. *Butcher* and the Doctrine of Mistake in Contract' (1987) 103 LQR 594 at p. 599; Lord Wright, *Legal Essays and Addresses* (Cambridge, 1939), p. 262; *Associated Japanese Bank (International) Ltd* v. *Crédit du Nord SA* [1989] 1 WLR 255 at p. 267.

[30] Lord Atkin at p. 217.

[31] At pp. 219, 221. See also Lord Warrington at p. 208 and Lord Thankerton at p. 233.

[32] Above, fn. 19.   [33] Above, fn. 9.   [34] At pp. 217, 218.

[35] Ibbetson, *Historical Introduction to the Law of Obligations*, ch. 12.

[36] R. J. Pothier, *Le traité des obligations* (Paris, 1761), para. 17.

L'erreur est le plus grand vice des conventions: car les conventions sont formées par le consentement des parties; et il ne peut pas y avoir de consentement, lorsque les parties ont erré sur l'objet de leur convention.

But this is too bold: even a system committed to assessing the existence of a contract by reference to a subjective assessment of the parties' intentions must draw the line somewhere – some mistakes will not suffice to invalidate the contract, otherwise the non-mistaken party's bargain is too insecure. Different systems may strike the balance in different ways, but nonetheless a balance has to be struck.[37]

The nineteenth-century judges never quite settled the question of whether mistake was an independent doctrine or just part of the analysis of the parties' agreement. This was an era when the parties' agreement was everything:[38] and so if there was a defect in the agreement which justified its avoidance, it was natural to present the solution as being embodied in the agreement itself. The parties' agreement must have been based on certain implicit assumptions: if those assumptions were not correct, then the agreement is avoided – but because the parties must have intended it to be so. As we have seen, the earlier cases had tended to find implied conditions in order to resolve issues of mistake. At the time of *Bell* v. *Lever Brothers* this was still a form in which an argument of mistake could be presented. In the case of one party's mistake about the other party's identity, it is natural to ask whether the one party intended to deal with (and only with) the person he mistakenly thought the other party to be – and, if so, to hold that the contract is void for lack of agreement.[39] But when the question is as to the existence or quality of the subject matter, it is not so clear whether the parties' 'intentions' – and therefore a term of the contract giving effect to those intentions – can so easily solve the matter. Sir John Simon KC, counsel for Lever Brothers, drew the analogy between mistake, frustration and implied terms, and suggested that all three were based on the intentions of the

---

[37] For a discussion of French law (which starts from a subjective theory of contract formation) and English law (which does not), see J. Cartwright, 'Defects of Consent and Security of Contract: French and English Law Compared' in P. Birks and A. Pretto (eds.), *Themes in Comparative Law in Honour of Bernard Rudden* (Oxford, 2002), p. 153.

[38] In addition to the doctrines of mistake and frustration, see *Lloyd* v. *Guibert* (1865) LR 1 QB 115 at pp. 120–1 (proper law of the contract attributed to the 'presumed intention' of the parties); *The Moorcock* (1889) 14 PD 64 at p. 68 (implied terms based on the 'presumed intention' of the parties).

[39] *Bell* v. *Lever Brothers* [1932] AC 161 at p. 217 (Lord Atkin). Mistake of identity is discussed further below.

parties – terms to be implied into the contract.[40] Lord Atkin responded
to this in his speech by agreeing that these issues can be said to be based
on a single principle:[41]

This brings the discussion to the alternative mode of expressing the result
of a mutual mistake. It is said that in such a case as the present there is to
be implied a stipulation in the contract that a condition of its efficacy is that
the facts should be as understood by both parties – namely, that the contract
could not be terminated till the end of the current term. The question of the
existence of conditions, express or implied, is obviously one that affects not the
formation of contract, but the investigation of the terms of the contract when
made. A condition derives its efficacy from the consent of the parties, express
or implied. They have agreed, but on what terms? One term may be that unless
the facts are or are not of a particular nature, or unless an event has or has not
happened, the contract is not to take effect. With regard to future facts such a
condition is obviously contractual. Till the event occurs the parties are bound.
Thus the condition (the exact terms of which need not here be investigated)
that is generally accepted as underlying the principle of the frustration cases is
contractual, an implied condition. Sir John Simon formulated for the assistance
of your Lordships a proposition which should be recorded: 'Whenever it is to be
inferred from the terms of a contract or its surrounding circumstances that the
consensus has been reached upon the basis of a particular contractual assumption, and that assumption is not true, the contract is avoided: i.e., it is void ab
initio if the assumption is of present fact and it ceases to bind if the assumption
is of future fact.'
I think few would demur to this statement, but its value depends upon the
meaning of 'a contractual assumption', and also upon the true meaning to be
attached to 'basis', a metaphor which may mislead. When used expressly in
contracts, for instance, in policies of insurance, which state that the truth of
the statements in the proposal is to be the basis of the contract of insurance,
the meaning is clear. The truth of the statements is made a condition of the
contract, which failing, the contract is void unless the condition is waived. The
proposition does not amount to more than this that, if the contract expressly
or impliedly contains a term that a particular assumption is a condition of the
contract, the contract is avoided if the assumption is not true. But we have not
advanced far on the inquiry how to ascertain whether the contract does contain
such a condition . . . Nothing is more dangerous than to allow oneself liberty to
construct for the parties contracts which they have not in terms made by import-
ing implications which would appear to make the contract more businesslike or
more just. The implications to be made are to be no more than are 'necessary'
for giving business efficacy to the transaction, and it appears to me that, both
as to existing facts and future facts, a condition would not be implied unless

---

[40] [1932] AC 161 at p. 166.   [41] At pp. 224–7.

the new state of facts makes the contract something different in kind from the contract in the original state of facts . . . We therefore get a common standard for mutual mistake, and implied conditions whether as to existing or as to future facts. Does the state of the new facts destroy the identity of the subject-matter as it was in the original state of facts?

This analysis pulls together three areas of the law of contract: mistake, frustration and implied terms. Lord Atkin's view was that it is possible to define by reference to the parties' 'intention' the circumstances in which a contract will be void for mistake, discharged for frustration, or subject to unexpressed (implied) terms. But he made clear that a test is still required to decide what it was that the parties intended. And in devising the test, we move away from the language of intention to a doctrine of mistake – just as frustration began its life in the nineteenth century on the theory that it was the (real) intention of the parties that the contract should terminate,[42] but during the twentieth century the courts began to admit that this 'intention' was a fiction, better replaced by a substantive test for the doctrine of frustration.[43] The test of the

---

[42] *Taylor* v. *Caldwell*, above, fn. 18. In 1931, when *Bell* v. *Lever Brothers* was decided, it was still common to speak of the basis of frustration as being the 'foundation' of the contract or an 'implied term': W. A. MacFarlane and G. W. Wrangham (eds.), *Chitty's Treatise on the Law of Contracts* (18th edn, London, 1930), pp. 828–32.

[43] *Davis Contractors Ltd* v. *Fareham UDC* [1956] AC 696 at pp. 728–9 (Lord Radcliffe): 'there is something of a logical difficulty in seeing how the parties could even impliedly have provided for something which ex hypothesi they neither expected nor foresaw; and the ascription of frustration to an implied term of the contract has been criticized as obscuring the true action of the court which consists in applying an objective rule of the law of contract to the contractual obligations that the parties have imposed upon themselves . . . By this time it might seem that the parties themselves have become so far disembodied spirits that their actual persons should be allowed to rest in peace. In their place there rises the figure of the fair and reasonable man. And the spokesman of the fair and reasonable man, who represents after all no more than the anthropomorphic conception of justice, is and must be the court itself. So perhaps it would be simpler to say at the outset that frustration occurs whenever the law recognizes that without default of either party a contractual obligation has become incapable of being performed because the circumstances in which performance is called for would render it a thing radically different from that which was undertaken by the contract. Non haec in foedera veni. It was not this that I promised to do.' Similarly, the old idea of basing the proper law of the contract on the 'presumed intention' of the parties (above, n. 38) was replaced by an objective test: L. Collins (ed.), *Dicey & Morris: The Conflict of Laws* (13th edn, London, 2000), § 32–004. And it became clear that it was not sufficient to claim that implied terms were necessarily based on the intentions of the parties: *Lister* v. *Romford Ice & Cold Storage Co Ltd* [1957] AC 555 at pp. 576, 587, 594.

doctrine of mistake was stated in *Bell* in different ways, but the principal expression is Lord Atkin's statement[44] that

Mistake as to quality of the thing contracted for . . . will not affect assent unless it is the mistake of both parties, and is as to the existence of some quality which makes the thing without the quality essentially different from the thing as it was believed to be.

This is not an easy test to apply, but it was intended to be restrictive, whilst still making clear that the doctrine of mistake extended beyond mistakes as to the identity of the other party or as to the existence of the subject matter of the contract to mistakes as to the qualities of the subject matter.

However, Denning LJ in *Solle* v. *Butcher*[45] sought to reinterpret the doctrine of mistake. In effect, he ignored the acceptance in *Bell* of a doctrine of mistake, and tried to sideline cases of mistake at common law to those where there is an implied condition. He appeared to want to interpret *Bell* – even though it was a decision with the authority of the House of Lords – as not having endorsed the development beyond the early nineteenth-century cases which had based mistake on implied conditions:[46]

Let me first consider mistakes which render a contract a nullity. All previous decisions on this subject must now be read in the light of *Bell* v. *Lever Brothers Ltd.* The correct interpretation of that case, to my mind, is that, once a contract has been made, that is to say, once the parties, whatever their inmost states of mind, have to all outward appearances agreed with sufficient certainty in the same terms on the same subject matter, then the contract is good unless and until it is set aside for failure of some condition on which the existence of the contract depends, or for fraud, or on some equitable ground. Neither party can rely on his own mistake to say it was a nullity from the beginning, no matter that it was a mistake which to his mind was fundamental, and no matter that the other party knew that he was under a mistake. A fortiori, if the other party did not know of the mistake, but shared it. The cases where goods

---

[44] [1932] AC 161 at p. 218. He said at p. 224 that his statement at p. 227, 'Does the state of the new facts destroy the identity of the subject-matter as it was in the original state of facts?' was an 'alternative mode' of saying the same thing.

[45] [1950] 1 KB 671. The question was whether a tenant could recover overpayment of the rent on a flat which the parties had agreed on the mistaken assumption that the flat was not subject to rent control. The court was divided; Jenkins LJ dissented, on the basis that the mistake was of law, not of fact; Bucknill and Denning LJJ held that the lease should be set aside for mistake, but Bucknill LJ did not discuss in any detail the general principles or the relationship between common law and equity. The only substantive discussion was therefore that by Denning LJ.

[46] At p. 691.

have perished at the time of sale, or belong to the buyer, are really contracts which are not void for mistake but are void by reason of an implied condition precedent, because the contract proceeded on the basic assumption that it was possible of performance.

One might have thought that this was the approach of a judge who wished to hold parties to their bargain, who took the view that mistake as a doctrine has no place in the law of contract because it would allow one (mistaken) party to deprive the other party of his bargain. But it was not. The approach of Denning LJ was to deny the existence of a doctrine of mistake *at common law*, but then to admit that a contract can be *voidable* for mistake in *equity*. He went on:[47]

Let me next consider mistakes which render a contract voidable, that is, liable to be set aside on some equitable ground. Whilst presupposing that a contract was good at law, or at any rate not void, the court of equity would often relieve a party from the consequences of his own mistake, so long as it could do so without injustice to third parties. The court, it was said, had power to set aside the contract whenever it was of opinion that it was unconscientious for the other party to avail himself of the legal advantage which he had obtained . . .

The court had, of course, to define what it considered to be unconscientious, but in this respect equity has shown a progressive development. It is now clear that a contract will be set aside if the mistake of the one party has been induced by a material misrepresentation of the other, even though it was not fraudulent or fundamental; or if one party, knowing that the other is mistaken about the terms of an offer, or the identity of the person by whom it is made, lets him remain under his delusion and concludes a contract on the mistaken terms instead of pointing out the mistake. That is, I venture to think, the ground on which the defendant in *Smith* v. *Hughes*[48] would be exempted nowadays, and on which, according to the view by Blackburn J of the facts, the contract in *Lindsay* v. *Cundy*,[49] was voidable and not void.

A contract is also liable in equity to be set aside if the parties were under a common misapprehension either as to facts or as to their relative and respective rights, provided that the misapprehension was fundamental and that the party seeking to set it aside was not himself at fault.

Far from rejecting the notion of a doctrine of mistake in contract, Denning LJ sought to shift it from a common law doctrine to an equitable doctrine. In the middle of the twentieth century, with the common law and equitable jurisdictions fused for 75 years, it might seem odd that a judge should want to re-draw the jurisdictional boundaries of

[47] At pp. 692–3.   [48] (1871) 6 QB 597.
[49] (1876) 1 QBD 348, p. 355; (1878) 3 App Cas 459. Mistake of identity is discussed further below.

the doctrine of mistake. But it was not just a jurisdictional matter, but substantive. This quotation from Denning LJ's judgment shows his view of the proper place for a doctrine of mistake as to the subject matter: as a doctrine of equity, not of the common law, it has the consequence that a sufficient mistake renders the contract voidable, not void; and it is within the court's discretion whether to grant the remedy or not – and, if so, on what terms. In consequence, as Denning LJ made clear, the contract will not be avoided in such a way as to prejudice innocent third parties. During the second half of the twentieth century the approach advocated by Denning LJ started to take hold. There were relatively few reported cases on mistake;[50] but both at first instance[51] and in the Court of Appeal[52] it became accepted that *Solle* v. *Butcher* was authority for a doctrine of common mistake under which a contract which was not void at common law could still be rescinded by the court in its discretion – and on terms if the court so decided. The final outcome at the end of the century was not, however, quite what Lord Denning had intended. *Bell*, and the common law doctrine of mistake, was not rejected altogether, but retained its authority. If, therefore, a mistake was not provided for in the contractual allocation of risk between the parties, it could still render the contract void if it fulfilled Lord Atkin's test – being so serious as to render the subject matter of the contract essentially and radically different from the subject matter which the parties believed to exist.[53] But Lord Denning had achieved the development of a *second* doctrine of mistake under which, if a contract did not contain an allocation of the risk of the mistake, and the mistake was not sufficiently serious to render the contract void under the *Bell* test, it could still make the contract voidable under the test stated in *Solle* v. *Butcher*.[54]

---

[50] Most cases of mistake are, in fact, litigated either as claims for breach of contract (e.g. for breach of description) or misrepresentation (since mistake commonly arises from the reliance on a false statement: above, text to fn. 8), depending on the remedy sought by the claimant.

[51] *Grist* v. *Bailey* [1967] Ch 532; *Laurence* v. *Lexcourt Holdings* [1978] 1 WLR 1128; *Associated Japanese Bank (International) Ltd* v. *Crédit du Nord SA* [1989] 1 WLR 255.

[52] *William Sindall plc* v. *Cambridgeshire CC* [1994] 1 WLR 1016. Other statements in the Court of Appeal were generally by Lord Denning himself, without explicit support from other judges in the case: see, e.g., *Magee* v. *Pennine Insurance Company* [1969] 2 QB 507 (where Fenton Atkinson LJ, who found with Lord Denning, appears to have based his decision on the common law); *Fredrick E. Rose (London) Ltd* v. *William H. Pim Jnr & Co. Ltd* [1953] 2 QB 450 at pp. 460–1; *Oscar Chess Ltd* v. *Williams* [1957] 1 WLR 370 at pp. 373–4.

[53] *Associated Japanese Bank (International) Ltd* v. *Crédit du Nord SA* [1989] 1 WLR 255 at p. 268 (Steyn J, drawing on the language of the frustration cases ('radically') as well as that of Lord Atkin in *Bell*).

[54] *Ibid.*, at p. 268.

The third life of mistake: the future?

Recently there have been further significant developments. In *The Great Peace*[55] the Court of Appeal has rejected the equitable doctrine of common mistake which was developed by Denning LJ in *Solle* v. *Butcher*. And in *Shogun Finance Ltd* v. *Hudson*[56] the House of Lords has reviewed the law on mistake of identity.

In *The Great Peace* the defendant resisted payment of the price agreed for the charter of the vessel 'Great Peace' on the basis that the vessel was not where the parties had thought it to be. The defendant had agreed to charter the Great Peace from the claimant in order to bring assistance to the crew of a vessel (the 'Cape Providence') which was in distress. From inaccurate information that the defendant obtained from a third party source, it thought that the Great Peace was about 35 miles away from the Cape Providence. In fact, the vessels were 410 miles apart. But, in the mistaken belief that the Great Peace was in a position to assist urgently, the defendant's brokers contacted a representative of the claimant's managers, told him that the Great Peace was in a position to assist, and negotiated a 5-day minimum charter of the Great Peace to escort and stand-by the Cape Providence for the purpose of saving life. When the mistake was discovered, the defendant did not cancel the charter immediately, but waited first to find another ship that was closer to the Cape Providence and could therefore bring help more quickly. On these facts, both Toulson J (the trial judge) and the Court of Appeal had no difficulty in deciding that the contract of charter was valid and the defendants must pay the agreed minimum hire. At both levels, however, the discussion went far beyond this and reopened the whole question of the place of the doctrine(s) of mistake in contract. Toulson J[57] re-examined the common law doctrine of mistake, vigorously criticised the judgment of Denning LJ in *Solle* v. *Butcher*, and rejected the idea that the court has an equitable discretion to grant rescission of a contract on the ground of common mistake. The Court of Appeal followed this and, broadly, confirmed it. In short, the Court of Appeal held, on the authority of *Bell* v. *Lever Brothers*, that there is a doctrine of mistake at common law; and the decision of Denning LJ in *Solle* v. *Butcher* should not be followed. If this decision is now the basis of the doctrine of

---

[55] *Great Peace Shipping Ltd* v. *Tsavliris Salvage (International) Ltd (The 'Great Peace')* [2002] EWCA Civ 1407, [2003] QB 679. The single judgment of the Court was given by Lord Phillips MR.

[56] [2003] UKHL 62, [2003] 3 WLR 1371.   [57] [2001] All ER (D) 152 (Nov), (2001) 151 NLJ 1696.

mistake[58] it has removed the 'equitable' doctrine, and taken us back to the law before *Solle* v. *Butcher* was decided. But why? And how far back?

There are two strands to the decision of the Court of Appeal in *The Great Peace*: the reassessment of the common law doctrine of mistake; and the rejection of the equitable doctrine. To take the second strand first: the Court found that there were reasons of authority to reject Denning LJ's development of a doctrine of mistake in equity: there was no evidence in the case law before *Solle* of an equitable doctrine of mistake wider than the common law doctrine, and *Solle*, in so asserting, was inconsistent with the earlier decision of the House of Lords in *Bell*.[59] Moreover, Denning LJ's judgment left unclear the precise parameters of the jurisdiction,[60] and its uncertainty brings confusion into the law of contract where certainty is essential. At the heart of the decision in *Solle* and cases which had followed it was a desire to remedy a particularly bad bargain for a party who could show a mistake which did not suffice under the common law test to render the contract void, and where the facts did not disclose any other ground of avoidance, such as misrepresentation or duress.[61] This is a strong, commercial approach to the law of contract: the emphasis on the importance of certainty, and the rejection of the courts' interference in the terms of the contract, belongs most particularly in the courts hearing commercial cases.[62] But it also repositions the doctrine of mistake back in the mainstream of English contract law. The courts cannot mend parties' bad bargains. It is for

---

[58] It is questionable whether the Court of Appeal in *The Great Peace* had the power to depart from its own earlier decision in *Solle* v. *Butcher*, and therefore whether future courts will necessarily prefer *The Great Peace* until the House of Lords has ruled on the matter: Midwinter, (2003) 119 LQR 180. However, it is more likely that judges will follow *The Great Peace*, given the strongly argued judgments of both Toulson J and the Court of Appeal: see, e.g., *EIC Services Ltd* v. *Phipps* [2003] EWHC 1507, [2003] 1 WLR 2360 at [155]–[158], [176].

[59] [2002] EWCA Civ 1407, [2003] QB 679 at [118], [126].

[60] At [131]: Denning LJ's test required the mistake to be 'fundamental': but how did this relate to the common law doctrine, which required a mistake to be as to a quality which made the subject matter essentially different? The language of a 'fundamental' mistake has also commonly been used in the common law test: e.g. in *Bell* v. *Lever Brothers* [1932] AC 161 at p. 208 (Lord Warrington), pp. 225–6 (Lord Atkin).

[61] At [155]–[156].

[62] For example, see *Associated Japanese Bank (International) Ltd* v. *Crédit du Nord SA* [1989] 1 WLR 255 at p. 268 (Steyn J: 'the law ought to uphold rather than destroy apparent contracts'); *EIC Services Ltd* v. *Phipps* [2003] EWHC 1507, [2003] 1 WLR 2360 at [168], [180] (Neuberger J, rejecting a claim that an allotment of bonus shares was void for common mistake).

statute[63] to regulate the substantive terms of the contract: the judges are able to police the parties' conduct through common law and equitable principles such as misrepresentation, duress and undue influence; but as was made clear by Lord Atkin in *Bell*,[64] the courts do not normally otherwise intervene to relieve one of the parties from the effects of the bargain.[65]

So after *The Great Peace* we are left with only the common law doctrine of mistake: but in what form? We saw earlier that there had been different ways of formulating the common law approach to mistake: within the (express and implied) terms of the contract; or as a doctrine that goes beyond the assessment of parties' intentions. The Court of Appeal saw itself as bound by, and giving effect by its restatement to, the decision of the House of Lords in *Bell*. It is therefore not surprising that it adopted a similar view of mistake to that which emerges from Lord Atkin's judgment in that case. The link between mistake and frustration is adopted; and mistake is based not on implied terms but is an independent doctrine. But, as in the case of frustration, the test cannot be applied without asking what the parties agreed. Mistake is still a doctrine, a rule of law; but it is rooted firmly in the parties' own agreement:[66]

73. . . . the theory of the implied term is as unrealistic when considering common mistake as when considering frustration. Where a fundamental assumption upon which an agreement is founded proves to be mistaken, it is not realistic to ask whether the parties impliedly agreed that in those circumstances the contract would not be binding. The avoidance of a contract on the ground of common mistake results from a rule of law under which, if it transpires that one or both of the parties have agreed to do something which it is impossible to perform, no obligation arises out of that agreement.

74. In considering whether performance of the contract is impossible, it is necessary to identify what it is that the parties agreed would be performed. This involves looking not only at the express terms, but at any implications that may arise out of the surrounding circumstances. In some cases it will be possible

---

[63] Principally consumer protection legislation such as the Unfair Terms in Consumer Contracts Regulations 1999. Cf. also *National Westminster Bank plc v. Morgan* [1985] AC 686 at p. 708 (Lord Scarman, discussing undue influence and rejecting Lord Denning's proposition in *Lloyds Bank Ltd v. Bundy* [1975] QB 326 of a general doctrine of 'inequality of bargaining power').

[64] [1932] AC 161 at 224, quoted above, text to fn. 41.

[65] See also *The Great Peace*, above, fn. 55, at [161] (Lord Phillips MR, suggesting that if a more flexible doctrine of mistake is required, it is for legislation to provide it).

[66] [2002] EWCA Civ 1407, [2003] QB 679 at [73]–[76].

to identify details of the 'contractual adventure' which go beyond the terms that are expressly spelt out, in others it will not.

75. Just as the doctrine of frustration only applies if the contract contains no provision that covers the situation, the same should be true of common mistake. If, on true construction of the contract, a party warrants that the subject matter of the contract exists, or that it will be possible to perform the contract, there will be no scope to hold the contract void on the ground of common mistake.

76. . . . the following elements must be present if common mistake is to avoid a contract: (i) there must be a common assumption as to the existence of a state of affairs; (ii) there must be no warranty by either party that that state of affairs exists; (iii) the non-existence of the state of affairs must not be attributable to the fault of either party; (iv) the non-existence of the state of affairs must render performance of the contract impossible; (v) the state of affairs may be the existence, or a vital attribute, of the consideration to be provided or circumstances which must subsist if performance of the contractual adventure is to be possible.

In relation to mistakes as to the subject matter of the contract, therefore, the doctrine of mistake at the start of the twenty-first century amounts to this: a mistake can, but rarely will, make the contract void (but never void*able*). The mistake must be shared by both parties. There are then two key questions. First, what have the parties agreed to? Second, is it possible to perform that agreement? The first question focuses on the parties' intentions, and so if, for example, the terms of the contract have expressly or impliedly[67] provided for the mistaken circumstances, then it is the parties' own agreement that determines the outcome of the case. But if there is no answer in the terms of the contract, then we move on to the doctrine of mistake: the contract is void if the agreement is impossible to perform. In cases where the subject matter of the contract has ceased to exist, it is generally easy to assess – as Lord Atkin made clear in *Bell*:[68] 'though the parties in fact were agreed about the subject-matter, yet a consent to transfer or take delivery of something not existent is deemed useless, the consent is nullified'. But the parties' shared mistake about the essential qualities of the subject matter can also, in law, make the agreement 'impossible' to perform. This will

---

[67] *William Sindall plc* v. *Cambridgeshire CC* [1994] 1 WLR 1016 at p. 1035 (implied allocation of risk to buyer under principle of *caveat emptor*); *Associated Japanese Bank (International) Ltd* v. *Crédit du Nord* [1989] 1 WLR 255 at p. 263 (on facts, risk of mistake allocated expressly or (if not expressly) impliedly by the parties).

[68] At p. 217. Similarly, where the contract is to transfer property rights which do not exist, as in *Cooper* v. *Phibbs* (1867) LR 2 HL 149: 'The parties intended to effectuate a transfer of ownership: such a transfer is impossible: the stipulation is *naturali ratione inutilis*' ([1932] AC 161 at p. 218).

always be difficult to assess on the facts of the case. But we are here back with the ideas which were brought into English law from the civil law. Roman law acknowledged a principle that a mistake as to the substance of the subject matter could affect the validity of a contract.[69] And French law took this up – in its *Code civil*,[70] the principle is:

1109 Il n'y a point de consentement valable, si le consentement n'a été donné que par erreur . . .
1110 L'erreur n'est une cause de nullité de la convention que lorsqu'elle tombe sur la substance même de la chose qui en est l'objet . . .

But although the English judges brought into English law the idea that the 'substance' of the subject matter was relevant to the test of the validity of a contract where mistake is alleged, the use made of this by the English judges has been very different not only from Roman law but also from their modern colleagues across the Channel. The French courts have interpreted the code in an expansive manner: where the code says 'la substance même de la chose' the judges read 'les qualités substantielles de la chose' – which sounds rather like the idea in the English cases that a mistake can be not only as to the existence of the subject matter but even as to its essential qualities. But the French judges have given a much broader interpretation to the *qualités substantielles* than Lord Atkin would have been prepared to do in *Bell*.[71] English law has kept an explicitly restrictive test of mistake, focusing on the parties' own agreement, and using the idea of the 'substance' of the subject matter to explain why the agreement is impossible to perform. This highlights the difference in approach of the two systems to contractual obligations. French law focuses not on the agreement but on the (subjective) consent of the party who is mistaken – and therefore admits unilateral mistake as to the subject matter, and a wider notion of 'mistake' than English law: the French starting point is to allow the mistaken claimant to revoke his consent because it was not complete.[72] English law, by contrast, focuses

---

[69] See above, text to fn. 21.

[70] This is not identical to Pothier's earlier view: above, fn. 22.

[71] For example, a mistake by one party as to the authenticity of a work of art is well established to be a sufficient mistake in French law: Civ 26 Jan 1972, D 1972 517; even if it is the seller's own mistake: Versailles, 7 jan 1987, D 1987 485. But even a shared mistake of authenticity is not sufficient in the common law: *Bell* v. *Lever Brothers* [1932] AC 161 at p. 224.

[72] The test for *violence* (≈duress and undue influence) also focuses on the subjective state of mind of the victim (his *crainte* – fear) without, as in English law, requiring that the source of the duress be the other party to the contract: Code civil, arts. 1111, 1112.

on the (in general terms, objective) agreement which embodies a bargain, and therefore tends to view things more from the defendant's point of view: why should the defendant be deprived of the bargain? It is therefore much more content to allow a mistaken claimant to avoid the contract by reason of the defendant's misrepresentation than simply for his own mistake.[73] Given this difference of approach, it is not surprising that the civil law influences on the English law which were evident in the development of the doctrine of mistake in the nineteenth and early twentieth centuries should have remained just that: influences – concepts, ideas, and a vocabulary to explain the unique view of the proper role of a doctrine of mistake in contract in English law.

However, the future of the doctrine of mistake may yet be subject to further development. The voice that has prevailed in the Court of Appeal in relation to mistakes as to the subject matter of the contract has been the commercial voice, reinforcing the traditional view that the law of contract protects the security of the parties' bargain (or, rather, protects one party against the other's claim that he made a mistake which affects the value of his bargain). We cannot exclude the possibility that the House of Lords, in an appropriate (non-commercial?) case might re-think some of the rules which are reasserted in *The Great Peace*. One particular problem is that under the doctrine of mistake a contract is either void or valid. And void contracts are particularly troublesome where third parties are concerned: that was one of the principal objections held by Lord Denning[74] to the common law doctrine of mistake, which led him to seek to shift the doctrine into equity, where the result could be a contract not void but *voidable* at the instance of the mistaken party, and at the discretion of the court. Another consequence of the contract being voidable, rather than void, would be that a party would be able to choose whether or not to invoke the mistake – either to affirm the contract, or to claim to rescind it. It should be noticed that French law takes this position, since the remedy (*nullité relative*) is designed to protect a party who gave his consent, but the consent was defective and so he can elect to revoke it.

The jurisdictional (and doctrinal) shift from common law (void) to equity (voidable) proposed by Denning LJ in *Solle* v. *Butcher* was not limited

---

[73] These are, of course, only the (rather stereotypical) starting points for each system's enquiry into the validity of a contract in the case of a claim based on mistake, and the complete picture is more nuanced: for a more detailed discussion, see Cartwright, 'Defects of Consent'.

[74] *Solle* v. *Butcher* [1950] 1 KB 671 at pp. 692–3, quoted above at text to fn. 47.

to the case of mistake as to the subject matter of the contract. It was also to apply to mistakes of identity – Denning LJ expressly rejected the idea that a mistake of identity makes a contract void, and therefore criticised the decision in *Cundy* v. *Lindsay*,[75] in which the House of Lords based its decision on the absence of agreement. The same position was stated by Lord Atkin in *Bell* v. *Lever Brothers*:[76] 'Thus a mistaken belief by A that he is contracting with B, whereas in fact he is contracting with C, will negative consent where it is clear that the intention of A was to contract only with B.' This was reviewed by the House of Lords in *Shogun Finance Ltd* v. *Hudson*,[77] and survived only by the narrowest margin. An unknown person (the rogue) dishonestly obtained the driving licence of one Mr Patel, and bought a car on hire-purchase from Shogun signing the hire-purchase agreement in Mr Patel's name. The majority of the House of Lords held that there was no contract between Shogun and either Mr Patel or the rogue: it was a contract in writing, and on its proper construction the offer of credit was addressed only to Mr Patel, and not to the rogue; but Mr Patel did not accept it because he knew nothing about the transaction. However, for us the significance is that two members of the House, Lord Nicholls and Lord Millett, dissented and would have overruled *Cundy* v. *Lindsay* and held that, as long as there is in fact an exchange of offer and acceptance between two persons there is (objectively determined) a contract which is at most voidable by the party who proves he was misled[78] as to the identity of the other contracting party. This was crucial on the facts of *Shogun*, because by the time the fraud had been discovered, the car had been sold on by the rogue to

---

[75] (1878) 3 App Cas 459. In a later case, *Lewis* v. *Averay* [1972] 1 QB 198 at p. 206, Lord Denning again rejected the idea that a contract could be void for mistake of identity: 'It has sometimes been said that, if a party makes a mistake as to the identity of the person with whom he is contracting, there is no contract, or, if there is a contract, it is a nullity and void, so that no property can pass under it. This has been supported by a reference to the French jurist Pothier; but I have said before, and I repeat now, his statement is no part of English law.' Notice that under the Code Civil a mistake of identity (*erreur sur la personne*, as long as it is *la cause principale de la convention*: Code Civil, art. 1110) makes a contract *nul* – but again it is *nullité relative*. However, in parallel with its broader view of actionable mistakes as to the subject matter, French law also gives considerably greater latitude to mistakes as to the person than English law: e.g. Soc, 3 July 1990, Bull civ V no 329 (employer's mistake as to the employment history of a new employee could be a mistake as to the person, although it was not actionable on the facts because the employer had failed to make adequate enquiries).

[76] [1932] AC 161 at p. 217.   [77] [2003] UKHL 62, [2003] 3 WLR 1371.

[78] Almost every case of mistaken identity involves fraud, and therefore the contract will be voidable for the misrepresentation of identity. Mistake need not, as such, be invoked.

Mr Hudson who knew nothing about the hire-purchase agreement. Lord Nicholls and Lord Millett found confusion and contradictions in the existing case law; but they were also very keen to protect innocent third parties and therefore not to allow contracts to be void;[79] and they noted that other jurisdictions also achieve a similar result in protecting the innocent third party.[80] Lord Millett went so far as to say that[81]

> German law reaches this conclusion by admitting a far wider exception to the nemo dat quod non habet rule than we accept, and this enables it to dispense with the need to decide the contractual effect of mistaken identity (and the meaning of 'identity' in this context) or to conduct a fruitless inquiry into the identity of the intended counterparty. Our inability to admit such an exception compels us to adopt a different analysis, but it would be unfortunate if our conclusion proved to be different. Quite apart from anything else, it would make the contemplated harmonisation of the general principles of European contract law very difficult to achieve.

The majority regarded this case as involving a straightforward application of the existing rules for the formation of contracts, and the interpretation of written contracts. So far, therefore, as we move into the twenty-first century we can say that the decisions in the courts – in relation both to mistakes as to the subject matter of a contract (*The Great Peace*) and to mistakes of identity (*Shogun*) – have reasserted the traditional common law rules, and have rejected the attempts of Lord Denning[82] during the last century to make a shift from common law to equity and from void to voidable. But there are still voices in the House of Lords who would prefer to reopen some, at least, of these questions; and the fact that they are looking to other jurisdictions to see how these issues are dealt with elsewhere shows that – as at its birth in the nineteenth century – there may yet be a place for comparative law in the development in the twenty-first century of the doctrine of mistake in English law.

---

[79] At [35] (Lord Nicholls), [60], [82] (Lord Millett).

[80] At [35] (Lord Nicholls: other common law jurisdictions, notably the Uniform Commercial Code in the US); [84]–[86] (Lord Millett: the US and Germany).

[81] At [86]. Lord Hobhouse at [55] took a very different view: 'to attempt to use this appeal to advocate, on the basis of continental legal systems which are open to cogent criticism, the abandonment of the soundly based nemo dat quod non habet rule (statutorily adopted) would be not only improper but even more damaging.'

[82] *Solle* v. *Butcher* [1950] 1 KB 671 (common mistake as to subject matter); *Lewis* v. *Averay* [1972] 1 QB 198 (mistake of identity).

4 Case studies

Case 1

Anatole v. Bob

Case

Anatole, an impressionist specialist at the Musée d'Orsay, put up for sale his own private collection of paintings. For a moderate price, Bob acquired two of them for his New York gallery, ballet scenes described by the catalogue prepared by Anatole as the 'charming work of an unknown artist'. Anatole has now learnt from the American press that the two paintings have been hailed by certain American impressionist experts as authentic Degas, hitherto undiscovered, and are to be resold at a breathtaking price. French experts, called in to give their views, are more reserved; the painting might not be the work of Degas himself, but could well have been carried out by a pupil under the master's supervision. If confirmed, such doubts as to the paintings' authenticity could well diminish their value as re-estimated in New York; however, it is also patently clear that Anatole's own initial judgement was inaccurate and that the price paid by Bob was in any event greatly below the one the work could now reach. What remedy, if any, is available?

Discussions

Austria

(i) Anatole made a mistake as to the content of the contract, such a mistake relates to the qualities of the subject matter of the contract and was an intrinsic element of Bob's performance.[1] Whether or not the paintings were by Degas himself or by one of his pupils is not important. Not every mistake as to the value, i.e. the market value of goods, is an

[1] *Irrtum über wertbildende Eigenschaften*, Koziol/Welser, *Grundriß des bürgerlichen Rechts* (10th edn, Vienna, 1995), p. 124, Rummel, *Kommentar zum ABGB I* (2nd edn, Vienna, vol. I 1990, vol. II 1992), vol. I Rz 10–12 to § 871.

important mistake as to the content of the declaration. The intention of the law is not and cannot be to release the parties from every potential economic risk. The right both to annul and adapt the contract on the ground of mistake should not be used as a means for getting out of contracts that turn out to be a bad deal later on. Therefore, mistakes as to value will often be seen as non-fundamental mistakes but this is not the case where the value of the contract – as here – is also part of the subject matter of the contract.

Anatole can only make a claim for his mistake as to the content of the declaration if and when the other party, namely Bob, does not deserve to be protected (§ 871 ABGB). Applying this article to the facts of the case, Bob neither (a) caused Anatole's mistake nor (b) should he have recognised the mistake nor (c) did Anatole notify his mistake in good time before Bob had relied on the contract, since Bob had already put the contract into effect (at least by transporting the painting to New York). Therefore, none of the three conditions mentioned in § 871 ABGB are fulfilled. If however, it is assumed that Bob did not know the real value of the paintings when concluding the contract and the fact that the paintings were very valuable and were worth a huge sum only became apparent to both parties afterwards, then in this case Austrian law qualifies such a mistake common to both parties. Such a common mistake is operative although this opinion is controversial[2] as the so-called common mistake is not expressly included in the cases mentioned in § 871 ABGB. Moreover, should both parties be mistaken then one party is not more or less worthy to be protected than the other.[3] However, according to the line of authority of the majority of legal scholars and case law, Anatole may be able to claim on the ground of common mistake. He can annul the contract or adapt it depending on whether he would still have concluded the contract if he had been aware of the true facts or whether both parties would have concluded the contract under different terms and conditions if they had known the true facts.

(ii) Even if a common mistake is not accepted, Anatole will have another remedy under *laesio enormis* (*Verkürzung über die Hälfte*, reduction

---

[2] According to the doctrine of the OGH (Austrian High Court) (e.g. SZ 36/22; SZ 44/59; JBl 1976, 646; SZ 53/108; SZ 56/96; SZ 61/53; but apparently not commented SZ 54/71) and to the majority of scholars, Gschnitzer in Klang, *Kommentar zum ABGB IV/1* (Vienna, 1968), pp. 133 ff.; A. Ehrenzweig, *System des österreichischen allgemeinen Privatrechts* (Vienna, 1951) I/1, pp. 238 f.; Mayer-Maly in *Klang IV/2*, pp. 218; E. A. Kramer, 'Zur Unterscheidung von Motiv- und Geschäftsirrtum', ÖJZ 1974, pp. 452 ff.

[3] Koziol/Welser, *Grundriß I*, p. 130; Rummel in *Rummel I* Rz 118 zu § 871; P. Rummel, 'Anmerkungen zum gemeinsamen Irrtum und zur Geschäftsgrundlage', JBl 1981, 1.

by less than half; §§ 934 f. ABGB), which provides that a person who receives consideration for his performance that is worth less than half the value of his own performance and has concluded the deal without knowing about the unequal disproportion has the right to annul the contract. The facts do not state the price paid nor the actual value of the paintings in case they are by Degas himself (or even by one of his students). However, one interpretation could be that Anatole has, in any event, received less than half of the value of the paintings. According to some scholarly opinion, this ground is, therefore, very closely related to the law of mistake, namely to the specific case of a mistake as to value.[4] It is not necessary to fulfil the same requirements set out in § 871 ABGB, the disproportion between performance and counter-performance suffices. Annulment on the basis of *laesio enormis* is easier for the claimant to prove than mistake insofar as only the disproportion between the value of the two performances needs to be considered. The disadvantage however, is that the other party, has the right to 'save' the contract by paying the difference between the two values. So he can prevent the other party from using the right to annul the contract. One proviso remains, merchants do not have the right to claim under *laesio enormis* (§ 351(a) HGB). This does not apply to Anatole as he is not running an art business but only selling some of his private collection.

(iii) Anatole's right to a claim for damages for lack of information about the value of the painting is only available if Bob can be blamed for the mistake he made when he made the contract, as the right to damages is conditioned by the fault of the party who caused the damages (see Cases 2 and 3).

Belgium

Three remedies are theoretically available to Anatole under Belgian law.

(i) Mistake relating to the substantial qualities in the subject matter of the contract (*erreur sur la substance*) under art. 1110 of the Civil Code ('fundamental mistake'). Mistake is defined as '*false or inexact representation of reality. It implies a lack of concordance between the true will and declared will.*'[5] Mistake is considered to relate to a substantial quality of the subject matter of the contract when it concerns an element that induces

---

[4] For this opinion of *laesio enormis* see P. Bydlinsky, 'Die Stellung der laesio enormis im Vertragsrecht', JBl 1983, 410.

[5] H. De Page, *Traité élémentaire de droit civil belge* (3rd edn, Brussels, 1962), vol. I, no. 37.

the mistaken party to contract, which he would not have done had he known that this element was absent.[6] Belgian law retains a *subjective* view of the substantial nature of a mistake: the parties' intentions must be examined *in concreto;*[7] some authors observe that mistake relating to substance amounts to a lack of (subjective) cause[8] to the contract. Moreover, in order to be considered in an action based on fundamental mistake, the quality must have 'entered into the contractual field', that is that this particular quality either is considered fundamental in general or that it is regarded as such by a party, the other party being aware of this fact or, that the party contracting with the *errans* should have known, in the circumstances, that this particular quality was substantial.[9] Annulment on the basis of a fundamental mistake will be excluded when the aggrieved party actually accepted the risk of a mistake occurring.[10] The burden of proving the existence of a fundamental mistake is on the *errans* but all types of evidence are admissible.[11] Finally, even when proven, a fundamental mistake will allow annulment of the

---

[6] *Ibid.,* no. 39.

[7] See, for instance, R. Kruithof, 'Overzicht van rechtspraak (1974–1980) Verbintenissen', TPR 1983, 548, no. 43; C. Goux, 'L'erreur, le dol et la lésion qualifiée: analyse et comparaisons' in *La théorie générale des obligations,* Formation permanente CUP (Liège, 1998), pp. 7 ff., no. 9: citing some recent case law, e.g. Mons, 31-3-1987 (JLMB 1987, 710) where the plaintiffs could obtain the annulment of a contract relating to the accomplishment of work on a building when they could demonstrate that the granting of a rehabilitation allowance from the public authority (which they in fact were not entitled to) constituted the character of a substantial quality without which they would not have contracted (the court had regard to the situation of the plaintiffs as a young couple at the start of their professional career); Liège, 11-12-1989 (Act. dr., 1991, 210) where the court decided that the quality of the land purchased as developable land was so important to the purchasers that it justified the annulment of the sale on the basis of a substantial mistake (since the land was in fact not developable). In both the cases described, it is clear that the 'substantial quality' of the subject matter of the contract had nothing to do with an objective quality of the thing itself.

[8] C. Renard, E. Vieujean and Y. Hannequart, *Théorie générale des obligations, Les novelles – Droit civil* (Brussels, 1957), vol. IV nos. 640–4.

[9] See De Page, *Traité élémentaire de droit civil belge,* no. 43; M. Coipel, *Théorie générale des contrats,* Book 29, *Guide juridique de l'entreprise* (Diegem, 1996), no. 390, C. Parmentier, 'La volonté des parties' in *Les obligations contractuelles* (Brussels, 1984), pp. 65–6; P. Van Ommeslaghe, 'Observations sur la théorie de la cause dans la jurisprudence et dans la doctrine moderne', note under Cass, 13-11-1969, RCJB 1970, pp. 353 ff., no. 18. For a summary, see Goux, 'L'erreur, le dol et la lésion qualifiée', no. 11. As to case law, see Trib. trav. Brussels, 3-9-1990, JTT 1991, p. 13; Brussels, 21-11-1996, JT 1997, 180; Cass, 27-10-1995, JT 1996, 61.

[10] See Goux, 'L'erreur, le dol et la lésion qualifiée', no. 10 *in fine* and see Case 3.

[11] Cass, 28-12-1882, Pas 1883, I, 11; Cass, 11-3-1960, Pas 1960, I, 811; Cass, 28-3-1974, Arr. Cass, 1974, 834.

contract only when it can be considered as excusable.[12] There is some dispute as to the *in concreto*[13] or *in abstracto*[14] examination of the excusable nature of a mistake.[15] However, even when the mistake is examined *in abstracto*, case law often considers personal characteristics of the *errans* such as his age, experience, degree of information on the subject matter, social status etc.,[16] which greatly reduces the practical significance of the controversy.

Applying these principles to the present case, it appears that Anatole has most probably made a fundamental mistake. Indeed, an action brought on the basis of fundamental mistake is the remedy most commonly applied in cases where a mistake bearing on the authenticity of a work of art has been made.[17] The fact that authenticity was substantial to Anatole and that he did not accept the risk of mistake could easily be inferred from the description of the paintings made in Anatole's own catalogue. Under the circumstances, it may also be assumed that it will be easily proven that the quality of the paintings (as non-authentic) had entered into the contractual field. However this mistake will probably not be held to be excusable, considering the fact that Anatole is, if not a professional seller of impressionist paintings, at least highly knowledgeable in this field.[18]

(ii) Fraud, a defect of consent that can lead to annulment of the contract under art. 1116 of the Civil Code, can be defined as 'the use of reprehensible means by a person who wants to deceive another and induce the latter into deciding to accomplish, under the influence of the mistake that was created in his mind, a detrimental act of legal

---

[12] See Goux, 'L'erreur, le dol et la lésion qualifiée', no. 12; Cass, 6-1-1944, Pas 1944, I, 133; Cass, 28-6-1966, JLMB 1997, 12.

[13] Would a 'reasonable man' (*bon père de famille*) have erred under the same objective as well as subjective circumstances?

[14] Where the criterion of the 'reasonable man' is being taken into account only abstractly.

[15] Goux, 'L'erreur, le dol et la lésion qualifiée'.

[16] *Ibid.*; C. Jassogne, 'Réflexions à propos de l'erreur', RGDC 1994, pp. 102 f., no. 3.

[17] M. Fontaine, 'Les aspects juridiques de la commercialisation d'oeuvres d'art', Ann. dr. Louvain 1988, pp. 383 ff., at p. 402.

[18] See for instance Antwerp, 22-4-1991, RW 1994–5, 405 (a mistake about the number of kilometres done by a used car is not excusable when it is made by a professional repairer of car parts); Civ Brussels, 19-5-1995, RGDC, 1996 (a purchaser who is a professional in the sale of works of art will not be allowed to annul the sale of a painting on the basis of mistake; even if it were admitted that the painting is not authentic, the mistake would be excusable for such purchaser); Fontaine, 'Les aspects', p. 404: 'A specialist who erred on the authenticity of the work of art that he sells or purchases will most frequently bear the consequences of his mistake.'

significance (contract, unilateral declaration of will) the profit of which will go to the author of the fraudulent behaviour or to a third party'.[19] This commonly used definition must be completed with the assertion that, in order to allow an action in annulment, the fraud must have induced the aggrieved party to contract.[20] It should be emphasised that it is not necessary that the aggrieved party suffer a loss in order for fraud to lead to the contract being annulled. If fraud can be proven, the *Cour de cassation* has held that a mistake caused by fraud does not need to satisfy the requirement of excusability although this position has been criticised by some authors.[21]

However, Anatole might find it difficult here to prove the existence of fraud consisting in Bob's intentional deceitful behaviour (the intentional element) made up either of positive manoeuvres (lies) or of fraudulent concealment (the material element),[22] knowing that the majority opinion in Belgian law decides that fraudulent concealment constitutes fraud only when there was an obligation to speak incumbent on the party alleged to have acted fraudulently derived from legislation, usage, the professional situation, the specific position of the defrauding party or the circumstances.[23]

(iii) Although Belgian case law[24] and majority authority recognise a more general principle of *lésion qualifiée* which applies to all kinds of contracts,[25] and can be broadly stated as the prohibition for a contracting party to take advantage of the other's inferiority to obtain engagements that are disproportional to his aim,[26] this doctrine clearly does

---

[19] Free translation of a definition formulated by authors and case law and cited by Goux, 'L'erreur, le dol et la lésion qualifiée', no. 2.

[20] Otherwise, we would have a mere incidental fraud (*dol incident*) that may only form the basis for an action in damages: *ibid.*, nos. 2 and 16.

[21] Cass, 23-9-1977, RCJB, 1980, 32; Cass, 29 May 1980, Pas 1980, I, 1190: 'when fraud induces consent the party who acted fraudulently may not invoke the imprudence or negligence of his contracting party (. . .) the said imprudence or negligence may not dispense the author of the fraud from compensating *entirely* the harmful consequences inflicted upon the victim' (emphasis added). See the authors and additional case law cited by Goux, 'L'erreur, le dol et la lésion qualifiée', no. 17.

[22] For a reminder of the intentional and material elements constituting fraud as a defect of consent: see Goux, 'L'erreur, le dol et la lésion qualifiée', no. 14.

[23] *Ibid.*

[24] Cass, 29-4-1993, JT 1994, p. 294. The *Cour de cassation* has not expressly admitted the concept but has accepted it implicitly.

[25] Civ Mons, 21-11-1990, JJP, 1991, 45.

[26] See Coipel, *Théorie générale des contrats*, no. 470; A. De Bersaques, 'L'œuvre prétorienne de la jurisprudence en matière de lésion' in *Mélanges en l'honneur de Jean Dabin* (Paris, 1963), vol. II, pp. 487 ff.; A. De Bersaques, 'La lésion qualifiée et sa sanction', note

not apply on the facts. Even if it could be asserted that there is some disproportion between the parties' respective performances, it cannot be maintained that it is a consequence of Bob's abuse of Anatole's weaker position.

Anatole's best chance on the basis of fraud does not look very hopeful as proving Bob's fraud might be difficult under the circumstances.

England

English law would not give Anatole any remedy on the facts as stated. The essence of the problem is a mistake made by the seller of an item where the buyer has not induced the mistake. English law will consider various possible remedies.

(i) Whether there is any contractual remedy available – typically, damages for breach. But here Bob is in breach of no obligation (express or implied) in buying the paintings at what turns out to have been an undervalue. He made no promise to Anatole that the paintings were not as Anatole had himself described them. And the mere undervalue is not a ground for interfering with the contract: the court will not concern itself with the adequacy of consideration in a contract as long as there *is* consideration – something of value which the law can recognise[27] – except sometimes where the undervalue might be evidence of

under Comm. Brussels, 20-2-1970, RCJB, 1970, 10; W. De Bondt, *De leer der gekwalificeerde benadeling* (Antwerp, 1985); D. Deli, 'De leer der gekwalificeerde benadeling en de verhouding tot de imprevisieleer', note under Antwerp, 21-1-1986, RW, 1986–7, pp. 1494 f.; P.-H. Delvaux, 'Contrats d'adhésion et clauses abusives en droit belge' in *La partie la plus faible dans les rapports contractuels* (Paris, 1996), nos. 19–20; E. Dirix, 'La réductibilité du salaire du mandataire: survivance d'une tradition', note under Cass, 6-3-1980, RCJB 1982, 537, nos. 14 ff., esp. note 62; R. Kruithof, H. Bocken, F. De Ly and B. De Temmerman, 'Overzicht van rechtspraak (1981–1992) – Verbintenissen', TPR 1994, pp. 394 ff., nos. 149–50; Parmentier, 'La volonté des parties', pp. 87 f.; J.-F. Romain, 'Regain de la lésion qualifiée en droit des obligations', JT 1993, pp. 749 ff.; S. Stijns, D. Van Gerven and P. Wery, 'Chronique de jurisprudence (1985–1995) – Les obligations: les sources', JT 1996, pp. 689 ff., no. 65; W. Van Gerven, 'Variaties op het thema misbruik', RW, 1979–80, col. 2485 f.; P. Van Ommeslaghe, 'Examen de jurisprudence (1974 à 1982) – Les obligations', RCJB 1986, pp. 33 ff., no. 24; M. Vanwijck-Alexandre, 'La réparation du dommage dans la négociation et la formation des contrats', Ann. Fac. Dr. Lg. 1980, 74, no. 42. Antwerp, 21-1-1986, RW 1986–87, p. 1488; Liège, 11-6-1986, RRD 1986, p. 240, JP Antwerp, 5-11-1986, RW, 1987–8, p. 1446; Trib. trav. Brussels, 5-9-1988, JTT 1988, p. 445; Trib. trav. Brussels, 26-9-1988, Chron. D. S. 1989, p. 58; J. P. Soignies, 17-5-1989, JJP, 1991, p. 42; Civ. Mons, 21-11-1990, JJP 1991, p. 45; Comm. Bruges, 7-1-1994, AJT 1994–5, p. 143; Civ. Brussels, 17-3-1995, RGDC 1995, p. 507; Liège, 17-10-1996, JT 1997, p. 569.

[27] *Thomas v. Thomas* (1842) 2 QB 851 at p. 859.

improper conduct on the part of the contracting party who obtains the benefit of an unusually good bargain: for example, the undervalue may be one element which raises a presumption of undue influence by a strong party over a weak party;[28] or where there is an 'unconscionable bargain' entered into by a 'poor and ignorant man at a considerable undervalue'.[29] But there is no such issue here, where the seller, the party seeking a remedy, is a specialist.

(ii) Remedies arising from misrepresentations made by the defendant in the action. The remedies will vary in their nature, and will depend on such things as the form and circumstances of the statement, and the state of mind (e.g. fraudulent or not) of the person who made it. But here the only relevant statement is made by Anatole ('work of an unknown artist') and there is no evidence of any statement by Bob. A party cannot use his own misrepresentation to claim a remedy. If, however, it could be established by evidence that Bob *also* made statements to Anatole that the paintings were not of a major artist, further issues would arise. In general, a contracting party can obtain a remedy for misrepresentation (whether damages or avoidance[30] of the contract) only if he can be shown to have *relied* on the statement in suffering the loss claimed, or in having entered into the contract. Here, Anatole would still have some difficulty, since he originated the mistake by his statement in the catalogue: on the facts as given, it would be difficult for him to establish that Bob's later statements (even if made) caused him to misunderstand what he was selling.

(iii) In English law, a contract is rarely vitiated by mistake. Where there is a claim that a contract was entered into on the basis of a mistaken understanding shared by the parties, one must ask whether the contract by its terms, express or implied, allocates the risk of the mistake to one of the parties: if so, the terms of the contract apply. If not, one asks whether the mistake is sufficiently serious to make the contract impossible of performance. This is not limited to literal, physical impossibility, but extends to the case where the contractual adventure, or purpose, cannot be fulfilled; but it is a narrow test, difficult to satisfy: the mistake must 'render the subject matter of the contract *essentially and radically different*

---

[28] *Allcard* v. *Skinner* (1887) 36 Ch D 145, as applied in *Royal Bank of Scotland* v. *Etridge (No. 2)* [2001] UKHL 44, [2002] 2 AC 773 at [29].

[29] *Fry* v. *Lane* (1888) 40 Ch D 312.

[30] For misrepresentation, the contract is voidable, but by the party without the need for a court order: *Car and Universal Finance Co. Ltd.* v. *Caldwell* [1965] 1 QB 525.

from the subject matter which the parties believed to exist'.[31] If the test is satisfied, the contract is *void ab initio*. Until recently it was thought that a less serious mistake might allow the court to declare the contract *voidable* in equity (that is, not automatically void *ab initio*, but to be set aside with retrospective effect, in the court's discretion, and on such terms as the court thinks fit), but this has recently been rejected by the Court of Appeal.[32] Even if it can be shown that the mistake here was shared – that is, that Bob too thought at the time that the paintings were minor works – then it is still not a sufficiently serious mistake to make the contract void *ab initio*. Lord Atkin in *Bell* v. *Lever Bros. Ltd.*[33] gave the example of a picture sold by A to B, both believing that it is the work of an old master but it turns out to be a modern copy: but 'A has no remedy in the absence of representation or warranty.' Although the facts here are the reverse (i.e. the parties wrongly believe the paintings *not* to be genuine) it seems that a court would follow the same line.

If it could not be shown that Bob shared the mistake, but instead realised that he might be buying paintings of a different kind from that which Anatole believed he was selling, then there would still not be a remedy for mistake. Anatole's mistake is then *unilateral*; such a mistake can generally be taken into account only if it related to the terms of the contract itself. But here there is no doubt about the terms of the contract (i.e. the promises by each party in the contract). The mistake relates to a quality (certainly a very important quality) in the subject matter of the contract. It has long been held that such a mistake is not sufficient, as long as it is not created by the defendant's misrepresentation: in *Smith* v. *Hughes*[34] Blackburn J said:

even if the vendor was aware that the purchaser thought that the article possessed that quality, and would not have entered into the contract unless he had so thought, still the purchaser is bound, unless the vendor was guilty of some fraud or deceit upon him, and . . . a mere abstinence from disabusing the purchaser of that impression is not fraud or deceit; for whatever may be the cases in a court of morals, there is no legal obligation on the vendor to inform the purchaser that he is under a mistake, not induced by the act of the vendor.

Given that Anatole would not have any remedy even in the situation where the paintings are authentic Degas, it follows that no remedy

---

[31] *Associated Japanese Bank (International) Ltd.* v. *Crédit du Nord S. A,* [1989] 1 WLR 255 at p. 268, approved in *The Great Peace* [2002] EWCA Civ 1407, [2003] QB 679, at [90]–[91].

[32] *The Great Peace,* above, fn. 31.   [33] [1932] AC 161 at p. 224.

[34] (1871) LR 6 QB 597 at p. 607. This statement confirms that the *seller* has no obligation to disclose defects to a *buyer: caveat emptor.* The position of the buyer is *a fortiori.*

would be given in the situation where the facts cannot be so strong as to fall within this, and the mistake is simply one as to value.

This area is predominantly a matter for case law, and so has been discussed in those terms. There are no legislative provisions, or other legal formants, which impact on the case law solution to Anatole's position, except that academic writing has sometimes been critical of the rigidity of the approach to *caveat emptor* in recent times. The most recent case law development,[35] however, has re-emphasised the courts' reluctance to allow mistake to vitiate a contract.

France

Under French law Anatole's only remedy would lie in asking the court to annul the sale[36] for mistake (*erreur*) relating to the substantial qualities in the subject matter of the contract under art. 1110 of the Civil Code.[37] The likelihood of this action succeeding is subject to two conditions:

(i) The mistake relates to whether the paintings can be attributed to Degas or one of his pupils. Is such a mistake fundamental so as to annul the contract?

(a) Does the mistake relate to a substantial quality? The mistake could be considered to be a mistake relating to a substantial quality since French case law has a subjective view of mistake and considers that it falls within the substance if it is of such a nature that 'without it one of the parties would not have contracted'.[38] Numerous cases have held that the artistic authorship of a work of art is a substantial quality under art. 1110 of the Civil Code, the most famous being the 'Poussin'[39] and

---

[35] *The Great Peace*, above, fn. 31. This case was, however, decided in a commercial context which may explain the tone adopted by the court: J. Cartwright, *Rewriting the Law on Mistake* [2003] RLR 93.

[36] Article 1117 of the Civil Code states 'la convention contractée par erreur [. . .] n'est point nulle de plein droit; elle donne seulement lieu à une action en nullité . . .' ('The contract contracted by mistake . . . is not void as of right; it only gives rise to an action to be annulled.') It is thus stricter than § 143 BGB, see the German report below. Furthermore, art. 1304 of the Civil Code states that such an action is prescribed five years after the mistake is discovered.

[37] 'L'erreur n'est une cause de nullité de la convention que lorsqu'elle tombe sur la substance même de la chose qui en est l'objet.' ('Mistake is only a cause for nullity when it relates to the substance itself of the subject matter of the contract.')

[38] Civ, 28 January 1913, Recueil Sirey, 1913. 1. 487, comp. Com, 20 October 1970, JCP 1971. II. 16916, note J. Ghestin; Civ 1, 8 March 1988, Bull civ I, no. 56.

[39] Civ 1, 22 February 1978, D 1978. 601, note P. Malinvaud, JCP 1978. II. 18925, Def 1978. 1346, obs. J.-L. Aubert, RTDCiv 1979, 127, obs. Y. Loussouarn; Civ 1, 13 December 1983, D 1984. 340, note J.-L. Aubert, JCP 1984. II. 20186, concl. Gulphe; J. Ghestin, note sous Com, 20 October 1970, JCP 1971. II. 16916.

the 'Verrou de Fragonard'[40] cases. Moreover, the fact that Anatole as the seller has made a mistake about the authorship of the paintings and that the mistake concerns the very subject matter of his own obligation does not preclude him from invoking the mistake, although the question has given rise to a great deal of controversy amongst scholars.

The case law definition of mistake is very wide and exceeds by far the apparent reach of art. 1110 of the Civil Code. Mistakes that case law considers to relate to 'the substance of the thing' are indeed very varied. The authenticity of a work of art is a good illustration. Very often, actions to annul the sale of works of art have been brought before the courts when their authorship was not that which a contracting party believed at the time of the sale.[41] The increasing risk of mistakes in the field can probably be explained by the variable attribution of certain works as a result of investigations carried out by experts.

In view of the risk that such a wide and subjective view of mistake may have on legal certainty, case law requires a further condition to be fulfilled, namely that the party contracting with the mistaken party (in this case Bob) was aware of the essential character which the latter (Anatole) attached to the litigious quality. It is said that the quality must 'have entered into the contractual field'[42] or have been 'agreed'.[43] According to general legal rules, the burden of proof lies on Anatole as the claimant.[44] Traditionally, the quality of the painting to which the mistake relates justifies annulling the contract. However, here the quality as to the paintings' authenticity is open to doubt.

(b) Do doubts as to authenticity disqualify the mistake? Mistake is defined as arising where a party's belief clashes with the reality. Although this is simple when the reality is clear,[45] it is less so when the reality is hedged with doubt.[46] This appears to be the case here as the expert opinions are contradictory.

---

[40] Civ 1, 24 March 1987, D 1987. 489, note J.-L. Aubert, RTDCiv, 1987. 743, obs. J. Mestre.

[41] See the abundant case law cited by J. Ghestin, *Traité de droit civil, La formation du contrat* (Paris, 1993), no. 502, p. 465.

[42] Y. Loussouarn, obs. RTDCiv 1971, 131.

[43] J. Ghestin, note sous Com, 20 October 1970, JCP 1971. II. 16916.

[44] He must prove that he thought that the painting was not by Degas and that the absence of this quality induced him to contract. He must also prove that Bob knew that the litigious quality was a determining factor. All kinds of evidence of mistake (examined *in concreto*) made at contract formation (e.g. by presumptions such as the moderate price paid for the paintings) and even the aid of elements which arose after the sale, such as the expert opinions are admissible.

[45] Anatole believed the painting was not by Degas whereas it is by Degas.

[46] Anatole believed the painting was not by Degas whereas the painting might be by Degas.

In this sort of case a further distinction may be drawn: either Anatole had accepted a risk about the paintings' authors, then the risk enters into the contractual field and 'chases away the mistake'[47] and there is no remedy available to annul the contract of sale. Or, as seems more likely since Anatole actually drafted the catalogue description, he had not accepted the risk.[48] The court's interpretation of the catalogue description will therefore determine the acceptance of the risk. In that respect, it is interesting to note a decree has been enacted in an attempt to define common ambiguous expressions.[49] Thus a remedy would still be available to annul the contract despite the subsisting doubt about the reality.[50]

(ii) Is a mistake excusable (*erreur excusable*) if it is made by a seller with professional experience? The fact that Anatole made a mistake and is a professional impressionist specialist may bar his claim. If it is generally admitted that contracting parties are obliged to disclose relevant factors about which they have knowledge,[51] namely those which may change the other party's behaviour, it is likewise considered that the latter has a duty to require information. These obligations to disclose and require information are all the more consequential here in that they lie on a professional in his field of speciality. This is the case for both Bob and Anatole and in this respect it makes no difference that the latter sold paintings from his private collection. Whether or not a mistake will be legally excused is decided *in concreto* with regard to the actual competence of the mistaken party and the fact that the contract had been concluded for his private needs is irrelevant.[52] It is arguable that Anatole did not carry out sufficient enquiries when he was compiling the catalogue and it is highly likely that the courts would dismiss Anatole's action on the grounds that his mistake is inexcusable.

---

[47] J. Mestre, obs. RTDCiv 1989, 740.

[48] The painting was presented as the 'charming work of an unknown artist' which excludes the possibility of it being attributed to a famous artist.

[49] Decree no. 81–255 of 3 March 1981. In addition, upon the buyer's request, the decree obliges sellers, even of private collections, as here, to deliver an invoice of sale specifying the painting's authorship etc. which constitutes preliminary evidence of the mistake – cf. J. Ghestin, *La Formation*, no. 530, p. 497.

[50] This results from the *Poussin* case, see above.

[51] M. Fabre-Magnan, *De l'obligation d'information dans les contrats, Essai d'une théorie* (Paris, 1992), no. 169, pp. 132 ff.

[52] In this sense a case which held that the mistake made by an amateur of art was unforgivable, when he had attached importance to the description 'attributed to Courbet' in order to believe the signature on the painting which he had bought: Civ 1, 16 December 1964, Bull civ I, no. 575.

(iii) In the alternative, Anatole could plead that Bob was in breach of his precontractual duty to inform, or that he was liable for deceitful manoeuvres on the basis of fraud[53] in order to claim damages in tort.[54] These actions can be claimed concurrently.[55] However, it is highly unlikely that this action will succeed on the facts as there is no evidence that Bob's fraudulent behaviour and intention have induced Anatole to contract. Moreover, the *Cour de Cassation* held recently that a professional buyer does not owe a duty to inform a seller who is not a professional, in a case similar to the facts here;[56] *a fortiori*, where both the buyer and seller have expertise in the field, as is the case here, it is most unlikely that Bob would be held to owe a duty to inform Anatole, the seller.

The last remedy which might be envisaged is on the grounds of *lésion*,[57] but it is emphasised that it is not available in the circumstances since art. 1674 of the Civil Code does not cover sales for movable goods such as works of art.

Germany

Under German law Anatole can try annulling on grounds of mistake and a claim to vary the contract because the basic contractual assumption has failed (*Wegfall der Geschäftsgrundlage*).

---

[53] Provided that the constitutive elements – the existence of deceitful manoeuvres which may result from mere silence and a breach of a precontractual duty of disclosure, intention to induce a mistake in the other party to the contract and the fact that these manoeuvres led the other party to make the contract – are proven (art. 1116 of the Civil Code).

[54] Com, 18 October 1994, Bull civ IV, no. 293, D 1995. 180, note C. Atias, 'Contrats, concurrence, consommation', 1995, no. 1, p. 3, note L. Leveneur, RTDCiv 1995. 353, obs. J. Mestre. Such an action in tort is possible even in the absence of a vitiating factor provided that the mistaken party proves that the other party has committed a fault; see Fabre-Magnan, *De l'obligation d'information dans les contrats*, no. 345, p. 277.

[55] Civ 1, 4 February 1975, Bull civ I, no. 43, p. 41, JCP 1975. II. 18100, note Ch. Larroumet, D 1975. 405, note C. Gaury, RTDCiv 1975. 537, obs. G. Durry.

[56] Civ 1, 3 May 2000, *Clin v. Mme Natali, the Baldus case*, RTDCiv 2000, 566, note. The seller had sold some Baldus photos to the buyer at a public auction. The seller then sought out the buyer for another private sale at the same price (per photo) as at the auction. The seller was unaware that the Baldus photos were of value whereas the buyer was clearly aware of their value and made a considerable profit on resale. Nevertheless, the court held that the buyer was not under a duty to inform the seller of their value. See note B. Fromion-Hébrard, Petites Affiches, 5 December 2000, no. 242, p. 14, who suggests that the court has favoured a liberal view of contract. This decision counters the criticisms made by B. Rudden, RTDCiv 1985, 91, that French law is inefficient in its outlook.

[57] Rescission of a contract for *lésion* is open to the seller when the sale is sold at an undervalue, i.e. seven-twelfths of the (market) value.

(i) From the facts there has been no mistake in declaration under § 119 I BGB. Anatole did not know who the painter of the two pictures was and therefore intended to sell the works of an 'unknown artist'. This is exactly what he has expressed; the declaration of intent and expression correlate. Nor would Anatole be able to claim that he had made a mistake as to the painting's value; an item's value – even if it is a work of art – is widely accepted as not amounting to an essential quality.[58]

According to case law, a painting's authorship is regarded as a substantial quality of the painting.[59] The German concept of 'mistake' means an 'incorrect understanding of the reality of the situation'.[60] Whether Anatole's understanding of the situation diverges from reality is, however, uncertain. As long as the artist's identity remains unclear it cannot be said that Anatole has made a 'mistake'. A German court would nevertheless be unlikely to employ this argument.[61] Rather, it would be guided by the fact that Anatole is an 'impressionist specialist'. A mistake made by a specialist is to be classified differently from that made by an uninformed lay-person. One would therefore be inclined to regard the continuing doubt as to the paintings' authorship as part of the balance of risk: if a specialist sells pictures, the origin of which specialists are in disagreement over, then he himself is to bear the risk of making an incorrect judgement. Some years ago, in a case exhibiting very similar facts, the *BGH* nevertheless allowed a claim for annulment on the ground of mistake.[62]

(a) Anatole may annul the contract of sale for both paintings which he has entered into with Bob as a result of his mistake relating to their authorship (§ 119 II). To annul the contract, Anatole can make a simple declaration (§ 143) addressed to Bob, he does not need to go to court as long as he is within the time limits (§ 121), the contract of sale is extinguished and Anatole may claim the surrender of the paintings together with title over them according to § 812 I 1 BGB. Nevertheless, Anatole is

---

[58] Cf. RG LZ 1926, 742, 744; BGHZ 16, 54, 57; BGH LM § 779 Nr. 2/2; BGH DB 1963, 285; BGH DB 1966, 379; critically on this T. Mayer-Maly, *Festschrift zum 65. Geburtstag von Mario M. Pedrazzini* (Bern, 1990), pp. 343 ff. and – because of other reasons – M. Adams, 'Irrtümer und Offenbarungspflichten in Vertragsrecht' (1986) ACP 186, 453, pp. 468 ff.

[59] BGHZ 63, 369, 371 = NJW 1975, 970; BGH NJW 1988, 2597, 2599.

[60] Staudinger/Dilcher, § 119 para. 1; similarly Larenz/Wolf, AT 664.

[61] The OLG Düsseldorf NJW 1992, 1326 avoided this argument, even though it would have been wholly appropriate; cf. however, E. Becker-Eberhard, 'Der nicht beweisbar echte Elvis' – OLG Düsseldorf, NJW 1992, 1326, in: JuS 1992, 461, 463: 'The mistake relating to the authenticity of the pictures requires that these are not authentic.'

[62] BGH NJW 1988, 2597.

liable to compensate Bob for the damage he has suffered arising from his negative interest (§ 122 I) if he did not know or could not have known of Anatole's mistake (§ 122 II). Negative interest 'is the damage which the aggrieved party suffers by his futile reliance on the validity of the declaration of intent which has been extinguished by the annulment'.[63] Bob should therefore be placed in the position he would have been in had he not relied on Anatole's declaration. Therefore, if Bob has had to terminate negotiations for sale with a third party or where a contract of sale has already been concluded with a third party which he can now no longer perform, he may demand that Anatole compensate him for all costs arising to him under the contract, all claims of the third party and the amount of the purchase price[64] he has already paid. § 122 limits the claim to the value of his positive interest. The damages demanded by Bob may therefore amount to the price the pictures were expected to fetch in America. In the worst possible scenario for Anatole he may of course demand the return of the paintings together with title over them (§ 812 I 1) but in return he must compensate Bob for the 'breathtaking' price which the latter has agreed upon in a contract with a third party.

If Bob has already transferred title to a third party it is no longer possible for Anatole to claim return of ownership. In this case, Anatole may claim compensation up to the value of the paintings (§ 818 II).[65] In the absence of any other criteria, the extent of this claim under unjust enrichment will normally be determined by the price that Bob expects the paintings to fetch. As far as Bob is concerned, he may demand the refund of the purchase price he paid Anatole (§ 122 I).

(b) Alternatively, it is arguable that annulment is not possible, in accordance with the theory of the distribution of contractual risk. Anatole is not simply an amateur art-lover; he is a specialist. Of course, even specialists can make mistakes and their mistake may justify annulment. However, having regard to the uncertainty which still persists as to the identity of the paintings' artist, great significance attaches to the seller's

---

[63] Cf. RGZ 170, 281, 284; on this: Soergel/Hefermehl, § 122 para. 4; Staudinger/Dilcher, § 199 para. 6.

[64] The claim for the return of the counter-performance is contained in § 122 and therefore need not be pursued under the law of unjust enrichment (§ 818 III); Erman/Brox, § 122 para. 5; Staudinger/Dilcher, § 122 para. 11.

[65] On the discussion concerning the obligation to restore possession under *lucrum ex negotiatione* briefly: Palandt/Thomas, § 818 para. 14; extensively – with criticism of the leading opinion: H. H. Jakobs, 'Lucrum ex negotiatione. Kondiktionsrechtliche Gewinnhaftung' in *Geschichtlicher Sicht* (Tübingen, 1992).

own expertise. One may therefore argue that Anatole was unaware of the suspicions other (French and American) experts entertained at the point in time when the pictures were sold to Bob. Therefore, he did not intend to assume any particular risk concerning the origin of the paintings. Yet precisely this dispute amongst these experts illustrates that it is not possible to ascertain the artist's identity with any degree of certainty and that, possibly some time later, Anatole's own opinion that the pictures were painted by an 'unknown artist' will be regarded as authoritative.[66] From this point of view,[67] Anatole's mistake becomes one that relates to the market price the two pictures expect to fetch at that particular moment in time.[68] By assessing the value himself, Anatole therefore bore the risk of making an incorrect evaluation. Due to this, it is not possible for him to claim annulment on grounds of mistake.

(ii) Anatole can also make a claim to vary the contract on the grounds that there is a failure of the basis of the transaction (*Fehlen der Geschäftsgrundlage*). Mistaken assumptions entertained by both parties may justify a claim to adapt the contract according to the principles of the doctrine of *Geschäftsgrundlage*. In contrast to annulment on the ground of mistake this claim would have the advantage for Anatole that the sale price would be adapted to the market price. Anatole would not have the paintings returned but he would not be bound to compensate Bob for the loss arising from his negative interest (§ 121 BGB). If one applies the *BGH*'s solution, which would allow annulment pursuant to § 119 II BGB, then it would be more sensible for Anatole to demand that the contract be adapted on the grounds of a failed basic contractual assumption. In all likelihood, he will be more interested in obtaining a good sale than having the paintings returned on the condition that he pays compensation.

From a mass of case law on this subject, German contractual theory has developed criteria governing the adaptation of the contract

---

[66] The evaluation of the numerous fakes of the works of A. Jawlensky is typical for this; cf. for example, A. Müller-Katzenburg, 'Die Akte Jawlensky' in *Frankfurter Allgemeine Zeitung* from 25.7.1998, 38 f.

[67] Similarly W. Flume, 'Der Kauf von Kunstgegenständen und die Urheberschaft des Kunstwerks' JZ 1991, pp. 633 f.; according to Flume in the case of an uncertain attribute rescission under § 119 II 'ought' not to be possible. Where a 'discovery' is later made then by analogy with the rule *casum sentit dominus* the person who is in possession of the work of art at the time should enjoy the benefit of an increase of value (634).

[68] The concept of an 'insignificant' mistake relating to value is similar.

according to the principles laid down by the doctrine of a failure of the basis of the transaction which is now codified in § 313. For a start, there must be a gross disproportion in the relationship of exchange between the performance and counter-performance (breach of the principle of equivalent exchange).[69] Our case fulfils this criterion: Anatole has received only a 'moderate price' for an extremely valuable pair of paintings. However, the next criterion causes problems. The limits of the contractual apportionment of risk must be exceeded by the loss or absence of a basis for the transaction.[70] In contrast to § 119 BGB, the apportionment of risk when assessing the basis for the transaction plays a large role in practice.[71] Anatole sold the paintings as the 'work of an unknown artist'. The unknown identity of the painter will hardly have formed the basis of the transaction. Rather, the wording indicates that both Anatole and Bob did not intend to rule out the possibility that the true identity of the artist would come to light later. In that respect, both have assumed a particular risk concerning the authorship of the paintings.

One could also argue however, that the relationship of exchange agreed upon by Anatole and Bob forms the transaction's basis. This basis would then fail once the American specialists had given their assessment and the value of the paintings had risen enormously. Mistaken assessments of the value or the price of an item made by both parties may in fact be taken into consideration as part of the doctrine of the basis for the transaction.[72] Nevertheless, in our case the determination of the paintings' sale price is inseparable from the assumption made concerning the artist's identity. If Anatole assumed responsibility for the fact that the pictures 'of unknown origin' could also have been painted by an artist of world renown then, at the same time, he assumed the risk of making an incorrect estimation of their value. Thus, it is not possible to adapt the contract owing to the loss or absence of a basis for the transaction.

---

[69] Cf. Palandt/Heinrichs, § 242 para. 125 (*Wesentliche Änderung*); MüKo/Roth, § 242 para. 518 ff. (*Objektive Unangemessenheit*); Larenz/Wolf, AT 715 (*Wesentliche Abweichung*). Now § 313 I demands that the circumstances have changed fundamentally (. . . *schwerwiegend verändert*).

[70] Palandt/Heinrichs, § 242 para. 126 ff.; MüKo/Roth, § 242 para. 537 ff.; Larenz/Wolf, AT 715 f. Now § 313 I: '. . . as far as adherence to the contract is unreasonable with regard to all circumstances, especially the balancing of risk intended by law or contract'.

[71] Cf. for example, BGHZ 74, 373; BGHZ 101, 152; BGHZ 107, 92, 104; BGH NJW 1992, 2691.

[72] In the famous cases RGZ 90, 268 ('Altmetallagerfall'), RGZ 94, 65 ('Börsenkursfall') and RGZ 105, 406 ('Rubelfall') the Reichsgericht still held that rescission (§ 119 I) was possible (doctrine of the 'extended mistake in content'); cf. however, BGH LM 1 on § 242; BGH MDR 1960, 580; OLG Köln WM 1991, 1463 = NJW-RR 1991, 1266. Further information in MüKo/Roth, § 242 paras. 636 and 666.

Greece

If the paintings prove to be authentic works of Degas, or one of his pupils, Anatole can ask for the annulment of the sale and the contract of transfer of ownership[73] on the grounds of mistake as to quality of the thing (art. 142 AK).[74] Mistake as to quality does not suffice for annulment; a fundamental mistake is required. The fundamental nature of the quality will be decided on the basis of two criteria, one objective, one subjective (art. 142 AK). Anatole's mistake is objectively fundamental as it relates to an important quality for the whole legal act[75] according to good faith and common usage. The authenticity of a work of art is considered an important quality on the basis of good faith.[76] The subjective criterion is also present here. It is clear that Anatole would not have agreed to sell the paintings, at least under these terms, had he known the true state of affairs.

If the paintings are finally judged not to be works of Degas, nor one of his pupils, and their value still remains much higher than what Bob paid, Anatole is not entitled to seek the annulment of the contracts on the grounds of his own mistake. His mistake concerns the economic value of the thing, which according to the prevailing view[77] is not a quality in the sense of art. 142 AK. Although this opinion is criticisable, since a mistake as to the value of the thing may result from a mistake as to quality, in this case it is correct. The paintings' high price does not

[73] The Greek Civil Code, following the German legal system, distinguishes between promissory contracts, by which the parties promise and bind themselves to perform an obligation and disposition contracts by which the disposal, i.e. transfer, charge, abolition or alteration of a right, is effected.

[74] Article 142 AK lays down that: 'A mistake as to the qualities of a person or thing shall be considered an operative mistake if such qualities are, according to the agreement of the parties or on the basis of good faith and common usage, of such importance in regard to the whole of the act that the mistaken person if he were aware of the true situation would not have entered into the act.'

[75] The term 'legal act' is somewhat inelegant in English but is retained to denote the conception of contracts as 'legal acts' known to certain civil law countries. For the sake of convenience and elegance, this term has often been replaced by that of 'contract'.

[76] A. Gazis, *General Principles of Civil Law, Juridical Acts* (1973), p. 68.

[77] Ap 268/1974, NoV 22, 1269; Gazis, *General Principles of Civil Law*, vol. C, p. 65; D. Bailas, 'Error as to the qualities a thing' in *Miscellany in Honour of Maridakis* (Athens, 1963), vol II, p. 335; I. Karakatsanis, in Ap. Geordiadis and M. Stathopoulos, *Civil Code AK 138–157* (Athens, 1978), AK 142 n. 4; K. Simantiras, *General Principles of Civil Law* (4th edn, Athens-Thessaloniki, 1988) n. 727; I. Spyridakis *General Principles*, (Athens-Komotini, 1987), p. 602; see, however, A. Georgiadis, *General Principles of Civil Law* (2nd edn, Athens-Komotini, 1997), p. 426; M. Karassis, *Manual of General Principles of Civil Law. Law of the Judicial Act* (Athens-Komotini, 1996), p. 103; D. Klavanidou, *Error as to the Qualities of the Thing in Sales* (Thessaloniki, 1991), p. 18; N. Papantoniou, *General Principles of Civil Law* (3rd edn, Athens, 1983), p. 396.

result from their authenticity as works of Degas but from other factors, such as the fact that long discussions have occurred about the paintings. In this case Anatole's mistake is one of motive. Anatole's estimate about the artistic value of the paintings proved to be inaccurate. In this kind of mistake there is a discrepancy between the will of the person making a declaration and the reality. Anatole's declaration of will coincides with his actual will to sell the paintings. Mistake as to motive is not fundamental according to art. 143 AK, and is therefore inoperative.

As to defects of consent the Greek Civil Code, like other European legal systems, follows an intermediate compromise between the will theory and the security of transactions. The mistaken person can under certain conditions invoke the fact that his will was defective and seek the annulment of the legal act (arts. 140f. AK). The Greek Civil Code's position closely resembles the German Civil Code but with some differences. Greek law (art. 154 AK) following the system of Roman law[78] requires the annulment to be pronounced by a court[79] and not by a simple declaration, as under § 143 BGB. Thus the law sacrifices simplicity and speed in the interests of the security of transactions.[80] The right to demand annulment is extinguished by the lapse of two years from the point when the state of mistake ceased and, at all events, within twenty years (arts. 154f. AK). Upon annulment, ownership of the paintings reverts *ipso jure* to Anatole (art. 184 AK), who is obliged to return to Bob the enrichment, that is the price of the paintings (arts. 904f. AK). Anatole is however liable for the loss sustained by Bob, unless the latter knew or should have known of the mistake (art. 145 AK). He is liable to pay the negative interest[81] that is the harm arising out of Bob's reliance on the contract.

Although Anatole was an expert on impressionistic art and an expert's mistake could be considered as inexcusable,[82] under art. 144 § 2 AK, it is considered that this article does not apply on the facts. Other factors such as the level of negligence and the damage which the mistaken

---

[78] See also French Civil Code arts. 1117, 1304.

[79] The right to seek the annulment of a juridical act may be exercised either by an action, a counterclaim, or an exception.

[80] See G. Maridakis, 'Introductory report on General Principles' in *Draft of the Civil Law – General Principles* (Athens, 1936) p. 201; Papantoniou, *General Principles of Civil Law*, p. 442; M. P. Stathopoulos, *Contract Law in Hellas* (The Hague, Boston, Athens, 1995), p. 114.

[81] AP 1030/1992 EllDik 36,75.

[82] See for example Stathopoulos, 'Mistake Crucial for the Annulment of the Juridical Act' in *Miscellany of N. Papantoniou* (Thessaloniki, 1996), p. 726.

person will suffer if annulment is refused[83] require that the sale and contract of transfer be annulled. In this case it would be contrary to good faith to refuse annulment. It is obvious that the issue of the authenticity of the actual paintings is debatable. Good faith does not demand an excessive research of the author of a painting when there are no apparent elements speaking for the painting's authenticity.

Ireland

It is difficult to see how there could be a remedy for Anatole under Irish contract law based on the facts. This is a case where the mistake is on the part of the seller who appears to be a man of some experience in his field and it does not appear that the mistake has been caused by any act on the part of the purchaser.

The mistake is one as to the quality of the goods and, as a general rule, the Irish courts will not hold a contract to be void where there is a mistake in respect of the subject matter or other attribute of the contract unless the mistake goes to the essence of the contract in question. In this regard the Irish courts have followed the decision of the United Kingdom's House of Lords in *Bell* v. *Lever Brothers*.[84] Further dicta from the judgment of Lord Atkin have often been interpreted as refusing to allow a mistake as to quality to render a contract void. Furthermore, in the instant case the seller has not been placed at any disadvantage as a result of undue influence. Nor is he in such a weak bargaining position that he might have been induced to enter into an 'unconscionable bargain'.

Italy

Under Italian law Anatole can try to annul the sale on the grounds of mistake (*errore*) (arts. 1427–33 of the Civil Code) or under the legal doctrine of '*presupposizione*' (basic contractual assumption).

(i) The Italian Civil Code says that a contracting party whose consent was given by mistake can ask for the contract to be annulled (art. 1427) when the mistake is fundamental (*essenziale*) and recognisable (*riconoscibile*) by the other contracting party (art. 1428).[85] The Code gives

---

[83] Criteria mentioned by Spyridakis, *General Principles*, p. 590.

[84] (1932) AC 161.

[85] The Italian Civil Code deals with mistake in the following articles:
   Article 1428 Relevance of mistake: 'A mistake is the cause of annulling a contract when it is fundamental (1429) and recognisable (1431) by the other contracting party.'

to the court a long list of cases in which the mistake could be considered fundamental; moreover, it requires that the parties were not able to recognise it by exercising reasonable and proper care at the time the contract was made. The Italian Supreme Court tends either to exclude the presence of a mistake or consider the mistake not essential when it is inexcusable (*inescusabile*).[86] The chance of Anatole's action succeeding depends on three conditions: (a) is the mistake about authenticity fundamental; (b) could Bob recognise the mistake; (c) is Anatole's mistake excusable, considering his professional expertise?

(a) It is important to point out that the authenticity of a painting is not always fully ascertainable; the attribution to Degas or to his pupil is something which definitely depends on the development of experts' studies and may be subject to change. Before the 1942 Code the Italian courts used to consider the sale of a painting as an aleatory contract (*contratto aleatorio*): 'someone who has sold an old painting ignoring its artistic value, cannot, once he has discovered it, plead to annul the sale for factual mistake'[87] or 'once he has sold an old painting without a warranty about the value (it was a Raffaello), there is neither fraud on the part of the vendor, nor a fundamental mistake that could annul the sale'.[88] This approach has not changed since the new Code,[89] but there have not been many cases in the last few years. An Italian court used both the former doctrine of an aleatory contract and the new doctrine of fundamental mistake as to the quality of the said object (art. 1429 n. 2 of the Civil Code) in a case of a Carraccio painting sold for a few

---

Article 1429 Fundamental mistake: 'A mistake is fundamental when it concerns:
    (i) the nature or the object of contract;
    (ii) the identity of the object of the performance or a quality of the said object which, according to common understanding or in the circumstances, should be considered to have determined consent;
    (iii) the identity or personal qualities of the other contracting party, so long as the one or the other induced consent;
    (iv) when the mistake was one of law and was the only or the principal reason for entering into the contract'.
Article 1431 Recognisable mistake: 'A mistake is considered recognisable when, with respect to the content, the circumstances of the contract, or the quality of the contracting parties, it would have been detected by a person of normal diligence'.
[86] Cass 16.5.1960, n. 1177, G.I. 1960 I, 1, 112 noted by G. Amorth.
[87] A. Firenze 18.7.1905 GI 1905, I, 2, 577.   [88] A. Firenze 15.3.1910 *Filangeri*, 1910, 459.
[89] A. Milano 12.6.1947 GI, 1948, I, 2, 193 noted by Grassetti, *Verità, errore ed opinione circa la paternità dell'opera d'arte compravenduta*.

liras by a Roman antique shop.[90] The discussion about the authenticity of the painting sold by Anatole seems to give the Italian court the possibility of maintaining the aleatory contract doctrine to refuse the action. Moreover, fundamental mistake may fail for the reasons given below.

(b) The fact that the mistake was recognisable could be inferred from the fact that Bob was an art gallery owner, he too was a professional. The criterion of fair dealing[91] used by the Italian courts is a very broad concept. The main characteristic of fair dealing should be seen in the fact that the courts mostly consider the 'status of the parties' and 'the contract's content' in order to decide if the mistake is recognisable or not.[92] The Supreme Court has recently stated that the analysis must be done case by case.[93] On the facts, it is pretty likely that an Italian court would be inclined to hold that Bob is not liable because the new information about the paintings' value was given by third parties. Moreover, it might have been difficult for Bob to recognise the mistake given Anatole's expertise.[94]

(c) Anatole's expertise will also play a role in relation to whether his mistake is inexcusable. The interpretation *in concreto* made by the judges, under the influence of Italian case law before the 1942 Code, strongly influenced by the French courts, will consider if Anatole, as an art expert, could have been mistaken about the attribution of the painting, in other words whether his mistake is excusable. The transition from the Civil Code of 1865 to the 1942 Code allowed the Italian legislator to prefer the rule of reliance (*affidamento*) instead of the will theory (*dogma della volizione o della responsabilità*).[95] Some authors, though, consider that the will theory is still firmly established in the Italian courts' tradition: it is thus necessary to examine if the mistake was excusable

---

[90] A. Roma 23.11.1948 RDCo 1949, II, 192 noted by Sacco; a Carraccio painting has been sold as an 'unknown maestro'.

[91] Cass 1991, n. 980,

[92] V. Pietrobon, *Errore, volontà e affidamento* (Padua, 1990, ried.), p. 225.

[93] Cass 1985, n. 3892.

[94] A. Milano 5.6.1951, FP 1951, I, 874. If a picture bought as a real Picasso turns out to be a forgery, the purchaser can only rescind if the vendor could have known that it was a forgery; this requirement was held satisfied in a case where the vendor himself was a painter!

[95] M. Allara, *Teoria generale del contratto* (2nd edn, Turin, 1955), pp. 148 ff.; F. Martorano, *La tutela del compratore per vizi della cosa* (Naples, 1959), p. 217; Pietrobon, *Errore, volontà e affidamento* nn. 29 ff.; for the Italian case law see Cass 9.2.1952, n. 316, GI 1952, I, 1, 162; Cass 20.5.1954, n. 1623 GI 1954, I, 1, 700; Cass 22.5.1958, n. 1721; Cass 9.10.1963, n. 2684 FI 1963, I, 2088, and RDCo 1963, II, 468; Cass 20.9.1978, n. 4240.

(*scusabilità*). Moreover it is arguable that the reliance principle does not exclude liability, because the courts sometimes use the inexcusable principle without saying so[96] by saying that there is no mistake or that the mistake is not about a fundamental subject matter.[97]

In the unlikely event that the courts were to find Anatole's mistake excusable, his right to annul is subject to Bob's claim under art. 1432 of the Civil Code to ask for the contract to be adapted.[98]

(ii) Another way to attempt to annul the contract is through the use of the doctrine of 'basic contractual assumption' (*presupposizione*),[99] a factual situation not related to one of the parties that the work 'of an unknown artist' is considered to be a basic assumption of the contract. One way of explaining this idea is that the contract is conditional, where the parties have negotiated under an implied condition that 'the contract will not stand if the work is attributed to a *maestro*'. The fulfilment of this condition annuls the contract.[100]

---

[96] R. Sacco and G. De Nova, 'Il contratto' in *Trattato di diritto civile/diretto da Rodolfo Sacco* (Turin, 1993), vol. 1, p. 378; There are, indeed, a number of articles in the Civil Code that consider the double principle of reliance and responsibility (arts. 1338, 1490, 1494, 1478, 1479, 1° and 4° co., 1481, 2° co.; 1909, 1° and 2° co.).

[97] Cass 16.5.1960, n. 1177, GI 1960, I, 1, 112 noted by G. Amorth; Sacco and De Nova, 'Il contratto' vol. 1; p. 378.

[98] Article 1432 of the Civil Code states: 'The mistaken party cannot demand annulment of the contract if, before he can derive injury from it, the other party offers to perform it in a manner which is pursuant to the substance and characteristics of the contract that the mistaken party intended to conclude'.

[99] The *presupposizione* doctrine has a German origin inspired by B. Windscheid, P. Örtmann, *Die Geschäftsgrundlage. Ein neuer Rechtsbegriff* (Leipzig, 1921) and Larenz, *Geschäftsgrundlage und Vertragserfüllung* (Munich, 1963). It is arguable that the English coronation cases, like *Krell* v. *Henry* (1903) 2 KB 740, offer a factual example of a situation in which the *Geschäftsgrundlage* could have been invoked in Italian law, see A. Pontani, 'La presupposizione nella sua evoluzione, con particolare riferimento all'errore ed alla causa', *Quadrimestre* 1991, 833. However, the Italian Supreme Court in *Roy* v. *Canessa* (3.12.1991, n. 12921) has held that: 'The doctrine [of *presupposizione*] must be considered as an autonomous doctrine; it has abandoned the theory of the implied condition and now, under the influence of the German doctrine of *Geschäftsgrundlage* we must think of it as a basic contractual assumption, formed by the contract's external circumstances, without which the contract itself could not exist; one can find the basis of this doctrine in art. 1467 of the Civil Code which strictly refers to the *rebus sic stantibus* principle.'

[100] Cass 17.9.1970, n. 1512, FI 1971, I, 3028; Cass 7.4.1971, n. 1025 FI 1971, I, 2574; Cass 22.9.81, n. 5168, FI 1982, I, 104; Cass 31.10.1989, n. 4554, RDC 1990, II, 350; Cass 11.8.1990, n. 8200; Cass 3.12.1991, n. 12921, GI 1992, I, 1, 2210 noted by ODDI: the latter is a case of a purchase of the stocks of a company annulled when the only immovable good in the company asset was under an action to obtain revocation (art. 2901 of the Civil Code); Cass 1995, n. 1040; Cass 1995, n. 8689.

The Italian courts often find a basic contractual assumption in contracts for the sale of land[101] and long-term contracts.[102] It would definitely be innovative if the court were to use this doctrine to annul the contract on these facts, but it is not logically impossible. Moreover, the Italian courts appear sometimes to use indifferently, *presupposizione*, the sale of *aliud pro alio*[103] or mistake[104] according to the facts of the situation. Anatole's position would be stronger if he could allege that Bob was in bad faith or that he did not adhere to a standard of fair dealing during the bargaining process.[105] This may be diffcult to prove on the facts. According to the Tribunale of Milan a basic contractual assumption and fundamental mistake are two different aspects of the same situation; the principle of good faith (*buona fede*, arts. 1337 and 1375) adds new strength to the argument favourable to the use of basic contractual assumptions when it is a practical criterion for the contract's interpretation.[106] If a basic contractual assumption is interpreted as a new kind of mistake[107] the contract could still be annulled (art. 1441 of the Civil Code); on the other hand, if it is considered to create

---

[101] Cass 1983 n. 6933, Cass 1984, n. 5512.

[102] Article 1467 relating to contracts for mutual counter-performance has been interpreted as an explicit adoption of the basic contractual assumption by the courts: Cass 1995, n. 1040; Cass 31.10.1989, n. 4554, RDC 1990, II, 350; Cass 1986, n. 20.

[103] Article 1497 Lack of quality. When the thing sold lacks the qualities promised or those essential for the use for which it is intended, the buyer is entitled to obtain termination of the contract according to the general provisions on termination for non-performance (*risoluzione per inadempimento* art. 1453 ff.), provided that the defect in quality exceeds the limits of tolerance established by usage. However, the right to obtain termination is subject to the forfeiture (2964 ff., 1495 co.1) and prescription (2946 ff., 1495 co.3) established in art. 1495.

[104] Trib. Napoli, 24.6.1970, in Giurisprudenza di merito ('Merito') I, 1972, 407 noted by Baldanzi; Cass 8.6.1948, n. 864 GI 1949, I, 1, 174.

[105] This argument favours an interpretation of the *presupposizione* doctrine as an application of the standard of good faith principle, inferred from art. 1337 of the Civil Code. Sacco and De Nova, 'Il contratto', p. 443, pleads for a flexible and adaptable rule in order to solve the case law.

[106] Trib. Milano, 11.10.1948, in DL II, 1949, 17, where the mistake was on the essential quality of the counterpart, but the judges used the *presupposizione* doctrine instead of the essential mistake rule; this favours a broad interpretation of *presupposizione* Cass 3.10.1972, n. 2828.

[107] See fn. 92 above following Pietrobon, *Errore, volontà e affidamento*, p. 357 and C. Massimo Bianca, *Diritto civile*, 3 (Milan, 1987), vol. 3: *Il Contratto*, p. 610 it is possible to create a new hypothesis of fundamental mistake independently from the numbers of art. 1429 of the Civil Code, Sacco and De Nova, 'Il contratto', p. 389 does not agree, submitting that there is a *numerus clausus* of kinds of fundamental mistake.

an impediment for the contract (*causa*) the contract itself will be void (*nullo*) following arts. 1418 and 1325 of the Civil Code.[108]

However as the use of this legal ground is speculative it is more probable that Italian law will not give Anatole a remedy on this ground nor for mistake.

The Netherlands

There is no remedy available to Anatole. This is a case of seller's mistake by an expert. Mistake is dealt with by the new Civil Code (1992) by art. 6:228 BW, which reads as follows:[109]

Article 6: 228 BW

1. A contract which has been entered into under the influence of error and which would not have been entered into had there been a correct assessment of the facts, can be annulled:
   a. if the error is imputable to information given by the other party, unless the other party could assume that the contract would have been entered into even without this information;
   b. if the other party, in view of what he knew or ought to know regarding the error, should have informed the party in error;
   c. if the other party in entering into the contract has based himself on the same incorrect assumption as the party in error, unless the other party, even if there had been a correct assessment of the facts, would not have had to understand that the party in error would therefore be prevented from entering into the contract.
2. The annulment cannot be based on an error as to an exclusively future fact or an error for which, given the nature of the contract, common opinion or the circumstances of the case, the party in error should remain accountable.

It is clear that Anatole 'would not have entered into this contract had there been a correct assessment of the facts': had he known that the painting was the work of Degas or of a pupil working under the master's supervision, he would not have sold it for a moderate price. However, under art. 6:228 BW this is in itself not decisive since the contract can only be annulled if one of the three situations mentioned under a–c has

---

[108] The difference between annulment and voidness, a subject of academic debate, depends on the way the judge interprets the facts.

[109] The translations are taken from P. P. C. Haanappel and E. Mackaay, *New Netherlands Civil Code/Nouveau Code Civil Néerlandais* (The Hague, 1990); the English version translates *dwaling* as 'error'. However, following the terminology adopted, it will be translated as 'mistake'.

occurred. The case states no facts as to statements made by the buyer (Bob). Therefore it must be held that (a) does not apply. Article 6:228 (1)(b) raises the question whether Bob should have informed Anatole. However, at the conclusion of the contract Bob did not know of the authorship (and, as a result, the real value) of the painting, nor ought he to have known.[110] Rather Anatole, as an expert, ought to have known what he was selling. Article 6:228 (1)(c), however, does seem to apply. Not only is the seller mistaken, but also the buyer. In a case of common mistake a party may in principle annul the contract. The exception in art. 6:228 (1)(c) does not apply: if both parties had known of the real author (Degas or his pupil) and the true value of the painting, Bob would have realised that Anatole would not sell the painting for this price.

However, the question arises whether this mistake does not amount to 'an error for which, given the nature of the contract, common opinion or the circumstances of the case, the party in error should remain accountable' and whether therefore the contract should not be held valid. In *HR* 19 June 1959,[111] the *Stevensweerd Kantharos* case, the *Hoge Raad* decided that in principle the seller has no remedy if he discovers after the sale that the object he sold had characteristics of which he had no knowledge.[112] In that case the seller had sold for a small sum a cup which turned out to be a unique Greek-Roman *kantharos* and was worth a fortune. It was held that the seller may not annul a contract on the mere ground that the object of sale turned out to have a quality which the seller could not have anticipated, because according to reasonable prevailing opinion a party that sells an object of his own for a certain price, by doing so gives up the chance that the object afterwards will appear to have such an unanticipated quality.[113] It is generally held that this rule still applies under the new code and should be regarded as

---

[110] A party is not only under a duty to inform if he has actual knowledge of certain fact, but may also be under an obligation to investigate in order to be able to inform, especially if he is an expert. Not knowing is, in itself, not always a defence. Cf. Asser/Hartkamp II (2001), no. 185.

[111] NJ 1960, 59, note Hijmans van den Bergh.

[112] This decision met with some critical reactions. Cf. e.g. A. H. M. Santen, *De Kantharos van Stevensweert* (rede UvA, Deventer, 1993), Ars Notariatus LX, and J. C. M. Leijten, 'De Kantharos van Stevensweert in het licht van de gerechtigheid' in W. M. J. Bekkers and A. A. H. Gommers (eds.), *De Kantharos: Over recht en onrecht in de rechtspleging* (Wijn & Stael bundel), (Deventer, 1998).

[113] It was also held that the result may be different if the buyer was under a duty to inform the seller (art. 6:228(1)(b) BW). As we have seen, in the mechanism of the new code this is a preliminary question which in this case must be decided in the negative.

being based on art. 6:228 (2) BW.[114] The underlying policy of this rule lies in the distribution of risks between the seller and the buyer: the risk of not knowing the true characteristics of the object of sale, typically is one which the seller should bear. Application of this rule means that the contract cannot be annulled for mistake and is therefore valid.

Some authors have argued that the rule that the seller should bear the risk of his own mistake (unless the buyer was under a duty to inform him) should not be absolute. They say that things should be different if the buyer was an expert and the seller was not.[115] Although this argument is convincing, this is not of much help to Anatole in this case since here we have the reverse case where the seller himself is the expert.

Since there is no other reason for the invalidity of the contract nor any other remedy available, Anatole has no remedy.

Norway

On the facts, Anatole, the seller, would scarcely succeed with a claim on the grounds that he was mistaken about the value of the painting.

(i) The conclusion is clear cut if the purchaser (Bob) is supposed to have had *knowledge* of the artist's (possible) identity only *after* entering into the purchase contract.[116]

(a) A remedy for *breach of contract* in this situation would not succeed. There is no breach of the duty to inform. Unforeseen events which occur after the time of delivery, and which influence the value of the object for sale, are the risk of the parties concerned (in this instance, the purchaser's profit). In other words, there is no defect in the item.

(b) Another approach is to consider the question in light of the set of rules leading to *invalidity*.

The doctrine of mistake as found in the common law and in continental law, does not exist in Scandinavia, only a 'mistake in transaction' is explicitly covered.[117] On the other hand, from the turn of the century, a doctrine of contractual assumptions (not implemented in law)

---

[114] Cf. Asser/Hartkamp II (2001), no. 195; Asser/Hijma 5-I (2001), no. 246; P. Clausing, 'De Kantharos en artikel 6:228 BW', WPNR 6357 (1999), pp. 385 f.

[115] A. G. Castermans, *De mededelingsplicht in de onderhandelingsfase* (Deventer, 1992) (diss. Leiden, 1992), p. 130; Asser/Hijma 5-I (2001), no. 246; Santen, 'De Kantharos', n. 124; Leijten, 'De Kantharos', n. 124; Clausing, 'De Kantharos', n. 126, p. 385.

[116] We are then facing a situation where both parties experience an identical mistake, in common law doctrine referred to as 'common mistake' or 'shared mistake'.

[117] The Scandinavian contract laws contain only one regulation that deals directly with mistake (not created by force or fraud). The Norwegian Contract Act, § 32, para. 1, regulates situations of mistake in the transaction. But mistake would naturally be an important element when the general invalidity regulations are applied, as, for instance, in the Contract Act, § 33.

was developed. It finds its roots in the theories put forward by the German legal scholar Bernhard Windscheid.[118] The doctrine of assumption entered Scandinavian law principally through Danish writing.[119] The doctrine deals both with wrong assumptions at the time of the contract (*uriktige forutsetninger* – initially failed contractual assumptions), and with later changes of conditions (*bristende forutsetninger* – subsequently failed contractual assumptions). A common term is failed contractual assumptions (*sviktende forutsetninger*).

The basic conditions for claiming failed contractual assumptions are that the assumptions have been a determining element in the contract (so-called fundamental assumptions) and that the other party was aware of the assumptions (but not necessarily of the mistake). Furthermore, an assessment of risk[120] should be made, which in practice is the chief obstacle to reaching a claim based on failure of assumptions. The principal rule in Scandinavian law has always been that each party should bear the risk of its own assumptions.[121] Only in special cases would the court judge in favour of the party making the assumptions.[122]

In the eighties, the so-called *General Clause* of Scandinavian law of obligations and property was incorporated into contract law (§ 36 of the Contract Act). The relationship between the older non-statutory doctrine of breach of contract and § 36 of the Contract Act has been problematic. In more recent Norwegian case law it might appear as if the older doctrine would particularly apply in situations concerning professionals only, whereas the Contract Act's provisions have greater significance in consumer relations.[123]

Based on the grounds that the purchaser had no knowledge of the identity of the artist at the time he entered into the contract, the General Clause should be used, possibly in combination with the older doctrine of assumption. The Norwegian version of the Contract Act, § 36, reads:

A contract can wholly or in part be set aside or changed if it would seem unreasonable or contrary to good business practice to insist on it. The same holds for unilateral contracts.

---

[118] B. Windscheid, *Die Lehre des romischen Rechts von der Voraussetzung* (Düsseldorf, 1850).

[119] A more recent description of the doctrine is found in the monograph, by B. Lehrberg, *Förutsettningsläran* (Uppsala, 1989).

[120] Particularly on the basis of Ussing's treatment of the doctrine of contractual assumption, H. Ussing, *Aftaler paa formuerettens omraade* (3rd edn, Copenhagen, 1974), pp. 459 ff., there has been agreement that the assessment of risk is essential.

[121] See NJA 1985.178, p. 191 (cf. NJA 1981.269) and Kjetil Krokeide, TfR 1977.569, p. 592.

[122] K. Krüger, *Norsk kontraktsrett*, (Bergen, 1989), p. 688.

[123] RT 1999, p. 922 and RT 2000, p. 806.

In making these decisions, attention should be paid not only to the content of the contract, the position of the parties, and the situation at the time of entering into the contract, but also to the conditions and other circumstances which subsequently emerge. The regulations of paragraphs 1 and 2 hold similarly when it would seem unreasonable to apply trade practice or other laws of contract traditions.[124]

This provision gives the courts jurisdiction to intervene in contractual matters if they consider the contract 'unreasonable'.[125] The intervention might require setting the contract aside or – what is most commonly the case – a modification of the contract. The decision is based on a broad, total evaluation of all aspects of the relationship between the parties. Both the circumstances at the time the contract was entered into and those arising later can be taken into account.

The present case concerns a sale between professional parties. The courts will, therefore, exercise care in applying the Contract Act, § 36. Furthermore, there is an element of speculation or risk involved in this type of contract. It would, therefore, be only in extreme circumstances that the Contract Act, § 36, would be applied.[126] It could also be argued that claiming invalidity in such cases would be regrettable as, in this way, the desire to track down undiscovered works by recognised artists could be discouraged.

The seller's own circumstances could be significant in assessing unreasonableness. If Anatole, himself, ought to have discovered the identity of the artist (or possible artists), this would not favour the application of the Contract Act, § 36. This is not conclusive, however, but the more the party that claims invalidity according to this provision is at fault, the less likely the claim will be accepted.

(ii) If Bob had *knowledge* of the seller's mistake *at the time he entered the contract* (which is not very likely in the present situation), the case would be somewhat stronger. Traditionally, a claim of invalidity would be applied in this type of case and not a breach of contract. Whether a legal contractual duty of disclosure by the *purchaser* exists is very unclear

---

[124] The Danish version of the General Clause originally differed from the Swedish and the Norwegian in that the courts were only given the authority to set the contract aside, either wholly or in part, and not to reword the contents of the contract. A more recent revision of the law has done away with this distinction.

[125] The expression 'contrary to good business practice' does not have a distinct meaning, and is covered by the criterion of unreasonableness.

[126] Ot. prp. no. 5 (1982–3) p. 36 reads: 'If the contract is characterised by speculation by both parties, this will not normally be considered as modifying the contract.'

in Scandinavian legal doctrine.[127] In the case where one of the parties has knowledge, § 33 of the Contract Act, would normally be applied together with § 36 of the Act (See Case 2).

The question hinges on the extent of the *duty of disclosure* in this type of contract. Probably, the courts would, to a large extent, let each party reap the fruit of his particular knowledge (such as the origin of the artist) as long as there is nothing else to object to in the setting out of the contract. In other words, an invalidity claim would not succeed. The actual facts also favour this solution. Anatole is an expert in his field. He has taken the initiative to make a sale, and such a situation is a well-known risk when selling objets d'art. Furthermore, the identity of the artist is still uncertain. Here, also, the question arises as to the seller's own situation. Normally, however, it is assumed that a failed duty of disclosure has greater weight than a failed duty of examination.[128] Only when the factual conditions are entirely obvious would the duty of disclosure be waived.

(iii) If the purchaser's actions concerning the sale could be considered both as a breach of contract and as a breach of the validity rules, the question arises as to the relationship between the two legal remedies. A number of Scandinavian authors have claimed that breach of contract should have priority over invalidity rules (the theory of consumption).[129] It is not for the aggrieved party to choose which remedy he prefers. This opinion, to a large extent, corresponds to the rule on mistake now incorporated in art. 3.7 of the UNIDROIT Principles of International Commercial Contracts.

The approach cannot be considered as having reached its final solution in Scandinavian law. Conclusive judgments relating to this matter do not, to my knowledge, exist,[130] and writers have been sceptical of the

---

[127] The question is touched on by C. Hultmark, *Upplysningsplikt* (Stockholm, 1993), p. 45, who is opposed to such duty of disclosure. The *seller's* duty of disclosure, on the other hand, is a well-established legal concept in Scandinavian law, see below.

[128] See V. Hagstrøm, *Fragmenter fra obligasjonsrett* (Oslo, 1992), vol. II, chs. 12 and 51, p. 34.

[129] See S. Jørgensen, *Kontraktsret, Aftaler* (Copenhagen, 1974), vol. 1, p. 120; K. Rodhe, *Obligationsrätt* (Stockholm, 1956), p. 345; A. Christensen, *Studier i köprätt* (Stockholm, 1970), pp. 4–5; B. Gomard, *Almindelig kontraktsret* (2nd edn, Copenhagen, 1996), p. 162; and K. Krokeide, TfR 1979.132, p. 154.

[130] On the contrary, some judgments take no account of the consumption doctrine. Hence, the Swedish Supreme Court in NJA 1985.178 gave the seller the right to demand the delivered goods returned from the purchaser's bankrupt estate as a result of invalidity based on the doctrine of contractual assumptions, something the seller could not have done by termination.

theory of consumption.[131] Seen realistically, the question about the relationship between the two legal remedies has to be considered in light of the individual type of invalidity in relation to the terms of the individual contract. It cannot be taken for granted that the findings will be identical in all these situations.

Portugal

According to Portuguese law, Anatole has a chance to get a court to annul the sale, if he proves he was under a mistake when he contracted. According to arts. 251° and 247° of the Civil Code, a party whose consent was given by a mistake relating to the object of the contract can demand its annulment if the other party knows or should not be unaware that the mistake was fundamental for him. It should be recalled that Portuguese law uses the criterion of the non-mistaken party's knowledge of the mistake and has not adopted the bar of an excusable mistake.[132] It follows that Portuguese law is highly protective of the mistaken party.

On an initial consideration of the facts, if the seller refers to the painting as a work of an unknown artist and the painting proves to be an authentic Degas, it would be easy for Anatole to obtain judicial annulment of the sale, because Bob could not ignore the fundamental nature of the mistake. Anatole referred expressly to the painting as a work of an unknown artist, and Bob made the acquisition with this in mind. If the painting proves to be a work of Degas, Anatole concluded the sale under a fundamental mistake, of the nature of which Bob could not be unaware.[133] In this case, the mistake would be considered as referring to the essential qualities of the object (*error in corpore*). A quality is essential when it is decisive to the contract, according to its economic or legal finality. The case law and doctrinal opinion state that the essentiality is given by the subjective point of view of the mistaken party and not by the objective point of view of the market.

However, under a secondary interpretation, which infers that the paintings were not by Degas himself, it would be a bit more difficult for Anatole to obtain the annulment of the sale, because of the nature of

---

[131] See, for example, Hagstrøm, *Fragmenter fra obligasjonsrett*, p. 23.

[132] See the explanation in the General Introduction above at p. 21.

[133] See 'Ac. STJ. of 4/1/1972', in BMJ 213, pp. 188 e ss., P. de Lima and A. Varela, *Código Civil Anotado* (4th edn, Coimbra, 1987), vol. I, p. 235, P. Nunes de Carvalho, 'Considerações sobre o erro em sede de patologia da declaração negocial', in ROA 52 (1992), pp. 169–82 (172) and D. Ferreira, *Erro Negocial. Objecto – Motivos – Base Negocial e Alteração das Circunstâncias* (Coimbra, Almedina, 1998), p. 23.

this mistake. In fact, if the paintings prove to be by a pupil under Degas' supervision, they are still the work of an unknown artist as stated by Anatole when he made the sale. However he is still under a mistake, and the mistake refers not only to the value of the object sold, but also to the qualities of the paintings, as he did not know the influence that Degas may have had on the paintings (*error in qualitate*).[134] To obtain the annulment of the sale on this basis, Anatole would have to prove in court that he would never have sold the paintings at this price if he had known of this quality (the fundamental nature of the mistake) and that Bob knew or should have known that the paintings would not be sold at a price so far below their real value, if Anatole had had known the true facts (arts. 251° and 247° of the Civil Code).

Scotland

The area of mistake in contract in Scots law is fraught with confusion and conflicting views. The approach adopted is the result of eclectic research.

Under Scots law it is not enough for a party challenging the validity of a contract simply to aver that one of the contracting parties consented under mistake. In order to be successful the pursuer must go through a number of steps. Mistake (*error*) operates in two ways; 'mistake in intention' and 'mistake in expression'. A 'mistake in intention' is when the pursuer asserts that one or both parties to the contract consented under mistake. As they did not intend so to bind themselves there has been no *consensus in idem*. The lack of consensus means the contract has never truly been formed, therefore it is treated as being *void ab initio*. A 'mistake in expression' is when the final embodiment of the contract does not accurately express the intent of the party or parties. Anatole's error is a 'mistake in intention'.

Mistake in intention is further divided into 'mistake in transaction' and 'mistake in motive'.[135] A mistake in transaction is when a party has misunderstood what she has bound herself to, or the contract has been interpreted in a way contrary to how she believed herself to be bound.

---

[134] Legal writers state that if the mistake only refers to the price in the market (A sells for a price because he does not know the price has increased), it is not a mistake about the qualities of the object, but only a question of usury. See M. de Andrade, *Teoria Geral da Relação Jurídica* (Coimbra, Almedina, 1992), p. 251; S. Vaz Serra, 'Anotação' RLJ 107° (1975), pp. 39–41 and D. Ferreira, *ibid.*, p. 23.

[135] J. D. Stair, *The Laws of Scotland. Stair Memorial Encyclopaedia* (Edinburgh, 1999), vol. 15 para. 686.

A mistake in motive is when a party is not disagreeing with the terms of the contract but that due to her misapprehension of the circumstances it is not what she intended. The distinction is not always clear. I believe Anatole's mistake was a mistake in transaction. His mistake in relation to the artist meant that he misunderstood what he had bound himself to sell. Another difference between mistake in transaction and mistake in motive is that there is only a remedy for mistake in motive if another party to the contract induced mistake.

Having classified the mistake as one of intention and transaction it must then be shown to be fundamental (*essential error*). Only a fundamental mistake will prevent formation of contract. The definition of what is fundamental has caused problems. Originally in Scots law the distinction was between a mistake that was 'substantial' and a mistake that was 'insubstantial'. A by-product of this is the continuing tendency in Scots law to refer to fundamental mistake (essential error) as 'error in the substantials'. This is just one example of the confused state of Scots law in this area. A distinction is also made between a mistake which excluded consent and that which did not exclude consent. This consensus approach was not without limits. To ensure objectivity the mistake had to be one of a recognised type. The categories represent the mistakes that the reasonable man would view as preventing consent. These were most famously stated by the Institutional Writer, Bell[136] as:

mistake as to the subject matter
mistake as to the person undertaking the obligation or for whom the
    obligation is undertaken
mistake as to the price or consideration
mistake as to the quality of the thing engaged for (quality being either tacitly
    or expressly agreed as being essential)
mistake as to the nature of the contract that was entered into.

This position was affirmed by Lord Watson in *Stewart* v. *Kennedy*.[137] A mistake which fitted one of Bell's categories was *prima facie* a fundamental mistake. However Lord Watson appeared to recant upon this definition in the later case of *Menzies* v. *Menzies*.[138] Instead of requiring the mistake to be one of Bell's accepted five, *any* mistake where '*but for this the party would not have entered*' the contract would be operative. Although still consensus-based, this introduced an element of

---

[136] G. J. Bell, *Principles of the Law of Scotland* (10th edn, W. Guthie, Edinburgh, 1899),
    Section 11.
[137] (1890) 17 R (HL) 25 at 28–9.   [138] (1893) 20 R (HL) 108 at p. 142.

subjectivity and appeared to extend the scope of mistake. As I will state later, other aspects of *Menzies* qualify this width. Whether or not Lord Watson intended to overrule his earlier approval of Bell is not clear. It has been argued that since the pursuer in *Menzies* limited his challenge to mistake in motive then the *Menzies* interpretation of essentials should be limited to that area. This would leave intact the general requirement of fitting the mistake into one of Bell's five examples. As I have already classified Anatole's mistake as one of transaction, Bell would be applied. As the parties were both agreed as to the subject matter being contracted for, Anatole's mistaken belief as to the identity of the painter affects only the *quality* of the pictures. Therefore he made a *mistake as to the quality of the thing engaged for.*

Merely establishing the mistake as fundamental is not enough. The principle of objectivity requires that the mistake is not only of a type that the reasonable man would see as vitiating consent, but that it did so apply in this contract. This can be shown by the consequences the mistake creates. Although two mistakes may fall into the same category as laid down by Bell, the courts will treat them according to the severity of the events that flow from them. This is particularly so in *mistake as to quality*, where it has been expressed that the resultant situation will have to be a fairly extreme case before the courts will intervene.[139] Such an extreme case was *Earl of Wemys v. Campbell.*[140] There the court held that the presence of deer on an estate was integral to a lease of a '*shooting of the deer forest of Dalness*'. Accordingly, the absence of stag during the shooting season constituted a sufficient *mistake as to quality* to invalidate the contract. Similarly, the terms of the contract must have sufficiently directed each party's mind to the essential quality[141] so that a reasonable man would see it as essential to the contract. Therefore, the validity of Anatole's contract with Bob will only be at risk if the identity of the painter (the quality of the subject matter) was an essential part of the agreement to which both parties directed their minds. The quality of the subject matter will most obviously be seen as essential to the contract if it has been expressly agreed to by the parties. However, its importance can also be inferred from the circumstances of the transaction. Then the parties are said to have tacitly agreed to the quality of the subject matter being essential. It is possible that Anatole falls into the latter case. Anatole and Bob are both what could be called professional

---

[139] W. M. Gloag, *The Law of Contract* (2nd edn, Edinburgh, 1929), p. 447.
[140] (1858) 20 D 1090.
[141] G. J. Bell, *Commentaries on the Law of Scotland* (7th edn, J. Meharen, Edinburgh, 1870), p. 314.

collectors. Presumably their predominant intention in dealing with a painting is its quality. This being so the error as to quality would be of a sufficient degree to challenge the validity of the contract.

However two factors could undermine this conclusion. First, as there is some doubt over Degas being the artist, the extent of the mistake is uncertain. If the painter was in fact only a student of Degas then this is possibly not an extreme enough difference in quality from what was agreed, to warrant a challenge to contractual validity. Secondly, if the artist is an anonymous student of Degas then depending on your interpretation of the catalogue entry ('charming work by an unknown artist') there would be no mistake as to quality. Although the painter being a pupil of Degas would make a difference to the value of the painting, there is a distinction between a mistake being in a *quality* of the object and a mistake as to the object's *value*. Mistake as to value is only given a remedy (i) if it would cause the contract to be different in kind; (ii) if the value was made a specific term of the contract;[142] or (iii) if the mistake was due to the misrepresentations of the other party.[143] On the facts given, Anatole could not fulfil these requirements. The contract is still sale, albeit now a bad bargain. The value does not appear to be an essential term of the contract. Finally, the only representations made have been by Anatole himself.

So far it has been assumed that there is a mistake as to the quality of the thing engaged for, because of the mistake as to the identity of the painter. This presupposes that the subject matter of the contract was 'a painting by x'. Therefore if x is not the painter, there is error as to quality. But in the present scenario where the artist is unknown it may be more appropriate to say that the subject matter is simply 'this painting'. In this case the identity of the artist is not part of the subject matter and consequentially the mistaken identity would not be an essential mistake. As the facts do not contain any other mistakes there would be no challenge to the validity of the contract.

To summarise, it has been established that Anatole's mistake in intention is a mistake in transaction and that it could be classified as being an essential mistake as to quality. However, there is doubt if the parties tacitly agreed to the quality of the subject matter being essential to the contract. Further, it is not clear what the subject matter was or if there is sufficient severity in the effect of the mistake. Assuming the mistake

---

[142] G. J. Bell, *Principles of the Law of Scotland*, section 11.
[143] Gloag, *The Law of Contract*, p. 450.

does pass these hurdles, it must be defined as either unilateral, common or mutual.[144]

In Anatole's case there are elements of both unilateral and common mistake. It is clear that Anatole was under a unilateral mistake. It could be inferred that Bob had relied on Anatole's catalogue for his knowledge of the painting; if so, Anatole's mistake would then be shared (common). The classification of the mistake affects the availability of a remedy. In common mistake the contract is *void ab initio*. Both parties were under a mistake which affected their intention, therefore they did not reach *consensus in idem*. As the contract is treated as if it never existed Anatole would not need to seek the court's intervention. Further, if Bob resold the painting as proposed, the ownership of it would not pass to the buyer, but remain with Anatole.

The effect of unilateral mistake is less certain. As it is still an example of a mistake in intention, the Institutional Writers such as Stair stated that because the consent of the party under mistake had been affected, then like common mistake the contract is *void ab initio*. However, there is a feeling that it is unfair on the innocent party that the other should be able to rely on his own mistake. This school of thought claims support in Lord Watson's dicta in *Stewart* v. *Kennedy*[145] and *Menzies* v. *Menzies*.[146] Lord Watson stated that onerous contracts reduced to writing,[147] where the mistake concerned the legal effects of the contract, would not be invalidated by a unilateral mistake, unless it had been induced by the misrepresentation of the other party. Further, the contract would be regarded as validly formed, but voidable. Therefore, unless the pursuer is granted rescission of his contract by the court, the defender remains the new owner and can pass on good title. In *Menzies*, Lord Watson applied *Stewart* v. *Kennedy* and required the mistake to be induced by the misrepresentation of the other party. This led to the view that an action for unilateral uninduced mistake is no longer competent except in gratuitous obligations. So, while *Menzies* on the one hand extended the scope

---

[144] In unilateral mistake, only one of the parties is consenting under mistake. In common mistake, the mistake is shared by both parties. In mutual mistake, while both parties are under mistake it is not the same mistake.

[145] (1890) 17 R (HL) 25.   [146] (1893) 20 R (HL) 108.

[147] *Stewart* v. *Kennedy* involved a different conflict with the principle of *consensus in idem*. The practice and sometimes legal necessity of putting some obligations in writing led the courts to refuse to look behind the four corners of the written contract to examine the true intent of the parties. As a result of the Contract (Scotland) Act 1997 s. 1, provided the contract does not express itself as being conclusive in its terms, extrinsic evidence is now admissible to prove additional terms of the contract.

of mistake by its subjective definition of essential, it limited its effect in cases of unilateral mistake.

On the other hand, MacBryde[148] argues that this conclusion takes account of the fact that *Stewart* v. *Kennedy*[149] was only concerned with onerous contracts and that it should be restricted in accordance with the rest of Lord Watson's dicta. Thus, only those contracts *reduced to writing* where the unilateral mistake is over the legal effect of the contract should require inducement. All other unilateral mistakes should operate to prevent formation, even if uninduced.

There is no case law in point with Anatole's situation, therefore it is uncertain which of the two views the court would adopt. Recent cases that have denied a remedy for uninduced unilateral mistake in relation to the legal effect of a contract, have concerned transactions where the contract has been reduced to writing and has been onerous.[150] The courts have made particular reference to the existence of these factors and have not excluded the possibility that there could be uninduced unilateral mistake in other onerous contracts resulting in their being void.[151] However, it has also been stated that the law in relation to uninduced unilateral mistake is too confused to give a conclusive statement of its effect.[152] Consequently, the theoretical approach that I have outlined causes great difficulty in practice. There is no clear statement on such definitive areas as what will be regarded as essential mistake, when it will be seen as sufficient or if there is a remedy for unilateral uninduced mistake. This situation has been recognised by the Scottish Law Commission in their Memo Number 37 on 'Constitution and Proof of Voluntary Obligations', but until it leads to fruitful reform, practitioners will continue to seek remedies other than in mistake.

To conclude, I do not think Scots law would provide a remedy for Anatole. Although his mistake is one of intention and in transaction it is not an essential mistake. The facts do not show that the identity of the painter was expressly or tacitly agreed as essential. In the absence of this, the subject matter of the contract would be more properly seen as the painting itself not the painter. Therefore the mistake as to the identity of the painter is not essential.

---

[148] See W. W. McBryde, *The Law of Contract in Scotland* (Edinburgh, 1987), p. 180.

[149] *Ibid.*, p. 2.

[150] *McCallum* v. *Soudan* (1989) SLT 522; *Royal Bank of Scotland plc* v. *Purvis* (1990) SLT 262.

[151] (1989) SLT 522 at p. 523 per Lord Morison and 1990 SLT 262 at p. 265 per Lord McClusky.

[152] *Steels Tr* v. *Bradley Homes (Scotland) Limited* (1972) SC 48 at p. 56 per Lord Dunpark.

Spain

As an introduction a brief analysis of defective consent under Spanish law as provided by art. 1365 of the Civil Code[153] will be outlined. Case law has adopted a strict approach to mistake which is subject to the following conditions: (i) a mistake must relate to the substance of the subject matter or terms of the contract which constituted the main reason for concluding the contract; and (ii) a mistake must be excusable, which means that it could not have been avoided by the mistaken party's average or normal diligence, according to principles of good faith. Diligence is assessed according to all the circumstances of the case, including the personal circumstances of both parties to the contract. The basic function of the idea that a mistake should be excusable is to prevent the mistaken party being protected where such protection is not deserved because of the mistaken party's negligence, in which case the protection shifts to the other contracting party under the principles of contractual liability, good faith and legal certainty.

(a) Applying these conditions to the facts it is therefore necessary to determine the scope of the mistake made by Anatole in this particular case. In this sense, clearly, what led him to describe the two paintings that are the subject matter of the contract as 'by an unknown artist' was his absolute ignorance of their possible author, whether the work of Degas himself or one of his pupils: this is a decisive factor in determining the price of a painting. Had Anatole known what he was selling, the price would not have been the same since his mistake arose from the conditions of the item which were largely the reason for concluding the contract so that, had they not been present, the contract would not have been concluded, at least not on the same terms. Therefore, the mistake of one of the contracting parties, the seller in this case, referred to the essence of the matter.

(b) Was Anatole's mistake excusable? The degree of diligence required varies according to the situation of the person claiming to have suffered a loss. This is therefore greater if a professional or an expert[154] has made a mistake, whereas when a layperson contracts with an expert, the standard of diligence required is less high. Finally, in assessing diligence, it is necessary to consider whether the other party assisted with its conduct, even though it may not have been fraudulent or at fault.

---

[153] Article 1265 of the Spanish Civil Code states: 'Consent given by mistake, under duress or intimidation or with fraud is null and void.'

[154] Supreme Court Ruling of 28/2/1974.

As an expert on Impressionism, Anatole should have known that the pictures he was putting on sale could have been worth far more than he had estimated in principle, thus demonstrating his complete absence of diligence in not checking the material in his private collection. On the other hand, there is nothing to enable us to establish that Bob was aware of the value and importance of the paintings he was acquiring or that he did anything to encourage Anatole to conclude the contract.

As an expert, Anatole is required to use a high degree of diligence and his mistake must be classified as inexcusable. He cannot, therefore, have the sale annulled.

Comparative observations

I – Four types of remedies are envisaged here, mistake, basic contractual assumption, *laesio enormis* and breach of contract.

Mistake

As a preliminary parenthesis, is should be noted that the fact that some countries recognise a mistake on the facts, whereas others do not, is not in itself decisive. Even where mistake is admitted, in practice bars operate in the majority of the legal systems, so that in reality, the legal qualification of mistake is of minor relevance.

Under a number of legal systems there is a mistake that can be characterised as to quality of the subject matter. This is the case in, Austria, Belgium, France, Germany, Greece, Italy, The Netherlands, Spain and Portugal. All these legal systems consider that the mistake is fundamental. A subjective criterion (a unilateral mistake even where the mistake originates in Anatole) suffices. In Italy the mistake must also be recognisable, but such a requirement is probably not fulfilled here. In Greece, an objective criterion (compliance with good faith and usage) is also fulfilled on the facts. However, in Austria, despite fulfilling these prerequisites, such a mistake is subject to a further condition, namely proving that the other party is not worthy of protection. Here this condition is not fulfilled as Bob had already taken action incurring expenses to evaluate the painting. The result is, therefore, to award protection to Bob, which thus precludes Anatole from annulling the contract. Moreover, in France, Belgium, Italy and Spain the mistake is subject to a bar, so that annulment would not be available. The mistake would be inoperative on the grounds that it is inexcusable since the seller is a professional. Such a bar is not always contained in the various Codes but has sometimes emerged as a result of case law. Greek law, which also recognises the excusable nature of the mistake, would not, as a matter of interpretation apply this condition on the facts. The only objection under Greek law to annulling the contract would be if it were not proven that the paintings were by Degas or one of his pupils, in which case the mistake would be disqualified, since a mistake as to mere value is insufficient to annul a contract. In the Netherlands, the bar to liability is based on the rule on risk allocation: the seller should bear the risk for a mistake concerning value. In all of the above-mentioned countries, the legal formants for the solutions are a combined result of articles in the Civil Code and case law interpretation.

To summarise, only Germany (according to one line of case law authority), Greece and Portugal would actually annul the contract for mistake. Moreover, in Germany and Greece, non-judicial and judicial annulment respectively, would be counterbalanced by Anatole paying Bob the negative interest suffered as a result of relying on the contract's validity. In practice, the German reporter has pointed out that this might make annulling the contract less worthwhile than is supposed at first sight.

Under an alternative legal analysis, there is no mistake on the facts. In English and Irish law there is no common law mistake, i.e. a mistake of fact shared by the parties, necessary to annul the contract. The absence of representation or warranty as to authorship (a condition which is not satisfied) and the fact that the mistake originated in the seller (a bar if the condition were satisfied) cumulatively prevent the mistake from being qualified as capable of annulling the contract. In addition, the presence of a (unilateral) mistake as to an important quality of the subject matter, absent a misrepresentation, does not suffice to annul the contract. Under Scots law, initially it may appear that Anatole has made a mistake in intention and transaction which could be qualified as an essential mistake as to quality. This interpretation closely resembles the civil law line of thought. However, two further obstacles then arise; first, it is not certain that there is an essential mistake as to quality here since the objective criterion is not met and in this Scots law diverges from a corresponding civil law reasoning, in the absence of express or implied agreement as to the identity of the painter. Secondly, if the mistake is not qualified as fundamental and also unilateral (as opposed to a common mistake) it is uncertain that such an uninduced unilateral mistake would suffice to justify annulling the contract. All countries rely on case law, and in Scots law on works of authority, to arrive at a similar solution.

Likewise, in Germany, and Greece if the authenticity of the paintings is not established, in the event that the mistake as to the authorship of the painting is qualified as a mistake as to value, and not to quality (the same solution is arrived at by following an objective line of interpretation under Scots law), the contract will not be annulled. Following a similar line of reasoning, under Portuguese law, the mistake would be requalified as one of the painting's qualities and not an essential quality and annulment might be more difficult to obtain. Ultimately, the question of whether annulment will be granted or not is not dependent on a purely conceptual analysis of mistake but is measured by other factors, see below (II).

Basic contractual assumption (clausula rebus sic stantibus, 'Geschäftsgrundlage')

In Germany, another legal doctrine may be invoked, that of the failure of a basic contractual assumption. Such a ground may suffice to vary or adapt a contract but the various conditions, developed by case law, are not met here. Likewise in Norway, Denmark and Sweden, influenced by the German doctrine in the absence of a legal concept of mistake developed their own Scandinavian doctrine of assumption. This has now to some extent been replaced by a 'general clause' of legislation relating to contracts (Invalidity and Contract Act). Here, however, the relevant section of the Act is not satisfied since the contract would not be considered unreasonable, i.e. not contrary to good business practice.

In Italy, also influenced by the German doctrine, the Italian courts sometimes invoke a similar concept (presupposizione) as an alternative version to mistake to annul the contract. This may be explained as another way of viewing mistake, which takes into account good faith. However, a subjective criterion is applied and not satisfied here.

Laesio enormis

In Austria, the sale could be annulled on the grounds of laesio enormis. Two cumulative conditions exist: that of an objective undervaluation of price of more than 50% and the seller's lack of knowledge of the undervalue. Such a remedy is derived from the Civil Code and distinguishes Austria from other civil law countries by its extraordinarily wide field of application. Similarly, Belgium has a wide-ranging doctrine of lésion qualifiée, but unlike under Austrian law, its conditions would not be met here.

Breach of contract

In Norway, were such a ground to exist, it is suggested by legal authorities that such a ground should be given priority over any invalidity doctrine for the simple reason that contractual remedies do not, unlike the latter, give priority to unsecured creditors. However, there is no breach of contract on the facts, in the absence of a breach of a duty of disclosure. Likewise, under English law there is no remedy for breach of contract. Bob is under no obligation to point out the undervalue to Anatole and the mere undervalue of the contract, i.e. inadequacy of the consideration, is not a matter of the court's concern.

II – The most obvious distinguishing features of this case are the fact that during a sale between two professionals a mistake is made by the seller as to the value and authorship of the object of the sale. It can be noted first that there is a divide between common law and civil law countries in relation to the status of the contracting parties. The professional status of the parties is not a relevant factor as far as common law countries are concerned, as it does not have any bearing on the qualification of mistake. As far as some civil law countries are concerned however (Belgium, France, Italy, the Netherlands and Spain), the status of the parties has an effect in relation to the operation of bars developed by case law, such as the inexcusable nature of the mistake. Under Greek law, the inexcusable nature of the mistake is recognised by a rule (§ 142 AK), although it was not held to apply in the circumstances. Under Austrian law, a similar idea is set out formally as a legal condition (§ 871 AGBG) and not as a bar developed by case law, namely the worthiness of the other non-mistaken party's protection. This concept puts to the forefront the notion of reliance. Reliance is also recognised by German and Greek law, though to a lesser extent, since annulment would be granted, counterbalanced by compensating the negative interest of the non-mistaken party who relied on the contract. The first feature (that of the status of the parties) is thus linked to the second: can the mistaken party claim for a mistake which is the subject matter of his own obligation, here the authorship of the paintings? Again, the civil law countries do not object to this in theory (e.g. the *Poussin* case in French law) although here its limits are defined by the seller's status. Interestingly, Greek law seems to be much less stringent as to the requirement of excusability, using a broader measure of compliance with good faith.

All legal systems agree that a mistake as to value does not suffice to annul the contract. The only exception to the rule is the alternative remedy of *laesio enormis* under Austrian law. Even though both parties have professional expertise, they are not acting in a business capacity and so the rule applies. Thus variants as to the reasoning lead to the same result in practice that mistake will not be operative in a majority of the civil law countries, except for Greece (if Degas's authorship is confirmed), Germany, according to a line of case law authority, and Portugal.

In the common law countries, as well as Norway, there is no initial qualification of mistake, for numerous reasons: either because Norway does not recognise mistake as a legal concept or because the mistake is uninduced, unilateral and thus inoperative (England, Ireland and Scotland). Nevertheless, in Norway, the status of the parties may be a relevant factor to assess whether the contract complies with business practice, as required by legislation. This question is less important in England, Ireland, Scotland and the Netherlands, which seem to concentrate more on how the mistake arose – whether it is unilateral and/or uninduced – rather than on the nature or status of the party causing it. This analysis relies quite explicitly on the underlying importance of the distribution of risks in contract theory and is also present both in one doctrine of mistake in German law[155] and in the German doctrine of failed contractual assumptions. It is submitted that the underlying value behind the requirement that a mistake must be excusable is implicitly directed at a concern to protect the security of transactions and confirm the allocation of risks made under the contract. It should be apparent that divergences do not divide neatly into the common law and civil law divide but are rather represented by underlying, and not exclusively legal, factors.

---

[155] See German report.

Case 2

Célimène v. Damien

Case

Célimène, a venerable old lady, put up a sign outside her house near Giverny, advertising the 'sale of attic contents'. Damien, an antiques dealer on his way to visit Monet's home, stopped to look and recognised one of the master's original works among the bric-a-brac. He bought it on the spot for twice the asking price, and then proceeded to resell it to the Louvre. What remedy, if any, is available?

Discussions

Austria

Célimène, who is no art expert, has made a mistake (as to the value of the painting, see Case 1) as to the content of the contract. The difference lies in the fact that only one party has made a mistake, whereas in Case 1 there was a common mistake. Damien, as an art expert, immediately recognises the artist. Damien is not worthy to be protected in accordance with § 870 and 871 ABGB. If § 871 ABGB accepts and recognises the fact that the mistake will have to be recognised by using proper alertness and due diligence in order to entitle the mistaken party to avoid or to adapt the contract, this is even more so if the mistake not only had to be recognised but in fact had been so recognised. Scholarly opinion accepts this analogy unanimously.[1] Célimène has, therefore, the right to annul the contract on the ground that she would not have sold the painting at all if she had been aware of the artist and its real value, or the right to adapt the contract on the basis that she would have sold the painting in any case but at a different, namely higher, price.

[1] Rummel in Rummel I RZ 4 § 870, Rz 16, Koziol/Welser, p. 136.

The right to claim under *laesio enormis* (see Case 1) is also available to Célimène.

In addition Damien is liable for damages in accordance with § 874 ABGB which is in favour of Célimène. This states that anyone who either deliberately deceives or misleads another person or (as in this case) deceitfully takes advantage and benefits from an existing mistake is liable to reimburse all losses that would not have occurred without the mistake (or without taking advantage of it). This liability for losses exists and remains irrespective of the existing rights to annul or adapt the contract and can be exercised by the mistaken party independently of the exercise of the other available remedies. The mistaken party in any case quite often obtains compensation by using the right to annul or adapt. Should such a party, however, have suffered a loss that cannot be compensated by annulling or adapting the contract, for example, expenditure carried out in reliance on the contract's validity, such costs will be reimbursed.

The fact that Célimène could have recognised the mistake by using proper alertness and due diligence and has acted negligently cannot be assumed under the circumstances. Even if that were so, she cannot be blamed for contributory fault and negligence (which might lead to reducing her claim for damages), as her lack of diligence would have to be assessed in comparison with Damien's fraudulent action.[2]

Belgium

Three remedies are theoretically available to Célimène, yet contrary to Anatole in Case 1, Célimène has a good chance of succeeding in her action based on any of these three grounds.

(i) An action based on fundamental mistake is the most commonly used remedy in Belgium when the controversy bears on the authenticity of a work of art. As far as the existence of a fundamental mistake is concerned, we have also seen that Belgian law uses a subjective view of mistake assessed *in concreto*. Therefore, Célimène's advanced age and lack of expertise as to works of art will be taken into account to her advantage. As to the excusability of the mistake here again, the age and inexperience of Célimène work in her favour. One uncertainty remains however: the fact that Damien spontaneously bought the painting for twice the asking price without even discussing it could eventually lead a judge to consider that Célimène should have had her attention drawn

---

[2] Rummel in Rummel I Rz § 874.

to the abnormal character of the purchaser's behaviour. If excusability is assessed objectively, this might be unfavourable for Célimène if the judge thinks that a reasonable man *in abstracto* should have paid attention to this circumstance.

A remedy based on mistake leads to annulment of the contract but this is impossible here as the new owner of the painting is protected by art. 2279 of the Civil Code which means that Célimène cannot recover the painting. Célimène will obtain, in lieu of annulment, the increase in value obtained by Damien. If Célimène wishes to obtain extra damages, she will have to prove, in addition, a precontractual fault committed by Damien based on art. 1382 of the Civil Code.[3]

(ii) Célimène could also base her action on fraud which appears to be a preferable solution since such an action entitles the successful aggrieved party to claim either annulment plus additional damages (and the fault, consisting precisely in the fraud committed, is here, contrary to an action based on mistake, already proven against the defrauding party)[4] or damages alone.[5] Another advantage of the remedies available for fraud consists in the distinction that is made between principal fraud (*dol principal*) and incidental fraud (*dol incident*):[6] if Célimène does not succeed in proving that Damien's fraudulent behaviour induced her into contracting in order to have the contract annulled, she will still be able to claim some damages on the basis of incidental fraud. The second reason for Célimène to prefer an action based on fraud is that the issue of excusability will not be raised. Finally, it will probably be easy for Célimène to demonstrate the existence of the intentional and material elements of fraud (see Case 1): there is some case law deciding that the abuse of the other party's old age and weakness constitutes evidence of these elements.[7] Here the fact that Damien spontaneously paid twice the required price for Célimène's painting works in her favour: it helps to show Damien's intent to deceive her.[8]

---

[3] Goux, 'L'erreur, le dol et la lésion qualifiée', no. 32; A. Meinertzhagen-Limpens, 'La vente: erreur, non-conformité et vices cachés' in A. Meinertzhagen-Limpens et al., *Actualités du droit civil* (Brussels, 1994), vol. II, pp. 5 f., no. 2.

[4] Goux, 'L'erreur, le dol et la lésion qualifiée', no. 28.

[5] *Ibid.*, no. 33.   [6] *Ibid.*, no. 16.

[7] Civ Brussels, 29-6-1995, Res Jur. Imm., 1995, p. 171; Brussels, 17-2-1989, JT, 1989, 291.

[8] See Fontaine, 'Les aspects juridiques de la commercialisation des oeuvres d'art', p. 407: the purchaser of a work of art who *deliberately* maintained the seller's ignorance in order to purchase from him at a low price a work of art that he recognised as authentic commits a fraud.

The only small risk that Célimène has to assume, basing her action on fraud, is that Damien's fraudulent behaviour consists here mainly in fraudulent concealment and we have seen that Belgian law generally recognises such 'negative' manoeuvre only when there is *in casu* an obligation to speak on the part of the defrauding party. Considering the parties' respective positions, ages and expertise (see Case 1), it is most probable that the judge will hold that such obligation exists here.

(iii) *Lésion qualifiée* may also be a ground of action for Célimène. The conditions are all fulfilled here,[9] there must be: (a) a manifest disproportion in the parties' respective engagements or performances, which is clearly the case here; (b) one of the parties is in a position of inferiority: here Célimène's old age and lack of expertise clearly place her in such a situation with regard to Damien; (c) the abuse of such a situation by the other party. It must be established that, without such abuse, the other party would not have contracted or would have done so under other conditions. Contrary to the remedy based on fraud, the abuse does not entail an intentional element: merely knowing and taking advantage of the other party's position suffices.[10] *Lésion qualifiée* can lead either to annulment of the contract or damages.[11] In the present state of the law, it is unclear whether the aggrieved party's negligence (which here would lie in Célimène's absence of reaction to Damien's spontaneous offer to pay more than required) would have some consequences on either the admissibility of the action or mitigate the amount of damages awarded.[12] To conclude, we would suggest that the remedies of fraud and *lésion qualifiée* constitute the best options for Célimène.

England

The starting point would be not to distinguish this case from Case 1, and so not to give Célimène any remedy on the facts as stated. On the general principles of mistake and non-disclosure, the distinction from Case 1 – that here the seller is a non-professional – makes it a hard case but the principles applicable are identical. The buyer would have no duty

---

[9] For a reminder of these conditions, see Goux, 'L'erreur, le dol et la lésion qualifiée', nos. 18–22.

[10] See for instance Liège, 17-10-1996, JT, 1997, p. 569, where the judge, from this point of view, clearly distinguishes *lésion qualifiée* from fraud.

[11] Civ Brussels, 17-3-1995, RGDC, 1995, p. 507.

[12] See Case 1 for the answer provided by the *Cour de cassation* in the similar debate concerning fraud, see Goux, 'L'erreur, le dol et la lésion qualifiée', no. 23.

of information; and as long as he made no misrepresentations about the work of art he was buying, he did not lay himself open to any remedy. A court looking sympathetically on Célimène might enquire all the more carefully into the facts to check that Damien did not make any express or implied misrepresentation, but if they could find no such statement, there is no basis on which to grant any remedy. There is clearly no remedy here for common mistake since the mistake was not shared: Damien realised what he was buying.

There is, however, a faint possibility of an alternative argument by Célimène which was not open to Anatole in Case 1: that the contract should be set aside as an 'unconscionable bargain'. The basic statement of principle is in *Fry* v. *Lane*:[13]

. . . where a purchase is made from a poor and ignorant man at a considerable undervalue, the vendor having no independent advice, a Court of Equity will set aside the transaction . . .

This is not a fully developed area in English law (although other common law jurisdictions have made much more of it),[14] but there have been signs of development which *might* allow an English court to treat Célimène as a 'poor and ignorant person' for the purposes of this rule.[15] If that is so, then the burden would shift to Damien to show that the transaction is 'fair, just and reasonable', which appears to mean, in essence, that he has not taken advantage of her weakness. It is, though, still rather unlikely that this case would fall under the principle, since it does not fit the fact-pattern of the (relatively few) cases: for example, Célimène took the initiative in the sale, which seems to be motivated more by a desire to clear her attic than by impecuniosity. Even if the court could hold this to be an unconscionable bargain, it would render the contract not void but *voidable*: that is, Célimène would be entitled to avoid the contract retrospectively, and obtain the return of the picture

---

[13] (1888) 40 Ch D 312, 322.

[14] *Commercial Bank of Australia Ltd.* v. *Amadio* (1983) 151 CLR 447 (Australia); *Knupp* v. *Bell* (1968) 67 DLR (2d) 256 (Canada); *Nichols* v. *Jessup* [1986] 1 NZLR 226 (New Zealand).

[15] For example, the principle was applied to allow a woman to avoid a conveyance to her husband of rights in the former matrimonial home, since she was 'poor' in the sense of belonging to the lower income group; and 'ignorant' in that she was not highly educated and could not be expected to understand the complex legal transaction: *Cresswell* v. *Potter* [1978] 1 WLR 255. How far this principle can be developed further in English law remains to be seen, but there have been recent (obiter) statements in the Court of Appeal that the jurisdiction is capable of adaptation to different transactions entered into in changing circumstances: *Crédit Lyonnais Bank Nederland NV* v. *Burch* [1997] 1 All ER 144 at p. 151.

(but with the requirement to return the price she received) – but (as is the general rule for voidable contracts under which property has passed) only as long as a third party has not purchased the subject matter of the contract, without notice of the defect in title. If the resale to the Louvre has gone ahead, and the Louvre had no notice at the time of the purchase that the circumstances under which Damien had obtained it from Célimène might render that earlier contract voidable, the Louvre's title to the painting prevails over Célimène's remedy.[16] In that situation, Célimène has no remedy, either against the Louvre (which has good title to the picture and has committed no wrong against her) or against Damien (since she has no other remedy, either in contract or in tort, if he has made no misrepresentation nor committed any other wrong. Even the purchase of the picture in circumstances amounting to an 'unconscionable bargain' would not of itself constitute an actionable wrong giving rise to a remedy beyond rendering the contract itself voidable).

Célimène therefore has no remedy under case law. As in the case of Anatole, there are no other relevant legal formants on these facts.

France

Despite his duty to contract in good faith, Damien did not inform Célimène who was the author of the painting he bought from her. Under French law, a remedy lies both in annulling the sale for mistake or fraud and in damages for breach of a duty to inform.

(i) Célimène's action in annulment could be based on fraud (*dol*) as a result of Damien's disloyal behaviour. Fraud includes all kinds of manoeuvres by one party inducing a mistake in the other party, and leading the latter to contract. On the facts, Damien did not use active deceit, nor did he lie: he remained silent as to the authorship of the painting. But as long as his silence was intentional, Célimène can bring an action in fraud (art. 1116 of the Civil Code) in order to annul the sale. According to established case law 'fraud can consist in one party remaining silent, thus dissimulating to the other party an element which could have led the other not to enter into the contract if it had been disclosed'.

Courts evaluate the essential character of fraud *in concreto*. To this end they take the personality of the victim into account: here they would consider Célimène's age, naivety and inexperience which render her particularly vulnerable, as well as Damien's expertise in the field of art. The fact that the mistake induced in the seller relates to the subject matter

---

[16] *White v. Garden* (1851) 10 CB 919.

of her own contractual obligation does not prevent the sale from being annulled; it is not even necessary that this mistake relates to a substantial quality of the painting: a mere mistake relating to the value[17] of the painting is sufficient since that mistake has been induced by deceitful manoeuvres.

In accordance with the general rules of French contract law and art. 1116–2 of the Civil Code, Célimène will have the burden of proving the fraud. Fraud is difficult to prove in the case of an omission as to the duty to disclose; but fraudulent intention is most often deduced both from the fact that the person with knowledge of the information remained silent and the importance that this retained information could have represented to the contracting party. Fraud can be proved by all kinds of evidence, including events prior to and subsequent to the formation of the contract since French law qualifies fraud as a legal event (*fait juridique*). In such a case, French law excludes the application of art. 1341 of the Civil Code which only relates to the admissibility of evidence in relation to written documents. If there were witnesses Célimène will therefore be able to plead the fact that Damien spontaneously offered her twice the price she originally set and that he immediately resold the painting to the Louvre Museum as evidence of his fraud.

(ii) It also seems that Célimène could base her action on mistake since the authorship of a painting is considered a substantial quality according to art. 1110 of the Civil Code.[18] The likelihood of this action succeeding is subject to two conditions being established (see Case 1): namely that the essential character of the authorship of the painting forms part of the parties' contract and that such a mistake could be excusable.

In order to annul the sale, Célimène will have to prove that her consent had been determined by the mistaken belief that the painting was not attributed to Monet. Like fraud, mistake can be proved by all kinds of evidence. To this end the mistaken party's age and inexperience as well as the price paid and the conditions in which the sale occurred can be taken into account.

On the basis of fraud and mistake, annulling the contract will be the first possible remedy. Because the sale will be annulled retrospectively Damien should normally return the painting to Célimène and the latter should reimburse the purchase price to him. However, as Damien has

---

[17] It should be noted that a pure mistake as to value does not, as a general rule, call for a remedy.

[18] Although as seen below, mere mistake will not give rise to a remedy in the form of damages.

already sold the painting to the Museum, reciprocal restitution would not be possible. As the Louvre Museum is a *bona fide* sub-purchaser, it is protected by the provisions of art. 2279 of the Civil Code according to which 'possession equals title as regards movable property'. Restitution will therefore consist of money and not the painting itself: Célimène, as the initial vendor, will be attributed the increase in value obtained by Damien in bad faith.

In addition, as his attitude was fraudulent Damien could even be ordered to pay damages. The *Cour de cassation* admits that an action in tort may be brought by the victim of fraudulent manoeuvres independently of the right to seek the annulment of a contract according to arts. 1116 and 1117 of the Civil Code. The purchaser's fault, even if it does not vitiate the other party's consent, consists in breaching the duty to inform and is analysed as a question of precontractual bad faith. Damages sought for independently on the basis of tortious liability (art. 1382 of the Civil Code) will compensate Célimène for all the losses arising. Practically this means that Célimène could obtain a kind of re-evaluation of the sale price as well as any losses incurred in making the contract.

Nowadays courts do not only disapprove of a person whose behaviour deliberately induces the mistake of the other contracting party, they also take into account the attitude of people who, even if they do not provoke the mistake, nevertheless make a profit out of it. The current case law requires increasing loyalty and scrupulously protects the principle of good faith in precontractual and contractual relationships. This situation differs from the traditional one according to which each party has to look after his own interests and must carry out his own enquiries. Now, a contracting party who possesses information must disclose it where it is likely to influence the other party's consent.

It is arguable that the solution that French law would adopt here is justified if Damien had used deceitful manoeuvres in order to make Célimène enter into the contract. It might also be justified on the basis that Damien did nothing (failed) to inform Célimène. Annulling the sale may be a fair remedy since it tends to prevent those who benefit from a superior knowledge from taking advantage of those who are unaware of this information. However this situation must be distinguished from another: such a remedy can seem inappropriate where the purchaser did not use any deceitful manoeuvres nor tried to take an unfair advantage of the seller. Indeed it could be unfair to a *bona fide* purchaser who only discovered the authorship of a painting thanks to his works and efforts.[19]

Germany

As in Case 1 Célimène, the seller, may demand the painting's return under the law of unjust enrichment if the contract concluded with Damien is void (§ 138) or if Célimène is able to annul it. Annulment is possible on two grounds: namely, mistake (§ 119 I and II) or upon evidence of Damien's fraudulent intent (§ 123).

(i) The Civil Code does not take breaches of the principle of equivalent exchange in the case of reciprocal agreements into consideration. A contract can, however, be immoral and thus void if the imbalance between performance and counter-performance arose through the reprehensible acts of the party which benefits from such imbalance. In a situation like this, § 138 I provides only a general statement that a contract which offends 'good morals' is void. The *BGH's* recent case law displays a tendency also to presume immorality (according to § 138 I) where the imbalance between performance and counter-performance is especially pronounced. Accordingly, it must be considered whether the contract of sale between Damien and Célimène is void according to either § 138 II or 138 I.

(a) A transaction is void according to § 138 II if a party to the contract 'by exploiting the predicament, inexperience, lack of judgement or considerable weakness of will of the other party, causes pecuniary advantages to be promised to or conferred on him or a third party in exchange for a performance whereby these pecuniary advantages are clearly disproportionate to this performance'. The section contains two elements that must be present in any given case: the objective element refers to the disproportionate relationship between the performance and counter-performance (absence of equivalent exchange), the subjective element requires that the party benefited has exploited the weakness of the other party ('reprehensibility').

In the present case one may think that Damien exploited Célimène's 'inexperience' in order to gain the advantage stated. However, only a lack of experience in life or business in general is understood as amounting to 'inexperience'.[20] The lack of specialist knowledge in a special

---

[19] See the case concerning 'Le Verrou' by Fragonard, Civ 1, 25 May 1992, Bull civ I, no. 165.

[20] Cf. Palandt/Heinrichs, § 138 para. 71; MüKo/Mayer-Maly, § 138 para. 125

field – here, for instance, the lack of specialist knowledge relating to the history of art – does not come under this concept.[21] Therefore, the contract of sale which has been concluded between Damien and Célimène is not void according to § 138 II.

(b) The *BGH* has mainly classified credit arrangements where the promisee agrees to extremely high rates of interest as immoral, even where it is not possible to prove conclusively that the lender has acted with an intention 'which is morally reprehensible' (§ 138 II). If the value of the counter-performance promised reveals that the lender has – through negligence at least – failed to recognise the predicament in which the debtor finds himself,[22] then the credit agreement will accordingly be held void (§ 138 I). Where the creditor acts as a consumer, then the *BGH* has renounced even this element of 'negligent exploitation' and argues that an interest rate of 100% indicates in any case that the lender has acted with a morally reprehensible intention.[23]

In this way, the courts have resurrected *laesio enormis* – a customary law institution – in § 138 I.[24] That said, the *BGH* has not completely renounced a subjective element: the court would like to deduce a morally reprehensible intention of the party benefiting from the objective disparity between the performances on a regular basis. It therefore proceeds on the basis of a legal fiction.[25] Moreover, case law relating to consumer credit agreements has been extended to other cases exhibiting a disparity between performance and counter-performance.[26]

However, in our case, the *BGH* would hardly classify the contract as immoral. The cases mentioned above in which the *BGH* accepted the subjective element of exploitation on the basis of an objective set of facts

---

[21] So, for example: BGH NJW 1957, 1274; BGH NJW 1979, 758; BGH WM 1982, 849; concerning this: Soergel/Hefermehl, § 138 para. 79

[22] BGHZ 80, 160; BGHZ 128, 257; for an overview of this see Palandt/Heinrichs, § 138 RZ 25 ff. In many cases (for example, BGH NJW 1951, 1274; BGH WM 1979, 966; BGH WM 1982, 849) the precondition of invalidity according to § 138 I is – with reference to the *dolus eventualis* of the party benefited – in fact derived from § 138 II ('. . . if one party to the contract . . . carelessly fails to recognise that the other party enters into the disadvantageous terms only on the grounds of his weaker economic position').

[23] BGHZ 98, 178; BGH NJW 1995, 1022; references to older judgments made by K. Hackl, BB 1977, 1412.

[24] T. Mayer-Maly, 'Renaissance der laesio enormis?' in K. Larenz and C. Canaris (eds.), *Festschrift für Karl Larenz zum 80. Geburtstag* (Munich, 1983), p. 395.

[25] For more exact details on this, see MüKo/Mayer-Maly, § 138 para. 102.

[26] RGZ 150, 6; BGH NJW 1992, 899 f.; BGH DB 1997, 92; OLG Stuttgart NJW 1979, 2409; quite extensive is also: KG Berlin BB 1985, 829; numerous further examples in: Palandt/Heinrichs, § 138 para. 34.

have in common that the disadvantaged party acquired an asset available on the market which had been greatly overvalued. In these cases, the courts attempt to remedy the disadvantage (or 'damage') suffered by the obviously weaker party with the help of § 138 I. From the point of view of common law, this concerns the problem of *damnum vitare* rather than – as is the case with Damien's profitable purchase – *lucrum captare*: Célimène was ignorant of the fact that she owned a valuable painting by Monet. Only Damien's knowledge led to its discovery. Therefore, why should Damien not profit from his discovery? Of course, Célimène loses a fortune by selling the picture but she could not have used this fortune in an economic sense had Damien not revealed to her that this picture was in fact a Monet. This reasoning – following an economic analysis[27] – argues that Damien should be allowed to profit from his discovery.

One may even deduce from the provisions regulating treasure trove (§ 984) that the law intends to reward the performance of the discoverer. Nevertheless in that case the treasure trove is to be divided between the finder and the land owner in keeping with Hadrian's division.[28] If one were to apply this principle to our case then Damien would have to set aside 50% of his takings from the painting's sale for Célimène. The device contained in the BGB does not offer such a solution however; to draw an analogy with treasure trove is daring by German standards.

(ii) Due to the fact that a mistake in expression (§ 119 I) has clearly not been made, only a mistake relating to quality can be considered as grounds for annulment. The origin of the painting is without a doubt a 'substantial quality'.[29] Célimène did not know that the picture which she had sold was in fact a Monet; therefore, she made a mistake relating to the artist's identity. She may therefore annul the declaration she made when concluding the contract with Damien and demand the return of the picture together with the rights of ownership.[30]

---

[27] Cf. for example, M. Adams, 'Irrtümer und Offenbarungspflichten in Vertragsrecht' (1986) AcP 186, 472, according to whom (in the case of an annulment for mistake) it ought to come down to whether the 'advantageous information of one party concerning the value of an object rests on a way of obtaining such information which is obviously socially damaging and which does not improve the allocation of goods (. . .)'.

[28] D. 41,1,63; Inst. 2,1,39.

[29] Cf. BGHZ 63, 369, 371 = NJW 1975, 970; BGH NJW 1988, 2597, 2599. Similar to this case is that in RGZ 124, 115 ('Ming-Vasenfall'), where a married couple inexperienced in such business matters sold two valuable vases dating from the Ming Dynasty at a ridiculously low price.

[30] For a fundamentally different view, however, see: RG JW 1912, 525 (on this Mayer-Maly, F. S. Pedrazzini, 346); here the Reichsgericht rejected a rescission on grounds of a

Damien does not have any claim against Célimène for compensation of negative interest. The unusually low price which Célimène had demanded and which Damien himself doubled in order to quell his bad conscience must have made him realise that Célimène had made a mistake about the picture's origin (cf. § 122 II). Therefore Damien could not justifiably rely on the contract's legal validity and accordingly is unable to claim damages from Célimène.

In contrast to Case 1, Célimène's claim to annul the contract concluded with Damien is also unaffected by the fact that she had assumed the risk of making a mistake about a characteristic of the painting. Even where a larger number of art objects or antiques were sold as part of a clearance sale, the seller would not necessarily assume a particular risk relating to the importance and characteristics of individual objects of sale. A case was recently decided by a German *Amtsgericht* on a different set of facts.[31] Notebooks and pages of notes were sold at a flea market: amongst them, unknown to the seller, was the original manuscript of a composition by W. A. Mozart. The seller annulled the contract once she had found out that she had practically given away a fortune for as little as 10 DM. However, the court dismissed her claim for annulment because a disparity between the value of a corporeal object and its asking price is typical at a flea market. Each of the parties to the contract therefore assumes the risk to acquire valuable things at little cost or worthless things at relatively high cost.[32]

In our case the facts are different. Neither the nature of the sale nor the nature of the goods which Célimène offers indicate that she had intended to assume a particular risk with regard to the price–value relationship. She is obviously not learned in matters of art history. Moreover, in contrast to Case 1 there appears to be no uncertainty in respect of the painting's origin. Célimène is therefore able to annul the contract for her mistake about the painting's characteristics.

(iii) At first glance, Damien appears not to have acted fraudulently. The law requires that fraudulent misrepresentation caused the declaration of intent to be given.[33] Célimène determined the price at which she wanted

---

mistake relating to a characteristic owing to the fact that the 'value' of a subject was not a characteristic.

[31] AG Coburg, NJW 1993, 938.

[32] The *ratio decidendi* of the decision does not come through so clearly as described here but can be perceived in the grounds of the *Amtsgericht's* decision; cf. NJW 1993, 939.

[33] Cf. § 123 I: 'A person who has been caused to make a declaration of intention by deceit . . . , can rescind this declaration.'

to sell the painting to the public in her *invitatio ad offerendum*.[34] It was not Damien's offer which induced her mistake. However, withholding facts may fulfil the conditions laid down in § 123 if one party to the contract is bound by a duty to disclose and deliberately fails to fulfil this duty.[35] According to the *BGH*, the causal requirement between the failure to disclose and the other party's decision to enter into the contract is fulfilled if the circumstances are such 'which may frustrate the (other party's) purpose of entering into the contract and which are therefore of significance to the latter's decision'.[36] The value of the picture is clearly of importance in Célimène's decision to sell. In that respect, Damien's silence caused Célimène to accept his purchase price.

Nevertheless annulment on grounds of fraudulent misrepresentation is only possible if Damien was bound to inform Célimène of the picture's value. Regarding this issue, the courts are guided by § 242: whether Damien was under a duty of disclosure is a question to be determined by asking whether Célimène could have expected disclosure according to good faith having regard to the generally accepted standards of business.[37] The *BGH* has only imposed a duty to draw a party's attention to the unusually high proceeds of a further sale if a special fiduciary relationship already existed between the parties to the contract.[38] Such a fiduciary relationship – for example, an already existing business relationship – does not bind Damien or Célimène. For that reason, Damien is certainly under no duty to inform Célimène of the painter of the picture. Basically, Damien ought to profit from his 'act of discovery'.

Damien is therefore not obliged to inform Célimène as to the identity of the picture's artist. In addition such a duty does not directly arise from § 138 and the arguments which oppose the immorality of the contract between Damien and Célimène also oppose the presence of fraudulent misrepresentation.[39]

---

[34] Concerning the nature of *invitatio ad offerendum* and its distinction from an effective declaration of intent to conclude a contract see, for example: Larenz/Wolf, AT 576; Flume, AT II, 636 f.; Brox, AT 91.

[35] Cf. RGZ 77, 309, 314.   [36] BGH LM § 123 BGB Nr. 45.

[37] RGZ 77, 309, 314; BGH NJW 1989, 764; BGH NJW-RR 1991, 440; cf. on this: Palandt/Heinrichs, § 123 para. 5; Larenz/Wolf, AT 697.

[38] BGH LM § 123 BGB Nr. 52.

[39] With the reprehensible intention which it is assumed Damien had (§ 138 II), one would also have to establish that he also had a fraudulent intent. Only if one assumes that Damien had a duty of disclosure may one see in his failure to do so the required elements of an immoral exploitation.

(iv) If Damien has negligently breached the duty of disclosure which he owed to Célimène then he is liable in damages according to the principles of *culpa in contrahendo*. Due to the fact that such a duty of disclosure does not exist (as shown in iii) Damien could not have breached this duty, even through his own negligence. Therefore, Célimène does not have a claim of damages according to the principles of *culpa in contrahendo* (and consequently no claim to have the property restored according to § 249).

Greece

Greek law gives Célimène several remedies. She is entitled to seek for the annulment of the sale and the contract of transfer on the grounds of mistake, fraud and the immorality of the contract.

(i) Célimène is mistaken as to the qualities of the object of the transaction, specifically as to the author of the painting. Whether this mistake is fundamental, that is justifying annulment of the contracts, will be decided by virtue of two criteria, objective and subjective (art. 142 AK). The objective criterion is present since the quality of the painting as an original work of Monet is of importance for the whole transaction according to good faith and common usage. Célimène's mistake is also fundamental according to the subjective criterion. It is obvious that Célimène would not have entered into the contract had she known of the true situation.

(ii) Célimène's declaration of intent was procured by Damien's fraud who acted with the purpose of reinforcing her erroneous representations (art. 147 AK). It is generally accepted[40] that fraud can take place by the concealment of true facts in respect of which there exists a duty to inform in accordance with the agreement of the parties, or by law (e.g. arts. 303, 304, 456 AK etc.), or according to good morals, good faith and common usage. Such an obligation is obvious in the above situation. The fact that Damien is a professional art dealer is crucial. The sort of transaction and the obvious importance of the concealed fact,[41] i.e. the quality of the painting as a work of Monet, impose an obligation on Damien to reveal the truth. As explained in Case 1, Célimène must

---

[40] AP 355/1968 NoV 16, 950; AP 249/1976 NoV 24, 785; Gazis, *General Principles of Civil Law*, p. 80; Georgiadis, *General Principles of Civil Law*, p. 432; Karakatsanis AK 147 n. 3; Papantoniou, *General Principles of Civil Law*, p. 410; Spyridakis, *General Principles*, p. 612; Karassis, *Manual of General Principles of Civil Law*, p. 107; Papachristou AK 147 n. 5; Simantiras, *General Principles*, n. 753.

[41] Karakatsanis AK 147 n. 3.

go to the court to annul the contracts of sale and transfer (arts. 150, 154 AK).

In case the transfer and delivery of the painting[42] to the Louvre has gone ahead, the museum acquires title according to art. 1036 AK, which protects a *bona fide* third party who acquires ownership of movable goods from a non-owner. In this case Damien, who is enriched without just cause at the expense of Célimène, is liable to return to her the equivalent of the enrichment, that is the purchase price from acquiring the painting (art. 908 AK). It is disputed whether the thing becomes lost for its owner if the contract by which it is transferred to another person is annulled on the grounds of a defect of consent.[43] Article 1038 AK excludes stolen and lost things from *bona fide* acquisitions. If this opinion were accepted, the Louvre would not become owner of the painting in spite of its good faith. The certainty of transactions would be in favour of the real owner's, that is Célimène's, interests. According however to the more persuasive view[44] the subsequent annulment of the contract of transfer cannot change the voluntary transfer of the thing into an involuntary loss of its possession. The special circumstances however under which the transfer has taken place may render the thing lost and thus entail the application of art. 1038 AK. In parallel with her rights to demand annulment by reason of fraud, Célimène is entitled to compensation in tort since fraud is of course a tort (arts. 149 and 914 AK).

(iii) The contracts concluded by Célimène and Damien are voidable and simultaneously void according to art. 179 AK. This provision stipulates that the act 'where a party through exploitation of need, mental levity or inexperience of the other party, stipulates or receives for his own benefit or the benefit of a third party, in consideration of a performance, pecuniary advantages which in the circumstances are obviously disproportionate to the performance' is contrary to morality and consequently null and void. The rule with its objective and subjective criteria refers

---

[42] According to a persuasive but not prevailing view for art. 1036 AK to be implemented the delivery of possession must be material, that is the third party must acquire physical power over the movable object – A. Georgiadis, *Real Property Law* (Athens, 1975), vol. II 1: Ownership, § 28 pp. 230 ff. See also Stathopoulos, *Contract Law in Hellas*, p. 49; for the opposite view: G. Balis, *Real Property Law* (4th ed, Athens, 1961), § 56; I. Spyridakis, *Real Property Law* (Athens-Komotini, 1983), p. 594; A. Toussis, *Real Property Law* (4th edn, R. Toussis, Athens, 1988), § 100 n. 3a.

[43] For the various views which have been supported see Simantiras, *General Principles of Civil Law*, p. 121 on the acquisition of ownership from a transferor not the owner; Vouzikas, on the acquisition of pledge not from the owner p. 98.

[44] Georgiadis, *Real Property Law*, pp. 249–50.

to contracts in which an abuse has occurred. The strict conditions laid down by the above articles are met here. Damien has taken advantage of Célimène's inexperience in the field of sales of works of art with the intention to exploit her. As to the obvious disproportion between performance and counter-performance, the Greek court[45] accepts it when the latter is about double the former, a criterion that resembles the *laesio enormis* of Roman Law. The fulfilment of the conditions of art. 179 AK entails, according to the prevailing view,[46] the nullity not only of the contract of sale but also of the contract of transfer. A void act, contrary to voidable acts, produces no legal effects and need not be judicially declared null (art. 180 AK).[47]

The same arguments raised above as to the consequences of annulled contracts are also valid here. Although doubts have been raised as to whether the annulment of a contract of transfer renders the transferred movable lost or not, neither the Greek courts nor Greek legal opinion have addressed the issue of whether an object transferred by a contract void for abuse could be considered lost. By analogy, the same argument may be submitted. Gazis[48] maintains that the provisions of fraud are not concurrent with the rule of art. 179 AK. The former, as special rule, precludes the application of the latter. There are however strong arguments against this opinion.[49]

Ireland

It appears from the facts of this case that the buyer has made no representation to Célimène as to the value of the object of art work he was purchasing. In Irish law silence will not, as a rule, amount to misrepresentation. On this basis, this case is not dissimilar to the previous one. However, the Irish courts have not been reticent in invoking their equitable jurisdiction to set aside contracts where there is an

---

[45] AP 416/1975 NoV23, 1173.

[46] Balis, *General Principles of Civil Law*, § 66; Georgiadis, *General Principles of Civil Law*, p. 394; Karakatsanis AK 179 n. 4; E. Kounougeri-Manoledaki, 'The Extent and the Consequences of the Nullity of the Improperly Exploitative Juridical Act' (1975) *Arm* 29, 569; for the different opinions which have been supported see Spyridakis, *General Principles of Civil Law*, pp. 670–1.

[47] The nullity of an exploitative legal act, according to the prevailing view, is absolute, which means that nullity may be invoked by anyone who has a legal interest. A minority view (cf. P. Papanikolaou, *Exploitative Juridical Act* (1984), pp. 230 ff. See also Spyridakis, *General Principles of Civil Law*, p. 670), based on the *ratio legis* of the provision – which is the protection of the victim of the exploitation – submits that only the victim can invoke the nullity of the legal act.

[48] Gazis, *General Principles of Civil Law*, p. 84.

[49] Karakatsanis AK 149 n. 12; Spyridakis, *General Principles*, p. 623.

unconscionable bargain. In this regard, the judgment of Shapely J in *Carroll and another* v. *Carroll*[50] is illustrative of the proactive approach of the courts in Ireland.

However, what makes this a difficult case is that the purchaser paid valuable consideration for the painting purchased, notwithstanding that it represented considerably less than the true value of the painting. In cases where Irish courts have set aside contracts on the basis of unconscionable bargain, there has generally been an absence of consideration, e.g. the judgment of Lynch J in *Noonan* v. *O'Connell*.[51] If the Irish courts were to hold that this is a case of unconscionable bargain, the contract would be set aside leaving Célimène with the option of avoiding the contract and having the painting returned to her. This, however, supposes that the painting has not been sold on to a third party who was without notice of the circumstances in which the picture was obtained. On the basis that the Louvre gallery had no knowledge of the circumstances in which the painting was purchased from Célimène, it would be difficult to see how a court would intervene.

Italy

It is important to remember, before dealing with the sale of a work of art that the discovery of historical, archaeological objects etc. or objets d'art falls under public law provisions and the goods may be taken by the competent authorities (art. 839 of the Civil Code; L. 1.6.1939, n. 1089 and modifications up to L. 1.3.1975, n. 44). As in Blackstone's commentaries: 'treasure belongs to the Crown'. Under regulations relating to works of art, the Italian National Museum (the Italian equivalent of the Louvre) will keep the painting independently from the circumstances in which the work of art was purchased from Célimène. That said, Célimène's case could be solved under Italian law both as a mistake (*errore*) and as fraud (*dolo*).

(i) It will be easier than in Case 1 to convince an Italian court of the presence of a mistake here. The fact that the mistake must be fundamental (*errore essenziale*) and recognisable (*riconoscibile*) will be immediately inferred by the judges in this situation. Damien immediately understood that Célimène was not an expert and could not understand the incredible treasure she was selling within the 'attic contents'. The

---

[50] Unreported judgment of the High Court which was affirmed by the Supreme Court in July 1999.
[51] Unreported judgment of the High Court.

difference in the parties' status could be a sufficient argument to enable the court to assert that mistake was recognisable.[52] Moreover accepting double the price is not enough to demonstrate that Célimène agreed that the painting she was selling was a valuable one. The theory of a sale of a work of art as a 'risk contract' (*contratto aleatorio*), which the courts use when both parties are professionals seems to be set aside in the presence of an unskilled party.[53] The contract will be annulled, and the *status quo* will be restored (arts. 1441 ff. of the Civil Code), unless Damien pays Célimène the difference between the price he paid and the real value of the painting (art. 1432).

(ii) The fact that Damien did not tell Célimène that she was selling a masterpiece among the bric-a-brac pieces could be seen as silence amounting to fraud (*dolo*).[54] If Célimène decides to choose this approach, she will face some difficulties in convincing the court! The fundamental requirement to obtain the annulment of the sale for non-disclosure could be found in a negative fraud (*dolo negativo*), that is fraud perpetrated by the failure to say something, although this solution has not yet been developed by the Italian courts.[55] The negative fraud would consist in Damien's non-disclosure to Célimène that the painting was an authentic Monet; had Célimène known this fact, she would have created a different kind of contractual obligation. Silence, by itself, does not amount to fraud unless there is a fraudulent concealment of true facts or a breach of an explicit duty to inform provided by law.[56] Italian scholars,[57] like the French, put the breach of the duty to inform in the

---

[52] Pietrobon, *Errore, volontà e affidamento*, pp. 220 ff.

[53] This is the solution adopted by A. Roma 23.11.1948 RDCo 1949, II, 192 noted by R. Sacco; a Carraccio painting has been sold as by an 'unknown maestro'.

[54] Article 1439 Fraud: 'Fraud is the cause of the annulment of the contract when the deception employed by one of the contracting parties was such that, without it, the other contracting party would not have entered into the contract. When the deception was employed by a third party, the contract is voidable if it was known to the party who derived a benefit from it.'
   Article 1440 Incidental fraud: 'If the deception was not such as to compel consent, the contract is valid, even though without the deception it would have included different terms; however, the contracting party in bad faith is liable for damages.'

[55] The criminal law courts use it; moreover the civil *dolo* and the criminal *truffa* are considered to be constituted by the same factual situation, see Cass 1986, n. 7322.

[56] This statement could be found in a decision of the Trib. Verona, 18 November 1946, in FP 1947, 199. The sale of a truck, without disclosing that it belonged to the State, was considered fraudulent and annulled. The Civil Code contains an explicit duty to disclose in arts. 1892–3 regarding insurance contracts.

[57] Numerous Italian authors have written on the subject but the case law is less abundant. The liability arising from non-disclosure is always dealt with along with

doctrine of defective consent and link it to art. 1439 of the Civil Code, according to which the contract is void 'when the deception employed by one of the contracting parties was such that, without it, the other contracting party would not have entered into the contract'; the text is not so different from art. 1116 of the French Civil Code. At the very basis of the idea of fraud, there is the postulate, the result of the will theory, in accordance with which consent must be free, otherwise it is vitiated.[58] However, there is still a very long way to go from the concept of fraud to that of duty to inform. As in France we have to distinguish between different stages in the development of liability for defective consent, injury or abuse of the other party.

(iii) In order to consider that a legal duty to disclose has been breached, Célimène must convince the court that art. 1337 of the Civil Code (providing for a duty to behave in good faith during negotiations and formation of contract) imposes a general duty to inform. This provision might be read in order to oblige the parties to inform each other when they discover the other party's mistake.

The 1960s gave rise to the birth of new cases in which the courts were asked to give more efficient answers to new defective consent situations. The courts have started to implement their decisions with the articles referring to the good faith principle (*clausole generali*). The most remarkable example of this trend can be found in the evolution of the doctrine of *culpa in contrahendo*[59] after Von Jhering's influence on the Code drafters, but has not yet given the results called

---

the precontractual obligations of good faith. The most recent works are by D. Caruso, *La culpa in contrahendo. L'esperienza statunitense e quella italiana* (Milan, 1993); G. Grisi, *L'obbligo precontrattuale di informazione* (Naples, 1990); L. Nanni, *La buona fede contrattuale* (Padua, 1988), pp. 1–143; F. Benatti, 'Culpa in contrahendo' in *Contratto e Impresa* (Milan, 1987), 287 ff.; F. Benatti, *La responsabilità precontrattuale* (Milan, 1963); G. Cuffaro, 'Responsabilità precontrattuale' in *Enciclopedia del Diritto* (39 vols., Milan, 1988), at pp. 1265 ff.; C. Chiola, *Informazione* in *Enciclopedia Giuridica Treccani* (Rome, 1990) at pp. 122 ff.; S. Ferrarini, 'Investment banking, prospetti falsi e colpa in contraendo' (1988) 2 *Giur. comm.* at p. 585; A. Fusaro, 'Fondamenti e limiti della responsabilità precontrattuale' (1984) I, 1 *Giur. It.* at p. 1199; M. L. Loi and F. Tessitore, *Buona fede e responsabilità precontrattuale* (Milan, 1975), at p. 146; Rasi, *La responsabilità precontrattuale* (1974) *Riv. dir. civ.* At p. 496; G. Visintini, *La reticenza nella formazione dei contratti* (Padua, 1972); M. Bessone, *Rapporto precontrattuale e doveri di correttezza* (1955) I *Riv. trim. dir. proc. civ.* at p. 360.

[58] R. Sacco and G. De Nova, 'Il Contratto', vol. I, p. 310. We agree with the authors that the 'complete freedom, the complete thought, the full consciousness of the party are unattainable ideals'.

[59] See the role of the *culpa in contrahendo* in Italy and the United States in the excellent work of D. Caruso, *La culpa in contrahendo*.

for by some authors.[60] There are in fact few decisions mentioning this article in order to oblige a party to disclose information, the courts tend to use it only to disapprove of an unjustified withdrawal from negotiations.

However, according to traditional doctrine, silence by itself does not mean fraud.[61] The only case in which a court has accepted a similar reasoning has been in *Banca Manusardi* (a bank which did not disclose the information concerning the economic situation of a company, whose convertible loan stocks it wanted to sell, was held liable for breaching art. 1337 of the Civil Code). The decisions of the Court of Appeals of Milan have a strong influence all over the country, but it should be pointed out that this case dealt with the liability of a professional institution towards consumers for the sale of securities.[62]

(iv) A final word must be said about treasure trove, which, as some authors have pointed out, offers a very similar situation to the one we are dealing with in this case.[63] Article 932 of the Civil Code considers as a treasure trove 'any movable thing of value, hidden or buried, of which nobody can prove he is the owner'. Arguably, the painting could be qualified by the courts as treasure trove as it fits this description. In that case the Code says that 'provided that [the treasure] is found only by accident, one half goes to the owner of the land and one half to the finder'.

The Netherlands

This is, like Case 1, also a case of seller's mistake. However, it is different in two significant respects: (i) the buyer knew of the characteristics the seller did not know of; (ii) the buyer was an expert. The combination of these factors means that Célimène may probably annul the contract for mistake.

Article 6:228 (1)(b) BW says that

a party may annul a contract for mistake if he would not have entered into the contract had he made a correct assessment of the facts and (. . .) b. if the other

---

[60] Sacco and De Nova, 'Il Contratto', vol. I, p. 356; Sacco foresees the development of art. 1337 as a contract liability threshold rule, giving all the protection needed through the comparative evaluation of the parties' behaviour; this would then be a means of preventing contractual unjustice.

[61] See fn. 56.

[62] App. Milan, 2 February 1990, in *Giur. It.*, 1992, I, 2, 49, note by M. Arietti.

[63] Fabre-Magnan, *De l'obligation d'information dans les contrats*, p. 162; J. Gordley, 'Equality in Exchange' (1981) Cal. L. Rev. 69, p. 1583.

party, in view of what he knew or ought to know regarding the mistake, should have informed the mistaken party.

Therefore if Damien was under a duty to inform Célimène she may annul the contract (subject to what is said in s. 2 of the same article). Was Damien under a duty to inform Célimène? In this case Damien knew that the painting was a Monet. He also knew that Célimène did not realise the painting was a Monet and therefore that she was mistaken and would probably not have sold the painting for the same price (or indeed not at all) if she had known better. However, does this mean that he had to inform her?

As mentioned under Case 1, in *HR* 19 June 1959 (*Stevensweerd Kantharos*) the *Hoge Raad* held that a seller, under a mistake as to the characteristics of the object he sold, may have a right to annul the contract if the buyer was under a duty to inform. Before the new code the precontractual duty to inform was based on precontractual good faith. Today the requirement of good faith is still said to explain why under certain circumstances a party may be under a duty to inform the other party.[64] It is generally held in legal doctrine, and it is confirmed by case law, that the question whether or not the buyer is under a duty to inform depends heavily on the expertise of both the buyer and the seller.[65] In this case the seller seems to be totally ignorant, whereas the buyer is an expert. In Dutch law there seems to be a general trend in case law to impose a duty more readily on experts and professionals to inform non-expert and non-professional parties with whom they are contracting.[66] In view of this trend it seems likely that in this case a court would recognise a duty to inform. However, the law with regard to duties to inform is under constant development and debate, particularly where experts are concerned. Therefore, it is difficult to establish where the law stands at the present moment. The representation given here may be too modern (i.e. too extensive a duty for experts).

---

[64] Cf. e.g. *HR*, 2 April 1993, NJ 1995, 94, note Brunner, and M. W. Hesselink, *De redelijkheid en billijkheid in het Europese privaatrecht* (diss. Utrecht), (Deventer, 1999), p. 261.

[65] Cf. J. B. M. Vranken, *Mededelings, informatie- en onderzoeksplichten in het verbintenissenrecht* (Zwolle, 1989), no. 170; Asser/Hartkamp II (2001), no. 186; *Verbintenissenrecht* (Hijma), art. 228, no. 86. On professionals cf. R. P. J. L. Tjittes, *De hoedanigheid van contractspartijen* (diss. Groningen), (Deventer, 1994), p. 47 e.v.

[66] Cf. e.g. *HR*, 1 June 1990, NJ 1991, 759, note Brunner, on a bank's duty, as a professional credit supplier, to inform a non-professional party generally on the risk concerned with giving a personal guarantee. Cf. on this case R. P. J. L. Tjittes, *Bezwaarde verwanten* (oratie VU), (Deventer, 1996), pp. 54 ff.

It is sometimes said that what matters is whether a person presents himself as an expert rather than his actual expertise.[67] However, here the dissimulation of his expertise should not favour Damien: had he presented himself as an expert of Monet paintings, Célimène might have become suspicious of his readiness to pay double the price.

As it is clear that Célimène 'would not have entered into this contract had there been a correct assessment of the facts' – had she known the painting was the work of Monet she would not have sold for the present price – she may annul the contract for mistake. She may do this, at her choice, in court, or by a simple declaration (art. 3:49 BW).[68] A party who has the right to annul the contract for mistake may, instead of annulling, ask the court to change the content of the contract in such a way that his loss is compensated (art. 6:230 BW).[69]

If Célimène decides to annul the contract for mistake, this means that, as a result, and due to the retrospective effect of annulment,[70] Damien had no title when selling the painting to the Louvre. This means consequently, that transfer of property did not take place (art. 3:84 s. 1 BW) and that Célimène, still owner, can demand her property back ex art. 3:84 BW or 6:203 BW. On the other hand, the Louvre, on acquiring the piece in good faith (as seems to be the case), can be protected by art. 3:86 BW.[71] It should be noted, however, that the (alleged) transfer of property of Damien to the Louvre could never influence Célimène's opportunity to annul her contract with Damien. If Damien is unable to return the painting, as he is obliged to on the ground of art. 6:203 BW (*repetitio indebiti: onverschuldigde betaling*), he is liable in damages under art. 6:74 BW, the general rule on liability for non-performance of an obligation.

Norway

Even if we here, also, have to deal with a mistake concerning the value of a work of art, the situation is different from the previous one. This

---

[67] *Verbintenissenrecht* (Hijma), art. 228, no. 86.

[68] Article 3:49 BW: 'Where a juridical act is subject to annulment it can be annulled either by extrajudicial declaration or by judgment.'

[69] On this article, see Case 3.

[70] Article 3:53 s. 1 BW: 'Annulment has retrospective effect to the time the juridical act was executed.'

[71] Article 3:86 s. 1 BW: 'Although an alienator lacks the right to dispose of the property, a transfer pursuant to articles 90, 91 or 93 of a movable thing, unregistered property, or a right payable to bearer or order is valid, if the transfer is not by gratuitous title and if the acquirer is in good faith.'

will possibly be sufficient for the question of legal claims to be resolved differently.

The *knowledge* possessed by the purchaser (Damien) at the time of entering into the contract is significant: the courts would in such a situation frequently make use of § 33 of the Contract Act (sometimes referred to as the 'Little General Clause'), either instead of, or in addition to, § 36 of the Contract Act.[72] The regulation reads:

Even if a declaration of intention otherwise had to be regarded as valid, it does not bind the person who has given it, if, owing to circumstances present when the other party received knowledge of the declaration and which it must be assumed that he knew of, it would be contrary to decency and good faith, if he claimed the declaration.

What might be contrary to 'honest behaviour and good faith', has to be determined after a concrete evaluation of the circumstances at the time of the formation of the contract. That we have here a professional purchaser who has done business with a non-professional, is likely to be decisive.[73] In the present case, the seller could demand that the entire arrangement be *revised*. Invalidity works *ex tunc* (retrospectively) and requires that a restitution settlement with exchange of goods be made. Invalidity is not automatic, but is an option for the person who has the right.[74] Since fault (*culpa*) lies with the purchaser, Célimène can, in addition to the claim of invalidity, demand *compensation*. It is, in this case, the reliance loss that has to be met.[75] The seller must be restored to the same financial situation as if the contract had not been entered into.

Portugal

Under Portuguese law this case would be considered as a case of mistake (*erro*) by Célimène and as a case of fraud (*dolo*) by Damien.

---

[72] Section 36 of the Contract Act has such a comprehensive wording that it also covers the situations described in § 33.

[73] A general increase in the value of objets d'art subsequent to entering into contract is, on the other hand, not sufficient reason to make a claim against the purchaser, see Rt. 1993.309.

[74] In conformity with 'common law' terminology, the contract is 'voidable' or, as expressed in German legal doctrine, the person has been granted '*ein Anfechtungsrecht*'.

[75] B. Gomard, *Alminnelig kontraktsret* (2nd edn, Copenhagen, 1996), pp. 139 ff.; V. Hagstrøm, *Fragmenter fra obligasjonsrett* (3rd edn, Oslo, 1992), vol. I, p. 202. H. Karlgren, *Avtalsrättsliga spørsmal* (2nd edn, Stockholm, 1954), p. 84, notes that the person suffering the damages can claim the expectation loss. See also C. Hultmark, *Upplysningsplikt* (Stockholm, 1993), p. 26.

(i) First, it is a question of mistake, because Célimène thought she was selling a piece of bric-a-brac and not a masterpiece. So her consent to sell was given on the ground of a mistake relating to the subject matter of the contract. The fact that Damien paid twice the asking price is not sufficient to exclude Célimène's mistake, and we must assume that Damien knew or should have been aware that the mistake was fundamental for Célimène's consent to sell. Therefore, according to arts. 251° and 247° of the Civil Code, Célimène can demand the annulment of the sale, which restores the painting to her with retrospective effect.

(ii) In the second place, this situation can be seen as a case of fraud (*dolo*) by Damien. According to art. 253° of the Civil Code there is a fraud when a party makes any suggestion with intention or knows he is inducing or keeping the other party under a mistake or does not disclose the other party's mistake. The non-disclosure of the mistake is not considered to be fraud when there is no duty to inform according to the law, the contract or prevailing doctrinal theories. However, according to the rules of *culpa in contrahendo* (art. 227° of the Civil Code), we must consider that there are duties to behave in good faith during negotiations and when the contract is formed and among these duties is a duty to inform, the breach of which constitutes fraud and can also incur liability for losses.[76]

Fraud is a sufficient ground for annulling the contract (art. 254° of the Civil Code), which restores Célimène's property to her (art. 289°). This is the position even though title has passed to a third party, the Louvre, since annulment is retrospective which means that no title passes to Damien and on the basis of *nemo pluris juris* nor to the Louvre. On this basis, Célimène will have her title restored and the sale to the Louvre will be considered as a sale by a non-owner and subject to a revindicatory action by Célimène. Restitution *in integrum* is still possible here,[77] it only becomes impossible when the third party has acquired *usucapio* or if the object of the sale has been registered before restitution is claimed (art. 291° of the Civil Code), which does not apply to the sale of a painting. Portuguese law does not therefore protect the rights of a *bona fide* third party purchaser.

---

[76] See C. Mota Pinto, *Teoria Geral do Direito Civil* (Coimbra, Almedina, 1984), p. 524 and M. Cordeiro, *Da Boa Fé no Direito Civil* (Coimbra, Almedina, 1985), pp. 574 ff.

[77] In the event that restitution is impossible a monetary equivalent would be paid by the buyer in substitution.

Scotland

There are similarities between Célimène's and Anatole's situations. Both involve a mistake in intention which is unilateral and uninduced. Therefore the same process of deduction is applied. First, as the dispute concerns the subject matter that Célimène has bound herself to deliver, it is, like Anatole's, classified as a mistake in transaction. As previously stated, the mistake does not therefore require to be induced.

Secondly, the mistake fits one of Bell's five essential mistakes, viz. mistake as to the quality of the thing engaged for.[78] Unlike Anatole, Célimène did not attach a description to the painting. However, I would suggest the reasonable man would identify Célimène's mistake as to quality of the painting from her apparent willingness to include an original Monet in an attic sale. As the facts do not contradict Damien's assessment of the work as a Monet, the difference in quality is clearer than in Anatole's case. Therefore, I believe Célimène has a stronger claim of essential mistake sufficient to prevent formation of contract.

Thirdly, the mistake is unilateral and uninduced. The arguments and implications noted above apply as before. Therefore depending on which interpretation of *Stewart* v. *Kennedy* and *Menzies* v. *Menzies* is followed either the contract is *void ab initio* or beyond challenge due to lack of inducement. The court will most probably favour the latter. It is unlikely that they would see the offer of twice the price as an operative misrepresentation.

There are two notable differences between Célimène and Anatole which could give Célimène a remedy if one for unilateral mistake is refused. Firstly, the doctrine of undue influence provides a separate ground of rescission. Although Célimène and Damien are both individuals they are not of equal bargaining strengths. Damien's skill as an antiques dealer would give him an advantage over Célimène. The courts have held that a difference in power does not of itself affect the validity of a contract. However, where a relationship of trust has grown up between the parties, abuse of that trust can amount to undue influence.[79] There is no such relationship in this case. Nor is it thought that there is any obligation of good faith on Damien to disclose the value of the painting to Célimène.[80]

---

[78] As above, the distinction between a mistake in quality and mistake as to value should be noted.

[79] *Honeyman Executors* v. *Sharp* (1978) SC 223.

[80] Cf. the obligation of a creditor to advise a wife to seek independent legal advice when she is prepared to act as a cautioner for her husband's debts. See *Smith* v. *The Bank of*

The second distinction is more important. Unlike Bob, Damien appreciated the bargain he was getting before the contract was formed. Since *Steuart's Trs* v. *Hart*[81] it has been a principle of Scots law that a party cannot 'snatch at a bargain'. In that case the pursuer sold a piece of his land in the belief that the feu-duty[82] for the whole area would fall to be paid by the purchaser of the plot. The land had been advertised on this basis and the terms of sale did not contradict the pursuer's belief. However, this intention was not achieved. Further, although the defender was aware of the pursuer's belief, he did not inform the pursuer that he was mistaken. As the mistake did not prevent the contract from being formed, it was still valid. The appropriate remedy for the court was to grant rescission.[83]

The First Division of the Court of Session[84] did not base their judgment on precedent nor classify the *nomen iuris* as either mistake or taking advantage of the other part. These omissions were highlighted in *Spook Erection (Northern) Ltd* v. *Kaye*.[85] Again, the pursuer was mistaken as to the quality of the subjects in a sale of land. He believed the property was under a 999-year lease. The defender, knowing the pursuer's belief, did not inform him that he had discovered that the term of the lease was only 99 years. Unsurprisingly, given the similarity of the facts, the pursuer relied on the *Steuart's Trs* principle that a person should not knowingly take advantage of another. However, while appreciating the argument, the court did not find the dicta in *Steuart's Trs* appropriate or sound in principle. Lord Marnoch questioned why favouring the seller, when the buyer had received a good bargain, should be seen as preferable. Therefore he refused to grant rescission.

In *Spook Erection* the court distinguished *Steuart's Trs* on the grounds that the earlier court had been influenced by the pursuer's uninduced, unilateral mistake and not simply because the defender took advantage

---

Scotland (1997) SC (HL) 111. The effect of this obligation based on good faith appears to be restricted to cautioners.

[81] (1875) 3 R 192.

[82] Feu-duty is a monetary burden on land in Scotland. The holder of the land is bound to pay a Superior the specified amount. Statutory intervention in the 1970s has decreased the number of properties so affected. The feudal system in Scotland is soon to be abolished: the Abolition of Feudal Tenure, etc. (Scotland) Bill 1999.

[83] Before rescission is granted, *restitutio in integrum* must be possible, i.e. the parties must be able to be restored to the positions they were in before the contract was formed.

[84] The Court of Session is the highest civil court in Scotland. The Inner House of the Court is divided into two divisions; First and Second.

[85] (1990) SLT 676.

of the pursuer's ignorance. Lord Marnoch also maintained that uninduced unilateral mistake was irrelevant after *Stewart* v. *Kennedy*. However
in *Angus* v. *Bryden*,[86] Lord Cameron of Lochbroon argued that *Steuart's
Trs* remained good law. He maintained that a party would usually be
personally barred from denying the terms upon which he was prepared to contract by pleading unilateral mistake. Therefore a purchaser
could accept a seller's offer despite his knowledge that the seller had
undervalued the goods. There would, however, be grounds for rescission
if the final offer that the buyer accepted was drastically different from
the offers being proposed during negotiations so that the buyer knew
the final offer was made under mistake. As there were no prior negotiations between Célimène and Damien, she would remain personally
barred from relying on her unilateral mistake.

However, by applying the alternative interpretation of *Stewart* v.
Kennedy, it could be argued that the principle against snatching at a
bargain survives despite *Spook Erection*. But this would not aid Célimène.
As stated, the remedy of rescission operates differently from declaring
a contract *void ab initio*. As Célimène's contract with Damien was validly
concluded, he was able to pass on his title to the Louvre. This third party
intervention prevents *restitutio in integrum* and thus bars annulment.[87]
Therefore the availability of a remedy for Célimène is dependent on an
interpretation of *Stewart* v. *Kennedy* which permits uninduced unilateral
mistake.

Spain

In the contract of sale Célimène made a mistake as to the essential
conditions of the subject matter, which were the main reason for the
contract. Célimène was unaware that there was a picture of great value
among the objects she was selling: this is a fundamental mistake which
comes under the second alternative in art. 1266.1 of the Civil Code.

As explained in Case 1 the excusable nature of the mistake is determined according to the following factors: (i) the diligence of the mistaken party *in concreto*, and the standard is less high when a layperson
contracts with an expert;[88] (ii) consideration must be given to whether
the other party collaborated in the mistake: the fraudulent or faulty
nature of that party's action is not an essential requisite.

---

[86] (1992) SLT 884.   [87] The Scottish term is 'reduction'.
[88] Supreme Court Ruling 4/1/82.

Clearly, on that basis, Damien did manoeuvre to bring the sale to fruition, intentionally concealing information known to him and in the knowledge that, had Célimène been aware of it, the contract would probably not have been made, at least not on the same conditions. While he did not contribute directly to the production of the mistake, he should have advised the seller of the information which he, as an expert in the field, had at the time when the contract was concluded (this may indeed amount to 'negative fraud' due to an omission).

On the other hand, given Célimène's personal circumstances, a high degree of diligence cannot be required since the information about the true value of the picture was not easily accessible to her. Added to this is that, as a non-expert in the field, she contracted with an antiques dealer who was fully aware of the true value of the painting, so that we must conclude that Célimène was the victim of an entirely excusable mistake.

Thus the requirements are met for Célimène's defective consent to be a cause for annulling the contract, pursuant to art. 1266 of the Civil Code. Célimène must bring the claim for annulment within four years, as provided for in art. 1301 of the Civil Code, which also establishes that time starts running from the moment when the contract was concluded.

Comparative observations

I – The salient features of this case, again concerning a mistake made by the seller in relation to the object of her sale, are as follows. There is a difference in the status of the contracting parties, one a professional with expertise in the field and the other a consumer, without specialist knowledge. The effects of the annulment of the contract for mistake, where mistake is operative, are conditioned by the protection of third party rights which have interfered in the initial sale. Furthermore, the non-mistaken party's behaviour (keeping silent about the object sold and paying twice the purchase price) are subject to a number of interpretations and inform us about different national laws' views about silence. Three possible remedies can be considered here, mistake, fraud/lack of good faith and variants of *laesio enormis*.

Mistake

There is a fundamental mistake here in Austria, Belgium, France, Germany, Greece, Italy, The Netherlands and Spain. Célimène can therefore ask for the contract to be annulled (or under Dutch law annul the contract herself) on this basis. As there is no ambiguity as to authorship and as the parties are in an unequal bargaining position, no bars will preclude Célimène from asking for judicial[89] annulment of the sale. In addition, the fact that Damien was aware of Célimène's mistake strengthens her case. As a consequence, no compensation or protection will be given to the non-mistaken party under Austrian, German or Greek law. The difficulties which arise will, therefore, be evidential (not substantial) and practical since the painting has now passed into the hands of a *bona fide* purchaser. All such legal systems (except for Portugal) have means to protect such a third party purchaser which means that in a majority of cases the consequences of the annulment will not be restitution *in integrum*. In France, Belgium, Italy, the Netherlands and Germany restitution of the subject matter of the sale is converted into its true monetary value, i.e. Damien will be ordered to pay the difference between the contract price and the real value of the painting to Célimène. In Austria, if the painting has been sold on, an alternative remedy to annulment lies in adapting the contract, namely obliging Damien to pay the higher price that he himself received. Again, the result is the same, despite the slightly different legal basis. It is submitted that in Greece, according to a somewhat controversial interpretation, if the annulled (void) contract of transfer of title is assimilated to a lost good, the rules protecting *bona fide* third party purchasers will not apply and Célimène will even be able to claim title over the painting itself. In the Netherlands, a similar solution as to the qualification of mistake itself is reached through a more causal analysis of mistake, namely that Damien should have informed Célimène as to the value of the painting. Conceptually this is a mistake, even though it overlaps with the next ground, since the duty to inform does not exist independently but is covered by both mistake and fraud.[90] In addition, even though mistake may be declared extra-judicially, Célimène may be obliged to go to court, thus making the solution converge even further, since if title has passed on to a third party, she will be entitled to restitution of the real value (which will be compensated in part with the price she received) and if Damien refuses to pay she will ask the court to order specific performance.

As for England, Ireland and Scotland, the legal analysis diverges. Under English and Irish law, the factual particularities have no bearing on the

---

[89] As stated, in the Netherlands, judicial annulment is not required.
[90] See introduction for an explanation of the different foundations of the duty to inform.

legal qualification, there is no mistake here just as in the previous case. The English view of mistake is certainly the most severe. In Scotland, however, there could be, according to a certain interpretation of case law, an essential unilateral uninduced error. In practice however, if such a mistake does not render the contract *nul ab initio* and where restitution is no longer possible since the property has been passed on to a third party purchaser, reduction or annulment is no longer an effective remedy. This seems to be an intermediate position since the equivalent of annulment cannot be converted into monetary restitution as under civil law.

Fraud/lack of good faith

For France, Belgium, Greece, Austria, Portugal fraudulent concealment of facts known by one party to be material to the other suffices to constitute a fraud by virtue of a case law interpretation of the provisions of the Civil Code on fraud. Silence by Damien who knew the true value of the painting gives rise to tortious liability on the basis of what could be called fraud by omission. A similar result can be obtained by an extensive interpretation of good faith provisions. It should be noted, for example, that under Portuguese law liability is implied not from the equivalent of fraud but from *culpa in contrahendo* and the duty to negotiate in good faith. However, the position in Italy is less certain as the case law on the point is sparse. An action in fraud gives rise to both annulment and damages but the remarks already made as to the effectiveness of a remedy in annulment apply, barring Portugal, which gives little protection to a third party in such a case and would consider that restitution *ad ante* is still possible. Likewise, in Norway, the solution can be assimilated with the above approach since a remedy would be available under § 33 of the Contract Act (and/or the more comprehensive § 36 of the same Act). As Célimène can prove that the contract is contrary to decency and good faith – the fact that Damien is a professional buyer dealing with a non-professional is decisive – she is entitled to ask for the contract to be annulled with restitution. However, the fact that the painting has passed into the hands of a *bona fide* purchaser means that restitution will be provided in its monetary equivalent. In addition compensation may be awarded; damages are meant to put the innocent party in the position she would have been had the contract not been made. Thus most reporters agree where both mistake and fraud are optional remedies, since fraud is easy to prove in these circumstances, it will be preferable as damages may be awarded as well.[91]

Conversely, in England, Ireland and Scotland, the law's view of silence is much more restrictive. There is no equivalent to fraud by omission. Damien's silence cannot be a ground for annulment and/or damages in the absence of a prior duty to disclose. Here a real divergence lies in the protection awarded to the victim of the other party's silence. It is somewhat difficult to give a satisfactory explanation of the unwilling-ness of the common law to protect such a victim although one could suggest that if the residue of the *caveat emptor* principle applies, *a fortiori caveat vendor*. In the same way, German law is more reluctant to impose a duty to disclose in these circumstances, a less extensive interpretation of § 242 BGB would apply under German law; absent a fiduciary relation-ship between the parties, there is no reason why Damien has acted con-trary to good faith and he should be able to benefit from his discovery. German law joins the common law position here, which may be expli-cable on the basis of underlying (and somewhat inexplicit) economic rationales.

Laesio enormis and unconscionability

Although a number of common law remedies may be invoked under the general heading of unconscionability, such as the rule in *Fry v. Lane* – sale by a poor and ignorant person under English law; snatching at a bargain – the rule in *Steuart Trs v. Hart* under Scottish law, in practice such a remedy is useless since it renders the contract voidable and once title has passed on into the hands of a third party, the contract is no longer capable of being annulled. In contrast, the remedy of *laesio enormis* may be successfully invoked under Austrian law as may qualified *lésion* under Belgian law. Greek law takes a similar view as the meaning given to immoral contracts coincides with the Roman law concept of *laesio enormis*. Conversely, German law will reject such an attempt, under § 138 I and II of the BGB, since once again a more economic analysis prevails: since Damien's behaviour has prevented Célimène from making a profit,

---

[91] On the additional question of damages for fraud, the conceptual evaluation of damages differs slightly. Under Austrian law, for example, the equivalent of 'reliance damages' may be recovered, namely reimbursement for expenditure incurred as if the contract were to be performed (§ 1874 ABGB). Whereas under French law, for example, the analysis varies: damages awarded on the basis of tortious liability compensate the victim for all the loss suffered as a result of the fraud (art. 1382 of the Civil Code).

as opposed to suffering a loss, which she would not have made except for his discovery, German law does not consider that Célimène can be deemed to have been exploited according to this doctrine.

II – Despite the similarities of legal analysis it is essentially the operation of a convergent legal bar, in the form of protection given to the *bona fide* third party purchaser for the object of the sale, which brings together the various different legal systems, but not always to the same conclusion. In the legal systems where there is a legal qualification of fundamental mistake it should be noted that the effectiveness of the remedy of retrospective annulment and restitution *in specie* is diminished as practically impossible. It is therefore possible to identify a similarity of outlook in relation to the limits of mistake; the protection of the mistaken party to what is essentially a unilateral mistake, does not prevail over the property rights of an innocent third party. However, differences may lie in the form in which restitution of the subject matter of the sale may be converted into monetary compensation. This possibility highlights the conceptual differences between annulment known to civil law systems and the void/voidable distinction known to the common law, since even where alternative remedies might lie in English and Scots law, on the basis of either unconscionability or snatching at a bargain, the material impossibility of awarding restitution, when a contract is voidable, precludes the operation of the remedy altogether.

More importantly, this case highlights a difference of outlook in relation to the parties' behaviour, status and in particular silence. Generous interpretations protecting the inexperienced seller given in a form of *laesio enormis*, under Austrian, Belgian and Greek law (see above), will treat severely the so-called exploitative behaviour of the buyer on this basis. Other systems resort to an extensive notion of mistake, fraud or lack of good faith to arrive at a similar, or even more generous result, since additionally, compensation may be granted. Obviously, the interpretation depends on its teleological aim (see, for example, German law's application of § 138 BGB). A divergence arises between systems protective of a deemed weaker party, whose interests are put to the forefront, and those which seem to prefer the research and discovery of economic values, albeit at an individual cost, where each party must bear the risks. The division between these competing values is not straightforward but arises out of a multiplicity of factors (legal theory, economic considerations etc.). In this case the national legal systems clearly do not all adopt one common legal value: priority given to economic considerations, or conversely, to protecting a party whose informational power (lack of expertise) does not match the other party's, highlights a clash in outlook. This can also be explained by a split in legal theory: some legal systems still cling to the idea (or the myth?) of contracting on equal footing (even if the parties are not, *de facto*, equal), while others admit this inequality and are more wary of how the stronger party can take advantage of the weaker.

It is interesting to note that the Italian and German reporters have made suggestions *de lege ferenda* that take us back to Roman law. If the rules relating to discovery are applied by analogy, maybe an intermediate solution would be the fairest (awarding half to both discoverer and owner). This is not, as yet, positive law!

Case 3

Emile v. Far Eastern Delights

Case

Far Eastern Delights, an ancient oriental art gallery, sold a Chinese statuette to Emile, an amateur art lover. The piece was described by Far Eastern Delights' catalogue as 'Tang dynasty, practically intact with very few restorations'. Emile has now discovered that the head and hands are in fact very recent, and that little remains of the original work. What remedy, if any, is available?

Discussions

Austria

(i) This case again covers a mistake as to the content of the contract (mistake as to the characteristics and qualities of the subject matter).

(a) On one view, there seems to be a common mistake to both parties, if it is considered that Far Eastern Delights did not know that the Chinese statuette sold had not been a pure and practically intact original statuette of the Tang Dynasty. This mistake common to both parties, however, is less problematic than in Case 1. As already described, the prevailing view and the unbroken line of authorities under which a common mistake is to be added to the cases named and recognised in § 871 ABGB and, therefore, entitles both parties to a right to annul or to adapt is criticised on the grounds that a mistake common to both parties does not fit with the system of § 871 ABGB which emphasises the importance of protecting the non-mistaken party since in case of a common mistake both parties are equally worthy to be protected. In Case 1 the parties are equal in that they both have more or less the same knowledge and business experience. Here however, the two parties are not equally worthy to be protected as the gallery is clearly a professional expert in ancient oriental art and Emile, an amateur art lover. Consequently and following the legal opinion of the minority, Emile is also entitled to annul or to adapt the contract respectively depending on whether the contract would not have been concluded at all or under other conditions (especially for another price) if the true and correct facts had been known.

(b) In this case the gallery is to be blamed for the mistake and the erroneous information given to Emile; if it should have noticed the true and correct value of the statuette because of its expertise, then Emile is entitled to damages under the *culpa in contrahendo* doctrine (see Case 2) in addition to the right to annul and adapt the contract for uninduced unilateral mistake. Recent case law has confirmed that liability for damages lies in cases of merely negligent as well as fraudulent misrepresentation.[1]

In the case of a contributory fault by Emile (where Emile could have noticed the mistake by using proper alertness and due diligence, therefore, being negligent himself) this might reduce the amount of the claim for damages against the gallery if it had not misled Emile on purpose (compare with Case 2).

(ii) The doctrine of the *laesio enormis* applies here as well. In the case the statuette was worth less than half the price paid, Emile is entitled to annul the contract. Far Eastern Delights, however, has the right and possibility to 'save' the contract – even against Emile's wishes – by paying the difference between the purchase price and the real value of the statuette.

Belgium

Four remedies are theoretically available to Emile. In spite of the variety of remedies available, chances for Emile to succeed appear as remote as in Case 1. The order of presentation chosen reflects the remedies least likely to succeed in increasing order.

(i) Emile could allege a breach of the statuette's conformity on delivery (art. 1604 of the Civil Code). This action is based on the obligation of the seller to deliver the thing in conformity with the contractual provisions.

---

[1] See generally Welser, *Das Verschulden bei Vertragsabschluß im Österreichischen Recht*, ÖJZ 1973, 281; Rummel in Rummel I Rz 2 to § 874; Koziol/Welser, p. 139; in contrast to on purpose only Gschnitzer in Klang IV/1, 145) and as to the latest case law (OGH SZ 48/102, SZ 49/94, SZ 51/26, JBl 1980, 316; the former case law recognised liability for damages only in the case of a mistake induced by a deliberate misrepresentation cf. OGH SZ 36/22.

Lack of conformity entitles the buyer to an action for termination of the contract with reciprocal restitution (art. 1610 of the Civil Code) and to any extra damages when the buyer incurred an additional detriment as a result of the non-conformity (art. 1611 of the Civil Code). Compared to an action based upon the seller's guarantee against hidden defects (see (ii), the action brought in non-conformity has two advantages: firstly, it entitles the buyer to total compensation for damages suffered, the seller's good or bad faith being non-significant in this respect; secondly, there is theoretically no time limit to bring this action before the court other than the limitation period of 30 years.[2] Here Emile could attempt to prove that the statuette delivered to him does not correspond to the thing agreed upon: an ancient statuette 'practically intact with very few restorations'.[3]

However, in spite of its attractions, lack of conformity does not give rise to many actions and case law awarding a remedy under this heading is rare.[4] The reason for this scarcity is explained by the crucial importance that Belgian law awards to the concept of approval or acceptance of the thing; such approval has the effect of barring actions based on lack of conformity.[5] Moreover, approval could amount to 'confirmation'[6] of a mistake or fraud, barring any action in annulment, if when Emile discovered the mistake he nonetheless tacitly approved the thing.[7] It is not

---

[2] A. Meinertzhagen-Limpens, 'La vente: erreur, non-conformité et vices cachés', no. 2. The prescription period for lack of conformity (ten years) is thus longer than the prescription period for an action brought in nullity.

[3] More precisely, Emile will have to demonstrate the non-conformity, the importance of additional damages and the causal relationship between the latter two: see Y. Merchiers and M.-F. De Pover, 'La vente – Les contrats spéciaux – Chronique de jurisprudence 1988–1995', Les dossiers du journal des tribunaux, no. 13, no. 44.

[4] Meinertzhagen-Limpens, 'La vente: erreur, non-conformité et vices cachés', no. 25 (case law as to non-conformity is far less important in terms of the number of decisions than case law centred on mistake or hidden defects).

[5] De Page, Traité élémentaire de droit civil belge, vol. IV, nos. 114, 128, 130 and 134. Approval may be express or tacit. See Merchiers and De Pover, 'La vente – Les contrats spéciaux', no. 42 (case law as to tacit approval). As to the time frontier between non-conformity and hidden defects through approval, see D. Deli, 'Afbakeningsproblemen tussen de vrijwaring voor verborgen gebreken en de niet-coforme levering bij het hanteren van een functioneel gebreksbegrip in de koop-verkoop', note under Gent, 24-6-1987, RW, 1987–8, p. 1363, at pp. 1366–7.

[6] Confirmation is the act, express or tacit, through which a person renounces unilaterally the right to avail oneself of a relative nullity (that is a cause of nullity that was created for the benefit of a protected party who may renounce to its benefit): see G. Cornu, Vocabulaire juridique (8th edn, Paris, 2000).

[7] Meinertzhagen-Limpens, 'La vente: erreur, non-conformité et vices cachés', no. 39 in fine; see also De Page, Traité élémentaire de droit civil belge, no. 134 (although this last edition seems to except fraud).

clear from the facts however, whether or not Emile did actually approve the thing: how long did he take before he actually protested about the restorations, did he 'use' the thing (i.e. did he exhibit it for some time in his house) etc.?

Moreover, a claim for non-conformity could be defended on the grounds that there was no non-conformity: Emile received the statuette he chose and saw in the gallery and not the one described in the catalogue.

(ii) The seller's guarantee against hidden defects, effective even after approval of the thing, is generally distinguished from an action based on fundamental mistake according to the nature of the defect. As far as mistake is concerned, the defect is extrinsic: it carries a subjective aspect inherent in the buyer's will as to the *specific* use he personally intends to make of the thing whereas the hidden defect is an intrinsic (sometimes referred to as structural) defect that affects the thing's so-called '*normal* use'.[8] This distinction became blurred once the *Cour de cassation* accepted the concept of 'functional defect' affecting the use that the purchaser intended, with the seller's knowledge, to make of the thing even if it does not intrinsically affect the thing.[9]

Should the restorations be considered an apparent or a hidden defect? A defect is considered apparent when it can be detected upon careful examination that a 'serious man' would devote to the affairs that are being dealt with by him.[10] If the restorations are to be considered apparent defects, Emile's case is weak if he has approved the statuette.[11] On the facts here, the outcome appears very doubtful for Emile: he might have been negligent in examining the statuette, especially since even if he is not a professional buyer, he is an amateur who is knowledgeable in the field.

[8] *Ibid.*, nos. 15–19.

[9] Cass, 18-11-1971, Pas, 1972, I, 258 (where a product, perfect in itself, could not stand up to the specific use, of which the seller was aware, that the buyer intended to make); Cass, 17-5-1984, RW, 1984–5, p. 2090, JT, 1984, p. 566, Pas, 1984, I, 1128; Comm. Charleroi, 12-04-1994, JLMB, 1995, 276 (where the concept of 'normal use' amounts, under a functional view of hidden defects, to the use that the buyer had in mind, provided that this specific use entered into the contractual field).

See H. Daco, 'Le régime des vices cachés' in H. Daco et al., *Unité et diversité du droit privé* (Brussels, 1983), pp. 498 ff. describing the evolution that led to the concept of 'functional defect'; P. A. Foriers, 'Les contrats commerciaux', RDCB, 1987, pp. 2 ff., nos. 60–2 (critical point of view on the notion of 'functional defect'); Meinertzhagen-Limpens,'La vente: erreur, non-conformité et vices cachés', nos. 33 ff.; Merchiers and De Pover, 'La vente – Les contrats spéciaux', no. 48.

[10] *Ibid.*, no. 201, Cass, 29-3-1976, Pas, 1976, I, 832.

[11] See D. Philippe, 'Les clauses relatives à la garantie des vices cachés', RGDC, 1996, pp. 173 ff., at no. 2.1.

In the alternative that the defects constitute a hidden, and not an apparent defect, four conditions must be complied with:[12] (a) the defect must impair the 'use' that the buyer can make of the thing. Here, Emile will have to prove that the use that he intended for the statuette is excluded by its having been recently restored. He might have a hard time in doing this, even with the help of the notion of a 'functional' defect (see above);[13] (b) the defect must be hidden, that is to say that it must not be apparent in the sense described above; (c) the defect must be of a certain importance (*De minimis non curat praetor*); and, (d) the defect must exist at the moment of the sale.

The burden of proof lies on the buyer and, thus, it appears that Emile might have serious difficulty in proving conditions (a) and (b). In a case decided by a court in Antwerp where a non-specialist buyer purchased antiques, that were delivered with a certificate of authenticity and of no-restoration, that actually appeared to be either from another (more recent) period or to have been restored, the court first held that the guarantee against hidden defects could work only if the restorations were not immediately visible to a normally careful buyer and then finally rejected the action on the grounds that the short time limit under art. 1648 of the Civil Code had expired.[14] In view of the harshness of such case law, where the facts were more favourable to the plaintiff than they are for Emile, the latter appears to have little chance to succeed.

(iii) The notion of fundamental mistake (under art. 1110 of the Civil Code) especially in the context of the sale of works of art has already been discussed in detail (see Case 1). Here Emile will have to prove that the absence of restorations was a decisive factor in his entering into the contract. Like Anatole, he might have difficulty over the issue of excusability: should he not have seen the restorations before the sale was concluded or should he not have refused to accept delivery of the thing especially when one considers that he has some knowledge in the field? It should also be pointed out that in a neighbouring sector, that

---

[12] De Page, *Traité élémentaire de droit civil belge*, no. 201.

[13] Fontaine, 'Les aspects juridiques', observes that the case law tends to reject actions on the basis of hidden defects in controversies pertaining to the authenticity of works of art.

[14] Antwerp, 20-1-1988, RGDC, 1990, p. 33 and note M. Dambre, 'Informatieplicht en actiemogelijkheden van partijen bij de aankoop van kunstvoorwerpen'; Antwerp, 3-1-1990, RGDC, 1993, p. 342 noted by W. De Bondt 'Over gedupeerde kopers, vervallen termijnen en teleurgestelde rechtzoekenden'.

is public sales of works of art, there is a usage stating that the buyer accepts (or assumes) the risk of mistake.[15]

(iv) As we have seen in Case 1, fraud is a useful avenue to explore in terms of remedies since it prevents, in principle, the issue of excusability from being raised. If Emile can prove that the seller intentionally deceived him in the catalogue, he might have a chance of succeeding.[16] However, Emile will probably have a hard time in proving that the seller's deceit was intentional simply by producing the latter's catalogue. Indeed, in the Antwerp case (see (ii) above) the court rejected the cause of action based on fraud, even though the seller was a professional antiques dealer, in the absence of satisfactory evidence that the seller's deceit was intentional ('conscious and voluntary').[17]

To conclude, the highest chance of success would be in an action based on fraud but the likelihood of success is not significantly higher, in our view, than in Case 1.

England

This situation is very different from Cases 1 and 2. Here, the seller makes a positive statement of fact which is inaccurate; and the buyer, rather than the seller, requires a remedy. Emile will consider a range of remedies arising out of the misrepresentation.

(i) Remedies for breach of contract, for which he must show that the statement of description was incorporated into the contract. He may show that there was an express guarantee in terms of the description – in establishing this, a court will ask whether the parties are to be taken to have intended this promise to be incorporated into the terms of the sale, and in this the fact that the seller is in a particularly favoured position to know the facts about what he is selling is relevant (although not conclusive).[18] Alternatively, if Emile can show that he bought the piece by reference to the description, it will (in the absence of stipulation to the contrary in the contract) be implied that there was a condition in the contract that the piece would comply with the description: Sale of

---

[15] Goux, 'L'erreur, le dol et la lésion qualifiée', no. 10; P. Van Ommeslaghe, 'Examen de jurisprudence', no. 15.

[16] See Fontaine, 'Les aspects juridiques', p. 407: if the seller consciously abused the buyer's incompetence to sell him a non-original work or if he deceived him on the basis of a false certificate, there is a cause of action on the basis of fraud.

[17] Antwerp, 20-1-1988, RGDC, 1990, p. 35.

[18] *Heilbut, Symons & Co.* v. *Buckleton* [1913] AC 30; *Dick Bentley Productions Ltd* v. *Harold Smith (Motors) Ltd* [1965] 1 WLR 623.

Goods Act 1979, s. 13. In such a case, Emile would be entitled to claim a reduction in the purchase price of the goods, or rescind the contract;[19] or reject the goods (as long as he has not yet 'accepted' them – a term which includes not only intimating to the seller that he accepts them in spite of the breach, but also the lapse of a reasonable time during which he could have examined the goods),[20] and sue for damages for breach of contract (or, if he preferred, just sue for damages). Damages in contract are calculated so as to protect the injured party's expectations: here, broadly, such a sum of money as would allow him to go into the market and obtain a piece equivalent to the one which Far Eastern Delights have failed to deliver.

(ii) Since the statement is a material misrepresentation on which he relied (or can be taken to have relied) Emile may be able to rescind the contract (the contract is *voidable* for misrepresentation). The fact that he *could* have discovered the truth will not limit this remedy, if he relied on Far Eastern Delights' statement. There are, however, restrictions on the remedy: here the most likely restriction is that of 'lapse of time' – the remedy is barred if Emile does not take steps to rescind the contract within a 'reasonable time'. The facts are not sufficiently clear to advise. We do not know how long it is since he bought the statuette (the notion of 'reasonable' time seems to be related to the idea that the misled party should have the time necessary to take steps to find out that the statement is false).[21] And even if some time has elapsed since the contract of purchase, Emile would still be entitled to rescind if he can show that the statement by Far Eastern Delights was fraudulent (that is, not made with an honest belief in its truth), since time cannot run against him in a case of fraud until he discovers the fraud (or, perhaps, ought to have discovered it, if it is by his fault that he failed to do so)[22] – again, we do not know the circumstances.

Emile might also consider seeking damages in tort for misrepresentation: these would not be calculated to fulfil his expectation

---

[19] Sale of Goods Act 1979, s. 48C (inserted by Sale and Supply of Goods to Consumers Regulations 2002, which implemented EC Directive 1999/44/EC on certain aspects of the sale of consumer goods and associated guarantees). A consumer buyer may require the seller to repair or replace goods which do not conform to the contract or, where those remedies are impossible or disproportionate, require a reduction in the purchase price or rescind the contract. These remedies are additional to the existing remedies for breach of contract (rejection of the goods and/or damages).

[20] Sale of Goods Act 1979, s. 35; *Bernstein v. Pamson Motors (Golders Green) Ltd.* [1987] 2 All ER 220. The timescale is unclear in the case of Emile and Far Eastern Delights.

[21] *Leaf v. International Galleries Ltd* [1950] 2 KB 86 at p. 91.

[22] *Armstrong v. Jackson* [1917] 2 KB 822 at p. 830; *Redgrave v. Hurd* (1881) 20 Ch D 1 at p. 13.

(as in a breach of contract), but to cover his losses: here, broadly, the diminution of his wealth as a result of entering into the contract to buy the actual, defective, statuette (and including any consequential out-of-pocket losses, such as fees paid to experts to establish the defects in description). Such a remedy can be obtained if he can show fraud on the part of Far Eastern Delights (the tort of deceit); or alternatively[23] under Misrepresentation Act 1967, s. 2(1), which imposes liability for pre-contractual statements without fraud, *except* where Far Eastern Delights can show that they had reasonable ground to believe, and did believe, the truth of the statements.

Emile must *choose* between remedies for breach of contract, on the one hand, and rescission/damages in tort on the other. His choice of remedy will depend, in part, on how favourable the contract would have been for him, had the representations about the statuette been true. If, on that basis, he had struck a good bargain, he is likely to prefer damages for breach of contract, since that gives him a higher measure to enable him to pay for a new, equivalent piece (although there is no requirement that he must so spend the damages once awarded). If it was a poor bargain, damages in tort (if he can establish a tort) are likely to be more favourable.

(iii) In accordance with the principles of mistake discussed above, in relation to Case 1, Emile will be able to rely on his mistake as to the qualities of the statuette only if there was no contractual provision governing the defects; and if he can show that Far Eastern Delights shared the mistake and that the defect was sufficiently fundamental to make the piece 'essentially and radically different' so as to render the contract void *ab initio*. There is no equivalent case: we are told that a contract for a horse believed to be sound but not in fact sound is not a sufficient mistake to render the contract void;[24] but there is a case where the purchase of a completely different quality of commodity was held to be sufficient.[25] It would be a question of fact for a judge to decide whether the mistake is sufficiently serious to pass the test, although in practice Emile would not rely on this remedy, since his claims for damages (and perhaps rejection) for breach of contract, or rescission and/or damages for the misrepresentation, are clearly adequate here.

---

[23] A cause of action in the tort of negligence is in practice not useful because the rules of the 1967 Act are here more favourable for Emile.

[24] *Bell v. Lever Bros.* [1932] AC 161 at p. 224.

[25] *Nicholson and Venn v. Smith Marriott* (1947) 177 LT 189: table linen sold at auction as being the property of King Charles I, although it was in fact Georgian; the main ground, though, was for breach of contract (misdescription).

The solution to this Case flows from the position taken by English law, discussed in relation to Case 1. Here, however, it is a case of *caveat emptor* since it is Emile, the buyer, who seeks a remedy. And the fact that Emile is an amateur, dealing with a professional, means that a court will tend to view him as more likely to be reliant on the seller (which is then shown in the legal rules for incorporation of the seller's statements into the contract).

France

Emile can first of all have the contract annulled by showing that he gave his consent by mistake (*erreur*) or fraud (*dol*). It is also necessary to consider whether he can seek termination (*résolution*) of the contract for hidden defects or for breach of non-conformity on the grounds of defective performance. Two potential causes of action are therefore available:

(i) Emile may be able to annul the contract on the grounds of mistake, the conditions of which have already been set out above and/or fraud.

(a) Mistake consists in believing true what is wrong and conversely.[26] Emile seems to have made such a mistake: he thought he was buying a Tang statuette almost intact and hardly restored whereas very little of the original work actually remained. Thus, there is a disparity between what Emile had imagined and the reality. However, things would be different if the catalogue had indicated that the statuette had been 'largely restored'. In such a case, Emile would be deemed to have accepted an uncertainty, which would have prevented him from invoking his own mistake (*L'aléa chasse l'erreur*).[27]

In order to succeed Emile will have to prove that he made a mistake and as already noted, the French courts have adopted a subjective view of substance.[28] Two potential obstacles remain, proving reliance on the mistake and that it induced consent. First, Emile must prove that he relied on the representation made by the seller (the catalogue). If he fails, the sale will not be annulled.[29] Secondly, he will have to prove that

---

[26] Ghestin, *Traité de droit civil*, no. 490, p. 455; F. Terré, P. Simler and Y. Lequette, *Les obligations* (8th edn, Paris, 2002), no. 208.

[27] Civ 1, 31 March 1987, Bull civ I, no. 115.

[28] Civ 1, 28 January 1913, S, 1913. 1. 487; Com, 20 October 1970, JCP 1971. II. 16916, note J. Ghestin. According to French legal theory, cf. R. J. Pothier, *Traité des obligations* (Paris, 1768), no. 18, for example, two interpretations of the concept of substance are possible; the first objective: the substance is the material from which the object is made. The second subjective: the substance is the main quality that the parties took into account when contracting. These two views can both coincide and diverge.

[29] For some examples, see Com, 20 October 1970, n. 33; Civ 1, 13 June 1967, Bull civ I, no. 215; Civ 3, 29 May 1970, D 1970.705.

the mistake induced his consent, that is to say, had he known that the statuette had been restored that much, he would not have contracted or would have contracted under different conditions. Emile will probably succeed on both these points if he refers to the gallery's catalogue. The latter indeed shows the characteristics of the statuette on which a buyer would reasonably have relied. However, Emile's success will depend on the interpretation of the facts by the trial courts.

Nonetheless, as seen in Case 1, the courts sometimes refuse to annul a contract when the buyer's mistake is inexcusable. The only issue which is controversial here is whether the mistake is the result of Emile's own negligence or thoughtlessness. Can Emile be blamed for not noticing at first sight that the statuette had been substantially restored or for failing to ask for more information? As already explained, in order to decide whether or not the mistake is excusable, judges will take into account the age, profession and knowledge of the buyer. In the present case, Emile is an art lover, and his mistake may therefore be considered inexcusable. On the other hand, even if Emile is an art lover, he is an amateur (consumer) dealing with a professional (the art gallery) and this fact may enable the courts to condone his mistake.

(b) Secondly, Emile may try to prove that the seller acted in bad faith, and especially that he made a fraudulent statement in the catalogue. This would enable him to bring an action under art. 1116 of the Civil Code.[30] There would be several advantages for Emile to claim fraud rather than mistake, as already seen. First, the former is easier to prove because it lacks the psychological aspect of the latter. Secondly, fraud enables remedies to be granted in cases of non-fundamental mistakes which do not normally lead to the contract's annulment. Thirdly, such an action would avoid discussion about the excusable nature of Emile's mistake. Last but not least, such a claim enables the plaintiff to be awarded damages in addition.

Emile has a fairly good chance of showing that the art gallery was liable in fraud. As already mentioned, the courts have interpreted the concept of fraudulent manoeuvres broadly: fraud can consist in a positive act (ploys or lies), or in an omission, as long as either is aimed at being misleading.[31] Thus, Emile can try to prove that the art gallery

---

[30] Article 1116: 'The contract can be cancelled for fraud when the behaviour of one party is such that, without this behaviour, the other party would not have contracted.' ('Le dol est une cause de nullité de la convention lorsque les manoeuvres pratiquées par l'une des parties sont telles, qu'il est évident que, sans ces manoeuvres, l'autre partie n'aurait pas contracté.')

[31] Civ 1, 10 July 1995, Rép. Def. 1995, 36210, no. 138, obs. J.-L. Aubert.

deliberately lied in the catalogue. A specialist in ancient oriental art, the latter, cannot possibly have not seen that the statuette had been restored. If Emile fails to prove that the gallery lied intentionally, in the alternative he may then plead that it committed fraudulent conceal-ment (*réticence dolosive*).[32] In the present case, the art gallery could be blamed for not informing Emile as to the extent of the restoration.

(ii) If Emile fails on either of the above-mentioned grounds, he may seek a remedy on the basis of the seller's defective performance.[33] He may well prefer to do so. The burden of proof is certainly less onerous but the choice is open to him only if he acts quickly (art. 1648 of the Civil Code). Under the law of sale two possible legal bases lie, on the grounds of arts. 1604 and 1641 of the Civil Code (see also Case 6).

First, Emile may allege a breach of the statuette's conformity on deliv-ery (art. 1604 of the Civil Code). Indeed, the statuette does not conform with the terms of the contract: little is left of the original work. The general rule is that the buyer can bring an action for non-performance within 30 years. However, in practice, conformity is checked much more quickly. The buyer has to accept or refuse the delivered goods at the place and time of delivery when possible, or after testing the goods.[34] In the case of non-conformity upon delivery, the buyer has a right to seek termination (*résolution*) of the contract (arts. 1184 and 1610 of the Civil Code).[35] It should be noted that under French law, termina-tion is retrospective and restores the parties to the position they were in before the contract was made.

(iii) In the alternative, Emile could try and make a claim under art. 1641 of the Civil Code (*garantie des vices cachés*) in respect of the seller's

---

[32] Civ 3, 15 January 1971, Bull civ III, no. 38: 'Fraud can result from the fact that a party hides to the other material fact in the knowledge of which the latter would not have contracted.'

[33] Concerning the distinction between mistake, latent defects and non-conforming delivery, see: J. Ghestin and B. Desché, *Traité des contrats, La vente* (Paris, 1990), pp. 818–56; Y.-M. Serinet, *Les régimes comparés des sanction de l'erreur, des vices cachés et de l'obligation de délivrance dans la vente* (thèse Paris I, 1996, 3 vols.).

[34] F. Collart-Dutilleul and P. Delebecque, *Contrats civils et commerciaux* (3rd edn, Paris, 1996).

[35] Article 1184: '. . . The aggrieved party can, at his choice, ask for specific performance when it is possible, or seek termination and damages.' ('. . . La partie envers laquelle l'engagement n'a point été exécuté, a le choix ou de forcer l'autre à l'exécution de la convention lorsqu'elle est possible, ou d'en demander la résolution avec dommages et intérêts.') Article 1610: 'If the seller fails to deliver within the agreed time, the buyer may, at his choice, seek termination or injunction if only the seller can be blamed for the delay.' ('Si le vendeur manque à faire la délivrance dans le temps convenu entre les parties, l'acquéreur pourra, à son choix, demander la résolution de la vente, ou sa mise en possession, si le retard ne vient que du fait du vendeur.')

guarantee against hidden defects.[36] To succeed, Emile must show that: (a) there is to be a hidden defect inherent in the goods, (b) the defect was not apparent but existed at the time of the sale, and (c) the defect made the goods improper for normal use. Moreover, Emile must bring the action within a short period of time (art. 1648 of the Civil Code). The redhibitory aspect of the defect will probably be the most difficult element to evaluate. In the present case, can the extent of the restorations make the statuette improper for its normal use? If it is to be a collector's item then the answer is yes. On the other hand, properly using a work of art may simply be a question of looking at it, but then, if the restorations are shocking to the observer because they appear at first sight, it follows that the defect is not latent, but apparent and Emile would be more successful invoking art. 1604 of the Civil Code.

Lastly, it should be noted that art. 1644 of the Civil Code[37] offers another remedy to Emile as the buyer, enabling him to keep the statuette and ask for a reduction of the price.

Germany

In contrast to the two previous cases this scenario deals with the situation where one party's performance diverges from what has been agreed in the contract. Therefore the first possible remedy which should be considered is Emile's guarantee claim that the goods are not of proper quality and fit for contractual use. Emile may choose termination of contract or reduction of the purchase price because repairing the statuette (according to § 439)[38] seems impossible.

(i) A claim to terminate the contract (§§ 437 Ziff 2, 440, 323, 326 I 3) or for a reduction of the purchase price (§§ 437 Ziff 2, 441) requires that the goods bought by Emile are defective. A defect can lie in the fact

---

[36] 'The seller is liable to guarantee if a latent defect in the goods sold makes it improper for its normal use, or alters this use so dramatically that the buyer, if aware of the defect, would not have bought the goods or would have bought it at a lower price.' ('Le vendeur est tenu de la garantie à raison des défauts cachés de la chose vendue qui la rendent impropre à l'usage auquel on la destine, ou qui diminuent tellement cet usage, que l'acheteur ne l'aurait pas acquise, ou n'en aurait donné qu'un moindre prix, s'il les avait connus.')

[37] Article 1644: 'Under arts. 1641 and 1643, the buyer can choose to give the goods back and be reimbursed, or to keep the goods and be reimbursed a part of the price . . .' ('Dans le cas des arts. 1641 et 1643, l'acheteur a la choix de rendre la chose et de se faire restituer le prix, ou de garder la chose et de se faire rendre une partie du prix . . .')

[38] The new regulation of warranty in the BGB (§§ 437 ff.) is accorded to the Directive 1999/44/EC (OJ 1999 L 171).

that the goods do not show the qualities agreed upon in the contract (§ 434 I).[39] The statuette was sold as a collector's item. The seller claimed in its catalogue that the item was a product of the Tang dynasty and preserved in its original condition. If it then turns out that the statuette was substantially made up of new parts then it will be at odds with the contractual description of its quality and therefore defective according to the subjective concept of a defect.[40]

Emile may therefore demand a reduction in the purchase price or termination of the contract. He is free to choose which of the two remedies to apply (§ 462) and – in accordance with modern opinion – may claim them immediately and without the seller's agreement.[41]

(ii) Emile may also demand damages for non-performance instead of the contract's termination or a reduction of the price, if the statuette lacks the special qualities guaranteed by the seller (§§ 437 Ziff 3, 440, 280 I, 276 I 1, 443). Up to now,[42] the assessment of warranties in the art trade has given rise to a great deal of controversy. Sometimes, the mere description of goods and a correspondingly high purchase price provided sufficient grounds to assume a warranted characteristic.[43] The BGH in its *Jawlensky* Decision[44] was of the opinion that including a picture in the catalogue of works by a certain artist may constitute an – implied – warranty as to a picture's origin. On the other hand, the BGH later[45] argued that the description of a painting as 'by the artist's hand' was insufficient to be regarded as a warranty relating to authenticity.

---

[39] According to the old § 459 it was discussed whether the sold good must be a 'defect' according to an objective or subjective standard; cf. for example, W. Flume, *Eigenschaftsirrtum und Kauf* (Münster, 1948), pp. 110 ff.; R. Knöpfle, *Der Fehler beim Kauf* (Berlin, 1989); Foerste, 'Der Fehlerbegriff im Kaufrecht' JuS 1994, 202; Palandt/Putzo, § 459 para. 8 ff.; Soergel/Huber, § 459 para. 32 ff.

[40] OLG Hamm NJW 1987, 1028: a grandfather clock had been sold as being '150–200 years old' but in fact it consisted – as the purchaser later found out – of substantially new replacement parts; OLG Karlsruhe NJW-RR 1993, 1138: in this case an 'original Harley Davidson' had been sold (but under the exclusion of warranty claims). The frame of the motorbike had been replaced without using an original Harley-Davidson component.

[41] Despite § 465 which expresses the theory of *contrarius consensus*.

[42] These and the following decisions circle around the old § 459 II, 463, but the problem (if special statements of the seller concerning the quality of the goods can be considered as a guarantee) will be the same according to the new law.

[43] OLG Frankfurt 1982, 651, 652 = EwiR § 463 BGB 1/93, 659 (with commentary, Braun); similarly ('echter Perser') OLG Koblenz MDR 1987, 322 und LG München NJW 1990, 1999.

[44] BGHZ 63, 369, 372 = NJW 1975, 970.

[45] In the second 'Burra-Entscheidung', BGH NJW 1995, 1673 = JZ 1995, 1015 (with commentary Braun) = LM § 459 BGB No. 124 (with commentary, Grunsky) = ZIP 1995,

However, the fact that the court was reluctant to impose liability to pay compensation in light of the common uncertainty surrounding the authenticity of paintings proved decisive for the judgment.[46] Thus, even in older judgments, a certain restraint was demanded when determining the existence of warranties in art trade transactions.[47]

Emile's case does not directly concern the authenticity of a work of art but rather the question as to whether the seller has given a guarantee that the item was in its substantially original state. To this extent, the case is comparable to warranties in the sale of used goods, in particular, the sale of road vehicles. Here statements of the seller concerning the age, condition and restoration measures undertaken are sufficient to be regarded as warranties relating to a characteristic because the (usually) inexperienced purchaser ought to be able to rely on the expertise of the road vehicle dealer.[48] Emile is also an 'amateur' and relies mainly on the statements of the seller (Far Eastern Delights), apparently a professional dealer in Asian artefacts. Thus, the description of the statuette as 'Tang Dynasty, practically intact with very few restorations' is not only a contractual agreement and as such decisive for the classification of a poor performance as 'defective' but is also a guarantee regarding a characteristic attributable to the object of sale. One may assume that Far Eastern Delights intended to assume a special liability relating to the statuette's condition.

Emile may therefore demand damages for non-performance together with the contract's termination or reduction in the purchase price (§ 437 Ziff 2 and 3 BGB). By so claiming, he may demand to be put in the same position as he would have been if the statuette had actually been only partially and diligently restored, as promised.[49] He may also demand lost profit (§ 252 BGB) if, for example, in the meantime he could have sold the statuette on at a profit.

(iii) According to leading German academic opinion,[50] annulment of the contract for mistake relating to a substantial quality (§ 119 II)

---

570. Cf. also the first 'Burra-Entscheidung' in NJW 1993, 2103; for a critical summary see C. Hattenhauer, JuS 1998, 186 ff.

[46] BGH NJW 1995, 1674 = JZ 1995, 1017.

[47] RGZ 114, 239, 241; BGHZ 63, 669, 372; BGH NJW 1980, 1619.

[48] A good overview of this is offered by: Staudinger/Honsell, § 459 para. 158 f.

[49] Cf. Palandt/Putzo, § 463 para. 14.

[50] Herrschende Meinung; vgl. nur Flume, *Eigenschaftsirrtum*, pp. 132 ff.; Flume, AT II, pp. 484 ff.; D. Medicus, *Allgemeiner Teil des BGB. Ein Lehrbuch* (6., neubearb. Aufl., Heidelberg, 1994), Rz. 775; Larenz/Wolf, AT 691; Soergel/Huber, Vor § 459 Rz. 187 ff.; MüKo/Kramer, § 119 Rz. 33 ff.; MüKo/Westermann, § 459 Rz. 74; Staudinger/Honsell, Vor

is excluded due to the fact that Emile may enforce warranty claims against the seller (see above at pp. 175–6). Because the legal provisions on warranties are regarded as *leges speciales* in contrast to the law on mistake, annulment of the contract on grounds of mistake ought not to play a role here.[51] The main argument in this regard has been that the seller should be secure from claims of the buyer when the 6-months' period for warranties on moveables had expired. This argument, however, will fall away according to the new law on warranties, which provides a 2-years' period for claims of the buyer (§ 438 I 3).

(iv) The contract may be void on the grounds of fraudulent misrepresentation (§ 123) if it is understood that Far Eastern Delights made incorrect assertions relating to the statuette knowingly and with the intention to cause Emile to enter into the contract.

Greece

(i) Both the contract of sale (art. 513 AK) and the contract of transfer by which the ownership of the statuette was transferred to Emile (art. 1034 AK) can be annulled for mistake. Emile's declaration of will was the result of a fundamental mistake as to quality (art. 142 AK). The two criteria, objective and subjective, are present here. Emile's mistake is objectively fundamental as the statuette's actual quality is of importance for the whole contract. It is not necessary to show that the parties expressly agreed on the quality of the statuette as a term of the contract. It suffices that parties tacitly agreed on the specific quality or it may be inferred from the preceding negotiations of the parties.[52] Here it must be accepted that the condition of the statuette as practically intact has been agreed by the parties. As to the fundamental criterion of mistake it is clear that Emile would not have made the sale had he known of the true situation. The objective difference in value between the object as agreed, a statuette practically intact, and the actual statuette favours recognising the subjective fundamental aspect of Emile's

---

§ 459 Rz. 23 und § 459 Rz. 19; Staudinger/Dilcher, § 119 Rz. 62 ff.; RGRK/Krüger-Nieland, § 119 Rz. 62 ff.; AK/Hart, § 119 Rz. 31; Erman/Brox, § 119 Rz. 6 und 19.

[51] Fundamentally, BGHZ 34, 32. Now critical however J. Wasmuth, 'Wider das Dogma vom Vorrang der Sachmängelhaftung gegenüber der Anfechtung wegen Eigenschaftsirrtums' in W. Erdmann, W. Gloy, R. Herbe (eds.), *FS für Henning Piper* (Munich, 1996), pp. 1083 ff.; P. Huber, *Irrtumsanfechtung und Sachmängelhaftung* (Tübingen, 2001).

[52] Spyridakis, *General Principles* p. 598; Georgiadis, *General Principles of Civil Law*, p. 426; see also Papachristou AK 141–142 n. 5 III.

mistake.[53] Article 145 AK providing for the compensation (negative interest) of the other party is not applicable if it is proved that Far Eastern Delights knew or should have known of Emile's mistake, that is of the inaccuracy of their own statement.

(ii) The contracts may also be annulled on the grounds of fraud practised by the gallery[54] (art. 147 AK). The fact that Far Eastern Delights were specialised in ancient oriental art would help Emile prove the gallery's fraud. The defendant however can rebut the allegation if it can prove that it believed that its statement as to the statuette's qualities was true. Fraud occurs with the purpose of creating an erroneous impression. It is obvious that Far Eastern Delights made fraudulent representations in order to induce future purchasers to enter into the sale of the statuette.

If the court accepts mistake or fraud, the contracts are reversed retrospectively and with effects *in rem* (art. 184 AK). The ownership transferred by the annulled contract reverts *ipso jure* to Far Eastern Delights. The purchase price will be sought by Emile on the basis of unjust enrichment (arts. 904 ff. AK). If the contracts are annulled on the grounds of fraud, Far Eastern Delights will be liable in damages under the general tort provisions (art. 149 subpara 1 AK). According to the prevailing view,[55] the damages will be for the negative interest suffered as a result of relying on the conduct of the other party, for example the expenses, e.g. fees Emile has incurred to conclude the sale.

(iii) The gallery is also strictly liable for the lack of agreed qualities of the thing sold (art. 535 AK). A quality is agreed not only in the case of an express agreement of the parties but also when it is concluded that the parties attached a particular importance to a specific quality.[56] The description or advertisement of the quality of the thing does not suffice.[57] Whether such an agreement exists is a matter of interpretation

---

[53] *Bailas*, 'Error as to the Qualities of a Thing', pp. 352, 353.

[54] It is assumed that Far Eastern Delights is a legal person. The fraud as well as other subjective factors which have been committed by one of its agents are judged by the person of the agent (arts. 68 § 2, 214 AK by analogy).

[55] See for example Karakatsanis AK 149 nn. 4, 5; K. Asprogerakas-Grivas, *General Principles of Civil Law* (Athens-Komotini, 1981), p. 322; Papantoniou, *General Principles of Civil Law*, p. 413.

[56] I. Deliyiannis and P. Kornilakis, *Law of Obligations. Special Part I* (Thessaloniki, 1992), p. 199; Stathopoulos, *Contract Law in Hellas*, p. 221; Klavanidou, *Error as to the Qualities of the Thing in Sales*, p. 76; contra Ef of Thessaloniki 138/1978 Arm 32 (1978), p. 228; K. Kafkas, *Law of Obligations. Special Part* (7th edn, Thessaloniki, 1993) arts. 534–5 § 11.

[57] Ef of Athens 9057/1986 Dni 28, 1285; Deliyiannis and Kornilakis, *Law of Obligations*, p. 199; P. Filios, *Law of Obligations. Special Part* (Athens, 1997), vol. 1/1, § 5 BII; Stathopoulos, *Contract Law in Hellas*, p. 221.

of the contract which will be solved on the basis of generally accepted views as to the purpose of the contract.[58] Emile can seek termination of the sale, a remedy similar to annulling the contract,[59] or the reduction of the purchase price, or damages for non-performance if the vendor is at fault. The damages (for the so-called positive interest) aim to put Emile in the position in which he would have been if the defect had not existed.[60]

Ireland

In this case Emile would have a remedy under Irish law. There has been an inaccurate statement of fact as to the condition of the statuette which misled Emile into purchasing the piece. Emile has a remedy for breach of contract. He relied on an express guarantee relating to the description of the statuette. The statement is more than a 'mere puff'. In addition, Emile has a remedy in Irish law under s. 10 of the Sale of Goods and Supply of Services Act 1980 where goods purchased fail to match the description of those goods. Under the statutory provisions, Emile has the remedy of suing for damages for breach of contract or avoiding the contract by rejecting the goods – *O'Connor v. Donnelly*.[61]

Emile also has a further remedy for misrepresentation. Under this head, he has the option of rescinding the contract as he relied on the misrepresentation. Like English law, Irish law requires that he should take steps to rescind the contract within a reasonable time. However, if he can show that the statement by Far Eastern Delights was a fraudulent one, he is entitled to rescind at any time once he discovers the fraudulent nature of the statement. It is also possible for Emile to seek damages under the tort of misrepresentation to cover the losses sustained by him as a result of the misrepresentation. Once again, it would be necessary for Emile to show fraud on the part of Far Eastern Delights.

Unlike Northern Ireland, there is no Misrepresentation Act in Ireland. Accordingly, the position in relation to misrepresentation is governed by the common law. As in England, Irish law requires that Emile should choose his remedy for breach of contract on the one hand or rescission and damages in tort on the other. Under the heading of mistake,

---

[58] Deliyiannis and Kornilakis, *Law of Obligations*, p. 199; Stathopoulos, *Contract Law in Hellas*, p. 221.

[59] Restitution has the consequence that the purchaser must return the thing and the vendor the purchase price.

[60] On the question of whether Emile can choose between defects of consent provisions and remedies for breach of contract, see Case 7.

[61] (1944) IR Jur Rep 1.

the contract is rendered void *ab initio* at common law if the mistake as to the quality of the statuette was deemed sufficiently serious and such mistake was shared by both parties. Under the last stringent criteria governing the equitable jurisdiction of the courts, the court might regard the mistake as to quality not to be so fundamental as to render the contract void *ab initio* at common law but sufficiently serious to render it voidable under equitable principles.

Italy

Emile has several actions against Far Eastern Delights under Italian law: two for defects of consent (mistake and fraud); three for non-performance of contract (guarantee against latent defects, lack of quality and impossibility).

(i) We are faced with mistake as to the quality of the said object (art. 1429 n. 2 of the Civil Code) and the fact that Far Eastern Delights is a professional dealer (there is a difference in the parties' status) will easily enable the court to consider the mistake recognisable (*riconoscibile*).[62] Emile's excusability is not an issue here.

(ii) Far Eastern Delights' statement should not have been 'the statuette is partially restored', but 'some parts are original': we are facing a typical situation of fraud (art. 1439 of the Civil Code) see Case 2. The simple falsity of a statement is considered *dolus malus* and will provoke the annulment of the contract.[63] A very interesting case is given by a decision involving the glorious and unlucky Torino Football Club: the purchase of a season ticket was annulled because of fraud, when the club president's declaration that a certain player would not be sold to another club, turned out to be false.[64] When fraud generates a fundamental mistake the plaintiff could be better off choosing mistake instead of fraud. The objective evidence of mistake is easier to adduce than the psychological evidence of fraud.[65]

Far Eastern Delights could, however, argue that 'partially restored' was not a false statement but a '*dolus bonus*' normally used in those kind of transactions. It must prove that the collectors are cautious of the seller's

---

[62] Pietrobon, *Errore, voluntà e affidamento*, pp. 220 ff.

[63] Cass 1996, n. 1955; Cass 1993, n. 10718; Cass 6.12.1984, n. 6409; Cass S Lav 22.12.1983, n. 7572; Cass 17.10.1969 e Cass 30.10.1969, n. 3609 entrambe in GI 1972, I, 1, 456; Cass 8.10.1955 n. 2925 all repeat the following 'even simple falsity provokes the annulment of contract for fraud when, considering the subjective condition of the party to whom it has been said, it is sufficient to deceive him'.

[64] Cass 26.1.1995, n. 975.   [65] Bianca, *Il contratto*, p. 628.

statements in this kind of business.[66] In *Manifatture Spugne* v. *Intermarittima* the Supreme Court said that in order to decide if there is fraud, the silence or concealment by one party must be considered according to the subjective conditions of the other.[67] In that case both parties were experienced business people and the court found no fraud, while in our case Emile seems to be a naive collector. Some authors think that the area for *dolus bonus* is losing ground following the idea that art. 1337 of the Civil Code and European legislation concerning misleading advertisements are enhancing the degree of intolerance towards any kind of falsity, even the slightest one.[68]

(iii) There is a guarantee against hidden defects in the thing sold. Article 1490 of the Civil Code states '[a] seller is bound to warrant that the thing sold is free of defects which . . . appreciably diminish its value' (*Garanzia per i vizi della cosa*). The Italian Supreme Court considers that the factual situation in which 'the quality of the thing or the characteristics giving it the value'[69] are lacking constitutes a standard case of breach of guarantee and because of that reason the object of the contract 'within the same kind of goods will belong to a lower type of it'.[70] In the case of breach, the buyer has to prove that the goods do not have the promised qualities; there is no need to demonstrate any fraudulent behaviour or negligence. Emile can at his choice demand termination of the contract (art. 1453 of the Civil Code) or reduction of the price; the buyer forfeits the right if he fails to notify the seller of the defects within eight days after discovering them.

(iv) Another way to terminate the contract is to prove that the restored statuette is a completely different object from a 'practically intact statue'. In this case Emile will claim that the statute lacks a fundamental quality (*Mancanza delle qualità essenziali*),[71] according to art. 1497 of the Civil Code

---

[66] Cass 1996 n. 3001 and Cass 1960 n. 2119; S. Gentilini, 'Dolus Malus' in *Enciclopedia Giuridica Treccani* (Rome, 1990), at p. 347 and F. Carresi, 'Il Contratto' in A. Cicu, F. Messineo and L. Mengoni (eds.), *Trattato di Diritto Civile e Commerciale* (Milan, 1987), at p. 109.

[67] Cass 12.1.1991, n. 257.

[68] Sacco and De Nova, 'Il contratto', pp. 436 ff.; Funaioli, I, *Enc. Giuridica Treccani*.

[69] Cass 1970, n. 2544.   [70] Cass 1982, n. 1839.

[71] Article 1497 Lack of quality: 'When the thing sold lacks the qualities promised or those essential for the use for which it is intended, the buyer is entitled to obtain termination of the contract according to the general provisions on termination for non-performance (art. 1453 ff.), provided that the defect in quality exceeds the limits of tolerance established by usage.'

However, the right to obtain termination is subject to forfeiture (2964 ff., 1495 co.1) and prescription (2946 ff., 1495 co.3) established in art. 1495.

this is tantamount to the adage *aliud pro alio*. The difference between this action and the previous one is considered irrelevant both by the courts and legal scholars.[72] Far Eastern Delights will try to bar the claim using the argument that the limit of tolerance (*limite di tolleranza*) has expired, but the facts will be decisive.[73] For example, in *Automega s.p.a.* v. *Pezzillo*, the Tribunale, the Court of Appeal of Palermo and finally the Italian Supreme Court[74] considered that the sale of a 'Mercedes Benz 190 with full options' was defective for a lack of quality since the air conditioning was not an original Mercedes option and had been installed in Palermo.

Actions to annul the contract, based on defective consent (arts. 1441–6 of the Civil Code) and actions based on non-performance (arts. 1490 and 1495 of the Civil Code) are independent and can be concurrent on the same facts.[75] As to which action is preferable, factors relating to evidence (fraud is harder to prove) and prescription (5 years for defective consent; time runs from the discovery of the defect; 8 days to notify the seller after discovery of the defect, in any event within one year after the sale) are relevant.

The Netherlands

Far Eastern Delights made statements that turned out to be untrue. If these statements made Emile buy the statuette for the price Far Eastern Delights asked for it – in other words: if Emile would not have bought this statuette for this price had he known that the statuette was in fact not 'practically intact with very few restorations' – there is a causal link between these statements and the mistake under which Emile has concluded the contract.

(i) In case the conclusion of a contract was caused by mistake (*dwaling*) and 'if the mistake is imputable to information given by the other party', the contract may be annulled by the mistaken party (art. 6:228 BW). Emile may, at his choice, annul the contract in or out of court (art. 3:49 BW). The annulment has retrospective effect (art. 3:53 BW) which leads to the retrospective cancelling of the transfer of property: Emile has never become owner (for lack of title: art. 3:84 BW) whereas the payment made by Emile was, with hindsight, undue and he can

---

[72] Cass 1981, n. 247; Cass 1969, n. 3695; Cass 1967, n. 2488; S. Rubino, 'La Compravendita' in A. Cicu, F. Messineo and L. Mengoni (eds.), *Trattato di Diritto Civile e Commerciale* (Milan, 1962), at p. 187; Bianca, *Il contratto*, p. 589.

[73] Cass 1995, n. 3550; Cass 1977, n. 4923.

[74] Trib. Palermo, 7.10.1989; A. Palermo, 7.06.1991; Cass 25.3.1995, n. 3550.

[75] Cass 1968, n. 1573.

therefore claim his money back (6:203 BW). The annulment may be avoided by Far Eastern Delights proposing a sufficient adaptation of the price. Cf. art. 6:230 BW, s. 1:[76]

The power to annul a contract on the basis of arts. 228 and 229 shall be extinguished when the other party in good time proposes to modify the effects of the contract which adequately removes the detriment which the person entitled to annul the contract would suffer by continuing the contract.

On the other hand Emile himself may, instead of annulling the contract, ask for a price reduction. Cf. art. 6:230 BW, s. 2: 'Furthermore, instead of pronouncing annulment the court may, upon the demand of one of the parties, modify the effects of the contract to remove the detriment.'

(ii) From the statement of facts it is not clear whether Far Eastern Delights knew that the statements they made were untrue. If they did Emile may also annul the contract for fraud (*bedrog*). See art. 6:44 BW:[77]

1. A juridical act may be annulled when it has been entered into as a result of threat, fraud or abuse of circumstances. (. . .) 3. A person who induces another to execute a certain contract by intentionally providing him with inaccurate information, by intentionally concealing any fact he was obliged to communicate, or by any other artifice, commits fraud. Representations in general terms, even if they are untrue, do not as such constitute fraud.

If Emile chooses this remedy he will have to establish that Far Eastern Delights gave the wrong information on purpose, which may be difficult. He may have an interest in doing so if he has suffered additional damage which would not be compensated by merely annulling the contract. If fraud is established a claim for damages in tort will easily be accepted since fraud, in principle, constitutes an 'unlawful act' in the sense of art. 6:162 BW, the general tort clause.[78] Another difference between mistake and fraud is that art. 3:44 BW does not contain a provision similar to the second section of art. 6:228 BW. This means that the possibility to annul a contract for fraud cannot be limited on the ground that 'given

---

[76] Cf. on art. 6:230 BW: M. W. Hesselink, 'Vragen bij de toepassing van artikel 6:230 BW', (1995) WPNR 6191–6192, pp. 541–5; 563–7; M. E. M. G. Peletier, *Rechterlijke vrijheid en partij-autonomie* (diss. VU) (The Hague, 1999), pp. 23ff., and *Verbintenissenrecht* (Hesselink), art. 230, with further references.

[77] See on fraud in general Asser/Hartkamp II (2001), nos. 199 ff.; *Vermogensrecht* (Hijma), art. 44; *Rechtshandeling en Overeenkomst* (Van Dam) (2nd edn, Deventer, 1998), pp. 208 ff., and on fraud in sales contracts Asser/Hijma 5-I (2001), nos. 253 ff.

[78] Cf. Asser/Hartkamp II (2001), no. 204; Asser/Hijma 5-I (2001), nos. 253 ff.

the nature of the contract, common opinion or the circumstances of the case, the party in error should remain accountable for its mistake'.

If fraud is established, the effects are similar to those of mistake. However, there is a difference: Far Eastern Delights cannot avoid the annulment by proposing a sufficient price adaptation: with regard to fraud there is no provision similar to art. 6:230 BW. The reason is that the legislator thought it would be unacceptable that a party should be obliged to remain in a contractual relationship with a fraudulent party.[79] Most authors are not convinced by this argument and favour application of art. 6:230 BW to fraud by way of analogy.[80]

(iii) Far Eastern Delights did not give Emile what they promised. Although they gave him the statuette which he had contracted for this statuette did not have the qualities Emile was entitled to expect. Emile was entitled to expect the qualities described in the catalogue.[81] There-fore there is a case of non-conformity (art. 7:17 BW).[82] Non-conformity constitutes a breach of contract which gives Emile all the specific reme-dies for consumer sales, sales in general, synallagmatic contracts, con-tracts in general and obligations (art. 7:22 BW), i.e. specific performance, repair, replacement, right to withhold performance, termination and damages.[83]

Norway

The Far Eastern Delights catalogue gave an inaccurate description of the statuette which had been sold. When a mistake about the contract offer is created by the other party, one would, in Scandinavian law, consider the situation as a breach of contract. There is a breach of the seller's legal duty to provide correct information about the object for sale. This duty is purely objective and is not dependent on the seller's fault.

This duty can (also) be seen as deriving from a principle of interpreta-tion. A contract is entered into based on the actual information given.[84]

---

[79] *Parlementaire Geschiedenis, Boek 6*, p. 914 (MvA II).

[80] Cf. Asser/Hartkamp II (2001), no. 481 and *Verbintenissenrecht* (Hesselink), art. 230, no. 36, with further references.

[81] Cf. Asser/Hijma 5-I (2001), no. 338.

[82] See art. 7:17 BW: '1. The thing delivered must conform to the contract. 2. A thing does not conform to the contract if it does not possess the qualities which the buyer was entitled to expect on the basis of the contract. The buyer may expect that the thing possesses the qualities necessary for its normal use, the existence of which is not open to doubt, and the qualities necessary for any special use provided in the contract. (. . .)'

[83] Cf. Asser/Hijma 5-I (2001), nos. 272 ff.

[84] Kai Krüger admittedly assumes that the misled person can only demand that the reliance loss be returned in such cases; see K. Krüger, *Norsk kontraktsrett* (Bergen, 1989),

Whether the seller should have realised that the information was misleading is irrelevant.

For Far Eastern Delights to be responsible for the contents listed in its catalogue, the assumption is either that it has provided the information itself, that the information has been provided on behalf of the firm, or that the information has been given by an earlier supplier.[85] The misleading information represents a significant defect in the objet d'art, and gives the purchaser the right to terminate the contract. Together with the termination of contract, the purchaser can also demand compensation. This presupposes, however, that there is a basis of liability for compensatory damages. If the seller ought to have known that the information given was inaccurate, the purchaser can demand that his full economic loss be covered (the expectation loss). Further, according to Norwegian and Swedish law, directly related losses can be claimed on an objective basis, the so-called 'control liability'.[86]

Portugal

(i) This case concerns the question of defects in the thing sold. According to Portuguese law (arts. 913° and 905° of the Civil Code), if the thing sold has some kind of defect which diminishes its value or prevents it from fulfilling its purpose, it does not have the qualities guaranteed by the seller and the contract is voidable on the grounds of mistake or fraud. So the same rules referred to in the previous case would apply, and Emile would be entitled to annul the contract. However, the defect must be communicated to the seller within thirty days after the buyer has discovered it and at the utmost within six months after delivery (art. 916° of the Civil Code). This provision, criticised by a number of scholars, includes an action which looks like a remedy for non-performance under the head of defects of consent. The justification for such a conceptual oddity lies in the fact that the seller is obliged to sell specific goods, if the goods are defective this affects the buyer's consent constituting a defect of consent. In case of fraud, Far Eastern Delights would also have to compensate Emile for the loss he has suffered as a

---

p. 296, and K. Krüger, *Norsk kjøpsrett* (3rd edn, Bergen, 1991), p. 120. However, this does not express the prevailing opinion.

[85] The Norwegian Sale of Goods Act, § 18, and the Swedish Sale of Goods Act, § 18. In Danish law, we find the same regulation in the Sale of Goods Act, § 76, regarding consumer sales.

[86] The Norwegian Sale of Goods Act, § 40(1) and the Swedish Sale of Goods Act, § 40, which is an implementation of CISG, art. 79.

result of the purchase (arts. 908° and 913° of the Civil Code). If there is no fraud, but only mistake, according to art. 915° of the Civil Code, Emile can still ask for damages (*damnum emergens*) but not for his losses (*lucrum cessans*), and damages would not be available if Far Eastern Delights was not at fault, in being unaware of the kind of defect in the statuette. In other words compensation is limited to the negative interest suffered by Emile.

(ii) If circumstances show that without mistake or fraud, Emile would have still acquired the statuette, but for a reduced price, he would not be entitled to annul the contract, but only to ask the court for the reduction of the price (arts. 913° and 911° of the Civil Code).

Scotland

In Cases 1 and 2, we have been concerned with uninduced mistake. When a mistake has been induced by an operative misrepresentation, the contract can be annulled even though it is an error in motive and does not go to the root of the contract, i.e. it is not essential.[87] Before a party can have a contract annulled on the ground of misrepresentation, the misrepresentation must be operative. To be operative the following criteria have to be satisfied: (i) the statement must have been made by the other party to the contract or his agent; (ii) the statement must be an inaccurate statement of fact. Where a mistake has been induced by a material misrepresentation, the contract can be rescinded; *restitutio in integrum* must be possible.

In the problem, the description in the catalogue is a false statement of fact. If Emile was in fact induced to purchase the statuette because of the description in the catalogue, then the misrepresentation is operative, as a mistake as to the quality of the object is clearly material. Emile can therefore have the contract annulled and recover the price. If the statement has been incorporated as a term of the contract, Emile could elect to keep the statuette and sue for breach of contract and recover the value of an original work.

If the statement was made negligently or fraudulently, in addition to rescission (should he so elect), Emile has an action for damages in delict: rescission is not a condition for a claim in damages. There is no claim for damages in delict if the misrepresentor honestly believed that what he was saying was true: *Boyd & Forrest* v. *Glasgow & S W Railway Co.*[88]

---

[87] *Stewart* v. *Kennedy* (1890) 17 R (HL)1; *Menzies* v. *Menzies* (1893) 20 R (HL) 108.
[88] (1915) SC (HL) 20.

Spain

(i) In cataloguing the item, the gallery (Far Eastern Delights) must have examined it and should have been aware that it had undergone major repairs. This is a case of deception or fraud by Far Eastern Delights, and Emile would be protected by the right to annul the sale contract due to defective consent based on that fraud (art. 1301 of the Civil Code). As already pointed out, fraud is not presumed and Emile must prove the deception, by adducing the catalogue and the evidence of the repairs to the statuette if the claim for annulment of the contract is to succeed.

(ii) In addition, and alternatively, Emile may also bring a claim for guarantee against hidden defects *actio redhibitoria* or *quanti minoris* as a result of latent defects in the acquired object (art. 1486 of the Civil Code) making the object unsuitable for its intended use, or diminishing such a use. These claims, which place a reduced burden of proof on the buyer, are subject to a 6-month limitation period (art. 1490 of the Civil Code): if they are successful, the object and price are returned or the price is reduced.

Comparative observations

In this classic example of sale of a work of art (false description of the subject matter in a professional's catalogue, ambiguity as to whether the seller knew of its falsity or not) to a non-professional buyer, the overlapping remedies for defective consent and/or breach of contract are highlighted.

Defective consent

In Austria, Belgium, France, Greece, Italy, Portugal and the Netherlands an action may lie for a fundamental mistake as to the quality of the subject matter entitling the buyer to annul the contract. Again, the legal analyses may vary – for example under French law the mistake is fundamental according to a subjective view of substance, whereas under Greek law an objective criterion – the importance of the quality according to the agreement of the parties – is also satisfied. The bar rendering a mistake inexcusable (in Belgium, France, Greece, and Italy for example) will probably not operate here since the mistaken party is a consumer, albeit with some amateur expertise in the field, dealing with a professional. Under Portuguese law the action appears to be a special category of mistake with more restrictive time limits for the buyer. In contrast Germany will not admit mistake because of the application of *lex specialis* concerning the law of sales.

Under Austrian law the mistake could be analysed as common to both parties, although this interpretation infers that the seller honestly believed that the content of its catalogue description was true. (If this is not the case, a remedy will still lie for unilateral mistake without compensation to the non-mistaken party as the conditions of art. 871 ABGB are fulfilled.) Likewise, under English, Scots and Irish law, precisely because the mistake is shared and not unilateral, a fundamental mistake may be admitted if it renders the statuette 'essentially and radically different' from that contracted for. Two conceptions of mistake may apply, a common law fundamental mistake which renders the contract void *ab initio*, which could be appropriate here or possibly, according to the Irish reporter, an equitable mistake making the contract voidable. However, it should be noticed that in practice, under English, Scots and Irish law, Emile is unlikely to pursue his claim on this basis since other easier and more adequate remedies lie.

Moreover, this case illustrates a divergent conceptual analysis in relation to mistake which reveals somewhat unexpected results. Misrepresentation clearly does not correspond to a positive duty to inform since it does not remedy a neutral (non-fraudulent) failure to disclose. Nonetheless, it would appear to bridge the gap between civil law and common law mistake; whereas the former is widely admitted, the latter is not. Applying this analysis to the facts, were it proved that the seller honestly believed that the contents of the catalogue were true, fraud would no longer be a possible route (see below p. 190) and Emile would have to rely on mistake. Under English, Irish and Scots law however, Emile would not rely on mistake but would choose rather to rely on innocent misrepresentation that would entitle him to annulment of the contract (absent operative bars) and/or damages.[89] If a misrepresentee claims damages in tort as well as annulling the contract, he will obtain restitution of the price paid (the immediate consequence of the annulment) as well as tort damages for additional consequential damages. In the event that the court awards damages in lieu under s. 2(2) of the Misrepresentation Act, instead of annulment, it is submitted that this remedy resembles the civil law monetary equivalent of restitution granted where restitution

---

[89] Under Irish law, damages cannot be awarded as an alternative to annulment since there is no Misrepresentation Act. Under English and Scots law, s. 2(2) of the Misrepresentation Act provides for such a technical remedy, termed 'damages in lieu', which allows the courts to award damages instead of annulment by exercising their discretion.

in integrum is no longer possible. These functional similarities indicate that the conceptual civil law/common law gap in relation to mistake is not as wide in practice as is often assumed.

If the seller's behaviour is interpreted as being fraudulent, then remedies will lie for fraud and fraudulent misrepresentation. Under this head the solutions are similar both in appearance and effect. Under English, Irish and Scots law, Emile could make a claim based on fraudulent misrepresentation. As stated, misrepresentation renders the contract voidable, time bars will not preclude annulment provided that action is taken within a reasonable time of discovery of the fraud. Damages are calculated on a tortious basis to cover losses, i.e. the price paid for the defective statuette and consequential losses, such as expenditure incurred to establish its defectiveness (experts' fees etc.).

On the basis of a Civil Code provision as to fraud (Austria, Belgium, France, Germany, Greece, Italy, the Netherlands, Portugal, and Spain) or by a case law extension of fraudulent concealment (e.g. France, Belgium) the seller could be held liable for failure of a duty to inform. Another means of arriving at a similar result can be achieved by treating the seller's behaviour as in breach of good faith on the basis of *culpa in contrahendo* (Austria, Portugal, Greece). As we have seen an action in fraud normally circumvents any allegations of the mistaken party's inexcusable behaviour, except if, under Austrian law, for example, Emile were held contributorily negligent (for failing to detect the extent of the restoration) which would thus diminish the amount of his damages.

Breach of contract remedies involve a guarantee against hidden defects and non-conformity with the description or lack of agreed quality

In some countries, such as France, Belgium, Italy and Spain, a claim may be brought under the contract of sale for breach of the guarantee against hidden defects.[90] Obstacles arising under this head are both procedural – the short time limit and on the facts substantial – it may be both difficult to prove that the goods are not fit for its normal usage and indeed that the defects are hidden.

An alternative remedy for breach of contract lies in France, Belgium, Greece, the Netherlands, Italy and Germany, under the heading of non-conformity on delivery or lack of an agreed quality respectively and in

---

[90] Notice that the Directive 1999/44/EC which, when transposed will change the answer here to some extent, has not been considered by the majority of the reporters, with the exception of Germany, since the Directive's provisions had not been transposed into national law at the date of writing the reports.

England and Scotland under breach of description – s. 13 Sale of Goods Act 1979 for the United Kingdom.[91] The operative bars are quite similar, the buyer will lose the right once the goods have been accepted. Belgium has a fairly severe attitude towards acceptance or approval, which means in practice this ground is rarely used. In Italy the seller can likewise raise the defence of 'limit of tolerance' to bar the claim which has arisen as a result of the principle of good faith contained in art. 1337 of the Civil Code which provides that contracts must be performed in good faith. If the goods have not been accepted, a claim can be made for both termination and damages. It should be pointed out that termination is retrospective in Austria, Belgium, France, Germany, Greece, Italy, Norway,[92] Portugal and Spain but not in England, Ireland, Scotland and the Netherlands. In the alternative, the buyer can ask for a reduction of the price (France, Greece, Portugal, the Netherlands, Germany) or the seller can offer to adapt the contract in certain circumstances (Germany, the Netherlands). Contractual damages will put the buyer in the position he would have been had the contract been performed, i.e. by an award of a sum of money enabling him to buy an equivalent statuette to the one promised but not delivered (the 'expectation interest').

The solution given in Norwegian law must be included in the above breach of contract remedies. Far Eastern Delights' inaccurate catalogue description could be analysed as a breach of a duty to disclose accurate information about the sale which enables Emile, the buyer to terminate the contract and claim damages provided that the seller ought to have known that the information given was inaccurate. This contractual remedy is distinct from a duty to inform which is imposed upon formation of the contract. It overlaps, therefore, with the precontractual duty to inform developed in some civil law countries, such as France, and the other contractual remedies which may be available elsewhere. A similar remedy would lie in England and Scotland if it were proved that the statement of description was incorporated into the contract which thus constituted an express guarantee.

The countries converge as to the choice of available remedies. In fact, the solutions are highly similar, the differences lie not in substance but in practice. Some of the practical reasons as to whether one remedy is preferable to another are thus emphasised. Two obvious factors may influence the injured party's choice: first, the procedural difficulties of

---

[91] In Ireland, the relevant statute is s. 10 of the Sale of Goods and Supply of Services Act 1980.

[92] Under Norwegian law, if restitution in kind is impossible, the creditor can normally only claim termination for the future.

short time limits, evidential obstacles, such as proving fraud or a party's subjective mistake; second, the crucial question of damages. If a claim is brought on one of the grounds of defective consent, damages will be tortious whereas on the grounds of breach of contract, contractual measures apply. The question of which measure is preferable will obviously depend on whether the buyer's bargain is a good or bad one.[93] It must be emphasised however that in Germany, which stands on its own here, the buyer cannot exercise a choice of remedy since the application of the *lex specialis* argument to the Code's provisions to remedies for breach of contract (and particularly warranties concerning the goods' characteristics) means that such remedies are exclusive. Nevertheless, in case of fraudulent misrepresentation by Far Eastern Delights the *lex specialis* argument would not apply and the contract would be void.

At the end of the day, the conceptual differences in legal nature of mistake – unilateral, shared or common, subjective/objective – have little bearing on the solution. Here the common core in terms of the solution is clearly identifiable.

---

[93] It is obvious that the buyer has made a bad bargain as he will have paid too much for the statuette.

Case 4

Mr and Mrs Timeless v. Mr and Mrs Careless

Case

Just as Mr and Mrs Timeless were ready to sign the contract of sale as purchasers, the vendors, Mr and Mrs Careless, found out that the right of way at the bottom of the garden had been varied by permission of the local authority to allow motor vehicles a right of way through the woods. One of the main attractions of the house and garden for Mr and Mrs Timeless was the quiet adjoining woods at the bottom of the garden. Anxious, however, to complete the sale Mr and Mrs Careless omitted to inform Mr and Mrs Timeless of the variation. After moving in Mr and Mrs Timeless complain of the substantial noise caused by vehicles crossing the woods. What remedy, if any, is available against Mr and Mrs Careless?

Discussions

Austria

(i) Mr and Mrs Timeless are entitled to annul the contract of sale for fraudulent misrepresentation in accordance with § 870 ABGB. Four cumulative conditions must be satisfied: (a) one of the parties has made a mistake, (b) there must be fraudulent intent of the non-mistaken party, (c) such intent causes the mistake, and (d) the misleading act is unlawful.

If one of the parties has been fraudulent in order to conclude the contract it is not necessary to differentiate the type of mistake. Both mistakes, as to the content of the contract and as to motive apply. Furthermore, the mistaken party is entitled to annul the contract even if the mistake is non-fundamental. In this case the purchasers are mistaken about the fact that the land is charged by a right of way. The vendors, aware of the mistake before the sale is concluded, have omitted to inform the purchasers. This behaviour has certainly induced Mr and Mrs Timeless to contract, as the main attraction of the house and the garden for them was the quietness of the adjoining woods and they would probably not have contracted, or at least not on these conditions, if they had been properly informed about the true facts. Withholding information can only be seen as unlawful where there is a breach of the duty to inform.[1] The existence of such a duty can be presumed, according to scholarly opinion and case law, if the party may expect proper disclosure under generally accepted business standards. In the case of contracts of sale, only minimal requirements are generally assumed in order to give the contracting parties the possibility to look after their own interests. The duty to inform, however, will always be assumed if and when the nature of the subject matter of the contract is concerned.[2] Concealing conditions that are relevant and important to the other party in order to induce them to contract can be seen as illegally misleading them. It also can be assumed that this was an intentional concealment in order not to put the conclusion of the contract at risk, since the vendors were perfectly aware that the quietness of the woods was important for the purchasers. Therefore, this can be seen as a fraudulent intention in accordance with § 870 ABGB. Instead of annulling, Mr and Mrs Timeless are also entitled to amend and adapt the contract,[3] i.e. to adapt the contract as it would have been concluded if the parties had known of the true facts. Such an adaptation of the contract, however, can only take place if the fraudulent party would also have concluded the contract under those changed circumstances.[4] To what extent the mistaken party can oppose the contract being adapted is examined according to the standards of an honest business party.[5] The mistaken party must prove the fraud and seek annulment or adaptation in court. The limitation is thirty years from the date of the contract.

(ii) Mr and Mrs Timeless can also claim for damages under § 874 ABGB which states that the person who has induced a contract with

---

[1] Dazu/Bydlinsi, 'Über lsitges Schweigen beim Vergtragsabschluß', JBl 1980, 383.
[2] OGH 2.5.1963 ÖRZ 1963, 154; OGH 26.5.1964 SZ 37/76; OGH 20.3.1968 SZ 41/33; OGH 23.12.1970 MietSlg 22069.
[3] OGH 21.3.1991 EvBl 1991/68.
[4] Gschnitzer in Klang IV/1 114, 136, 143; Iro, JBl 1974, 233; OGH 27.4.1976 SZ 49/56.
[5] OGH 10.7.1986 SZ 59/126.

fraudulent intent is liable for the disadvantageous consequences. Mr and Mrs Timeless are, therefore, entitled to damages arising out of the contract, that is the loss incurred by their relying on the contract. These damages will include expenditure which would not have been necessary had proper disclosure been made, such as the cost of making the contract. The gravity of Mr and Mrs Careless' fault is taken into account to assess the extent of their liability. In the case of fraud they are also liable for loss of profit (*lucrum cesssans*), such as missing the opportunity to conclude another contract.

(iii) Mr and Mrs Timeless also have a concurrent claim to terminate the contract for breach of a guarantee against defects in accordance with § 932 ABGB. Mr and Mrs Timeless have the right to choose between these two available remedies. In case they base their claim on a guarantee, they are entitled to terminate the contract *ex tunc*.

The following conditions must be met: (a) a material defect or defect as to title must have existed when the goods were transferred, (b) the relevance and importance of the defect must be proved, and (c) the defect was irremediable.

A defect of title is only operative if the seller does not transfer the legal title to the buyer. Mr and Mrs Careless are liable by the contract to transfer the property to Mr and Mrs Timeless, subject to an easement, the right of way. In fact, this easement had been varied. This is definitely a limitation on title as agreed in the contract of sale and, therefore, title is defective. This defective title already existed when the property was transferred, as the permission of the local authority had already been given and existed prior to the contract's conclusion. The defect (as to material or as to title) is important if and when it does not allow the proper and ordinary use of the goods. This is examined according to generally accepted business standards or by the actual contract. Restrictions of the right of way are to be seen as an important defect and the defect is clearly irremediable as the local authority has already granted permission for vehicles to use the road. As all the conditions are met Mr and Mrs Timeless are entitled to terminate on this ground. According to the former prevailing scholarly opinion[6] it was not possible to ask for a price reduction instead of termination in the case of an important and irremediable defect. It was feared that the uselessness of the goods could lead to a very considerable price reduction that could not be demanded

---

[6] Gschnitzer in Klang IV/1, 535.

of the seller. Present scholarly opinion and case law, however, allow the price to be reduced insofar as the defective good is still of some value to the buyer.[7] A claim to terminate the contract or for a reduction in the price must be made before the courts within three years of the contract.

(iv) In addition to termination, Mr and Mrs Timeless can also claim damages in accordance with § 1295 ABGB on account of the material defects. The concurrence of actions for a claim in damages and for a guarantee was not accepted by the former prevailing scholarly opinion[8] and case law[9] by arguing that the seller had not caused the defects innocently or fraudulently. The present view and case law[10] offer the buyer the choice of these two remedies. Here, however, as the defect is irremediable, only a claim for reliance damages on the basis of breach of a duty to inform lies (see above pp. 194–5).

Belgium

Two remedies are available to Mr and Mrs Timeless and they have a fairly good chance of succeeding under either of these remedies.

A claim lies for fundamental mistake (art. 1110 of the Civil Code), moreover here the mistake can also be considered a mistake of law. A mistake of law can be defined as a lack of knowledge and/or false opinion as to the existence and/or the meaning and/or the applicability of rules pertaining to the law, that influenced the *errans'* behaviour and led or contributed to a result that was not wanted by the *errans*.[11] Nowadays, the same rules apply to mistakes of law[12] and so-called mistakes

---

[7] Jabornegg, JBl 1976, 184; OGH 14.2.1991 SZ64/15.   [8] Gschnitzer in Klang IV/1, 547.

[9] OGH 4.4.1973 SZ46/39; OGH 30.4.1975 SZ 48/56, JBl 1975, 600.

[10] Welser, JBl 1976, 127; (1974); R. Welser, *Schadensersatz statt Gewährleistung. Konsequenzen aus der neueren Judikatur* (Vienna, 1994) OGH 7.3.1990 JBl 1990, 648. If the defect is remediable, a claim in damages lies for non-performance of the contract.

[11] B. Bouckaert, 'Verdwaald in de jungle van de wet. Biedt rechtsdwaling een uitkomst?', TPR 1993, pp. 1347 ff., at p. 1354.

[12] Thus, for instance, a mistake of law must also be excusable in order to allow the annulment of the contract. Bouckaert, *ibid.*, pp. 1377 ff.: see for instance Cass, 23-1-1984, Pas, 1984, I, 560; Cass, 31-10-1994, RW, 1994-5, p. 1122, Pas, 1994, I, 879 (an admissible mistake of law is a mistake that would have been made by any other reasonable and prudent person placed in the same situation, the fact that this person had been badly informed, even by a qualified person, is not enough to constitute in itself an admissible mistake of law). For examples of mistakes of law coming close to the Timeless case, see Bouckaert (pp. 1389–90): purchase of land in the false belief that a building permit could be obtained from the authorities; purchase of land in the false belief that a right of way-out is attached thereto.

of fact, with the result that the distinction has become irrelevant.[13] So we shall focus on the relevant case law dealing with the most comparable factual situations to those here without paying attention to the fact that they concern a mistake of law. There are several recent cases where a fundamental mistake was admitted, provided that the quality 'entered into the contractual field' (see Case 1). Here the quietness of the property (as guaranteed by the absence of a right of way for motor vehicles) could be considered to be such a quality. Case law has admitted a mistake as to quality (*qualité substantielle*) in cases for the sale of land where for example, land was stated to be developable land on the basis of a certificate delivered by the planning authority that was revoked after completion of the notarised contract.[14] Or where, after signing a preliminary contract for a holiday chalet, the purchaser learned, upon reading the draft notarised contract that the property was sold as forest land without planning permission for the chalet.[15] Or in the sale of developable land on a housing estate where the building permission had expired, thus preventing the purchasers from obtaining new permission.[16] In this case, the purchasers were also awarded damages for costs incurred.[17]

The purchasers' mistake must however be excusable and this is probably Mr and Mrs Timeless' weak point since in another case where the building permission had expired the court held that the purchaser's mistake was not excusable, he should have known this.[18]

The requirement for the mistake to be excusable implies that the court will take into account the obligation of the aggrieved party to inform himself in the circumstances of the case.[19] Therefore, there is a risk that a court might hold that Mr and Mrs Timeless should have checked as to the nature of the right of way on the property themselves. However, the mistake would be considered excusable if the right

---

[13] Bouckaert, 'Verdwaald in de jungle van de wet. Biedt rechtsdwaling een uitkomst?', TPR, 1993, no. 3, p. 1354.

[14] Antwerp, 22-2-1989, T. not., 1990, p. 27.   [15] Mons, 17-3-1998, RGDC 1999, p. 197.

[16] Civ Namur, 4-12-97, Amén. 1998, p. 165 and note O. Jamar.

[17] If damages are awarded as well as annulment, this is on the basis of tortious liability under art. 1382 of the Civil Code, see Case 1.

[18] Gand, 25-4-1997, T. not. 1998, p. 148: perhaps the court's decision was influenced by the circumstance that the transfer of property contained a no-guarantee clause as to the developable nature of the land sold. For another example, see Antwerp, 12-11-1996, AJT 1997–8, p. 41. where an enterprise purchased land on an agricultural zone (and erected a building without permission). The purchasers' mistake was not excusable.

[19] See Goux, 'L'erreur, le dol et la lésion qualifiée', no. 12.

of way was changed shortly before completion of the notarised contract (as the facts suggest), since it was then not materially possible for Mr and Mrs Timeless to find out about this change. Finally, it must be ascertained if the buyers did not incidentally confirm the mistake (see Case 3) with the effect of barring their action to annul the contract: such confirmation could occur if they continued to behave as the owners of the property after they were put on notice of the existence of the problem.[20]

(ii) As already pointed out (see Case 1), the issue of excusability will normally[21] not be raised if Mr and Mrs Timeless bring their action under the head of fraud (art. 1116 of the Civil Code). There is some case law where fraud has been held to exist and the sale annulled in circumstances that can be compared to the present one. For example, in the sale of property where the seller abstained from mentioning the existence of a registered lease;[22] or in the sale of a French fries-snack place where the seller did not inform the purchaser that, by virtue of an earlier court decision, the place had to be rendered in spotlessly clean condition;[23] or in the sale of a business where the seller did not mention the existence of a non-terminated commercial lease, the court expressly ruled out the possibility for the seller to plead the purchaser's negligence to excuse his own behaviour.[24]

To conclude, Mr and Mrs Timeless have a good chance of obtaining satisfaction, fraud being the best remedy that allows them to circumvent the issue of excusability.

---

[20] See Civ Namur, 27-5-1993, Rev. not. b. 1995, p. 308: the buyer was mistaken about the content of the immovable property that he purchased but his action to annul was dismissed, the nullity having been cured by the fact that he continued to behave as the owner of the property after he knew about this.

[21] The word 'normally' is used because the decisions of trial courts are not always consistent with the position of the *Cour de cassation*: see, for instance, Civ Hasselt, 3-10-1989, RGDC 1990, p. 367: building land was purchased with the intent to build thereon but the land was improper due to the exploitation of a mine, the court held, against the assertion of fraud of the seller who did not inform the buyer about this peculiarity of the land sold, that the purchaser's mistake was not excusable because he could easily have ascertained himself the state of the thing. In our view, the court could have avoided the use of the excusability criterion merely by holding that the elements constituting fraud were not fulfilled here (i.e. that there was no obligation of the seller to speak; the state of the land being obvious).

[22] Brussels, 5-4-1993, JT 1993, p. 667. It is significant here that the court complied with the position of the *Cour de cassation* as to exclusion of the issue of excusability: the lease being registered by a public authority, the buyer could have ascertained its existence.

[23] Antwerp, 1-4-1992, RW 1994–5, p. 783.   [24] Mons, 10-2-1992, JT 1992, p. 777.

England

There are two possible issues here. If the 'right of way at the bottom of the garden' is over *adjoining land*, and not over the land itself being purchased, the mistake is only as to the quietness of the location. However, the mistake may be about the extent of a right of way over the purchased land itself, which raises an issue of a mistake about the rights purchased (it is difficult to see how in English law such a change to a right of way could come about on the facts stated, but the case will be discussed on the basis that Mr and Mrs Timeless are purchasers of land burdened with the obligation of a right of way greater in extent, and therefore in substance of a different kind, than they had believed).

In both cases, Mr and Mrs Timeless have no remedy against the vendors[25] in the absence of breach of contractual warranty or misrepresentation (neither of which is clear on the facts). Following the principles set out in Case 1 (which are not specific to contracts for the sale of goods, but also in general extend to contracts for the sale of land):

(i) they have a *contractual remedy* only if they can show that there was a promise in the contract that is broken by virtue of the changed circumstances relating to the use of the right of way. There are no grounds for any such promise being implied here (no statutory provision, for example) and so an express promise must be found. It is therefore a question of fact as to what was in the documents by which the contract was formed (a contract for the sale of land must be in writing, containing all the expressly agreed terms.[26]) It is common in practice for contracts for the sale of land to be on, or to incorporate, standard terms; however, the standard terms currently published do not include any term which would cover the case of a mistake as to the quietness of the location. The question is therefore whether any reference to the right of way and its impact on the quality of the land being purchased was included as a particular term of the contract. If it was (although this seems unlikely) Mr and Mrs Timeless would have a remedy in damages. However, if the mistake is about the terms of the right of way over the land sold, it is more likely that this would form the basis of a term in the contract, since it is common for contracts to affirm that the land is sold subject only to specified third party rights.

---

[25] They may, though, have a remedy against those responsible for causing the noise: this would depend on establishing a claim in the tort of nuisance, which protects a landowner against unreasonable interference with the exercise of his rights of ownership.

[26] Law of Property (Miscellaneous Provisions) Act 1989, s. 2(1).

(ii) they have a remedy in *misrepresentation* only if they can show a statement, made by the vendors (or their agents), which is false. Although it is unlikely that any statement would have been made about the quietness of the location, the information which is customarily asked of sellers of land by purchasers[27] does include questions about such things as rights of way over the land being sold; there may well therefore have been a statement made about the extent of the right of way. If such a statement was made here, it will have been made innocently, and perhaps when it was still true. But by the time of the contract, it had certainly become false, to the knowledge of the vendors. A precontractual statement is regarded as continuing up to the time of the contract, and (at least where the party making the statement *knows* of the change of circumstances) giving rise to an obligation to inform the other party that the statement is no longer true.[28] The vendors here did not correct their earlier statement (if made), and so would be liable to remedies for misrepresentation: rescission of the contract, and/or damages in tort (either in the tort of deceit or under the Misrepresentation Act 1967, s. 2(1), as discussed in relation to Case 3). The fact that the contract has been performed by the execution of the conveyance of the land is not of itself a bar to rescission.[29]

(iii) there is no sufficient *mistake* here, following the rules for mistake set out in relation to Case 1. At the time of the contract, the vendors had discovered the problem, and so the mistake was unilateral, and not shared. The mistake about the quietness of the location is a mistake only of the quality of the subject matter of the contract, not as to the terms of the contract; and on the facts given there is nothing to suggest that the mistake about the rights in the land purchased would be a mistake as to the *terms* of the contract. No remedy is therefore available unless a misrepresentation can be found: the *caveat emptor* rule applies.[30]

The general principles here are similar to those in Case 1. The fact that the contract is for the purchase of land, rather than goods, does not change the general principles, although the practical solution may have different elements. Whereas in relation to contracts for the sale of goods there are some statutory provisions which allocate risks (for example, as regards the quality of goods, under Sale of Goods Act 1979,

---

[27] National Conveyancing Protocol of the Law Society (4th edn, London, 2001).
[28] *With v. O'Flanagan* [1936] Ch 575.   [29] Misrepresentation Act 1967, s. 1(b).
[30] *William Sindall plc v. Cambridgeshire County Council* [1994] 1 WLR 1016 at p. 1035.

s. 14) there are no such general provisions for land contracts, and the general rule of *caveat emptor* is strictly applied. All therefore depends on the statements made by the vendors before the contract was concluded, and on the terms of the contract itself.

However, the importance and frequency of land transactions has led to the development of standard conveyancing procedures (including standard questions to be asked of sellers)[31] and standard terms which are used by practitioners as the basis of contracts for the sale of land, at least in the case of routine domestic land contracts. The current standard form of contract is the Law Society's Standard Conditions of Sale (4th edn, 2003), which does not reverse the allocation of risks in a case such as that of Mr and Mrs Timeless' mistake as to the quietness of the location, although the standard questions and standard forms of contract do cover such issues as the right of way over the land being purchased.

France

The purchasers may try to have the contract annulled for defective consent as well as damages on the basis that the sellers are liable in tort. First of all, it should be underlined that the fact that the house is no longer in a quiet residence could be analysed as a mistake of law (concerning the legal nature of the right of way) or a mistake as to the quality of the land sold. As far as a mistake of law is concerned, French law generally assimilates this to a mistake of fact.[32] Such a mistake can therefore lead to the contract being annulled. In relation to the attributes or quality of the land sold, two legal bases may be invoked: fraud and mistake as to the substantial qualities of the subject matter of the contract.

(i) First, the purchasers may avoid the sale on the grounds of fraud and more precisely, fraudulent concealment.[33] As we have already seen they will have to prove that the sellers voluntarily kept silent (the material requirement) about subjectively material facts (the psychological requirement) in order to induce them to enter into the contract for the sale of the house and the garden (the intentional requirement). Therefore, provided that it was legitimate for them to have been unaware of this information,[34] the purchasers may be able to annul the sale under

---

[31] National Conveyancing Protocol of the Law Society.

[32] Ghestin, *Formation du contrat*, no. 505, p. 469. An exception exists for settlements (*transactions*).

[33] See Case 2.

[34] Cf. Fabre-Magnan, *De l'obligation d'information dans les contrats* (1992), no. 253, pp. 197 ff.

art. 1116 of the Civil Code. Indeed, the *Cour de Cassation* has recently granted such a remedy in a case similar to the facts here.[35]

However, the whole question will depend on whether or not the buyers' reliance on the sellers' attitude was legitimate, in other words, was a duty to disclose incumbent upon the latter? Was the information available to the public at large or only to the sellers? If the former, for example the road was a public highway, arguably it was not (objectively) legitimate for the buyers to have trusted the sellers since they could and should have made the necessary enquiries about the right of way. If, however, only the sellers as owners of the property had access to the information (without investigating further as to why this might be the case), the purchasers would have a much greater chance of succeeding with their claim. All these variables boil down to questions of fact, to be assessed by the trial courts, and the solution is, therefore, unpredictable. As explained above, concealing material information is qualified under French law as a fault (*faute*) which gives rise to an action for damages on the ground of tortious liability under art. 1382 of the Civil Code. If the two claims were made simultaneously, the purchasers might also obtain the reimbursement of the expenses incurred in order to enter into the now annulled contract. If the purchasers were only success- ful under the second head, the action in tort would enable them to be compensated for the loss resulting from the failure of the expected quality.

(ii) Another ground for annulling the contract may be mistake. The purchasers will thus have to prove that, for them, the missing qual- ity (the quietness of the wood at the back of the garden) was essential and material to their entering into the contract, and that this mate- riality had been agreed upon by the parties and had thus become a term of the contract. They will also have to prove that the mistake was excusable.

Germany

The central question in this case is whether the quiet adjoining woods that Mr and Mrs Timeless expected are contractually stipulated in some form or other. If this is so, then warranty claims could be considered

---

[35] Civ 3, 20 December 1995, Bull civ II, no. 268, Cont. Conc. Cons., 1995, no. 55, obs. L. Leveneur, about the silence kept by the sellers of a flat about the existence of a possible adjoining construction project; comp. Civ 1, 13 February 1967, Bull civ I, no. 58, about the concealment of a project to enlarge a road.

which would exclude annulment on the grounds of § 119 II BGB[36] or claims under *culpa in contrahendo* (§§ 311 II, 241 II BGB, 280 I).[37]

(i) In order to claim termination of the contract (§§ 437 Ziff 2, 440, 323, 326 I 3 BGB) or a reduction in the purchase price (§§ 437 Ziff 2, 441 BGB), Mr and Mrs Timeless must prove that the house purchased is defective because it does not possess a warranted characteristic. It does not matter whether there is a defect in characteristic of the land sold (*Sachmangel*) or a defect in legal title (*Rechtsmangel*), both forms of defect give rise to the same legal consequences (§§ 437, 434, 435 BGB). New law does not distinguish the type of defects; it only concentrates on the question of whether the land comes up to the terms of the contract. In addition, if Mr and Mrs Careless have acted negligently, Mr and Mrs Timeless can also claim damages for breach of contract.

Applying objective criteria, the house which has been sold to the purchasers is not defective simply because the road in its vicinity is being used. It can still be occupied. Therefore, the house could be considered 'subjectively' defective[38] with regard to the contract. The 'quiet surroundings' were not however made a particular 'precondition' of the contract but the amount of the sale price agreed could point to such contractual preconditions. This is unclear on the facts. According to Flume certain characteristics of the object of sale are deemed to have been agreed if they are referred to in the contract.[39] The fact that the sellers feared that the purchasers would not enter into the contract if they became aware of the new circumstances indicates that here the contract made explicit reference to the particularly quiet situation of the property.

The courts have also adopted Flume's opinion.[40] In the case of BGHZ 34, 32 on a similar set of facts, the courts clearly had no difficulty in holding there to be a problem relating to warranty.[41] More recently the *BGH* has expressly held even those characteristics as contractually agreed

---

[36] See Case 3.

[37] Only the seller's *dolus in contrahendo* gives the purchaser an individual claim for compensation of negative interest; BGH NJW 1992, 2564; Staudinger/Honsell, Vor § 459 para. 33.

[38] Which is decisive according to new § 434 I.

[39] Flume, *Eigenschaftsirrtum*, pp. 20, 31 ff., 47 ff. *passim*.

[40] On the leading opinion cf. for example, H. Brox, *Besonderes Schuldrecht* (23rd edn, Munich, 1998), para. 62.

[41] K sold to B a piece of land which was situated in the immediate vicinity of a planned main road – a fact known to K but not to B. The purchaser's claim for repudiation was however rejected in this case because the contract of sale contained a clause excluding warranties; cf. BGHZ 34, 33.

which both parties tacitly presupposed.[42] It must also suffice, for the existence of such an implied agreement by both parties on a particular characteristic relating to the object of sale, that the vendors recognised the fact that the quiet surroundings were especially important to the purchasers. Therefore, because both parties included the quiet situation of the house in the contract they designated this characteristic of the house as a subject of the contract. If it is now the case that vehicles crossing the woods cause substantial noise then the property sold is defective in relation to the content of the contract. Thus, the purchasers may demand termination of the contract or a reduction in the purchase price.

(a) Mr and Mrs Timeless are not able to claim damages on grounds of non-performance due to the fact that Mr and Mrs Careless have not given any guarantees relating to particular characteristics of the house as discussed above (§§ 437 Ziff 3, 440, 280, 276 I, 283). The courts had been very reluctant to accept implied guarantees relating to characteristics. A characteristic of the object of sale is only deemed to be 'warranted' if the seller indicates that he intends to vouch for the presence of the characteristic under all circumstances.[43] The BGH has usually only accepted the assumption of such liability if the buyer is a layperson and the seller an expert;[44] otherwise implied warranties are only accepted in exceptional cases.[45] In our case the facts do not indicate that the seller particularly intended to vouch for the property's quiet situation. Accordingly, Mr and Mrs Timeless cannot rely on §§ 437 Ziff 3, 280, 281, 283, 276 I BGB to support their guarantee claims.

(b) But the buyers may nevertheless be able to claim damages because the sellers have fraudulently withheld the fact that the road that had previously only been used as a footpath has now been opened to motor traffic (§§ 437, 440, 281 I, 280 I BGB). They knew that Mr and Mrs Timeless intended to purchase the house primarily because it was situated in a quiet area. In order to avoid endangering their decision to purchase they deliberately withheld the presence of a defect (cf. above (i)) in the house. By their act, Mr and Mrs Careless fulfil the requirement of fraud (§§ 276 I, 280 I BGB).

---

[42] BGH NJW-RR 1995, 364; similarly ('Assumptions . . . of both parties . . . elevated to the content of the contract') but see also, earlier BGHZ 16, 54, 57 f.; BGH BB 1961, 305; BGH NJW 1984, 2289.

[43] Cf. Palandt/Putzo, § 459 para. 15.

[44] BGH NJW 1981, 1269; BGH NJW 1996, 836 and 1962; for further references see Palandt/Putzo, § 459 para. 17.

[45] The so-called 'Kunstharz-Entscheidung', BGHZ 59, 158 is therefore seen as unusual.

(c) The buyers may alternatively claim damages on the ground of §§ 437 Ziff 3, 311 a: that it was initially impossible to deliver house and garden according to the contractual conditions. The sellers knew of the impossibility (§ 311 a II). Therefore they have to compensate the buyers' damage.

The buyers can combine their claim for damages with termination of the contract or the reduction of the price (§ 437 Ziff 2 and 3 BGB). If Mr and Mrs Timeless wish to keep the house then they may also claim the difference in value between the 'quiet' house they expected and the 'noisy' house they in fact acquired.[46] Alternatively, should they wish to rescind the purchase then they could demand the purchase price as compensation in return for transferring ownership over the house. Besides this, they may claim compensation for other damages such as the cost involved in making the contract, the cost of surveys and similar outlays.[47]

(ii) Being *leges speciales* the rules governing warranty (guarantee) contained in the law on sales take precedence[48] over annulment on grounds of mistake relating to a substantial quality of the object of sale (§ 119 II BGB). Because the concept of 'defect' contained in § 434 BGB is determined by the same definition which applies to 'characteristic' in § 119 II,[49] annulment for mistake is commonly ruled out as soon as a defect in a characteristic has been established.[50]

In contrast to this, the purchaser is able to annul the contract for fraudulent misrepresentation (§ 123) despite his claim of compensation according to §§ 437 Ziff 3, 440, 280. The seller who committed the fraud is not to profit from the fact that the purchaser is denied one of several possible remedies. We have already established that the sellers acted fraudulently ((ii)(b)); the 'silence' is reprehensible *per se* because they should have disclosed to the buyers the defect in the object of sale of which they were aware. For the purposes of § 123 however, it must

---

[46] Cf. the evidence in Palandt/Putzo, § 463 para. 18 concerning the extent of this so-called 'small claim of compensation'.

[47] Cf. the evidence in Palandt/Putzo, § 463 para. 19 concerning the extent of this so-called 'large claim of compensation' (*Großer Schadensersatz*); now (since 1.1.2002) compensation for outlays is regulated by § 284 under the same conditions; §§ 280 ff. grants compensation of damages.

[48] According to the leading opinion; cf. at length in Case 3.

[49] First RG JW 1906, 378; later also BGH NJW 34, 32, 41; later, for example BGHZ 79, 183, 185; BGH NJW 1990, 1658, 1659; BGH WM 1997, 272 and more frequently.

[50] Cf. Staudinger/Köhler, § 440 para. 15; MüKo/Kramer, § 119 para. 33; more recently K. Flesch, *Mängelhaftung und Beschaffenheitsirrtum beim Kauf* (Baden-Baden, 1994), pp. 100 ff.

in particular be established whether the silence constitutes an act of fraud. Therefore, it must be asked whether the party making the mistake may have expected disclosure according to the principles of good faith taking into account the generally accepted standards in business.[51] In the present case however, this requirement which is orientated around § 242, may be complemented by the evaluation established by §§ 437 Ziff 3, 434 I: Mr and Mrs Careless must disclose the defect in the house to Mr and Mrs Timeless if they know of this defect and are aware that it plays a role in the purchasers' decision to enter into the contract.

Therefore, because the buyers may expect disclosure, the sellers' fraudulent silence fulfils the condition in § 123. The buyers may accordingly annul the contract of sale and (by virtue of § 812 I) demand that the price they have paid for the house be refunded.

(iii) Another way of annulling the contract is to treat the sellers' fraudulent behaviour as giving rise to tortious liability. The courts regard the requirement of immorality contained in § 826 as being satisfied by many cases of fraudulent behaviour when concluding the contract.[52] Thus, the OLG Hamm has deemed silence fraudulent when concluding a contract in relation to factors which contribute considerably to value as immoral pursuant to § 826.[53] Accordingly, it is wholly probable in the present case that a German court would also allow Mr and Mrs Timeless' claim under § 826.[54] On the basis of their claim in tort, Mr and Mrs Timeless could demand to be placed in the position they would have been had the sellers not committed their tortious act. Nevertheless, it is easier for the buyers to prove that the sellers withheld information than to prove that they wanted to deceive them.

To conclude, Mr and Mrs Timeless could bring a variety of actions: on the grounds of warranty claims, fraudulent misrepresentation or on the basis that the fraudulent silence constitutes a tort.

---

[51] BGH NJW 1989, 764; BGH NJW-RR 1991, 440; cf. Case 2.
[52] For information on this cf. Palandt/Thomas, § 826 para. 22.
[53] OLG Hamm NJW 1997, 2121.
[54] If the buyers had known that the right of way had been opened to motor traffic then they would not have entered into the contract. Accordingly, their 'damage' arises by their concluding the contract. Therefore, in cases such as this, the view is generally taken that the sellers are liable to compensate the buyers for the latter's negative interest. This is imprecise; in the case before us the damage which may be compensated under tortious liability in fact overlaps with the negative interest – which is to be compensated according to the principles of *culpa in contrahendo*, for example. Therefore, according to the general principles (§ 249) the buyers can demand that the contract be reversed.

Greece

(i) Mr and Mrs Timeless are entitled to sue to annul the sale on the basis of fraud under art. 147 AK.[55] The following conditions are fulfilled:

(a) Misleading conduct has taken place by concealing the true facts about the variation of the right of way. The vendors are under a duty to inform the purchasers of the true facts in accordance with good faith and common usage (art. 288 AK).

(b) The vendors have concealed the truth with the purpose of reinforcing the purchasers' erroneous impression. They will be liable under art. 147 AK, even if they did not intend to mislead the purchasers, since it is generally accepted[56] that *dolus* is present not only when the culprit willed the unlawful result but also when he accepted the consequences of his conduct (wilful conduct).

(c) There is a chain of causation between the vendors' conduct and the purchasers' declaration of will. In the case of fraudulent concealment, a hypothetical chain of causation suffices,[57] i.e. the fact that the victims of the mistake would not have entered into the contract had they been informed of the true state of affairs.

(ii) Mr and Mrs Timeless' claim will fail on the grounds of mistake. Their mistake refers exclusively to their motives which affected their intention to contract; here their declaration coincides with their will, but there is a discrepancy between their will and the reality. Such a mistake as to motive is not fundamental according to art. 143 AK. Another way of characterising the mistake could be on the basis of art. 142 AK – a mistake as to the quality of the thing contracted for – but the quietness of the property cannot be qualified as a quality of the thing since qualities of a person or a thing are considered to be all the real and legal features by which the person or the thing is individualised in the transaction.[58]

(iii) As Mr and Mrs Timeless' mistake is not fundamental (under art. 148 AK) if Mr and Mrs Careless accept what Mr and Mrs Timeless really

---

[55] Article 147 AK lays down that a person who has been led by fraud to make a declaration of will shall be entitled to seek the annulment of the act.

[56] Georgiadis, *General Principles of Civil Law*, p. 433; Karakatsanis AK 147 n. 5; Karassis, *Manual of General Principles of Civil Law*, p. 107; Papantoniou, *General Principles of Civil Law*, p. 108; Spyridakis, *General Principles*, p. 613.

[57] Karakatsanis AK 14, n. 7.

[58] See for example Georgiadis, *General Principles of Civil Law*, p. 426. The qualities of an immovable include its position, the fact that it may be built on, the consistence of the soil etc.

wanted, the court is free not to annul the contract. It has been sub-mitted[59] that the court's decision not to annul does not mean that the contract is maintained but is amended. The judge will mainly base his decision on the rules of good faith and common usage. For example if the purchasers had not been defrauded they would have possibly still entered into the contract but under different terms, i.e. for a lower pur-chase price and if the vendors accept this the sale would be valid at this lower price.

(iv) Mr and Mrs Timeless may seek compensation under the general tort provisions cumulatively with or without annulment (art. 149 AK). In the latter case the reversal of the sale, analysed as compensation *in natura*, cannot be sought after the two years'[60] prescription provided by art. 157 AK.[61]

Ireland

There is an issue in this case as to whether Mr and Mrs Timeless intended to purchase a house with a garden or a house with a garden in a quiet location. The mistake in this case is one as to the quality of the land being purchased. We are not aware whether there has been any misrep-resentation in the case, i.e. whether there has been a positive statement of fact on the part of the vendors that the property was located in a quiet location when they knew or ought to have known that such a statement was inaccurate. Even if there was not a positive misrepresentation as to the quality of the property during the contractual negotiations, it behoves the vendors to inform the purchasers of the material change in relation to the quality of the property once they learn that the right of way at the bottom of their garden has been varied.

On the other hand, the change in the status of the right of way has been effected by an act of the local authority and not due to any action on the part of the vendors. As such it is a public act and it is arguable that there is an onus on Mr and Mrs Timeless to inform themselves of such a change. However, in *Gahan v. Boland*,[62] the defendants falsely

---

[59] Spyridakis, *General Principles*, n. 214 p. 620; see also Georgiadis, *General Principles of Civil Law*, p. 435.

[60] Karakatsanis, AK 149 n. 6.

[61] Article 157 AK lays down that: 'The right to claim annulment shall be extinguished at the expiration of two years from the transaction. If the mistake, fraud or threat have continued after the conclusion of the legal act the two year period shall begin to run after the cessation of this condition. In any event annulment shall not be allowed when twenty years have elapsed since the date of the legal act.'

[62] Unreported judgment of the Supreme Court (20 January 1984).

represented that their property would not be affected by any new roads to be built in the area in reliance on which representation the plaintiff purchased the property. After completion the claimant, a practising solicitor, sought to rescind the contract of sale on the grounds of a contractual misrepresentation. The defendants argued that the claimant as a solicitor and an intending purchaser was obliged to make his own enquiries which would have led him to be informed of the true position. The Supreme Court granted rescission, holding that only actual and not constructive notice would debar a purchaser from annulling a contract on grounds of misrepresentation.

A more harsh reading of the facts of the case would lead one to surmise that the Irish courts might hold that the principles of *caveat emptor* holds good in relation to this case.

Italy

(i) Article 1489 of the Civil Code provides[63] that the buyer can request termination of the sale if when he entered into the contract he did not know that the thing sold was encumbered by burdens or by real or personal rights which were not apparent and which would diminish its free enjoyment and were not declared in the contract (*Cosa gravata da oneri*).[64]

This is a case of *evizione* (eviction of the thing) and scholarly opinion considers the case either as a right of way due to administrative regulations; or a right of way due to a private agreement or as a *de facto*

---

[63] Article 1489 Thing encumbered by burdens or rights of enjoyment of third persons: 'If the thing sold is encumbered by burdens or by real (art. 810 of the Civil Code) or personal rights which are not apparent, and which diminish its free enjoyment and are not declared in the contract, the buyer who did not have knowledge of them can demand termination of the contract or reduction of the price according to the provision of art. 1480'.

Article 1479 Good Faith of Buyer: 'A buyer can request termination of the contract (art. 1453) if at the time it was concluded, he did not know that the thing was not owned by the seller, and if the seller meanwhile has not caused him to acquire ownership of it.

Subject to the provisions of art. 1223, the seller is bound to restore to the buyer the price paid, even if the thing has diminished in value or has been damaged; he shall furthermore reimburse him for all expenses and payments legitimately made under the contract (art. 1475). If the diminished value or damage is caused by the buyer, the value of the use of the thing by the buyer shall be deducted from the said amount.

The seller is, furthermore, bound to reimburse the buyer for necessary or justifiable expenses incurred for the thing and, if he was in bad faith, also for unnecessary expenses.'

[64] Cass 1985, n. 1215.

compulsory pre-emption situation (arts. 1051–5 of the Civil Code).[65] The courts, on the other hand, do not think that a remedy will be admitted to protect the buyer from an encumbrance due to an act of the public authorities, considering, as we have already said, that the law is supposed to be known by everybody: *ignorantia legis non excusat*[66] (though the principle has been weakened by a Constitutional Court decision[67]). There is in fact considerable discussion about whether there is a duty to inform about legal regulations: the common cases deal with the duty of the seller of property to disclose the existence of new planning zones relevant for that piece of property.[68] There is only one decision by the *Tribunale di Roma*[69] where the court, applying an equitable approach, said that the knowledge of the law cannot be imposed on everybody in the same measure.

The purchasers can claim to terminate the contract (art. 1453 of the Civil Code) or reduce the price (art. 1480 of the Civil Code), moreover they can claim damages (art. 1479) or can refuse to pay the price raising a defence based upon non-performance (art. 1460). The buyers have the burden of proof if the right of way was visible; the opposite rule applies if the right was not visible.[70]

(ii) The purchasers can claim against the seller that the property does not have the quality that was promised to them (*mancanza di qualità promessa*) when they bargained for it (cf. Case 3),[71] or that there was a basic contractual assumption (*presupposizione*)[72] that the quiet adjoining woods were their main reason for choosing that property (cf. Case 1).

---

[65] Rubino, *Compravendita*, Tratt. Cicu Messineo, and Bianca, *Il contratto*.

[66] Cass 1993, n. 1469; Cass 1991, n. 7639; Cass 1982, n. 6935, contra Cass 1992, n. 253 where the Supreme Court applied the provisions of art. 1489 of the Civil Code in a case in which land sold as having the right to be constructed on, turned out to have this right subject to modification according to a zoning plan.

[67] Cort. Cost., 24.3.1988, n. 364, FI 1988, I, 1385.

[68] Cass 30.12.68, n. 4081, *GCR, Vendita*, 23; Cass 4.1.1966, n. 47, GC, 1966, I, 13; Cass 30.1.65, n. 6, GC, 1965, I, 224; Cass 30.5.59, n. 1638, FI 1959, I, 1280 see Carresi, 'Il Contratto', p. 735 and Benatti, 'Culpa in contrahendo' in *Contratto e Impresa* (hereafter CI), p. 294.

[69] Trib. Roma, 14.5.1980, *Temi Romani* (hereafter TR), 1980, 531, noted by Dell Rocca.

[70] Cass 1975, n. 2947; Cass 1982, n. 4458.

[71] The case law is mostly on mistakes about the existence of planning permission on real property (*edificabilità del terreno*): Cass 1991, n. 13578; Cass 1991, n. 4984; Cass 1990, n. 2518; Cass 1974, n. 4020, in *Giustizia Civile* (hereafter GC) 1975, I, 779.

[72] Cass 1987, n. 718; Cass 1961, n. 2632.

The Netherlands

As a preliminary remark, it is crucial in this case to ascertain what is meant by the right of way. Under Dutch law, in order to be valid such a 'real' right must be recorded on the public registers (*openbare registers*) and can therefore be known by any member of the public including Mr and Mrs Timeless. In practice, therefore, they would have found out either at the conclusion of the contract or at the moment of transfer of the property because the notary would have informed them of the variation. However, it does not seem likely that 'right of way' here indicates a real right because such a right would be given to one or more specific persons whereas the facts suggest that this right is given to any member of the public. The type of case closest to the one given here is the one where the public authorities change the zoning plans (*bestemmingsplan*). In the following it will be assumed that before the conclusion of the contract the public authorities have changed the destination of the woods at the bottom of the garden: they plan a road through the woods where motor vehicles are allowed to drive.

Mr and Mrs Timeless will probably maintain that they were mistaken with regard to the silence in the adjoining woods. Is their mistake legally relevant? If it is, they can choose either to annul the contract (art. 6:228 BW) or claim a reduction of the price (art. 6:230 BW). It is clear that Mr and Mrs Timeless were mistaken: they expected quiet woods and got noisy cars instead. The causation requirement also seems to be met. One of the main attractions of the house and garden for Mr and Mrs Timeless was the quiet adjoining woods at the bottom of the garden. In other words, had they known of the substantial noise caused by vehicles crossing the woods, they would probably not have bought this house, or at least not for this price.

Mr and Mrs Careless knew of the variation. If they were under a duty to inform Mr and Mrs Timeless, then the latter can, in principle, annul the contract for mistake (art. 6:228, S. 1(b) BW). A bar to such a duty could be that Mr and Mrs Careless did not know nor should have known that Mr and Mrs Timeless would not have concluded the contract had they known of the variation (art. 6:228, S. 1(b) BW). It is, therefore, crucial to ascertain whether Mr and Mrs Careless knew that the quietness of the woods was important to the buyers (the apparent knowledge requirement (*kenbaarheid*)).

Assuming that Mr and Mrs Careless knew that the quietness of the woods was important to the buyers the following question as to whether they actually were under a duty to share their knowledge about the variation with Mr and Mrs Timeless needs to be examined further. Whether a duty to inform exists in a specific case depends very much on the circumstances of the case.[73] A relevant (though not, in itself, decisive) factor would be whether either the buyer or the seller was an expert. In this case neither of the parties is said to be an expert. In *HR*, 18 April 1986,[74] Spaai, a professional seller of immovable properties, sold, on behalf of Crombag, a house and garden with a nice view. Before the conclusion of the contracts the buyers asked whether the premises were included in a zoning plan (*bestemmingsplan*). Spaai answered that 'as far as he knew' they were not. After the conclusion the buyers found out that they were and disputed the validity of the contract under the doctrines of fraud and mistake. The Court of Appeal held that if it was established that Spaai positively knew of the zoning plan the contract could be annulled for mistake. However, the plaintiffs did not succeed in establishing this. Before the *Hoge Raad* the plaintiffs argued that a professional seller has a duty to inform the prospective buyers about whether there is a zoning plan (*bestemmingsplan*), and, where necessary, to make investigations, and that the buyer may expect he will do so. However, this argument was rejected by the *Hoge Raad*.[75] This case differs from ours in two respects: in our case the sellers were not professionals and the sellers did know of the relevant facts. In *HR* 30 November 1973,[76] the seller sold an apartment without telling the buyer that the public authorities had decided not to allow it to be used for habitation any longer. The Court of Appeal held that the seller was under a duty to inform the buyer of this but that such a duty does not diminish the duty of the buyers to investigate the public registers to see whether there were any obstacles. However, the *Hoge Raad* quashed the decision after having held that for a party who is under a duty to inform the other party, it would in principle be contrary to good faith to invoke a duty to investigate incumbent on the first party. This case is mainly known for the balance between duties (cf. below p. 213). However, what is of interest here is that a party who knows of a decision by the public authorities which is publicly known, may be under a duty to inform the other. Were our sellers here under a

---

[73] Cf. *Verbintenissenrecht* (Hijma), art. 228, aant. 84.

[74] NJ 1986, 747 note Van der Grinten (Ernst en Latte/Crombag-Spaai).

[75] This decision was criticised by several authors. Cf. for references *Verbintenissenrecht* (Hijma), art. 228, aant. 91.

[76] NJ 1974, 97, note G. J. Scholten, *AA* XXIII (1974), note Van der Grinten (Van der Beek/Van Dartel).

duty to inform? In legal doctrine it is said that, although limitations by the public authorities on the enjoyment of an immovable are in principle at the buyer's risk, the risk must shift whenever these facts are positively known to the seller.[77] It is likely that a court would decide accordingly in this case. The buyers did not know but could have known since zoning plans (*bestemmingsplannen*) are public. Were they under a duty to investigate? In principle, a duty for one party (here the sellers) to inform outweighs a duty for the other party (here the buyers) to investigate. The *Hoge Raad* has held this in various cases.[78] It is often said that the duty for one party to inform and the duty for the other to investigate are two sides of one coin: there is an inadequacy of information and one party is held responsible (is attributed the risk) for it.[79]

Only the mistake about the variation of the right of way, which had already occurred at the moment of conclusion of the contract, can be relevant. The quietness of the woods, that apparently changed after the conclusion of the contract is, in itself, irrelevant, because it is a future circumstance (cf. art. 6:228, S. 2 BW).

In case the buyers are entitled to annul for mistake they can also, at their choice, ask for the contract to be adapted (art. 6:230, S. 2 BW), e.g. for a reduction of the price.

If Mr and Mrs Careless had explicitly guaranteed that there would be no traffic in the adjoining woods, of course, Mr and Mrs Timeless would have a claim in damages for non-performance of that collateral contract. However, this does not seem to be the case here. Recently, in a series of cases where land sold for construction turned out to be polluted, the *Hoge Raad* has accepted the (highly fictitious)[80] implied guarantee that the land is in every respect suitable for building.[81] And in another case it has accepted that a seller of a car implicitly guarantees that the number

---

[77] Van Rossum (1991), p. 162.

[78] First in *HR* 30 November 1973, NJ 1974, 97, note G. J. Scholten, *AA* XXIII (1974), note Van der Grinten (*Van der Beek v. Van Dartel*).

[79] Cf. Castermans, *De nededelingsplicht in de onderhandelingsfase*, pp. 23 ff., with further references. However, in a recent case (*HR*, 10 April 1998, NJ 1998, note Klein (*Offringa/Vinck en Van Rosberg*)) the *Hoge Raad* said that a duty to investigate for the buyer does not exclude a duty to inform for the seller. Cf. *Verbintenissenrecht* (Hijma), art. 228, aant. 87. However, this case could also be interpreted differently: the presence of a duty to investigate for the buyer, violation of which would prevent them from invoking mistake, does not exclude fraud (*dol par réticence*) by the seller.

[80] Cf. for criticism on the legal technique of an 'implicit' guarantee in these and similar cases, Hesselink, *De redelijkheid en billijkheid in het Europese privaatrecht*, pp. 166 ff.

[81] *HR*, 9 October 1992, NJ 1994, nos. 287 and 289 (*Steendijkpolder*).

of kilometres indicated on the meter is correct.[82] It is possible that a Dutch court would accept other implicit guarantees, although it does not seem likely that in this case an implicit guarantee of absence of traffic in the adjoining woods would be accepted.

A reform with regard to the sale of immovables contained in art. 7:2 (2) BW has come into force introducing a 'cooling off period' of three days.[83] Under the new law therefore, if Mr and Mrs Timeless found out about the right of way within three days they could terminate the contract.[84]

Norway

This type of question (an encumbrance on the property) is discussed in relation to the *breach of contract doctrine*.[85] There is no tradition for applying the invalidity doctrine. As mentioned in Case 1, it is not clear whether any limitations have been established to claiming invalidity. Nonetheless, applying the breach of contract regulations would normally serve the aggrieved party best.

Hence, the real issue is whether Mr and Mrs Careless should have informed the purchasers about the new use of the road, and whether this created a *defect* in the property. Regulations governing the purchase and sale of property are, in Scandinavian countries, less uniform than, for instance, those regarding the purchase and sale of goods. The description given below is intended primarily to provide a picture of Norwegian law. However, I shall refer to Danish and Swedish law. The likely result of the case will be discussed at (iv).

(i) According to *Norwegian law*, the Sale of Property Act[86] has to be our point of departure. The act deals generally with the sale of property (with or without buildings), not only in respect to consumer situations. The duty to inform is here regulated in the Sale of Property Act, § 3-7, which reads:

---

[82] *HR*, 25 June 1993, NJ 1994, 291, note Brunner (*Kilometerteller*).

[83] Article 7:2(2) BW came into force in October 2003.

[84] See Asser/Hijma 5-I (2001), nos. 133 ff.; S. E. Bartels and J. M. van Buuren-Dee, 'Woningkoop door consumenten', and M. W. Hesselink and H. J. van Kooten, 'De rechtspositie naar art. 7:2 BW (Nieuw) van de consument die bij mondelinge overeenkomst een woning heeft gekocht', both in J. M. van Buuren-Dee, E. H. Hondius and P. A. Kottenhagen-Edzes (eds.), *Consument zonder grenzen* (Deventer, 1996), all with further references.

[85] See as examples the following judgments: Norway – RT 1997.70 (antiquities), RG 1983.592 (smell), and RG 1987.760 (sound); Sweden – NJA 1982.894 (noise) and NJA 1986.670 (radon gases in homes); and Denmark – U 1968.272 H (pesticides).

[86] Sale of Property Act, 3 July 1992, no. 93.

The property has a defect if the purchaser has not been informed about conditions which the seller knew of or could not have been unaware of, and of which the purchaser had reason to believe that he should have been informed. This, however, is only relevant if one could assume that the non-provision of information has influenced the contract.

In other words, there are three conditions for applying the duty to inform. First, a subjective condition should be present – 'knew or could not have been unaware of'.[87] Second, the purchaser's need for information should be worthy of protection – 'had reason to expect to be provided with'. Third, a criterion of cause (an inducement) should be present – 'influenced the contract'.

In principle, the duty to inform covers all types of situations provided these three conditions are fulfilled, including the disadvantages affecting the new owners of the property in our case.[88] The statute does not require that the duty to inform should be essential.[89] But the purchaser 'must have reason to expect to be provided with' the information, and that such information would 'influence the contract'. Whether this represents an actual extension of the seller's duty to inform in relation to earlier legal situations, is not clear. Another characteristic of the Sale of Property Act is that the seller's duty to inform has priority over the purchaser's right to examine, cf. the Sale of Property Act, § 3–10(3).[90] However, since it is a requirement that the purchaser should have 'reason to expect to be provided with information', the possibility for his obtaining the necessary information should, nonetheless, be considered.

(ii) Until 1995, the purchase and sale of property was not regulated by law in *Denmark*. Hence, the legal background was developed based on case law and theory. The extent of the duty to inform has been a much debated topic in Danish law. In the standard work on the purchase of property, Vinding Kruse states concerning this duty:

---

[87] It is not clear if the alternative 'could not have been unaware of' is only a regulation relating to proof linked to intent, or if it gives indication of a certain normative requirement as to perception.

[88] Questions of municipal assessments and restrictions relating to the use of property are examined according to the Sale of Property Act, § 3–7, cf. § 4–18. However, defects in performance (i.e. the rights of third persons to the property), are specifically regulated in the Sale of Property Act, § 4–17.

[89] The reason for not including a fundamental criterion was 'a fear that this might be considered as a too severe limitation', see Ot. prp. no. 66 (1990–91), p. 89.

[90] Compare what has been said in Case 1 about the relationship between the promisor's own situation and the duty to inform.

Based on legal experience, I find it most fitting to explain the duty of disclosure as follows: the seller must inform the purchaser about all the conditions and defects regarding the property which he knows of or should not have been unaware of (or had suspected), and which he must assume is of substantial interest for the purchaser's evaluation of the property, and of which he cannot assume that the purchaser is aware.[91]

By law no. 391 of 14.6.1995, 'the law on consumer protection in acquiring property', conditions for the sale of housing were changed dramatically. The law introduced an insurance regulation in respect of the sale of property: a claim should initially be presented to the insurance company. It would not be appropriate at this point to enter into details regarding this consumer law. Which claims (for defect) may be presented to the insurance company are, however, not specified in the statute.

(iii) The purchase and sale of property is, in *Swedish* law, regulated in the '*Jordabalken*' (JB), chapter 4 on Purchase, Exchange and Gift.[92] Responsibility for the defect is described in chapter 4, § 19, of the JB. The regulation does not mention specifically the duty to inform, but it is clear that the seller must comply with it.[93] Because the property in all circumstances should correspond to 'what the purchaser with reason could expect from the purchase' (i.e. without regard to the seller's good or bad faith), the duty to inform has less significance.[94] The interaction between objectively and subjectively based defect regulations is also a condition of considerable importance in Danish and Norwegian law.

(v) The *resolution* of the disagreement would presumably depend on the degree of noise and on the disadvantages to which the new use subjects the purchaser. If the disadvantages are moderate and the motorised traffic more or less a natural development in the area, the condition would presumably not be considered a defect in the property. A similar case appeared in the Swedish Supreme Court.[95] This also concerned traffic noise. An apartment was sold without information being given about a deregulation of traffic which would lead to the purchaser being subjected to increased noise levels. Distance to a roundabout was reduced from 20 m to 3 m. The seller knew of the deregulation of traffic but did not pass the information on to the purchaser. In line with the

---

[91] A. Vinding Kruse, *Ejendomskøb* (6th edn, Copenhagen, 1992), p. 112.
[92] The new JB of 17 December 1970, see SFS 1971: 1209.
[93] See J. Hellner, *Speciell avtalsrätt* (2nd edn, Stockholm, 1993) vol. II: Kontraktsrätt, part I, pp. 58 ff.
[94] See C. Hultmark, *Upplysningsplikt* (Stockholm, 1993), pp. 40 ff.
[95] NJA 1981.894.

purchaser's claim, a price reduction of SKR 60,000 was granted. The apartment was purchased for SKR 535,000. The Supreme Court maintained that 'the risk of this kind of deregulation was of considerable significance to the owner wishing to speedily divest himself of the property'. If the changed use is considered a defect, the usual remedies for breach of contract are applied, such as the right to terminate the contract (if the defect is fundamental), claim a price reduction, or claim compensation.

Portugal

This case concerns the question of encumbrances on the thing sold. According to art. 905° of the Civil Code if the thing sold has some kind of encumbrances or limitations which exceed the normal limits of rights of that kind, the contract can be annulled on the grounds of mistake or fraud.

(i) There is a mistake relating to the object of the contract, because Mr and Mrs Timeless did not know of the existence of the right of way for motor vehicles on the land, so the rules of arts. 251° and 247° of the Civil Code would apply, and Mr and Mrs Timeless can ask for the contract to be annulled, as Mr and Mrs Careless knew or should not have been unaware that the mistake was fundamental for them.

(ii) There is a question of fraud, because Mr and Mrs Careless omitted to inform Mr and Mrs Timeless of the variation of the right of way, which constitutes fraud in the sense of art. 253° of the Civil Code, as art. 227° of the Civil Code recognises the existence of duties to behave in good faith during negotiations and the formation of the contract and among these duties is a duty to inform, the breach of which constitutes fraud and can also give rise to liability for damages.

So Mr and Mrs Timeless would be entitled to annul the contract within a year after the conclusion of the contract (art. 287° of the Civil Code). But if circumstances showed that without mistake or fraud, they would still have acquired the land, but for a reduced price, they would not be entitled to annul the contract, but only to ask the court for a reduction of the purchase price (art. 911° of the Civil Code).

Besides the annulment of the contract or the reduction of the price, in case of fraud, Mr and Mrs Careless would also have to compensate Mr and Mrs Timeless for all the expenses (*damnum emergens*) and losses (*lucrum cessans*) incurred as a result of the acquisition (art. 908° of the Civil Code). If there is no fraud, but only mistake, according to art. 909°

of the Civil Code, Mr and Mrs Timeless can still ask for damages even if there was no fault by the vendors in addition to annulling the contract.

Scotland

It is a rule of the law of misrepresentation in Scotland that there is in general no duty of voluntary disclosure. There are exceptions to this rule, the main example of which is a contract of insurance. The general principle, however, is that of *caveat emptor* or buyer beware, as was noted by Lord Trayner in *Murray* v. *Marr*[96] where he stated that,

there may be many things which, if disclosed on one side or the other, would prevent a party from entering into a contract, but the non-disclosure of which will not affect the validity of the contract.

In the present example, there is no duty of voluntary disclosure. Therefore there will only be a remedy if the question is asked of Mr and Mrs Careless, and they either assert that it is not the case, or attempt to conceal the existence of the right of way. This does not appear to be the case given the facts as presented, and therefore there is no remedy available as there is no misrepresentation by non-disclosure in the sale of heritable property, and the principle of *caveat emptor* means the buyers must inform themselves of such rights of way. It is likely that in most cases a clause in the missives would require the sellers to reveal the fact to the purchasers. If such a clause was in place and they failed to inform them, the contract would be voidable due to their misrepresentation.

Spain

The ground of fraud as a defect of consent is in the idea of deception, implying an intentional manoeuvre designed to give the mistaken party information about a particular reality. Accordingly, the result of the fraud is always a mistake and there is a very close relation between the two types of defective consent. The basic difference in the legal treatment of both is that the second considers, above all, the formation of the mistaken party's knowledge and its own liability for the mistake, while fraud is appraised, legally speaking, in terms of the conduct of the party causing the deception.

What is essential here is that the sellers knew some of the basic reasons why the buyers wished to acquire the house, i.e. the quietness of the

[96] (1892) 20 R 119 at 125.

adjacent wood and, fearful that the contract might not be concluded, failed to advise them of the new easement which was to affect the woods. This conduct is absolutely contrary to the principles of good faith which must govern the conclusion of contracts.

It is not necessary therefore to ascertain whether the fraudulent conduct of the sellers produced the buyers' mistake, thereby rendering their consent defective but rather, given the gravity of the sellers' fraud (negative fraud, see Case 2) and considering that had Mr and Mrs Timeless been duly informed of the actual situation, the contract would probably never have been concluded, this fraudulent concealment is sufficient to invalidate the buyers' consent, entitling them to bring a claim for annulment under art. 1265 of the Civil Code.

Comparative observations

The important features of this case are that it contains a mistake about rights in land, the consequences of which are as follows: the mistake can be qualified as a mistake of fact and/or law – more significantly, is the qualification legally relevant? In addition, the sellers knew something about the land which they failed to disclose to the buyers, such a failure highlights the different legal views as to the obligation to disclose and the balance between conflicting duties to inform (on behalf of sellers and buyers). Lastly, since the mistake concerns land, *lex specialis* arguments, in relation to codification containing guarantees owed by an owner of land in relation to the title or hidden defects of the land sold, may be raised. The available remedies are summarised in the laws of mistake, fraud and duties to inform and breach of contract.

1. There are two mistakes conceivable here: a mistake as to the right of way and a mistake as to quality of the land. Even though the former may be qualified as a mistake of law, in most civil law systems, such a mistake can be assimilated to a mistake of fact and give rise to annulment.

As to a mistake to quality under English, Scots and Irish law there is no remedy for a unilateral mistake as to quality, whereas it may be possible for such a mistake to give rise to annulment in some civil law countries partly due to the fact that the conception of mistake is more subjective. This would be the case in Austria, Belgium, France, Portugal and the Netherlands. In France and Belgium the interpretation of mistake diverges, whereas the Belgian reporter considers that the mistake is inexcusable, the French reporter does not. A similar position could be reached in Italy on the ground of a basic contractual assumption (i.e.

the quietness of the property constituted the buyers' main reason for entering into the contract). In Greece, in contrast, the quality of the property fails to qualify for mistake since the purely subjective aspect of the mistake does not render it sufficiently fundamental here. In Germany, a mistake could not be admitted, not for reasons arising out of the qualification (fundamental or not) of the mistake but simply according to the application of *lex specialis* rules. In the countries admitting mistake the remedy would consist in annulment and perhaps damages (Portugal) or adapting the contract consisting in a reduction in the purchase price (Portugal, the Netherlands).

2. Another ground, possibly more popular, would lie in fraud and breach of duties to inform.

This case is a good illustration of the three different conceptual foundations of the duty to inform. First, in some legal systems this duty is subsumed into defective consent provisions. Secondly, in others, it is treated as a ground of independent precontractual liability (*culpa in contrahendo*, art. 1382 of the French Civil Code etc.). Thirdly, the fraudulent aspect of silence can also be envisaged independently as a tort. One importance difference may be procedural, as suggested by the German reporter: it is no doubt easier to prove that a party has withheld information (under the head of precontractual liability) than to prove fraudulent intent.

(i) In Austria, France, Belgium, Germany, Greece, the Netherlands, Portugal and Spain, a remedy would lie more easily on the basis of a fraud consisting in a failure to disclose incumbent on the sellers. Similarly, under German, Greek, Portuguese and Austrian law, fraudulent concealment could also be inferred either by combining articles on fraud and good faith/common usage to give rise to an obligation to disclose (previously § 242 BGB, now codified in §§ 311 II, 241 II, 280 I BGB, arts. 147 and 288 of the Greek AK and arts. 227 and 253 of the Portuguese Civil Code) or by simply concentrating on the fraudulent behaviour of the sellers which induces a mistake in the buyers (§ 870 ABGB). Likewise it should be added that the Dutch version of mistake is based on a failure, deemed incumbent on the sellers, to inform the purchasers, constituting an induced mistake. In all its varieties such a claim gives rise to annulment and/or damages as discussed. In addition, under Austrian law, Dutch, Greek and Portuguese laws, it is possible to ask the courts to adapt the contract as if it were concluded in the light of the actual circumstances. This remedy would presumably consist in reducing the sale price and thus resembles the contractual remedies (below pp. 221–2).

(ii) If the sellers' silence constitutes a tort this entitles the buyers to bring an action under this head regardless of a claim under defective consent. This analysis is suggested by the German and Greek reporters. The remedy will be the same; for example, Greek law provides as a remedy in tort that the contract can be reversed by virtue of compensation *in natura*.[97]

However, a clear-cut divergence in the civil law/common law approach arises here since in common law countries no remedy will lie for misrepresentation in the absence of a duty of voluntary disclosure. Once again, attitudes towards silence diverge. Thus the principle of *caveat emptor* applies firmly here unless a positive statement of fact has been made by the vendors which subsequently turns out to be false. Only in these circumstances would a claim lie for innocent misrepresentation – if the vendors knew of the change of circumstances but failed to inform the buyers – or fraudulent misrepresentation, if the tort of deceit could be proved. The buyers' remedies would then be annulment of the contract and/or damages in tort respectively, such remedies being the result of legislative provisions in England and Scotland (Misrepresentation Act 1967).

3. Breach of contract claims can be characterised as a (i) contractual duty of disclosure, (ii) guarantee of good title and (iii) warranty as to characteristics or quality.

(i) Under Scandinavian legal systems, a breach of contract consisting in the failure to disclose would, under specific and fairly recent legislation relating to the sale of property give rise to the right of termination (providing the defect is fundamental), reduction in the purchase price or damages. In Norway the seller's actual or constructive knowledge is weighed up against the buyer's expectation that he should have been informed, such a requirement being subject to the buyer's own worthiness of protection. This rationale is comparable to that contained in French law, where a precontractual obligation to inform, often derived from an extensive view of fraudulent concealment, is cumulatively conditioned by the buyers' legitimate unawareness of the material information and of their reliance on the sellers to inform them.

In a similar vein, in Germany, a contractual claim for damages (this time compensation for positive interest) for fraudulent non-disclosure could be made, under § 463 BGB, now §§ 437 Ziff 3, 434 I, 280, 281, 283, 276 I 2 BGB or §§ 437 Ziff 3, 311 a. BGB. Likewise under Austrian law § 1295 ABGB damages can be claimed for the loss incurred for breach of

---

[97] See also German report.

non-disclosure since the buyers have relied on the contract where the thing transferred contains irremediable defects (whether material or in title).

(ii) A different contractual remedy also lies, namely that of transferring the property with good title. In Italy (art. 1489 of the Italian Civil Code) and Austria (§ 932 ABGB), the right of way could be qualified as an encumbrance on the land and thus the sellers are in breach of their duty to sell the property free from encumbrances, thus entitling the buyers to a choice of contractual remedies, termination, a reduction in the sale price and/or damages for a defect in title.

(iii) Under German law a similar result can be achieved for breach of contract in a warranty claim. The quietness of the property is a subjective defect (§ 434 I BGB) for the buyers and they can terminate the contract or ask for a reduction in price. In contrast, under English law a contractual remedy would only lie if it could be proven that the contract contained an express term as to the quality of the land, which is unlikely on the facts. This is also probably the case in the Netherlands.

Once again the qualification of an initial mistake as to the quality of the property, the subject matter of the contract of sale, gives rise to a number of overlapping remedies; some of which are specific to the type of contract (sale of land – guarantee of good title), others, being more general, relate to the process by which the contract is formed and concentrate more on the fairness of the parties' conduct towards one another. In circumstances which apparently indicate an equality of the contracting parties (two sets of individuals) the common law/civil law systems clearly perceive this equality differently. Whereas the classical principle of *caveat emptor* continues to prevail in the common law systems, the civil law takes into account the presence of information as a source of inequality, thus leading to a redistribution of the parties' obligations. First, it appears that possession of material information should be disclosed, thus leading to a higher standard of fair dealing between the parties. Secondly, this higher standard of fair dealing is further reflected by giving a remedy for a failure to disclose, on the basis that silence constitutes a fraudulent concealment.[98] It should be underlined that such a perception of the parties' unequal access to material information for the contract's formation has arisen as a result of case law but has also been incorporated into specific legislation under Scandinavian law.

---

[98] Compare art. 4:106 PECL.

A number of observations can be made from this case. First, in the absence of fraud (by the sellers), the same underlying values (as to the relative strength of the parties) are not shared by all legal systems. Secondly, a further difference arises within the legal systems offering protection for the buyer: for some legal systems the duty to inform is precontractual; for others it is contractual.[99] Moreover, it is interesting to note that when an obligation to inform is imposed, this has the effect of putting the risk on the shoulders of the 'stronger' party who is in possession of the information, rather than leaving the risk systematically to the buyer. An economic analysis has inferred that the criterion of risk can be linked to the access and cost to each party of acquiring the information,[100] rather than focusing on their status (seller or buyer; professional or consumer). It has also been suggested that a criterion lies in the extrinsic or intrinsic nature of the information.[101] The results of this case show that the choice as to whether the risk should lie on the buyer or seller is economical and political. The classical theory preconises that the risk lies on the buyer whereas a more modern approach allocates the risk to the seller via the obligation to inform. Whether the re-allocation of risks has an uneconomic effect on the market, a criterion considered essential according to the classical vision of contract, remains to be seen.

[99] See Comparative Conclusions at pp. 399–400 for a further discussion on this point.
[100] A. T. Kronman, 'Mistake, Disclosure, Information and the Law of Contracts' (1978) 7 J. Leg Stud. 1.
[101] R. E. Barnett (ed.), *Perspectives on Contract Law* (Boston, 1995), pp. 342 ff.

Case 5
Bruno v. The Local Garage

Case

Several months ago, Bruno bought a second-hand car from his local garage, who assured him that it was a 1995 model 'as good as new'. He has now discovered that the car is unroadworthy and the motor needs replacing. What remedy, if any, is available?

Discussions

Austria

Bruno's claims lie in mistake and breach of contract.

(i) Bruno can allege that he made a mistake when concluding the contract, as provided for in § 871 ABGB. As Bruno assumes that the car is capable of being used on the roads and is in good working order for a 1995 model, both of which turn out not to be the case, he has made a mistake; that is a mistake as to the important qualities of the subject matter of the contract.[1] One out of the three conditions stated in § 871 ABGB applies since Bruno's mistake has been caused by the seller's promises.

The right to annul (§ 871 ABGB) or the right to adapt (§ 872 ABGB) is available by considering respectively the importance of the mistake. If Bruno would not have bought the car if he had recognised its defects, namely the poor condition of the car, the mistake is fundamental. The

---

[1] An objective promisee who knows when the car was manufactured considers this statement as an advertisement more than a promise; compare Reischauer in Rummel §§ 922–3 RZ 5; OGH IN HS 135/51. As Bruno assumes the car has already been used, the statement has to be seen as indicating that the car has no severe defects and is in working order like any used car.

contract can then be judicially annulled in accordance with § 871 ABGB[2] and he is entitled to the reimbursement of the purchase price at the same time as returning the car to the seller in an action under § 877 ABGB (*condictio sine causa*).

(ii) As long as a period of six months has not yet passed since the actual delivery of the car (the so-called '*Fallfrist*' or expired term in accordance with § 933 ABGB) Bruno can also make a claim on the basis of a guarantee against defects (§§ 923 ff. ABGB). Since the defects are sufficiently serious to render the car unroadworthy they must be considered important (compare § 932 ABGB). However, the facts do not indicate if these defects can be remedied (can the condition of the car be improved?). If they can be remedied by (economically) reasonable means (compare § 1167 ABGB), Bruno can ask for a price reduction or adjustment (§ 932 ABGB). Only in the case of important and irremediable defects[3] is Bruno entitled to ask the court for termination of the sale with retrospective effect which would also lead to the restitution of the car and the purchase price (§ 1435 ABGB).

(iii) Contrary to termination, the right to annul a contract for fraud or mistake has an impact on the law of property.[4] Annulling the contract implies that the acquisition of title (the title for actual delivery) required for the transfer of the purchase price is set aside (especially § 380 ABGB; the so-called '*Prinzip der kausalen Tradition*'). As the purchase price has already been transferred to the seller, Bruno cannot ask for repayment of the purchase price by using an action *in rem* (*rei vindicatio*) (§ 370 ABGB).

Belgium

Bruno's claims lie in defective consent (mistake or fraud) and breach of contract (lack of conformity or guarantees against hidden defects).

(i) There are numerous cases involving controversies as to the sale of used cars but very few use a fundamental mistake as the basis for the buyer's action. The point is that the issue of excusability (see Case 1) can constitute an extremely difficult obstacle to overcome when the sale of a *used* good is at stake: the buyer is not supposed to have expected the delivery of goods in perfect condition and the judge will often impose a

---

[2] Compare Gschnitzer in Klang IV/1 113f; Koziol/Welser, *Bürgerliches Recht*, I 131; OGH in SZ 50/35; JBl 1976, 240; JBl 1980, 424; JBl 1982, 36.

[3] For more details of this concept see Case 4.

[4] Compare Gschnitzer in Klang, IV/1538; Koziol/Welser, *Bürgerliches Recht*, 1 256; H. Mayerhofer, 'Schuldrecht Allgemeiner Teil' in vol. II/I of A. Ehrenzweig (ed), *Systeme des österreichischen allgemeinen Privatrechts* (Vienna, 1986), 1 444.

stricter duty on the buyer to inform himself about the actual condition of the car.[5]

(ii) Here the case law on fraud (art. 1116 of the Civil Code) is more helpful. In 1988 the *Cour de cassation* approved[6] a Court of Appeal's decision that held, first, that a garage is, as a professional seller, supposed to know all the characteristics of the vehicles that it sells, with the sole exception of non-perceptible characteristics. Secondly and consequently, that the court, having ascertained that the mileage recorder had been manipulated, considered that the garage should have detected the manipulation and, by concealing it from the buyer, committed fraudulent manoeuvres to the effect of intentionally deceiving the buyer and inducing the latter into contracting upon more onerous conditions (incidental fraud was retained *in specie*). The *Cour de cassation* therefore seems to infer fraud from the presumption of the ability of the professional or specialised seller (cf. Case 3), to discover hidden defects.[7] Even if it is submitted that this decision of the *Cour de cassation* should rather be taken as an isolated instance, it nevertheless indicates a tendency of the courts to be rather lenient in admitting the existence of fraud in the context of the sale of motor vehicles by professionals to non–professionals.

In Bruno's case, there will however be one preliminary obstacle to overcome: the combination of the age of the car (that was not concealed to Bruno) and the assertion that it was 'as good as new' seems to reveal some kind of gross exaggeration that a strict judge might perceive in terms of a *dolus bonus*. However, if Bruno's garage pretended that the engine of the car was new when actually it had just been repaired, there is some case law holding the seller liable for fraud.[8] Again, the issue of excusability will normally not be raised when the action is brought in fraud[9] (see Case 3).

---

[5] See, for instance, Liège,14-5-1986, JL, 1987, 173: a used car was sold as dating from 1975 whereas it actually dated from the year 1974; the judge held the purchaser's mistake not excusable for he should have been aware of the real year when, upon delivery of the car, he was given the registration certificate along with the certificate from the automobile inspection authority that both mentioned this year.

[6] Cass, 21-04-1988, *RDC*, 1991, p. 203 and note C. Jassogne, 'Observations sur le dol du professionnel'.

[7] Jassogne note under Cass, 21-04-1988, *ibid.*, p. 205.

[8] Comm Liège, 24-1-1991, JT, 1991, p. 526.

[9] *Ibid.*, in this decision the commercial tribunal of Liège expressly ruled out the possibility of seeing the fraud wiped out by an eventual demonstration of the buyer's imprudence or technical knowledge in the field. Compare however Brussels, 27-6-1996, AJT, 1997–8, 329: an intentional transmission of erroneous information is reprehensible on the basis of fraud but, however, there is a certain obligation incurred by the deceived party to inform him- or herself, account being taken of his or her competence.

(iii) Making a claim on the basis of non-conformity is unlikely to succeed as it is very likely that Bruno has accepted the car since he needed to use it before he could discover the defect and this has the effect of barring such an action (see Case 3).

(iv) Bruno could bring a claim based upon the seller's guarantee against hidden defects and the most abundant case law as to the sale of used cars is to be found under this ground (arts. 1641 ff. of the Civil Code) as discussed in Case 3. If Bruno can prove the hidden defect, he will have the choice between terminating the contract (with reciprocal restitution) and asking for a reduction of the price corresponding to the diminution in value of the thing sold (art. 1644 of the Civil Code). Additionally, the purchaser will be awarded damages when the seller acted in bad faith (art. 1645 of the Civil Code), which is 'presumed' to be the case when the seller is a professional or specialist except if the latter can prove the non-perceptible character of the defect (which is hard to prove[10]).

Recent case law contains several decisions, the factual situations of which are similar to Bruno's case, where an action was successfully brought on this ground. For example it has been held that the fact that the car sold is a used car does not exclude the seller's guarantee against hidden defects; one cannot object that the purchaser did not get an expert to carry out a report on the car;[11] a used engine must be able to provide satisfaction for several thousands of kilometres.[12] If Bruno continues to use the car (here it would obviously be after repairs) during the time that his action is pending, he is estopped from exercising his right to terminate the contract but he will still be able to obtain a reduction of price and additional damages under art. 1645 of the Civil Code.[13]

---

[10] P. Galand, 'L'appréciation des vices cachés en cas de vente de véhicules automobiles', RGAR, 1992, no. 12024, E observes that the requirement for the defect to be non-perceptible has the effect, as to transactions for the sale of cars, of bringing Belgian case law closer to the position of the French *Cour de cassation* that does not allow contrary evidence against this presumption.

[11] *Ibid.*, no. 3: generally speaking there is no obligation for the buyer to have an expert analysis conducted upon the car nor to undertake a specific enquiry in order to discover eventual hidden defects (see also J.P. Zele, 6-9-1989, JJP, 1991, 442). Also the fact that the vehicle was presented to the automobile inspection authority (not giving rise to any observations on this occasion) does not in itself constitute an argument in favour of the seller (see also Antwerp, 30-3-1988, DC/CR, 1990–91, p. 716 and note B. Tuerlinckx).

[12] Liège, 20-6-1996, JLMB, 1997, p. 17.

[13] Civ Verviers, 16-10-1995, RGDC, 1996, 161; Comm Hasselt, 13-6-1995, Limb. Rechtsl., 1995, 246, Pas, 1995, III, 22; Civ Bruges, 6-9-1989, RW, 1991–92, p. 95, note EMS.

As explained in Case 3, Bruno must prove the importance of the defect; the fact that Bruno bought a used car will be taken into account because he may not require the car to have the same qualities as a new one.[14] But, as seen above, Bruno may expect the engine of a car, even a used car, to work, at least for some time. However, if Bruno purchased the car at a very low price, he will be deemed to have accepted the risk of potential hidden defects existing.[15] In any event Bruno must comply with art. 1648 of the Civil Code's requirement of a short time limit.[16]

To conclude, fraud looks like a good ground to invoke since the case law appears to be lenient with regard to proving the intentional element of fraud when the seller is a professional. However, the seller's guarantee against hidden defects appears to be the most commonly used and satisfactory remedy for the buyer in such cases.

England

Bruno's claims lie in breach of contract and misrepresentation. The principles are as set out in Case 1:

(i) the *contractual remedy*, if any, will be damages or the right to require the garage to repair or replace the car. There was an express assurance about the age and quality of the car, which will be incorporated as express terms of the contract if it can be said that, in the circumstances, the parties so intended;[17] but there will also have been implied conditions in the contract that the car complies with the description by reference to which it was bought, and that it was of satisfactory quality.[18] It is not clear from the facts whether the statement as to age is false: if so, there will be a breach of contract in relation to description. The unroadworthiness of the car will also be a breach of contract, as long as it can be established that the quality of the car was unsatisfactory at the time of the contract, and not merely because of what has happened

---

[14] Galand, 'L'appréciation des vices cachés', no. 5.

[15] Comm Hasselt, 12-1-1987, Limb. Rechtsl., 1987, p. 164.

[16] Case law concerning this time limit shows that each case is very much judged on the facts and that the courts interpret this provision to be enacted in the interest of both buyer and seller. Note that if the buyer brings an action not against the immediate seller but against the person who sold the car to his seller on the basis of arts. 1382–3 of the Civil Code (action in tort), he does not have to comply with the requirement of a short time limit under art. 1648 of the Civil Code (Liège, 26-5-1992, JLMB, 1995 and note P. Henry.

[17] See discussion under Cases 5 and 6.   [18] Sale of Goods Act 1979, ss. 13 and 14.

to it in the 'several months' which have elapsed since then. Although breach of condition (such as under ss. 13 and 14 Sale of Goods Act 1979) gives rise to a right to reject the goods, the time lapse will here mean that Bruno cannot any longer reject the car.[19] He may however claim damages on the contract measure, which will be the difference, at the time of contract, between the value of a car such as the dealer promised it to be, and the value of the car as it was in fact. Alternatively, he may require the garage to repair or replace the car.[20]

(ii) The *misrepresentation* claim depends on Bruno establishing that a false statement was made, either as to the age or simply as to the quality of the car. The statement 'as good as new' might not be a sufficiently precise statement of fact but the claim is certainly arguable.[21] If the misrepresentation is established the remedies have been described in Case 3: damages on the tort measure is the most likely remedy, since the lapse of time will have barred rescission unless Bruno can establish that the garage was fraudulent in making the statement(s) – time running from the contract in the case of non-fraudulent misrepresentations, but only from the date of discovery of the falsehood if fraud can be shown.[22]

(iii) No case of *mistake* could be made out here: the mistake would be as to quality, and is not sufficiently serious to fall within the established case law. Nor is it clear that the mistake was shared with the garage.

This case is a further illustration that a purchaser of a chattel must normally find a false statement or an unperformed promise by the vendor before he can complain of defects in what he has bought; and statements made during the negotiations ('sales talk') have to be analysed with some care to see whether they are sufficiently serious to bind the representor (either as a misrepresentation or as a contractual promise). Some assistance is given to a purchaser by the implication of contractual conditions (and therefore allocation of risk in favour of the purchaser) by the Sale of Goods Act 1979; but the basic principle of *caveat emptor* survives.

---

[19] See discussion under Case 3.

[20] Sale of Goods Act 1979, s. 48B. He may not claim a reduction of purchase price or rescind the contract under s. 48C, discussed under Case 3, because repair or replacement is here possible.

[21] See discussion under Case 6. In *Reece v. Seru Investments Ltd* [1973] EGD 152 it was held that an estate agent's assurance about a property being 'as good as it looks' was, on the facts, an actionable misrepresentation.

[22] See discussion under Case 3.

France

Bruno's claim against his seller could be based upon non-performance of the contract of sale (i) as well as on defective consent (ii).

(i) Article 1641 of the Civil Code provides that the seller must guarantee against all latent defects of the goods which might render them unfit for their intended use or which may diminish their use to a point that, had the buyer known about them, he would not have bought the goods or would have paid a lower price for them. The cause of action is distinct from simple non-conformity with the terms of the contract. For the first action to succeed, two main sorts of conditions (substantial and procedural) must be fulfilled:

(a) Bruno has to show that the defects of the car he bought (the fact that it is unroadworthy and that the motor needs replacement) were hidden at the moment of the sale, i.e. that they existed at that time but were not apparent (cf. art. 1642: the seller is not liable for any apparent defects which the buyer might have known about). Obviously, this is the case since the seller assured Bruno that the car was a 1995 'as good as new'. Bruno had no reason to be suspicious, since as a consumer he was dealing with a professional. The main rule created by case law applies here: as a professional, the seller is supposed to have known of the defect, i.e. he could not be unaware of it because of his professional expertise.[23] This rule arises from the presumption of the seller's knowledge of the defect, from which his bad faith is inferred. The presumption cannot be rebutted which has had the effect of converting an evidential rule into a substantive rule of law. Bruno then has to show that these defects render the thing 'unfit for its intended use'. Here again, the condition is satisfied and there is no need to show any specific use of which the seller may have been unaware: objectively a car must be roadworthy and the motor should not need to be replaced. Bruno can base his action on numerous precedents.[24]

(b) The main procedural condition, which has given rise to abundant litigation, is related to the interpretation of art. 1648 al. 1, which provides that such an action must be commenced by the buyer shortly after he has discovered the defect, according to the nature of this defect. What is mainly at stake here is the line that must be drawn between the action

---

[23] See Civ 1, 24 November 1954, JCP 1955.II. 8565, note HB.

[24] In relation to cases concerning cars, see Paris 3 May 1967 (Gaz. Pal. 1967.2.34, note J-P. D) or Paris 11 June 1970 (*ibid.* 1971.1. Somm.47, RTD civ 1971.389, obs. Cornu) retaining the excessive consumption of a car as a hidden defect; Civ 1, 23 May 1995 (Bull civ I, 217, 1996. Somm.15, obs. Tournafond) about the defective conception of a motor.

based on art. 1641 and the action for non-conformity, i.e. breach of the seller's duty to deliver the goods (see below (ii)).[25] The question as to when the short limitation period starts running is a matter of fact, decided by the trial judges.

Finally, it should be underlined that as the claimant Bruno has the burden of proof, which means that he must adduce evidence of the existence of the defect; the fact that the defect was prior to the sale; and if he wants damages, the bad faith or the professional quality of the seller. A recent decision of the *Cour de cassation* highlights the first condition by holding that the fact that the seller had voluntarily – at his own expense – replaced a part of a machine, was clear evidence, in the absence of other elements, of the existence of the defect (a kind of rebuttable presumption of the existence of a hidden defect).[26]

If Bruno's action succeeds, he may choose between two different types of remedies. According to art. 1644 he may either choose to return the car to the seller, in which case he shall be reimbursed; or he may choose to keep the car, in which case experts will determine its real market value and Bruno would be entitled to a reduction of the price. Of course, the second hypothesis is not convenient at all for Bruno, except if he wants to collect unroadworthy cars!

(ii) Bruno could also base his claim on the non-conformity of the car (see art. 1604 of the Civil Code). There is a concurrence of actions with the claim under (i) above. Either Bruno could allege that the seller's oral stipulation is deemed to be incorporated into the contract, and the car that has actually been delivered clearly fails to match up to its description, or that the non-conformity of the car delivered is understood as being unfit for the purpose. In a recent case the *Cour de cassation* decided that a failure to deliver a car capable of being used to transport disabled persons (and contractually agreed for this use) was a failure by the seller of his obligation to deliver goods in conformity and not a hidden defect.[27] However, a relative uncertainty remains for two main reasons. First, the *Cour de cassation's* attitude is not always as clear as it should be;[28] secondly, in some cases, it may still be difficult to distinguish the 'normal use' from the contractual description of the goods.

---

[25] If Bruno has just discovered the defect, he can ask for (but not require) a court-ordered expertise and the short limitation period will run from the date when the expert's report is delivered.

[26] See Com, 1 April 1997, *Dalloz Affaires* 1997, n. 20, p. 632.

[27] Civ 1, 17 June 1997, *Dalloz Affaires* 1997, p. 1218.

[28] See e.g. Civ 1, 5 November 1996, *Dalloz Affaires* 1996, p. 1410; JCP 1997.II. 22872, note Rade: adde D. 1998, Jault – Sczeke.

(iii) Bruno could also claim he has made a mistake as to a substantial quality of the subject-matter of the contract, under art. 1110 of the Civil Code. Actions pursuant to art. 1641 and mistake are theoretically very different: the former refers to the performance of the contract and is based on an objective approach (the car must objectively be unfit for its intended purpose); the latter is related to the formation of the contract and is a mixture of objective–subjective criteria. The distinction is clear where the mistake concerns a quality without any link with the use of the thing, for instance the authenticity of a painting (see Case 1). However the frontier is less clear-cut where the mistake is a consequence of a hidden defect, which might be the case here: one could easily argue that the hidden defect of the car has led Bruno to have a mistaken idea of the reality, and furthermore that he has been victim of fraud (art. 1116 of the Civil Code).[29] Some recent case law suggests that an action may well lie for a breach of the duty to inform on the basis of fraud if the seller fraudulently concealed the condition of the car.[30]

As the above-mentioned actions are concurrent, Bruno will have to make a choice according to the procedural and substantive advantages of each action. He will have to consider whether it is easier to prove mistake, fraud or a hidden defect of the goods. It could be argued that evidence of mistake or fraud is more difficult to establish than the objective criterion of art. 1641 of the Civil Code. However, according to the recent decision of the *Cour de cassation*, in an action for fraud concealment, the seller has the burden of proving that he has discharged his duty to inform, thus reversing the burden of proof. This obviously alleviates the evidential difficulties of an action based on fraud. In the end, it depends on what Bruno wants – to keep the car with damages or to return it to the seller and get his money back, with damages.

Germany

Because the car is defective Bruno (under §§ 434, 437, 439, 440 BGB) can claim his warranty rights (repairing the car, termination of the contract, reduction of the purchase price). He can also claim for damages

---

[29] See Case 3 for example.

[30] For example, Civ 1, 19 June 1985, Bull civ I, no. 201 where the seller was held liable for concealing the condition of a second-hand car and even more to the point, Civ 1, 15 May 2002, RTDCiv 2003, 84, where the *Cour de cassation* held that the seller had the burden of proving that the duty to inform had been fulfilled, thus reinforcing the duty incumbent on him, as opposed to the claimant proving the seller's fraud (in relation to the seller's concealing the fact that the second-hand car for sale had been in an accident).

for breach of contract if the seller knew or should have known of the defect (§§ 437 Ziff 3, 440, 280). It is not clear whether Bruno may claim for damages also from the fact that the car does not show the guaranteed characteristic (§§ 437 Ziff 3, 280, 276 I, 311a BGB). The courts have often assessed statements concerning the age, condition and roadworthiness as guaranteed qualities – mostly in cases where a dealer sells used cars. However, the statement that the car is 'as good as new' is too indefinite to invoke the seller's special liability for the damage caused by his breach. The seller has not given a warranty relating to a particular quality but on the contrary, has only touted the apparently good condition of the car.[31]

If the seller had nevertheless been aware of the fact that the car was in fact unroadworthy and that the motor needed replacing, then Bruno may nonetheless seek to enforce his claim for damages under §§ 437 Ziff 3, 440, 280. The seller is then liable on the grounds that he fraudulently withheld a defect in the object of sale. The knowledge of the seller also determines whether Bruno may, besides this, annul the contract under § 123 (fraudulent misrepresentation) and whether he can in addition seek to enforce a tortious claim for damages. The seller is also made liable under § 826 if he intended wilfully and knowingly to injure Bruno by selling him the used car.

Bruno's claims under *culpa in contrahendo*, however, are ruled out; they become subsidiary claims if the purchaser is able to assert his special warranty claims.[32] The same applies to a claim to annul the contract of sale on grounds of mistake as to quality (§ 119 II).[33] If the promise that the car is a 1995 model turns out to be incorrect, then things would differ: the *BGH* does not see any defect of quality in the age of a used vehicle, but rather a characteristic as to quality. According to this view, the purchaser who makes a mistake as to the year of a car does not have a warranty claim but may annul the contract on grounds of mistake.[34]

Greece

When Bruno bought the car he had made a fundamental mistake as to the car's qualities, more specifically as to its roadworthy condition.

---

[31] On the wealth of decisions concerning warranties in used goods trade cf. Palandt/Putzo, § 459 paras. 30a and 31.

[32] Cf. R. Knöpfle, 'Zum Verhältnis zwischen Gewährleistungsansprüchen und Ansprüchen aus culpa in contrahendo oder positiver Forderungsverletzung' NJW 1990, 2497 ff.

[33] Cf. Case 3.

[34] RG LZ 1929, 547 and 1931, 240 ('Rohilla-Case'); BGHZ 72, 252; BGHZ 78, 216 ('Mähdrescher-Case'); OLG Stuttgart NJW 1989, 2547.

Therefore according to art. 142 AK, he can seek judicial annulment of the sale. Both the objective and the subjective criteria are met.[35] Bruno's mistake is due to the local garage's inaccurate declarations which were made with intent. As fraud is recognised by law (art. 147 AK) as a special ground for the annulment of a legal act, Bruno can seek the annulment of the sale and, in parallel, damages in tort, since fraud is a tort (art. 914 AK). Bruno can ask for the return of the purchase price, as the seller has been unjustly enriched to Bruno's detriment (arts. 904 ff. AK) and he must return the car.

The good condition of the car is a specific quality expressly agreed by the parties. Bruno may also make a claim for breach of contract (termination, reduction of purchase price or damages under arts. 543–4 AK). However, as Bruno discovered the non-conformity several months after the conclusion of the sale, it must be presumed that this claim is time barred, since arts. 554 ff. AK provide for a short limitation period of six months from the delivery of movable goods.

It is disputed whether the above rights of the purchaser are concurrent with his right to annul the sale on the grounds of mistake (art. 142 AK). According to the predominant opinion[36] the purchaser cannot seek the annulment of the sale, because the provisions of arts. 534 ff. AK, as *lex specialis*, exclude the application of the general provisions on mistake.

The opposite view[37] submits that, as the two legal institutions have different goals – the provisions on mistake secure the autonomy of the will while those on the vendor's liability for defects of the thing and lack of conformity aim at avoiding the harmful consequences of the

---

[35] On the question of prescription, see Case 1.

[36] AP 463/61 NoV 10, 166; Balis, *General Principles of Civil Law*, § 42; D. Bosdas (1964) ArchN 15, 373; Filios, *Law of Obligations*, Special Part § 1; Gazis, *General Principles of Civil Law*, § 16 III 3; I. Karakatsanis, 'Concurrence of annulment in the grounds of fraud with the rights of the purchaser which arise from art. 543 AK' (1975) EEN 42, p. 854; A. Ligeropoulos, 'Concerning the sale of goods chapter of the draft of the law of obligations' (1937) *Themis* 48, p. 638; K. Spiliopoulos, in A. Litzeropoulos, A. Gazis and G. Rammos (eds.), *ErmAK Introd. Notes to Arts* 534–56 (Athens, 1972), n. 65.

[37] AP 706/85 Elld 27, 91; I. Aravantinos, *Mistake as to the object of the performance* (Athens, 1954), p. 89; P. Doris, 'Concurrence of the action for annulment on the grounds of mistake as to quality with the claims which arise from hidden defects and absence of agreed quality' (1968) EEN 35, pp. 703 ff. who however accepts that the purchaser's right to annul the contract is subject to the brief six months prescription of art. 554 AK; Kafkas, *Law of Obligations*, pp. 534–5 § 7; Spyridakis, *General Principles*, p. 602; Stathopoulos, *Contract Law in Hellas*, p. 221; P. Zepos, *Law of Obligations. Special Part* (2nd edn, Athens, 1965), p. 80; see also Klavanidou, *Error as to the Qualities of the Thing in Sales*, pp. 222 ff.

disproportion between performance and counter-performance which is due to the defect or non-conformity – the purchaser can have recourse to either provision without one excluding the other.

Ireland

In this case the fact that the car was unroadworthy gives rise to a breach of contract between Bruno and the local garage. Under the Sale of Goods and Supply of Services Act 1980, s. 13 imposes an implied term into contracts relating to the sale of motor vehicles. Such contracts carry an implied condition that on delivery, the vehicle is free from any defects which would render the vehicle unsafe or dangerous to occupants, to road users or to the public in general. This is quite an onerous condition and exposes the seller to considerable liability as was the case in *Glorney* v. *O'Brien*[38] where a car sold for £250 rendered the vendor liable for damages in excess of £18,000 when the suspension collapsed in the vehicles injuring the occupants. There would also be potential liability under s. 39 (goods of merchantable quality) and s. 40 (goods fit for the purpose for which they are intended) of the 1980 Act.

Whilst the Sale of Goods and Supply of Services Act 1980 provides a purchaser with the remedy of rejecting the goods, the facts of this case show that there has been a considerable lapse of time (several months) since Bruno purchased the car. It may be that this lapse of time would prevent him from rejecting the goods but would allow him a claim in damages.

Bruno also has a remedy under misrepresentation. In this case, there appears to have been a misrepresentation as to the quality of the motor vehicle and as to its age. Again, given the amount of time that has elapsed since the purchase of the motor vehicle, Bruno's most likely remedy under this head would be in damages, as he may have lost his rights to annul under the Act.

Italy

(i) As stated in Case 3, the provisions of art. 1490 of the Civil Code containing a guarantee against hidden defects (*Garanzia per i vizi della cosa*)[39] are currently interpreted to be useful even in the sale of second-hand objects so that in Italy there is no difference between new and

---

[38] Unreported judgment of the High Court (14 November 1988).   [39] See Case 3.

second-hand things.[40] In such cases the buyer only has to prove that the goods do not have the promised qualities; there is no need to prove any fraudulent behaviour or negligence. The fact that the engine has been found broken after several months does not bar the action because time runs from discovery of the defect (art. 1495 of the Civil Code).[41]

(ii) In the case of fraud, if the factual evidence proves that the car was not at all in good condition, as assured by the garage, the court could find elements of deceit (art. 1439 of the Civil Code).[42] In case Bruno decides to raise such a claim the presence of an express promise of 'good condition' would enable him to use the precontractual liability action. There is a general precontractual duty of good faith (according to arts. 1337 and 1338) and the promise made by the seller that the car was in 'good condition' amounts to a breach of this duty.

The Supreme Court[43] says that a buyer can claim damages with or without claiming annulment as cumulative actions are allowed by Italian case law; scholars analyse this as a precontractual liability although 'negative interest' (reliance) damages are allowed.[44] The way Italian courts assess damages in precontractual liability cases does not follow the straight distinction between reliance and expectation damages; generally they provide an equitable assessment and even if in theory only negative interest can be claimed, there are cases where greater compensation can be obtained.[45] This kind of case is very frequent in the small claims court 'giudici di pace' and are generally handled through a pre-trial examination of the vehicle made by an expert who will take an oath out of court to fulfil his duty correctly.

The Netherlands

Bruno has several remedies.

(i) The local garage assured Bruno that the second-hand car he bought was a 1995 model 'as good as new'. Does this amount to a guarantee? If it is, and if the statement turns out to be untrue Bruno can claim

---

[40] Cass 1995, n. 806, Cass 1979, n. 2167.

[41] Article 1495 of the Civil Code. The limits and conditions of action: 'The buyer forfeits the right of warranty if he fails to notify the seller of the defects in the thing within eight days from their discovery, unless a different time limit is established by the parties or by law. Notification is not necessary if the seller has acknowledged the existence of the defect or if he has concealed it. In all cases, the action is prescribed in one year from delivery; but the buyer who is sued for performance of the contract can always plead the warranty, provided that the defect in the thing was notified within eight days from the discovery and within one year from delivery.'

[42] Cass 1996, n. 3001; Cass 1960, n. 2119.   [43] Cass 1968, n. 2445.

[44] Bianca, Il contratto, p. 1 77.   [45] See D. Caruso, La culpa in contrahendo, pp. 118 ff.

damages on the basis of breach of the guarantee, which is a separate contract.[46]

Under the old Code, which was applicable until 1992, and which may still be applicable to some cases decided today,[47] the question whether there was a guarantee was of particular interest. The *Hoge Raad* had held since 1963 that in case of *species* objects the rules on hidden defects[48] excluded the applicability of the general rules on non-performance (liability for breach, possibility of termination etc.), thereby effectively turning the rules on hidden defects from a protection device for the buyer into a doctrine that favours the seller, because the buyer had to complain very quickly (within a short delay) and if he did not he would lose his claim. However, the rules on hidden defects did not preclude the buyer from making a claim on the basis of a guarantee made by the seller.[49] Therefore in cases of hidden defects it was crucial for the buyer to establish that the seller guaranteed the absence of hidden defects.[50] This also explains why the courts sometimes applied the rather artificial doctrine of implied warranties.

The present 1992 Code no longer contains a specific doctrine of hidden defects. It was replaced by the general doctrine of non-conformity, similar to the Vienna Sales Convention. Therefore the doctrine of explicit and implicit guarantees is no longer needed to circumvent the obstacle of the requirement of short delay for a claim for damages or termination to succeed in case of hidden defects (see below (ii)). Nevertheless, in the case where an explicit or implicit guarantee can be established the buyer is free to base his claim on that rather than on a (possible) ground of non-conformity.

Does the garage's assurance that the second-hand car sold is 'as good as new' amount to a warranty? The statement 'as good as new' is definitely far too general but the claim that the car was a 1995 model might amount to a warranty.[51]

(ii) Article 7:17, s. 1 BW says that the object delivered must 'conform to the contract' (conformity). Section 2 explains when this requirement is not met:

A thing does not conform to the contract if it does not possess the qualities which the buyer was entitled to expect on the basis of the contract. The buyer

---

[46] Cf. Asser/Hijma 5-I (2001), no. 338.   [47] See art. 182 *Overgangswet*.
[48] Articles 1540 ff. old BW.   [49] *HR*, 10 May 1963, NJ 1963, 288 (*Vouwapparaat*)
[50] Cf. Asser/Hijma 5-I (2001), no. 365.
[51] Compare the examples in Asser/Hijma 5-I (2001), no. 338.

may expect that the thing possesses the qualities necessary for its normal use, the existence of which is not open to doubt, and the qualities necessary for any special use provided in the contract.

Did the car conform to the contract? This requirement does not seem to have been met. In other words: there seems to be non-conformity. The car does not seem to have the qualities the buyer was entitled to expect. It does not have the qualities necessary to allow an ordinary use of it and Bruno was not expected to have any doubt about the presence of these qualities. The ordinary way to use a car is to drive it on the public roads. Here the case *HR*, 15 April 1994, (*Schirmeister/De Heus*)[52] is of particular relevance. In that case the *Hoge Raad* made the following general considerations:

Whenever the seller knows that a (second-hand) car is bought in order to use it, as the seller knows, on the public roads, it will have to be held in general that the car is not in conformity with the contract in case, as a result of a defect that cannot be easily discovered nor repaired, such use of the car would lead to a dangerous traffic situation. It is not to be excluded that exceptions have to be made to this rule, e.g. when the buyer has accepted the risk of the presence of such a defect. The latter may occur, for transactions like the one under discussion here, in the situation, among others, where for a buyer the state of the carrosserie of the car is more important than its suitability for circulation. However, it should be taken into account that, statements by the seller regarding that condition, depending on their content, may be a bar to such an acceptance of the risk of defects.

Applying this rule to Bruno's case there seems to be a case of non-conformity. If Bruno intended to use the car on the public roads and the seller knew this – which seems likely in this case, and which, unlike the case of *Schirmeister/De Heus* that dealt with the sale of an 'old timer' (a 20-year-old Citroen DS), may probably be presumed – the car does not correspond to the contract if using it on the public roads would cause danger to traffic. This seems to be the case here. The car is likely to cause danger to traffic since it is said to be 'unroadworthy', and the defect cannot be easily repaired since it is said that the motor needs replacing.[53] The exception to the rule indicated by the *Hoge Raad* in its decision does not seem to apply. There are no facts stated

---

[52] NJ 1995, 614, note Brunner.
[53] It seems likely that the *Hoge Raad* intends the expenses of the reparation to be decisive rather than the amount of work and time it will take.

that suggest that Bruno had accepted the risk of the presence of the defect.

Bruno does not seem to have lost his right to invoke non-conformity on the basis of limitation set out in art. 7:23, s. 1 BW.[54] So, regardless of whether or not the statements made by the seller amounted to a guarantee, Bruno may opt for several remedies on the basis of non-conformity, i.e. repair and replacement, terminate, and ask for specific performance and claim damages. In principle the remedies may be combined to the extent that they do not logically exclude each other (e.g. specific performance and termination).

As the contract comes within the definition of a consumer sales contract,[55] Bruno has a number of additional rights and remedies as a consumer which cannot be limited or excluded in the contract (art. 7:6 BW). According to art. 7:21 BW, s. 1, in case of non-conformity the buyer may, in principle, at his choice, claim delivery of missing parts, repair of the object, or replacement of the object.[56] Since the problem is not one of a missing part, the first remedy does not apply, but the second and the third may be of interest for Bruno. He may claim repair or replacement of the car. However, if he does, because it is a consumer sale, the seller may choose either to replace the car or give back the price Bruno paid.[57] Of course the consumer-buyer does not only have these specific

---

[54] The first sentence says: 'The buyer may not claim that delivery does not conform to the contract, unless he has notified the seller thereof promptly after he has, or reasonably should have, discovered this.' The second sentence of art. 7:23, s. 1 BW says: 'Where, however, it is established that the thing lacks a quality which according to the seller it possessed, or where the variance pertains to facts of which the seller was aware or ought to have been aware but has not communicated, the notification must take place promptly after the discovery.'

[55] A contract of consumer sale is defined in art. 7:6 BW as a contract of sale between a professional seller and a non-professional buyer.

[56] Article 7:21 BW, s. 1: 'Where the thing delivered does not conform to the contract, the buyer may demand: a. delivery of that which is missing; b. repair of the thing delivered, provided the seller can reasonably comply therewith; c. replacement of the thing delivered, unless the variance from what was agreed is too insignificant to justify this, or unless, after the buyer should reasonably have taken into acccount the right to set it aside, the thing has been lost or has deteriorated because the buyer has not ensured its safekeeping as a prudent obligor.'

[57] Article 7:21 BW, s. 2: 'If, in a consumer sale and pursuant to subparagraph b or c of paragraph 1, the buyer demands the repair or replacement, the seller is entitled to choose between replacement or reimbursement of the purchase price. The seller must make this choice within a short period, and, subsequently, he must perform his obligation within a reasonable period, failing which the buyer may enforce his rights to demand repair or replacement.'

remedies given to him in art. 7:21 BW; he also has the other general remedies,[58] so he may, in principle, terminate the contract as explained above.[59]

Bruno may also claim damages (see arts. 6:74 BW and 7:24 BW). As to damages he may claim both damages that replace the performance by the seller and damages for delay for the period for which the seller was in *mora* (art. 6:85 BW). As said, remedies may be combined. Bruno could, for example, choose to terminate the contract and at the same time claim damages for delay.

(iii) Depending on whether the seller knew that the car was not a 1995 model 'as good as new' but in fact unroadworthy Bruno may annul the contract for fraud (art. 3:44 BW). Bruno will then have to prove intentional deceit. It does not necessarily follow from the facts that the seller deceived Bruno intentionally.[60] If intentional deceit is established Bruno may eventually claim for recovery of damages in tort.

(iv) Bruno may annul the contract for mistake. If Bruno entered into the contract on the basis of the seller's declarations he may annul the contract for mistake. The seller made statements which turned out to be untrue. This makes the contract voidable (art. 6:228 (1)(a) BW). A potential duty for Bruno to investigate is outweighed by the seller's duty to make correct statements. In principle, a party may expect the statements made by the other to be true.[61] If Bruno was not induced to conclude the contract by the statements of the seller he may nevertheless annul it for common mistake if he would not have concluded the contract had he known that the car was unroadworthy and the motor needed replacing. In the *Schirmeister/De Heus* case mentioned above,[62] the *Hoge Raad* quashed the decision on this point: the reasons given were insufficient to shift the risk of the mistake to the buyer. In Bruno's case there seems to be no reason why the common mistake should remain at his risk. Thus, he may choose to ask for a reduction of the price or for the car to be repaired on the basis of art. 6:230 BW.[63]

---

[58] Article 7:22 BW: 'The rights mentioned in articles 20 and 21 may be exercised by the buyer, without prejudice to all other rights or actions.'

[59] See art. 6:265 BW.   [60] See above pp. 184–5, Case 3.

[61] See *HR Booy/Wisman* etc. See on this, Case 11.

[62] The Court of Appeal gave as reasons for their decision the fact that the car was 22 years old; the characteristics of the parties (both were amateur enthusiasts of old Citroens) and the fact that the defect had become apparent only a year after the conclusion of the contract and the buyer had used the car for some time.

[63] See on this article, Case 3.

Norway

Whether Bruno can claim breach of contract against the seller may be answered using two different legal principles:

(i) One may ask if the car could be seen as corresponding to the *information* provided by the seller, cf. Norwegian Sale of Goods Act, §§ 17 (1) and 18. The description 'as good as new' is general and vague, but still gives the impression that the car is in (relatively) good condition. The description is, therefore, not without content and, as such, cannot be regarded as a 'mere puff'.

Somewhat earlier legal practice seems to have favoured a more liberal attitude towards the seller. Reference may, for instance, be made to U 1961.143 H and U 1975.84 H. It would seem that there has been a tightening up in this area. Even if the purchaser of a nine-year-old car has to be prepared for considerable wear and tear, the claimed defects are so serious that the description 'as good as new' appears to be a misrepresentation. There is consequently a defect in the car, and the purchaser can present the usual claims for breach of contract. In this case, termination combined with damages seems reasonable.

(ii) A judgment of defect can be made *independently of the information* the seller has given the purchaser about the item for sale. If a judgment is given which is not closely related to the circumstances of the sale, it is often termed an abstract or general judgment of defect. The judgment must then be based on a general standard of quality – an implied term.

It is somewhat unclear what can, generally, be expected by the purchaser from an item for sale. In the Swedish Sale of Goods Act, § 17, para. 3, the criterion is 'what the purchaser with reason could expect'.[64] Regarding the sale of fungible goods, one speaks in Norwegian theory of the requirement for delivering 'a reasonably good item' or an item having 'a normal functioning capacity throughout a reasonable operating period'.[65,66] Especially when considering brand new goods, such a view could be of value. With the sale of unique items, this approach would

---

[64] J. Nørager-Nielsen and S. Theilgaard, *Købeloven med kommentarer* (2nd edn, Copenhagen, 1993), p. 708, consider that the commonly used defect term 'is based on the purchaser's expectation of an item having the same use and value as items of a similar kind'.

[65] See RT 1974.269, p. 276 and ND 1979.231 Wingull, as well as V. Hagstrøm, *Fragmenter fra obligasjonsrett* (Oslo 1992), vol. II, chs. 12 and 51, p. 34, and K. Krüger, *Norsk kontraktsrett* (Bergen, 1989), p. 213.

[66] The requirements of the Norwegian Sale of Goods Act, § 17(2) (a), that an item should be suited to the same purposes as similar items and (2)(d) should be packaged in a regular or secure way, can be seen as resulting from more stringent norms.

be less fruitful, and (each situation) would need to be more individually determined. Not least, the price of the item would influence judgment. It is emphasised that 'the decisive factor is whether the creditor has adequate grounds to be concerned about the item'.[67] This is actually the same thinking as we found in the Swedish Sale of Goods Act, § 17, para. 3.

The flaws found in the car are probably more serious than what the purchaser could reasonably expect at the time of the signing of the contract. On these grounds, a defect is present, and regular defect remedies can be used.

Used goods, such as second-hand cars, are normally sold in 'as is' condition. The Norwegian Sale of Goods Act, § 19(1)(c) indicates, in such a case, particular limitations that hold regardless of any disclaimer of liability. The goods should not be in 'substantially worse condition than the buyer had reason to expect in view of the price and other circumstances'. Because a purchaser normally has to be prepared for a deterioration of quality in used goods, the criterion of essentiality would probably not lead to conclusions noticeably different from what follows from the general principles.

Portugal

This case would be considered as a case of defects related to the working order of the thing sold, which the seller guaranteed was in proper working condition. Therefore, the law (art. 921° of the Civil Code) states that if the seller was obliged by agreement or usage to grant the good working order of the thing sold, he has to repair or substitute it, even if he committed no fault nor was the buyer mistaken. The law provides for this guarantee and does not distinguish between new and second-hand things. However, the guarantee is only valid for six months after conclusion of the sale unless common usage has established a longer period (art. 921°, 2 of the Civil Code). Provided that Bruno brings a claim within six months of the sale, he can ask the seller to repair or replace the car.

Scotland

Whether a remedy is available to Bruno or not depends on how the statement from the garage is classified. A statement that a second-hand car is 'as good as new' would appear to be an expression of opinion. An opinion has been held not to give rise to any obligations and cannot be relied upon. This point was made by Lord Mackenzie in the

---

[67] Hagstrøm, *Fragmenter fra obligasjonsrett*, vol. p. 41.

case of *Gowans* v. *Christie*,[68] where he argued that: 'such representations are, it is thought, a mere matter of opinion, which even if erroneous, could not form a good ground for reducing the lease'. In the case of *Flynn* v. *Scott*,[69] a statement that a vehicle was in good running order was held to be an expression of opinion which could not be relied upon.

The statement can be treated as a fraudulent misrepresentation of fact if it can be established that the opinion that the car was as good as new was not honestly held by the proprietor, or that no reasonable person in the defender's position could have held such a view. Further support for Bruno's case can be found in the case of *Smith* v. *Land and House Property Corpn*,[70] where Bowen LJ stated that 'if the facts are not equally known to both sides, then a statement of opinion by the one who knows the facts best involves very often a statement of a material fact, for he impliedly states facts which justify his opinion'.

In the present case, the garage is likely to have had more chance to assess the condition of the vehicle than Bruno and is also likely to have more expertise in the relevant field. It therefore may well be that their statement that the car was 'as good as new' will be treated as a statement of a material fact, and therefore Bruno will be able to have the contract rescinded on the grounds of the misrepresentation.

Alternatively, since the statement was made in negotiations close to the time at which the contract was formed, by a party in a better position to know the accuracy of the facts, it could be regarded as a term of the contract, and an action would lie for breach of contract.

Spain

(i) In such circumstances, the Spanish Civil Code allows the buyer to seek annulment of the contract of sale on the basis of a fraud by the seller. Articles 1300 and 1301 thus provide that contracts can be annulled: there is a four-year time limit.

Our point of departure must be the presence of possible fraud in the seller's conduct. In this case, clearly the buyer would not have acquired the car but for the seller's declaration that it was in perfect condition, as if it were new. There is clear precedent on this matter (the Supreme Court Ruling of 4/12/56), where an automobile was sold as if it were in good condition when that was not the case, the court concluded that this was a fraud.

For this reason, we consider that a claim to annul the sale contract pursuant to art. 1301 of the Civil Code before the Courts of first instance

---

[68] (1871) 9 M 485 at p. 487.   [69] (1949) SC 442.   [70] (1885) 28 Ch D 7 at p. 15.

would be quite likely to succeed so that the seller would have to return the money received for the car and the buyer would have to return the car.

(ii) Legal theory and case law also admit another approach for the buyer in the form of the redhibitory action under art. 1486 of the Civil Code in the case of hidden defects in the item sold which render it unsuitable for its use. It could also be considered here that there are hidden defects since the buyer and perhaps the seller are unaware of the true state of the automobile, which stopped running shortly after it was bought. Bruno could also bring an action under this head within six months following the sale, pursuant to art. 1490 of the Civil Code, in order to return the car and recover the price paid.

Comparative observations

The panoply of available remedies under a contract of sale is highlighted here; the case is simpler than the hypotheses under Case 1 since doubts as to the quality, value or authorship of the subject matter of the contract are not an issue. The significant characteristics of this case are: the consumer/professional inequality of information; the fact that a false representation was made orally prior to making the contract; the fact that the subject matter is second-hand and the fact that the altered quality of the goods seriously affects their usage.

Once again, all legal systems offer a variety of remedies, both for defective consent as well as for breach of contract. These options will be summarised briefly.

(i) Under Austrian, Dutch, French and Greek law there will be a remedy for mistake which entitles the buyer to annul the contract and claim restitution of the purchase price. For the most part, no bars or conditions operate to restrict the claim, save under Belgian law where it is suggested that the mistake may be inoperative since a purchaser of a second-hand car has to comply with a more onerous duty to inform himself about its condition; failure to do so renders his mistake inexcusable.

(ii) Subject to the proviso that a representation must be a statement of fact (made by one party to the other prior to the contract), an action could lie for fraudulent or innocent misrepresentation, under English, Irish and Scottish law. However, only damages will be available, since the lapse of time will bar a claim in rescission, except if fraudulent misrepresentation is proven, in which case time only starts running from the discovery of the fraud. Likewise, under Belgian, Dutch, French, German, Greek, Italian and Spanish law an action will lie for fraud, giving rise to annulment and/or tortious damages.

(iii) Again, several types of breach of contract are identifiable: breach of a contractual duty to inform the other contracting party, breach of a guarantee against hidden defects, breach which may be described as non-conformity in contracts of sale (relating to the quality and fitness for purpose of the goods) and breach of description.

(a) *The contractual duty to inform.* Once again under Norwegian law, the breach of contract is qualified as a contractual failure to disclose since the breach is based on the falseness of the seller's statement (the serious-ness of the defect renders the statement untrue). This kind of breach of contract can be assimilated to a precontractual obligation to inform (or a fraudulent concealment) and gives rise to termination and damages. The similarity of the solution as under (ii) is striking except that the remedy is qualified as contractual. The practical difference lies in the assessment of damages: contractual damages (combined with termination and resti-tution in kind) enable the aggrieved party to claim expectation damages (putting him in the situation he would have been had the contract been performed) whereas tortious damages have a different end-purpose.

(b) *Guarantee against hidden defects and non-conformity.* Under Austrian, Belgian, Dutch, French, Italian, Portuguese, and Spanish law a claim can be made for breach of a guarantee against hidden defects within a short time limit. The remediable aspect of the defect affects the choice of remedy under Austrian law (retrospective termination or price reduc-tion). The fact that the car is second-hand does not affect the existence of the remedy. Remedies consist in termination, price reduction or dam-ages. This was the case in German law (up until 31 December 2001).[71] Under the new law, the buyer's remedies are strengthened, since he can now claim for the car's repairs[72] as well as damages.[73] Under Greek law, the absence of the good condition of the car, a quality agreed by the

---

[71] Such damages were awarded either as the car lacked a guaranteed quality (former § 463, 1st sentence), which is not applicable here or whenever the seller had concealed a defect and deceived the buyer (former § 463, 2nd sentence); this being a question of evidence.

[72] If repairing the car is useless or impossible, the buyer can fall back on termination of the contract or reduction of the price because the car's condition does not correspond to the contract (cf. §§ 434, 437 Ziff 1 for the provisions on repairs; §§ 434, 437 Ziff 2 for termination or reduction of price).

[73] Damages for breach of contract can be awarded because the seller knew or ought to have known that the car is defective (§§ 434, 437 Ziff 3, 440, 280) or if the seller made a guarantee as to the quality of the car but the quality is lacking (§§ 434, 437 Ziff 2, 280, 276 I, 311 a). The latter provision is not fulfilled on the facts.

parties, constitutes a breach of contract under arts. 543–4 AK. This action looks similar to those above, described as a guarantee against hidden defects, the remedies are identical and a short time limit of six months also applies.

Furthermore, a remedy, which may be considered somewhat similar, lies in English and Scots law under s. 14 SGA 1979 (as amended) and in Irish law under s. 13 SGSA 1980 for breach of satisfactory quality. In a similar vein, under Swedish law and other sections of the Norwegian Sale of Goods Act, the seller's conduct can be qualified as a breach of contract independent of the information given to the buyer, since the goods do not comply with what the purchaser was expecting. Special provisions apply in relation to second-hand goods under Norwegian law. Termination and damages are thus available. This presents non-conformity against an objective criterion as that which could be reasonably expected by the buyer.

(c) *Breach of description.* Likewise, if the statement 'as good as new' is deemed to be incorporated into the contract itself, an action for breach of description will lie. Such an action giving rise to termination and damages is recognised by English, Irish and Scots law.[74] Here however, the lapse of time is such that it will bar the claim for termination, since the car has been accepted. This action appears to resemble that of § 463 BGB (new law: §§ 434, 437 Ziff 2, 280, 276 I, 311a) an action for damages in respect of breach of what is described as a 'guaranteed characteristic' and that of express warranties in the Netherlands. Furthermore, under Norwegian law, an action for breach of description (§§ 17 and 18 of the Sale of Goods Act) will also lie, giving rise to termination and damages.

The cumulative nature of remedies for defective consent and breach of contract has been the subject of academic controversy.[75] This case exemplifies one of our original hypotheses that fact-hypotheticals that can be qualified as mistake often give rise to an overlap between the two types of remedies. Here the similarity of available remedies is noticeable and one might ask therefore whether this is because the sale of goods is a relatively codified area of the law in all legal systems (including the common law countries!). Another explanation would be not to rely on the legal formant but to highlight the underlying value which may

---

[74] Section 13 SGA 1979 for English and Scots law; s. 13 of SGSA 1980 for Irish law.

[75] Note that in Austria, France and Greece a concurrence of actions is admitted whereas the strict interpretation given to the *lex specialis* rule in the law of sales means that this is not the case in Germany, except for fraud.

be similar here: it is plausible that there is a similarity in outlook in relation to the law's expectation of the seller's obligations. This may be expressed, conversely, by the idea that all legal systems lay down a minimum objective standard in the contract: the buyer is entitled to a car that can be used on the road. In the end, the buyer's choice of remedy is based on factual considerations such as prescription, evidential difficulties to prove the seller's statement and on his personal preference: repair, replacement, price reduction or termination in order to go to another seller. The fact that the car is second-hand has little bearing on the buyer's remedies in view of the fact that the contract is categorised as a consumer sale. This factor would be relevant in some systems, however, if the sale took place between two individuals. Whether on the legal ground of the falsity of the information given or on the basis of the non-conformity of the goods with the buyer's expectations (in a variety of forms), all systems are in agreement that the risk lies clearly on the seller when the goods do not correspond to what had been contractually agreed (and can be reasonably expected) and what is actually delivered.

It is probable that the harmonisation of rules as to consumer guarantees[76] may have the effect of simplifying the available remedies and replacing remedies for defective consent with the action for non-conformity in the future. The action for non-conformity is intended to alleviate procedural difficulties for the buyer (such as the burden of proof) although the Directive leaves some leeway on a number of important points.[77]

---

[76] See EC Directive 1999/44.

[77] For example, the Directive allows member states to opt out of the guarantee in respect of second-hand goods. The question of concurrence of actions is left open for member states to implement as they think fit, so harmonisation is aimed at a minimal protection. Furthermore, no precision is given as to the mechanism of termination so it can be inferred that termination will continue to be judicial or unilateral according to present national rules.

Case 6

Emmanuel v. The Computer Shop

Case

Emmanuel, a gifted philosophy student but not much of a handyman, bought a computer from a shop specialising in the sale of quality second-hand office equipment. He chose a model that was fairly expensive, but, as he informed the salesman, he recognised the brand and preferred to pay extra as he was acquiring the benefit of a proper maintenance contract. The salesman made no comment. However, when, on encountering various technical difficulties, he applied to the manufacturer for help, he was informed that the maintenance contract had expired before the sale. What remedy, if any, is available?

Discussions

Austria

Emmanuel's reason for buying the fairly expensive computer was in order to have a proper maintenance contract with the manufacturer of a recognised brand mark. Even if Emmanuel had informed the salesman about his motives it is uncertain and questionable whether these motives had been agreed upon by both parties (in the sense of § 901 1st sentence ABGB) as a condition relating to the subject matter of the contract. If not, such motives have no influence on the validity of a legal transaction for payment (§ 901 2nd sentence ABGB). Such an agreement must be made expressly and prevailing scholarly opinion interprets 'expressly' in the sense of 'sufficiently clear and evident',[1] which

---

[1] Gschnitzner in Klang 2 IV/1 335; Rummel 2 § 901 Rz 2; OGH in SZ 35/7 = JBl 1962, 606; SZ 35:47; JBl 1987, 378.

can already be assumed under the general legal provisions (compare § 863, § 914 ff. ABGB).

The fact that Emmanuel recognises the brand is very clearly to be seen as a mere motive. The question arises as to whether the comments about the maintenance contract made to the salesman had to be understood as an offer for a subject matter to be included in the contract. This has to be answered by considering the actual circumstances and facts given at the moment of concluding the contract, where no doubt may remain (§ 863 ABGB). In that respect the salesman is not just 'silent',[2] his behaviour indicates that he has accepted Emmanuel's offer. Thus the maintenance contract is included as a condition of the contract.

Even if the manufacturer refuses the maintenance no permanent obstacle[3] for performing the contract exists, as the maintenance could also be proved by another expert. The salesman therefore, caused and is liable for partial non-performance. Emmanuel is entitled to claim performance in accordance with § 918 ABGB and is entitled to damages for the breach. The seller is liable to provide the maintenance of the computer as agreed upon, either by the manufacturer or another expert. In this case the technical difficulties and obstacles are to be considered hidden defects at the moment of transfer and Emmanuel is entitled to claim a guarantee against defects against the salesman (see Case 4).

Belgium

It is well established as a result of case law that computer sellers owe a specific duty to inform non-specialised purchasers, since the particular nature of their activity requires a special technical expertise.[4] More specifically, this comprises the following duties: (i) to be informed about the actual needs of the customer and to help the customer to define them; (ii) to inform his prospective purchaser about the characteristics and modalities of use of the proposed hardware or software; (iii) to advise the customer as to the most appropriate solutions taking into account the latter's possibilities, needs and wishes and (iv) to warn the prospective buyer as to the restrictions and limits in the use of the proposed acquisition (requiring the seller to draw the purchaser's attention

---

[2] As to the prevailing opinion, cf. Gschnitzner in Klang 2 IV/1, 79; Koziol/Welser, *Bürgerliches Recht* 10 I 88; Rummel 2 § 863 Rz 15; OGH in JBl 1993, 78; ÖBA 1993, 908 (P. Bydlinski); WBl 1994, 23. Keeping silent cannot constitute acceptance since there are different reasons for keeping silent.

[3] Compare Koziol/Welser, *Bürgerliches Recht* 10 I 233.

[4] See generally E. Cannart d'Hamale, 'Le devoir de conseil du fournisseur en informatique', *RDCB* 1989, pp. 568 ff., with the case law cited.

to his own mistakes).[5] However, the purchaser incurs a correlative obligation to inform him or herself and to decide finally about his computer project as the seller's failure to provide adequate information may not be the consequence of the customer's own obvious incompetence.[6]

As far as consumer law is concerned, art. 30 of the law of 14 July 1991[7] provides that the seller must, at the latest upon entering into the contract, provide in good faith the consumer with correct and useful information pertaining to the characteristics of the product or of the service and the conditions of sale.

In the present case, three remedies are more specifically available to Emmanuel:[8]

(i) In a recent case (sale of computer software where the purchaser changed his printer after the software had been satisfactorily demonstrated and before its delivery and the new printer was not compatible with the said software), the judge held that the seller did not comply with his duty since he did not inform the purchaser about the software's printing possibilities. As a result, the contract was annulled on the basis of a fundamental mistake that was considered excusable, taking into account the technical complexity of the thing sold.[9] In this case, general rules applied since the purchaser could not be considered a consumer in the sense of the law of 1991.

(ii) The duty to inform may be analysed under two heads, by taking into account either:

(a) the nature of the seller's duty, especially that of warning the prospective buyer: here the seller should have informed Emmanuel that the maintenance contract had expired) and his failure to do so would constitute a fault under art. 1382 of the Civil Code or fraudulent concealment (cf. Case 1); or

(b) the content of the seller's obligation to inform Emmanuel as a consumer under art. 30 of the law of 1991. Emmanuel could allege that the seller has breached this duty and under Belgian law a breach of a

---

[5] *Ibid.*, nos. 3–15.

[6] *Ibid.*, no. 28; E. Davio,'Obligation de renseignement et vices du consentement', note under J. P. Wervik, JJP, 1996, pp. 263 ff., no. 8.

[7] The law relates to commercial practices and the information and protection of the consumer.

[8] The two other remedies for the seller's failure to comply with his counselling duty are termination of the contract under art. 1184 of the Civil Code and the seller's guarantee against hidden defects (see Case 3).

[9] J. P. Wervik, JJP, 1996, p. 261.

statutory duty is deemed to be a fault within the general provisions of art. 1382 of the Civil Code.[10]

England

Emmanuel will have a claim only against the shop from which he bought the computer (since he had no dealings with the manufacturer and therefore has no cause of action against him); and the claim will only be for breach of contract arising out of his mistake as to the terms of the purchase, unless Emmanuel can show a misrepresentation. On the facts stated, the salesman appears by his silence to have made no false representation, although if he reacted to Emmanuel's own statements in any way (e.g. a nod) which could be taken to have confirmed them, that would be sufficient to constitute a representation. However, Emmanuel may have an arguable claim that the salesman by his silence caused Emmanuel to believe that one of the terms on which he was buying the computer was that it would have a warranty. If it can be shown that Emmanuel believed that this was to be a term, and that it was reasonable in the circumstances for him so to believe, the shop will be precluded from denying that this became one of the terms of the contract.[11] Emmanuel's claim against the shop would then be for damages on the contract measure, based on the sum necessary to give him what he had been led to believe he was buying (i.e., a computer with a maintenance contract).

France

Emmanuel can bring an action against the seller for breach of the latter's duty to inform. Here, Emmanuel could argue that the seller is liable for fraudulent concealment; as already observed,[12] the *Cour de cassation* has held that fraud can be constituted by the silence of one party dissimulating to the other a fact, that would have prevented the other party from contracting, had he known of this fact.[13] This fits Emmanuel's situation exactly. However, Emmanuel may have evidential difficulties proving the

---

[10] Emmanuel could also bring an action against the seller for breach of contract, see Case 3.

[11] *Smith v. Hughes* (1871) LR 6 QB 597. The mistake is then about the terms of the contract, rather than simply about the factual quality of its subject matter: cf. discussion to Case 1.

[12] See Cases 2 and 4.

[13] Cass civ 3, 15 January 1971, Bull civ III, no. 38, p. 25, confirmed since.

fraud, since there may be no witnesses to verify the salesman's silence.[14] Should he overcome these difficulties, he will of course be entitled to both annulment of the contract and damages.

In this context it should be pointed out that the duty to inform incumbent on a professional seller dealing with a consumer is now incorporated in specialised legislation. Articles 111–1 and 111–3 of the Consumer Code contain a duty to point out the essential characteristics of the goods or service, as well as the price, limitations of liability and the special conditions of sale. By remaining silent about the maintenance contract's expiry date, the seller is clearly in breach of such a duty. Moreover, some professionals see their duty to inform extending beyond the simple precontractual duty to inform. This is the case for computer sellers, because their field is complex and because they often deal with lay persons. Scholarly opinion often refers here to a 'counselling duty' (*devoir de conseil*) which is a kind of reinforced duty to inform.[15] Here the breach of such a duty is not really relevant since the initial duty to inform has obviously been breached. It should be procedurally easier for Emmanuel to rely on the provisions in the Consumer Code than on the general defective consent provisions since he does not have to prove the existence of the duty to inform, nor fraud, he merely has to prove the seller's breach of that duty, i.e. that the necessary information has not been provided. This could be analysed as analogous to strict liability. However, if Emmanuel chooses this ground, he will only be entitled to damages and not annulment, in the absence of fraud. It has been suggested[16] that another remedy could be provided by incorporating the maintenance contract into the contract, if it is reasonable for Emmanuel to expect the maintenance contract to form part of the contract of sale and if it is within the seller's power to provide the maintenance then Emmanuel could enforce the seller's obligation, i.e. oblige him to maintain the computer. This might be a preferable remedy for Emmanuel (rather than annulling and/or damages) and would amount to a contractual remedy for enforced performance.

---

[14] On the question of the rules of evidence in cases of fraud, see the explanation given in Case 2.

[15] Paris 12 July 1972, JCP 1974.II. 17603, note NS; a computer unfit to the needs of a firm had disorganised it; the judge decided that the professional had to orientate his client's choice toward equipment capable of executing the foreseen task (confirmed since).

[16] See Fabre-Magnan, *De l'obligation d'information dans le contrat*, who talks of the '*effet obligatoire*' of the duty to inform.

Germany

The seller's silence in response to Emmanuel's statement is the point upon which this case turns. According to Oertmann's definition this is a classic case of the basis of the transaction being absent.[17] Nevertheless, academics and the courts have recently developed other instruments which may be used to help Emmanuel. In the case before us, no court would venture to adapt the contract to changed circumstances by reason of the fact that a (subjective) basis for the transaction (§ 242) is absent. Today, this method is only adopted if both parties to the contract made a mistake concerning an important condition of the contract (§ 313 II).

(i) First of all – for reasons of conflicting claims – Emmanuel's guarantee remedies will be examined. If the computer does not correspond to the condition described in the contract, Emmanuel could either demand the cost of repairs (§§ 437 Ziff 1, 434 I) or termination of the contract or reduction of the price (§§ 437 Ziff 2, 434 I). The normal characteristics do not have to be expressly agreed in order for the purchaser to assert his warranty claims upon discovering their absence.[18] Maintenance contracts however, are not usually included in the purchase of a used computer. But the high price of the computer as well as Emmanuel's statement that he was also acquiring a valid maintenance agreement indicate that the contract of sale also included the acquisition of a maintenance contract. However, the salesman's silence is not automatically to be regarded as confirming Emmanuel's assumption. Due to the fact that as seller and specialist he owes Emmanuel the duty to clarify any possible misunderstandings with respect to maintenance contracts his silence may be interpreted as a confirmation that the contract for the sale of the computer also extends to the provision of a maintenance contract. The most important argument in this regard is that the salesman himself must have realised Emmanuel's assumption. It can be argued therefore, that this assumption entered into the contract.[19] Accordingly, Emmanuel's claim may well succeed.

---

[17] P. Oertmann, *Die Geschäftsgrundlage – ein neuer Rechtsbegriff* (Leipzig, 1921), p. 37, defined the basis of the contract as: 'The basis of the transaction is the assumption or expectation of one party or the mutual assumption or expectation of several parties relating to the existence or the intervention of those circumstances constituting the basis for the intention underlying the transaction which arises at the conclusion of the contract and the importance of which is recognised and not objected to by the other party.'

[18] Cf. particularly D. 18,1,45; D. 19,1,21.   [19] Cf. BGHZ 109, 177, BGH NJW 1995, 953.

(ii) Because Emmanuel may assert his claims of warranty under sales law, annulment on grounds of mistake (§ 119 II) is excluded.[20] If it were the case that the seller had acted fraudulently however, then Emmanuel could annul the contract according to § 123. A person also acts fraudulently if he does not fulfil his duty of disclosure with the purpose of causing another to make a declaration of intent. We have already established that the seller is subject to a duty of disclosure in relation to the fact that the sale of a used computer does not automatically include the provision of a maintenance contract. From the facts of the case however, it is not exactly clear why the seller kept silent when Emmanuel explained his reasons. Did he in fact fail to understand what he meant by this? Was the seller not informed as to whether a maintenance contract was still valid for the computer that Emmanuel had chosen? Or did he in fact remain silent in order to leave Emmanuel labouring under his mistake? Only if the last scenario was in fact the case would Emmanuel be able to annul the contract under § 123 and claim for the refund of the purchase price under § 812 I.

(iii) As a rule, claims arising from the negligent breach of a duty of disclosure, which are judged according to the principles of *culpa in contrahendo*, are also excluded if contractual remedies are available to the mistaken party. Recent case law has allowed claims for compensation of negative interest under *culpa in contrahendo* (now: §§ 311 II, 241 II) besides those remedies arising from warranties if the seller assumed a special advisory duty.[21] The courts accept that such a special duty in excess of the usual advisory duties under contractual sales law exists in the sale of computer equipment and computer software.[22] Special advice is considered necessary in these cases because only rarely do the purchasers of computers and software have the relevant basic technical knowledge. If such purchases become usual then this special advisory duty will probably no longer be imposed.

Today, Emmanuel could still argue that the seller, through his own negligence at least, has infringed his advisory duty. If the seller had properly disclosed the facts to Emmanuel then he would not have believed he was also acquiring a maintenance contract and the contract of sale would possibly not have been entered into at all or concluded at a lower purchase price. If Emmanuel cannot assert a claim for negative interest

---

[20] On this conflict of claims see Cases 3 and 4.
[21] BGHZ 88, 135; lastly BGH NJW 1997, 3227. Or also, if the seller acted with malicious intent: BGH NJW 1992, 2564.
[22] BGH NJW 1984, 2938; OLG Köln NJW 1994, 1355.

in excess of this then his claim for compensation under *culpa in contra-hendo* (§§ 311 II, 241 II) would therefore lead to the same result as the warranty claim for termination of the contract or a reduction in the purchase price.

Greece

Emmanuel is not entitled to sue for the annulment of the sale by reason of his mistake which pertains exclusively to the shaping of his will, or motives and therefore is not fundamental according to art. 143 AK.

If the salesman was aware of the fact that the maintenance contract had already expired and he did not inform Emmanuel of the truth, he has deceived him (art. 214 AK[23]). Emmanuel informed the salesman that he would pay extra for this specific model only because he was interested in acquiring the benefit of a proper maintenance contract. In this case fraud has been committed by being silent about the true facts. It is obvious that the rules of good faith and common usage, as formulated in art. 288 AK,[24] impose a duty on the seller to tell Emmanuel the truth. It is obvious that Emmanuel's declaration of will was procured by fraud (art. 147 AK) and he therefore can ask for the sale to be annulled.[25] In addition or even without annulment, Emmanuel is entitled to compensation under the general tort provisions (art. 149 AK).

In the case where the salesman was unaware that the maintenance contract had expired he also made a non-fundamental mistake as to motive. In the case of a common mistake it is accepted that annulment is possible if the mistake relates to a fundamental element of the contract, that is the basis of the transaction.[26] Though this important element has not entered into the content of the agreement, the fundamental nature of the common mistake as to the basis of the transaction is generally accepted. The doctrine stems from the principle of good faith

---

[23] The salesman is the seller's representative for this purpose and art. 214 AK provides that in the case of representation, defective consent must be evaluated in relation to the representative.

[24] Article 288 AK lays down that: 'The debtor is obliged to effect the performance as good faith requires, after consideration of common usage.'

[25] A two-year limitation period runs from the date of discovery of the fraud (arts. 154, 157 AK).

[26] For the basis of the transaction, which is not regulated by the Greek Civil Code, see Gazis, *General Principles of Civil Law*, § 16; Georgiadis, *General Principles of Civil Law*, pp. 466 ff.; Papantoniou, *General Principles of Civil Law*, pp. 401 ff.; Simantiras, *General Principles of Civil Law*, nn. 737 ff.; Spyridakis, *General Principles*, pp. 607 ff. Cf. the corresponding German theory on '*Geschäftsgrundlage*' and the French theory on '*cause de l'engagement*'.

and common usage contained in art. 288 AK. The consequence of the non-existence or collapse of the underlying basis of the transaction is, according to the prevailing scholarly opinion, applicable by analogy with art. 388 AK. This provision, one of the most forward-looking of the Greek Civil Code, provides for the dissolution or adjustment of a synallagmatic contract if an unforeseen change in circumstances, which has occurred after the conclusion of the contract, has destroyed the balance of the contract to the detriment of one of the parties. It is maintained[27] that the other contracting party, here the shop owner, should be entitled to a reasonable compensation, a solution imposed by the rule of good faith (art. 288 AK).

Emmanuel's mistake has found expression outside his inner world and is known to the vendor. Stathopoulos[28] submits that in cases like the above where the mistake as to motive is not an inner personal matter of the mistaken person but concerns the other party (his quality as a professional is significant), the substantial criteria that justify annulment are met, since the mistake is objectified. Consequently, Emmanuel can seek the judicial annulment of the sale. He is however liable for the loss sustained by his contracting party but the award of damages cannot exceed the amount the other party would have received if the sale were valid (art. 145 AK).

As a result of judicial annulment the sale becomes void *ab initio* (art. 184 AK). This means that Emmanuel is obliged to return his title to the computer on the basis of unjust enrichment (arts. 904 ff. AK). The independent transfer agreement of the computer is not affected by the annulment of its cause, i.e. the promissory contract of sale.

Ireland

Under Irish law, Emmanuel's claim lies against the shop where he bought the computer. This is a breach of contract arising out of Emmanuel's mistake as to the terms of the purchase.

With regard to misrepresentation, it is possible that Emmanuel would have a claim where he can show the salesman, by his silence, led him to believe that one of the terms on which he was buying the computer was that it was still under guarantee. Where the courts agree that it was reasonable for Emmanuel to have such a belief, thereby making it an integral part of the agreement, he would be entitled to claim damages. However, as a rule, silence will not amount to misrepresentation with

---

[27] Spyridakis, *General Principles*, p. 611.   [28] Stathopoulos, *Contract Law in Hellas*, p. 104.

the Irish courts tending to follow the decision of *Smith* v. *Hughes*[29] in this regard.

Italy

Emmanuel has a slight chance of being successful against the seller. The relevant facts are the 'non-disclosure' by the computer store salesman and the fact that the 'maintenance contract had expired before the sale'. There is however no duty to disclose and the salesman might not have known that the maintenance contract had expired. If liability is established, the computer shop will be liable for the act of the salesman.[30]

(i) This could be considered to be a case of fraud (*dolo*) using art. 1337 and arts. 1339 and 1440 of the Civil Code (duty of good faith in precontractual negotiations and negative fraud), but there are no precedents. Once again we have to deal with a negative fraud when there is non-disclosure of an element, which if it were known, would have induced the party to enter into a different kind of contract or, in this case, to buy another computer. Silence by itself does not mean fraud,[31] unless there were a fraudulent concealment of true facts or breach of an explicit duty to inform required by law.[32]

(ii) This could also be considered to be the tort of negligence (*Fatto illecito*): the salesman has caused an injury by not correcting Emmanuel's false statement thus making him liable for the harm caused (art. 2043 of the Civil Code). Using a very innovative approach[33] we could say that we can derive from the new legislation's rationale (protection of consumers) a new tortious liability that could fit into the open provision set out in art. 2043 (*neminem laedere*). If such a provision were applied, the seller would be liable for tortious damages but arguably the obligation to pay damages could be transformed in order to annul the contract by the application of art. 2058 of the Civil Code, providing for specific

---

[29] (1871) LR 6 QB 597.

[30] Article 2049 of the Civil Code provides for the vicarious liability of masters and employers for damage caused by an unlawful act of their servants or employees acting in the course of their employment.

[31] This statement could be found in a decision of the Trib. Verona, 18 November 1946, in *Foro Pad.*, 1947, 199. The sale of a truck, without disclosing that it belonged to the State, was considered fraudulent and annulled.

[32] The Civil Code contains an explicit duty to disclose in arts. 1892–3 concerning insurance contracts.

[33] Sacco and De Nova, 'Il contratto', pp. 429–30; Bianca, 'Il contratto', pp. 614 ff., takes a position similar to Sacco.

relief.[34] The only cases that could be used in this latter approach are cases considering false information given by a company specialised in the collection of business information[35] or by a journalist when the information in the newspaper damages someone's reputation.

(iii) It may be possible to convince the court that the duty to behave in good faith (art. 1337 of the Civil Code) entails an obligation by one party to inform the other when the former discovers the other's mistake. The same article can be considered as a basis for *culpa aquiliana*; the Italian *giurisprudenza* (case law) and legal theorists have considered the breach of precontractual duties as tortious liability, as under French law.[36] Article 1337 is thus considered a specific example of the *neminem laedere* principle used by art. 2043 of the Civil Code. The Italian courts are open to creating new types of tortious liability. It could be easier for a court to take an innovative decision on the basis of the wide principle of 'unjust harm', than to create a new kind of negative fraud.

The Netherlands

Emmanuel's only possible claims must necessarily be against the shop that sold him the computer. Whether there is non-performance by the seller of his obligations will depend on the facts. The computer may not be what Emmanuel was entitled to expect on the basis of the contract (non-conformity) in which case Emmanuel may resort to the remedies for non-performance (repair, replacement, withholding his own performance, termination and damages), subject to the requirements discussed in Cases 3 and 5, above. Also the seller may be under an explicit (depending on the conditions of the contract) or implied (i.e. heteronomous, based, for example, on good faith (art. 6:248 BW)[37]) obligation to help.

---

[34] Article 2043 Compensation for unlawful acts: 'Any fraudulent, malicious, or negligent act that causes an unjustified injury to another obliges the person who has committed the act to pay damages.'

Article 2058 Specific redress: 'The injured party can demand specific redress when this is wholly or partially possible.

The judge, however, can order that the redress be made only by providing an equivalent, if specific redress would prove to be excessively onerous for the debtor.'

[35] Cass 1984, n. 94.

[36] Sacco and De Nova, 'Il contratto', p. 255; Cass 4.10.1948, n. 1667, in GI, 1949, I, 1, 29; and nine other decisions up to Cass 11.5.1990, n. 4051, in FI, 1991, I, 184; the opposite solution similar to the German tradition, where precontractual liability is considered as a breach of a contract has been followed in Italy by Mengoni, in RDCo, 1956, II, 365.

[37] See on this Hesselink, *De redelijkheiden in het Europese privaatrecht*, pp. 173 ff.

Did the parties agree on the sale of a computer which was covered by a maintenance contract with the manufacturer? In that case there is another ground for remedies for non-performance: i.e. breach of the obligation to deliver a computer covered by a maintenance contract. This is a matter of interpretation (arts. 3:33 and 3:35 BW). When determining the proper interpretation of the contract, among other things, the fact that the seller remained silent when Emmanuel informed him he preferred to pay extra as he was acquiring the benefit of a proper maintenance contract, could be taken into account. In legal doctrine it is maintained by some authors that interpretation may go further. They accept a 'normative' method of interpretation which does not aim merely at determining which obligations the contract agreed on in the view of the parties (subjective interpretation) or of an outsider (objective interpretation) but on which obligations it would be fair to deduce from this contract in this particular case.[38] Others regard this approach of so-called normative interpretation as fairly artificial.[39] It would be more straightforward to recognise an obligation laid on the parties by the law (in fact: the courts) rather than to try to attribute it to the contract.[40]

Emmanuel probably can annul the contract for mistake. The seller knew that the buyer thought he was acquiring the benefit of a maintenance contract and that this was crucial for him. If the seller knew that the contract had expired he was under a duty to tell this to the buyer, especially if he presented himself as a quality shop and as a specialist (art. 6: 228 (1)(b)). Probably only the seller knew whether the maintenance contract had expired (the buyer probably was not in a position to find it out himself). This explains the seller's duty to inform the buyer once he had become aware that the buyer was wrong on a point that he knew to be crucial to him.

Norway

The purchaser (Emmanuel) presumed there was a maintenance agreement with the purchase of the computer, which did not turn out to be the case. The question is whether the seller should have *disclosed* this. As

---

[38] J. M. van Dunné, *Normatieve uitleg van rechtshandelingen* (diss.) (Leiden, 1971), Verbintenissenrecht deel I, pp. 125 ff., H. Schoordijk, *Contractenrecht* (3rd edn, Deventer, 1997), Verbintenissenrecht pp. 21–43. Compare M. W. Hesselink, *The New European Legal Culture*, p. 16.

[39] See Asser/Hartkamp II (2001), no. 198 with further references.

[40] See Hesselink, *De redelijkheden in het Europese privaatrecht*, pp. 131 ff.

with property sales (see Case 4), a specific duty to inform rests upon the seller of the goods. The wording of this duty varies a little among Scandinavian countries, and is dependent on whether or not one is dealing with a consumer purchase.

(i) The duty to inform in *Norwegian* law has developed based partly on the theory of invalidity and partly on contract law.

(a) Section 33 of the Contract Act has been central to the *invalidity-based* duty to inform (see Case 2). Breach of this section leads to invalidity. We shall see below in (ii) that this could create some uncertainty in respect of the consequences of a breach of the legal duty to inform. However, § 33 of the Contract Act has not had great significance in legal practice. As regards professional business people, there has not been a single example of the use of § 33 in Supreme Court practice during the period 1945–91.

(b) The duty to inform has a much more important basis in *contract law*. It is generally accepted in Norway and the Scandinavian countries that a certain duty rests with the actual debtor to reveal 'negative' aspects of the item referred to in the contract. This duty is now regulated by law when, among other things, it concerns the purchase and sale of goods and property.

As a consequence of the EC Directive 1999/44 of 25 May 1999 on certain aspects of the sale of consumer goods and associated guarantees, Norway passed a law relating to consumer sales in 2002 (Consumer Sales Act of 21 June 2002, no. 34). The law came into force on 1 July 2002.

This Act contains a general rule about the seller's duty to inform, see § 16 (1)(b). Here it is stated:

The item has a defect if the seller at the time of the purchase has omitted to provide information about the condition of the item or its use which he ought to have been aware of and which the purchaser had reason to expect to be provided with, and if the omission can be assumed to have influenced the sale.

Three conditions for imposing upon the seller a duty of disclosure are listed. First, the seller ought to have been aware of the condition of the item or its use, secondly the consumer must have reason or expect to be provided with the information and finally the omission must be assumed to have influenced the sale.

(ii) In Sweden and Denmark the Contract Act, § 33, has, as a basis for the duty to inform, played an even more subordinate role than in Norway. It is primarily the contract-based duty of information which has attracted attention.[41] The general *Swedish* Sale of Goods Act is, to a large extent, framed along the same lines as the Norwegian. There are, however, specific regulations pertaining to consumer situations, see the Consumer Sales Act (1990.932). The Act contains a specific regulation pertaining to the seller, cf. § 16, para. 3, no. 2. The regulation is generally framed in such a way that it applies irrespective of whether or not an 'as is' condition is present. It reads:

> The item shall be considered defective if the seller prior to the purchase has neglected to inform the purchaser about a particular condition concerning the nature of the item or its use, which he knew or ought to have known of and which the purchaser could reasonably be expected to be informed about, providing the neglect can be seen as having influenced the purchase.

No duty of essentiality is stipulated. But failure to provide information about the condition must be assumed to have influenced the purchase (the requirement of hypothetical causality), and the purchaser must have had reason to expect to be provided with the information. It is further worth noting the normative character of the regulation. The duty to inform is applied if the seller knew or ought to have known of the condition.

(iii) The *Danish* Sale of Goods Act has incorporated specific consumer regulations into the general Sale of Goods Act, see §§ 72–86. In § 76, para. 12, we find, similarly to the Swedish Consumer Sales Act, a generally formulated regulation about the duty to inform on the part of the seller. The regulation reads as follows:

> There is a defect in the sale item if the seller has neglected to provide the purchaser with information on conditions which may have had a bearing on the purchaser's evaluation of the item and which the seller knew of or ought to have known of.

Even if there is a slight difference in wording between the Danish and Swedish regulations, it may be assumed that in respect to content they are closely related.

(iv) In the present case, the question arises as to whether Emmanuel's misunderstanding regarding the existence of a maintenance agreement creates a duty to inform on the part of the seller. It is clear that the seller was aware of the suppositions of the purchaser and that this was a motivating factor for entering into the contract. The criteria of

---

[41] See J. Hellner, TfR 1987.301, particularly pp. 307 ff.

knowledge ('ought to have been aware of') and causality ('be assumed to have influenced the sale') are thus fulfilled.

The question that remains to be answered is whether the purchaser had reason to expect to be provided with the information. Normally a maintenance contract is of importance to a purchaser of computers. The seller was therefore under an obligation to inform Emmanuel of his mistake.

The obvious thing for Emmanuel to do would be to invoke the contractual duty of disclosure, and not the invalidity doctrine. Pursuant to § 36 of the Act he can terminate the contract unless the defect is characterised as inessential (not fundamental).

Portugal

This case can be analysed as a case of mistake by Emmanuel, as well as a case of fraud committed by the salesman.

(i) Emmanuel has made a mistake because he was convinced he was simultaneously acquiring the benefit of a proper maintenance contract which turned out to be untrue. Such a mistake constitutes a mistake related to the subject matter of the contract. As the salesman was expressly informed of the fundamental nature of the mistake in Emmanuel's decision to purchase that computer at that price, Emmanuel will be able to obtain in court the annulment of the purchase, and the restitution of the price (arts. 251°, 247° and 289° of the Civil Code).

(ii) This is also a case of fraud by the salesman. In fact, according to art. 253° of the Civil Code the non-disclosure of a mistake can be considered a fraud when there is a duty to inform according to the law, the contract or legal authority. Emmanuel would therefore be able to obtain the annulment of the contract based upon fraud (art. 254° of the Civil Code) and ask for the restitution of the price (art. 289° of the Civil Code). Legal writers state that according to the rules of *culpa in contrahendo* (art. 227° of the Civil Code), parties have a duty to behave in good faith during the negotiation and formation of the contract and among these duties is a duty of information, the breach of which constitutes fraud and liability for loss.[42] Even if the salesman had no knowledge of the date on which the maintenance contract expired, he could be still liable in damages for not fulfilling his precontractual duty to inform. However, in this case

---

[42] See C. Mota Pinto, *Teoria Geral do Direito Civil*, p. 524 and M. Cordeiro, *Da Boa Fé no Direito Civil*, pp. 574 ff.

Emmanuel could combine this with a claim to annul the contract for mistake but not for fraud.

Scotland

There is no remedy available to Emmanuel because, as was noted above, there is in general no duty of voluntary disclosure and misrepresentation is therefore not established by the non-disclosure of a fact by the seller. It would have been a misrepresentation had he either failed to reply or replied inaccurately to any question put to him by Emmanuel about the warranty.

Spain

This is a case of negative fraud, arising when the buyer opts for a more expensive model because this allows him to benefit from an appropriate maintenance contract and the seller deliberately conceals from the buyer the fact that the maintenance contract has already expired. There is no difficulty under current Spanish law to accept fraud by omission, also known as 'negative fraud' and the Supreme Court has, on many occasions, ruled that fraudulent conduct occurred when a party failed to speak or did not provide due warning.[43]

Because the seller's failure to speak out was fundamental to Emmanuel's acquisition, we consider that he should be able to annul the contract under art. 1301 of the Civil Code.

Comparative observations

This case, concerning a contract of sale between a professional and a consumer of a computer, an object which requires technical expertise after sale, focuses on an omission on the part of the seller at a decisive moment just before the sale. The seller's omission, his silence, is characterised by some civil law systems as fraudulent concealment or a failure to inform his co-contractor of information which clearly induced the buyer to contract (namely the presence of an existing maintenance contract for the computer), whereas under the common law conception, silence is not remedied by the law and gives rise to no liability. Why then is silence to be treated oppositely, confirming here a presumption of divergence between civil law and common law conceptions of the law of contract? Nevertheless, despite this apparently striking

[43] Rulings of 6/6/53, 20/1/64.

difference, by comparing the whole range of remedies available, it transpires that contractual remedies may provide a complementary alternative for the aggrieved party, when defective consent remedies are interpreted more restrictively. Here a relative harmony of solution is achieved by very different means.

(i) First, the buyer can rely on a number of remedies for defective consent, namely mistake, fraud and the duty to inform. Relatively few countries prefer to rely on mistake but it has been admitted under Belgian and Portuguese law. In Greece, as an exception to the rule that a mistake as to motive is inoperative, the mistake is admitted since it was declared and known to the other party but the mistaken party must pay negative interest to compensate the seller for his losses. It may not be necessary to have recourse to this theory since under Greek law the mistake could be characterised as a common mistake as to the basis of the transaction – a fundamental mistake – sufficient to annul the contract. Interestingly, under Dutch law, the contract can be annulled for mistake but the mistake is characterised by the seller's knowledge of the buyer's reliance on the existence of the maintenance contract and his subsequent failure to inform the buyer of the truth (namely that the said contract has expired). This ground, qualified as mistake, looks more like a failure to inform than a more traditional version of mistake.[44] A comparable legislative duty to inform, the object of consumer protection law in France and Belgium for example, is distinct from both mistake and fraud. Under Belgian law, for example, the duty gives rise to tortious liability, on the basis that breach of a statutory duty constitutes a delict (art. 1382 of the Civil Code).

Along the same lines, certain legal systems, namely France, Belgium, Germany, Greece, Portugal and Spain prefer to concentrate on the remedy of fraud. Fraud gives rise to both annulment and damages. Fraud can be characterised here as fraudulent concealment, a failure of the duty to inform, as in French, Belgian, German, Greek, Portuguese and Spanish law. German law requires that the silence had a decisive effect on the mistake in the buyer's mind. Greek and Portuguese law explain the fraud in terms of a failure to disclose in accordance with good faith *culpa in contrahendo* rules. German law now conceives of the basis of good faith provision (§ 242 BGB) as a precontractual duty to inform. Exceptionally, in German law the *lex specialis* rule of contractual remedies is circumvented if the seller has assumed a special advisory duty

---

[44] Compare in the same vein, art. 4:103 of the PECL.

towards the purchaser in relation to advising him about the technical complexities of the subject matter of the sale. In the same vein, Italian law, although reluctant to admit a version of negative fraud, might admit precontractual liability on the basis of good faith, although it is suggested that this would work better as a specific example of a general tortious liability not to cause unjust harm (*neminem laedere*) than as a type of fraud. To conclude on fraud similes, Norwegian law provides an invalidity-based duty to inform under § 33 of the Contract Act but this suggested ground of action must be treated with caution since it has rarely been invoked in practice. The reason why Norwegian law has chosen not to use its invalidity-based remedy is that contractual remedies are a preferable alternative.

(ii) Once again, the same set of facts can be treated in a majority of countries under the head of contractual remedies for non-performance. Legal characterisation of the grounds of non-performance and the content of available remedies differ slightly. Under Austrian, German, English and Irish law the existence of the maintenance contract may be described as a condition or term of the contract, incorporated into the contract by the seller's silence. Remedies are also available under Dutch law on the basis of non-conformity. More significantly, under Scandinavian law, a contractual remedy lies for failure of a duty to inform. This contractual duty to inform, which provides a high degree of protection for the purchaser, is found both in general contract law legislation and in specific consumer provisions. The existence of this duty is based on four cumulative conditions: (i) the seller must possess the knowledge; (ii) there is a lawful need to give the information, i.e. the purchaser can be reasonably expected to be provided with the information; (iii) the information can be expected to influence the sale, i.e. a requirement of causation; and (iv) the information is essential. This contractual duty to inform looks quite similar to a precontractual duty, if the causation condition is examined, for example.

This case exemplifies different attitudes of the law in relation to the silence of one of the parties to a contract. The case here is even stronger than in Cases 2 and 4, in the sense that a consumer sale for an expensive luxury good[45] could be considered to be a relatively ordinary occurrence; the hypothesis is not far-fetched, on the contrary, it is highly plausible. These findings of a diverging underlying value towards silence raise a normative question: should the seller be under a duty to inform, i.e.

---

[45] Some people might not consider a computer is a luxury good but a necessity!

should the buyer be awarded protection in a case like this and if so, how? A preliminary answer may lie in both a technical approach and an enquiry into what might be considered fair. Several reporters have highlighted the fact that an advisory duty is necessary in contracts of sale where the parties have imbalanced specialist knowledge. In Germany, for example, this advisory duty has displaced the *lex specialis* rule on sales but it is contended that the new duty may disappear when such sales become more commonplace. This contention supports the hypothesis that duties to inform can play a pre-emptive role in contract law and in regulating standards of behaviour expected of contracting parties.

A further answer may be found if this case can be contrasted with another hypothesis where the parties are on equal footing and there is no imbalance of specialist knowledge. Are the legal rules as to silence different in the latter case? In legal systems where no protection is given on the facts here, *a fortiori* no protection would be given where parties are on equal footing. Moreover, in the majority of legal systems, no duty to inform would be imposed where the parties are on equal footing and there is no imbalance of information.[46] An inference could be drawn that imposing a duty to inform should be limited to specific contracts where a special need to protect one of the parties arises. This merely proves the point that it is a question of legal policy whether protection should be facilitated or increased, *de lege ferenda*.

Technical questions also arise in connection with the more substantive normative question. We have seen that a duty to inform can be imposed under heads of contractual and precontractual liability. There are then different types of duties to inform. Is the precontractual duty to inform, provided for in special legislation (e.g. in French and Belgian consumer law), comparable to a contractual duty to inform provided for in specific, or general contract legislation (e.g. in Scandinavia)? It is submitted that the difference is one of means and not of finality.[47] Does a duty to inform incorporated in legislation provide 'better' protection[48] for the party claiming a breach than that provided in the remedies for

---

[46] Take the example of a sale of business between individuals dealing in the course of business where the buyer fails to carry out the necessary enquiries about the value of the business and the seller is not obliged to inform him on the basis of *caveat emptor*. In other words, in a situation where the seller's silence would not be considered reprehensible and he could not be accused of any foul play.

[47] See Comparative Conclusions below pp. 399–400.

[48] From the point of view of the claimant, 'better' must mean there are procedural advantages in relation to the burden of proof and limitation but also that the remedy is (more) satisfactory.

defective consent? One could surmise that if legal systems have thought it worthwhile to implement the duty to inform in specific or general legislation (a policy choice), this is precisely with the aim of reinforcing such a duty. It can be deduced that the duty to inform is perceived as a means of protection for a contracting party who does not have the same informational strength as his co-contractor. It can also be inferred that remedies for defective consent are perceived as inadequate when such protection is considered necessary, thus confirming one of our initial hypotheses.[49]

[49] See in General Introduction, pp. 8–12.

Case 7
Cinderella

Case

Cinderella, a prosperous businesswoman, bought on the stock market a large number of shares in a company of growing reputation. The sale had hardly been concluded when it was revealed in the press that the company had already lost various important contracts to a Japanese competitor. The value of the shares dropped abruptly. What remedy, if any, is available?

Discussions

Austria

According to the predominant scholarly opinion each party is obliged to give full information to the other party if so required.[1] The obligation to provide information is partly derived from the contract, partly by law. As far as precontractual obligations are concerned a legally requested obligation for disclosure about important aspects of the subject matter of the contract can be assumed by analogy with the doctrine of *culpa in contrahendo*.[2] Cinderella, therefore, has a remedy against her business partner only if he breaches his duty to disclose.[3] However, the facts and circumstances do not indicate this to be the case. One would expect Cinderella to know how to take care of her business and it is generally known that shares do include such a risk. If Cinderella had

---

[1] Compare Koziol and Welser, *Bürgerliches Recht*, I, 194.

[2] Compare F. Bydlinski, *Juristische Methodenlehre und Rechtsbegriff* (Vienna, 1991), pp. 478 ff.

[3] For the bank's duty to inform about the risk of investments compare OGH in ÖBA 1993, 987, RDW 1993, 331 ecolex 1993, 669: ÖBA 1994, 156; SZ 67/54 ÖBA 1994, 558 EvBl 1994/137 WBl 1994, 237 ecolex 1994, 460; EvBl 1995/56 ÖBA 1995, 317 RdW 1995, 136 ecolex 1995, 171; ÖBA 1995, 990 ecolex 1995 797: ecolex 1996, 740.

false expectations about the increase in the value of the shares she has made a non-fundamental mistake as to motive (§ 901 ABGB). As the duty to inform cannot be interpreted extensively the bank would have been obliged to inform only if the news in the press had already been known to the bank. In that case a mistake as to motive can lead to annulment as it has been caused by the other party's intention to deceive (§ 870 ABGB).

Belgium

Three remedies might be considered:

(i) Cinderella may bring a claim against the company on the basis of its failure to provide occasional information as set out in art. 5 of the royal decree of 3 July 1996[4] (enacted pursuant to art. 19 of the law of 6 April 1995 relating to secondary markets, the status and control of investment enterprises, intermediaries and counsellors as to investments). This decree transposes into Belgian law some of the provisions deriving from EC directives as to the obligations imposed upon the issuers of securities listed with the stock exchange relating to annual, periodical or *occasional information* to the public.[5] Non-compliance with this obligation is a criminal offence under art. 148 10° of the law of 1995.

It is quite arguable that the company, as issuer of the shares, did not comply with its obligation to provide occasional information under the royal decree. We do not know however whether the publication in the press occurred upon the company's initiative[6] or whether the company obtained an exemption from the managing committee. If Cinderella can nonetheless prove that the company retained significant information for an excessive period of time and can show the chain of causation between the company's omission and the loss (in value of the shares)

---

[4] Article 5 § 1 provides that: 'The companies will make public without delay:

1° Any fact or decision of which they are aware and which, if made public, would be susceptible of influencing significantly the quotation on the stock exchange of the financial instruments. (. . .)

The directing committee may however exempt a company from the obligation mentioned at al. 1, 1°, when the publication of some information is susceptible of jeopardising the legitimate interests of the company (. . .)'

[5] See B. Feron and B. Taevernier, *Droit des marchés financiers* (Brussels, 1997), pp. 172 ff., the EC directives being referred to are: 79/279/EC of 5 March 1979 modified by 82/148/EC of 3 March 1982 and 88/627/EC of 12 December 1988.

[6] Publication in the press being considered as the normal way of providing occasional information according to art. 7 of the royal decree of 3 July 1996.

she suffered, she might be able to invoke the company's tortious liability on the basis of arts. 1382–3 of the Civil Code since breach of a statutory provision is generally considered to be a fault under these general provisions (see Case 6). Cinderella will probably have a hard time in proving the company's fault, especially if its legitimate interests might have been endangered by revealing information prematurely and, even more so, if the company obtained an exemption from the managing committee. Chances of success might also be greatly reduced if the company itself took the initiative to publish except if Cinderella can show that the company acted too late.

(ii) Cinderella can also bring an action against the directors of the company based on their negligence in managing the company (that led to the loss of important contracts to a competitor) but this avenue is not very promising for an individual shareholder like Cinderella. Indeed, the action against the directors is reserved for the majority of the shareholders, under art. 527 of the Companies Code, with the only alternative of the 'minority shareholders' action' (art. 562 of the Companies Code) requiring in short that Cinderella must hold either 1% of the voting power in the company or, alternatively, securities amounting to 1,250,000 Euros in the company's capital. Furthermore, even if Cinderella succeeds in bringing a shareholders' action against the directors, the damages will be given back to the company, since both these actions are derivative in nature.

Apart from these derivative actions of little interest, Cinderella will only succeed in an action brought in her capacity of individual shareholder if she can prove the existence of a loss which is her own that is not reducible to a fraction of the so-called 'social damage' incurred by all the shareholders.[7] This is obviously not the case here since all the shareholders will have to bear the loss in value of their shares.

(iii) Cinderella can also bring an action against the intermediary, who acted as Cinderella's financial agent, for non-compliance with his contractual obligation to inform his client. Recourse to an intermediary to purchase securities listed on a stock exchange is not compulsory when the transaction relates to the transfer of securities representing at least 10% of the voting rights in the relevant company (art. 2 § 3, 2° of the law of 6 April 1995). It will be assumed, for the sake of the following analysis, that this was not the case here.

---

[7] For a reminder of this principle, see note under Brussels, 7-2-1939, RPS, 1939, no. 3799, p. 160.

Whatever the status of the intermediary (stock exchange company, fortune managing company[8]), it will normally be considered to be Cinderella's agent, either acting in the name and for the account of Cinderella (*contrat de mandat*) or acting in its own name and for Cinderella's account (*commissionaire*).[9]

As such, the intermediary is under an obligation to inform its clients prior to entering into the transaction so that the said clients might arrive at a 'well thought-out decision' as to the purported investment (art. 36 § 1, 5° of the law of 1995). In complying with its duty to inform, the intermediary must take active steps in order to obtain useful information for its clients about the subject matter, the price and the risks attached to the transaction but may not be liable when no significant information on the transaction appears to be available.[10] Recently, the commercial court of Brussels held that the mere fact that a portfolio suffered a loss in value does not, in itself, constitute a fault committed by the intermediary.[11] Indeed, the risk-related nature of such operations, of which the purchaser is deemed to be aware, will be taken into account[12] and will generally lead the courts to be extremely prudent in deciding against the intermediary.[13] A possible clash between the intermediary's duty to inform and its obligation not to behave as an insider dealer may arise: the intermediary may not be obliged, in obtaining information for its clients, to go as far as gathering 'inside information' that might make it criminally liable.

To conclude, Cinderella's chances of obtaining the annulment of the sale appear almost non-existent (a paradoxical consequence of a market intended to be 'transparent') and her chances of being awarded damages are also remote, unless the circumstances are sufficiently favourable to alleviate her evidential difficulties.

England

This case concerns a contract where the thing purchased is, unknown to the buyer, of considerably lower value than the buyer had believed,

---

[8] '*Société de bourse*' or '*société de gestion de fortune*'.
[9] See Feron and Taevernier, *Droit des marchés financiers*, p. 269.
[10] *Ibid.*, pp. 298, 303.   [11] RDCB, 1996, p. 1072.
[12] Feron and Taevernier, *Droit des marchés financiers*, p. 347.
[13] In the decision of the tribunal of commerce of Brussels (cited above), the judge went as far as saying that such liability will be retained only in cases of fraud, bad faith and *gross* negligence whereas the principles would normally allow such liability to be sought even under mere (light) negligence (cf. Feron and Taevernier, *Droit des marchés financiers*, pp. 350–1).

although there is no evidence of any misrepresentation of facts relevant to the assessment of the value. And, here again, since the buyer is dealing as a professional at arm's length in entering into the contract, the undervalue cannot lead to a remedy. Nor is there a remedy for mistake: even if the mistake as to the company's business can be shown to have been shared by the person who sold the shares to Cinderella (which is necessary if the mistake is one as to the quality of what is bought: see Case 1) the shares are still the same shares she intended to buy – they are just of reduced value. A case in 1867 decided just this: *Kennedy v. The Panama, New Zealand and Australian Royal Mail Co.*[14] and there is no evidence that the courts would relax this approach today in a case such as Cinderella's.

The general rules described in relation to Case 1 apply equally to contracts for the purchase of shares in the stock market. There are also statutory provisions relating to the public issue of a company's shares: company directors and others have statutory duties to include information about the company in the listing particulars or prospectuses relating to the shares, and are liable to pay compensation for untrue or misleading statements, or the omission of matters required to be included.[15] This liability is however unlikely to apply here, since the duty only extends to statements which were untrue or misleading (or should have been made) at the time of the first dealings in the shares. It seems likely that, although the company had already lost important contracts to its Japanese competitor by the time Cinderella bought them, this all happened after the shares were already being traded on the stock market.

France

There is no duty of disclosure on the company to inform investors of the value of the shares, except in relation to fulfilling legal requirements as to the content of prospectus information, which it is assumed is not an issue here. Moreover, since buyers and suppliers do not deal directly with each other[16] on the market, no action based on ordinary remedies[17] can

---

[14] (1867) LR 2 QB 580.   [15] Financial Services and Markets Act 2000, s. 90.

[16] G. Ripert, R. Roblot, M. Germain and L. Vogel (eds.), *Traité de droit commercial* (17th edn, Paris, 1998) vol. 1, no. 1841.

[17] M. Cozian and A. Viandier, *Droit des sociétés* (16th edn, Paris, 2004), no. pp. 899 ff. Ripert et al., *Traité de droit commercial*, no. 737 ff.; J. Paillusseau, 'La cession de contrôle et la situation financière de la société cédée', JCP éd. G, 1992, I, 3578; Cass com, 12 December 1995, D 1996, 277, note J. Paillusseau; Paris 5ème ch. B, 2 May 1997, Bull Joly 1997, 783, n. P. Pigassou.

be brought against the seller (2 July 1996 law[18]). It is, however, possible for a buyer to take proceedings directly against the director of a company whose mismanagement has contributed to the fall in value of the shares. Such a hypothesis may be envisaged, i.e. that the directors were guilty of mismanagement, since it is stated that the company lost some important contracts. Nevertheless, even if this were the case, it should be noted that such actions are of little help to a disappointed shareholder, such as Cinderella. First, as for individual actions, their scope is relatively limited, since the shareholder must prove that he or she has suffered a special loss.[19] As an alternative, Cinderella, as a shareholder, could bring a derivative action,[20] but in practice this would not be of any help to her since any damages awarded would be of benefit to the company.[21]

The only claim Cinderella may have therefore, would lie against the intermediary, her financial agent, for failure of a duty to disclose. Under the agency agreement between Cinderella and her financial agent a duty of disclosure does indeed lie on the latter. The courts have imposed a duty of disclosure upon a bank, for example, in relation to the risks taken.[22] Moreover the agent cannot escape liability by showing he has merely carried out the principal's instructions. It is not sufficient to inform the client of the dangers of the market in general when he considers making a risky transaction, he must also be informed about the exact operations or markets.[23] The burden of proof lies on the agent to show that the obligation has been respected.[24]

If Cinderella can prove that as such her agent was under such an obligation (to some extent the variables depend on the kind of agency agreement in question as well as the client's relative expertise or absence

---

[18] M. Germain et M.-A. Noury, 'La loi du 2 juillet 1996 de modernisation des activités financières', JCP, éd. G, 1997, I, 4022, spec. no. 24 s.; JCP 1996, éd. E, III, 68046.

[19] Cass Com, 18 July 1989, Mme Bich v. Coquerel, Rep. Def. 1990, 633, obs. J. Honorat.

[20] Ripert et al Traité de droit commercial, vol. 1, no. 1372.

[21] Y. Guyon, Droit des affaires (12th edn, Paris, 2004), vol. 1: Droit commercial général et Sociétés no. 462.

[22] Cass Com, 5 November 1991, Bull civ, IV no. 327 the court held that 'whatever the contractual relations between a customer and his bank may be, the latter must inform the former of the risks taken as far as the speculative transactions are concerned on the stock market, except for case where he already knew about them'.

[23] Cass Com, 10 January, pourvoi no. 92-13. 172; Cass Com, 23 February 1993; Bull Civ, no. 68; D 1993, 424, n. I. Najjar.

[24] Cass Civ 1, 25 February 1997, Bull civ I, no. 75: 'celui qui est légalement ou contractuellement tenu d'une obligation particulière d'information doit rapporter la preuve de l'exécution de cette obligation'; 14 October 1997, JCP 1997, II, 22942, rapp. P. Sargos.

thereof) and that it has been breached, she can claim damages on the grounds that she lost the chance of making a profit.[25]

Germany

Cinderella has no possibility of withdrawing from the purchase of the shares if the sale had arisen without any fraud by the bank or the dealer selling them. Annulling on grounds of mistake fails due to the fact that when Cinderella bought the shares she also assumed the risk of the exchange rate. Whoever assumes a contractual risk infringes the principle of good faith if he attempts to free himself from the contract simply because the risk assumed has materialised.[26] Nevertheless, the courts have hitherto only applied the theory of the burden of risk in the case of a mistake in declaration (§ 119 I) but not, however, in the case of a mistake relating to a quality made by the plaintiff.

A well-known case is that of RG LZ 1926, 742: in the inflation-ridden years of the 1920s a dealer sold furniture instead of unstable paper currency in return for shares. The value of the shares calculated did indeed correspond to the exchange rate, yet they were, as the dealer later claimed, already reduced in value at the time the contract was concluded and subsequently fell further. The Reichsgericht declined to rescind the contract according to § 119 I on the grounds that trading in shares carried with it the risk of making losses on the stock exchange. However, it was more difficult for the RG to reject an annulment on the grounds of mistake relating to quality. Here, it simply argued that the value of the shares was not one of their qualities and that – if in fact it was one of their qualities – it resulted indirectly as a consequence of developments on the financial market.[27] The justification given is not intended to confuse; according to the correct view an annulment on grounds of mistake as to quality – being a special case of a mistake in declaration – is to be rejected along with the same arguments as an annulment for a mistake in declaration: whoever assumes a risk is bound to bear it should it materialise.

For the same reasons an adaptation of the contract in view of the absence or loss of the transaction's basis also fails.

The case would only be decided differently if Cinderella had acquired the shares on the basis of a sales prospectus issued by the public

[25] Terré, Simler, Lequette, *Les obligations* (2002) no. 701, pp. 679 ff.; Cass Com, 10 December 1996, Bull Joly Bourse 1997, 206, n. H. de Vauplane; Paris, 12 April 1996, JCP 1996, II, 22705, n. P. Le Tourneau.

[26] § 242; so-called *venire contra factum proprium*.   [27] RG LZ 1926, 744.

limited company or the bank controlling the sale on the stock exchange. If the company or the bank making the sale knew or should have known that internal occurrences would have had negative effects on the shares' market price then they would be liable by reason of failing to provide disclosure. According to the principles relating to 'liability for legal statements made in a prospectus'[28] – which are orientated around the liability imposed by duties of disclosure – it would be possible for Cinderella to claim compensation for negative interest. In connection with this claim for damages she may also seek to have the contract set aside §§ 311 II, 241 II, 249, 280 BGB.

Greece

Cinderella's mistake relates exclusively to her motives, consequently it is not a fundamental operative mistake (art. 143 AK).

It could be submitted that Cinderella was mistaken as to the intrinsic value of the shares. It has been said[29] that the economic value of a thing or its price is not a quality in the sense of art. 142 AK, consequently a mistake as to the value of a thing is not considered fundamental. This is not entirely accurate. In most cases it is true that a mistake as to the value of a thing will not be fundamental according to the criteria of the law. It will relate to the contracting party's motives for entering into the contract. If however the false representations of the mistaken person about the economic value result from a mistake as to the qualities of a thing, not necessarily the subject matter of the transaction,[30] here of the enterprise, which affect its value, the mistake may be operative. Here, however, Cinderella was not mistaken as to the company's qualities, e.g. its prosperity and thus annulment according to art. 142 AK is not possible.

Cinderella is not entitled to demand the annulment of the sale for fraud either. The company was not obliged in accordance with good

---

[28] See, finally, for example E. v. Heymann, 'Die neuere Rechtsprechung zur Bankhaftung bei Immobilien-Kapitalanlagen', NJW 1999, pp. 1577, 1584 ff.

[29] AP 268/1974 NoV 22, 1269; Gazis, *General Principles of Civil Law*, p. 65; Bailas, 'Error as to the Qualities of a Thing', p. 335; Karakatsanis AK 142 n. 4; Simantiras, *General Principles of Civil Law*, especially on the value of shares n. 727; Spyridakis, *General Principles*, p. 602; see however Georgiadis, *General Principles of Civil Law*, p. 426; Karassis, *Manual of General Principles of Civil Law*, p. 103; Klavanidou, *Error as to the Qualities of the Thing in Sales*, p. 18; Papantoniou, *General Principles of Civil Law*, p. 396.

[30] Spyridakis, *General Principles*, p. 601; for the opposite view cf. Karakatsanis AK 142 n. 4 who maintains that the term thing in art. 142 AK refers only to the object of the transaction.

faith and common usage to reveal that it lost the actual contracts to a competitor. On the contrary, the principles of good faith and common usage impose that the purchaser bears the risk of a transaction concluded in the stock market field of intense competition and conflicting interests.

If a company which provides investment services (EPEY) has mediated for the conclusion of the sale, it could be liable, under specific conditions which are not met here,[31] to compensate Cinderella according to art. 8 L. 2251/1994 on consumer protection. If however the financial intermediary was aware of the truth, i.e. that the company had lost many contracts to a competitor, and this was confidential information to which the financial intermediary had access, it would not be liable to Cinderella's compensation, since PrD 53/1992, aiming mainly to protect the market's function and not the protection of private interests, prohibits 'insiders' from disclosing confidential information. It is submitted[32] however that if the confidential information may lead to an abrupt fall in the shares' value, as is the case here, the advisor should warn future investors of the risks which threaten the investment.

Ireland

Cinderella purchased the shares she intended to buy. There is no possible recourse to a remedy due either to mistake or misrepresentation under Irish law, purely because the shares were not of the value she believed them to be. She purchased her commodity/product without assurances and the undervalue of that commodity is not something which changes the nature of that commodity in itself. Furthermore, there has not been any mistake as to the substance or subject matter of the contract. Accordingly, Irish law recognises no remedy in such circumstances.

Italy

Cinderella's case can be seen as affected by a basic contractual assumption (*presupposizione*) that 'important contracts would not be lost' and we could have the solution similar to the one offered by the Supreme Court[33] where the purchase of the stocks of a company was annulled

---

[31] For example, if the financial intermediary has violated the duties imposed by the code of deontology of EPEY (see arts. 10, 11 of the corresponding Directive of 10/5/1993 93/22/EC) for instance by omitting to make enquiries and collect information from the press concerning the object of the investment.

[32] Triantafyllakis ChID A p. 28.

[33] 3 December 1991, n. 12921, see GI 1992, I, 1, 2210 noted by ODDI.

because the buyer was not aware that the only immovable good in the company assets was subject to a pending action brought by the administrator in liquidation (art. 2901 of the Civil Code).

A different solution could be reached if the 'prospectus' about the company concealed the 'loss of important contracts'. Then, Cinderella would have a claim against the company in respect of its untruthful prospectus (*Responsabilità da prospetto*). There are usually two kinds of prospectus: one is offered by the merchant bank proposing the investment, the other is issued by the company itself.[34]

The misstatement in the prospectus drafted by the underwriter of the investment was considered in the *Banca Manusardi* case, decided by the Court of Appeals of Milan,[35] to create a precontractual liability (art. 1337 of the Civil Code) where 'a bank did not disclose some information concerning the economic situation of a company, whose convertible loan stocks were proposed to the investors'. In the *Manusardi* case damages were awarded for the 'negative interest', consisting in the losses occurred for not investing the money in a different object. Thus, the court decided to award the plaintiffs what they would have earned if they had bought Italian State Bonds for the same amount of money they had invested in the bad bargain.

The misstatement in the prospectus drafted by the company itself and certified by the accountant could entail both the precontractual liability of the company (art. 1337) and the civil liability of the accountant according to securities sales regulations,[36] the requirement to certify and publish accounts[37] and the duty to provide a truthful prospectus.[38] There are only two cases of accountants' liability in Italy, both consider the accountant liable for a misstatement in the books, but not for general information about the company's business prospects. However, the *Manusardi* case result leads to speculation that the solution may be different in the future.[39]

The Netherlands

Cinderella has no remedy. I presume that shares were not sold by the company which – e.g. as a result of regulations of the stock market – was

[34] See Ferranini, 'La responsabilità da prospetto delle banche' in *Banca Borsa e titoli di credito* (hereafter BBTC) 1987, I, p. 437.

[35] A. Milan, 2 February 1990, in *Giur. It.*, 1992, I, 2, 49, note by M. Arietti.

[36] L. 2 January 1991, n. 1, in GU 4 January 1991, n. 3.

[37] D.p.r. 31 March 1975, n. 136.

[38] EC Directive 80/310, L.4 June 1985, n. 281 and L.29 December 1990, n. 428.

[39] Trib. Torino, 13.6.1993; Trib. Milano, 16.11.1994, noted by Santaroni.

under a duty to disclose these facts to the public (in its prospectus), nor that they were sold by a seller (e.g. by a member of the board) who in another capacity had knowledge of the fact that the company had already lost various important contracts to a Japanese competitor, which would trigger other specific regulations. Therefore this is a case of common mistake. In such a case, in principle art. 6:228, s. 1(c) BW, applies.

However, this common mistake could never lead to annulment of the contract since it is one for which Cinderella should remain accountable (see art. 6:228, s. 2 BW).[40] First, because of the nature of the contract (sale of shares).[41] Secondly, because Cinderella was mistaken with regard to an exclusively future fact. Although the company had already lost the important contracts to a Japanese competitor before the conclusion of the contract, the value of the shares dropped after it. If Cinderella had resold immediately, before the *revelation in the press*, she would have obtained a good price.

In this type of transaction the courts are very reluctant to accept remedies for disappointed buyers. Accepting a remedy here would be a serious threat to the proper functioning of the stock market.

Norway

Two potential issues arise here, that of the relationship between purchaser and seller and between the purchaser and the company.

(i) The selling of shares on the stock market is normally characterised by the purchaser and the seller having no knowledge of each other, and the seller is often without specific information about the companies in which he has shares. For these reasons, it would be difficult to establish breach of contract against the seller based on the insufficiency of the information provided.[42]

Whether a breach of contract can be based on objective defect criteria is rather doubtful.[43] The purchase of larger holdings would, on the other hand, be negotiated on an individual basis. If it is presumed that this is the case in the present situation, and that the seller possessed the necessary information about the loss of the contracts, the question of the duty of disclosure is extremely pertinent.

---

[40] Cf. Asser/Hartkamp II (2001), no. 189.   [41] Cf. Asser/Hartkamp II (2001), no. 194.

[42] For the same reasons, invalidity would not apply, cf. J. Hellner, TfR 1987.313 ff.

[43] For a monograph on the sale and purchase of stocks and shares in Swedish law, see C. Hultmark, *Kontraktsbrott vid köp av aktie. Särskilt om fel* (Stockholm, 1992).

The Stock Exchange Act contains a specific regulation about a business' duty of disclosure to the stock exchange, see § 47.[44] Businesses have, according to the regulation, 'a duty to provide the stock exchange with information necessary for a true evaluation of the stock'. Extensive guidelines are provided in the Stock Exchange Regulations, § 5–2.

There is reason to believe that the seller's duty of disclosure to the purchaser to a large extent corresponds to a business' duty of disclosure to the stock exchange. Individual conditions relating to the purchase situation can, however, be considered as extending or limiting this duty. According to this, the point of departure for judgment is whether the loss of the contracts would have any bearing on the value of the shares ('correct evaluation of the shares'). Since this concerns the loss of important contracts, the duty of disclosure is to be expected.

(ii) Furthermore, a tortious claim against the company or even the company's representatives could be entertained if this duty of disclosure according to the Stock Exchange Act has not been complied with. For the representatives of the company etc. this responsibility has been codified.[45]

Portugal

Cinderella's chances of obtaining judicial annulment of the contract are very slight. The only possibility is a mistake about the contractual basis (art. 252°, no. 2 of the Civil Code), as stated above, but it is difficult not to see this case as a situation covered by the normal risks of the contract, which exclude the application of art. 437°.

The only remedy I see in this case is the liability for the prospectus about the sale of shares in the stock market, if the prospectus concealed the loss of important contracts. Articles 160° and following of the Securities Code set out a liability for truthful information in the prospectus which involves simultaneously the company itself, its corporate members or the financial intermediaries of the purchase. More specifically, art. 161° of the Securities Code states that if anybody has suffered harm as a result of insufficient, false or non up-to-date information in the prospectus relating to a sale on the stock exchange market, then he can bring an action asking for damages.[46]

---

[44] The Stock Exchange Act of 17 June 1988, no. 57.
[45] Section 17–1 of the new General Companies Act adopted 13 June 1997 corresponding to §§ 15–1 and 15–2 of the old Companies Act of 4 June 1976, no. 4.
[46] See A. J. Ferreira, *Direito dos Valores Mobiliários* (Lisbon, 1997), pp. 368 ff.

Scotland

In order for Cinderella to have a remedy under the Scots law of mis-representation, there must have been a misrepresentation made by the defender to the pursuer, as established in the case of *Forth Marine Insurance Co* v. *Barnes*.[47] In that case, the law-agent of the company assured the defender that the company was prosperous. This did not amount to misrepresentation by the company as the law-agent was neither acting as an agent for the directors nor authorised to make any representation. As Lord Curriehill stated,

> there must be representation by the company itself. No doubt the company could not make representations, except through its functionaries; and if these parties as such made a representation, then there may be liability but not otherwise.

In the present example, it does not appear that the company made any misleading statement, nor indeed a statement of any kind, to Cinderella before she purchased the shares. There is no duty of voluntary disclosure in the law of Scotland.[48] Therefore the company was under no obligation to disclose the information regarding the contracts, and no remedy is available to Cinderella.

Spain

In this case, I think it unlikely that Cinderella could annul the contract for the sale of shares listed on the Stock Exchange for the following reasons:

(i) Permanent surveillance is essential to the operation of these financial products. Shares listed on the Stock Exchange involve serious risk if not correctly managed, and profits can quickly change to losses for a variety of reasons, so that operations with this type of product require know-how and good judgement which, given Cinderella's business status, she would have been assumed to possess.

(ii) In order to annul the contract for defective consent, Cinderella would have to prove her mistake and, as we have already indicated, such a mistake must be fundamental and excusable. We think her mistake here is inexcusable since her education and social standing should have meant that she was aware of the risks inherent to such products,

---

[47] (1848) 10 D 689, affirmed (1849) 6 Bell 54.   [48] *Murray* v. *Marr* (1892) 20 R 119.

meaning that her mistake could have been due to negligence or a lack of diligence, which does not annul a contract.

(iii) Another possibility might be that the National Stock Market Commission had 'privileged' information on these securities which it failed to make known to the shareholders: this would make the Commission liable for the loss caused to Cinderella and any other affected party.

Comparative observations

Here the sales contract concerns shares of a company listed on the stock market and the object of the sale has a direct effect on the solutions.

No country admits mistake here. In Austria and Greece the buyer's potential mistake is qualified as a mistake as to value and thus a mistake as to motive which is not fundamental to lead to annulment. Other analyses (Germany, The Netherlands) deny mistake on the basis that the buyer has tacitly accepted the risk or that her failure to be aware of the risk amounts to inexcusable behaviour (Spain).

England, Ireland and Scotland go one step further in refusing any remedy: there is no question of mistake nor misrepresentation. This bloc is not, however, restricted to the above-mentioned countries since Dutch law takes a similar view that the buyer assumes the risk and that the proper functioning of the stock market assumes a minimal interference.

As far as the imposition of a duty to inform is concerned, the majority of countries are also in agreement that no such general duty exists on the seller of shares of a listed company. The question then arises as a matter of factual interpretation: who exactly is the seller of the shares? The way in which reporters interpreted the facts reveals information about the various ways the stock market operates and is controlled in each country.

(i) If the sale is made by the company

Liability may be admitted by a number of countries, mostly on the grounds of specialised 'prospectus liability' contained in specific legislation, although it was considered that non-compliance had not been proven on the facts (Belgium, England, Italy, France). In contrast, Germany, Portugal and Norway consider that liability under this head could arise.

(ii) If the sale is made by a director of the company

In contrast, a claim made by a shareholder against a director of the company as seller (conceivable under French and Belgian law) would fail for practical reasons: any damages would be given back to the company as such an action is derivative in nature, and of little comfort to the purchaser as a result. In addition, if the purchaser tried to bring an individual shareholder's action she would fail since she would be unable to prove her personal loss.

(iii) If the sale is made by a financial intermediary

Certain differences as to result emerged under this particular hypothesis. Under French and Belgian law such a contractual duty to inform could plausibly lie on the intermediary to inform the client of the risks of the operation envisaged. However if the duty is interpreted strictly so as to expect the purchaser to make enquiries, as under Belgian law, it was suggested that such a duty had not been breached here. Under French law, according to a protective and thus more lenient interpretation of the purchaser's corresponding duty to inform herself, the seller could be liable; but at the most for damages would lie for loss of opportunity. Italian case law has gone even further in a similar case and imposed a general precontractual liability (art. 1337 – good faith) on an underwriter though it must be emphasised that the case is an important but isolated instance.[49] A similar result would be arrived at under an analogous argument used by the Norwegian reporter: it is argued that the seller has a duty to disclose which is analogous to that incumbent on the company, under specific provisions, to disclose to the stock exchange. It is assumed the argument by analogy will only succeed if the breach of specific company legislation is demonstrated.

Despite the complex legal analyses offered on the question of the seller's identity, two main issues emerge here. The presence of specific company legislation is the first. In the majority of countries that examined the existence of a specialised duty to inform, it was held not to apply on the facts (for exceptions, see (i)); it might be inferred that the end-purpose of such legislation is aimed more at fulfilling standards of apparent transparency than at protecting agents in the market. The second issue is one for economic, rather than purely legal consideration. It is clear that the majority of legal systems gave no remedy to the purchaser on these facts. Although some legal characterisations are more blunt about the reason than others this is surely because the object of the sale is a high risk contract subject to fluctuations in value, and that there are strong economic reasons for minimising interference. The

---

[49] *Manusardi* case, see Italian report.

consequence is manifested either by not imposing a duty to inform or by imposing a specific duty and interpreting it restrictively so that it does not apply. The prevailing values illustrated by this case are the contractual allocation of risks without outside interference and maintaining the security of transaction with the net result that party autonomy continues to apply.

Case 8
Estella v. Uriah Heep

Case

Estella opened the door to Uriah Heep, who was selling steam-operated pans that cook without fat. Estella, who has few pounds in her purse but rather too many elsewhere, could not resist the temptation and accepted Uriah's offer of a special credit arrangement. In her haste to begin cooking, she signed various documents full of small print without reading them. She later discovered to her cost, that the pan could only be used on a gas ring whereas her kitchen was entirely electric. However, when she contacted Uriah for help, he was less than friendly. He told her that her statutory rights were written out in the documents he had supplied, and that as she had not returned the pan within the period indicated, she could no longer cancel the sale. He also reminded her that her first monthly instalment on the loan was due. What remedy, if any, is available?

Discussions

Austria

(i) In accordance with § 3 *Konsumentenschutzgesetz* (the law regulating consumer rights) the consumer is entitled to cancel the contract upon written notice within one week after the purchase in the case of a so-called door-step sale. The seller must send a document to the buyer identifying the subject matter of the contract as well as informing him about the right to cancel; time begins to run when this document is sent. The law is considered (relatively) mandatory (*ius cogens*) in the sense that a different – probably shorter – period of time for the right of cancellation agreed upon between the two contracting parties is invalid.

284

In case Estella has actually received such a document it is necessary to ascertain whether or not the one-week period has already expired.

(ii) If the legislative time period has already expired then the question whether Estella is entitled to annul the contract on the ground of mistake arises. In accordance with § 6 subsection 1 figure 14 *Konsumentenschutzgesetz* the right to annul on the ground of mistake can neither be limited nor excluded by a contractual agreement. Annulling the contract is available only in case of an *important mistake*. The following conditions have to be fulfilled: (i) a mistake as to content of the contract in the wider sense exists; (ii) the mistake is fundamental; (iii) one of the three possibilities under § 871 ABGB exists, namely that (a) the mistake was caused by the other party; or (b) the other party should have recognised the mistake due to the circumstances; or (c) the mistake was notified on time.

In accordance with § 871 ABGB Code a contract can be annulled in the case of a mistake as to the important and fundamental nature of the subject matter of the contract. The term 'important and fundamental nature' does also include the usage of a physical good.[1] The importance of a certain quality of the goods is primarily to be considered in accordance with generally accepted business usage.[2] Since it is important that a cooking pan can be used on a common stove, the mistake is, therefore, a *mistake as to the content of the contract*. The mistake is *important*, as Estella would not have bought a cooking pan that she could not use if she had known the true circumstances. Furthermore, the mistake has been *caused* by Uriah Heep as he was obliged to provide full information (precontractual duty to inform) about the usefulness of the goods' characteristics. Estella can thus successfully annul the contract. In addition she can sue Uriah Heep for damages incurred as a result of her reliance on the contract in accordance with the rules under *culpa in contrahendo*.[3]

(iii) The usefulness of the cooking pan for an entirely electric kitchen has to be seen as a generally recognised qualification of a cooking pan as to the large range of usage of that generally recognised form and method of energy. Therefore, this has to be seen as a material defect for which the seller is liable. The material defect is relevant and important as the defect does not permit the proper use of the goods, but the defect is removable. Estella, therefore, is entitled to claim termination on account of a material defect within a period of six months.

[1] Pisko in Klang II, 118.   [2] Gschnitzer in Klang IV/1, 124.
[3] OGH 8.10.1975 JBl, 205 note by Bydlinski; Koziol and Welser, *Grundriß des Bürgerlichen Rechts* I 138.

She may also claim for damages in accordance with § 1295 ABGB (see Case 4).

Belgium

Four remedies will be considered:

(i) The peculiarity of this case is that it does not only constitute a door-step sale[4] but also, more specifically, an instalment sale as defined by art. 1,9° of the Consumer Credit Law. Article 87(g) of the law of 14 July 1991 provides that its provisions are not applicable to consumer credit door-step sales dealt with by consumer credit law. As a result, the time limit (seven working days after the contract has been signed) for cancelling the contract provided in art. 89 of the 1991 law does not apply here.

The relevant cancellation provisions are, in my view,[5] to be found in art. 18 of the Consumer Credit Law,[6] which gives the buyer similar, if marginally shorter, rights.[7] Although there is some controversy over the interpretation of these provisions,[8] this discussion is of mere theoretical

---

[4] A sale entered into outside the seller's enterprise, according to the terminology used in arts. 86 ff. of the law on commercial practices and information and protection of the consumer of 14 July 1991.

[5] The history of the Consumer Credit Law (the so-called 'travaux préparatoires') also points in that direction: see Projet de loi relatif au crédit à la consommation, Documents parlementaires, *Sénat*, sess. 1990–1991, no. 916–2 (1989–90), pp. 92–3.

[6] Article 18 § 1. '*Except for instalment sales* and for leasing contracts, the consumer has the right to cancel the contract within a 7 working days time limit starting on the day of signature of the contract, when the latter has been entered into on the day when the [credit] offer became valid (. . .).

§ 2. The consumer has the right to cancel the contract within a 7 working days time-limit starting on the day of signature of the contract, when the contract was entered into by both parties being present outside the enterprise of the lender or of the credit intermediary (. . .).'

[7] F. Domont-Naert, 'L'information du consommateur et l'obligation de renseignement dans la loi du 12 juin 1991', Colloque CIEAU, 17 October 1991, Brussels, p. 67, no. 3.2 (reprinted in the review DA/OR); E. Balate, P. Dejemeppe and F. De Patoul, *Le droit du crédit à la consommation* (Brussels, 1995), no. 241.

[8] P. Lettany, *Het consumentenkrediet. De wet van 12 juni 1991* (Antwerp, 1993), no. 131; L. De Brouwer, 'Le délai de réflexion. Variations d'une protection dans les lois sur les pratiques du commerce et le crédit à la consommation' in *Formation permanente CUP. Pratiques du commerce* (Liège, 1997), vol. xvi, pp. 121 ff., p. 135. ('Sauf s'il s'agit d'une vente à tempérament (. . .), le consommateur peut exercer son droit de renonciation 'pendant un délai de sept jours ouvrables à dater de la signature du contrat lorsque ce dernier a été conclu le jour à partir duquel l'offre est valable (. . .) ou lorsque le conclusion du contrat a eu lieu en présence des deux parties en dehors de l'entreprise du prêteur ou de l'intermédiaire de crédit.')

value in the present case since it appears that the time limit (supposing that one applies) has already expired.

(ii) Estella was mistaken about a substantial quality of the pan: she thought she could use it on electric equipment whereas it was only suitable for a gas ring. Estella will however have to face two evidential obstacles in that she will have to prove that the substantial quality (that is fitness of the pan to be used on electric equipment) entered into the contractual field (see Case 1); and that her mistake was excusable.

Interestingly, in that respect, Estella might be in a better situation than if her contract had been governed by the law of 1991 since the latter provides that the contract must mention the precise description of the product along with its main characteristics: in that case, Estella would normally have been put on notice of the ability of the pan to work only on a gas ring and it would have been difficult for her to assert that the electric suitability of the pan entered into the contractual field and that her mistake was excusable. But here the contract does not need to describe the thing sold precisely: the instalment sale provisions of the Consumer Credit Law require a description of the financial aspects of the transaction but not of the thing sold itself.

(iii) Again, the issue of excusability will not normally be raised if Estella bases her action on fraud (see Case 1). Is it plausible to assert that Uriah Heep committed some fraudulent concealment in not drawing Estella's attention to the fact that the thing offered was not suitable for use on electric equipment? Normally, a seller ought to provide information only about the so-called 'normal use' of the product[9] but this should probably have included mentioning, even incidentally, that the pan is only fit for use on a gas ring. If Uriah Heep actually saw Estella's kitchen it may not be feasible to raise the defence that he did not know that Estella's equipment was all electric, but this will depend on the circumstances of the sale.

The fact that Uriah Heep arguably complied with the statutory requirements as to instalment sales will not normally have a negative impact on Estella's claim because Belgian authors are generally favourable to a cumulative application of the general rules on defective consent protective of the consumer and specific consumer law provisions.[10]

---

[9] Merchiers & De Pover, ' La vente – Les contrats spéciaux – Chronique de jurisprudence 1988–1995', no. 35.

[10] See, for instance, H. Cousy, *Problemen van produktenaansprakelijkheid* (Brussels, 1978), no. 191 who suggests that the policy underlying this position is to protect the consumer by offering him the greatest variety of actions.

(iv) Estella can also bring an action against the seller for breach of guarantee of hidden defects (art. 1641 of the Civil Code). We have seen already that the concept of 'functional defect' comes very close to the notion of substantial defect. Indeed, a functional defect is one that affects the use that the purchaser intended, with the seller's awareness (i.e. it must have 'entered into the contractual field'), to make of the thing even if it does not intrinsically affect the thing itself (see Case 3). As the *Cour de cassation* has admitted that a hidden defect might be a functional defect, Estella might try to construct an argument under this head. The specific obstacles that she will have to overcome are that the alleged defect might be considered as apparent and the short time limit expressed in art. 1648 of the Civil Code may have expired.

Despite the presence of specialised consumer protection legislation, it would seem that the general rules (on defective consent or breach of contract) appear to be the most promising remedies although a favourable outcome is far from certain.

England

Two separate issues arise here: Estella's remedies in relation to the unsuitability of the pan; and the loan. These must be addressed separately because the fact that the contract involves a credit facility means that additional statutory rules apply.

The first issue is whether there was (apart from the 'small print') any remedy arising from the unsuitability of the pan. The facts are not sufficiently explicit. It is not clear whether Uriah made any misrepresentation about the pan (if he did, the remedies for misrepresentation discussed under Case 1 – rescission and/or damages – will be relevant); or whether the pan could be held to be not 'fit for any particular purpose for which the goods are being bought' with the result that Uriah would be in breach of an implied term under the Sale of Goods Act 1979, s. 14(3) (which implies such terms into contracts of sale of goods entered into by sellers in the course of a business where the buyer has expressly or impliedly made known the purpose. It will therefore depend here on whether Estella made clear to Uriah that she needed a pan suitable for an electric cooker); or whether any express right to return the goods within a particular period was given in the contract (if so, she would have to exercise it within the given time period). If no right to reject the pan (or other remedy, such as damages) arose under any of these heads, then Estella has no remedy under the contract of sale. If, however, she did have such a remedy, the next question would be whether she had deprived herself of that remedy by signing the 'small print' which (it appears) placed a time limit on the exercise of remedies. At common law[11] the approach has been to say that a signature on a document containing terms is sufficient to incorporate the terms into the contract, whether or not the party has read them (and even where the other party knows that they have not been read). But there are statutory provisions which might prevent Uriah relying on the written terms. Any claim Estella may have for misrepresentation can only be restricted by the 'small print' if Uriah establishes that the restriction is reasonable;[12] under the Unfair Contract Terms Act 1977,[13] Uriah cannot exclude his liability for breach of the term implied by s. 14 Sale of Goods Act, and he cannot exclude his liability for other breaches of contract unless he establishes that the exclusion is reasonable;[14] and under the Unfair Terms in Consumer Contracts Regulations 1999[15] any term which Uriah included in the 'small print' will not bind Estella if it is 'unfair' – in the sense that 'contrary to the requirement of good faith, it causes a significant imbalance in the parties' rights and obligations arising under the contract, to the detriment of the consumer'. Depending on the precise details of the term in the 'small print' Estella's remedies may therefore not be restricted, although this (together with the assessment of the 'reasonableness' of the term and whether it is 'unfair') depends on the facts.

Given the credit arrangements here[16] there is a statutory regime, under the Consumer Credit Act 1974,[17] which, in the case of a door-step

---

[11] *L'Estrange* v. *F. Graucob Ltd.* [1934] 2 KB 394. This has been strictly applied in England, although there are signs in other common law jurisdictions that the rule might not be so absolute: in Canada, for example, it has been held that where a car hire company held itself out as offering a speedy service and so knew that a hirer would not have the opportunity to read all the small print, the hirer was not bound by unusual terms: *Tilden Rent-a-Car Co.* v. *Clendenning* (1978) 83 DLR 3d. 400.

[12] Misrepresentation Act 1967, s. 3 (as replaced by Unfair Contract Terms Act 1977, s. 8).

[13] Section 6(2), since Estella is a 'consumer' within the meaning of the Act. If she were entering into the contract in the course of business, there would still be a restriction on the effectiveness of the 'small print' but then Uriah would have to establish that the exclusion of remedy was 'reasonable': s. 6(3).

[14] Section 3(2)(a).   [15] Implementing Council Directive 93/13/EEC.

[16] The Consumer Protection (Cancellation of Contracts Concluded Away From Business Premises) Regulations 1987, implementing Council Directive 85/577/EEC, impose a cooling-off period of 7 days in the case of contracts for goods over £35 between a trader and a consumer following an unsolicited visit to the consumer's home. However where, as here, there is a credit agreement governed by the Consumer Credit Act, the Act takes effect *in place of* the Regulations.

[17] Sections 67–73. For the purposes of this Act, the agreement must be a 'regulated' agreement: a credit agreement in favour of an individual, not exceeding £15,000. It is assumed that Uriah is both creditor and supplier of the goods (and therefore the contract is a 'debtor-creditor-supplier' contract within the meaning of the Act).

contract where the price of the goods is greater than £35 (which we do not know here), requires the creditor to give the debtor a 'cooling-off' period during which she has the right to cancel both the credit agreement and the linked sale contract. A prescribed notice detailing, *inter alia*, the cancellation right must be given on the spot, when the contract is concluded; and a copy must be sent by post, within seven days. The consumer's cooling-off period is 5 days from receipt of the posted copy. Estella's right to cancel therefore depends on whether the documents supplied by Uriah complied with the Act, and whether the cooling-off period has now expired. If the prescribed notice was not served by Uriah within the period required by the statute, the cancellation right is prolonged indefinitely. If she has the right to cancel the credit agreement and the sale contract, Estella would have the right to refuse to pay, and to require Uriah to take back the pan.

France

The case of Estella is a typical example of door-step sale to a consumer. Two kinds of provisions concerning protection against vitiated consent are cumulatively applicable. Special protection is granted by the Consumer Law Code provisions which are to be added to the general remedies offered by the general law of contract for defective consent. Moreover, the whole field is subsumed under the doctrinal concept of the duty to inform.

(i) As far as the adequacy of a remedy provided by the Consumer Code is concerned, reference has to be made to arts. L121–21 ff.[18] The Consumer Law of door-step protects individuals, to whom a seller (or his employee) pays a visit for selling purposes, to offer goods or services.[19] These three requirements are satisfied in the case of Estella.

Moreover, the special protection against vitiated consent is guaranteed by a series of prerequisites, the absence of which gives rise to the annulment of the whole agreement. Among them certain information must clearly feature in writing in the contract (art. L121–23), including

---

[18] Statute of 22 December 1972 as modified by the law of 1989 and introduced in the Consumer Code in 1993.

[19] Article L121–21: 'The provisions of the subsequent section are applicable to any person who sells or appoints to sell door to door to an individual, at his residence or place of work, even when asked, in order to offer him a purchase, sale, a lease, or a hire-purchase agreement of goods or services.'

a description of the item or service subject to contract, the payment facilities and the option to cancel.

In our case this would seemingly apply to the ability of the pan to be used only on a gas ring as the statute demands 'a precise description of the nature or features of the proposed item or service',[20] the absence of one of the above-mentioned characteristics rendering the contract voidable.[21] Besides, the remedy is available even if the cancellation option has expired.[22] The formal requirement has been also interpreted by the courts as including a requirement of legibility, subject to the same remedy.[23]

Estella's case does not at first sight satisfy any of these conditions for annulment. Although the documents are written out in 'small print', nothing really suggests that they are not legible (if they were then the contract could be annulled no matter the delay). It can be assumed on the facts that all the legislative provisions have been complied with.[24]

Focusing now on the key element of the statutory protection, i.e. the cancellation option, art. L121–25 offers a seven-day delay (not open to any agreed suppression or reduction) within which the client can retract his consent. Here too Estella will not be able to take advantage of it if Uriah Heep is right in saying that she has not returned the pan soon enough, the time limit being supposedly the statutory one.[25]

Thus it seems that Estella will not be able to avail herself of any protection provided by the Consumer Code. It is accordingly crucial to determine whether she could have recourse to the general provisions of the Civil Code for defective consent.

(ii) Actually and perhaps surprisingly[26] the specific protection of the Consumer Code is not exclusive of the general protection of arts. 1109 and following of the Civil Code.[27] Is an action based upon mistake

---

[20] Article L121–23, 4°.

[21] Cass Civ 1, 30 March 1994, no. 92–18. 179, See G. Lamy, *Droit économique* (Paris, 1998), no. 2765.

[22] CA Versailles: 1st division, 12 April 1996, MHT Case, Lamy cit. no. 338.

[23] Cass Com, 23 October 1984, D 1985.IR.74: pale grey ink on the back of the document, the contract was annulled.

[24] As she has signed 'various documents full of small print' presumably fulfilling the statutory requirements. If not, again the agreement is voidable and also the loan.

[25] Note that the delay is postponed by bank holidays: art. L121–25 cited.

[26] The relationship is indeed controversial – the principle of *specialia generalibus derogant* could provide an argument for the opposite solution.

[27] CA Versailles, 8 July 1994, RTDCiv 1994.97, obs Mestre, granting a remedy based upon the general provisions of the Civil Code.

doomed to failure? As already observed, to be actionable, it is not enough that the mistake must have induced the mistaken party's consent; it is also necessary that the substantial quality concerned has entered the 'contractual field'.[28] In addition, the unfitness of the thing bargained for to achieve the desired end has to be inherent to the item itself, and must not result from the personal situation of the party concerned unless within the 'contractual field' (see also Case 4). Estella could claim she was so mistaken: she thought that she was buying a device which could be used on electric equipment in her kitchen when it was only suitable for a gas ring and this has implicitly entered into the contractual representations of the parties.

Nevertheless, the success of Estella's claim will still depend upon two successive hurdles. First, she will have to defeat the seller's allegation that the written provisions of the contract mention the ability of the pan to be used on a gas ring only. Secondly, the seller could allege that Estella had made an inexcusable mistake.[29] In that respect Estella could perhaps rely on an *a contrario* interpretation of a decision of the Court of Appeal of Paris[30] which held that 'despite the clear provision of an advertising order, a confusion occurred in the client's mind, such a mistake is not excusable on the part of a tradesman who is under an obligation to read the written or printed writing under which he lays his signature'. Conversely, the consumer's mistake (as opposed to the professional tradesman's) may not result from the sole fact that he did not read carefully all the documents that he has signed. Here the problem will boil down to the free assessment of the judges who may also take into account the circumstances of the door-step sale. Estella might thus show that her mistake was justified and the contract may be annulled.

(iii) Lastly, Estella might try to allege fraud. But this is unlikely to work as Estella would have to plead the seller's fraudulent concealment. As already seen, fraudulent concealment depends in most cases on the prior existence of a duty to inform.[31] The duty to inform has been incorporated in a specific duty in the Consumer Code.[32] In that respect the *Cour de cassation* has decided that when the debtor under such a duty, i.e. Uriah Heep – has fulfilled the statutory requirements, no fraudulent

---

[28] See Ghestin, *La formation du contrat*, nos. 500 ff.

[29] 'Mistake is a cause of nullity only if it is excusable' Cass Soc, 3 July 1990, D 1991, 507.

[30] CA Paris 24 April 1984, RTDCiv. 1985, 572 obs. Mestre.

[31] Cf. Ghestin, *La formation du contrat*, nos. 571 ff.   [32] See above pp. 290–91.

concealment can be claimed against him.[33] The whole question would depend again on whether or not the statutory provisions have been fulfilled.

Germany

The more recent legislation on consumer protection which has in part been prompted by European Directives[34] in this case offers Estella two possibilities to cancel the contract – independently of her mistake concerning the use of the pan: according to § 1 of the *Haustürwiderrufgesetz* (*HaustürWG*: Law on Doorstep Sales)[35] the customer (consumer) may in the case of a contract concluded away from the seller's business premises, revoke his acceptance within a period of one week from when the contract was concluded. According to § 2 HaustürWG the period begins to run if the seller has distributed a 'printed, clearly formulated, instruction of his right to revoke in writing'. Section 7 of the *Verbraucherkreditgesetz* (*VerbrKrG*: Law on Consumer Credit Arrangements) provides a similar right of cancellation.[36] Because Estella and Uriah have agreed payment by instalments then under certain circumstances (§ 1 II and § 3 *VerbrKrG*) the Law on Consumer Credit Arrangements is also applicable to the contract of sale. Uriah replies in his defence that he had provided Estella with all the necessary contractual documents prescribed by statute. However, the facts of the case make reference to the 'small print' which could – according to the way in which the contractual documents have been formulated – infringe the requirements of clarity in § 2 of the Law on Doorstep Sales and § 7 of the Law on Consumer Credit Arrangements, thereby granting Estella a right of cancellation. Due to the fact that the case lacks sufficient evidence to support this claim such a possibility will not be considered.

(i) Estella might claim either for repair (i.e. exchange of the pans, §§ 437 Ziff 1, 434 I, 439 BGB) or for termination of contract or reduction in the price (§§ 437 Ziff 2, 434 I, 440). But neither the pan's normal

---

[33] Cass Civ 1, 14 of June 1989, Bull civ I, no. 240. JCP 1991 II, 21632 obs. Virassamy, Dalloz 1989, Somm. Comm. p. 338, Aubert.

[34] The German laws on consumer protection are as a rule older than the relevant Directives of the EC but it has been necessary to change certain details to bring them into line with these Directives.

[35] *Gesetz über den Widerruf von Haustürgeschäften und ähnlichen Geschäften* (Law on the Revocation of Doorstep Sales and Related Transactions) from 16.1.1986 (BGBl I 122); corresponds to the Directive 1985/577/EEC (OJ 1985 L 372).

[36] *Verbraucherkreditgesetz* from 17.12.1990 (BGBl I 2840); corresponds to the Directive 1987/102/EEC (OJ 1987 L. 42).

use nor its use as prescribed by the contract is impaired; it may be used without any problem with gas stoves. Even if Uriah must have known that Estella intended to cook on an electric stove the limited possibility to use the pan has not become a component of the contract. It is not apparent from the facts of the case that Uriah actually knew that Estella intended to use the pan with her electric stove. Therefore the pan that Uriah supplied is neither objectively nor subjectively defective. Accordingly, Estella is unable to enforce any guarantee claims.

(ii) According to Flume's view of mistake relating to characteristics in business transactions, the conditions set out in § 119 II are only fulfilled if the properties of the corporeal object provided diverge from those which have been agreed in the contract. The courts substantially follow this view but not without allowing exceptions.[37] However, in order to accept it as a 'normally substantial quality' they require that the party making the mistake 'perceivably' rooted the contract in his expectation of this quality being present.[38] According to both views it would not be possible for Estella to annul for such a mistake. The pan's suitability for use on electric stoves was neither made a condition of the contract nor did Estella make it clear at the conclusion of the contract that she intended to use the pan on an electric stove. Both Flume and the BGH would consequently classify Estella's mistake as an insignificant mistake as to motive.

I have already criticised this view a number of times; it does not take into account the fact that the laws on mistake and warranty use different evaluations. To be sure, here as there the absent 'quality' occupies centre stage but the perspectives are different: in the law on warranty the principle of equivalent exchange is in the foreground whereas in the law on mistake the question concerns a party's mistaken assumption or expectation. In practice, the fact that the party claiming annulment is liable towards the other party for the latter's negative interest (§ 122) deters the mistaken party from annulling his declaration.

When assessing a mistake as to quality, it is more appropriate to draw upon the evaluation criteria contained in § 119 I. Estella can annul the contract of sale for the pans if her mistake relating to the use of the pans caused her to conclude the contract not only in her case (subjective) but also in the case of other purchasers (objective) and if she did not assume any particular risk concerning the use of the pans. The criterion that

---

[37] Especially well-known instances are the so-called 'Baujahr-Cases'; cf. above at Case 5.
[38] BGHZ 88, 240, 246.

Estella's mistake would also have proved substantial for other purchasers of the pans causes difficulties. This criterion helps to differentiate mere 'mistakes as to motive' from mistakes which may typically occur in the conclusion of such contracts. The assumption that the pan which Uriah sold can also be used on electric rings is not Estella's exclusively subjective expectation; the mistake which Estella made may also induce other users of electric kitchens to enter into such a contract with Uriah. For this reason, Estella should be able to annul the contract of sale. That said, she must compensate Uriah's negative interest (§ 122 I) if he could not have known of Estella's mistake (§ 122 II).

(iii) Instead of annulling the contract, Estella may claim that Uriah compensate her negative interest in the case, if Uriah through his own fault failed to fulfil his duty in informing Estella that the pan's use was qualified. Such a duty of disclosure will mainly be implied if Uriah was bound to have taken into account the fact that his customers use electric stoves.[39] Assuming that Uriah has negligently breached such a duty of disclosure, when assessing his obligation to pay compensation it should also be considered whether Estella should have enquired whether the pan sold could also be used on electric rings. Uriah's duty to inform and Estella's duty to obtain further information therefore supplement each other: the sooner Uriah had to take into account that his customers use electric rings the sooner he comes under a duty to inform; vice versa, Estella is especially expected to obtain further information in the case where gas rings are mainly used in her area; she cannot therefore expect Uriah to provide clarification on this matter. However these two considerations are weighed up – with regard to the actual circumstances – Estella's claim for compensation according to § 254 will either be reduced or fail altogether.

Greece

Greek law gives Estella several remedies. The contract which she has concluded with Uriah Heep falls under the scope of application of art. 3 of the L.2251/1994 for the protection of consumers who have concluded contracts outside business premises. A right to cancel without reason is provided by art. 3 § 4 which must be exercised within 10 working days from the delivery of the contractual document or the later delivery of the thing. If it is assumed that Estella's statutory rights have expired,

---

[39] The predominance of gas ovens varies greatly both on a regional and national level; to my knowledge gas ovens are seldom used in Germany.

the contract is valid as the fact that her rights were written in small print is not crucial.

(i) Estella can however ask for the termination of the contract on the grounds of a defect of the thing sold (art. 534 AK). Such a defect must be accepted because the quality of the pan as suitable only for gas appliances and not the usually used electrical ones affects its usefulness, in accordance with the content of the contract but also generally accepted views (subjective-objective theory). The defect is substantial. The question whether 'the usefulness of the thing is eliminated or substantially diminished' (art. 534 AK) will be judged on the basis of the usefulness that the parties intended. Finally, it is a matter of interpretation of the contract, which will be carried out with the use of the subjective and objective interpretative criteria of arts. 173 and 200 AK.[40] This means that the pan, in the absence of express provision, must have the usual qualities of its category,[41] i.e. it should be suitable for use on an electric stove, a perfectly normal feature of modern kitchens. Remedies under this head, actionable within six months of delivery (arts. 554 ff. AK) are alternatively termination, reduction of the purchase price or damages.[42] Uriah Heep is not liable if he can show that Estella knew of the pan's defect or that her lack of knowledge amounts to gross negligence. Negligence on Estella's part cannot be established from the fact that it was written somewhere that the pan is only fit for gas rings and she did not read it before the conclusion of the contract.

(ii) Estella can also claim the annulment of the sale on the grounds of mistake as to the qualities of the thing (art. 142 AK). The two criteria, objective and subjective, of the fundamental nature of the mistake as to quality are satisfied here. With regard to the objective criterion, the quality of a pan as suitable for electric appliances is of importance for the whole legal act on the basis of good faith and common usage. The effects of annulment have already been discussed.[43] If the pan has suffered harm because of the use Estella made of it she may be liable to pay negative interest damages to Uriah as owner of the pan (art. 145 AK).

(iii) Annulment on the grounds of fraud (art. 147 AK) could be sought only if Uriah Heep concealed the truth as to the pan's qualities (a duty to inform must be established first) with the purpose of inducing Estella to conclude the sale.

---

[40] I. Spyridakis, and E. Perakis, *Civil Code Law of Obligations. Special Part* (Athens, 1978), AK 534 n. 6.

[41] Filios, *Law of Obligations*, Special Part § 5 A IV.

[42] See Cases 3 and 5.   [43] See Case 2.

Ireland

It is necessary to ascertain whether Estella actually told Uriah Heep that she required a pan that would work on an electric cooker or whether Heep made a representation to her that the pan would work on such a cooker. If she did not make explicit her requirements to him, it may be that her right to redress is limited to a situation where the pan is actually defective. In such circumstances, the implied warranties under s. 39 and s. 40 of the Sale of Goods and Supply of Services Act 1980 come into play. If Estella bought the pan based on a misrepresentation by Heep that the pan was suitable for use on an electric cooker, Estella would be entitled to rescind the contract or sue for damages. However, she may have restricted her remedies by signing the small print in the contract. Irish law presumes that people understand the 'small print' of a contract and in *Carroll (A Minor) v. Budget Travel* (Unreported judgment of Morris J in the High Court), the fact that the mother of the infant plaintiff had failed to read the small print in the contract because such had not been explicitly brought to her attention did not render the contract inoperable. The court held that as a reasonable person, she should have read the small print and informed herself of the consequences of entering into the contract. Furthermore, the approach of the Irish courts has been that while clauses in a contract which exclude a party's statutory rights are not permissible, clauses which limit those rights can be allowed. In Ireland, the issue as to whether such a term in a contract is fair is governed by common law principles and EU legislation in the form of the Unfair Terms in Consumer Contracts Regulations 1994.

A further possible method of redress for Estella arises under the Consumer Protection (Cancellation of Contracts Concluded Away From Business Premises) Regulations 1987. These apply where the value of the goods purchased is in excess of £35.00 and require a trader who deals with a consumer on foot in an unsolicited visit to the consumer's home to give the consumer notice of her right to cancel the contract, which right can be exercised within seven days of the contract being entered into. If such notice was not brought to Estella's attention however, she has a right to refuse to pay and hand the pan back to Uriah Heep.

Italy

This is a typical case of door-step sale,[44] the new legislation provides the consumer with five days to make up his mind. Furthermore, in case the

---

[44] L. 7 June 1974, n. 216, DL 8 April 1974, n. 95, modified by the EEC Directive 89/298, enacted by the d.lg.vo 25 January 1992, n. 74, L. 29 December 1990, n. 428.

five days have expired without notice of cancellation, Estella could take advantage of the consumer contracts regulations[45] introduced in the Civil Code (arts. 1469 *bis*–1469 *sexies*). Following the EC Directive 93/13, the new regulations on unfair contract terms provide the consumer a way out from unfair terms[46] (such as the one that fixes a shorter time limit for cancelling the contract); in other words, unfair terms are not considered as part of the contract, while the contract itself will stand in its fundamental provisions.

Moreover, Estella might find some grounds for recovery under the provisions of arts. 1519 *bis*–1519 *nonies*, recently introduced in the Italian Civil code by Dlgs 2/2/02 n. 24.

In fact, art. 1519 *ter* Civil Code imposes on the seller the obligation to supply the buyer with goods that conform with the contract. Goods do conform if two criteria are met: (a) they are fit for the purposes for which goods of the same description would ordinarily be used; and (b) they possess the qualities necessary for their normal use. Thus, a saucepan is expected to be used on an electric stove if the seller does not mention the fact that the item might have a more restricted range of use than similar products have.

It follows that Estella could claim either for repair (i.e. exchange of the pans) or for termination of the contract or for a reduction in price (art. 1519 *quater*).

The Netherlands

Estella may terminate the contract on the basis of the statute on door-step sales, and may probably also annul the contract on the basis of mistake.

This is a case of door-step selling to which the *Colportagewet* of 1973, which was adapted several times (amongst other reasons for the implementation of the Directive 85/577/EC), applies (see definition in art. 1). The general rules on door-step sale in the *Colportagewet* apply. Article 25 says that the buyer may unilaterally cancel the contract within 8 days

---

[45] The new section of the Civil Code has been enacted by art. 25 of L. 6.2.1996, n. 52.

[46] V. Roppo, 'La nuova disciplina delle clausole abusive nei contratti fra imprese e consumatori', RDC 1994, I, p. 277; R. Pardolesi, 'Clausole abusive, pardon vessatorie: verso l'attuazione di una direttiva abusata', RCDP 1995, p. 523; C. Alpa and C. M. Bianca, 'Le clausole abusive nei contratti stipulati con i consumatori. L'attuazione della direttiva comunitaria del 5 aprile 1993', 1995; G. Cian, 'Il nuovo Capo XIV-bis del codice civile' in *Studium Iuris*, 1996, pp. 415–16; G. De Nova, *Le clausole vessatorie* (Milan, 1995).

after the seller has registered his copy of the contract document at the Chamber of Commerce (*Kamer van Koophandel*) (cooling-off period).

Therefore, if registration has not been effected or the 8-day period has not yet passed Estella may cancel the contract unilaterally (art. 5 *Colportagewet*). Therefore Uriah's claim for payment of her first monthly instalment on the loan (and any other claims based on the contract) will fail. It also means that if she has paid some money, this becomes retrospectively undue. She can claim the money back on the basis of art. 6:203 BW (*onverschuldigde betaling*). The right to claim her money back cannot be limited in the contract (art. 3, s. 5, *Colportagewet*).

In the event that the cooling-off period has already expired, Estella can only rely on the following remedies.

(i) Estella made a mistake. She thought that she could use the pan she bought, whereas she could not, since, as she later discovered to her cost, the pan could only be used on a gas ring and her kitchen was entirely electric. Apparently the seller did not tell her that the pan could only be used on a gas ring. Was he under a duty to do so? If he was, Estella may annul the contract for mistake (art. 6:228, s. 1 sub. b BW).[47] She then should do so within 3 years after she discovered her mistake (art. 3:52 BW). Was the seller under a duty to inform the buyer that the pans could only be used on a gas ring? In this case there are several circumstances that point towards such a duty. First, the seller was a professional and the buyer a consumer.[48] Secondly, the pan was sold at the door step and therefore the buyer was ill-prepared and was not in a position to ask the right questions immediately. Finally, today it is quite normal to have an electric, induction or other hob; a seller can therefore be expected to warn the buyer. Although not certain, it seems likely that a Dutch court would allow Estella to annul the contract for mistake. This would have the same (retrospective) effects as termination under the *Colportagewet* discussed above.

Uriah argues that Estella's statutory rights were written out in the documents he had supplied, and that, as she had not returned the pan within the period indicated, she could no longer cancel the sale. Upon one interpretation of the facts, this could be taken to mean that the

---

[47] It should be noted that the *Colportagewet* should not be regarded as a *lex speclialis* of the doctrine of mistake. If it were so, on the basis of the principle *lex specialis derogat legi generali*, Estella would not be able to invoke the doctrine of mistake.

[48] Some authors hold, on law and economics grounds (efficiency), that a seller should in principle be under an obligation to inform the buyer with regard to the qualities and characteristics of the object he is selling. Cf. Barendrecht.

document actually includes a limitation of the right to invoke annulment for mistake. If the latter is the case the question arises whether such a limitation is valid, particularly if the 'various documents full of small print' are in fact general conditions in the sense of arts. 6:231 ff. BW in which case it may be contrary to good faith (arts. 6:2, s. 2, and 6:248, s. 2, BW) to invoke the limitation in the circumstances of this case.[49] However, the facts do not allow us to pursue the discussion any further.

The *Wet op het consumentenkrediet* of 1990, which has been adapted several times, among other reasons for the implementation of the Directive 85/577/EC, is not of any help to Estella. As far as this statute is concerned this is a valid contract and the statute does not provide a cooling-off period similar to the one in the statute on door-step sale.[50]

(ii) Article 7:17, s. 1, BW says that 'the thing delivered must conform to the contract' (conformity). Section 2 says when this requirement is not met:

A thing does not conform to the contract if it does not possess the qualities which the buyer was entitled to expect on the basis of the contract. The buyer may expect that the thing possesses the qualities necessary for its normal use, the existence of which is not open to doubt, and the qualities necessary for any special use provided in the contract.

This requirement does not seem to have been met, since the pan does not have the qualities that are necessary to allow an ordinary use of it. Estella was not expected to doubt that it would be possible to use the pan on an electric ring. Therefore Estella can terminate the contract (art. 6:265 BW).

However, the buyer must make his claims based on non-conformity within a reasonable delay ('*binnen bekwame tijd*') (art. 7:23 BW). It is unclear on the facts exactly when Estella protested and therefore it is difficult to establish whether she did so within a reasonable time. If she did so within days or few weeks she will probably not have lost her claim.

(iii) As suggested earlier, if the documents where her rights were written are to be regarded as general conditions in the sense of arts. 6:231 ff. BW, which seems likely since they seem to be meant to be used in

---

[49] Cf. Asser/Hartkamp II (2001), no. 195.
[50] This was a deliberate choice by the legislator. Cf. N.J.H. Huls, *Wet op het consumentenkrediet* (Deventer, 1993).

contracts with others as well,[51] they cannot limit her right to terminate the contract. Clauses which limit a party's right to terminate the contract for non-performance are on the so-called black list. All the clauses on that list are deemed to be unreasonably onerous.[52] And unreasonably onerous clauses can be annulled on the basis of art. 6:233 (a) BW.[53]

Norway

In the present case, the product does not meet the purchaser's intended area of use, namely on an electric stove. Assuming that the seller (Uriah Heep) was unaware of the purchaser's misunderstanding, the question regarding the placing of the risk must be decided by purely objective criteria.

The Sale of Goods Act, § 17 (2)(a) reads: 'Except as otherwise provided by the contract, the goods shall be fit for the purposes for which goods of the same description would ordinarily be used.'[54] In other words, the seller carries the risk that the item might have a more restricted range of use than similar products have. A saucepan can normally be used on an electric stove (at least in Norway where electricity is the common source of power). If neither its shape nor other characteristics made it reasonably clear that its area of use was restricted to gas stoves, there is a defect in the item. The regular remedies for defect could, therefore, be applied. In the present case, termination of contract seems appropriate. Limitations to the purchaser's rights cannot be agreed on when it comes to a consumer sale.[55] An agreed timeframe for termination of contract is, therefore, invalid.

---

[51] Cf. the definition in art. 6:231 BW: 'In this section: a. general conditions mean one or more written stipulations which have been drafted to be included into a number of contracts, with the exception of stipulations going to the essence of the prestations.'

[52] Article 6:236 sub b, says 'In a contract between a user and the other party, where the latter is a natural person not acting in the course of a business or profession, the following stipulations contained in general conditions are deemed to be unreasonably onerous: (. . .) b. a stipulation limiting or excluding the other party's right to set aside the contract, as provided for by section 5 of title 5.'

[53] Article 6:233 BW: 'A stipulation in general conditions may be annulled: a. if it is unreasonably onerous to the other party, taking into consideration the nature and the further content of the contract, the manner in which the conditions have arisen, the mutually apparent interests of the parties and the other circumstances of the case; b. (. . .).'

[54] Similar regulations are found in the Swedish Sale of Goods Act, § 17, para. 2, no. 1 and the Swedish Consumer Sales Act, § 16, para. 2, no. 1. A similar regulation must be assumed to apply in Danish laws relating to the sale of goods.

[55] See the Norwegian Sale of Goods Act, § 4(1), the Swedish Consumer Sales Act, § 3, and the Danish Sale of Goods Act, § 1, para. 2.

From the information given, it appears that the transaction concerns a sale on credit terms. Even if a person other than the seller gives the credit, or the seller has transferred the claim, the purchaser could claim his losses from the third person, cf. the Norwegian Sales on Credit Terms Act, §§ 8 and 8 (a).[56]

Portugal

This is a door-to-door sale contract governed by a law implementing the EU Directive 97/7. Article 18° of DL 143/2001 of 26 April 2001 gives the consumer fourteen working days to cancel the contract without giving a reason.

As far as the general rules of mistake are concerned, there is also a possibility for Estella to obtain the annulment of the sale because there is a mistake related to the object of the contract concerning the qualities of the thing purchased (*error in qualitate*). To obtain the annulment of the sale, Estella would have to prove in court that she would never have bought the steam-operated pans if she had known they only worked on gas rings (the fundamental nature of the mistake) and that Uriah Heep knew or should not have been unaware that the sale would never happened, if she had knowledge of these facts (arts. 251° and 247 of the Civil Code).

The use of general clauses, classified as unfair terms, by the seller is relevant to the extent that Portuguese regulation of such general clauses (DL 446/85, of 25 October 1985 and DL 220/95, of 31 August 1995) establishes special duties to disclose and inform on the party who uses this kind of clause (arts. 5° and 6°). If the seller has not fulfilled his duty imposed by law, the clauses will be deemed void (art. 8°).

Scotland

I believe Estella's remedy is more likely to lie in statute than the common law of mistake in contract. She has had a mistaken belief as to how the 'steam-operated pan' can be used. It is possible that this could be classified within Bell's 'mistake as to the quality of the thing engaged for'. However, to succeed she would need to show that the wording of the documents that she signed was wide enough to allow her to hold this belief. If they stated that the pan could only be operated on gas or some other indication that electricity was not suitable then the fact that

---

[56] The Act relating to Sales on Credit Terms etc. of 21 June 1985, no. 82. Similar legal regulations are to be found in Danish and Swedish laws relating to such sales.

Estella did not read them would be immaterial. It is a general principle of Scots as well as English law that you are presumed to have read and accepted a contract by signing it.[57] In the absence of written statements, any verbal communications of a similar nature made by Uriah before the contract was concluded would be similarly incorporated into the contract. Assuming that such clauses as to use are absent, then Estella's uninduced unilateral mistake as to quality would not be operative.

The requirement that the pan be returned within a specified time period in order to receive a refund is an example of an exemption clause. In consumer and standard form contracts these are governed by s. 17 Unfair Contracts Terms Act 1977. In the event that Estella can show there has been a breach of contract the exemption clause can only be enforced if Uriah, the relying party, can show that the clause is reasonable.

When Estella agreed to pay for the pan by accepting Uriah's offer of credit she formed a consumer credit agreement with him. Such agreements are governed by the Consumer Credit Act 1974. I believe the Act may provide a remedy for Estella. Firstly, as Uriah approached Estella at her home without her prior invitation the contract has been formed off trade premises. Consumer credit agreements are divided into different categories. A debtor-creditor-supplier agreement is when the person offering the credit is also the supplier of the goods. If the contract between Uriah and Estella is a debtor-creditor-supplier agreement then the fact that it was formed off trade premises is irrelevant. However, if Uriah, the supplier, is not also the creditor, the contract of credit is independent of the sale of goods. Such contracts are debtor-creditor contracts. Section 48 of the Act provides that it is a criminal offence to conclude a debtor-creditor agreement off trade premises. The facts state that Estella accepted Uriah's offer of credit. This would tend to suggest that the contract is debtor-creditor-supplier. If not, Uriah would have committed a criminal offence in the formation of the credit agreement. Under Scots law the credit agreement would be a *pactum illicitum* (an illegal contract). Uriah, the one labouring under the illegality would not be able to enforce the agreement against Estella. As the illegality affecting the contract is the commission of a criminal offence it is no defence that Uriah was unaware of the criminality of his act. Therefore Estella could withhold payment of the instalments of credit.

Secondly, the Act provides further protection for contracts formed off trade premises by setting a statutory cooling-off period. Section 68 states

---

[57] *L'Estrange* v. *F. Glaucob Ltd.* [1934] 2 KB 344, *Parker* v. *S. E. Railway* (1877) 2 CPD 416.

that the duration of the relevant cooling-off period for Estella would be from the date of signing the documents until the fifth day after she is given notice of her right of cancellation. The facts do not state the time elapsed, but if Estella is still within her statutory period then, regardless of the interval prescribed by Uriah, Estella could cancel the credit agreement.

Lastly, Uriah stated that the documents contained notice of all Estella's statutory rights. Further, as the contract was executed by Estella on it being presented to her she should have been furnished with a copy of the agreement immediately. If these formalities[58] were not complied with then the credit agreement is unenforceable by Uriah and Estella can withhold payment of the instalments.

Therefore although Estella may have recourse to the common law of mistake in contract her remedies are most likely to lie in the Unfair Contract Terms Act 1977 and the Consumer Credit Act 1974. The 1977 Act would apply if Uriah is relying on an exemption clause which is not reasonable. The 1974 Act establishes the procedure that must be followed before the consumer credit contract could be enforced against Estella.

Spain

The contract of sale between Estella and Uriah concluded outside business premises is governed by the Law No. 26 of 21 November 1991. The Act was the upshot of Directive 85/577/EC and extends protection for consumers. It regulates the formal requirements for such contracts and even grants consumers the right to cancel without giving a reason within seven days of the contract's conclusion (art. 5). The formal requirements are set out in art. 3 (e.g. the contract must be in writing and include the right to cancel); if these are not complied with art. 5 of the Act provides that the contract can be cancelled on the consumer's initiative. Estella signed a number of documents, possibly including the cancellation option. However, the facts state that the information was written in small letters so that the requirement in art. 3 for a clear and precise reference to the right of cancellation appears not to have been met. In addition, if Uriah Heep did not deliver a copy of the contract to Estella she would be entitled to annul the contract, since non-compliance renders the contract void (art. 1301 of the Civil Code).

---

[58] Section 65 of the Act requires that the documents also contain all the terms of the agreement, follow the prescribed form and be duly executed.

However if Uriah had complied with all the requirements of the 1991 law, it would be unlikely that Estella might have the sale contract annulled based on a defect of consent, since her mistake cannot be qualified as excusable. It is inexcusable since had she acted diligently, she would have read the terms of the sale contract which she signed. It stated the terms for use of the product and the deadlines granted to the buyer to cancel the contract. However, she acted with very little diligence and did not read the contract she had signed: furthermore, the deadline indicated in the contract for cancellation has passed. As a result, her conduct cannot at any stage be considered excusable.

According to case law, mistake as a defect of consent must be dealt with particularly carefully and as an exception in the interests of legal certainty. Spanish law would not treat Estella's behaviour with much indulgence.

Comparative observations

This case puts to the trial the overlap between general remedies for defective consent and consumer legislation inspired by European Directives.

Total harmony is thus achieved through the operation of the transposition of European Directives on door-step sales. In all countries automatic cancellation is granted as a result of a cooling-off period which entitles the buyer to cancel the contract within a short period of 7 days (subject to minor variations of little interest) from receipt of the contract.

Application of the consumer legislation works on two levels; first, has the statutory cancellation period expired? Assuming it has, the next step is to examine whether any other of the law's provisions may be of help: briefly these may be summarised as the duty to provide certain necessary information, the use of small print and the impossibility of limiting termination and other such protected rights, which would amount to unfair contract terms. It is therefore important to ascertain whether the seller was under a statutory duty to provide the crucial information about the pan's suitability on gas rings only. It appears, as a matter of interpretation, that the statutory duty to inform may not descend to this level of detail and the question is rendered more complex by the additional application of legislation relating to consumer credit as well as door-step sales. For the sake of argument it will be assumed that statutory compliance is not an issue, since this highlights the overlap with general remedies more acutely.

If we turn to the application of remedies for defective consent, the picture becomes more familiar, correspondingly more complex and less harmonious! Under Austrian, Belgian, French, German, Greek, Portuguese and Dutch law a mistake could be qualified here but is not necessarily operative. The Spanish reporter considered the possibility but rejected it: Spanish law interprets the excusable nature of the mistake quite severely and would consider the buyer's behaviour inexcusable. This interpretation resembles the French and Belgian analyses. German law could contrive to find mistake whereas only Austria, Greece, Portugal and The Netherlands were really comfortable about admitting mistake here.

Another possibility presented itself in the form of contractual remedies. The question of whether there was a breach of contract was therefore considered by some countries that did not even consider mistake for obvious reasons, i.e. Norway and England, and also Austria, Belgium, and Greece on the basis of a hidden defect in the goods. Only Austria, Belgium and Greece considered a remedy would lie under this head. Likewise, Germany and the Netherlands considered whether non-conformity would give rise to a remedy; the former rejected the possibility whereas the latter admitted it.

Last, but certainly not least, there was a discussion raised by a number of reporters as to the relevance of fraud and/or good faith provisions as founding a duty to inform. Under Austrian and German law a claim would lie under the *culpa in contrahendo* provisions, subject to the usual balance between the duty to inform and the duty to make enquiries being met. Greece thought that if a duty to inform was established and the seller had actually concealed the information there would also be a case for fraud. A divergence of interpretation arises under Belgian and French law: the Belgian reporter thought there probably would be fraud here whereas the French analysis, arguing backwards from the compliance with statutory requirements suggested that the conditions of fraud might not be met.

This case produces some interesting and perhaps surprising results. Greater harmony has been achieved by the transposition of European directives, but not without cost. First, general remedies for defective consent appear to have been subsumed. This may be quite normal if they are considered to be subsidiary remedies. Secondly, however, one may wonder if the character of these remedies, not just their availability, may be changing. If the French illustration is a precursor of this evolution we might ask whether the general remedies for defective consent are going to be judged by the criteria of *lex specialis*, in which case their disappearance may just be a question of time. Lastly, a more harmonious result may go hand in hand with less overall protection if we count the number of legal systems that gave a remedy on the facts: four or perhaps five countries would admit a remedy in mistake and four (two of which admit both) in fraud or on good faith provisions. Are the objectives of consumer protection being met? If so, it is not clear that we have moved a long way away from the common law's position of *caveat emptor*, which is somewhat surprising.

Case 9

Nell v. Scrooge Bank

Case

When Scrooge Bank told David it was not prepared to give him a loan for his business without a personal guarantee, he did not dare tell his wife Nell. Instead, he explained that he was taking a short-term loan from the bank that required her to sign the loan document as secretary of his one-man company. Trusting David, Nell went to the bank and signed what subsequently proved to be a personal guarantee for David's business. Now that David's business has been declared insolvent, Scrooge Bank has called in the guarantee against Nell. What remedy, if any, is available?

Discussions

Austria

(i) In the case in discussion Nell has made a *mistake of expression* which is also a mistake as to the content of the contract in the broad sense. However, the question of whether the mistake is fundamental must be considered. The mistake will be considered important if the mistaken party, namely Nell, would not have concluded the contract had she known the true facts. Clearly, here Nell would not have agreed to conclude the contract of guarantee. Nell cannot, however, hope to succeed in contesting the validity of the contract, since none of the requirements stated in § 871 ABGB is fulfilled. The persons acting for Scrooge Bank were in no way responsible for causing Nell's mistake. Moreover they could not have been aware that Nell had made a mistake since she did not mention her intentions to them. Finally, Nell did not point out her mistake in time, since the bank has already paid out the loan by relying on the fact that the contract of guarantee is valid.

(ii) Nell's mistake was not caused by the other party to the contract but by a *third* party, namely her husband David. Generally the validity of a contract will not be influenced by the behaviour of a third party even when this influence leads to a contracting party making a declaration with defective consent as a result of a fraudulent misrepresentation (§ 875 ABGB). This is the result of the so-called 'reliance theory'[1] whereby a declaration of intent has to be seen and understood according to the standard of an honest recipient's behaviour. There are exceptions but only in cases where the other contracting party is not worthy of protection. § 875 ABGB therefore entitles the mistaken party to annul if the other contracting party has participated in the third party's behaviour or should obviously have known about it. According to prevailing scholarly opinion and case law, people who are used as a sort of accomplice by one of the contracting parties during the negotiation of the contract are not to be considered third parties in the sense of § 875 ABGB.[2] As David is not an accomplice of Scrooge Bank and none of the requirements of § 875 ABGB is fulfilled, Nell cannot invoke the invalidity of contract of guarantee on this ground.

(iii) Under § 25c KSchG (Law regulating consumer rights) the owner of a business, which extends or gives loan facilities (the 'lender'), is obliged to refer to the economic situation of the debtor in the case of a consumer becoming a co-debtor or a surety and in this case the lender is aware or should be aware that the debtor is probably not able to repay his debts in whole or in part. If the lender does not disclose this information then the consumer is only liable if he would have assumed the same liabilities despite being properly informed. In the present case Nell was given no information at all by Scrooge Bank about David's financial situation, yet the bank, must, however, already have been aware of the critical financial situation of David's one-man company. As already stated, it must be assumed that Nell did not intend to sign a contract of guarantee, all the more so if she had been informed about David's critical financial situation. Therefore, Scrooge Bank cannot enforce the guarantee against Nell since they have not complied with the disclosure requirements under specific legislation.

---

[1] Rummel, § 871 Rz 1.
[2] Gschnitzer in Klang IV/1, 129: Iro, JBl 1982, 470 and 510; OGH 19.10.1989 JBl 1990, 175; OGH 21.3.1991; JBl 1991, 584.

Belgium

Two general remedies may be considered since Belgian law has not experienced the same case law's development of art. 1326 of the Civil Code as in France, and no specific obligation incumbent on the bank to inform its customers exists either:

(i) Can Scrooge Bank be considered liable for fraud (see Case 1) toward Nell? The problem here is that fraud must emanate from a party to the contract, which does not appear to be the case at first glance here since the fraudulent statements emanated from a third party to the contract, that is the principal debtor, David. There are, however, two ways out for Nell to show that (a) the bank was in some way an accomplice to David's fraud;[3] and (b) the bank had committed fraudulent concealment when entering into the contract. We have already seen that the existence of an obligation to inform incumbent upon a party derives from legislation, usage, the professional situation or the specific position of the defrauding party or circumstances. Thus, a contract of guarantee made by an institution of public assistance (Centre public d'aide sociale) was annulled on the ground that the guarantor was not in a position to assess the extent of his obligation correctly and that the CPAS should have carried out an enquiry and should have informed the guarantor.[4] This case is however very specific on its facts: the guarantor was probably in a very weak position and the CPAS is not supposed to act like a bank. In Nell's case, it seems quite unlikely that a court will hold the bank liable for fraudulent concealment. Therefore, where a mistake provoked by a third party to the contract (here David) excludes an action based on fraud, only an action based on mistake is admissible.[5]

(ii) The difficulty here lies in the requirement that the mistake be excusable (see Case 1). In an unreported decision[6] of the Court of Appeal of Brussels,[7] a contract for a joint and several loan facility had been entered into between a bank and a married couple, the wife having been led to sign in the belief that she did so only to satisfy some (non-existent) requirement of authorisation relating to the law on matrimonial property. When an action was brought by the bank against the wife after her

---

[3] Goux, 'L'erreur, le dol et la lésion qualifiée', no. 15.

[4] Antwerp, 4-11-1997, RGDC, 1998, p. 367.

[5] Goux, 'L'erreur, le dol et la lésion qualifiée', no. 28.

[6] Unreported decisions are equivalent to reported decisions in Belgium since case law reporting is not official. This may be contrasted to the situation in France where unreported decisions do not enjoy the same value as reported cases.

[7] Brussels, 3-11-1993, RG 476/91.

husband's insolvency, she invoked a fundamental mistake (insisting on the fact that the loan was obviously devoted to cover the needs of her husband's business and not her own). The court held that the existence of a mistake was not proven and, even if it had been, it would have been inexcusable, considering that the wife was a sufficiently well-educated person (she was a maths teacher in a secondary school) to have informed herself as to the extent of the obligation that she undertook. In Nell's case, the problem of excusability is even more troublesome because, as a secretary of her husband's company, she might be considered even more capable of informing herself about the meaning of business transactions for which her cooperation is required. Nell's remedy based on mistake is therefore unlikely to succeed.

England

It seems likely that Nell can resist payment under the guarantee. The starting point is to observe that there was no misrepresentation made by Scrooge Bank to her, which might found a remedy under the principles discussed in Case 1; nor is there a sufficient mistake here: the bank knows the real transaction and – we may assume – does not know of her mistake. English law recognises a doctrine of *non est factum*, under which a written contract can be void if the party was unable to understand the document, and the document embodied a radically different transaction from that which he thought he was signing,[8] and he was not careless in making the mistake: but this is difficult to establish and appears not to be satisfied here.

However, a contracting party (such as the bank here) might be affected by a misrepresentation made by a *third party* (here, David). If the bank used David as its agent in obtaining Nell's signature, it would be treated as if it had itself made the misrepresentations: but this appears unlikely here, since Nell attended at the bank to sign. Alternatively, Nell could avoid the guarantee against the bank if the bank had knowledge or notice of the misrepresentations made by David. The courts have developed a special rule for cases involving bank guarantees: in addition to the general rule (under which a contracting party is affected by *actual* knowledge of a misrepresentation or undue influence by a third party), in the case of a bank guarantee where – as here – the relationship between the surety and debtor is non-commercial, the bank is 'put on inquiry' of the risk that the debtor might have made misrepresentations to, or

---

[8] *Saunders v. Anglia Building Society* [1971] AC 1004.

exercised undue influence over, the surety; and therefore it must take steps to bring home to the guarantor the risks that she is running by standing as surety – and if the bank does not take these steps it is deemed to have notice of any claim that the guarantor might have that the transaction was procured by undue influence or misrepresentation on the part of the debtor.[9] On the facts here, therefore, Nell will be able to avoid the guarantee on the basis of David's misrepresentations unless Scrooge Bank discharged its duty to bring home to her the risks that she was running by signing the guarantee. The bank is not required to interview Nell privately (without David being present) and explain to her the nature of the transaction, although it can discharge its duty in this way. But it is sufficient if the Bank advised her to take independent advice, and received confirmation from a lawyer acting on her behalf that he has advised her. It appears that Scrooge Bank did not explain the document to Nell when she attended to sign it; nor did they advise her to obtain independent advice about the transaction. If so, the bank is unable to enforce the loan against her.

France

In this case Nell, the guarantor, signed the contract of guarantee after her husband's lie had induced a mistake in her mind as to the true nature of her commitment. She may therefore invoke remedies under specialised legislation as well as for defective consent.

(i) Articles 341-2 and following of the Consumer Code (in force since 5 February 2004 and incorporated in the Code by the Law 'Dutreil' of 1 August 2003) give a reinforced protection for 'all physical persons' guaranteeing a loan, regardless of its nature, whether for business or consumer purposes.[10] Nell can therefore rely on the protection offered by the Consumer Code which first imposes that a certain number of formalities be respected when the contract of guarantee is signed.[11] If the necessary formalities have not been respected, the guarantee will be

---

[9] *Royal Bank of Scotland plc* v. *Etridge (No. 2)* [2001] UKHL 44, [2002] 2 AC 773 at [87] developing and explaining the earlier decision of the House of Lords in *Barclays Bank plc* v. *O'Brien* [1994] 1 AC 180, after which this special rule is often named.

[10] Before this law, art. 313-10 of the Consumer Code applied a similar protection to guarantors guaranteeing a consumer credit loan or guaranteeing a loan relating to real property given by a professional lender to a consumer.

[11] Article 341-3 states that the amount of the capital, and interest of the loan guaranteed as well as the amount of liquidated damages, payable on late repayment, must be preceded by a manuscript note to ensure that the surety is aware of the amount of the guarantee and what it entails.

void. As it is not clear from the facts whether or not this is the case, further possibilities must be considered.

(a) Nell may be able to invoke art. 341–4 of the Consumer Code, which states that if the guarantee is disproportionate to her capital and income at the time the contract was concluded, the lender cannot rely on the guarantee and call it in after the principal debtor's, i.e. David's, default. There is insufficient information to determine whether this is the case here and this is a question of fact. It is plausible to argue that Scrooge Bank would have checked Nell's financial situation otherwise there would have been no point in asking her to guarantee the loan. In any event, under the new law, Scrooge Bank should have verified Nell's situation otherwise it runs the risk of not being able to rely on the guarantee contract.

If Nell can prove that the guarantee was disproportionate to her capital and income when she entered into the contract, the guarantee is not void, but Scrooge Bank cannot call in the guarantee.[12] It is not yet clear to what extent this new concept of proportionality differs from that created by case law under the general provisions of the Civil Code in the case of *Macron*,[13] although a certain amount of speculation as to the differences exists.[14]

(b) Article 341–6 of the Consumer Code puts Scrooge Bank under an obligation to inform Nell annually, by 31 March at the latest, of the outstanding amount of the loan guaranteed as at 31 December of the previous year, i.e. the capital and interest etc. due as well as the length of the remaining term. If the loan has been guaranteed for an indeterminate period then the lender must remind the surety of his option

---

[12] The lender's inability to rely on the guarantee means that it is deprived of its right and this constitutes a kind of '*peine*' or punishment, called a '*déchéance*' in French law. For an example of the mechanism, in the context of a surety given for a consumer credit loan, see Civ 1, 22 October 1996, JCP 1997, jp. 22826, note S. Piedelièvre.

[13] Com, 17 June 1997, D. 1998, jp. p. 208, note J. Casey. RTDCiv 1998, p. 157, 935 ff., obs. P. Crocq. The lender was held liable for a *faute* and was liable in damages to the guarantor, which had the effect of reducing to nearly nothing the amount of the guarantee due, since the damages offset the amount due under the guarantee. The *faute* of the lender was not a failure to inform but the very fact of asking for a guarantee that was disproportionate for the guarantor was held to be contrary to good faith and meant that the lender must bear the risk, not the surety. This imposes a high standard of behaviour on the bank which was considered not to have acted in good faith.

[14] It appears that the remedy is different since case law allowed the courts to adjust the amount owing whereas the new law has the effect of abolishing the guarantor's liability. See for a very helpful overview, D. Fenouillet, *Revue des contrats* 2004 (2), pp. 305 ff.

to revoke the guarantee. If the bank fails to respect this obligation, it cannot claim interest due or a penalty for late payment until it fulfils its statutory obligation to inform.

However this will not help Nell much since the guarantee contract is not annulled. A breach of this obligation simply means that the bank will lose a penalty and/or interest for late payment and Nell will still be liable under the guarantee.[15]

(ii) Nell can also try to annul the guarantee and/or claim damages on the grounds of defective consent.

(a) Nell may first think of claiming that she made a mistake when she signed the guarantee contract. If Nell is considered to be a layperson, rather than acting in the course of business since she is secretary of the company, her chances of success will be higher. If Nell can prove that she was mistaken as to the nature of the document she might succeed, provided that it is not held that her mistake is inexcusable. However, it is going to be difficult to prove that she was mistaken; if the document clearly indicated the nature of her undertaking, how can Nell prove that she did not read it? By analogy, if Nell could prove that she thought she was signing a loan document that was given to David who was solvent, she could try and prove she had only signed on the condition that David was solvent whereas in fact he was not.[16] However, it is not clear from the facts that David was insolvent when the contract of guarantee was concluded so this argument might not succeed. To resume, Nell's chances of proving mistake are slight.

(b) Nell could allege that the bank has deliberately failed to inform her of David's irremediable financial situation and has thus fraudulently concealed the truth thus provoking a mistake, under arts. 1116 and 1134, line 3 of the Civil Code.[17] She cannot of course allege David's dishonesty since he is not party to the contract and his behaviour cannot bind Scrooge Bank except if they were acting in collusion and the bank knew of David's fraudulent manoeuvres. By extension to fraudulent concealment, it has even been inferred, *a contrario*, from the *Cour de cassation's*

---

[15] See V. Avena-Robardet, 'Reforme inopinée du cautionnement', D 2003, p. 2083, especially pp. 2086 ff.

[16] The *Cour de cassation* has recently been more generous with this argument and has finally admitted that a mistake about the solvency of the principal debtor may be operative even if it is a tacit condition of the guarantor's engagement; see Com, 1 October 2003, D 2003, jp. p. 1607, note Y. Picod.

[17] For an example, see Civ 1, 13 May 2003, D 2003, jp. p. 2309. In this case even though the bank had included an exclusion clause about the condition of the guarantor's engagement, it was still held liable for fraudulent concealment.

decision in *Nahoum*,[18] that a lender may have a positive duty to inform a guarantor if the latter was not aware of certain information relevant to signing the guarantee. To succeed, Nell will need to show that her ignorance of the true situation was legitimate, i.e. as secretary of the company she was not expected to know about its financial situation.[19] However, once again, it is not clear that the bank knew that David's situations was disastrous, nor even that it was in fact disastrous at the relevant time, so it might be difficult to prove fraudulent concealment or a positive duty to inform incumbent on the bank.

It is too early to tell whether the case law decided before the new law will be relegated to history or in other words how the general and special law now fit together. The recent provision protecting sureties has been criticised because it has been inserted into the Consumer Code whereas its scope is much wider than consumer protection. Has the development of the duty to inform been instrumental in making the law recognise the idea of a general contractual imbalance? In any event, the new duty to inform, contained in the Consumer Code, is pretty limited and would not be that helpful to Nell who would remain liable for most of the principal debt. Paradoxically, the old general law of defects of consent might be more protective, in the event that she could not rely on other provisions of the Consumer Code.

Germany

This case touches on two legal issues: first whether and how the fraud of a third party enables the contract to be annulled and secondly, whether a statement of guarantee given by an impecunious close relative is immoral.[20] Because the facts of the case do not indicate whether Nell has her own income or property this second question will not be analysed.

(i) Nell was certainly induced into giving the statement of guarantee to Scrooge Bank by David's misrepresentation. However, she cannot automatically annul her statement. If misrepresentation was made by a third party then § 123 II only allows annulment if the recipient of the declaration was aware or must have been aware of the misrepresentation. The facts do not offer any evidence that this was the case. Nevertheless, the requirement that Scrooge Bank must at least have been aware

---

[18] Com, 8 October 2002, D 2003, p. 414; note Koering. Confirmed in Com, 25 March 2003, Com, 11 June 2003. See D. Fenouiller, *Revue des contrats* 2004 (2), pp. 315–16.

[19] Com, 5 December 2000, see V. Avena Robardet, D 2003, jp. 2308.

[20] Cf. numerous instances of this in the BGH's case law in Palandt/Heinrichs, § 138 para. 38–38c.

of the misrepresentation would disappear if David was employed as a representative (§ 166 I) or if he had performed an obligation for which Scrooge Bank was vicariously liable (§ 278). David certainly acted at the request of Scrooge Bank but not, however, as its representative; rather, he acted in his own interest. Moreover when he persuaded his wife, Nell, to make the contract of guarantee, he was not performing an obligation on behalf of Scrooge Bank for which it was vicariously liable; that is to say, Scrooge Bank was not connected to Nell so that David could have acted in 'discharge of her liability' (§ 278). Thus, Nell may not annul the contract of guarantee on this ground.

(ii) § 119 I actually contains two grounds of annulment, a 'mistake in substance' (*Inhaltsirrtum*) and a 'mistake in expression' (*Erklärungsirrtum*).[21] A mistake in substance is made if the declaration – according to the objective meaning of the declaration – is understood differently from the way that it was intended; a mistake in expression on the other hand, is made if the declarer makes a mistake in his choice of symbols with which he makes the declaration: if he makes a slip of the tongue or the pen, or if – as in our case – he signs a document without knowing that he is making a statement of guarantee. This distinction between mistakes in substance and expression is academic and does not offer any reference points for different evaluations.[22] In both cases the declarer did not intend – as expressed by the wording of the definition contained in § 119 I – to '[make] . . . a declaration of this substance'. Therefore, it is also unnecessary to attribute the mistake that Nell has made to one of these two instances of mistake. As to the operativeness of the mistake, it is only important to ascertain whether it subjectively and objectively caused Nell's mistake and whether Nell had assumed a particular risk in making the declaration.

(a) Nell believed when she signed the document given to her by David that she was signing a loan document; not in a capacity as a future borrower but for all intents and purposes as the acting representative of David's company. Her mistake therefore related to the meaning of her signature. Accordingly, Nell may annul the contract if she would not have signed the document which David presented to her had she

---

[21] Cf. for example Flume, AT II, 449 ff.; Bork, AT 303 ff.; MüKo/Kramer, § 119 para. 46 ff. and para. 55 ff.

[22] Their roots lie in the psychological 'Doctrine of Intent' by A. Brinz, *Pandekten* (2nd edn, Brussels, 1892), vol. IV, pp. 1393 ff. and E. Zitelmann, *Irrtum und Rechtsgeschäft* (Leipzig, 1879), the effects of which still influence German legal theory (especially with regard to the 'mistake in motive').

been aware that it was in fact a contract of guarantee. From the facts it appears certain that this would have been the case (subjective causation criterion). Likewise, it is also certain that another person making the same mistake would not have made the contract in full knowledge of the facts (objective causation criterion).

(b) In apparently signing a document without having read it, Nell could have assumed the risk of making a mistake in the substance of this document. In this case she would not be able to annul the guarantee.[23] However, when she signed the document presented to her by David she believed she was entering into a loan agreement in her capacity as representative. Therefore, she did not intend to make any old declaration and thereby assume the risk of the declaration's meaning diverging from what she believed it meant, but rather she thought she was making a declaration that was precisely defined in content. In such cases, the person making the declaration will be allowed to annul where, contrary to his belief, he actually makes a different declaration.[24]

(c) Nell can of course free herself from the obligations under the contract of personal guarantee but she will then be liable to compensate the bank's negative interest (§ 122). That is to say, that if Scrooge Bank neither knew of her mistake nor could have known of it (§ 122 II), she has to compensate the bank for the damage it suffered arising from its reliance on her statement of guarantee being valid. Due to the fact that Scrooge Bank would not have authorised credit to David if Nell had not entered into the guarantee then its negative interest amounts to the sum of the loan which was paid to David. Thus Nell is now liable under § 122 and no longer under the statement of guarantee which was effectively annulled – for the satisfaction of the amount to which she would have been liable under the guarantee. Annulment is therefore also worthless for Nell due to the obligation it carries with it, to compensate the non-mistaken contracting party for his negative interest.[25]

Greece

Nell signed the document unaware that she was undertaking a legally binding obligation, she merely believed that the requirement to sign the

---

[23] BGH NJW 1951, 705; BGH DB 1967, 2115.

[24] RGZ 62, 201, 205; RGZ 77, 309, 312; RGZ 88, 278, 282 f.: RAG JW 1930, 2729, 2730; BGH WM 1956, 316 f. = BB 1956, 254 = DB 1956, 228; BAG NJW 1971, 639, 640; BGJH BB 1994, 2439, 2440; in overview and (with further references) MüKo/Kramer, § 119 para. 52; cf. also Henrich, Rabelsz 35 (1971) 55 ff.; Soergel/Hefermehl, § 119 paras. 11 ff.; Flume, AT II, 450 and 453.

[25] BGH WM 1984, 27 f. comes to the same result.

loan document as secretary of the borrower was a common practice in banking business. It is controversial whether in this case the contract must be regarded as non-existent[26] or having binding force.[27] In the latter case the contract can probably be annulled on the grounds of mistake. If, however, the first view is adopted, the bank is entitled to be compensated by Nell on the grounds of precontractual liability since her negligent behaviour is in breach of the principles of (objective) good faith and common usage. In accordance with the express provision of art. 198 § 1 AK she is liable to compensate the bank for its negative interest or damage resulting from its reliance on her behaviour.

An intermediate view submits[28] that the issue whether or not behaviour should be considered as a legal act is a matter of interpretation. Interpretation is effected on the basis of the criteria laid down by the two general provisions, arts. 173 and 200 AK. More specifically, it is submitted[29] that if the person could with some attention realise that third parties might consider his conduct as a declaration of will, the act must be considered as legally binding. It is obvious here that the existence of a contract is not in dispute. It is however necessary to examine whether it remains possible for Nell to annul the contract of guarantee that she did not realise she had made.

Nell can seek to annul the contract on the basis of mistake. There is an involuntary discrepancy between the meaning of her declaration and her will (art. 140 AK). Her mistake is fundamental according to the objective and subjective criteria of art. 141 AK. Nell's mistake affects such an important element of the contract that she would not have concluded it had she known the true state of affairs. However, once again, Nell is obliged to compensate Scrooge Bank since it was not at fault in being unaware of her mistake (art. 145 AK).

As Nell signed the document without having read it, the bank could allege that annulment is excluded as contrary to good faith (art. 144 § 2 AK), since Nell has shown negligence without which she would have avoided making the mistake. The special conditions of the case however, the fact, for example, that she trusted David because he was her husband would, I think, justify annulling the contract by giving priority

---

[26] See for example Gazis, *General Principles of Civil Law*, p. 58. With reservations E. Michelakis, in *ErmAK Intr. Notes to Arts 127–200* (Athens, 1954), n. 102.

[27] Karakatsanis AK 140 n. 7; Spyridakis, *General Principles*, p. 579.

[28] M. Stathopoulos, 'On the Method of Interpretation of the Declaration of Will' (1969) NDiK 25, p. 6, Papantoniou, *General Principles of Civil Law*, p. 293.

[29] Papantoniou, *General Principles of Civil Law*, p. 294.

to the will theory to the detriment of the security of transactions. Nell was induced into the contract by David's fraud, but she is not however entitled to annul on this ground as the fraud was committed by a third party.[30] According to art. 147 AK annulment can only be sought if the other party to the contract, here the bank, was aware or should have been aware of the third party's fraud.

Annulment has retrospective effect, so that when the guarantee contract becomes void this means that Scrooge bank granted the loan without the guarantee. In turn, the Bank could therefore, seek to annul the loan agreement on the grounds of mistake or fraud.

As to whether a duty to inform or ensure that Nell is informed lies on the bank, it is submitted[31] that good faith imposes on the lender a duty to inform the guarantor about any fact that could affect his decision to provide the guarantee, e.g. information about the extent, nature and importance of the principal obligation. Thus, if the creditor has concealed from the guarantor the real economic situation of the debtor with the purpose of inducing him to give the guarantee, the provisions on fraud (art. 147 AK) may be applicable. However, case law holds[32] that in view of the nature of a guarantee as a unilateral contract, a duty to inform only exists when the guarantor declares that providing the guarantee depends on the information given to him about the economic situation of the principal debtor.

Ireland

Owing to the fact that there can be said to be no misrepresentation made by the bank, there are no remedies available to Nell. Neither can the bank be held to be aware of a mistake. Similar to law in England, Irish law recognises the doctrine of *non est factum* (this is not my deed). This doctrine applies in relation to a written contract that can be avoided in circumstances where one party to the contract was unable to understand the document and was in ignorance of its character and he was not unduly irresponsible in making the mistake. The doctrine is narrowly construed by the Irish courts and has tended to be successfully invoked only in extreme cases such as where one party was suffering from a disability such as illiteracy – see *Bank of Ireland* v. *McManamy*.[33] Nell will have difficulty in convincing an Irish court that she should be protected by this doctrine.

---

[30] See Karakatsanis AK 147 n. 12; Spyridakis, *General Principles*, p. 616.
[31] Kafkas, 847 AK p. 440 note 1a.
[32] AP 194/1956 EEN 24, 710; Ef of Athens 1177/1956 EEN 24, 156.   [33] (1916) 2 IR 161.

The Irish courts tend to be concerned that adequate protection is given to an 'innocent' party such as Nell when such cases arise and would frequently expect banks to shoulder the loss, which results as a consequence, on the basis that banks must share a measure of culpability in failing to make sufficient investigation in a case such as this to ensure that Nell understood what she was doing.

Italy

Nell is in a bad position, she can sue David for delictual liability (art. 2043 of the Civil Code) for he induced her to sign a guarantee pretending it was an extra document for the mortgage but the burden of proof will be very onerous and David will not be able to compensate her. Nell cannot claim she was mistaken since mistake is assessed objectively in Italian law and *prima facie* she is capable and had she read the guarantee contract, she should have been able to understand it.

Until recently, according to a decision of the Supreme Court, the only way to obtain the guarantee's annulment was provided by arts. 1325 (conditions of validity) and 1418 (causes of nullity of contract) of the Civil Code:[34] 'when a party signs a contract drafted by the other, under a misrepresentation about the real nature of the obligation arising out of it, there is not fraud but an absolute lack of conditions, i.e. absence of *causa*'.[35]

The Netherlands

Nell may challenge the validity of the contract but this may be unnecessary.

Nell was mistaken as to the content of the document she signed. She thought that she signed the loan document for a short-term loan from the bank in her capacity as secretary of her husband's one-man company,

---

[34] Article 1325 Indication of conditions: 'The conditions of validity of the contract are:
    (i) agreement of the parties (1326 ff.)
    (ii) *causa* (1343 ff.)
    (iii) object (1346 ff.)
    (iv) form when prescribed by law, under penalty of nullity (1350 ff.).'
  Article 1418 Causes of nullity of contract: 'A contract that is contrary to mandatory rules is void, unless the law provides otherwise. A contract is rendered void by the lack of one of the requisites indicated in art. 1325, unlawfulness of *causa*, unlawfulness of the motives in the case indicated in art. 1345, and lack of the object of the requisites set out in art. 1346. A contract is also void in the other cases established by law.'
[35] Cass 1977, n. 163.

whereas she actually signed a document for *what subsequently proved to be* a personal guarantee for David's business. Is she now personally bound by a guarantee contract (*borgtocht*) for the debts of her husband's one-man company?

It could be argued that no guarantee contract was concluded since there was neither consensus nor was Scrooge Bank justified in relying on the fact that Nell wanted to conclude such a contract. There is no *consensus ad idem* since Scrooge intended to conclude a contract of personal guarantee whereas Nell intended to contract a short-term loan on behalf of David's one-man company. Under Dutch law this is a case of 'mistake improper' (*oneigenlijke dwaling*).[36] Proper mistake is a defect of will: a party intends to conclude a contract, but his will was formed in a defective way: he would not have wanted had he known better. Improper mistake is the case where a party did not intend what he declared; he said one thing but he wanted another.

Here Nell declared (by signing the document) that she wanted to be bound to an agreement of personal guarantee but actually she did not want to be bound at all; she only wanted to bind her husband's company, and she wanted that company to be bound to a different type of contract, i.e. a short-term loan. In other words she wanted to conclude a different type of contract and in a different capacity. Therefore no contract was concluded on the basis of consensus (*wilsovereenstemming*) (art. 3:33 BW).[37] However, what if the bank did not know that Nell was mistaken? No evidence is given that the bank knew that the husband had misled his wife. Can the bank argue that its reliance should be protected? Under the Dutch Civil Code reliance is protected in principle if it is reasonably justified in the circumstances (art. 3:35 BW).[38] However, is the bank here justified in its reliance? Probably not since the bank was under a duty to investigate whether Nell knew what the object of the document she was signing was and what the consequences of her signature would be. Sometimes a party is only justified in its reliance if it made some investigations before.[39] Such a duty is more likely if

---

[36] Cf. on the distinction between mistake and mistake improper, and on its origins (Savigny) Asser/Hartkamp II (2001), no. 174.

[37] Article 3:33 BW: 'A juridical act requires an intention to produce juridical effects, which intention has manifested itself by a declaration.'

[38] Article 3:35 BW: 'The absence of intention in a declaration cannot be invoked against a person who has interpreted another's declaration or conduct, in conformity with the sense which he could reasonably attribute to it in the circumstances, as a declaration of a particular tenor made to him by that other person.'

[39] Asser/Hartkamp II (2001), no. 110.

that party is a professional and the other a non-professional.[40] And in the particular situation of a private person giving a personal guarantee to a bank for the debts of one of his beloved ones the courts seem to want to protect that person. This was explicitly decided for mistake in the proper sense (see the case *Van Lanschot/Bink*[41] that I will discuss in a moment), but the same must hold for a case of improper mistake like this one. In legal doctrine it is even argued that there should be a general protection of guarantors for relatives' debts ('*bezwaarde verwanten*') against banks in the form of a stricter duty to inform persons who are about to give guarantees for their relatives.[42]

Could Nell also annul the contract on the basis of mistake in the proper sense? She probably could, because even if she did not argue that she thought she had signed a document to a different effect and thus would not challenge that consensus was reached and a contract concluded, she would be protected by the law because she could challenge the validity of the contract on the basis of mistake. She could invoke the decision in the *Van Lanschot* v. *Bink* case. In that case it was held:

A contract of personal guarantee like the one at hand may be annulled for mistake, if the guarantor when forming his opinion on the likelihood that he would be called upon, based himself on such an erroneous perception of the state of affairs that, had he had a correct perception of the situation, he would never have been prepared to stand surety. This rule also applies in case the mistake was not induced by the other party.

In our case Nell could equally argue that the bank should have informed her as to the risks related to the personal guarantee she was about to give.

From the statement of facts it seems that Nell went to the bank alone. This raises an interesting question. Article 1:88 s. 1 sub. c BW says:

One partner needs permission from the other for the following legal acts: [a, b] c. contracts with the effect that he will bind himself, outside the ordinary course of his business or profession, as a surety or joint and several debtor [. . .].[43]

Article 1:89 BW says that the partner may annul the contract concluded in violation of art. 1:88 BW. If the bank cannot prove that the husband actually gave his permission, he could annul the personal guarantee. He would probably not do this immediately, of course, but he may have

---

[40] Asser/Hartkamp II (2001), no. 110.   [41] *HR* 1 June 1990, *NJ* 1991, 759, note Brunner.
[42] Tjittes (1996), pp. 53–7.   [43] My translation.

an interest in doing so when the bank invokes the personal guarantee. Would the law allow him to do so? The principle *nemo auditur turpitudinem suam allegans* would probably be a bar but that principle is not generally accepted by Dutch law.[44]

Norway

Two sets of invalidity rules could be applied to the question as to whether fraudulent misrepresentation by a third person (David) can be pleaded by Nell, the guarantor against Scrooge Bank.

(i) The first set of rules relates to *fraudulent misrepresentation* as given in the Contract Act, § 30, para. 1, second clause, which reads:

The same applies [namely, the promise is invalid] in cases where a third party has obtained a declaration of will by fraud, and the second party was, or should have been, aware of the fact.

Fraudulent misrepresentation is applied here to a so-called invalidity, which may only be pleaded against bad faith addressees of a contractual promise: in Scandinavian theory called 'relative invalidity' (*relativ ugyldighetsgrum*) as opposed to 'strong invalidity' (*sterk ugyldighetsgrum*), which operates against parties in good faith, see below. If there were no conditions attached to the signing of the guarantee, which should have raised the bank's suspicions, Nell is bound according to this rule. She cannot invoke David's fraudulent misrepresentation against the bank as it was in good faith. She can, of course, present a claim for compensation to David, but this would probably not have much point.

(ii) The other set of rules that are relevant, the principles relating to forgery (*falsk*) are not laid down by statute. According to Norwegian and Scandinavian law, the pseudo-declarer is not bound by false or forged declarations. This rule involves a strong invalidity objection, that is, that it could also be applied against an addressee acting in good faith. According to this principle, Nell is not bound by her declaration.

(iii) The question, then, is *which of the two sets of rules* should be applied. If David had signed Nell's name, a classical forgery would have been present. The problem is that Nell, herself, has signed the guarantee. We are then, formally, within the area of fraudulent misrepresentation under the Contract Act, § 30.[45]

---

[44] Cf. H. J. Van Kooten, *Restitutierechtelijke gevolgen van ongeoorloofde overeenkomsten* (diss., Utrecht 2002).

[45] It might also be appropriate to consider the situation a mistake in the transaction, cf. the Contract Act, § 32, para. 1.

Nonetheless, there is in theory a tendency to judge cases, where the promisor does not realise that a promise has been given, according to the law of forgery.[46] This means that the promisor for a start does not become bound, regardless of the addressee's good or bad faith. The thinking is supposedly that the same conditions apply in these situations as with real forgery, namely, that one has few chances to protect oneself against this type of misuse. There is, to my knowledge, no firm legal position regarding this question.

If the pseudo-declarer had behaved negligently, this person would presumably still not be considered bound.[47] However, it would generally be a common understanding that the promisee in such a case can claim compensation through the reliance interest.[48] It is beyond doubt that Nell has acted negligently in signing the guarantee, and therefore can be made liable to pay damages to the bank.

In the present case, the rules governing compensatory damages completely eliminate the protection provided by the invalidity regulations. The reliance interest corresponds to the size of the loan. The rules regarding contributory negligence of the party suffering the loss (the bank) can, however, apply. According to the Damages Act, § 5–1, compensation in these cases can be reduced or cease to apply, if this seems reasonable.[49]

Portugal

In this case, David has committed a fraud (*dolo*). According to art. 253° of the Civil Code there is a fraud when someone makes a suggestion or acts deceitfully with the intention of inducing or not disclosing one of the parties' mistake. Article 254° specifies that the fraud can be performed by a third party, but in this case the contract can only be annulled if the other party knew or should not be unaware of the fraud. However, if anyone acquires a benefit as a direct consequence of the fraud the contract is voidable in relation to that benefit, where it concerns the author of the fraud or someone who knew or should not be unaware of it.

Therefore, if Scrooge Bank knew or should not be unaware of the existence of the fraud, Nell would be able to obtain the judicial annulment

---

[46] See H. Ussing, *Aftaler* (Copenhagen, 1974), p. 159; L. L. Andersen et al., *Aftaler og mellemmænd* (Copenhagen, 1991), p. 228; as well as A. Adlercreutz, *Avtalsrätt* (9th edn, Lund, 1991), vol. I.

[47] According to J. Hov, *Avtalerett* (Oslo, 1992), p. 212. In cases of gross negligence (*culpa lata*), the validity of this position might be questioned.

[48] See Hov, *Avtalerett*, p. 212 and Ussing, *Aftaler*, p. 42.

[49] The Damages Act of 13 June 1969, no. 26.

of the guarantee. However, it is far from certain that the bank knew or ought to have been aware of David's fraud on Nell. This means that she would only have an action against David to make him liable for the damages caused to her which would not, of course, be helpful in practice.

Scotland

In this example, there has been no misrepresentation by the bank, but rather by David, who is not a party to this action. The example is almost identical to the facts of *Mumford/Smith* v. *Bank of Scotland*.[50] The facts concerned wives who were misled by their respective husbands into signing forms granting a heritable security over the matrimonial home. They sought to have the mortgage rescinded in so far as it related to their interest in the property, relying on the English case of *Barclay's Bank* v. *O'Brien*.[51] However, the Lord Ordinary (Johnston) held that the law of Scotland does not infer constructive notice of a misrepresentation to somebody wholly ignorant of it simply because of the surrounding circumstances. There is an exception to this in the law of agency, but the husbands were not the agents of the bank. It was similarly held that in the absence of actual knowledge of undue influence, the lenders were under no duty to explain the nature of the transaction to the wives, or to advise or require them to take independent legal advice.

The decision of the Lord Ordinary was upheld by the Inner House on appeal. However, in the House of Lords,[52] it was held that the law of Scotland should be altered to allow protection to wives in such cases. Lord Clyde held[53] that the creditor was obliged by the doctrine of good faith to tell the wife, as a potential cautioner for her husband's debts, to seek independent legal advice. Since this was not done in this case, the guarantee could be annulled. It should be noted that the doctrine only applies when the wife has been a victim of her husband's misrepresentation.

Spain

(i) At first sight, this might appear to be a case of fraud or deception, by inducing Nell to sign the contract of guarantee. However, the Spanish Civil Code treats fraud as a defect of consent of the parties when it occurs between the parties, in other words, there is no such thing as third party fraud but merely *dolus adversarii*. In the case of David and

---

[50] (1994) SCLR 856.   [51] [1994] 1 AC 180.   [52] 1997 SC (HL) 111.   [53] *Ibid.*, at 121.

Nell, David duped his wife, who signed the contract with the bank. Thus the fraud was not between the contracting parties but between one of the parties and a third party.

(ii) Secondly, we may ask whether this is a case of mistake. It has already been shown how, for mistake to annul a contract, it must relate to the substance of the object of the contract, and it must be excusable. Here, Nell's mistake was evidently induced by her husband and does concern the substance of the contract: she believed she was signing a loan document for his company purely as a formality, whereas she was actually committing herself to a personal guarantee. I am, however, unable to find a basis for asserting that this mistake may be considered excusable in order to invalidate the contract. There was a minimum requirement of diligence on the part of Nell before signing a loan document, whether as a secretary or as a private individual. It might be argued that she acted with the confidence that it had been her husband who was asking her to sign and that she should have believed him unquestioningly. However, the bank would be defenceless against such conduct by a married couple who might easily agree on such a strategy. I think it difficult to plead in the court of first instance that there was mistake in order to annul the guarantee contract.

(iii) Finally, given David's action, we may ask whether Nell would have any claim against her husband, who tricked her. Under the general tort provisions (art. 1902 of the Civil Code), Nell could claim damages against her husband who acted not just negligently but also fraudulently, but in practice, this will not be of much help to her.

Comparative observations

This case inspired by *Barclays Bank* v. *O'Brien*,[54] concerns a guarantee given by one spouse to guarantee the other spouse's business. The enquiry is thus aimed at finding out if this kind of guarantee is considered in a particular way by the law in view of the special relationship of dependency between spouses. In addition, the facts illustrate a three-party situation which has long been a subject of enquiry: if a third party fraudulently induces a contracting party to contract, can the third party's behaviour vitiate the contracting party's consent? The answers to these questions reveal divergence as to result and as to the legal concepts used to arrive at a solution.

[54] [1994] 1 AC 180.

(i) Is there an operative mistake here? Under Austrian law, there is a qualified mistake but the conditions of § 870 ABGB are not fulfilled, likewise under French, Belgian and Spanish law, the mistake would be considered inexcusable. Under English, Irish and Scottish law there would be no mistake. In contrast, under German and Greek law, the mistaken party (Nell) could plead mistake but in practice the remedy is unhelpful, since Nell would have to pay negative interest to the other contracting party (the bank). There is quasi-unanimity that mistake is not a probable nor efficient remedy; indeed many reporters did not even consider invoking mistake! Two important exceptions exist: the Netherlands and Norway.

(a) In the Netherlands, Nell could perhaps claim proper mistake (a defect of the will) or mistake improper, described as a case where the party did not intend what he declared, he said one thing but he wanted another: there is therefore no *consensus ad idem*.[55] The mistake is clearly unilateral and it is thus arguable that the bank's reliance should be protected. Here however, Dutch law shows itself to be progressive since a reinforced duty on the Bank to investigate whether Nell knew what she was doing (a duty to inform itself, not to inform the other contracting party) may work in Nell's favour.

(b) Once again, in the absence of a theory on defects of consent Norway has developed an original variant, based on case law that might interpret Nell's promise as a case of forgery. This is clearly a legal fiction. The result looks rather similar in practice to German and Greek law's position as regards mistake. Although the forgery will entitle the person to claim the contract is invalid, if it is argued that the 'pseudo-declarer', i.e. Nell was negligent, she must compensate the bank for her negligence. Obviously, in practice this would eliminate all practical effects of the protection.[56]

(ii) A more obvious avenue for Nell would be to try and rely on the fraudulent behaviour of her spouse, David, the third party to the contract. There is a consensus that if David (third party and principal debtor) is not an accomplice of the other contracting party – the bank – David's fraud, namely his misrepresentation about the nature of Nell's undertaking, cannot be invoked by her: this is the case in Austria, Germany, Belgium, France, Germany, Greece, Norway, Portugal and Spain.

---

[55] This may be compared to a *Smith* v. *Hughes* situation or an *erreur-obstacle* under French law.

[56] Unless contributory negligence on the bank's part is proven, thus reducing the quantum of damages.

The same rule basically applies in England except that an exception has been invented for this particular kind of case. It could be expected that Ireland would follow but Irish law does not appear to have adopted this approach. Because of the non-commercial relationship between Nell and David, the case falls straight into the rule set out in *Barclays* v. *O'Brien*,[57] thus enabling Nell to annul the guarantee contract. The reason why she can do so is not directly on the basis of David's fraudulent misrepresentation but linked to the omission by the bank to take the necessary steps to bring home to Nell the risks that she is running by standing as surety. It is considered that this constitutes a reinforced duty on the bank, which is designed to provide protection for a party in a weak informational position, due to her relationship with the principal debtor. Whether the bank's duty to inform the dependant party is sufficient or adequate protection is controversial.[58] In that respect, a comparison with the protection awarded by Dutch law is instructive: the result is fairly similar in that the law protects guarantors guaranteeing relatives' debts. Arguably, however Dutch law is more protective in its reinforcement of the bank's duty to investigate the guarantor's situation: this is surely more efficient than merely telling the potential guarantor to take advice since the onus is on the bank to carry out its enquiries. French law may make use of the general principle to contract in good faith, coupled with an allegation of fraudulent concealment by the bank, if it is considered that the bank should have informed Nell about David's financial situation before she signed the guarantee. However, the burden lies on Nell to adduce evidence that the bank fraudulently concealed such information or did not contract in good faith, so it could be contended that the law offers a qualified protection for the guarantor. Nevertheless, it can be inferred that this case is particularly interesting from a comparative point of view since the protection offered by England is apparently considerable, thus contradicting the assumption that civil law systems are more protective than common

---

[57] As developed and explained by *Royal Bank of Scotland plc* v. *Etridge (No. 2)* [2001] UKHL 44, [2002] 2 AC 773.

[58] Feminist criticism suggests it does not go far enough to protect sexual inequality; others may suggest it is just a panacea for the sake of appearances, since the subsequent cases applying the rule admit a minimum compliance by banks (it will suffice for the bank to tell the interested party to take advice, even if the advice is not obtained). Furthermore, of what real protection is advice which needs paying for anyway? See for example, B. Fehlberg, *Sexually Transmitted Debt: Surety Experience and English Law* (Oxford, 1997); R. Auchmuty, 'Men Behaving Badly: An Analysis of English Undue Influence Cases', (2002) *Social and Legal Studies* 11(2), 257.

law systems of 'weak' parties. Moreover, Scots law arrives at a similar conclusion by the use of good faith.

(iii) Protection may, however, be provided for by consumer protection legislation (suggested by the Austrian and French reporters) although French law will be of limited value in practice, since it will not entitle Nell to annul the contract. It is suggested that under Austrian law, the legislative duty on the bank to inform the guarantor about the principal debtor's financial situation is highly protective and will enable her to claim the guarantee is unenforceable on the basis of the bank's failure to inform. This is comparable to or perhaps even stronger than the protection provided under Dutch law. It is interesting then to compare the levels of protection, layer upon layer, granted either by defective consent doctrines or by a *lex specialis*.

(iv) Two last heteroclite suggestions: under Italian law it has been suggested that there is an absence of conditions – *causa* (art. 1325 of the Civil Code) – which would enable Nell to annul the contract. Under Dutch law, the provisions of matrimonial law may entitle the principal debtor, Nell's husband, to annul the contract, since it was guaranteed without his permission!

To conclude: in Austrian, Dutch, English, German, Greek, perhaps Italian, Norwegian and Scottish law, Nell could annul the contract. In some cases annulment is tempered by Nell having to pay negative interest damages to the bank (Germany, Greece, Norway). These legal systems concede a degree of individual protection, which is counterbalanced by reliance, a concept used to protect a conflicting value, namely that of the security of transactions and the allocation of risks. Only five legal systems allow Nell to annul the contract outright. To achieve this aim, three mechanisms, or protective devices, can be identified: (i) the bank should advise or inform the guarantor; (ii) the bank should make its own enquiries; and (iii) the Bank should advise the guarantor to take independent legal advice. These may be variations on a theme. It is difficult to ascertain which mechanism gives greater protection to the surety, but the case shows that the duty to inform does indeed play a protective role in this instance. This comparative enquiry also confirms that this is a hard case where conflicting priorities are obvious: there are clearly no easy answers, policy not legal logic determines the outcome.

Case 10

Zachary

Case

Zachary, delivery boy for Red Hot Pizzas, uses his own vehicle for his work. Believing himself bound to do so, he took out a motor insurance policy without realising that the same risks for liability were covered by the insurance taken out by his employer. What remedy, if any, is available when Zachary's insurance policy is with (a) the same insurance company as his employer and (b) a different company?

Discussions

Austria

(a) § 59 of VersVG, Austrian Insurance Contract Law of 1959,[1] provides for double insurance when the insurance is concluded with two different insurers.[2] In my opinion § 60, which allows the insured to terminate the insurance contract concluded at a later point in time, cannot be directly applied. This provision requires that the insured is obliged to terminate immediately after he has recognised that there is double insurance. Application of this provision by analogy seems to be pretty reasonable, although unfortunately no comments could be found in case law nor in scholarly opinion.

In addition, annulling on the grounds of mistake (a mistake shared by both parties) is possible according to scholarly opinion and case law.[3]

[1] BGBl 1959/2.
[2] Compare M. Schauer, *Das österreichische Versicherungsvertragsrecht* (3rd edn, Vienna, 1995) pp. 181 ff.
[3] OGH SZ 36/22; OGH JBl 1976, 646; OGH SZ 61/53; Gschnitzer in Klang, Kommenta IV/1, pp. 133 ff.

According to the prevailing view, annulment would have effect *ex nunc*.[4]

(b) Zachary can terminate the contract with another insurer as a result of §§ 59 ff. VersVG. Moreover, Zachary is obliged to cancel the second contract immediately after he has found out about the double insurance.

Belgium

(a) Article 42 of the law of 1992 dealing with over-insurance by the insured in good faith applies. According to this provision, Zachary is entitled to a reduction of the premium in keeping with the insured interest.

(b) When the contracts have been concluded with different insurers, art. 42, line 2 of the 1992 law applies.[5] Assuming that the policy subscribed by Zachary's employer was sufficient to cover the risk, compliance with the 1992 law will lead, in the absence of an agreement intervening between the different insurers, to avoiding the most recent contract that is precisely the insurance contract that Zachary took out.

The question as to whether Zachary might invoke an absence of cause (arts. 1108 and 1131 of the Civil Code) appears quite academic when one considers the detailed rules of protection of the insured's interests laid down in the 1992 law. In any event, a *lex specialis* argument might also be raised against the continuing application of the general rules of defective consent.

England

The general position is that the double insurance of risks does not automatically invalidate either insurance policy: unless one or other policy contains conditions against overlapping policies (or otherwise regulating the consequences of double insurance – for example, the proposal for one policy requires express disclosure of other policies) both policies are valid. If, however, the risk materialises and claims arise under both policies, the insured has the right to claim under either policy but not to recover more than his loss by a double claim. (This is, however, subject to

---

[4] Koziol/Welser, *Grundriß*. I 129 mwA in n. 61.

[5] Article 42 line 2 of the law of 1992 provides: 'When the insured amount is spread among several contracts entered into with *several insurers*, the said reduction is to be operated, in the absence of an agreement between all the parties, on the amounts insured by the contracts *in the order of their date beginning with the most recent* and eventually generates the *avoidance* of one or more contracts of which the insured amount would thus be rendered void.'

the terms of each policy: it is not uncommon for insurance contracts to provide expressly that, in the event of double insurance, the insurer shall be liable only for his rateable proportion of the loss.) The insurer who pays then has the right to make a restitutionary claim for contribution from the other insurer, a claim which arises independently of contract but can be modified by contract between the parties.[6] In the absence of specific contractual provision, the insured has no claim to recovery of any part of the premium paid to either insurer, since both insurers were on risk and the premium is generally regarded as indivisible.

(a) Zachary might argue that the insurer had a duty to disclose the other, overlapping policy, since an insurer has the duty to disclose material facts. There appears, however, to be no case law to indicate how the courts would view this: there are very few cases on the insurer's (as opposed to the insured's) duties of disclosure and it might well be thought too onerous on insurers to have to check whether there are other policies with other clients that cover the same risks. And it is unlikely that Zachary can successfully plead mistake: if he had himself entered into a second insurance policy with the same insurer, he and the insurer both forgetting the earlier policy, there might be an arguable case of common mistake. But the fact that his policy just overlaps with another policy taken out by his employer makes this case quite different.

(b) Where Zachary's policy is with a *different* company from that used by his employer, there can be no question of either the insurer or Zachary having had a duty of disclosure since neither knew the circumstances of the overlapping insurance policy. And Zachary cannot claim mistake: although there does not appear to be guidance in the case law, it is not likely to be arguable that the (shared) mistake was sufficiently fundamental to make the contract void, since the double insurance of risks, with different insurers, is not uncommon in practice; and the insurer would not have been likely to refuse the risk just because there was another insurance policy, between different parties, which covered it.

France

Zachary will want to try and allege that the insurance policy to which he subscribed for his vehicle is void, which would enable him to recover the amounts already paid. To do so, he could try to claim *absence de cause*

---

[6] *North British and Mercantile Insurance Co.* v. *London, Liverpool and Globe Insurance Co.* (1876) 5 Ch D 569.

of the second contract (art. 1131 of the Civil Code), since a mistake about his personal reasons for contracting (*erreur sur les motifs*) is an inoperative mistake.

Zachary may allege that the contract has no cause since an identical insurance contract for the same purpose exists already. There is a certain amount of case law where this argument has been invoked, though not always with success.[7] The case law is somewhat contradictory, for example, the independent purchase by husband and wife of tickets for the same theatre performance was annulled on the grounds of mistake whereas double insurance is not always annulled on the basis of absence of cause.[8] Some scholars suggest this is because double insurance does not eliminate the counterpart of the insurer's obligation, on the contrary it reinforces his likelihood of guarantee, and if the cause is assessed objectively, this suffices. In other words, the fact that the insurance contract has no subjective utility for Zachary is irrelevant. This position is, however, subject to academic criticism on the basis that it takes the idea of utilitarianism too far.[9]

Germany

Double insurance policies are quite common and are normally caused by the policy holder's absent or incorrect information. Nevertheless, it is basically up to the policy holder to inform himself about the type and extent of the risks insured against and about the insurance policy he enters into for this purpose. The insurer is not under a duty of disclosure – even if in the meantime many insurance companies offer to thin out the 'private insurance policy jungle' as an individual service – except in the case where the policy holder is insured with the same insurance company twice against the same risk.

(a) In this case § 60 VVG, which gives the policy holder a right to terminate the contract, would not apply, because this provision is designed for cases in which the same risk is insured by different insurers. But because the insurance company is supposed to know everything that its employees know, it is supposed to have entered a second insurance contract on the same risk intentionally.[10] As a consequence, Zachary can set

---

[7] See for a full discussion of the question, Ghestin, *La formation du contrat*, no. 854, pp. 853 ff.

[8] *Ibid.*, for an explanation of the case law.

[9] See P.-Y. Gauthier, 'Contre Bentham: l'inutile et le droit', RTDCiv 1995, pp. 797 ff.

[10] E. Schilken, *Wissenszurechnung im Vertretungsrecht* (Bielefeld, 1983); R. v. Book, *Allgeméiner Teil des Bürgerlichen Gesetzbuches* (Tübingen, 2001), 610 ff., Larenz/Wolf, AT 885 ff.; cf. for example BGHZ 132,30 = JZ 1996, 731; BGH NJW 1999, 284.

aside the insurance contract he entered due to a fundamental mistake (§ 119 II) without having to indemnify the insurer (§ 122 II).

The crucial question at a German court would be if Zachary has actually made a mistake as to quality (§ 119 II): a 'quality' for the purposes of § 119 II could only be found in the fact that Zachary's risk that he has insured against with the insurer has already been insured against by his employers. However, whose 'quality' is it? That of Zachary, of the vehicle he uses or even a 'quality' of the employment contract he concluded with Red Hot Pizzas? This uncertainty illustrates that § 119 II is a flawed provision that only covers the problem of a mistake relating to the facts of the case in a small section.[11] In fact, it cannot be a question of to whom the 'substantial quality' – i.e. the fact that Zachary is already insured against accidents – is to be attributed. Despite this, a German court would probably employ the concept of mistake and, because Zachary's mistake cannot be described as a 'mistake relating to a quality', reject the claim for annulment. In order to avoid this consequence the court will probably apply the doctrine of a common mistake about the basis of transaction (lack of the basis of transaction, *Fehlen der Geschäftsgrundlage*), which will not lead to nullity *ex tunc* of the second policy (like the annulment according to §§ 119 II, 142) but to the cancellation of the policy *ex nunc* (§ 313 III). The same solution would be reached by cancelling the contract according to §§ 59, 60 VVG if they were applicable (see (b) below).

A more favourable solution can be reached by granting Zachary a claim in damages against the insurer who did not inform him about the policy held by Red Hot Pizzas. As mentioned before, the insurance company is supposed to know about the policy held by the employer and was therefore bound to inform Zachary. Having failed to do so it committed *culpa in contrahendo* and therefore has to indemnify him. Zachary's damage is the insurance policy itself (i.e. the obligation to pay the premium) and the premium he has already paid. Restitution in kind (§ 249) therefore means that the insurance company has to set aside the second policy from the very beginning and to refund the insurance premium paid by Zachary.

(b) If Zachary and Red Hot Pizzas entered into their insurance policy agreements with different insurance companies, then Zachary is entitled to demand cancellation of his (later contracted) insurance policy *ex nunc* (§§ 59, 60 VVG).

---

[11] An opinion shared by MüKo/Kramer, § 119 paras. 110 ff.

Greece

According to art. 15 L 2496/1997 double insurance is valid. Both insurers are liable jointly up to the extent of the insured value.[12] Zachary took out a motor insurance policy for his own vehicle, because he believed he was bound to do so. If he took out an insurance with a different insurer, he has made a mistake as to motive which is not fundamental (art. 143 AK). If however he took out an insurance with the same insurer who was aware of the first insurance, Zachary's mistake will enable him to annul the insurance contract on the grounds of fraud (art. 147 AK). His mistake is due to the insurer keeping silent about a fact as to which there exists a duty to inform by law according to morality and good faith.[13]

As the law gives annulment retrospective effect (art. 184 AK), Zachary is entitled to the restitution of the premium paid to the insurance company on the grounds of unjust enrichment (arts. 904 ff. AK). It is however controversial whether the insured person who annulled an insurance policy is entitled to the premium if the insurer has already incurred expenses for performance.[14] Since the insurance contract is a long-term contract, it is more correct to accept that annulment is precluded according to art. 144 AK as contrary to good faith. It is generally submitted that if a long-term contract has functioned for a certain time its annulment is equivalent to termination, that is it takes effect *in nunc*. Otherwise annulment would conflict with the security of transactions.

Ireland

The fact that there are two insurance policies governing the same risks will not render either or both invalid under Irish law. In this case, there seems to be no obligation to disclose the other policies of insurance and both remain valid. However, in the event of the insured risk occurring, there is no right to recover under both policies. The claimant cannot find himself in a better position than if only one policy covering the risk was extant.

---

[12] For the problems arising from double insurance see V. Kiantos, *Insurance Law* (7th edn, Thessaloniki, 1997), pp. 225 ff.

[13] R. Chadzinikolaou-Angelidou, *Insurance Contracts* (Athens, Thessaloniki, 2000), p. 114 on the duty of the insurer to inform the insured as a means of consumer protection. See also art. 4 LD 400/1970.

[14] See Z. Skouloudis, *Private Insurance Law* (3rd edn, Athens, 1999), p. 175.

Italy

In Zachary's case the mistake of law provisions could be used successfully; he can annul his insurance contract claiming that he was mistaken about the law regarding his employer's duty to insure. The condition that a mistake of law must be the only or principal reason for entering into the contract in order for annulment to be admitted is met.[15] It makes no difference whether Zachary's insurance was made with the same or a different insurance company.

The Netherlands

In principle, an insurance contract concluded after another insurance contract that covers exactly the same risk to the very same interest in the same object is void (art. 252 WvK[16]).[17] If his employer has taken out the insurance for his employee (i.e. in order to cover his risk) the second contract is void. It does not make a difference whether the insurance policy is with the same or with a different insurance company.

However, there is an exception: if the first contract was concluded without a mandate from the insured and without his knowledge, the first contract is void if the conclusion of that first contract comes to the knowledge of the insured only after the conclusion of the second contract (art. 266 WvK).[18] That is what seems to be the case here. Therefore, not the second contract (between the insurer and Zachary) but the first one (between the insurer and Red Hot Pizzas) is void. Here also the law says nothing on whether it would make a difference whether the insurance policy is with the same company or with a different insurance company. However, one could argue that in the former case the insurance company is under a duty to inform the prospective insured (Zachary) that it has already covered the same risk (Zachary's risk of damage to his car) in an insurance contract with another party (his employer, Red Hot Pizzas), and that if it does not do so 'it would be contrary to good faith (art. 6:2, art. 6:248 BW) to invoke' the invalidity of the (first) insurance contract. In other words, one could argue that there should be an exception for the case when it is the same insurer in both contracts.

---

[15] The condition is laid down by case law, Cass 1963, n. 1233; Cass 1971, n. 1194; Cass 1977, n. 4977; Cass 1981, n. 180; Cass 1982, n. 2688; Cass 1995, n. 2340.

[16] See art. 7.17.2.24a NBW, which adopts a different principle: the insuree may, at his choice, invoke the one or the other insurance.

[17] Cf. Asser/Clausing/Wansink (1998), no. 279.

[18] Cf. Asser/Clausing/Wansink (1998), no. 283.

Norway

The meaning of double insurance must first be clarified when an insurance case arises. This is regulated in the Insurance Contract Act, § 6–3. The insured can choose which company he prefers, but double insurance does not give him the right to any form of double coverage. The right to choose holds only until the insured 'has been awarded the compensation he or she in total can claim'.[19] Generally, it can be stated that the insured would normally have no interest in a double insurance. Zachary has two remedies in this situation.

(i) According to the Insurance Contract Act, § 3–2, para. 2, the insured can cancel the insurance contract with immediate effect. Both the alternatives 'if the need for insurance no longer exists' and 'if other specific reasons exist', can be employed. When an insurance contract is terminated, a financial settlement should subsequently be arranged between the parties. The insured shall be granted the return of 'excess premium', cf. the Insurance Contract Act, § 3–5. Detailed rules for settlement are given in the insurance regulations.

(ii) The taking out of the insurance policy has occurred based on mistake (mistake as to motive). The insured himself carries the risk for this mistake and consequently cannot claim return of the premium for the time the insurance had been running. Exceptions might be made if the company ought to have discovered that a double insurance existed. This would primarily be the case with insurance policies held in the same company under hypothesis (a). Whether on a purely objective basis one can succeed with a request for exemption from paying a double premium because the company, in reality, has not had an increased risk, is unclear.

Portugal

The insurance made by Zachary is void because art. 434° of the Commercial Code prohibits double insurance of the same risks.

Scotland

Zachary's mistake is one of mistake as to motive; he agreed with the terms of the contract but due to his mistake of the circumstances he has not achieved the result he intended. Therefore in absence of inducement he has no remedy in mistake in contract.

---

[19] See NOU 1987: 24, p. 128.

Similarly I do not believe unjustified enrichment would provide relief. The appropriate remedy would be repetition. However, the '*condictio sine causa*' would not apply as when Zachary paid the insurers they were entitled to such premiums under the contract of insurance. The insurer would pay up if his car was damaged. The other possible *condictio*, '*condictio indebiti*', would be similarly unhelpful. It operates when the defendant has been given money under a mistake that the money was due. Although Zachary mistakenly thought that he had to effect a contract of insurance, once he did so, there was no mistake that the money was now due. Therefore both insurance policies are valid. It would make no difference if Zachary's insurance policy was with another company.

Spain

In this case, if not more than twenty days have elapsed since either of the insurance policies has been effected, Zachary could attempt to cancel his policy, with payment to the insurance company of the proportional part of the insurance premium for the period used (art. 32 of the Law on Insurance Contracts).

Otherwise, it would be complicated to try to declare either of the insurance policies void: case law and legislation are very strict in admitting mistake as a defect of consent, and always seek to protect the security of transactions. It would be difficult for Zachary to prove that his mistake was excusable since, if he had acted diligently, he would have asked Red Hot Pizzas whether or not he was obliged to insure his vehicle.

Comparative observations

This case concerns double insurance, a common enough occurrence no doubt, and the central issue raised is whether there is a duty on the insurer to inform the insured that his insurance constitutes a double insurance. If a duty were to exist, it could only really be expected under hypothesis (a) where the same insurer has been used by the employer and employee. The diversity of answers given show once again that national laws are more protective of insurer than the insured and that very few countries actually allow the contract to be annulled for defects of consent.

(i) Where special rules are laid down by law, two types of situation exist:

(a) In cases where the insurance is taken out with a different insurer the insured is allowed to avoid the second insurance policy. This is the case in Austria, Belgium[20] and Germany.

(b) Some countries consider double insurance is impossible. This is the case in Portugal and the Netherlands and means that the second (Zachary's) insurance contract is void. Dutch law contains an exception that works to the detriment of Zachary in the case where insurance is taken out with a different insurer, since it is the first insurance taken out by the employer, without the employee's authority, and not Zachary's second insurance, that is void. The Dutch reporter has suggested that an exception to the exception would probably exist when the second insurance is made with the same insurer under hypothesis (a).

(ii) In a number of systems the double insurance is valid. This is the case for England, France, Ireland, Norway, Scotland and Spain. In England and Norway it was pointed out that Zachary can always terminate his contract but he will not necessarily be entitled to the return of the premium. If two insurance contracts for the same insured interest are valid, two further related points need to be examined: (a) should the insurer have informed the potential insured that he was taking out a redundant policy? This question can only be raised if it is the same insurer; and (b) can double recovery be made if a claim is brought? Inevitably the second question is of less immediate concern regardless of the fact that it is most significant in practice, but we will see that for some systems the questions are connected. Under English law the answer to the first question is that the insurer, as well as the insured, can have duties of disclosure in this type of contract, although the insurer's duty appears to have been raised only rarely in litigation. The approach of English law to double insurance is, on the whole, to allow the contracts (both formed properly according to the normal common law rules) to stand, but not to allow the insured to benefit from the double insurance (indeed, the insurers gain, because both insurers keep their respective premiums in full). There has been no attempt, though, to provide general rules of priorities of claim between the overlapping insurance policies, which might be more efficient from an economic perspective.[21] Conversely, under German law taking a strict

---

[20] Under Belgian law this situation differs if the policy is made with the same insurer, here the insured who took out the second insurance is entitled to a reduction of the premium.

[21] See M. A. Clarke, *The Law of Insurance Contracts* (3rd edn, London, 1997), pp. 784–5.

view of the insurer's knowledge, it was considered that the insurer would be liable for damages *in culpa contrahendo* since it was supposed to know about the employer's insurance policy and failed to inform the insured. The insurer will cancel the contract and repay the insured in full.

(iii) The possibility of claiming annulment for a mistake may also exist. France rejects this option since the mistake was one of motive. Under Austrian law, the mistake qualified as a shared mistake would be admitted by the courts. Likewise under German law, a common mistake as to the underlying basis of the transaction would be admitted. Under Greek law, two paths are possible: either a fundamental mistake as to quality constitutes an operative mistake leading to annulment or a shared mistake, that the basis of the transaction was lacking, so that it would be contrary to good faith not to allow annulment. Spanish law considered the mistake inexcusable. Italy was the most positive about using the special mistake of law provisions here, which would entitle Zachary to annul his insurance contract.

(iv) French law might also allow a claim not based on defects of consent but on *absence de cause*. It is worth mentioning, since it is of doctrinal interest that a claim for *absence de cause* seems to be functionally equivalent to the absence of the basis of the transaction (under German law) and to the lack of object (Dutch law) in certain circumstances. The point should not be laboured since in this context French case law is somewhat ambivalent about whether the foundation can be satisfactorily invoked in the case of double insurance.

In conclusion and to return to the duty to inform, one could now justifiably ask why the insurer is not under a duty to inform the insured about double insurance. The sole exception is Germany which is highly protective of the insured's interests in this case. The following remarks only apply to systems that do not consider double insurance void. One can only guess at the answer which is probably economic; if it is true that the duty to inform is often imposed for protective end-goals, the object of its protection is perhaps the insurer and not the insured. Looked at from this point of view, double insurance is a windfall for insurers and unacceptable for the insured especially when it is the same insurer who knows about the existence of both insurance policies. This is a significant factor if the roles of the parties are reversed. It has been held in French law, for example, that the insured has a duty to inform the insurer of the existence of cumulative insurance policies that he wishes to pay for, as this affects the insurer's evaluation of the risks.[22] Less cynically, it might be noted that the duty to inform oneself is perhaps not too heavy a burden for the insured employee to bear in this context. If the question of double insurance were considered more generally, and not only in situations where a relationship of employer and employee is also involved, this might not always be the case. A law and economics analysis would suggest that the most significant question is to assess the relative cost involved to each party to inform the other, since in practice, an insurer may not know that double insurance is effected by several clients on the same risk. The German solution seems to take no notice of such considerations since a duty to inform is imposed arising out of the constructive knowledge of the insurer.

To summarise, this case clearly shows that the duty to inform has its limits. It also raises the crucial question: whom is the duty to inform really protecting? Finally, economic analyses may elucidate that the duty to inform is not always efficient.

---

[22] See for an example of this principle, Civ 1, 13 May 1997, RTDCiv 1997, 923, which constitutes a *'revirement'* of previous case law.

Case 11

Monstrous Inventions Ltd v. Mary Shelley

Case

In order to encourage management staff to retire early, Mr Dracula, managing director of Monstrous Inventions Ltd, sends out an internal memo without informing the personnel department and Mary Shelley, eligible for the proposal, accepts the 'package'. A settlement is thus concluded. Unknown to both of them, the personnel department was investigating an allegation of Mary's dishonesty, and Mr Dracula was advised the same day that there was sufficient reason to terminate Mary's contract. What remedy, if any, is available?

Discussions

Austria

(i) Although Mr Dracula made a mistake as to the important qualities of the other contracting party (§ 873 ABGB), namely as to her honesty, it is questionable whether Mary had been aware of this mistake at the time of contracting and had taken advantage of this fact and, if so, she was obliged to disclose the true facts to Mr Dracula. Although Mary had probably been aware of her misbehaviour, it cannot be assumed that she was aware of the consequences of the 'package'. Only fraudulent intention is retained, gross negligence is not sufficient.[1] Even if it is assumed that Mary recognised Mr Dracula's mistake and failed to disclose the proper facts on purpose, her non-disclosure does not amount to fraudulent misleading in the sense of § 870 ABGB. Despite an employee's duty of special loyalty to the employer, the employee has no duty to disclose

---

[1] OGH 27.5.1959 JBl.

information to his employer which would lead to his or her dismissal.[2] If however, Mary has attempted to gain an advantage with fraudulent intention, Monstrous Inventions Ltd is no longer obliged to pay under the terms of the settlement[3] and can raise *exceptio doli* as a defence.[4]

(ii) The contract between Mary and Monstrous Inventions Ltd is a settlement agreement. By retiring early, Mary may suffer a loss of income as pension payments are generally lower than a salary. To compensate the difference Mary receives a certain amount from her employer. In settlements only the mistake as to the content of the contract is considered important. A mistake in motive, does not, therefore, entitle the company to annul the contract (§ 901 ABGB). A mistake as to the person (§ 873 ABGB) is examined by analogy with a mistake as to the importance of the quality of physical goods (§ 871 ABGB). The importance of the person is thus examined in accordance with business usage and the intention of the parties.[5] The honesty of an employee is a very important aspect for such a settlement and is therefore part of the subject matter of the contract. The mistake is therefore as to the content of the declaration. The mistake is *important* as Monstrous Inventions Ltd would not have concluded the contract if it had known the true facts, particularly since if it had known the true facts it could have dismissed Mary immediately. Because of this, Mary should in any case have recognised the mistake. Therefore, it is a fundamental mistake in the sense of § 871 ABGB.

Belgium

As a preliminary observation, it is worth noting that Monstrous Inventions Ltd cannot derogate from employment law in its settlement,[6] nor can it benefit from its mandatory provisions contained designed for the exclusive benefit of the employee.[7]

---

[2] RG 22.12.1925 JW 1926, 795 commented on by Stoll, see also J. Taupitz, *Die zivilrechtliche Pflicht sur unaufgeforderten Offenbarung eigenen Fehlverhaltens* (Tübingen, 1989), p. 72.

[3] OGH 7.10.1974: Bydlinski, *Juristische Methodenlehre und Rechtsbegriff*, p. 493; Mader, *Rechtsmißbrauch und unzulässige Rechtsausübung* (Vienna, 1994), p. 237.

[4] See RG 22.12.1925 JW 1926, 795.   [5] OGH 30.11.1960 EvBl 1961/76.

[6] And see, for the same observation as to the entering into of a settlement contract relating to an employee's rights or obligations: F. Spanoghe, 'Van het water, de wijn, het zand en . . . oude koeien. De dading in het Belgisch recht' in Flemish Bar Association, *La fin du contrat – De behoorlijke beëindiging van overeenkomsten* (Brussels, 1993), nos. 68–75.

[7] Arguably Mary would herself not even be entitled to do so, provided that the agreement is more favourable to her than the statutory regime resulting from the 1978 legislation.

Monstrous Inventions Ltd might consider two types of remedies.

(i) Monstrous Inventions Ltd did make a mistake in awarding a supposedly juicy financial retirement package to Mary whereas Mary had been dishonest enough to provide the company with a sufficient reason to terminate her contract. In fact, Monstrous Inventions Ltd erred on the moral character of the contracting party. This particular type of mistake is qualified to be a mistake as to the person of the contracting party and, in Belgian law, it is generally admitted as a vitiating factor in *intuitu personae* contracts. As an employment contract is qualified as *intuitu personae*, there is no doubt that the package offered is qualified in the same way.

Monstrous Inventions Ltd will, however, most probably not pass the test of excusability: it acted through Dracula, its – competent – managing director whereas the investigation as to Mary's dishonesty had been led by one of its also competent departments. Monstrous Inventions Ltd is therefore deemed to have known about the investigation made concerning Mary. The circumstance that Dracula did not *in fact* know may not, therefore, be considered as ignorance on his part but as an act of mismanagement (especially since he acted without consulting with the personnel department). As a result, Dracula may be liable to the company (art. 7 of the Companies Code) but the company itself will not be entitled to avail itself of such ignorance.

(ii) As we have seen in Case 1 the remedy based on fraud normally avoids the issue of excusability. The question however is to determine whether Mary was, according to the circumstances, under an obligation to reveal her dishonesty. It probably will depend upon the importance and the nature of what she actually did.

It does not seem therefore that Monstrous Inventions Ltd has much chance of annulling the contract.

England

Once the contract to terminate Mary's employment has been concluded, it is too late for Mr Dracula to use the allegation of dishonesty to terminate the employment. On the facts given, the employer enters into a contract to terminate the employee's contract by making various payments, but without realising that he might have been able to terminate it without payment. It is not clear whether Mary had her own dishonest acts in mind (we are only told that she did not know of the investigation) but this would not, in any case, affect the position since there is no duty on an employee to disclose his or her own misconduct to his or her employer.[8] There would also be an argument that Mr Dracula should, in any case, be affected by knowledge of the dishonesty held by others in the company, since the contract to terminate Mary's employment is made by Mr Dracula on behalf of the company. But, quite apart from this, it was held by the House of Lords in *Bell* v. *Lever Bros.*[9] that a contract to terminate an employment contract by payment, which could (unknown to the employer) have been terminated without payment, was still a valid contract: the mistake was not sufficient to make the contract void, since the employer received essentially what he bargained for (i.e. the termination of the contract). This case shows the reluctance of the law to intervene on the ground simply of mistake. The analysis does not hinge on it being a settlement: simply a contract entered into under a mistake.

France

The question in this case is whether a contract formed between Monstrous Inventions Ltd and Mary can be annulled on the basis of mistake or fraud. We will assume that Mr Dracula could validly act on behalf of his company.

(i) At first sight, it is obvious that Mr Dracula made a mistake. Indeed, Mr Dracula made the offer because he was not aware that there was a valid cause for dismissal. In addition, the fact that he was not aware of this information induced him to make the offer, since had he known that Mary had a reprehensible attitude, he would not have made the offer. However, under French law, only a mistake as to the subject matter of the services to be provided renders a contract void. Consequently, a mistake as to mere motives, i.e. motives which are not directly linked to the nature of the services to be rendered, does not render the contract void. The courts have very solid views on this point. Had the parties intended differently, they would have included a term or condition in the contract. And, in this case, Mr Dracula's mistake consisted in his motives for contracting since he made Mary the offer because he was not aware of her reprehensible conduct.

(ii) However, such a mistake would have rendered the contract void if it had been induced by fraud. To uphold such an argument, it is submitted that Mary's failure to disclose the facts that were revealed by the investigations amounted to fraud (*réticence dolosive*). If such an

---

[8] *Bell* v. *Lever Bros* [1932] AC 161; *Sybron Corporation* v. *Rochem Ltd* [1984] Ch 112.
[9] [1932] AC 161.

argument were to be accepted, the contract could be annulled on the basis of art. 1116 of the Civil Code (see Cases 2 and 6 for examples).

Could it be argued therefore that Mary was under an obligation to disclose the fact that she was guilty of misconduct? The argument is both plausible – in terms of the duty of cooperation between employer and employee – and preposterous. It is thus perhaps more reasonable to clothe the duty to inform in terms of a more traditional version of fraud, rather than an independent obligation to provide information that does not make sense when the debtor under the obligation (Mary) is already liable for misconduct within the framework of the employment contract.

Germany

Monstrous Inventions Ltd could annul the agreement it concluded with Mary on the grounds of a mistake as to characteristic (§ 119 II): the fact that Mary may be dismissed is one of her characteristics or qualities. The mistake made by the representative (Mr Dracula) will be attributed to the legal person represented (i.e. the company) according to § 166. This provision, which derives directly from Roman law (D. 18, 1, 12) also states however, that the party represented is to be imputed with the representative's knowledge in addition to the latter's mistake. Owing to the fact that two representatives act for the company here, of which one (the personnel department), knew that Mary could be dismissed, the company will also be imputed with this knowledge.[10] If a person has knowledge of a circumstance however, he or she may not at the same time be mistaken in respect to it; the company may not annul on this ground the agreement it entered into with Mary by reason of having made a mistake.

The claim for compensation arising from *culpa in contrahendo* for neglecting to disclose the reason for dismissal also fails due to this imputation of knowledge; in any event, one will not be able to substantiate the argument that Mary was under a duty to have informed Mr Dracula about the reason for her dismissal.[11]

Greece

Greek law gives Monstrous Inventions Ltd a remedy arising from the theory of the basis of the transaction.

---

[10] On attributing knowledge, see generally, Schilken, *Wissenszurechnung im Zivilrecht* and – dealing with aggregation of knowledge in an undertaking – Larenz/Wolf, AT 886 ff.

[11] See generally on the duty of disclosure Taupitz, *Die zivilrechtliche Pflicht zur unaufgeforderten Offenbarung eigenen Fehlverhaltens.*

Both the contracting parties have mainly based the conclusion of the contract on a point, which turned out to be false. They shared the same mistake which was not fundamental as it referred to their motives for contracting (art. 143 AK). As the common mistake refers to a fundamental element of the transaction, it is considered operative. The fundamental aspect of their shared mistake as to the basis of the transaction,[12] is founded on the general clause of good faith of art. 288 AK and particularly on the more specific provision of art. 388 AK which provides for annulment or adjustment of a synallagmatic contract in case of a subsequent unforeseen change of the basis of the transaction.

The consequence of the lack of the basis of the transaction is, according to the prevailing view,[13] to apply art. 388 AK by analogy as this provision presupposes the collapse of the basis *ex post facto* and not a change already existing at the time of the contract's conclusion. This means that Monstrous Inventions Ltd has the right to seek the adjustment of the contract as appropriate, i.e. by reducing its performance or annulling the contract. If it chooses the latter Mary Shelley is obliged to return the enrichment received under art. 904 f. AK since the cause of the enrichment no longer exists.

Ireland

Similar to English law, in Irish law a contract to terminate an employment contract by payment continues to be a valid contract even where unknown to the employer, the contract could have been terminated without payment. Such a contract would not be void at common law for mistake because the employer obtained the benefit he had been seeking under the transaction – the termination of the contract of employment. The law as contained in the House of Lords decision of *Bell* v. *Lever Brothers* represents the situation in Irish law in this regard.

There may be a good argument for this position to be somewhat relaxed so as to provide for such a contract to be *voidable* at the court's discretion or possibly to be rescinded. However, such an approach has not proved attractive to the Irish courts.

---

[12] See the corresponding theories in Germany on subjective *Geschäftsgrundlage* and in France on the *cause de l'engagement*.

[13] Georgiadis, *General Principles of Civil Law*; Karakatsanis in Georgiadis and Stathopoulos, *Civil Code* (Athens, 1978), vol. 1, AK 143 n. 8; Papantoniou p. 403; Spyridakis, *General Principles*, p. 610; Stathopoulos, *Contract Law in Hellas*, p. 102.

Italy

The Mary Shelley settlement will stand notwithstanding the result of the investigation, in principle, such a contract cannot be annulled if one party turns out to have concluded it under a mistake with regard to its rights. In this case, moreover, there is a 'settlement' that cannot be annulled on grounds of a mistake of law (art. 1429 of the Civil Code) when relating to the questions that were the subject of litigation between the parties (art. 1969 of the Civil Code), only if one of the parties was aware of the lack of foundation of his claim, can the other ask for the annulment of the settlement (art. 1971). In this case, though, it will be impossible to take proceedings against Mary on the basis of the Civil Code, for we are facing an employment contract situation where ordinary contract rules do not apply.

The Netherlands

First, the company may argue that they were mistaken in reaching the settlement: had they known of Mary's dishonesty they would have fired her instead of offering her this (apparently favourable) retirement settlement. Therefore, they will argue, the contract may be annulled on the ground of mistake or fraud. Under Dutch law a contract may be annulled for mistake (art. 6:228 BW): (a) in the case where the company concluded the contract on the basis of incorrect information given to them by Mary; (b) in the case where Mary was under a duty to inform the company and she violated this duty; and (c) in the case of common mistake. Much depends here on what 'Mary's dishonesty', the sufficient reason for firing, means, but whatever it means there does not seem to be a case of common mistake because Mary knew she was dishonest. If Mary told lies to the company and if these lies also made the company conclude the settlement, the company may have a chance, since in principle the company was not under a duty to check whether the information actually given to them by Mary was correct. They may rely on its accurateness.[14] However, if Mary did not lie and instead she was guilty of some other type of dishonesty (e.g. she had stolen money from the company) the question arises whether Mary should have informed the company of her dishonesty. The problem seems to be here that at the moment of conclusion of the settlement the company knew of Mary's

---

[14] HR, 15 November 1957, NJ 1958, 67, note Rutten, AA 1957/1958, 103, note Van der Grinten (Baris/Riezenkamp); HR, 21 January 1966, NJ 1966, 183, note G. J. Scholten, AA 1967, 161, note Van der Grinten (Booy/Wisman).

dishonesty. Although Mr Dracula was not aware, the personnel department knew. Does this mean that Mary was no longer under a duty to inform? In principle a party is not under a duty to inform the other party of facts the first party may expect the second party to know of. Thus, much depends here, in principle, on whether Mary was aware of the fact that the company had found out about her dishonesty. This would be the case if the personnel department had explicitly told her, e.g. when they questioned her in the course of their investigation. In that case, in principle, she was not under a duty to inform. However, some courts may accept that in this case good faith even required Mary to tell Mr Dracula what the rest of his company already knew.

In the case that the contract can be annulled for mistake, i.e. if Mary's lying or violation of a duty to inform can be established, the contract may probably not only be annulled for mistake, but also for fraud. The company would opt for annulment for fraud if there were additional damages that they would wish to be compensated for.

If the employment contract has not yet been terminated, the company may dismiss Mary with immediate effect if the ground for termination is important enough (arts. 6:677 and 6:678 BW). Would this have any effect on the settlement? Dracula may try to rely on art. 6:229 BW.[15] At the moment that the settlement should take effect the contractual relationship (employment contract) that the settlement is based on no longer exists. However, they will probably not be successful because it is generally accepted that art. 6:229 BW is only meant for cases where the underlying relationship did not exist from the outset, i.e. the cases where under the old code the contract would be void for lack of *causa*.[16]

Finally, the company may ask the court for the adaptation or termination of the settlement on the ground of unforeseen circumstances. Article 6:258, § 1, BW says:

Upon the demand of one of the parties, the court may modify the effects of a contract or it may set it aside in whole or in part, on the basis of unforeseen circumstances of such a nature that the other party, according to standards of reasonableness and fairness, may not expect the contract to be maintained in unmodified form. The modification or setting aside may be given retrospective effect.

---

[15] 'A contract in furtherance of an existing legal relationship between the parties can be nullified if the relationship does not exist, unless, in view of the nature of the contract, common opinion or the facts of the case, the non-existence should remain for the account of the person who invokes it.'

[16] Cf. *Verbintenissenrecht* (Hesselink), art. 229, aant. 23.

Unforeseen means here: not taken into account by the parties when concluding the contract, not accounted for in the contract. That seems to be the case here: the contract does not say anything about what would happen in case Mary turned out to be dishonest or indeed if she should be fired. As to the first circumstance (Mary's dishonesty), this circumstance already existed at the moment of conclusion of the contract and it is generally accepted that a contract can only be adapted or terminated on the basis of art. 6:258 BW in case of an unforeseen *change* of circumstances.[17] However, if Mary were fired after the conclusion of the contract that would constitute a change of circumstances that a court might find serious enough to justify adaptation or termination of the contract for change of circumstances.[18]

Norway

The present case concerns a promise given without knowledge that Mary Shelley's employment contract could be terminated on grounds of dishonesty. Legal procedures in this situation are based on the invalidity regulations, and not on the doctrine of *condictio indebiti*. Whether or not a retirement compensation or similar allowances have been paid, is here irrelevant.

The question should be decided according to the Contract Act, § 33, possibly together with § 36. As previously indicated, the problem is, first, whether the person to whom the promise was made (the promisee) had knowledge of the conditions, and secondly, whether, because of these conditions, it would be contrary to 'honest behaviour and good faith' to ask for the promise to be honoured. In the present case, the question of knowledge is not in debate: Mary Shelley (the promisee) was aware of her dishonesty. The case would, therefore, depend on the interpretation of honest behaviour. How would regard for 'good faith and fair dealing' ('*Treu und Glauben*') stand in relation to the offer of early retirement?

If proof of dishonesty can be shown, which gives the right to dismiss the employee with immediate effect (termination), the employer would normally be able to free himself from this type of promise. The reason for dismissal is directly related to the giving of the promise in the sense that it clearly would not have been given if the employer had known

---

[17] Cf. *Parl. Gesch. Boek* 6, p. 969 (T.M.); *Verbintenissenrecht*, art. 258 (valk), aant. 21; Hesselink, *De redelijkheiden in het Europese privaatrecht*, p. 344; and HR, 20 February 1998, RvdW 1998, 55C.

[18] See on the German law in this kind of case, Hesselink, *ibid.*, p. 367.

of the situation. Furthermore, it concerns circumstances relating to the work performance of the promisee.

Portugal

If the proposal of early retirement has already been accepted it cannot be overruled if reasons to fire the employee are discovered subsequently. Fraud is irrelevant because Mary's dishonesty has nothing to do with the company's decision to offer her early retirement. Fraud would only have been relevant if the company had known about Mary's dishonesty before making her an offer but this would have constituted a mistake as to motive, inoperative unless the parties have agreed it is relevant before the agreement was concluded (art. 232°, no. 1, of the Civil Code).

Therefore, the only remedy against Mary Shelley is based on her liability to the company for damages if her dishonesty has caused it a loss. Such a claim must be brought within one year after the termination of her employment contract.

Scotland

When Mary accepts the package, a binding contract is formed entitling her to the early retirement package. There is no Scottish authority on the point, but it is thought, however, that the mistake as to the subject matter of the contract, that is to say to purchase the remainder of Mary's contract of employment, does go to the root of the contract. This means that there is an essential mistake as described in Case 1. If unilateral, uninduced mistake (error) is still operative in Scots law, it is submitted that the package could be annulled on the ground of mistake. This solution is, of course, inconsistent with the controversial decision of the House of Lords in *Bell v. Lever Bros*,[19] which was, of course, an English case.

Spain

According to Spanish employment law, in these circumstances the employer should have reacted immediately and should have dismissed the employee immediately for disciplinary reasons (art. 54 of the Labour Reform Law 1994).

Although the facts are improbable under Spanish law as a number of procedures would need to be followed before the settlement could be

---

[19] [1932] AC 161.

signed, it would be valid. The company would have the option to try claiming for damages caused by the employee's dishonest conduct.

Comparative observations

This case concerns a settlement in the context of employment contracts in which Mr Dracula, managing director and authorised agent of the employer, Monstrous Inventions Ltd, is mistaken as to the attributes (the honesty) of its employee, Mary Shelley. The case combines a number of factors relating to mistake, first can the employer rely on his own unilateral mistake in view of the fact that the company (via its personnel department) knew about Mary Shelley's dishonest behaviour? Secondly, did Mary have a duty to inform the company about her own improper behaviour, in view of the relationship of trust and loyalty which may sometimes be inferred from a relationship between employer and employee? Although at first glance it might seem as though the different faces of the company complicate these issues, the company's constructive knowledge is only partially relevant. Testing the limits of the duty to inform shows up once again its casuistic and versatile nature. It is, as one reporter expressed it, preposterous[20] to imagine that Mary should be expected to inform the company about her own misconduct while negotiating the settlement. Moreover, it could be submitted that her failure to inform is not necessarily deceitful or fraudulent. This might lead to an enquiry about whether a non-fraudulent failure to inform should ever be contested. This case would suggest that such a positive duty to inform will probably only lie in very limited circumstances. It could equally be inferred that the relationship of good faith that is said to exist under some national laws[21] between employer and employee is relative. Finally, this case suggests that not many laws push the duty to inform so far as to oblige a contracting party to give information against his own interests.[22] The majority of reporters were in agreement that the company had no remedy; exceptionally certain systems inclined towards very high standards of good faith suggested the contrary.

---

[20] See French report.   [21] See for example French and Austrian reports.

[22] This may be an illustration of the dialectic demonstrated in contract law between heteronomous and autonomous principles of good faith cf. M. Hesselink, 'Good Faith' in A. Hartkamp et al. (eds.), *Towards a European Civil Code* (2nd edn, Nijmegen, The Hague, Boston, 1998), pp. 285–310; G. Teubner, 'Legal Irritants: Good Faith in British Law or How Unifying Law Ends Up in New Divergences' MLR 61 (1998), 11.

(i) Not many countries were prepared to admit the company's mistake here. Under Belgian law, the mistake was analysed as inexcusable. A similar type of argument has been constructed under German law, by virtue of the laws on representation; the company is deemed to have constructive knowledge of Mary's past behaviour and thus no mistake has been made. Under French law the mistake was categorised as an inoperative mistake as to motive (and also under one analysis in Austrian law). This would also be the case under Portuguese law unless the parties had agreed that the motive was essential to their agreement. Under English, Irish and Scots law, the case is reminiscent of a leading authority on the law of mistake – *Bell v. Lever Brothers*,[23] also concerning a mistake arising over a settlement agreement, considered inoperative, although it was suggested that the fact that a settlement was involved was somewhat irrelevant here. In a sense, for English, Irish and Scots law this case does not have any distinguishing factors, it is merely a straightforward application of the law's reluctance to admit unilateral mistakes. Under Italian law, the mistake is qualified as a mistake of law and is inoperative but the *lex specialis* rules of employment law override the general rules in any event. Under Dutch law a mistake may possibly be successfully invoked, but in relation to Mary's duty to inform (see below (iii)).

(ii) Only Austria and Greece were really positive about using the remedy of mistake here. Under Austrian law, it was suggested that there was not a simple illustration of a mistake as to the quality of the person (§ 873 ABGB), but rather that the mistake relates to the content of the settlement agreement and that Mary's honesty is analogous to the importance of a quality of physical goods under § 871 ABGB. Moreover, under this article, Mary should have recognised or been aware of Mr Dracula's mistake, therefore she does not deserve to be protected. A rather different analysis is put forward under Greek law, the remedy is not for mistake but for the absence of the basis of the transaction as it was submitted that both parties have made a mistake, and that on this ground following art. 388 AK, the company can ask for the settlement agreement to be annulled or adjusted. Similarly, Dutch law may apply art. 6:258 BW and adopt or terminate the contract for an unforeseen change of circumstances.

(iii) A version of good faith, combined with Mary's duty to inform, might also be the basis for annulling the contract. This suggestion was made under Norwegian law, that Mary's conduct might be considered

---

[23] (1932) AC 161.

as contrary to honest behaviour and good faith and thus in violation of § 36 of the Contract Act. Likewise, under Dutch law the company just might be able to annul either for mistake or fraud if it was held that Mary had breached a duty to inform her employers, although the issue was not definitively determined since it was pointed out that although some courts might expect Mary to tell Mr Dracula what the rest of the company already knew, on another contrasting interpretation it might not be expected of her to inform the company of facts of which it was already aware.

Does this case show that there is not inevitably a correlation between breach of good faith and fraud? It would seem here that if Mary was held to have breached a standard of good faith in some countries, this does not mean that her non-disclosure of information amounted to fraud. Moreover, as in most countries it was not really suggested that a duty of good faith had been breached, this case might seem to suggest that it would be excessive to expect information to be given, absent either of these two elements in circumstances when the content of the information is self-incriminating! In other words, a certain amount of self-protection is justifiable.

Case 12

Lady Windermere v. Angel

Case

As her daughter Angela was due to be called to the bar, Lady Windermere decided to make Angela a present of her own diamond-studded fan and instructed her lawyer to draw up a deed of gift.[1] Arriving in a hurry before the ceremony, she signed the deed without more than a glance, only to discover later that the gift had been made in favour of her own estranged brother Angel. After her departure but before Lady Windermere's discovery, Angel formally accepted the gift but has not yet received the fan. What remedy, if any, is available against Angel?

Discussions

Austria

The wrong person has been declared the beneficiary of the gift due to the lawyer's mistake. This could be qualified either as a mistake as to identity (§ 873 ABGB) or a mistake of declaration (§ 871 ABGB) but as the conditions and results are the same the qualification is unimportant. This mistake is fundamental but neither provision on mistake applies because the three alternative conditions of § 871 ABGB are not fulfilled: (i) Angel did not cause the mistake; in fact Lady Windermere was careless when signing the deed so it was she who caused the lawyer's mistake; (ii) Angel did not notify the mistake nor should he have done; and (iii) the mistake was not declared in good time.

---

[1] A deed of gift is the name of the instrumentum. Each reporter has understood this term to designate the appropriate legal act and that the requisite formalities have been complied with under national law.

As the mistake regards a party's name, the doctrine of *falsa demonstratio* may be considered. However, this doctrine gives a remedy if the wrong declaration has been made but not when the wrong idea is behind the declaration as is the case here. As Lady Windermere wanted to give the fan to Angela and not to Angel, this does not constitute a *falsa demonstratio*. There is no remedy for mistake.

However in Austria the validity of a gift depends on two formal conditions: the execution of a deed of gift and the physical transfer of property (if movable property). Since Angel has not actually received the fan, the gift is not valid anyway.

Belgium

Assuming the formalities have been complied with the gift is a valid contract. Lady Windermere can therefore invoke two remedies.

(i) As a donation is an *intuitu personae* contract (see Case 11), mistake as to the person of the donee is admissible in order to annul the gift.[2] The mistake will however have to be excusable and the fact that Lady Windermere acted in quite an off-hand manner when entering into such an important contract is certainly not in her favour.

(ii) Lady Windermere could allege that the contract is void for absence of *cause* (arts. 1108 and 1131 of the Civil Code), if she could prove that she only gave the fan away because she wanted to give it to her daughter and that there is an absence of this decisive reason inducing her to contract.[3]

Lady Windermere will probably not have too much trouble in obtaining the annulment of the donation.

England

Lady Windermere is entitled to ask the court to rectify the deed so as to confer the gift on Angela, or to rescind the deed altogether. In either case, the gift conferred on Angel by the deed is revoked.

A deed is a formal document, which must make clear on its face that it is intended to be a deed, and must be signed and the signature witnessed.[4] If a promise is contained in a deed, it obtains its

---

[2] E. De Wilde d'Estmael, *Les donations, Repertoire notarial* (Brussels, 1995), vol. III, book VII no. 56.

[3] *Ibid.*, at nos. 56 and 108.

[4] Law of Property (Miscellaneous Provisions) Act 1989, s. 1. No publicity or registration is necessary, and the beneficiary of the deed need not accept its benefit, nor even know of its existence, for it to create the obligation. A deed can also be used to effect a transfer of property rights.

binding force by virtue of the deed, rather than the general rules for contract: consideration is not required (and so a deed can create a wholly *gratuitous* obligation, as here, where a simple contract cannot).

Rectification will be granted in the discretion of the court if the deed did not reflect the donor's true intention, and as long as the donee cannot show a reasonable objection to the order.[5]

As for the claim to rescission: whilst the courts start from a position of assuming that the deed is valid and binding, it is possible to seek rescission where the mistake is sufficiently serious.[6] A recent case spoke in terms that 'wherever there is a voluntary transaction by which one party intends to confer a bounty on another, the deed will be set aside if the court is satisfied that the disponor did not intend the transaction to have the effect which it did. It will be set aside for mistake whether the mistake is a mistake of law or of fact, so long as the mistake is as to the effect of the transaction itself, and not merely as to its consequences or the advantages to be gained by entering into it.'[7]

This case involves a voluntary transaction, rather than a contract: a deed of gift where the mistake is as to the person to whom the gift is to be made. It is an error of drafting in the deed; and it is easily remedied. If, however, the transaction had been not voluntary, but in a contract under which Angel had given consideration, the approach to both rectification and rescission would have been different. Although the courts are not disposed to overturn a voluntary transaction easily, and so require evidence of a serious mistake affecting the nature of the transaction, the approach is certainly much more restrictive where a contract is to be set aside. The doctrine of *non est factum* is available to make a contract (and a deed) void for mistake, but only under much more stringent conditions, requiring the claimant to show a misunderstanding of the nature of the transaction and an absence of negligence on his or her part.

---

[5] It is not entirely clear what will constitute a 'reasonable objection'. In *Re Butlin's Settlement Trust* [1976] Ch 251 it was said that rectification of a voluntary settlement might be refused in the court's discretion if there was a reasonable objection by the trustees of the settlement. Perhaps a court would refuse rectification if Angel had acted to his detriment in reliance on the undertakings in the deed being carried out; but there is no evidence of this anyway. The courts are much more reluctant to rectify a written contract, or a deed which contains a bargain, since the defendant's position merits greater protection by virtue of his having given consideration.

[6] *Lady Hood of Avalon v. Mackinnon* [1909] 1 Ch 476: deed executed in favour of X, 'in utter forgetfulness' of the fact that the gift had already been made by an earlier deed: second deed set aside.

[7] *Gibbon v. Mitchell* [1990] 3 All ER 338 at p. 343 (Millett J).

France

Under French law, Lady Windermere's remedy would lie in asking the courts to annul her settlement either for mistake (*erreur*) or for absence of *cause*.

(i) As already seen, the likelihood of an action based on a mistake as to the person is subject to two conditions: the situation must fit within the framework of such a mistake and must be excusable. Mistakes as to the person are generally considered inoperative[8] by French law. However, such mistakes are essential when contracts are *intuitu personae*, which is generally the case for gifts.[9] A mistake relating to the person will justify annulment if the donor's belief that she contracted in favour of a specific person induced her consent and the mistake related to a substantial quality of the donee.[10] The courts examine the first element *in concreto*,[11] and the second *in abstracto*.[12] Thus Lady Windermere could annul her gift since these two requirements are fulfilled. Indeed, the fact that she believed she was giving the fan to her daughter Angela induced her to sign the deed.[13] Secondly, the substantial quality of the donee inducing her to contract consists in Angela's success in passing the bar exam.

On the other hand, the requirements that the mistake must be excusable render the chance of success of this action less certain. In certain circumstances the mistake is considered to be so gross that it will bar the

---

[8] Terré, Simler and Lequette, *Les obligations*, no. 220, p. 223, 'mistakes which are not a source of annulment are considered ineffective, i.e. mistakes as to a non substantial quality of the obligation, the person in non *intuitu personae* contracts, the economic evaluation of the object of a contract and the motives having led a person to enter a contract'.

[9] P. Voirin, *Droit Civil* (26th edn, Paris, 1997), vol. I no. 727, '*Intuitu personae* contracts are either motivated by benevolence, such as settlements, deposit, gratuitous agency, suretyship and free loans, or are based on a fiduciary relationship, for example partnerships, contracts with doctors, solicitors, artists, etc.'; Talleur, *L'intuitu personae dans les contrats* (diss., Paris, 1938); M. Contamine, *L'intuitu personae dans les contrats* (diss., Paris, 1974).

[10] Such a substantial quality can be the donee's talent, skill, reputation.

[11] Judges will analyse what induced Lady Windermere's consent at the moment the contract was formed; Civ 1, 26 October 1983, Bull civ I, no. 249; but evidence of the mistake when the contract was formed can be proved by elements subsequent and prior to the formation of the contract, Civ 1, 13 December 1983, D 1984. 340, note Aubert.

[12] Judges analyse the qualities that have been considered as substantial by the parties, Civ 1, 26 February 1980, Bull civ I, no. 66.

[13] It induced her all the more since she had no justification for giving the fan to her brother with whom she does not have a friendly relationship.

annulment.[14] It is arguable that in this case Lady Windermere behaved so rashly – by not verifying that the document she signed did not conform to her wishes – that she might not be excused by the judges.[15] However, it is important to note that the mistake was due to a typographical error outside Lady Windermere's control. It is thus submitted that the fact that Lady Windermere's mistake was induced by the notary's mistake, whom she could legitimately trust, may diminish the allegation of her negligence. Indeed the judges could well take this factor into account.

(ii) In the alternative, Lady Windermere may be able to plead absence of *cause*. Under French law the *cause* of a gift has long been identified as the intention to give. As far as gifts (gratuitous contracts) are concerned, this intention has been interpreted subjectively by the courts, that is, by looking at the reasons for making the gift.

In this case the reason why Lady Windermere intended to give a fan to her daughter was presumably because she had successfully passed the bar exam. Traditionally, it may have sufficed to plead that she had the intention of giving the fan, thereafter the mere fact that she did not give it to the right person would not have been a cause of action. Nowadays, however, it is admitted that the reasons that motivated Lady Windermere should be examined more closely. Therefore it seems that the fact that the fan was to be given specifically to Angela, and not Angel – Lady Windermere's estranged brother – is sufficient to ascertain that there is an obligation without *cause*. The burden of proof lies on Lady Windermere to prove absence of *cause*.

Germany

In Germany, a notarised instrument is necessary to make a promise of a gift valid (§ 518 I). Apart from this, then according to German law there is no mistake relating to the identity of a person: that is to say, Lady Windermere does not make a mistake concerning the person to whom she wishes to give the present but rather what she states in the contract of donation. The question whether the signature made under a text that has not been read is voidable where the text diverges from the signatory's

---

[14] Terré, Simler and Lequette, *Les obligations* no. 223, p. 225 'by not taking the elementary precautions before entering into the contract, (Lady Windermere) [. . .] was negligent. (Her) negligence will be punished by the court refusing to annul the contract: *de non vigilantibus curat praetor.*'

[15] The excusable character of the mistake is analysed *in concreto*, i.e. according to the circumstances of the case, the age, experience and profession of the *errans*.

intention in making a declaration is a situation also discussed in relation to a notarised instrument.[16] Thus, Lady Windermere's mistake can also be framed as a mistake according to German law.

In any event, the contract (or the notarised instrument) is not automatically voidable: Lady Windermere signed a contract that was presented to her without even reading it through once. In so doing, she – as it later turned out – made a declaration that she had not intended to make; yet could she have assumed the risk of making such a mistake due to the fact that she gave up reading through the contract on account of her haste? The Reichsgericht itself had already limited the possibilities of annulment in the case where a signature was made under a declaration that had not been read. Since then, a distinction has been made between situations where the declarer made a certain assumption relating to the content of the instrument he signed and where he did not.[17] When drawing this distinction, it is correct to say that the person who does not consider the contents of the text and signs under the text without hesitation normally also assumes the risk of making an incorrect assumption about the contents of the text. However, in every case exactly which risk it was that the declarer actually intended to assume must be examined.[18]

Because Lady Windermere was under the understanding that she had signed a contract of donation for the benefit of 'Angela', annulment of the contract in 'Angel's' benefit would be allowed. Flume has nevertheless pointed to the fact that this rule is violated in cases where someone has entrusted someone with the preparation of text of a contract: if the person relied upon was authorised to this end, then the principal is forbidden from relying on a mistake made in respect of third parties. On the contrary, he must hold to the actions of the person relied upon.[19] Only if, as in our case, the person relied upon (the lawyer) made a mistake himself is the principal (Lady Windermere) able to annul the declaration (§§ 119 I, 166 I). Because the lawyer obviously confused 'Angela' with 'Angel' then, according to this view, Lady Windermere could annul the gift. Certainly, she has to indemnify Angel if he suffered damage by relying on the gift (§ 122 I).

---

[16] Cf. BGHZ 71, 260, 263.   [17] Cf. above in Case 9.

[18] Even if he thought that the text reflected his belief he may assume a risk relating to the declaration if he gave his signature under the unread text; for example, where he was bound to take into account that a mistake occurred in the writing down of the document.

[19] Flume, AT II 454; following his opinion Soergel/Hefermehl, § 119 para. 16; MüKo/Kramer, § 119 para. 53.

Greece

The contract of donation can be annulled for mistake. When Lady Windermere promises to give the fan without any *quid pro quo* to Angel, she has made a mistake as to declaration (art. 140 AK). According to art. 141 AK, such a mistake is fundamental when it affects a point of such importance for the contract that the party making the declaration would not have made it, had he known the true state of affairs. As already seen, the mistake must fulfil subjective and objective conditions both of which are met here. It is clear that subjectively Lady Windermere would not have made the donation had she known the true state of affairs. The objective criterion is that the identity of the person is important for the donation according to good faith and other generally accepted usage. It is accepted[20] that in the case of a donation, a mistake will be more easily admitted than in the case of a synallagmatic contract. Lady Windermere's fundamental mistake will enable her to ask the court to annul the donation.

Ireland

This is a case where Irish law is quick to provide a remedy for Lady Windermere. In this case, Lady Windermere may seek rectification of the deed so as to give effect to her original intention that the fan should be gifted to her daughter Angela rather than her brother Angel. Alternatively, she can annul the contract.

Italy

Article 1376 of the Civil Code provides that a gift is a contract but in order to be valid, a gift must fulfill certain formalities. Not only must the gift be made by a notarised act, which is the case here, but the donee must also accept the gift using the same formalities. If the gift has not been accepted by Angel it is therefore void. Moreover, even if the gift has been accepted, it is not perfect until the donor is notified of the donor's acceptance and the donor may revoke the gift up until the moment when the gift is perfected (art. 782 of the Civil Code). Lady Windermere might still have time to revoke the gift or it might not be valid as Angel has not yet accepted it. If the gift has been perfected and Lady Windermere can no longer revoke the gift, she will have to try another legal ground. As a donation is a contract in which the motive must be taken into account, mistake as to the person of the donee is admissible

---

[20] Stathopoulos, 'Mistake Crucial for the Annulment of the Juridical Act', p. 726.

in order to annul the gift. In this case a mistake in the declaration might also be raised as an argument (also art. 1433 of the Civil Code). The Code's provisions on mistake apply both in cases where there is a mistake in the declaration or where the declaration has been incorrectly transmitted.

The Netherlands

In principle, Angela has no remedy against Angel. Lady Windermere signed a deed in which she expresses the gift of her own diamond-studded fan to her brother, Angel, and if the deed was signed by her brother, before or afterwards, she is bound to the contract (art. 7A:1719 BW). From art. 184 Rv jo. 183 jo. 178 Rv it follows that proof by a notarised deed is binding. This is consistent with the character and purpose of a deed. If a notarised instrument were challengeable it would be useless in addition to any other written document. However, she may be able to rectify the deed. Since the statement of facts does not say that she has done so, for the time being the deed is binding. However, she may have a remedy against the notary if she establishes that she had properly instructed him and that it therefore was his fault that the wrong name was on the document.

Norway

For a start, a promise of a gift is as binding as other promises. In Scandinavian law, there are no requirements as to form that apply to such promises.[21] A consensus exists that this is the general understanding, though with certain modifications. For instance, it is assumed that the donor, to a greater extent than with synallagmatic promises, can plead a mistake.[22] In line with this, a mistake in the transaction[23] as in the present case to a large extent could be pleaded even when the recipient has no knowledge of the situation.[24]

---

[21] As far as gifts between spouses are concerned there are however strict regulations as to form.

[22] See, for instance, R. Knoph, *Knophs oversikt over Norges rett* (10th edn, Oslo, 1993), p. 533; Ussing, *Aftaler*, pp. 476–7; B. Gomard, *Almindelig kontraktsret* (2nd edn, Copenhagen, 1996), pp. 53–4; and L. L. Andersen et al., *Aftaler og mellemmænd* (2nd edn, Copenhagen, 1991), p. 175.

[23] See the Norwegian report on Case 1 for an explanation of the term.

[24] From the drafts for the Danish, Norwegian and Swedish Contract Acts, which have been put together by Scandinavian cooperation, it appears that the wording in the chapter on invalidity has been chosen, among other things, not to obstruct such a solution.

There is little doubt that, in Scandinavian law, one would consider Lady Windermere not bound by the declaration she had signed since Angel had not acted in reliance on the promise. Angel's acceptance of the gift has no bearing in Scandinavian law since a non-synallagmatic promise binds regardless of acceptance. Angel has not actually relied on the promise and in addition, it could be reasonably asked if he should not have realised that this was a mistake.

Portugal

This is a case of mistake in the declaration. Therefore, according to art. 247° of the Civil Code Lady Windermere can demand the annulment of the contract if the other party (Angel) knows or should not be unaware that the element in which the mistake occurred was essential for her. It was obvious for Angel that the gift could not have been made in his favour. Therefore, the gift can be annulled.

Scotland

Lady Windermere's mistake has not been on her intention but in the expression of it. This problem is also known as 'defective expression'. There is no general remedy at common law under which the document can be rectified. However, the courts can use their equitable jurisdiction to achieve this result. An example of the courts using their equitable jurisdiction is *North British Insurance Company v. Tunnock*.[25]

To produce greater certainty in the courts' use of their equitable powers, the Law Reform (Miscellaneous Provisions) (Scotland) Act 1985 was enacted. Under s. 8 a document transferring a right, here the right of ownership of the gifted item, which fails accurately to express the intention of the granter can be rectified so that it does so conform. On doing so the document is treated as if it was always so expressed.[26] In ascertaining the true intent the court will refer to all relevant written and verbal evidence.[27] However, the court will not alter the deed if it would adversely affect the interests, to a material extent, of one who was in ignorance of the defect but has had their position materially affected due to reliance on the deed.[28] Therefore if Angel has acted, or omitted to act, in some way due to his belief that he is the owner of the gift and his position has altered as a result, the court will not intervene. Before

[25] (1864) 3 M 1.   [26] Law Reform (Miscellaneous Provisions) (Scotland) Act 1985 s 8(3).
[27] Law Reform (Miscellaneous Provisions) (Scotland) Act 1985 s 8(2).
[28] Law Reform (Miscellaneous Provisions) (Scotland) Act 1985 s 9(1).

refusing to so act, the courts would have to be satisfied that Angel's reliance was reasonable.[29]

Alternatively, Lady Windermere could rely on *Hunter* v. *Bradford Property Trust Limited*.[30] This held that in a gratuitous obligation the grantor's error as to the legal effect of the contract was sufficient grounds for annulment. While the mistake must be essential, as the contract is gratuitous it is a recognised exception to the general rule against a party relying on her own uninduced mistake.[31]

Therefore, Lady Windermere could either seek the rectification of the deed under statute or have it rescinded at common law. The success of both is reliant on Angel's behaviour; in statute his consent may be required if he has acted upon the gift and the common law rescission will be thwarted if he has acted in a way that prevents *restitutio in integrum*.

Spain

According to art. 623 ff. of the Civil Code, donations are only valid if the donee accepts the donation, if chattels are transferred in writing, the donee must accept the gift in writing. As Angel has not accepted the gift, it is invalid. In addition, art. 1274 of the Civil Code concerning the cause of contracts states that the cause of a gratuitous contract is the will of the donor. It would also seem that the contract could be annulled for lack of cause as Lady Windermere did not want to give the fan to Angel.

Comparative observations

This case concerns a mistake made by a donor about identity of the beneficiary upon making a gift. The first comparative question that comes to mind is whether a gift is a contract. It is worth mentioning that in England and Ireland a promise of a gift is not classified as a contract, it is a voluntary transaction. If a gift is made by deed, it does however have binding force. In all other countries a gift is classified as a contract. However, in a sense the different legal classifications of a gift are irrelevant for the outcome of the case. This is significant as it would suggest that there may be a common underlying rationale that helps explain

---

[29] Law Reform (Miscellaneous Provisions) (Scotland) Act 1985 s 9(3)(a).
[30] 1970 SLT 173.   [31] See Cases 1 and 2.

the solution, even though legal categories differ. Secondly, however, the fact that a gift has been made raises the question of formalities. In some legal systems it has been emphasised that formalities prevail over issues of defective consent. Thus under Austrian and Spanish law, for example, the gift will be invalid because the donee has not accepted it in accordance with formal requirements. The third feature of this case relates to the type of mistake made – is the legal categorisation significant? – and the suitability of the remedy. The mistake here is entirely unilateral, the other party has not caused the mistake in any way, however in some countries the wrongly named beneficiary's knowledge that he should not and could not be intended as the true beneficiary may have a bearing on the mistake. This is an example of how the term 'unilateral' can be somewhat ambiguous, only one party – the donor – has made a mistake, yet the donee may be, or even should have been aware of it.

France, Belgium, England, Germany, Italy, Ireland, Norway, Portugal and Scotland will allow the donor Lady Windermere to annul the gift on the grounds of mistake. In Germany, Greece and Italy the mistake is classified as a mistake in the declaration. Scots law refers to 'defective expression', Norway to a mistake in the transaction. It is interesting to note that German law could have come to the opposite solution, concentrating on the fact that the donor could have assumed the risk of the mistake, but each case is assessed on its facts, and the question of risk was considered inapplicable on these facts. Portuguese and Norwegian law stressed the fact that the donee should have known that the donor made a mistake. Belgian and French law have analysed the mistake as a mistake as to the identity of the person, which is essential when making a gift. Under English and Irish law, two remedies are available. The deed of gift can be rectified so as to substitute the material mistake (Angel) with the intended beneficiary, Angela. Alternatively, the gift may be annulled for mistake, since the mistake is sufficiently serious and affects the nature of the transaction. This formulation (that the nature of the transaction is affected) appears to be similar to the explanation offered by Belgian, French and Spanish law, that the contract may be annulled for *absence de cause*. Rectification may also be possible under Dutch law. Scots law offers the same two remedies of rectification or annulment (properly called reduction). However the legal formants are different from English and Irish law, since a statutory provision exists,[32] giving

---

[32] Section 8, Law Reform (Miscellaneous Provisions) Scotland Act 1985.

rise to the right to rectify errors failing to conform to the donor's intention subject to the beneficiary's lack of reliance on the deed. Otherwise, the right to annul exists as a result of case law[33] and is a perfect example of Scotland as a mixed legal system. Since the mistake is essential, unilateral and uninduced (terms reminiscent of civil legal terminology) annulment may be granted as an exception to the general rule because the 'contract is gratuitous'.

The mistake made in this case is distinct from the mistakes treated in all the other cases as the mistake relates to the terms of the contract. This kind of mistake is treated under art. 4:104 of the PECL as 'inaccuracy in communication' and assimilated to mistakes under art. 4:103. Arguably, since the PECL does not contain a consideration requirement, art. 4:104 could apply to gifts anyway.

Two salient features have been picked up by certain reporters. First, the question of the knowledge or constructive knowledge of Angel, the unintended beneficiary of the gift. If this approach is emphasised, it could be maintained that the mistake is not purely unilateral, since the other party knew about it.[34] Secondly, the reliance (or lack of) made by Angel on the deed. This is mentioned indirectly under English law since it would affect the right to rectification (if the donee has a reasonable objection) whereas reliance has become a statutory requirement under Scots law. It is likewise taken into account in Scandinavian law. Why is reliance expressly invoked here? Normally protection is given to a contracting party who has given value and thus remedies for mistake are restrictive. Since the donee has given nothing and got something in return, the general reason is inapplicable. However, if the donee has relied on the gift, it will no longer be true to state that he has given nothing. In this case, the donee is not deprived of all protection, his reliance on the contract is an antidote. A similar approach is taken by Austrian, German and Greek law on mistake which constantly balances up the need to protect both parties by compensating the negative interest of the non-mistaken party or excluding annulment under Austrian law if reliance on the contract has actually occurred. Reliance apart, it could also be submitted that the protection of the donor and donee is based on moral considerations, i.e. that making donations should be encouraged – or not discouraged – and the will of the donor is paramount.

---

[33] *Hunter v. Bradford Property Trust Limited* (1970) SLT 173, see Scottish report.
[34] See Kotz and Flessner, *European Contract Law*, pp. 189 ff.

Finally however all analyses point to the same underlying rationale here – the law can afford to be more flexible and less severe about admitting a mistake made in a deed of gift, since the economic considerations about disturbing the security of market transactions is irrelevant. Contract or no contract – making gifts does not have the same economic impact on legal certainty.

5 Comparative conclusions

Ruth Sefton-Green

In the context of a study made within the framework of the Trento group known as the 'common core of European private law', the first question that needs to be answered is whether there is a common core in the area of mistake, duties to inform and fraud in European contract law, the object of our enquiry. In order to provide an answer we must first look at the empirical results of our study. At the same time we will bear in mind a second critical methodological question, namely what we mean by a 'common core'.

At the outset we stated that one of our objectives was to investigate the reality of the civil law/common law divide. Taking stock empirically of our answers enables us therefore to assess the facts. The reply is of course highly complex and neither black nor white. First, is it true that there are no differences between common law and civil law countries, hence is there a common core? We are not able to reply affirmatively without qualification. Second, if there are differences, we have shown that they do not necessarily arise where expected. Does it follow that there is no common core? The answer will depend to some extent on the meaning given to 'common core'.

A quantitative criterion, namely that a majority, as opposed to una-nimity, suffices to constitute a common core, has been adopted. Nonethe-less, there may be a great deal of crucially important diversity contained in a majority solution admitting or refusing a remedy. If the common-ality is identified merely by its solution, this still may not suffice to confirm the presence of a common core. In how many cases, for exam-ple, can a general rule be induced from one particular situation? Often, the solution to the problem case is derived from casuistic considerations and more importantly, a general rule cannot be induced at all, since a consensus as to the solution does not indicate a common underlying

369

reasoning nor a commonality of legal concepts. It is for this reason that it has already been suggested that a truly common core directs itself not only at the commonality of the solution but also at the path by which the solution has been reached.[1] It has been extremely important to detail and explain the number of different lines of reasoning used to reach each solution; if this divergence of reasoning is disregarded the value of comparative law would be diminished. That said, evidence suggesting that in eleven out of twelve cases, a majority out of thirteen different legal systems agree on the same solution and so share, to a certain extent, their attitude of what is a fair and just solution is valuable and important. Of the eleven cases that correspond to the defined common core, Case 10 was the sole exception where such a criterion cannot be identified. That said, our empirical observations are purely descriptive or 'topological'.[2] There is of course a great deal of controversy about whether the function of comparative law is positivist or normativist.[3] To put this another way, it is clear that finding a common core is only one step of a process (or perhaps several processes) and does not inevitably lead to the inference that the solution is better or even desirable. A quantitative criterion is in this sense both misleading and insufficient. This highlights the meta-legal nature of the project.

At this stage our lines of enquiry may appear self-contradictory. How can we destroy the common law and civil law wall without producing a common core? Surprisingly, the results allow us to do just this: we have seen that the frontiers lie not in terms of legal traditions[4] or legal families[5] (although of course this sometimes occurs) but mostly in terms of legal values. To be more explicit, we have shown that clusters of replies can be found within each case, but the basis of the cluster is often difficult to identify. It may be due to philosophical, political, economic, social and moral values: all of which one could call

---

[1] See R. Sefton-Green, 'Le défi d'un droit commun des obligations' in M. Delmas-Marty, H. Muir Watt and H. Ruiz-Fabri (eds.), *Variations autour d'un droit commun. Premières rencontres de l'UMR de droit comparé de Paris* (Paris, 2002), pp. 443 ff.

[2] The epithet was coined by M. Bussani and U. Mattei in their article, 'The Common Core Approach to European Private Law', *Journal of European Law*, 1997–8, pp. 339 ff.

[3] See for example, U. Mattei, *Economic Analysis and Comparative Law* (Ann Arbor, 1998).

[4] See P. H. Glenn, *Legal Traditions* (Oxford, 2000). No suggestion that legal traditions do not exist should be drawn from this statement, since their existence or their historical and contemporary significance are in no way denied.

[5] See K. Zweigert and H. Kötz, *Introduction to Comparative Law* (Oxford, 1998); R. David and C. Jauffret-Spinosi, *Les grands systèmes de droit contemporain* (11th edn, Paris, 2002).

extra-legal or extrinsic considerations.[6] It is of course one thing to identify these common characteristics, which often create groups, the pattern of which sometimes requires explanation: for example, why does German law side with England, Ireland and Scotland in Case 2? Why do England and the Netherlands sit side by side producing comparable results in Case 9? Our first step will consist in presenting the evidence, the second in attempting to explain it. In this respect our aims are relatively modest and are confined to speculative inductive observations.

Empirical results: conclusions on the cases

Case 1: Anatole v. Bob

Three legal systems admitted mistake (Greece, Germany and Portugal) but if the mistaken party pays negative interest (Greek and German law solutions) then the remedy is ineffective in practice. Austrian law coincided with the remedy given by Portugal, this time under the head of *laesio enormis*.

The majority of legal systems (in which we would include Germany and Greece for the reasons explained above) did not award a remedy to the purchaser here. It should be noticed that the minority does not consist of common law countries.

There is a common core of eleven legal systems where no remedy is available to the seller, Anatole.

Case 2: Célimène v. Damien

Nine legal systems admitted a remedy on the grounds of mistake (Austria, France, Belgium, Germany, Greece, Italy, the Netherlands, Portugal and Spain). The actual remedy on the facts would not be annulment but either restitution of the monetary equivalent (France, Belgium, Germany, Italy, Portugal and Spain) or by adapting the contract (Austria and the Netherlands). Exceptionally, under Greek law the seller might be awarded restitution of the paintings, although the analysis is controversial.

Another group of two is formed by Austria and Belgium that would grant annulment on the basis of *laesio enormis* or its equivalent.

---

[6] See the guidelines given to the Trento working groups. A civilian lawyer may well call these considerations or values 'extra-legal', although this could provoke a jurisprudential debate, since it is quite conceivable to explain these values as forming an intrinsic part of what the law is.

Four legal systems gave no remedy for mistake (England, Ireland, Norway and Scotland). The statement needs further qualification. Norway does not know and use the concept of mistake as such. English and Irish law did not recognise that there is a mistake here. Scots law may admit a mistake here but failed to give a remedy in practice because the rules on restitution are more severe and are barred by the passing of property to a third party.

Nine legal systems, but not exactly the same nine as under mistake (Austria, France, Belgium, Greece, Italy, Norway, Portugal, Spain and the Netherlands), admitted a remedy on the basis of fraudulent non-disclosure. Fraud is preferable to mistake for evidential reasons and, in addition, damages may be cumulated with a claim to annul the contract.

Four legal systems (England, Germany, Ireland and Scotland) did not admit fraudulent non-disclosure on the facts. Three of the four do not recognise this concept and German law would not give a remedy in these circumstances. The attitude of these countries can perhaps be explained on the basis of an economic rationale, but this is to some extent speculative. In any event, this cluster destroys the common law/civil law dividing line.

If a practical approach is taken there is a common core of nine legal systems admitting a remedy but under three distinct legal grounds.

Case 3: Emile v. Far Eastern Delights

Three hypotheses are possible here, the second of which gives rise to a practically unanimous answer.

(i) If the seller honestly believed the contents of its sale catalogue were true, seven legal systems (Austria, Belgium, France, Greece, Italy, Portugal and the Netherlands) would give a remedy for mistake and three (England, Ireland and Scotland) for innocent misrepresentation. It is relatively uncontroversial that innocent misrepresentation overlaps conceptually with other (civil law) versions of mistake so this constitutes a common core. Again, the minority is not easily explicable. A cluster made up of Germany, Norway and Spain does not fit into a pattern and a variety of factors may be invoked to explain why these three legal systems diverge from the majority in their solution (e.g. no concept of mistake for Norway, *lex specialis* rules prevent mistake being invoked in Germany etc).

(ii) If the seller was fraudulent, e.g. knew that the contents of its catalogue were untrue, there is unanimity (except for Norway, see (iii)) that a remedy lies to the purchaser on the ground of fraud (Austria, Belgium,

France, Greece, Italy, Portugal, Spain, the Netherlands), or fraudulent representation (England, Germany, Ireland and Scotland). In English law the seller's suspicion that the statement was untrue would suffice. In a sense the solution is unsurprising and wholly unobjectionable since a fraudulent disclosure is a clear-cut example. One could ask whether art. 4:107 of the Principles of European Contract Law represents a fusion of the various legal concepts as it would clearly apply here. One important difference must be highlighted: the PECL provisions treat liability as contractual not as precontractual (see (iii)).

(iii) The choice of remedy between defective consent and breach of contract has also been examined. In most legal systems a remedy will also lie for the purchaser for breach of contract. Norway provides a contractual remedy which is distinct from other contractual remedies in that it specifically covers the seller's duty to disclose accurate information about the sale. Such a provision, imposing strict liability on the seller, avoids the purchaser having to invoke fraud, as above.

There is a common core for mistake and fraud; Norway is the exception. Norwegian law converges on the actual solution but note that the legal categorisation is quite distinct: the seller is under a strict liability to inform the buyer and his liability is contractual (as opposed to precontractual).

Case 4: Mr and Mrs Timeless v. Mr and Mrs Careless

(i) If the seller was not fraudulent, mistake could be invoked and was admitted by Austria, France, Portugal and the Netherlands. Italy might give a remedy on the basis of a fundamental contractual assumption. If these remedies are cumulated, four legal systems might give a remedy to the buyer on these facts.

In contrast, eight legal systems did not give a remedy under mistake, but once again the cluster is somewhat heterogeneous. England, Ireland and Scotland did not recognise a unilateral mistake as to quality; Greece considered the mistake too subjective. The prevalence of *lex specialis* prevented mistake operating under German law and Norway did not recognise mistake. In Austria and Belgium the mistake was barred as inexcusable. There is a common core that no remedy is available under mistake.

(ii) If the seller was fraudulent, fraudulent non-disclosure would take over from mistake for Austria, Belgium, France, Germany, Greece, Spain, the Netherlands, Norway and Portugal. Two distinct categories can be observed: Germany awards a contractual remedy (damages to cover the expectation interest) on the basis of contractual fraud as does Norway (on the basis of a breach of a contractual duty to inform), whereas all the other systems grant a remedy on the basis of precontractual liability. In contrast, the same does not hold true under English, Irish and Scots law. This case shows that certain countries impose a 'higher' standard of dealing or behaviour between the parties. This behaviour requires parties to consider one another's interests (as well as their own). It has been suggested elsewhere that such an attitude can be explained on moral grounds and that the common law attitude is probably explained by a prevailing priority given to economic considerations.

A majority of legal systems would give a remedy for fraudulent concealment or breach of a duty to inform.

(iii) Austria and Germany and Italy also gave a contractual remedy for breach of the obligation to transfer the property with good title.

Case 5: Bruno v. The Local Garage

Solutions to this case were examined under the head of (i) defective consent and (ii) breach of contract.

(i) Ten legal systems admitted a remedy for fraud. Three admitted mistake and three innocent misrepresentation (see the remarks made in Case 3 on the functional equivalence of these two concepts). It is interesting to note that the mistake/misrepresentation cluster breaks through the common law/civil law wall.

(ii) Breach of contract remedies, variously defined as a guarantee against hidden defects, non-conformity or breach of description, also give rise to a majority solution admitting a remedy, if once again functionally equivalent comparisons are drawn. Comparing the different national concepts used to found breach of contract is admittedly speculative. The complexity of harmonising such conceptually diverse legal concepts may perhaps explain the presence of Directive 1999/44/EC.[7] Subsequent case law interpreting the transposition of the above Directive will enable us to consider more clearly how or whether such functional equivalence can be made. In any event, before European attempts to harmonise,[8] one of the issues raised by this case was that of determining the availability and reasons for choosing a remedy for defective consent or for breach of contract. It can be inferred that once the European

---

[7] It should be pointed out that not all national reporters have incorporated this Directive as it had not yet been transposed at the time of writing their report.

[8] Harmonisation will certainly not be total as art. 7.1 of the Directive allows a derogation in relation to time limits concerning second-hand goods.

Directive has been transposed, such a choice will be displaced to a certain extent. This induction confirms the increasingly residual nature of defective consent remedies observed in this study. Although the choice may not be entirely eliminated[9] by the implementation of the Directive, it will inevitably be altered in the future.[10]

Case 6: Emmanuel v. The Computer Shop

A division as to legal concepts used is balanced against a certain harmony of solution.

(i) As far as remedies for defective consent are concerned, nine legal systems provided relief as follows: Belgium, Portugal, Greece and the Netherlands admitted mistake. France and Belgium raised the possibility of relying on a statutory duty to inform. Belgium, France and Spain admitted a variety of fraud. Germany, Greece, Italy and Portugal relied on breach of good faith *culpa in contrahendo*, now a precontractual duty to inform in Germany. Norway could invoke a statutory invalidity provision although this would not be used in practice.

(ii) Some of the systems provided remedies for breach of contract as an alternative; others provided remedies under both heads. Austria, Germany, England and Ireland might provide a remedy on the basis of a breach of collateral contract (relating to the existence of the maintenance contract). The Netherlands would provide a remedy for non-conformity. Furthermore, Norway and the Netherlands would grant a remedy on the basis of a contractual statutory duty to inform or help the other contracting party.

Only Scotland does not provide a remedy here. Twelve legal systems provide a remedy to the claimant with a considerable diversity of legal grounds.

In addition, a major enquiry as to whether priority should be given to precontractual or contractual remedies needs to be considered (see below).

Case 7: Cinderella

The solution reached by a majority that there is no remedy for the buyer is achieved by a number of analyses. It was unanimously agreed

---

[9] This statement should be qualified: the concurrence of such an action is considered to be of more concern in some legal systems than in others. To take an example, the French Law Commission of October 2000 explicitly proposed maintaining concurrent actions for non-conformity and mistake.

[10] It is suggested that the presumption of conformity (a concept open no doubt to multiple interpretations) would push a claimant to choose a contractual remedy since evidential difficulties will be alleviated.

that mistake is not operative here. Only exceptionally would a duty to inform be imposed as a result of a general clause, as opposed to specific provisions contained in legislation. Three factual interpretations were feasible. It was a deliberate choice to leave a margin of factual ambiguity in the cases at times, since all cases that come to court inevitably contain a degree of factual ambiguity and the interest of this study has been to reveal this process, and to examine how national reporters interpret the case.

More precisely, if the sale was made by the company, only three legal systems would award a remedy (Norway and Portugal under specific company law provisions; Germany under the *culpa in contrahendo* doctrine). If the sale was made by a director of the company, no remedy would be granted. If the sale was made by a financial agent, three legal systems might give a remedy (France, Italy and Norway), although this interpretation was admittedly strained, the result rather of an isolated instance than a general rule.

To conclude, the underlying explanation for this solution lies in economic considerations that condition the functioning of the stock market.

Case 8: Estella v. Uriah Heep

European legislation on long-distance and credit sales results in a unanimous solution in favour of the buyer invoking her rights to cancel the contract.

Under defects of consent or remedies for breach of consent only a minority were prepared to grant a remedy. Five legal systems (Austria, Germany – subject to reservation, Greece, the Netherlands and Portugal) admit an operative mistake. Four (Austria, Belgium, Germany and Greece) would admit a breach of the duty to inform. Three (Austria, Belgium and Greece) would give a remedy under the action for a guarantee against hidden defects.

The main point of this case is to expand our enquiry into the overlap between remedies under *leges speciales* and those for defects of consent. The result of this case, as already mentioned, is that it appears that the consumer will have less protection than before the introduction of consumer protection laws. This conclusion is not only startling but also a cause for concern. Is European harmonisation working? On one level, the answer is positive since as seen above harmony has been achieved. On another, if the end-goal of such legislation is to protect consumers, the reply is less certain. The hypothesis that a consumer fails to act within the cancellation time limits is more than plausible.

Case 9: Nell v. Scrooge Bank

(i) Austrian, Dutch, English, German, Greek, Italian, Norwegian and Scottish law admitted that the contract can be annulled, but Germany, Greece and Norway rendered annulment ineffective by the requirement to pay negative interest damages. In practice, then, a satisfactory remedy would be available in five legal systems.

(ii) The solutions given to this case break down any preconceptions leaning in favour of the idea that certain legal systems are generally more protective than others. Moreover, the perennial difficulty of how to catch the fraud of a third party to the contract remains unanswered by the majority of countries. Three important and highly instructive exceptions exist.[11] The English solution requires the lender to tell the guarantor of the extent of her liability as a surety, to warn her of the risk she is running and to take independent legal advice.[12] This cannot be characterised as a duty to inform although it serves a similar purpose. The solution provided by the Netherlands is even more progressive since it puts the onus on the lender to make enquiries; such an obligation arises under general provisions relating to defects of consent; the final exception, under Austrian law, provides for the same obligation incumbent on the lender as a result of a *lex specialis*.

It appears that this case would not give rise to a remedy if the provisions concerning mistake in the PECL were applied. Fraud cannot be invoked because of the third party question discussed above. In relation to discussions about a European Civil Code the result of this case may sound a note of warning. If it is suggested that principles for the Code should be determined according to the positive law of the majority of member states, there is a flaw. This case shows that this criterion is not the only guiding factor for law-making, since it is quantitative and not qualitative. To put it another way, will adopting the majority solution produce 'better law' here?

---

[11] Those provided by England and the Netherlands will be the object of more general concluding observations below.

[12] See the English report. It has recently been submitted in *The Royal Bank of Scotland* v. *Etridge (No. 2)* (2001) UKHL 44 that 'the protection needed by wives differs from, and goes beyond, the disclosure of information', per Lord Nicholls at para. 81.

Case 10: Zachary

A variety of reactions to double insurance can be seen. The Netherlands and Portugal consider double insurance invalid. Austria and Belgium allow the insured to cancel or invalidate the insurance policy, if made with a different insurer. Five legal systems considered that the contract could be annulled on the ground of mistake (Austria, Greece and Italy), the lack of basis of the transaction (Germany) or perhaps for absence of *cause* (France). England, France, Ireland, Norway, Scotland and Spain consider that double insurance is valid. Several reporters have admitted more than one hypothesis. To summarise: the majority view is not clear and will depend on whether the French hypothesis of *absence de cause* is recognised or not.

No doubt economic considerations, namely the cost of making enquiries, helps to explain the solution: only Germany as an outstanding exception suggested that an insurer should be obliged to inform the insured about the existence of the double insurance policy in cases where the insurance is effected with the same insurer. Generally, legal systems providing protection for the insured party have chosen to do so through other means. This case confirms two recurrent themes observed throughout this study (see below in general conclusion). First, that the duty to inform is not always efficient (this may explain why certain legal systems do not favour it). Secondly, that by imposing the duty to inform, the obliged party has a reinforced standard of behaviour. One way the law can attempt to raise behavioural norms is to deem that the party under the duty to inform has knowledge, i.e. possesses the relevant information. Advancing one step further implies that this information must be disclosed to the other party.

Case 11: Monstrous Inventions Ltd v. Mary Shelley

A majority of nine legal systems did not allow the company to annul the contract. Only Austria was prepared to admit a mistake, and Greece and the Netherlands relied on the absence of the basis of the transaction and an unforeseen change of circumstances. As for the duty to inform, only Norway (and perhaps the Netherlands) accepted that the employee's behaviour amounted to a breach of good faith and honest behaviour.

This case illustrates the limits of the duty to inform when the information is personal in content (for the person possessing it). The law does not expect people to behave against their own self-interest, absent fraud or bad faith. This shows the very open-ended norm of good faith,[13] which some would argue renders it somewhat unhelpful as a guideline.

Case 12: Lady Windermere v. Angel

This case has produced quasi-unanimity since nearly all countries agreed that the gift could be annulled or rectified for mistake. A number of explanations may help. The mistake in question relates to a mistake in terms. The transaction under consideration is a gift, the donee is generally considered less worthy of protection since he has given no value. In certain legal systems the absence of reliance by the donee is emphasised, thus suggesting that, *a contrario*, if the donee had relied on the gift, this would be sufficient to disregard the nature of the voluntary transaction and provide a good reason for protection. Other legal systems focusing on the behaviour of the parties, note that the donee knew or should have known that the gift was not meant for him. Economic and moral considerations may also be invoked in order to explain the solution of this case.

Four observations can be inferred from these empirical results. First, in only two cases out of twelve was there unanimity over the solution and the legal techniques used to achieve the solution. Of these two, Case 3 was based on fraud and Case 8 on the basis of harmonising European legislation. As already noted a majority agreement on the solution of the cases has been identified in eleven out of twelve cases. Secondly, the consensus on result (be it in favour of or against a remedy being granted) is qualified by a major reservation: an incredible diversity and richness of legal concepts have been employed to reach each solution. This is of course unsurprising and can be resumed by stating the obvious: there are many different ways of looking at the same object. Thirdly, mistake is used decreasingly, it is becoming a subsidiary remedy in the face of *leges speciales* or is being taken over, to a varying extent, by the duty to inform. Conversely, the duty to inform is on the increase, either as a result of *leges speciales* or as a result of case law constructions.

Finally, at the outset, it was stated that one of the aims of this study was to investigate the accuracy of preconceptions about the dividing line between civil law and common law countries. This aim has been achieved as this study has demonstrated that dividing lines exist but they do not always fall where expected. It is submitted that the legal

---

[13] R. Zimmerman and S. Whittaker (eds.), *Good Faith in European Contract Law* (Cambridge, 2000), pp. 30–2.

concepts are insufficient by themselves to explain the similarities and differences. We shall therefore attempt to explain the dividing lines by examining the underlying rationales of the law (or of the national laws).

Explaining the dividing lines: underlying rationales

This study has demonstrated that the legal systems considered each have a different conception of mistake. Four main features can be extracted from each different viewpoint. These focus points represent each law's emphasis or priority in terms of how mistake is envisaged. The first points to the role of causation – how was the mistake caused? This viewpoint looks at the behaviour of the non-mistaken party. The second examines the question of fault – whose fault was it that the mistake occurred? Looked at from this angle, the law tends to concentrate rather on the mistaken party's behaviour (was it excusable or not?). The third concentrates on the knowledge of the parties; this viewpoint looks at both parties' behaviour and state of mind and also focuses on the importance to the parties of certain information about the contract's content. The fourth examines the distribution of risks. The parties' behaviour is no longer relevant, it is their economic choice that matters. It is submitted that the duty to provide information (informational power) is a key factor to understanding these viewpoints and may explain why certain countries admit mistake more easily than others. In order to confirm this hypothesis, an attempt to identify the underlying rationales will be made which will allow us to find a place for the duty to inform.

In order to identify the underlying rationales of mistake, a conceptual distinction proposed by Zweigert and Kotz will be adopted: that of focusing on the mistake itself and that of emphasising how the mistake was caused.[14] The former will be called a static view of mistake; the latter dynamic since the focus is on the way in which the mistake arose. It may be that these two viewpoints represent two extremes. It may also be true that the tendency to adopt a static view is evolving towards a more dynamic view of mistake. Starting from the static view of mistake, four main underlying tendencies will be further outlined, some of which may overlap and illustrate a progression, a change in attitude towards dynamic mistake.

---

[14] Zweigert and Kötz, *Introduction to Comparative Law*, pp. 423 ff.

Underlying tendencies in the static view of mistake

At the outset, it is possible to identify a mistake that occurs before a party's intention has been fully formulated. If such a mistake were recognised it could be explained as an extreme form of intention-based protection. In this instance party autonomy is exaggerated, since protection is given to what is in a party's mind, before the mistake has been declared (externalised). It is perhaps for this reason, as well as for evidential ones, that this can be qualified as the weakest type of mistake that is the least justified in being a ground for annulment. As outlined above, no system qualifies such a mistake as operative.

Moving on from a mistake in the party's mind, the next stage is to identify mistakes made that affect a party's intention. This shall be called intention-based protection. Whether the mistake is identified in the declaration of intent as in German law (§ 119 BGB) or as vitiating the party's will, as in French law (art. 1110 Code Civil), the mistaken party's interests are prominent. This is the best example of static mistake since the mistake itself is emphasised and little attention is paid to how it was caused. The importance of the parties' intentions and the will theory justify annulling the contract on this ground since to be properly bound a party's intention or will must be clear and free from defects. The emphasis is quite clearly on the mistaken party, to whom the law gives priority.

This viewpoint nevertheless admits a variety of degrees. French law probably provides the most extreme version since the mere fact of a mistake can suffice to annul the contract, and the interests of the non-mistaken party are overridden. German law will annul under § 119 BGB but § 122 BGB puts a limit on annulment, which is not, therefore, absolute. As already seen, the same is also true of Greek and Portuguese law. The qualification is that the mistaken party must compensate the negative interest suffered by the non-mistaken party. It may be that German law is thus a half-way house or a transition towards the next category.

Proceeding from an enquiry that concentrates on the mistaken party, the next tendency is to seek to protect the other (non-mistaken) party's reliance. This will be called reliance-based protection. Here more emphasis is given to the position of the non-mistaken party in the sense that annulment will be given at the cost of compensating the non-mistaken party and his reliance on the contract's validity. It may be misleading to term this reliance-based[15] since we are also looking at the question

---

[15] In other words, the term reliance is used *sensu lato* in this context.

of whether it is unfair to dash the non-mistaken party's expectations of the contract's fulfilment.

As stated before, German law creates a nuance between intention-based and reliance-based protection since a mistaken party may have to compensate the non-mistaken party. Austrian law goes one step further towards what can be clearly termed a reliance-based attitude since it examines to what extent the non-mistaken party is worthy of protection. Protecting the non-mistaken party's reliance may even be a reason for refusing the claim for annulment (§ 871 ABGB). If, for example, the non-mistaken party has acted in reliance on the contract, e.g. by incurring expenses, this will prevent the contract from being annulled. Austrian law protects the non-mistaken party more than German law in this respect. However, the non-mistaken party will not be protected if no reliance damages have actually been suffered or if the non-mistaken party caused or knew of the mistake. Here a new element is introduced, that of the circumstances of the occurrence of the mistake – a focus on the causing of the mistake. This element is to some extent shared by the common law's attitude to mistake.[16]

At the opposite extreme is the view which prefers that security of transactions be upheld over and above annulment on the basis of mistake (referred to as 'commerce-based protection'). This underlying rationale cares less for the mistaken and non-mistaken party and concentrates on the overall effect on the market of annulling the contract, not from one or both of the contracting parties' points of view. According to the common law's point of view, only a factual fundamental common mistake (shared by the parties) will annul the contract since the danger of impugning transactions and disturbing the market balance prevails. This extreme position does not give preferential treatment either to the mistaken or non-mistaken party. Arguably the emphasis is different for an additional reason, that of analysing the question in terms of the risks to be borne by each party. Taking into account the question of risks is a sign of a more general shift in contractual values and one which is increasingly recognised by legal systems (but not all of them) away from the contract based on the will theory.

A movement of change: dynamic mistake

Although it is more common to recognise that the English law of mistake takes into account the way in which the mistake was caused,[17] this is

---

[16] See (b) below.   [17] Zweigert and Kötz, *Introduction to Comparative Law*, p. 420.

true of other national laws as well. Although some authors relegate the narrow version of English mistake to what we have called static mistake and misrepresentation to the dynamic part of mistake, this may not be the only place where dynamic mistake can be identified. In order to explain where dynamic mistake can be found in other legal systems, it may be helpful to isolate some uses of terminology that have the effect of bringing the contrast between static and dynamic mistake into the open. So far, we have chosen to denominate the parties as the 'mistaken party' and the 'non-mistaken party'. This is no accident, since identifying the mistaken party as promisor or promisee does not really help matters. If we look at § 119 BGB in German law, for example, the law of mistake speaks of the mistake of the person making the declaration, but does not differentiate as to whether the declarer is the promisor or promisee since the term 'declaration of intent' covers a wide variety of juridical acts.[18] Likewise, in French law, since the accent is on the mistaken party, it is important to notice that as a mistaken party the claimant may be either the promisor[19] or the promisee.[20] In any event, neither French law nor German law looks under the law of mistake to see how (i.e. by whom, in what circumstances) the mistake was caused. It follows logically that unilateral mistakes will be admitted.

It has already been suggested that the emphasis on the causing of the mistake will, to some extent, be linked to what sort of mistakes (made by one or both of the parties) will be recognised. In contrast to French and German law, Austrian law, for example, does look at whether the non-mistaken party caused the mistake (or should have known of it) in determining whether the non-mistaken party's interests should counterbalance or override those of the mistaken party (§ 871 ABGB). Under this interpretation, either mistaken party could claim to annul the contract for its mistake, although both of them may be protected for their reliance on the validity of the contract.[21] A similar emphasis on whether the non-mistaken party knew or should have known of the mistake is made under Italian, Portuguese and Dutch law.[22]

---

[18] See further the explanation given in Chapter 2, pp. 60–61.

[19] The legendary example is that of the *affaire Poussin* – the sellers, as promisors, were entitled to annul the sale in which they were mistaken about the subject matter of their sale. See French report, Case 1.

[20] Another standard example would be of the buyer (promisee) who annuls the contract due to his mistake as to the object of the sale.

[21] This opinion is subject to criticism from scholars, for a new view that common mistake should be dealt with under, and not in addition to, the provisions of § 871, see Rummel Koziol and Honzell (see the Austrian report in Case 1).

[22] See General Introduction, p. 21.

At the other end of the spectrum, in legal systems where shared mistakes are expressly recognised, i.e. under English, Scots and Irish law, it is somewhat inevitable that the law takes into account the way in which the mistake was caused and not only in the realm of a misrepresentation-induced mistake. As an illustration, the Court of Appeal has held that a common mistake of fact is required to annul a contract.[23] However, a qualification must be made: a shared or common mistake will only be an illustration of dynamic mistake if the mistake has been caused by one of the contracting parties (as opposed to a third party). One of the questions raised by our enquiry is to examine whether looking at how mistake is caused is a trend that is being increasingly used.

One of the results of this study has shown that the law is putting more emphasis on the parties' behaviour. This emphasis on the parties' behaviour has also been called an awareness or a raising of standards of contractual behaviour more generally. This may be a natural or at least predictable consequence arising from the move away from intention-based protection (denial of the will theory as the basis of contract). This shift is represented by the two focus points of causation and fault since whether or not some legal systems admit mistake depends on one of these two factors or sometimes both. We have ascertained that some legal systems focus on how the mistake was caused by the non-mistaken party, i.e. by the other party's statements or silence;[24] others consider whether the mistake was caused by the mistaken party itself, or to put it another way, was it the mistaken party's fault? This viewpoint is more often framed in terms of the excusability or inexcusability of the mistake.

This change in focus once again explains the initial choice to examine mistake and the duty to inform concurrently, as it is believed that the

---

[23] *The Great Peace* (2002). See Chapter 3, pp. 79–85.

[24] It is of course debatable whether silence, i.e. non-disclosure can cause a mistake in the same way as a positive statement, i.e. disclosure may cause a mistake, as in the case of misrepresentation under English, Scots and Irish law. John Cartwright has expressed his scepticism to me but I consider that an omission can cause a mistake. Imagine the case where the failure to provide information leads to the mistake (see Case 6 on the sale of the computer and the salesman's silence as to the existence of the maintenance contract). Is it misleading to say that the failure to provide information caused the mistaken party's mistake? If the argument is reversed, the chain of causation may be proven. If the information had been provided (that the computer sale did not include a maintenance contract) then the mistake would not have been made. It was therefore caused by the omission to provide information along the lines of a 'but for' criterion of causation.

emergence of the duty to inform may be a decisive factor in the change. The effect of the change can be summarised as a move from intention-based protection where the emphasis is on the consent of the party to the contract to reliance-based protection where the emphasis is on the content of the contract. The results of this study have demonstrated this change of perspective yet one rhetorical question remains: is the relationship between static and dynamic mistake one of cause and effect? Is the fact of attributing knowledge and consequent risks to the parties a cause of the change towards a dynamic mistake or is it the effect of such a change?

The PECL provisions on mistake are in this respect revealing. Article 4:103 clearly puts the emphasis on the information provided by the contracting parties and the knowledge of the parties of the importance of this information.

PECL 4:103 MISTAKE

1. A party may avoid a contract for mistake of fact or law existing when the contract was concluded if:
   a) (i) the mistake was caused by information given by the other party; or
      (ii) the other party knew or ought to have known of the mistake and it was contrary to good faith and fair dealing to leave the mistaken party in error; or
      (iii) the other party made the same mistake, and
   b) the other party knew or ought to have known that the mistaken party, had it known the truth, would not have entered the contract or would have done so only on fundamentally different terms.
2. However a party may not avoid the contract if:
   a) in the circumstances, the mistake was inexcusable, or
   b) the risk of the mistake was assumed, or in the circumstance should be borne, by it.

This emphasis is outlined in the three alternative conditions for mistake to be operative as follows: (i) the causation criterion (did the other party cause the mistake?); or (ii) the knowledge criterion (did the other party know of the mistake or should he have known?) linked to the parties' behaviour interpreted through good faith and fair dealing; or (iii) the fact that the mistake is made by both parties. One of these conditions is cumulated with a further knowledge criterion by the non-mistaken party of the significance of the mistake. Furthermore, a claim to avoid for mistake is barred either by the fault of the mistaken party or when the risk of the mistake was assumed or should have been assumed in the circumstances.

The causation criterion is potentially quite wide. On one reading it would cover mistakes caused by information given negligently or innocently by the non-mistaken party. For some systems this might be considered as an overly-generous protection. This is of course a question of policy. The knowledge criterion linked to good faith and fair dealing includes actual and constructive knowledge.[25] It clearly imposes a standard of behaviour on contracting parties to act honestly and fairly with one another. In order to understand the implications of this provision it is crucial to consider whether this provision is aimed at reliance-based or commerce-based protection. As it is clearly not aimed at intention-based protection, that question will not be considered. Moreover, it is not necessarily the case that the purposes of reliance-based and commerce-based protection are opposed to one another. The drafting seems to be sufficiently wide to allow judicial interpretation to take into account both underlying rationales, although this does not necessarily mean that both rationales will always be admitted. If the text does not dictate the rationale that some may consider objectionable,[26] it follows that if judges were to employ this provision they would sometimes be obliged to choose one of these rationales. In other words, when presented with a dispute, the judges will determine what is contrary to good faith and fair dealing (either on the basis of reliance or commerce or both) in order to decide whether or not the mistake is operative. Judicial interpretation will no doubt be coloured by national legal concepts as well as extra-legal considerations (social, political, economic, cultural etc.). If such a hypothesis is not refuted, arguably, judges will carry on doing what they did before the introduction of such a provision. The main practical benefit would be to have evacuated intention-based protection on the grounds that it no longer corresponds to our conception of the contract nor of contract-making.

Bearing these underlying rationales in mind, the prevalence of the duty to inform and its significance in the law of contract needs further consideration. If a shift in underlying rationales has been identified, inevitably legal concepts must adapt as well.

---

[25] It is beyond the scope of this study to assess whether this criterion is useful and workable. On good faith, see Zimmerman and Whittaker (eds.), *Good Faith in European Contract Law.*

[26] Certain authors have recently expressed the desire for a text if incorporated in a code to be more and not less political: see U. Mattei, 'Hard Minimal Code Now' in S. Grundmann and J. Stuyck (eds.), *An Academic Green Paper on European Contract Law* (The Hague, Boston, London, 2002), p. 215.

General conclusions

Extrapolating from the duty to inform: the present and the future

The main preoccupation of this enquiry has focused on duties to inform and their relationship with mistake and fraud. We have seen that the scope of duty to inform is broader than that of mistake and fraud; while overlapping these two concepts it also widens their range since it includes negligent behaviour, which is not admitted by all legal systems under consideration; moreover duties to inform differ from traditional defects of consent. One difference lies in the source of duties to inform, which can arise in three ways. First, duties to inform have been derived as a result of case law interpretation of codified provisions: these provisions concern legal concepts belonging to the defects of consent, i.e. mistake and fraud. On one view this is a duty that has used an existing legal concept as a stepping stone. Secondly, also as a result of case law interpretation, duties to inform have been inferred from general clauses also present in codified systems, the most obvious example of which is the old § 242 BGB (now §§ 311 II, 241 II, 280), now classified as a precontractual duty to inform. In one sense, the distinction between these two sources of duties to inform is rather fine since arguably both categories are just examples of extensive case law interpretation of codified concepts. Thirdly, duties to inform have been imposed by specific legislation, either by national legislation or by the transposition of European Directives. A question then arises as to why case law and also, to an even greater extent, European legislation[27] have used duties to inform. Does the duty to inform fulfil a particular purpose not fulfilled by existing legal concepts and does it function well?

In the light of the empirical and comparative observations made throughout this study, it may now be useful to identify what function the duty to inform is fulfilling in European contract law. This will enable us in turn to reassess our initial hypothesis, namely that the duty to inform has a protective function.

This study has shown that duties to inform are indeed protective, but not along the lines of the classical model. First, if the legislative source of the duty to inform is considered, protection is directed at certain

---

[27] Emphasising the legal formant is critical here since it is submitted that specific duties to inform imposed by legislation may fulfil a different purpose than duties derived from case law. The reason is that legislative duties are general in their application, as opposed to casuistic and moreover, they are limited to certain types of contractual relationships.

categories of persons in specific contracts (special relationship theory). Secondly, and consequently, duties to inform have been shown to set standards of behaviour. This is substantiated by the recent green paper of the European Commission on Consumer Protection which includes the duty to disclose as one of the relevant elements of fair dealing.[28] A further question follows: why is this necessary, why should the law tell contracting parties how to behave? Thirdly, the requirement of a duty to inform illustrates the shift towards focusing on *the content of the contract and not the quality of the party's consent*. The emphasis lies not on informed consent but on being informed about the contract's content.[29] One explanation of this tendency would be to classify this as an effect of the standardisation of contracts: as contracts are increasingly standardised, the duty to inform helps guarantee that a minimum contractual content exists and that the parties know about it. It is suggested that these three functions of the duty to inform are interrelated.

(i) The first assertion that the duty to inform is directed at certain categories of persons can be substantiated by the examples in cases where the party who is the recipient of the information is in a special relationship with the other party. A special relationship may be expressed by law. The person to whom the information is owed may be a consumer in a contract of sale or credit (Cases 6 and 8); a guarantor (Case 9); or an insurer (Case 10). A special relationship, expressed by case law, can also be inferred from the status of the parties. The presence of a duty to inform owed by an employee to his employer was not demonstrated on the facts (Case 11). At first sight, this finding is surprising in view of the relationship between employers and employees, generally presumed to comport a reinforced duty of cooperation[30] and considered to belong to a special relationship either by law or from the status of the parties. However, it appears that an employee's duty to disclose to the employer is not absolute. This contrasts with an insured's duty to inform the insurer, which is practically unlimited. It may be inferred first that a duty to inform cannot be deduced from every special relationship, the relation between the two criteria is not deductive but subject to casuistic

---

[28] See *Follow-Up Communication to the Green Paper on EU Consumer Protection*, Com (2002) 289 Final, containing proposals for a framework directive for consumer protection.

[29] *Ibid.*, again, the Commission's Green Paper illustrates this nicely.

[30] This may be expressed in some jurisdictions under the wide heading of good faith, it could also be expressed in terms of a fiduciary relationship or by the presence of an obligation of confidentiality between the parties.

considerations. Second, it should be noticed that the special relationship does not necessarily give rise to an equal bilateral duty to inform the other party. For example, in a contract of surety the duty to inform is clearly one-sided (any information required to be given goes from the lender to the guarantor). In insurance and employment relationships, a duty to inform may lie on both parties, though not necessarily to the same degree. Indeed Case 10 highlights the asymmetrical nature of the duty to inform incumbent on the insurer and insured. It is submitted that emphasising that the parties are in a special relationship might be a way of taking the unilateral and asymmetrical nature of this relationship into account. Furthermore, it is contended that the laws' awareness of the parties' asymmetry may be an attempt to recognise that the parties are not equal.

This study has focused to some extent on examining the status of the parties and it is therefore important to examine the relevance of this criterion. First, as already suggested, it may be inferred from the results that the criterion is mainly casuistic and is thus used for a number of purposes. For example, Case 1 has shown that the status of the parties can operate as a bar on the question of whether or not a mistake is excusable. As far as the duty to inform is concerned, the status of the parties may be posited as a condition for the existence of the duty (Case 2 is a good illustration). It is submitted that this is a way of emphasising the person in the contractual relationship.[31] An objective version of contract might not focus on the status of the parties in quite the same way; rather the main question is whether the contract complies with business practice – fair dealing and business usage. Here the emphasis is on the contract, the parties' status is contingent on this. The emphasis is different but that does not mean that the status of the parties is irrelevant to the requirement to impose a duty to inform, as the solution under Norwegian law illustrates.[32] To summarise, in order to determine the existence of a duty to inform both the status of the parties and their relationship to one another may be helpful indices but not necessary conditions.

---

[31] See H. Maine, *Ancient Law: its Connection with the Early History of Society and its Relation to Modern Ideas* (1861) (Everyman's Library Edn, London, 1917) 'from status to contract'. It is open to debate if it is now more appropriate to reverse the phrase 'from contract to status'.

[32] See the Scandinavian report where duties to inform are imposed, because one party has less knowledge and the other party has knowledge or should have had the requisite knowledge, see Case 2 for an example.

(ii) This study has demonstrated that there is a link between imposing duties to inform and raising the standards of behaviour expected
of contracting parties. The relationship may be one of cause and effect:
by imposing duties to inform, certain standards of behaviour are set.
Or it could be the inverse. Since the law purports to raise standards of
behaviour to a certain level, it has achieved this end by means of the
duty to inform. However, this is not the only means: for example, laying
down a requirement that the *errans* has to use a minimum standard of
care, i.e. his behaviour must be excusable, is another way of raising the
standard of behaviour expected of the parties, particularly the *errans*.
Furthermore, this goal is partially achieved through the use of good
faith as a barometer for precontractual behaviour, through (fraudulent)
concealment etc. Apart from concerns that may be raised as to whether
good faith provides a workable and useful standard for contracting parties and the courts,[33] a preliminary question needs to be addressed. Why
is the law concerned with raising standards of behaviour? Is this part of a
standardisation process? This may be part and parcel of the law's
changing view of contract law. A further explanation will be offered
below.

(iii) It is submitted that the objective of contract-making has changed
so that its aim is to achieve a certain minimum content of the contract, judged by an objective standard, to ensure that it corresponds
to the parties' expectations. Duties to inform can be seen as means to
achieve objective standards of contract (if you are properly and sufficiently informed you know what is in the contract) and fair standards
of contract-making. The instrument is novel since it aims to cover both
the content of the contract and the contract-making process (procedural
and substantive fairness).

In the light of the above, the purposes of duties to inform must be
reassessed.

Initially, it was suggested that duties to inform have a protective end-
purpose. This study has demonstrated that there is a connection between
imposing duties to inform and setting standards of behaviour incumbent
on contracting parties. In the light of these findings the nature and the
efficacy of this protection can now be reconsidered.

---

[33] The literature on this question is too abundant to be cited here. See for example G. B.
Teubner, 'Legal Irritants: Good Faith in British Law or How Unifying Law Ends up in
New Divergences', (1998) 61 MLR 11 ff. For a more favourable view of good faith, cf.
Zimmerman and Whittaker (eds), *Good Faith in European Contract Law*.

If the duty to inform forms part of the pattern to protect the reliance of a party, as suggested above, then certain controls are needed. In order to protect reliance, *post hoc facto* protection, as traditionally provided by defects of consent such as mistake and fraud, is insufficient. As already mentioned, annulment is a drastic remedy, it 'protects' too late, it upsets the security of transactions etc. If all three identified functions of the duty to inform are considered, it can be seen that its purpose is not exclusively protective. Indeed, if the duty to inform contributes towards setting standards of behaviour, it can be inferred that its purpose is also normative.[34] Certain behaviour (failing to inform when the duty lies) is thus discouraged since a breach leads to liability. It may be preferable to refer to this as a disincentive measure, prophylaxis rather than punishment. As suggested elsewhere, punishment has criminal or moral overtones that do not fit with all legal systems' conception of contract law.[35]

It has been suggested that the third function of the duty to inform is linked to changing views of contract law where the content of the contract lies at the core and not the unvitiated consent of the parties. The purpose behind this function is rather difficult to characterise; indeed it might not be feasible to do so. Perhaps this is a side effect of the standardisation of contracts that norms must be set for behaviour and content. Perhaps there is no relation of cause and effect. However, the relationship between the duty to inform and the content of the contract, namely the impact of the information on the contract, clearly exists. Rather than speculating on the nature of this relationship, it may be more helpful to examine its content, nature and efficacy.

The content of the duty to inform

The material content of information provided in accordance with a duty to inform can be divided into (a) procedural rights (e.g. cancellation) about the dynamic process of contract-making and (b) the content of the contract itself. This distinction is highlighted in the case where the

---

[34] Some might prefer to suggest that this is an example of the regulatory effect of private law on the market. See H. Collins, *Regulating Contracts* (Oxford, 1999). See also, in a similar vein, for an account of how private law could enforce rules on marketing information, T. Wilhelmsson, 'Contract Law Enforcement of Provisions on Marketing' in H. Collins (ed.), *The Forthcoming Directive on Unfair Commercial Practices: Contract, Competition and Consumer Law Implications* (The Hague, London, New York, 2004), pp. 223 ff.

[35] See in General Introduction, p. 9.

transposition of a European Directive has resulted in harmonised solutions (see Case 8). Breach of the second category entitles the consumer who ought to have received the information to prolong the former category, i.e. cancellation rights. This illustrates that certain information is considered crucially important for the contracting parties to perform the contract (otherwise their contractual relationship is suspended or discontinued).

The nature of duty to inform: reliance-based liability

Examining the content of the duty to inform raises further enquiries into the nature of this duty. This study has demonstrated that the duty to inform is a negative and positive duty: the national legal systems' various attitudes to silence have been compared, e.g. in Cases 2, 4 and 6. Requiring a party to disclose information is a way of admitting the parties' inequality: this may be deduced, *a contrario*, from treating silence as reprehensible. The inequality itself is engendered by the presence of materially important information affecting the contract to which only one party has access. At least two explanations are possible: a moral explanation and an economic efficiency argument.

The moral explanation would suggest that imposing a duty to provide information is evidence of, or can be measured in terms of a norm of behaviour. A stark example can be given by referring to Case 4. According to the common law's interpretation of these facts, relying on the *caveat emptor* principle and allowing the seller to remain silent implies that the parties behave on an equal footing. It is plausible to suggest that this allows the parties to behave in a self-interested fashion, i.e. they are allowed to look after their own interests. There is no value statement attached to this observation. The contrary view adheres to a morally different view of human nature. If the seller is obliged to inform the buyer about the changes to the right of way affecting the property, arguably this forces the party in possession of the information to take into account the other party's interests. It could be submitted that this raises the standard of behaviour between the parties, or to put it another way, the level of what constitutes 'fair dealing' is placed at a higher rung up the ladder. Once again, no value statement is intended. The induction is empirical and not normative. Another way of looking at this is that it is not only a moral issue but also a political one. Kennedy explains these two opposing sets of moral values or codes as individualism versus altruism, suggesting that the law makes inherently political choices about its priorities.[36] To summarise: the presence or absence of a duty to provide information can be measured in moral terms relating to behavioural norms.

The economic efficiency argument concentrates not on how contracting parties behave or should behave but on how allocating the information inequality is measurable on the market. The first question is whether or not it is efficient[37] to require the party with the information to provide it to the other uninformed party. Of course numerous economic analyses of law[38] have already pointed out an important differentiating factor: whether the party who possesses the information has acquired it casually or deliberately (at a cost). According to Kronman, for example, it is clearly not cost-effective to require the party possessing the information to disclose it if he has acquired it at a considerable cost or personal investment as this would act as a disincentive to acquire valuable information. It has been shown that Kronman's analysis leads to eliminating duties to inform in the majority of cases.[39] However, this leads to a clash with other economic dictates in that perfect competition of the market requires parties to have equal access to information. If duties to inform are not imposed, inevitably there will be informational asymmetry and the goal of perfect competition will never be attained.[40] Cooter and Ulen[41] have proposed another distinction in terms of productive, redistributive and destructive facts. This distinction has also been criticised as it is unclear that the criterion is workable in reality.[42] Furthermore, a transaction-costs analysis suggests that the cost of acquiring information is relative and not absolute. It is therefore the lowest cost-avoider who should bear the brunt of providing information. Fabre-Magnan's analysis incorporates the transaction-costs analysis, albeit implicitly. She submits that if the law requires parties

---

[36] D. Kennedy, 'Form and Substance in Private Law Adjudication' (1976) 89 Harvard LR 1685.

[37] I am assuming for the sake of argument that efficiency is measurable in terms of cost-effective rules.

[38] A. T. Kronman, 'Mistake, Disclosure and the Law of Contracts' (1978) 7 J. Legal Studies, 1; R. Posner, Economic Analysis of Law, (5th edn, New York, 1998), pp. 122ff.

[39] See M. Fabre-Magan, 'Duties of Disclosure and French Contract Law: Contribution to an Economic Analysis' in J. Beatson and D. Friedmann (eds.), Good Faith and Fault in Contract Law (Oxford, 1995), pp. 99 ff at p. 110.

[40] See for example, M. Trebilcock, The Limits of Freedom of Contract (Cambridge, MA, 1997), ch. 5 on Asymmetric Information Imperfections, pp. 105 ff.

[41] R. Cooter and T. Ulen, Law and Economics (3rd edn, Reading, MA, 2000), pp. 275–6.

[42] See Fabre-Magnan, 'Duties of Disclosure and French Contract Law'.

to disclose information about their own obligations (e.g. the seller in relation to the condition of his house; the insured in relation to the condition of his health or car etc.), the duty is efficient. In addition, the economic and moral criteria converge.[43]

To summarise, the distinction proposed by Fabre-Magnan, of emphasising the nature of the information coincides with the transaction-costs analysis since the person required to provide information about his own obligation or the subject matter of the contract to which he has easier or better access is also the lowest cost-avoider. It follows that, duties to provide information can be convincingly explained by coinciding economic and moral considerations.

It was suggested earlier that the relationship between the three functions of the duty to inform (special relationships, standards of behaviour and content of the contract) are interrelated. This assertion requires further consideration. It is submitted that the link is provided by examining the concept of reliance-based liability. Reliance-based liability may be induced from a special relationship between the parties. Moreover, such liability actually is induced from special relationships.[44] This proposition is sometimes formulated the other way round: it has been suggested for example in English law that the existence of a 'special relationship' is a criterion for grounding liability for misleading statements.[45] Or again, that certain contracts, categorised in English law as *uberrimae fidei* require that the parties behave in a certain way with reinforced duties to disclose. Or even, more recently, that a certain contract (of surety) not belonging to any previously recognised category submits the parties to a special duty to disclose information.[46] Other legal systems may express a similar idea somewhat differently, since the point of departure is inverted. In systems where the general rule is to provide information, certain contractual relationships will simply reinforce the existence of

---

[43] See Fabre-Magnan, p. 119 who suggests that duties of disclosure (sic) are 'morally very satisfactory in that they prevent people from trying to obtain fraudulently more than they deserve from the contract, but they are economically efficient in that people pay only for what they receive and no more'.

[44] See above, when a duty to inform is imposed in a special relationship. This is because the nature of the relationship entitles one party to rely on the other, thus giving rise to a duty to inform in the presence of material information. If the party possessing the material information breaches the standard of expected behaviour that involves disclosure, and thus breaches the reliance the other party put in him, he will incur liability.

[45] *Hedley Byrne* v. *Heller* (1964) AC 465.

[46] See *Etridge* v. *Bank of Scotland (No. 2)* (2002) UKHL 44. This is one interpretation of Lord Scott's opinion, at paras. 181 ff.

a general duty, e.g. the professional seller must inform the consumer. In contrast under English, Irish and Scots law, the duty to inform is not the general rule but the exception. This is why the law highlights certain contractual relationships, to impose a special duty to inform. It makes sense then that the law should influence the way parties behave in certain relationships in order to protect the parties' reliance on one another. If contracting parties respect the law's incentive or deterrent (depending on which way you look at it) this should have the effect of reducing the incidence of reliance-based liability. Certain empirical observations may follow from this proposition.

Some legal systems lean towards recognising what might be identified as reliance-based liability even if it is not denominated as such. Austrian, German, Greek and Portuguese law all explicitly recognise reliance-based liability in the form of negative interest.[47] Norway, and Scandinavia in general, explicitly recognise reliance between contracting parties (take Case 12 as an example where the absence of reliance is a determining factor) as does the Netherlands (see below). It is suggested that other systems implicitly recognise such a basis for liability by using the duty to inform as a means to achieve this end. This could help explain why French law imposes a duty on contracting parties to provide information to the other party (see Cases 4 and 6 for example) since if information in the possession of one party is not disclosed, the other party is entitled to annul and/or claim damages. Recognising a right to annul and claim damages may amount to admitting that the relationship between the parties justifiably induces reliance. Moreover, English, Irish and Scots law recognise that certain special relationships give rise to extra protection. There is of course nothing new about this; contracts of insurance were designated *uberrimae fidei* as early as the eighteenth century.[48] It is in this sense that it has been suggested that there is a strong link between the duty to inform and reliance. The nature of the link is more complex: is it because the parties rely on one another (bilaterally or unilaterally) that a duty to inform is incumbent on one (or both) of them?

Two observations, the first descriptive, the second speculative, follow. This study has shown that duties to inform are increasingly being used. To take a legislative example, European Directives frequently have

---

[47] L. Fuller and W. Perdue, 'The Reliance Interest in Contract Damages' (1936) 46 Yale LJ, pp. 52–96. For a historical explanation of Fuller and Perdue's transposition, see D. Friedman, 'The Performance Interest in Damages' (1995) 111 LQR 628.

[48] *Carter v. Boehm* (1766) 3 Burr. 1905 per Lord Mansfield at p. 1909.

recourse to such a duty:[49] critics have queried the truly protective nature of this measure and several law and economics analyses have been carried out regarding what has been called the 'information overload' in the context of consumer transactions.[50] Put simply, the criticism of information overload suggests that consumers are not able to process the information given to them and market failure arises as a result of their failure. In reply, one might argue that market failure also arises as a result of imperfect information, and that it is important not only to assess how consumers process the information but also to note the fact that insufficient or incomplete information is provided in the first place. This argument is both hypothetical and speculative since it may be difficult to prove whether the market would function better if more complete information was provided. Who can say whether a better-informed consumer may be able to make better-informed decisions? This would imply that the 'typical consumer' actually exists. Another reply contests the relevancy of information overload and submits that consumers are able to process information adequately, even if they satisfice rather than optimise the information given to them.[51] However, the end-result of providing information appears to be more formalistic than content-based. Often consumers will have great difficulty in processing the information that is given to them in order to assess its relevance,[52] and so if a consumer cannot use the information, the duty to inform is nothing more than window-dressing and providing information is clearly not a panacea to consumer problems.[53]

It is plausible to conclude that imposing the duty to inform does exactly what it is designed to do; it is simply that we are mistaken about its aims. The results of this study allow us to infer that the duty to inform acts pre-emptively. However, its pre-emptive virtues are not exclusively

---

[49] Take food-labelling, information about cancellation rights, information about interest calculations for credit-sales; information about timeshares purchases, information by travel agents about package holidays etc.

[50] See W. Whitford, 'The Function of Disclosure Regulation in Consumer Transactions' (1973) 68 *Wisconsin Law Review*, pp. 400–70. D. M. Grether, A. Schwarz and L. Wilde, 'The Irrelevance of Information Overload: an Analysis of Search and Disclosure' (1986) 59 *Southern California Law Review*, pp. 277–303.

[51] See Grether, Schwarz and Wilde, 'The Irrelevance of Information Overload'. Satisfice means maintaining or reaching a satisfactory level as opposed to optimising that implies multiple objectives.

[52] Take the calculations of interest rates as an example.

[53] I am grateful to Christian Twigg-Flesner for having pointed this out to me.

for the benefit of the consumer or supposedly 'weaker party'.[54] Indeed it should be emphasised that the relative 'strength' of the parties includes, in effect, what may be called 'informational strength'. The object of the protection is meant to enlighten the consent of the party not in possession of the material information. That party is not necessarily the weaker party. For example, the insured is in some respects the weaker party but he has informational strength over the insurer since he has access to information which is highly material for the insurer (in terms of the risks engendered by the contract). Conversely, a seller may be the stronger party in relation to a consumer buyer and he also has informational strength in relation to the other. This seems to show that the stronger/weaker categorisation of persons is an unhelpful criterion. The emphasis is not on a party's informed consent at the time of making the contract but on its consequences on the contract itself, and indeed it may affect the contract's very existence. To put it another way, the pre-emptive virtue lies in allowing the uninformed party to know more about the contract's content. If the content of the information is relevant and material and not just formal, the consequences will affect and indirectly benefit the stronger party as well as the law. As Whitford has pointed out in the context of consumer transactions, '(. . .) despite appearances to the contrary, precontractual disclosure regulation is enacted precisely because it is expected to have little impact on consumer purchasing decisions'.[55] Although the proposition was made somewhat cynically and must be read in its context (i.e. of State legislation in the USA, subject to political demand for consumer legislation) it is submitted that there is some truth in this assertion. Protective legislation is inevitably a response to political pressure; Whitford merely suggests that a disclosure regulation pays lip service to keeping the consumer happy since the consumer does not realise that the legislation will not have the impact he is seeking.

How though can providing information benefit the stronger contracting party? Take the example of consumers. It has been suggested that consumers cannot always make use of the information given by the seller, manufacturer, lender (the 'stronger party'). This position of strength is exacerbated by the duty to provide information, since the

---

[54] In this respect, I adhere to the criticisms about the supposed virtues of the duty to provide information, see above.

[55] Whitford, 'The Function of Disclosure Regulation in Consumer Transactions', at p. 436.

party who possesses it can also use it as a defence against the other, i.e. if it is proven that the required information was actually provided then the transaction is unimpeachable.

To rebut the suggestion that the law is not truly helping persons such as consumers by imposing information requirements, it may be submitted that such regulation does indeed benefit the law, since by encouraging parties to provide information in certain circumstances litigation might be avoided or reduced. In a perfect world, if incentives are given so that parties behave towards one another so as to reduce or avoid mistakes occurring (recall that mistakes endanger the security of transactions), reducing their likelihood must be beneficial for contracting parties, the market and indirectly the law.

To conclude, it should be clear that this study has revealed the increasing use made of duties to inform but that its aim is not to promote the use of this duty at all costs. However, this study has demonstrated that the duty to inform may be displacing concepts such as mistake and fraud. This conclusion was reached in the cases where the law has been harmonised as a result of European legislation. An examination of the PECL is also revealing in that the duty to provide correct information (art. 4:106) is inserted between the provisions of mistake (art. 4:103) and fraud (art. 4:107). Article 4:106 of PECL states:

A party which has concluded a contract relying on incorrect information given to it by the other party may recover damages in accordance with article 4:117(2) and (3) even if the information does not give rise to a fundamental mistake under article 4:103, unless the party which gave the information had reason to believe that the information was correct.

This provision clearly covers information given negligently or carelessly. It is intended to cover what is presently included in French law, under the head of French precontractual liability (art. 1382 Code civil); liability under the *culpa in contrahendo* doctrine and innocent misrepresentation. The commentary informs us that the person giving the information does not guarantee its truthfulness; therefore damages are awarded to compensate the party for the position he is in now and the position he would have been in had he known the truth. Remedying the provision of incorrect information is not exactly the same as, though overlaps with, the duty to provide information, as already stated throughout this enquiry. The actual content and formulation of art. 4:106 of PECL is in itself uncontroversial. Attention must be given to comment G, however, which states that such liability, if the contract is governed by PECL, should be contractual.[56] This raises a much thornier issue which can only be addressed briefly here.[57]

Should liability arising out of the duty to inform, which has been identified as reliance-based liability, be contractual or precontractual?

Our aim is not to attempt to answer this question but simply to open the debate. The question can be looked at from two perspectives. Firstly, from an economic point of view, it might be useful to investigate if it would be better (more efficient?) for the aggrieved party (and for the market) if the duty to inform gives rise to precontractual or contractual liability. Secondly, from a conceptual point of view, is it better for contract law that such liability is precontractual or contractual? In reply to the latter, some have suggested that for the sake of the internal coherence of contract law, reliance liability is extra-contractual.[58] Others have argued that reliance is the core of the contract.[59] Some legal systems do not explicitly recognise that reliance forms part of contract law at all.[60] As already stated, the differences between the two lie in practical considerations and will also hinge on an evidential choice. PECL's proposal that such liability should be contractual is subject to reservation, since this mainly makes sense in order to ensure a coherent application of its own rules. This contrasts starkly with the empirical conclusion drawn from this study where the vast majority of legal systems (all but one, to be precise) consider that such liability is precontractual. This is the positive law.

---

[56] Articles 4:103 and 4:106 must also be read in conjunction with art. 6:101: 'Statements giving rise to Contractual Obligations'. In the case of a professional supplier giving information about the quality or use of goods or other property, the buyer may choose either of these provisions. Since the thrust of art. 6:101 is to treat such statements as contractual, it follows that a claim under art. 6:101 also gives rise to remedies for breach of contract.

[57] This no doubt will be dealt with by J. Cartwright and M. Hesselink, authors of the forthcoming Trento Common Core Project on precontractual liability.

[58] S. A. Smith, 'The Reliance Interest in Contract Damages and the Morality of Contract Law', (2001) *Issues in Legal Scholarship*, online bepress.com. See for example P. Mitchell and J. Philipps, 'The Contractual Nexus: Is Reliance Essential?' (2001) 22 OJLS 114 ff.

[59] P. S. Atiyah, 'Fuller and The Theory of Contract', p. 73 and 'Consideration: A Restatement', p. 179, both in P. S. Atiyah, *Essays on Contract* (Oxford, 1986). For a recent formulation, see P. Jaffey, 'A New Version of the Reliance Theory', (1998) NILQ 107.

[60] The concept of reliance, as such, is not recognised by French law, although I would not suggest that it is truly unknown to French law. Cf. H. Muir Watt, 'Reliance et définition du contrat' in J. P. Bertrel (ed.), *Prospectives du droit économique, Dialogues avec M. Jeantin* (Paris, 1999), p. 57.

It could be argued that the option is a question of policy or of legal coherence and mentality. The results of this study have shown for example that legal systems that emphasise the duty to inform (and impliedly give a high degree of protection), to take Norway and Germany as examples, are not characterised by the fact that liability for the failure to inform is contractual or precontractual respectively. However, both Norway and Germany do recognise explicitly the concept of reliance. Is it conceivable, in the face of discussion about a European Civil Code, to imagine changing the face of the law so as to insert a concept (reliance)[61] and alter the nature of liability upon which the duty to inform is based? Only the future can tell.

[61] The statement holds for several countries where no legislative provision mentions the concept of reliance (England, Belgium, France, Ireland and Scotland).

Index

Note: Reference should also be made to the Index by Country and the Tables of Legislation and Cases

absence de cause 23–4, 332–3, 340, 365, 378: *see also* variation or annulment of contract in case of frustration/change of circumstances caused by common mistake (*Wegfall der Geschäftsgrundlage*)

acceptance/allocation of risk: *see also* consumer credit contract/consumer sales by financial institutions, guarantor, obligations towards; mistake, annulment for, requirements, acceptance/allocation of risk, effect

economic basis 25, 34–5, 161, 162–3, 223, 372, 374, 380, 382

as underlying rationale 14, 21–2, 329

Aquinas, St Thomas 48–9

basic contractual assumptions doctrine: *see* contractual assumptions doctrine (*presupposizione/sviktende forutsetninger*)

breach of contract/guarantee/warranty as basis for damages, requirements 176–7, 180, 185–9, 191–2, 196, 203–4, 205, 222, 233, 246, 258, 285, 296: *see also* consumer credit contract/consumer sales by financial institutions; termination of contract for non-performance (hidden defects, non-conformity with description or lack of agreed quality)

alternative remedies; cumulative nature of remedies/factors determining choice 191–2, 196, 246–7, 373, 374–5; specific performance 249, 252

dolus bonus/seller's puff and warranty distinguished 233, 241, 242–3

duty to inform/disclose and 245

expertise/knowledge/professional status, relevance 177, 186, 191, 204, 227, 232–3, 243

incorporation of description in terms of sale; acceptance/time to examine goods 169–70, 187, 231; express 169, 191, 222, 228, 234; implied 169–70, 176–7, 204, 228, 233, 251, 265, 375; verbal communications 303

incorporation of maintenance contract into contract of sale 252, 258–9, 265, 375

motive for purchase as condition of contract, requirements; clear and evident agreement 248–9; implied 249

second-hand goods 33, 233, 244, 374–5

time limits 177–8, 183, 225, 228, 234, 245–6

breach of contract/guarantee/warranty giving rise to duty to repair or replace, requirements 185, 232, 239, 242, 245–6, 253, 258

annulment for mistake distinguished 294

duty to inform/disclose and 253, 265, 375

fault, relevance 242

incorporation of warranty in contract of sale 253

mistake, relevance 242

second-hand goods 33, 242

time limits 242, 245–6

burden of proof

consumer credit contract 287

deed of gift, requirements 359, 361, 362

duty to inform/disclose 273

Printed in the United States
125795LV00001B/125/P

9 780521 093101